Life Aboard a
Coast Guard Lightship

by George Rongner

Copyright © 2007 by George Rongner

ISBN 978-0-7414-3862-1

INFINITY PUBLISHING

Toll-free (877) BUY BOOK
Local Phone (610) 941-9999
Fax (610) 941-9959
Info@buybooksontheweb.com
www.buybooksontheweb.com

Contents

Foreword

Life Aboard a Coast Guard Lightship was a delightful manuscript to read, edit and transcribe to a computer disk. As the officer in command of a Cape Cod light vessel during the mid 1950s, my dad captures in descriptive detail the mundane and not so mundane day to day experiences of those relegated to a 28 day vigil at sea. The numerous episodes of humorous and dramatic life on board the *Buzzards Lightship* is sure to capture the interest of the casual reader as well as those who have served in the military in a similar capacity, perhaps even some who are well versed in lightship duty. Because of modern technological advances, the lightship no longer serves as an aid to navigation in U.S. waterways, but the services of those who experienced such duty will, and should, not be forgotten. Such a recollection as *Life Aboard a Coast Guard Lightship* possesses historical and literary significance. Not merely a well crafted narrative shared from the memories of the now retired vessel commander, much of this text is written in the present tense, capturing events in detail as if they were recently experienced, drawing the reader into real time drama. Such writing captures and maintains the reader's interest throughout the 247 page document causing future as well as present generations to benefit as they vicariously experience life on board an anchored vessel in Nantucket Sound.

Bob Rongner
Maple Falls, WA

Chapter I

"The Ship"

It was a horror to step aboard the *Buzzards Bay* lightship, a red-hulled, rust-streaked ship docked at the Coast Guard base in Boston. All was a mass of confusion. The crew were dirty. The ship looked worse. Civilian and uniformed workers were everywhere, for the *Buzzards* was on availability, receiving badly needed attention. Electronic equipment, engines and furnishings were all over the place. Unopen and partially opened crates filled the far end of the wardroom, itself grime covered, dark, and most unappetizing in appearance. The galley deck was torn up to make way for new linoleum. Tables and stools were stowed carelessly in an adjacent compartment. Bulkheads were covered with grime and smeared with greasy fingermarks. There seemed to be no system to anything, and yet everyone appeared to be intelligently engaged in work.

It was a ghastly day to assume command. Earlier, I had driven three hours over soaked highways crammed with early morning traffic. Rain had fallen in sheets and the closer to Boston the more congested the streets. Cars crawled for miles as four traffic lanes converged into a single artery at a bridge undergoing repairs. Roads were slippery, the tempers of drivers striving to reach their place of occupation were unfriendly, and I was not in a pleasant mood myself when the comparative sanctum of the Base was reached.

In order to reach the personnel office from my parked car I had to dash two hundred feet through torrents of rain. So severe was the downfall, the fringe of an offshore hurricane, I was soaked to the skin before reaching the building. What a bedraggled appearance I must have made, in my wet baggy uniform.

1

Thus my introduction to the *Buzzards* was clouded by the elements and a tiresome drive. Bob Dean, the senior engineer and a lifelong friend, introduced me to Bill Burroughs, the Chief boatswain's mate. Together they showed me the ship from one end to the other. I met and talked briefly with other members of the crew but was most unimpressed with everything, and couldn't refrain from thinking, "Oh, God almighty!" It was a nightmare, all right, but I did not awaken from it. It was to be my home for twenty-one months.

My luggage was taken to my quarters on the first deck, which we inspected first. My cabin measured six feet by twelve feet, minus eight square feet claimed by the wheelhouse. I noted a comfortable looking built-in bunk on the port side, with an inner spring mattress. Underneath were two spacious drawers. Alongside the bunk was a nightstand and radio. At the end of the cabin, that is, in the direction of the foot of the bunk, was a large CPO type metal locker for uniforms and coats. At one side a metal desk contained two small and three full sized drawers. These, with a wardroom chair and a single radiator, completed the furnishings except for the photo of a naked female, once part of a calendar, suspended above the bunk.

Off from the cabin was a small toilet, containing a hopper, sink, and medicine cabinet. There was hardly room to turn around, the floor space of four feet by three feet being decreased further by a triangular section of three feet square where a portion of the forward passageway intervened. A sliding metal door shielded the user from the outside world. My wife accompanied me to Boston that horrible first morning and was the first of my family to make use of this interesting section of the ship. To make matters even more interesting, a folded piece of cardboard, apparently used to muffle a rattle, jammed the door shut, leaving my spouse trapped within. No amount of tugging and pulling would cause the door to slide and finally, in embarrassed desperation, I asked for assistance. Chief Burroughs appeared, eventually, with a crowbar. Even then the door was reluctant to release its victim. At last, as a pile of paint chips grew, the door finally opened. Several weeks later the door was to trap me in exactly the same manner, and I had to remain there nearly half an hour before I could attract attention.

The remainder of the ship was as uninspiring as the weather as we continued our tour. The radio room, also on the first deck, was a maze of electronic equipment. Radios, radio beacons, transmitters, receivers, and alarms filled the entire space, with just enough room to walk between the equipment, plus a single chair in front of the radio transmitters. This compartment is most awesome to every new man, regardless of rank or rating, who suddenly finds himself assigned to a lightship. One wonders if he ever will be able to conquer his psychological misgivings about learning to handle the equipment properly under all conditions of weather or emergency.

The second deck contained spaces allotted to personnel. Starting forward was the windlass room which, with two engine room fidleys, comprised the sole compartment not of a personnel function. The windlass room, like that of any ship, housed the equipment used to lower and raise anchors. A small seabag locker was located on the port side and a laundry, with washing machine and one stationary metal tub, was on the starboard.

Going aft, we came to the crew's sleeping quarters, roughly five hundred square feet of deck space, containing six double bunks and twelve metal clothes lockers. The crew's washroom, a square measuring nine feet along each side, held a single shower, two hoppers, and three stainless steel washbowls with mirrors above. This was situated on the starboard side of the ship.

Still going aft, we retraced our steps to the port side of the berthing spaces and entered the library, where two automobile type seats were permanently installed abreast Formica covered tables. A glass enclosed bookcase brimmed with over a hundred bound novels. A fleeting glance revealed several well-known classics among the sundry volumes, which pleased me immensely.

Next came the recreation deck, a narrow space only eight feet wide but twenty-seven feet in length. It was explained that movies were shown nightly in this area when the ship was at sea. Another auto seat was installed at the far end, against a transverse bulkhead. A movie screen hung above a seventeen inch television set. Eight wardroom chairs completed the furnishings. A large bulletin board adorned the starboard bulkhead, adjacent to one of the engine room fidleys.

Crossing again to the starboard side we came to the galley and then to the mess deck. The eighty-eight square feet of galley space housed the usual electric range, cupboards, counter space, and a three-compartment stainless steel sink. A hatch led aft to the crew's mess deck which was receiving a new layer of linoleum. There were three tables here, sixteen oak topped stools, a refrigerator, and a combination bread and potato locker. This compartment was similar in construction to the recreation deck, measuring seven and a half feet by twenty-three.

Leaving the commissary spaces, we entered the recreation deck briefly to view the CPO-Officer shower room. The thirty square feet were devoured by a shower, s hopper, and a built-in closet. The tile deck glistened, and it was the cleanest place I had yet seen on the vessel.

Immediately aft on the same side was the ship's office, a space of forty-eight square feet into which was crammed a built-in desk, typewriter, bookshelves, file cabinet, safe, adding machine, and one chair. Tiny though it was, the office was handy and well planned. From the single chair, a man could reach all the equipment, files, safe, and shelves. If anything else was needed, a sound-powered telephone was readily available on the starboard bulkhead.

The remainder of the second deck was consumed by wardroom spacers. The mushroom shaped wardroom looked contented in spite of the accumulation of grime and litter. A rectangular table and four chairs in the center of the room,

4

with a skylight directly overhead, offered a cheerful appearance. Two luxurious easy chairs and a semi-circle of installed cushions, all in green, matched the linoleum of the deck and the painted bulkheads. A permanently installed table, at the head of the wardroom, carried a small television set, a toaster, and a coffee maker. In addition, there was a lone bookshelf constructed above the arc of cushions, a filing cabinet, a locker containing the ship's small arms, a medical locker, and a stationary closet.

The Chief petty officers' quarters, each measuring nine by five, opened from the starboard side of the wardroom. Each contained a clothes closet, bunk with inner spring mattress, four drawers constructed beneath each bunk, individual washbowls, and a small medicine cabinet. In addition, the chief engineer's room had desk, typewriter, and a chair, it being the engineer's office, so-called, because it was here that the engineers transacted the greater portion of their administrative functions.

Off the port side of the wardroom was its galley, identical in size to the CPO quarters. This compartment contained a stainless steel sink with shelves, counter space, a wall cabinet, and a refrigerator.

Our tour next was extended to the engine room area, where I was introduced to a spacious domain of thirty-two engines and generators, a large storeroom, a spare parts section, electrical lockers, the shaft alley, compressors, air tanks, fuel tanks, water tanks, a lathe, storage batteries, and a maize of pipes and wiring. I shuddered as we made our way over, across, through, atop and under the equipment that was being disassembled, assembled, replaced, repaired, cleaned and installed. My first reaction, which I kept to myself, was, "What a mess! How can anyone possibly know what's going on here? It doesn't seem that they ever will get everything back together again." It was a relief to leave the engine room and, under the guidance of Chief Burroughs, have a look at more of the area for which he was responsible.

Climbing the ladder back to the second deck, we walked forward past the crew's quarters, then down into the main hold. Here was a combination workshop, passageway, and catchall. Many repairs and alterations were underway, and civilian machinists, electricians, and welders were busy every place we looked. The hold itself contained carpenter tools, a commissary storeroom, a large walk-in refrigerator, and three lockers filled with housekeeping supplies. There were hatches leading to the water tank spaces and to the chain locker. Here again stores were piled confusion, portable fire extinguishers were being prepared for recharging, and there seemed to be a general lack of system to anything. In all fairness, of course, many ships do look this way during their availability period.

The last compartment was the paint locker. To reach this we had to return to the crew's berthing spaces, go forward to the windlass room, then down a narrow hatch. The same conditions existed here, and I could not help but think of the tremendous amount of work in store for all of us. Below the paint locker was the forward peak tank which held four and a half thousand gallons of fresh water. A remote control fire extinguishing system was being installed in the paint locker and we did not linger, for we obviously were in the way of the workers.

This, then, was my first inspection of the *Buzzards* lightship, and I was to make many more before my assignment was completed. I was not at all happy to be suddenly thrust onto this grimy hulk, but resolved to consider it a challenge.

Chapter II

Hurricane "Ione"

Time hastened ever onward, and three weeks later, repairs completed, we left Boston behind as we sailed to the open sea. We resumed the *Buzzards Bay* lightship station on September 7, 1955, and became a floating lighthouse. Living aboard an anchored vessel was a new experience for several of us, but soon we became accustomed to a routine, a routine that was to become a monotonous bore. After the first few days of nausea and being fitted with "sea legs," we began to wax interest in other details, especially in broadcasts of weather information, for this was the hurricane season. Several disturbances of a cyclonic nature already had been reported to the public. While they were of some interest to us, there was no immediate concern for they were still in the area of their origin or had swerved sharply seaward.

As a newly appointed "Captain," my thoughts turned to accounts of the great northeasters, common to this coast, that had driven men and ships to their death, but I was unprepared for a skirmish with a tropical lady - Hurricane Ione - whose portentous beginnings we heard about nine days after we dropped anchor.

Friday, September 16, 1955

2230: "This serious storm is located 650 miles southeast of Florida. It might pose a threat to the southeastern seaboard if it continues its present course."

An exchange of glances spoke the words we never uttered.

Saturday, September 17, 1955

0830: The news commentary was startling: "Ione is now centered 500 miles east of Miami and poses a definite threat to Florida, Georgia, and the Carolinas. The storm is moving northwest at 12 miles per hour, and growing in size and intensity. Winds now reach 90 miles per hour."

0900: The sea was a profound blue as it stretched toward the horizon. As it approached the ship, it became an eerie black. There was a bathtub ripple over the entire area with interlocked patches of smooth glassy water. It was almost as though oil had been dropped in spots to pacify its alarm. The brown banks of the mainland were visible through a deepening haze. Four white herring gulls loitering atop the water half a mile away appeared magnified in proportion. The sky was a pale transparent blue along the horizon increasing to a mottled hue overhead. The deep blue indication of good weather was obvious by its complete absence. Nowhere was it to be found. The clouds were light, practically without substance, rising from an ivory where sea met sky to a dull white directly above. They were in patches. Not fog, not haze, not "regular" clouds even, but were low at a fifteen hundred foot elevation. Shadows took on definite patterns, clear in depth and design.

1000: The sky is the same. The gulls continue to drift lazily, the four white ones still companions. A seaman on deck is catching fish which he calls squirrel hake. They bite practically as soon as the line hits the water. Now the glassy oily appearance of the water has won its duel, and the rippled areas are in a minority. A few remain in the distance where the tidal effects are more prominent. There is a light zephyr of a breeze from the southeast. A piece of driftwood bobs complacently astern. No tenseness or air of expectation is perceivable as yet.

Herbert Ressler, a seaman from Miami, expressed the feelings of all with a simple remark: "God, I hope we don't get it. It's bad enough on land."

1230: The wind has increased to four or five knots. The rippled areas of the sea now dominate, yet they contain currents of smooth rivers. Visibility has improved greatly, although the beach five miles away is indistinct except for the brown cliffs. A few sports fishermen nearby are making good catches. An auxiliary sloop to the north has taken in her sail and is proceeding under power. The color of the water is the same. The clouds, thickest in the south, are spreading into a broad mackerel back formation. Objects on the sea are magnificently distinct. Several of the crew fish off the stern, catching flounder, skate, and squirrel hake.

1300: The radio booms again with the report that a formal hurricane alert has been issued along the southeastern coast: "Ione could hit from southeastern Florida to North Carolina by tomorrow night. Winds are now up to 100 miles per hour."

1345: A strange mass migration of jellyfish is underway. The tide is running at two and a half knots from bow to stern or from southwest to northeast. Off our port side tens of thousands of white transparent fish, about three inches in diameter, move with the tidal flow. The mass follows a heavily populated line some four feet in width, while stragglers accompany the rank and file to the right. This regimented phenomena lasts fully ten minutes, and stragglers follow for another half hour.

Is this the usual action of these fish? Are they preparing to hibernate for the winter? Has some strange insight warned them of the impending fury of a storm and urged them to seek shelter? Is it perhaps normal for them to travel thusly?

We watched the procession in awed silence. The ways of nature are ever of keen interest. How beautiful and how varied her innumerable complexities of evolution and survival. Will man ever fully comprehend the completeness of the life cycles of the thousands of forms of life on this earth?

1515: The wind has freshened from the southwest. The sea is a mass of short irregular swells with occasional whitecaps. Visibility remains the same.

2300: The TV news informed us that "Ione, now 350 miles from the coast, is a definite threat to Florida, Georgia, and the Carolinas. A high pressure area to the north will prevent the storm center from changing course for the next six or eight hours."

On deck visibility is good to fair with a clear overhead. The seas are serene, but the ship has begun an unusual rolling motion, slowly moving from side to side. There is a heavy dampness in the air that gathers in large globules on the deck superstructure.

Sunday, September 18, 1955

0800: We turned on the television. "Ione is now centered 350 miles east of Daytona Beach with winds of 125 miles an hour, moving northeast at 13 miles per hour. Winds are expected to reach hurricane force along the Carolina coast, with high tides and rough seas. Ione may begin to affect sea and tides in the New England area tomorrow. Watch for further advisories."

Three parts of the advisory were of definite interest to us. Ione obviously would strike the coast. In fact, hadn't we heard that the Carolina coast already was receiving the preliminary effects? Secondly, we could expect, soon, to feel the first buffeting of the seas ourselves. Thirdly, the ominous suggestion to "watch for further advisories" did not escape us.

The sea has roughened into two foot swells with an accompanying addition of whitecaps. It is a murky blue-green, heavy in color and lacking clarity of depth or perception. The sky is covered with a low film five hundred feet in altitude. A damp southwest wind churns at ten miles an hour. Visibility is lessening to four miles.

0830: The island of Cuttyhunk no longer is visible, and our fog signal shrieks its long shrill warning. These deafening blasts are nearly unbearable in my cabin. The effect of the first forcible stream of air is startling, particularly at the beginning of each cycle. Gulls leave the rigging as the clarion tones cause the yardarms to vibrate. The genus of Laridae obviously object to this sensation, and with a protesting flap of wings they evacuate to the water.

We continue to listen to weather advisories. The reports are not inspiring. On board, all loose objects below decks are being lashed - just in case. The paint locker is a scene of aggravated activity as we prepare for the worst while hoping for the best. Cans of paint, thinner, linseed oil and turpentine are re-stowed and lashed. The tops of used cans are carefully sealed. Tools, paddles, and similar equipment are gathered and placed in a container already made fast to a stanchion. The top of the fore peak tank holding fresh water is checked for loose bolts. Lastly, the hatch leading to this compartment is dogged tightly. Now we can divert our attention elsewhere.

1430: A tanker passes in a southeasterly direction. Where is she going? Where is her home port? Has her captain not been informed of the disturbance that approaches menacingly from that direction? The tanker disappears into the fog and haze a few minutes after being prominently in sight off our beam.

Our foghorns have been blowing incessantly. Seas are picking up steadily, now reaching a height of three to four feet. We feel a long rolling sensation, caused by swells from the southwest. The wind is southwest, fifteen miles per hour. The water is an unfriendly medium green blending to a bluish-green a hundred yards from the ship. The sky, seen though the haze, is a milky blue. The sun is a bright yellow orb and can be seen by looking a few degrees to either side of its brilliance. A small fishing boat scoots for cover in the direction of the mainland, casting much spray in the process. We have flies for the first time in several days. They are here in abundance, making futile attempts to get through the porthole screens. The ship begins to pitch slightly.

1625: "Ione is 325 miles east of Georgia, moving northwest at seven to eight miles per hour, with winds of 125 miles an hour! Hurricane alerts are extended north as far as Atlantic City. It still is too early to tell if Ione will strike New England."

2000: Our foghorns still sound their powerful chatter. We watched a movie which ended a few moments ago, and all hands are on deck looking for visible landmarks, hoping that we may be able to secure the horns. A large freighter passes to starboard, heading south. The winds from the southwest have decreased to eight miles an hour. The seas are smoother. The overhead is clear, and stars are plainly visible directly above and for thirty degrees to either side. The horns and continuous radio beacon transmittals interfere with radio reception, hence we are receiving no hurricane news via that media. We expect momentarily to receive an official alert from our District office in Boston, for the last news was not favorable.

The horns, after twelve hours of steady bellowing, are becoming obnoxious. When on deck, walking from the radio room to my cabin, I wait until the final second of a blast and then dash quickly and close the hatch rapidly to avoid the drum shattering screams and reverberations.

There was one bright note in the day. Late in the afternoon Arthur Denault, a fisherman from Westport, MA, picked up our outgoing mail.

2110: A television program was interrupted by a special bulletin from the New York weather bureau: "The entire Atlantic seaboard is alerted as far north as Provincetown. High winds in the center of Hurricane Ione reach 125 miles an hour, and gale force winds extend as far as one hundred and seventy-five miles from the center. All shipping interests are cautioned to be on the alert."

2213: The radio room receiver crackled with our first official communiqué, an alert from Watch Hill, Rhode Island to Quoddy Head, Maine, acknowledging the possibility that a hurricane existed that might pose a definite threat to that area.

2320: A news bulletin on television likewise acknowledged that "Ione is a possible threat to southern New England. Winds can be expected to increase tomorrow morning."

2335: Thick fog has reduced visibility to a scant one hundred yards. The stars are visible directly overhead and for five degrees away from the center. The temperature is sixty degrees Fahrenheit.

Monday, September 19, 1955

0300: A second official communique from Boston headquarters indicated that a hurricane probably could be expected within forty-eight hours. This alert was passed to all planes, ships, and shore stations: "Radar reports this storm center as being very close to Morehead City."

0700: Another television alert: "Ione is considered one of the deepest storms of the season. The barometer is lower in the center of this storm than in the others. Hurricane winds extend seventy-five to one hundred miles from the center. Gale force winds extend up to two hundred miles. Winds of 125 miles per hour are recorded near the center. This dangerous storm is centered southwest of Cape Hatteras, moving fifteen to eighteen miles an hour in a north northeasterly direction."

Here the seas have become much calmer, with long rolling swells four to five feet high. There are no whitecaps. The foghorns continue their warnings, with a visibility of perhaps a mile. There is no sign of sky or sun through the heavy damp fog. The water is a mixture of dark blue and green hues. A small yellow warbler is resting on the rudder quadrant. He is tame, and we are able to approach within three feet before he scurries in alarm.

0705: Northeast storm warnings have been received and the appropriate daytime signal elevated, for the *Buzzards* is one of the daytime display stations cooperating with the weather bureau. Lightships do not indicate storm warnings at night.

0715: Everywhere on board there is a flurry of organized activity. Engineers are double-checking their engines, verifying oil levels, securing last minute items. On deck the boatswain's mates and seamen are passing additional lines around the boats in order that the canvas covers won't be blown off. Other lines are being rigged fore and aft to assist in holding the boats in place. Lifelines are being rigged, for our life may depend on them. An engineer is checking damage control gear. Another is preparing bags of oil to help make a slick alongside, should it become necessary. The foghorns have been sounding now for twenty-four hours, and the men walk topside with wads of cotton protruding from their ears.

0930: The radio is bristling with hurricane alerts, probabilities, and possibilities: "Southern New England probably will feel gale force winds by early evening."

1000: Official orders, received by radio, have instructed us to seek shelter near Bird Island WHEN directed. Bird Island is near the western entrance to the Cape Cod Canal in Buzzards Bay. Thick fog remains with us.

1015: Visibility is somewhat improved. Rhythmic rolling ground swells up to ten feet now approach from the south, along with a freshening wind. For the first time in two days the sun can be observed, appearing as a white disc through the thinning fog. Two thin shafts of sunlight appear on the water half a mile to port. The sea is a murky and turbulent bluish-green. I go to my cabin to shave, perhaps to show my disdain for misgivings unknown even to myself. Yet it makes me feel better, and I am more eager to battle the challenge that looms portentously ahead.

1115: Emergency hurricane alert: "From weather bureau, Boston. Boston weather bureau alert bulletin, 10:45 A.M. Ione near Cherry Point, North Carolina or about one hundred and forty miles south southwest of Norfolk, Virginia, moving toward the north northwest at twelve to fifteen miles per hour. Highest winds continue up to 125 miles per hour, and gales extend outward to the north and east three hundred miles. This severe storm is expected to continue its north northwest movement at fifteen miles an hour during the next twelve hours with a tendency to move towards the north northeast the following twelve hours. Southern New England will begin to feel the effects of increasing winds and rising seas this afternoon with steadily increasing winds and tides all along the New England coast tonight. High tides along the Maine, New Hampshire and Massachusetts coasts occur between 2:00 and 3:00 daylight time tonight and Tuesday afternoon, and 11:00 tonight and 11:00 to 11:30 Tuesday morning along the Buzzards Bay - Rhode Island coast area. Seas will become rough early tonight and will be extremely rough late tonight and Tuesday along and off the New England coast. Small craft should remain in port until further notice. Every precaution for the protection of life and property should begin immediately."

1130: The barometer reads 29.83, a drop of .06 during the past four hours. This is a particularly useful instrument to the mariner, since its fluctuations provide an index in predicting weather. Bad weather usually is associated with regions of low pressure, and conversely good weather is associated with high pressure. The standard atmospheric pressure at sea level is 29.92 inches, and the rapidity with which the barometer rises or falls is a key to the probable state of weather to be anticipated.

1135: A fifty foot auxiliary ketch slithers by, heading north.

1230: We have the radios and television in constant use. The reports are not encouraging. The storm is lashing the Carolinas, and a lightship has been torn loose from its mooring off Cape Hatteras. We are of one thought as we silently pray for the lives of the men on board as, with a stark reality, we suddenly are aware of the dire peril we face. It is not at all stimulating to realize that a lightship was lost in a previous hurricane just two miles from our own position. It sank without its crew having a chance to escape. Now, though, thoughts of the ship being battered and smashed off Cape Hatteras are as realistic as they are morbid. We picture the storm-tossed lightship, battling heroically for its very life. We picture huge seas engulfing the entire vessel, trying to push it down, down, down. Still she clings to life. The seas batter her again and again. What of the men on board? What are their thoughts at this hour? Will we undergo the same experience? Are we, too, destined to be a victim of the onslaughts of this fierce raging storm? A hundred thoughts flash through one's mind, simultaneously, at times like this. We think of our childhood, our home, our loved ones. Some of our thoughts are completely unrelated and insignificant. Strangely, though, most are disciplined and coherent rather than fantastic or terrorized.

1300: Once more visibility has closed to practically nil. The wind has shifted to the northeast, at five miles an hour. Southerly swells are increasing in height and rhythm. The barometer is falling ever so slowly, and stands at 29.83.

1330: Chief Burroughs, Chief Dean and I suppress news of the misfortune of the lightship off Cape Hatteras. We don't wish to alarm our crew members who are quietly making final preparations, as we await further developments. The man on watch in the radio room has his ear glued to the receiver.

I am thinking of requesting authority to proceed to our prearranged shelter, although I am torn between a desire to remain on station as long as possible and the wish to move the ship before conditions worsen too seriously. If I do make a formal request, will the District office think we are frightened and undependable? If I do not make such a request, am I being fair to my crew? They all wish to go, justifiably. Am I alone in presuming that our primary duty as an important aid to navigation calls upon us to remain on station as long as possible? Would we, by remaining, possibly be the guide that would lead some vessel to safety? If we were to leave prematurely and a ship was lost in this locale because our signals were unavailable, what of my conscience?

My thoughts drift to home and family. I wonder what preparations they are making. Here on board we are cognizant of their worry about our safety, and yet it is far less agonizing, at the moment, to be here in the ocean knowing what to expect. At home our families are thinking, wondering, dreading the developments about to engulf their loved ones at sea. We KNOW what is taking place out here, aboard ship, but they can only allow their pessimistic thoughts to run rampant. A twinge of pity surges through me as I picture the torment they must be experiencing. How distressing, indeed.

We all will be happy when this is over. How torturous this waiting, watching, wondering. Waiting and watching for what? How do we know what will happen? We wonder if - but, no, let's not become incoherent. Oh God, why doesn't it get here? Let's start this show, if this is the way it must be. We are prepared, as much as possible. What is worse, the actual fight or the slow ticking of the seconds that separate us from this great force wallowing along the coastline? Stop playing cat and mouse with us. Come on and fight! Has time stopped completely? Is the world at a standstill? A glance at my watch reveals the time to be 1355.

1400: I have requested authority to move to the shelter area. Meanwhile, everyone is busily engaged, with a two-fold purpose. The first is the last minute checks for the showdown with "Ione" - a battle that will see us emerge victoriously or be claimed as a victim. The second is to keep our thoughts from ruling our minds - to keep from thinking about this great unknown monster poised to strike.

There is a heavy oppressiveness in the air. We are like small boys about to walk through a dark graveyard where specters hover behind the shadowy trees and tombstones, ready to grasp frightened invaders. We are neither happy nor unhappy, for these two moods could not correctly describe our innermost feelings. It is stupid to worry, for when humans allow worry to dominate, they may panic, become upset, and become added burdens to their cohorts. We must all retain our strong senses of responsibility, to ourselves and to one another.

What has happened to our companions, the gulls? Nowhere is one to be seen. They are not tempted when Clem, the cook, disposes of his garbage. This indeed is an unparalleled rarity. Has Mother Nature already impressed them with the impending gloom of the terrific lashing she presently is to unfold? Have they gathered safely inland to avoid a dispute with atmospheric activity? Have they flown to warn coastline inhabitants to seek shelter? Do any of these reasons account for their being AWOL? And is their abrupt departure intended to serve notice to us on the lightship that peril brews?

One thing we know for certain is that "Ione" is a vixen-ish lady, terribly forward with her spasms of temper and destruction to all who dare take a stand before her. Another we know is that she is getting closer to us with the passing of each minute and that soon she may grasp us with her twisted, straggling, outstretched fury. Let us hope we will be unfettered prior to her approach so that we won't be the ones to stand in her path and argue that she is trespassing. Does the ancient axiom "We were here first" (and intend to stay) hold true? That is a matter of opinion. We think not. The right of way is hers, and so we acknowledge.

The sun is trying to break through the blanket of fog that insists on remaining with us. What a friendly sight! Perhaps this will be our sole amicable vision during the next twenty-four or thirty hours. How we would enjoy seeing the sun win her duel with the fog, but, alas, the wind first must lend a helping hand by shifting to a different quarter.

Hurricanes oftentimes have a way of accelerating their speed as they approach the northern latitudes. Are we to be trapped thusly?

We are increasingly curt with our responses to one another and extremely selfish with our smiles. Waiting, waiting, waiting.

Chief Burroughs reads our "hurricane preparation" instructions again. Nothing must be overlooked, no matter how relatively insignificant it may appear. The crew are bearing down on the more morbid details, checking painters on the life rafts and seeing that their life preservers are in readiness for any eventuality.

1435: Hooray! A dispatch from headquarters in Boston authorizes us to leave station at 1630 to seek shelter. Suddenly the crew is relaxed. The laugh and shout good-naturedly at one another. It is a great thrill to witness this evolution. A young seaman pats me on the back. It is good to know he is reassured.

Orders, orders, orders. The chief boatswain's mate is preparing to take in the main anchor. The chief engine man is constantly at work in the engine room, now getting the compressors and main engine ready. These two chiefs are standing up exceedingly well, and I am fortunate to be gifted with two men so responsible, logical, and imbibed with a sense of duty, especially when the going gets tough.

1445: The barometer is dropping faster but not dangerously so. The seas are picking up a chop and are a dark muddy green, almost black. The sky can not be studied because a layer of fog lies suspended a few hundred feet above.

It is well to note here that at the time of "Ione" the *Buzzards* lightship was not equipped with an anemometer or a radar. All observations as to wind velocity were strictly calculated guesses. All movements of the ship in poor weather were by dead reckoning. That is, our position was known by the course and speed from a definite point of departure.

1615: The barometer reading is 29.74. The fog has taken on a pinkish coloring, especially when one stares at the water's edge for a few moments. This is due to the sun reflecting off the fire-red hull. Visibility remains extremely poor. There is no ceiling now, not even the several hundred feet we had an hour and a half ago. The seas are roughening and resemble long rolling pasture lands of wheat. The chop is like grain waving before the wind.

We are taking in our anchor, and the clang, clang, clang of chain going around the wildcat into the chain locker is pleasing to the ear. Each link is "rung out" as it comes aboard, that is, struck with a hammer to test it for strength or weakness. A ringing sound indicates strength, while a dull thud indicates a probable weakness that should be investigated. It's a lonely feeling out here, with fog and water as sole neighbors.

1700: We're underway. The anchor is in the hawse, our aids to navigation signals have been shut down and "old faithful," the main engine purrs like a kitten. Conditions are worsening all around us, sea and wind operating with greater bravado.

One senses a difference and gropes for the answer. We're underway, but that's not it. The main engine is throbbing and the whole ship is pulsating, but that's not it either. Oh, of course! The fog signal has been discontinued. We have our underway blast, once every minute, but the on-station signal no longer vexes our auditory systems. What a relief, to be away from those six shattering blasts timed through every sixty seconds.

A small sandpiper plays around the bow, seeming to enjoy his ride. We also have a lone herring gull for an escort, the first to visit us all day.

1725: I note signs of tension again as I eat supper. Half eaten food, lack of chatter, sober faces are all clues.

1740: We are searching for a channel buoy, with binoculars as our sole offensive weapon. As one searches, trying to pierce the fog, mirages appear and disappear rapidly. A buoy seems to be dead ahead and then suddenly it vanishes. It plays on one's imagination. Chief Dean made the same observation.

1815: Barometer reads 29.71. Visibility improving. A crow flies across our bow from port to starboard, towards the south. That's odd. Why doesn't he fly AWAY from the path of the storm? Oh well, it's his business and we attach no omen to his flight.

Definite cloud formations with tinges of blue sky show through the thinning overhead. There are no swells in Buzzards Bay as we head easterly away from the open sea. The water is a rippled dirty bluish-green. We have four bow lookouts helping to locate buoys, and one of them spots the shores of Nashawena Island to starboard.

1823: We are passing "Traffic lighted buoy no. 6." The fog is dispersing in layers, showing, to the east, an aqua strip of sky surrounded by beds of gray stratus which in turn is transforming into willowy wisps of white. To the north lies a washboard effect of cirrocumulus. To the south and to the west fog still shrouds the atmosphere. Now, dead ahead, the stratus has lifted further, showing a variation of color and elements. We see, combined in one alluring setting, aqua sky, gray fog, ridges of white and grayish purple in rippling waves similar to wind blown sand dunes in dead of winter.

1832: Fog is closing in again.

1838: Visibility is one hundred yards with a zero ceiling. We are moving slowly, at 400 RPM.

1900: There is a small break in the fog. A section of sky to the northwest has a mackerel appearance, pinkish on th broad part of the back disappearing into a light gray inside the tail. Cleveland Ledge Light Station is sighted by the bow lookouts with a loud hurrah. It is dead ahead, 052 degrees on the magnetic compass. Dark layers of stratus hover beneath altostratus and we increase the RPM.

1915: It's clear, as though a curtain has been raised. Shore lights on Naushon Island twinkle across the five mile separation. Unusual segments of cloud are all around, with long black swordfish-like beaks. To the west the beauty is

21

unbelievable and breathtaking as we see splotches of aqua. Above the distant horizon lie alternate layers and various shades of blue, black, green, black and rose. Now they are being encompassed by a depressing bank of dark ominous nimbostratus.

1925: The sky to the northwest is taking on the shape of a huge and angry swordfish with the body and sword being represented by dark gray clouds, the open mouth by a stretch of medium blue, and the tongue by an elongated splash of pink. Scud, loose vapory clouds driven swiftly by the wind, which are the forerunner of a hurricane, present their first appearance to the southwest. The rest of the sky is mainly overcast, showing occasional glimpses of blue and green.

2000: The barometer reads 29.67. It continues to drop, slowly, steadily.

2030: We are at anchor in the vicinity of Bird Island, with three other Coast Guard ships as overnight bedfellows. The water is smooth. We have two shots of chain out, the lead line showing a depth of thirty feet. We are 200 degrees, magnetic, from Cleveland Ledge. This is a most satisfactory arrangement.

2100: Everyone breathes huge sighs of relief. We are much more relaxed. Grins caress the faces of the crew, who are taking more interest in pleasure, watching television, listening to the radio, reading, yakking, writing letters. A booming announcement reports, "The hurricane is sixty miles south of Norfolk, moving north northeastward at ten miles per hour. If it holds the same course, it is expected to skirt the coast and pass over Long Island." If this holds true, it can't miss us.

The barometer reads 29.67, identical to the reading of an hour ago. There is no wind, only the slightest murmur of a southerly breeze. Visibility is excellent as shore lights show clearly and distinctly. Hurricane warnings are now being displayed as far north as Block Island.

2300: Television report: "Ione now is in the vicinity of Norfolk, moving north northeastward at ten to twelve miles per hour. Millions of dollars of damage in the Carolinas. Communications in Morehead City available only through an amateur radioman. Boston weather bureau reports that Ione probably will pass fifty to a hundred miles south of Cape Cod with winds of gale force and possibly stronger. Strong precautions are still urged."

A scraping of chairs signaled the end of our relaxation and we go to bed for we know not how long. "Call me if there is any appreciable change in the weather. Maintain an especially alert radio watch. Check our bearings every hour."

Tuesday, September 20, 1955

0630: I awakened with a start, for it was morning. Where was Ione? What was the latest advisory? I dressed hurriedly and went below, to the wardroom. Glad tidings welcomed me. "The full fury of Ione will miss this area. Torrential rains are moving towards New England, but the hurricane has lost some of its intensity. It is due to pass one hundred miles south of Nantucket."

0830: "Ione still is a dangerous storm, and the New England coast should not relax as long as it is south of the area."

1100: The hurricane alert is terminated! "The storm will pass well south and well to sea. Northeast storm warnings remain in effect."

Soon we were underway, to resume station. Enroute we encountered an abundance of kelp and seaweed. The sea is a myriad of mill ponds as small snappers (bluefish, family of Lutjanidae) frolic everywhere. Our friendly gulls have returned as a welcoming committee and fly ahead of us, leading the way "back home."

Although we were not called upon to do hand battle with Ione, she gave us some oppressive moments. In declining a visitation she nevertheless punished us with her vehemence, for we did not realize peace of mind for several

23

days. As we took station again, the fog took station also, and the wearisome horns went to work.

What did the crew have to say? "Well, after this experience, we'll take the foghorns any day!"

Chapter III

"Noise"

Few realize that noise aboard a ship can become most vexing. People have said to me, "How nice to be anchored miles away from the din of modern civilization. You hear no automobile horns or train whistles, no roar of traffic. How peaceful and quiet it must be." They are mistaken, for they cannot possibly conceive the abundance or variation of noise encountered in our daily existence. It is with us perpetually. It shadows us every minute of every day of every week. There is no escape from it.

Your introduction to the ship is accompanied by the melancholy throb of a generator. Its presence is noted from the moment you first step on board. As long as you remain, whether it be an hour or a month, the generator remains activated. There are two exceptions. It may be stopped for a few minutes to have its oil thirst quenched on a rare occasion when its twin standby also is resting. Secondly, it is stopped during the annual in-port period for overhaul.

The generator furnishes electrical power for the ship. We hear the combustion occurring in the upper one-fifteenth of the cylinder. Air brought in by the upward stroke of the piston is compressed near the top. Its heat ignites the injected fuel oil which explodes and pushes the piston back down. Then ignition, or combustion, takes place the instant before the downward stroke commences, and it is at this precise moment the noise is produced.

The orderly firing of the generator can be heard from every deck, from every compartment. There is no place of refuge, in normal weather. The blast of a foghorn is overpowering, and, from the main deck, so is the piecing scream of a stormy wind. Otherwise, the throbbing and humming is everywhere. You awaken to it, shower with it, eat with it, work with it, read with it, and go to sleep with it. One soon becomes accustomed to the tonal inflections emanating from the engine room, however, and the gyrating dandles of the generator are accepted, not too agreeably, but with a sullen understanding. We get so used to the steady firing of pistons that we do not actually hear it as a deflection. We are able to converse in a normal tone of voice. It is not so loud or upsetting that it impairs concentration, ordinarily. It does not spoil mealtime like a tiny band in a cheap hotel. It fails to prevent the capture of sleep. The only time it becomes malignant is when one attempts to shut out all sound in thinking out the answer to some complex problem requiring temporary intense reasoning. This does not happen often or for any prolonged period of time, as the necessity of absolute silence is purely psychological and quickly passes, but during such a brief interim the generator seemingly becomes insolent and audacious. Its noise is a loud-mouthed foe. One's vein of thought is interrupted by a desire to curse. Just as quickly you realize that cursing at an innocent engine is an admittance of your own shortcomings and inabilities. Your impending maledictions evaporate; your mental distress vanishes; the complexity of your problem decreases; your answer is readily forthcoming. The generator drones on endlessly, but becomes less unpleasant and soon is forgotten.

Generator noise reaches its highest crescendo in the engine room. There the engineers must necessarily talk with less subdued voice. This becomes natural and established, for they must overwhelm the roar of the motors. The men are relatively unaffected by noise in motorized areas, for it is a natural occurrence, and it is part of engine room etiquette to speak loudly. Thus, little or no thought is given to conversational difficulties here.

On deck, as one approaches the radio room, he hears different noises, a mass of confused sounds emitting from various pieces of electronic equipment. There are beacons, timers, supervisors, radio receivers, radio transmitters, and an alarm that rings like a fire bell. To the layman or a man first assigned to a lightship this room is awesome and extremely puzzling. The noises are like nonsensible garble. One could hear static, code, voices, keyed transmissions from radio beacons and a vigorously clanging bell, all at one time, although it is extremely unlikely that all would combine in a simultaneous wave of frenzied outcries. It could befall the lot of a newcomer, however, to walk into such a mixture of jargon.

The usually reaction to the raucous protestations of the radio room is similar to that of Chief William Burroughs, the day he was assigned to the *Buzzards*. He walked along the main deck, quite unimpressed and not a little unhappy, for it was raining. He lifted one foot to step inside, stopped unbelievingly, gaped dourly, turned sadly and asked, "What the hell is this?"

Here again noises are transmitted and received twenty-four hours daily. The radio receiver is the loudest and can be heard to advantage from the wheelhouse to the stern. It may carry static, morse code, or an assortment of voices. Each sound may be individual or all three may, and frequently are, combined. It also is punctuated at regular intervals by the shrill passage of radio beacon signals. These transmissions, in series of dots and dashes, penetrate radios, direction finders, TVs, and any human ear in the proximity of the radio room.

Any error in radio beacon transmission timings exceeding five seconds is unmistakably announced by the urgent summoning of an automatic alarm bell. Many an unwary daydreamer has been frightened back to the world of man by vigorous pumping of its clapper, for this shrill noise invites instant attention by the watch standee who usually leaps to the rescue of the sinning beacon.

Noone possesses a desire to listen, at close hand, to a bell that tolls and clangs with such ear-shattering rouses, a bell that can be heard on the second deck anywhere abaft amidships, and most perceptibly in the wardroom directly below. It continues to ring until the beacon error has been reduced to five seconds or less.

The greatest combustion of sound, the grandfather of all lightship noise, is the foghorn. The effects of the horn are explained in another chapter and will be giving only fleeting mention here. It does, of course, cower all other noises into meek submission. It subdues any combination of noise. It travels to all sections of the ship. It will not be denied. The first blast to which a new member of the crew is subjected never is forgotten. It may affect him in an assortment of ways. It may scare Hell out of him. It may make him wish he were miles away, in any direction. It may cause him to converse with his conscience. It may cause him to bump his head as his nerves snap to attention. It may cause him to drop his coffee, the shattering of the cup adding to his woe. No matter what happens to the surprised individual, he never forgets the awful moment he first listened to the foghorn.

Going down the ladder to the second deck, which consists chiefly of dwelling spaces, one notices the apparent bustle of everyday routine. Noise comes from everywhere. From the ship's office the clickity clack of a typewriter passes through the louvre of a closed hatch. There follows a muffled bell and the sound of a platen being turned a notch. The carriage is moved to the right, and the clickity clack resumes.

The library radio offering rock and roll cannot be seen from the base of the ladder, but an amplifier wafts the notes from one end of the deck to the other. The younger element of the crew are jive enthusiasts and stoutly defend the present day popularity of this thundering jumble of sharps and flats.

Proceeding forward, toward the bow, the galley and mess deck are the scene of the next expression of harmonics. The chirping of pots and pans is indicative of a meal being prepared. Each cook (commissary man) had his own system, but an orderly clinking of cooking utensils might indicate organized preparations unnerved by proximity to a meal hour. A confused jangle, in the other hand, could well be informative of hurried attempts to avoid a tardy serving of ulcers. On the *Buzzards* we were most fortunate in having cooks who were highly efficient, conscientious, and took great pride in their culinary offerings.

China and silver erupt three times daily as they are placed on tables, used with spirited attention, removed, scraped clean, washed and placed in a drying rack. Oddly enough these implements are noisier in good weather than in bad. This is because rubber mats are used as table cloths when seas are rough, helping to soften the sound and, more importantly, preventing the assortment of gastric materials from gliding into space.

A daily recurrence is the expression of the gallery vent fan, used to clear smoke and fumes. Situated directly over a sturdy range, its rapidity of motion produces a very loud whir, likened to the scream of a siren with the shrillness siphoned off. It also has been described as similar to the acoustics in a subway station at the moment a train approaches the station stop. Individualistic in noise yielding qualities, it cannot be mistaken for anything else. To an early riser, the exhaust fan denotes stirrings significant of a new day. Its diurnal labors begin at five-thirty in the morning and continue irregularly for some twelve hours, and its whir can be noticed in a broad amidships area, on both the main and second decks.

The hubbub of voices, clanging of tools, and slamming of hatches being opened and closed is distinguishable throughout the ship. Voices waver in crescendo and diminuendo in proportion to the amount of electronic or mechanical competition, the desire to be noticed, or the relative excitability of the conversing parties. They may be alto, tenor, or bass and may carry the vastness of the southwest, the "y'all" of the south, or the "ayah" of New England.

The jingle-jangle of keys is all over the place, since seventy-one and four tenths percent of the crew carry keys at their side. The reason for key toting is not clear, but apparently it makes some men feel important. Perhaps a few, musicallly inclined, love the discordant notes that accompany their every step. Others, accustomed to the roar of urban existence, perhaps enjoy the noise created when their keys strike against a railing or bulkhead as they propel themselves rapidly on foot. Physical magnitudes of key soundings seem to indicate the relative importance of a man aboard ship, according to his own specifications. If he has only a couple of keys that jingle apologetically, he probably carries only the ones to his own locker. If the clinking is somewhat more strident, the man's self-nature increases in similar sequence, for he probably has been entrusted with the key to the cleaning gear locker. This man may carry as many as three of these instruments of admittance in addition to a knife that noisily helps announce his approach. The chief man of the moment is one who carries a dozen keys, a knife, a fingernail clipper, a small crescent wrench he never uses, and a beer can opener used solely to attract attention. Half of his keys fit nothing, but their bulk add to the welter of confused tinkling that herald him as a "big wheel," the man who has access to the bucket locker or a tool box. Others must ask him to unlock the door to the bos'n locker for a box of soap powder or a piece of sand paper. The key transporter thrusts his chest forward, looks wryly at his "inferior," and enjoys the opportunity of asking why the soap powder or sandpaper is to be used. The answer invariably is, "The Chief told me to get it." Key-toting is a popular recreation on the *Buzzards*, and the results can be heard on every deck at frequent times of day or night. These sonorous sounds are not particularly offensive to the ear. In fact, they are most amusing, especially when one realizes the impression the bearers are attempting to create.

Any sudden thrashing of gears in the engine room is caused by either of two clanking monstrosities. The fresh water pump which sends water from the tanks to the various outlets and the sanitation pump that groans in disgust whenever a toilet is flushed are of ancient vintage. They do their part flawlessly, but the commode sounds like a one-lunger saw used on farms to cut firewood. Their sounds are alike and can be detected throughout the second deck and the engine room. Their dull bass groaning deadens even the emissions of the foghorn.

Three times daily the dinner bell is thrust to life. This object resembles the school bell used in little red schoolhouses of a bygone era, where its tolls signified the start and termination of school and recess. On the Buzzards it beckons us to the mess deck for our intake of vittles. When the tables are ready for the chow hounds, the cook shakes this metallic summons vigorously for about five seconds and then stands adroitly to one side to avoid being swallowed in a stampede. The ringing can be heard everywhere in good weather, but distance seldom is a factor, for most of the crew mill alertly well within its limit of audibility.

Gulls scream with delight when the bell announces meal hours. They seem to talk to one another as if they were saying, "Come on, guys. It's mealtime on the *Buzzards.* It'll soon be mealtime for us, too, so let's stand by." A mild flapping of wings brings them closer, and they settle in eager vigilance not far from the mess deck portholes.

During warm weather, electric fans, adding their individual tones to the aggregate, hum a welcome breeze.

Every morning brings forth the capers of a deck polisher, for daily shining of all waxed areas is part of our routine. The buffer is practically silent as the brush swirls around and around, but a sudden lurch of the ship may cause momentary loss of control by the operator. The machine may crash into a table leg, a chair, the bulkhead, or a stanchion. The resounding smack then is recorded in numerous tones, depending upon the object struck, the force of the unscheduled conflict, and the temper of the operator.

Monday through Friday the complacency of everyday routine is shattered by the shrill persistency of the warning alarm. On these days emergency drills are held, usually at 1:00 P.M. although at other hours when the surprise element is accentuated. The warning device is similar in sound to that produced by early bicycle horns except that it is much louder and considerably more urgent. It is capable of instantly

31

awakening a man from deep slumber, even though the foghorn may be blowing. It is most startling when heard unexpectedly; it demands immediate attention; its pressing irreverence infiltrates every compartment on the ship. Only the foghorn or the southwest winds have been called a "son of a bitch" more often than the alarm. This seems to be the favorite vocal expression of men who lash out in retaliation when their ears suddenly are filled with this urgent invitation to get on deck in a hurry. Men roused from slumber thus instinctively grab a life jacket and utter blasphemous oaths as they scramble up a ladder to the main deck. The alarm, however, could well signal us to safety in time of emergency, and the importance of having it available is fully realized.

Noise is increased considerably in rough weather, both in substance and in variation. The dreary sometimes frightening wind is the primary source. It can be heard to best advantage on the main deck, but the sounds for which it is responsible are indiscriminately manifested in abundance in every nook and cranny. Wind produced anti-tranquility is no member of a caste system.

The piercing shriek of the wind reaches its peak on the main deck where it whistles past the bow, through the stays and antennas, around the masts and deck structures and sets in motion other objects that add to the din. The wind howls, moans, screams, whispers, blusters, puffs, shrieks or drones, according to the velocity and direction of approach. Its outcries are especially weird in the dark, being most voluminous when arriving from the southwest. The assemblage of associated vibrations, wind forced, angrily assail us in group onslaughts.

By day, flags and pennants flap briskly, giving off a wash on the clothesline effect. Storms greatly shorten their life spans. Signal halyards beat a rapid staccato tattoo against the masts. Television lead-in wires slap against the superstructure. A "Danger-High Voltage" sign on the antenna unit housing raps a sharp metallic rat-a-tat-tat. These sounds can be, and often are, bitter opponents of sleep. Their convulsions carry to the sleeping quarters and to my cabin. At night, when one is nestled in the arms of Morpheus, a sudden vigorous renewal of the slap, slap, slap or the rat-a-tat-tat causes eyes to open, peaceful minds to become active, and brawling of wind blown equipage seem more pronounced, more disturbing. The filibustering of the wind seems endless, a dozen other sounds are magnified, and one is wide awake. Finally, after doing prolonged mental battle with these intrusions, we usually drift back to slumber land. Upon awakening in the morning or to go on watch, we are immediately informed through our ears of the state of weather, for if the racket has decreased, there is little wind. On the other hand, if the wind is fresh, the rumpus will have increased in frenzy.

A second major contributor to noise during bad weather is the sound of the ocean. Breakers form and spill alongside the ship in much the same way as at the shore. Wind waves, caused by the motion of wind on the water, dissolve themselves in this manner. Swells, wind waves that have traveled out of a stormy or windy area, also crest and spill with a roaring mass of foam, although less frequently. Whitecaps, short-crested waves formed by winds in excess of twelve miles per hour, break in deep water, adding a hissing tone of their own as trapped air seeks to escape.

Seas, especially the swells, ofttimes smash against the bow with a tremendous thud. The ship shudders briefly from the impact as tons of water are diverted from their advance. Water engulfs the entire bow area; wheelhouse portholes are saturated with brine; the flying bridge is coated with a layer of salt spray; decks are drenched; waterways spring to life as they conduct the sea water back to its origin. The vibration from such a contact is felt all over the ship. The noise rises from a muffled moan near the stern to a resounding WHACK near the bow. If the wind is traveling in the same direction as the swell, the impetus is considerably heavier.

Seas can also be heard breaking around the stern, where they converge after being knifed by the bow. There is a great mass of agitation and confused noisy currents as the seas swish mightily into one another. From the engine room they can be heard wallowing against and along the hull with a frantic splashing as they make haste to be on their way. From the wardroom the seas make an indistinct gurgling as they round the stern. It is not unusual to have a sea strike against the region of the stern with such force that it feels and sounds as though a huge section of driftwood or wreckage has found its mark.

The wallowing seas cause vigorous activity where the anchor chain runs through the hawse pipes, tubes that lead the chain from the deck on which the windlass is located, down and forward through the ship's bow plating. Here the sledge hammering seas strike the openings with brute force; the ship's bow rides savagely up and down; the anchor chain becomes taut, moves violently from side to side and vibrates with a shuddering groan. The sound travels from link to link all the way from bow tp pawl, the short piece of metal hinged to engage an anchor link or prevent strain on the windlass gears. The chain slackens, becomes taut, slackens, becomes taut. Following a short lull the series refreshens, and the heavy low rolling sounds continue. On particularly heavy seas the slack is taken up more rapidly; the bulky weight of the ship tugs on the anchor and the chain resists with a rankling disapproval. Sometimes the chain merely fraps moderately at the opening of the hawse before the full force is received. Then, when it straightens abruptly, it quivers with deep rumblings. Rebellious thunderings of the anchor chain can be heard clearly in my cabin, in the crew's quarters, and on the main deck. Vibrations can be felt in every compartment.

When winds have lessened to the extent that the ocean makes no noise near the ship, but sizeable swells still exist from the southwest, mighty breakers can be heard smashing against the rocky west coast of Cuttyhunk, four and a half miles away. This rather uncommon occurrence can be witnessed only from the extreme stern of the ship, away from all ship-generated disturbances. It jolts a man to the stark realization of the tremendous power capable of being set in motion by an angry Atlantic.

In addition to the assortment of noise available topside, the remaining decks also offer variations. Bulkheads, where steel and wood meet, creak and groan indignantly. Hatches (doors) rattle and squeak. Ill fitting latches bang incessantly. Reels of film, enclosed in boxes, thud and bump as they shift to and fro in the movie locker. Loose gear everywhere slides, bangs, clicks, rasps and thumps as it demonstrates against the oversight of good seamanship. Calendars and clipboards swing with a gentle scraping effect. Dishes rattle in their galley racks. A chair with one leg shorter than the others performs a semi-athletic ballet, cavorting briskly in the process. From the main hold comes the sound of fresh water sloshing in the tanks. The same intonations can be heard by listening to the engine room bilges. In my cabin I hear wind whistling through an unused voice tube that leads from the windlass room to the wheelhouse. Radiators sizzle when hot, and they ping when getting that way. Air, trapped in hot water pipes by the motion of the ship, pops mightily when it gets free. If one listens closely, with his ear pressed firmly against the insulation, he can hear water boiling in the hot water tank.

There are more sounds on the *Buzzards* which might be classified as secondary noises because they are not heard daily or solely on occasions of heavy weather. The most important of these is the clattering of the air compressor which is used when fog envelops us. The compressor, when started or stopped, sounds like a motorcycle or a foreign sports car and about twice as loud. A novice on watch in the radio room, not far from the compressor's exhaust, has even suspected, on his first exposure to this experience, that one of the engines has gone completely out of control and has hastily made his report that "something is wrong in the engine room." To the more informed, the activating of this piece of equipment is an acknowledgment of poor visibility, and they know the foghorn will follow suit in a matter of minutes.

In the aft fidley one encounters the gentle clicking of the main light relay. This electronic apparatus times the flashes of the light in proper sequence, the slight sharp clicks being effected at the instant the contact points close. The points, of course, open and close, the light being on when they are closed and off when open. The noise making qualities of the relay might well go unnoticed unless all engines were stopped and there was no nearby talking.

The first few drops of rain are followed by the closing of portholes by the radio room watch stander, this being one of his responsibilities. He has help by day, but at night he is alone. The task is a noisy ritual in itself, ports being slammed shut with a thump that is closely followed by the squealing of dogs being tightened. (Portholes, correctly known as air ports, are circular openings in the side of a ship fitted with a hinged frame in which a thick glass is secured. The purpose of portholes is to provide light, ventilation, and vision. The hinged frame usually opens upward and is suspended from a hook to keep it from falling. Dogs are devices, usually four in number to equalize the pressure, that hold the frame firmly in place when the port is closed.) Closing of ports, then, is acclaimed by a single, solid thump pursued by a succession of squeals. The task occupies from one to ten minutes, depending upon the season of the year, the intensity of the rain, sleet, hail, or snow, and the vivacity of the barricader.

A torrential downpour results in a drip, drip, drip of raindrops that somehow penetrate the deck and find their way to the crew's berthing quarters. One section of the compartment canvas shields, placed strategically to intercept the descent of such drops, gives vent to a splattering somewhat more harsh than that yielded by soggy blankets or clothing. In any event, this invasion calls for a quick review of anti-influx measures. Clothing is removed, canvas shelters are readjusted, and sometimes a scurried redeployment of sleeping areas takes place.

From these same quarters strange nocturnal sounds emit. Some men talk in their sleep. Some mumble while others say unusual things. One night one of the crew, while he was fast asleep, held a conversation with his buddy. "God damned you, Hoople." he threatened, "the next time we're in Boston together and you hide my bottle I'll kick the hell out of you. Now where'd you put it?" He obviously was greatly distressed by the incident as he flailed his arms, stirred uneasily and tensed his face muscles. Another man constantly had gun battles, possibly as the result of reading material perused just prior to his retiring. "There's a machine gun down there. Get it! You'll never take me alive, you stinking bastard!" He shouted his epitaphs with great fervor. Still another, a ladies man, drooled sweet nothings, such as, "Honey, you've got me all wrong. Oh honey, you injure me when you say that." Attempts to engage these sleeping beauties in spontaneous conversation failed utterly.

Another bunk time noisemaker was the thrasher who tossed violently during slumber and who should, to all appearances, awaken more exhausted than when he went to bed. This disturbance results in a subdued rustling of bedding and once in awhile a crisp shudder as a hand accidentally strikes a locker. The restless one sometimes causes a humorous situation. For example, Ralph S. awakened one night to discover the sleeping Willie W., in the adjacent bunk, snuggling closely with an out stretched arm holding him in loving embrace. Ralph wasn't about to be loved by his shipmate. He indignantly thrust the arm away, awakened Willie, and demanded, "What the hell is going on?" Willie groggily apologized when the situation was explained and revealed that he had been dreaming of his wife-to-be. Ralph replied, "Well, I'm not her, so stay in your own bunk." Willie retorted smartly, "How the hell do you think I feel?" A roaring "Pipe down, you guys" from the boatswain's mate abruptly ended the bickering.

Number three in the procession of sleeping turbulence is the snorer. There are many types, ranging from the heavy breather with the "excuse me" beep to the professional whizbang snorter who has perfected his guttural utterances with disagreeably harsh intensity. The expert is the more disturbing, for his ratchet-like extortions are not easy to live with. Quite often his rasping efforts are delivered in conjunction with a swift pitter patter of feet, after which the snores cease for a short while. Thus, the man who raced over to awaken the snorer has an opportunity to return to his own bunk, hastily scramble beneath covers and to try to get to sleep before the offender returns to action. One of the most unhappy snorers I saw on the ship was one who awakened brusquely to the taste of a shaving brush, laden with lather, thrust between his teeth.

One of the signs of early morning life on the *Buzzards* during good weather was the docile snick snick of a metal sounding tape as an engineer measured fuel in the tanks. The sounding tube, a small pipe leading from the tank and arranged with the lower end opening into the tank so that liquid rose in the pipe in order that its height could be measured, was situated near my cabin. I found the noise particularly friendly, probably because it was a clue that the waters were smooth, and I enjoyed its soothing pacifism. From the crew's quarters the plumb bob could be heard lightly tapping against the side of the tube.

During clear weather, a whistle buoy moans its position two miles northeast from us.

Cries of the sea birds, mostly herring gulls and great black-backed gulls, give vent to the feelings of appreciation for garbage jettisoned by the cook. They flock to the scene in great numbers, bickering more often than not over a single morsel, even when there is plenty for all. During winter, they fly so close to the ship in pursuit of food that the flapping of their wings is nearly as melodic as their crabby shrieking.

Foghorns of passing vessels frequent the vicinity during fog and haze. They vary from a deep "Woooooooooooooo" of a large freighter to a shrill "Yahhhhhhhhhhhh"of a fishing vessel. These horns always create an uneasiness until their origin is traced to ascertain that a ship either has passed well clear of us or will not be a collision risk. The sounds are muffled or intensified according to pitch, distance, wind direction, wind velocity, or atmospheric conditions causing limited audibility. A vessel approaching from leeward, that is, from the side directly opposite from which the wind is blowing, might not be noticed until it was within half a mile. A vessel advancing from the windward might be heard several miles away. The height of anxiety is reached when our own signal ricochets off the steel hull of a nearby vessel whose position and course we have not yet catalogued.

The friendliest horn of all was the three-tone exhaust fed whistle of Arthur Denault's fishing boat. This melodious outburst was informative of mail from home, for Arthur, a local fisherman, always let us know when to pass the heaving line to receive a mail bag. He sounded his whistle when he was about half a mile away; word then quickly spread concerning the good news, and excited men rushed to the main deck with faces swathed with smiles. I must confess to having relaxed a bit after the 7:00 A.M. reveille on several Sabbath mornings during summer to be deliciously alerted to life by the joyous tooting of the three-toner.

I had a memorable experience with sound one night. I was in my cabin reading when the wind began to howl. This was not too uncommon, and yet the ship remained motionless. "Oh well," I thought. "The breeze just sprang up. We'll begin to pitch shortly." The noise continued for perhaps twenty minutes. A glance through an open porthole revealed nothing unusual except that the wind was NOT blowing with much force. The moonlit seas were serene, and no wind could be felt. "Hmmmm. That's odd." A shrug of the shoulders indicated that the howling was accepted as a freakish whim of nature. A bare two minutes after it ceased I heard a dog yipping. "But that is impossible! The is no dog out here." Curiosity soon overpowered me, so I walked out on deck. The yipping stopped, and I heard nothing but the gentle flow of the northerly current trickling into the night. I took a complete turn about the decks, chattered briefly with the man on watch and returned to my cabin. Almost immediately the howling was renewed. I was perplexed but once more shrugged it off. The howling persisted, however. Being unable to concentrate on my book I again went on deck. Nothing! I loitered several minutes and still heard nothing. Defeated, I returned to the cabin. Five minutes passed. Ten minutes. I began to relax. At the same moment I leaped to my feet with a start as the howling resumed a third time. "It's coming from somewhere near this cabin. By God, I'm going to locate it this time if it takes all night." Cautiously I made my way to the wheelhouse, passed through the starboard hatch and began to walk aft. Sure enough, that moaning wail was at work this time! As I walked toward the radio room, it grew fainter. I retraced my steps to the starboard corner of the cabin where the noise, whatever it might be, was intensified. Pressing my ear close to the deck I was rewarded with partial success. The forward engine room ventilators emerged from the deck near the rear of the cabin, and it was through here that the groans were rising. I scurried to the engine room, walked forward and entered the machine shop. There, making rings from scraps of metal, were two of the crew. They were "turning down" their jewelry on a lathe which was making the groans, moans, howls, and yips that had escaped to haunt me. When they had stopped to examine the products of their endeavors, it had been at those precise moments that I had chosen to inaugurate my searches!

After living with and becoming accustomed to continuous noise, I noticed that a sudden exposure to silence can become downright eerie. The lack of generator combustion at sea, for example, causes a ghostly atmosphere in the engine room of a lightship. This equipment is stopped every night at midnight, if it appears to be running normally, to have the oil checked. If the standby is not placed in operation at this time, electricity is received from the ship's storage batteries. The generator, reduced gradually in speed, is slowly brought to a complete stop. Multiple noises, previously drowned by the generator, spring to life. Water gently slaps against the hull on both sides. The main light timer clacks from the fidley. A boiler motor hums softly. Hot water gurgles in the tank. A TV converter whirs scratchily as it changes electrical current from DC to AC. Wind whistles and moans through the rigging. One becomes aware of a strange panicky emptiness. Footsteps of the man checking machinery trod heavily on deck plates. Men chat without hollering. The uncanny stillness lasts for about five minutes, and it actually is a marked relief to hear the generator back in operation.

Much the same experience is felt in port, during the first few hours when all machinery and electronics are secured. The crew say it's fun, though, getting oriented to peace and quiet.

Chapter IV

"Fog"

Of all the scourge of the sea, fog is by far the most contemptible. On the lightship *LV 511* (*Buzzards* Lightship station near Cape Cod, MA) sailors learned to distrust for more than the dreaded southwest wind – detested its influx. It was an unwelcome visitor. It became a hated arch-enemy. Most preferred the hoisting of storm warnings to the invasion of fog, which was cursed more than any other single object, condition or person.

There are several types of fog, several known causes for its formation and various reasons why it was so unpopular. First, then, let us deal with types of fog.

Dense or "Pea Soup" Fog

Dense or "pea soup" fog, the kind proverbially sliced with a knife, is the most accepted, recognized and understood. There can be no mistake when one is encompassed in the swirls of this form; you know you're in fog. Out there on the lightship station, this dense fog enveloped us completely. It was never so compact that one couldn't see the bow of the ship from the stern, but you couldn't see much further than perhaps the length of the ship. Only on a couple of nights was the stern greatly obscured when one looked aft from the wheelhouse. Those were abnormal conditions. The "soupy" fog, however, for all practical purposes, cloaks one entirely, day or night. It hides everything but moisture. At night, deck lights cast grotesque shadows, and encountering a shipmate on deck is similar to encountering an apparition.

We were alone out there on station, a tiny blob upon a great ocean. Occasionally, during this type of fog, there was a southwesterly swell, but the seas were seldom rough. A combination of the two can be particularly maddening. When you curse the motion of the ship, your voice is drowned by the roar of the fog horn. Conversely, if you curse the unbearable sound, a tilting deck may throw you off balance. If lucky, you might land against a bulkhead; if not, you might stumble over a chair, a table, or a deck fitting. Then you curse at both elements. A person has to learn to channel energy into something constructive. But, it's not always easy.

Soupy fog is definite in its characteristics. When it exists, it is everywhere. When it leaves, it disappears completely. It may return, but will do so as a body. It does not disintegrate to a point and then mold together again. Ordinarily the sun cannot be seen through this type of fog except when at or near its highest point in the sky. This is not the only time the "soup" becomes thin enough to lessen in texture. Otherwise, when it disburses, it leaves abruptly. The line of demarcation between it and good weather is distinct.

Those aboard willingly accept their lot when weather conditions envelop the ship. The horn is the lifeline, protection against huge vessels that may be bearing down on the lightship. Of course, it is distracting and wears on the nerves, but it is acknowledged, to a man, as a necessary safety factor. Radar is far from a cure-all, as collisions between new modern vessels equipped with radar have occurred. The horn, then, was our main protection. It served as a protection to others as well, and a cautious mariner will grope along, listening for our blast to verify his position. Unfortunately, mariners are not always cautious or wise.

Ground or Layer Fog

The second type of fog, for want of a better name, is "ground" or "layer" fog. This can be divided into two branches, one a low layer hugging the water and the other a thin layer suspended a few feet above the water. The former is the more common.

Layer fog is found primarily on cold nights that follow warm days. It is a close relative of water vapor that forms when air temperatures dip well below the temperature of the water, and is the coldest of the types. During periods of low layer fog, masts of ships often appear as floating perpendicular sticks without a base until the rest of the superstructure ultimately emerges.

Fog of this type frequently as observed on the *Buzzards* station. We saw the flash of the Gay Head Lighthouse on Martha's Vineyard, ten miles away, and the red topped antenna poles in Mattapoisett on the Massachusetts mainland, twenty miles away, all the while squinting unsuccessfully through binoculars for a buoy two miles from our ship's station.

When a stratum of layer fog lies on the water, a land-lubber, safely ashore, might think a night completely devoid of fog. To him, the twinkling of starlight available to his untrained ayes might lull him into a false sense that the weather is clear. Even if he is looking seaward, the lights of large vessels may come into sight, and he would assume that the night were perfectly clear, without a trace of fog. He would be only partly correct, for the fog would be upon the water!

Although the mainland was visible when layer for surrounded our ship, the fog signal was placed in operation for the benefit of small craft. Anyone who has ever been at sea in a small boat under theses conditions can well appreciate the comfort such a signal provides. The sailor is reassured at the sound, and sometimes might even become convinced that he indeed is a great navigator. "There I was," he might relate later to a disinterested acquaintance, "in my little boat and the fog shut in tight! And do you know what? I hit the lightship right on the nose!" We are not specifically opposed to using our fog horn during periods of layer fog because we know it's of short duration. We do not even dignify it by classifying it as a nuisance. It invariably dissipates before the warming sun and soon vanishes.

The second branch of layer fog is that which remains suspended a few feet above water. This type is rare. I saw it only twice when I was on the lightship. It is an actual layer of cloud likened to smoke emitting from a train or a chimney on a windy day when it is blown horizontally. When observed aboard the *Buzzards*, the water was uncovered for many miles, and the nearest buoys could be easily seen. The hull of a freighter two miles away was clearly sighted, but the superstructure of the vessel was not visible. The mainland and the top of Cuttyhunk Island loomed boldly. Thus we had two extremes, top and bottom in view, but not the narrow belt in the middle. The life expectancy of this particular form of fog is short. It passes so quickly one wonders if he has actually witnesses it.

Haze

A third type of fog is haze. We called it "halo" fog or "discouraging" fog. It resembled a huge halo as viewed from the *Buzzards*, with the ship being in the center of a perfectly clear area of four-to-six miles, that area, in turn, being surrounded by a wide band of haze, or fog. It was discouraging because it lingered and aggressively refused to leave. When Cuttyhunk Island, 4.6 miles to the east, no longer was visible from our ship, we turned on the foghorns. It was most exasperating to assume viability to be 4.5 miles, the final tenth of a mile being held prisoner by the haze. It meant the difference between shutting off the blasted horns and being compelled to endure them.

Haze may linger for several days, particularly during summer and autumn. Never completely obscuring, it impedes vision somewhat less drastically than other types of fog. It can make solo visits, or it can bring along a companion – a southwest wind. Smoky southwesters are common to the northeast section of the country and are miserable to endure aboard an unsheltered lightship. Haze without wind is bad enough, for it means that the fog signal must be sounded. With a violent pitching due to wind, it becomes even more disheartening.

On such days it would appear, at first glance, that the visibility was fair-to-good. However, you cannot see the shoreline or familiar landmarks lying just beyond the fringe. It's maddening. Looking through an open porthole on the second deck, and it seems as if you can see for miles.

"Why, I can almost see Cuttyhunk. By golly, of course I do. Or is it a figment of my imagination? No, of course not. There it is!" The man on watch is accused of not paying attention.

"What's the matter? Are you falling asleep? Can't you see Cuttyhunk yet? Do you think we want to listen to those damn horns forever? Here, let me take the binoculars. I'll show you."

Eyes were strained in vain. There was nothing to see except the disappearance of water as it faded into the haze.

"Well, you're right. I thought I saw it, but I must have been mistaken."

When this type of fog finally leaves, it may be for days or it may be for mere moments. Many times a joyous watchman has phoned the engine room to discontinue the air compressor because the fog cleared. A few minutes later the same man, now disconsolate, requests resumption of pressure. The fog returned. There is nothing more cheerless than the dreary reactivation of a foghorn before it has had time to stop vibrating. The crew sometimes referred to haze as a female fog because "it can't make up its mind." It leaves and returns, leaves, stays little longer, returns again. Indecision is one of its irritating traits.

Reasons for Fog

There are several known causes for the formation of fog. It may form when warm air, sufficiently high in vapor content, flows over water or land that is cooler than the air. The reverse sometimes occurs when very cold air lies just above warm water or land areas. It can be by the cooling of the earth's surface throughout the night. This is more common over land than over water. Radiation fog, when mixed with smoke, can cause smog that is so common in some of the larger cities. Another way in which fog is created is when warm, moist air moves from low to high altitudes and becomes sufficiently cooled in the process. Still another is rain falling through cool air that has high vapor content.

Two Aids for the Mariner

Before launching into a discussion of the reasons why fog was unpopular, it's necessary to note our defense against the element. We called it a defense because we were living aboard a ship located in harm's way. The *Buzzards* station was strategically located at the western entrance to Buzzards Bay to provide the mariner with a means of determining his position by our fog signal when visual signals were obscured by inclement weather. Whether the signals were considered an aid or a defense depended on where one was situated, that is, on the lightship or on another vessel. Regardless of the point of view, there were two such signals on a lightship, radio-beacons and fog horns.

Radio beacons were the most valuable of the fog signals. Beacons of the type on the *Buzzards* had a transmitting power capable of being heard from fifty to one hundred fifty miles.

For station identification, most beacons transmitted a Morse signal (combinations of dots and dashes) which was heard on radio direction finders of other vessels. Direction finders were instruments used to determine the direction from which a signal originated, and by obtaining a signal from several different radio beacons a mariner was able to fix his position on a chart. Radio beacons operated continuously, day and night, clear weather and during fog.

The following warning was quoted from the Coast Guard Light list:

"Caution must be used in approaching radio beacons on radio bearings [All Coast Guard radio beacons have been discontinued and replaced by more accurate electronic aids to navigation], and care must be taken to set course to pass safely clear. The risk of collision will be avoided by insuring that the radio bearing does not remain constant. This caution is applicable to those lightships and stations on submarine sites which are passed close to."

Unfortunately, this warning sometimes was unheeded by a careless mariner, and danger of collision was possible. On some occasions mariners remained on a constant bearing until the last possible moment, changing course barely in time to avert a disaster. Ships passed close to the *Buzzards* in bad weather, much too close for comfort or safety. This sobering occurrence was experienced by most men who served on a lightship.

Second in importance (but first in distraction to those on board) is the fog horn. Ours was a triplex diaphragm type which produced a chime signal by means of compressed air. The fog signal was distinguished from others by its assigned characteristics, such as tone, type and number of sound emissions, and intervals of time between these emissions. Fog signals on lightships provided a designated number of blasts and silent periods each minute to provide identification, much as different flashes identify lighthouses from each other. This data was obtained from a chart or Light List of the area to which a lightship was assigned.

On the *Buzzards* we listened to the horn eighteen seconds out of every minute the signal operated. It sounded in groups of two blasts every twenty seconds. There was a three second blast, a silent period of two seconds, another three second blast and then a silent period of twelve seconds. From there the cycle repeated itself, over and over and over. During a twenty-four hour period of thick weather the horn actually bombarded the crew a total of seven hours and twelve minutes.

Should both the starboard and port horns have become inoperative at the same time, the ship's bell was used as a standby signal., Strokes on the bell were manually sounded in groups of two every thirty seconds.

The Light List provides several warnings to mariners concerning the audibility of fog signals.

"Caution, Mariners are cautioned that the hearing of fog signals cannot be implicitly relied upon. Experience indicates that distance must not be judged only by the intensity or apparent direction of the sound. Occasionally there may be areas close to a fog signal in which it is not heard, and, that the mariner must not assume that a fog signal is not operating because he does not hear it. Fog may exist not far from a station, and yet not be seen from it, and that, therefore, the signal may not be in operation."

The influx of fog in our immediate vicinity was always dreaded for a variety of reasons: the feeling of being isolated from the world, the grating and constant sound of the horns, and the ever constant danger of collision.

Isolation

While on board for our customary twenty-eight day tours, we realized and accepted our isolation from civilization. But, when fog set in, the operation seemed more extreme, and it was difficult to take.

We began to feel hemmed in, shunned by the outside world. A claustrophobic person would be very uncomfortable in this situation. One could not see the mainland or any of the islands. Aircraft could sometimes be heard but not seen. We saw no boats or ships except for the few that passed close by and were quickly gone. At times we couldn't even see the sky or the sun or the clouds. We saw nothing but ourselves, our ship, and a minute portion of the Atlantic ocean.

Occasionally a gull's wings came into view, hoping for a morsel of food. That's it. That's all we saw! We were indeed locked in a closet, with strict limitations of freedom and movement.

We walked along the deck looking seaward, or we gazed dejectedly through a porthole. The same sights were out there -- fog and water, nothing more. During periods of fog, we watched through the portholes more than at any other time, as though some great unseen force was drawing us.

Hour after hour passes and a sailor continues his frequent vigil at a porthole. How we longed for a view of the mainland. A glimpse of anything would be so welcome! We realized how grand, after all, to be able to see lights and land and objects. On clear nights the beach appeared so tantalizingly close, and yet it was a forbidden fruit and we became morose. How lovely to be able to have that feeling right now, if only the damned fog would go away – fog and water, water and fog. Let's go on deck. We'll be able to see better. No, that gray blanket still persists – fog and water, water and fog.

This segregation became depressing. Our ability to think was dulled. Our concept of life was lusterless. We became spiritless. Constructive thinking was relegated to the dark recesses of our mind. Fog, fog, fog. If we were ashore, we could have gone someplace. We could have talked to somebody different. We wouldn't experience this acute craving for a change of scenery. Out here we talked to the same old shipmates. We could go from the main deck to the second or third decks and back again. Tiring of this, we walked from bow to stern, covering an overall distance of one hundred twenty-nine feet and nine inches. Ship's work continued unenthusiastically. During off-hours we wrote to our families or acquaintances, but our letters were vague and poorly worded. Some read, but remembered little of it. A few watched television, unimpressed, or listened to the radio, discovering no joy in what was heard. Besides, the radio beacons interfered with television and radio reception. The television screen flickered, the picture became slightly distorted, and a scratching noise was clearly audible, all at the beginning of each coded groups being transmitted by the beacon. The radio became a receiver of beacon tones. Dit-dar-dit-dit, thirty times a minute every minute. It jumbles the program. If only the fog would lift, our spirits would surge. Fog and water. Fog is everywhere – infiltrating our very souls. The outside world? Where was it? It must have been there, but certainly we couldn't see it. We remained locked in our closet. We busied ourselves in work or a personal; project, trying to forget our enforced isolation. But we did not forget, as we continued to look through a porthole, hoping, hoping.

Distressing Sounds

The fog signals are the most distressing elements aboard ship. Although the horn possesses the greater influence, the continuous transmittal of radio beacon signals also becomes wearisome. The first few hours are insignificant in their effect. The first twenty-four hours, in fact, didn't seem to be a bother. Beyond that, the constant dit-dar-dit-dit, dit-dar-dit-dit, dit-dar, dit-dit begins to assert itself. It became offensive to the man on watch in the radio room. It became objectionable to those who would like to hear a radio. The exasperating interference brought minds sharply into focus only to the fog that still encompassed the ship.

This irritation is mild, however, to that produced by the great booming sound of the foghorn. If you ever stood on a pier and heard the harsh resounding signal of a ship about to leave for sea, you probably were startled. If you can picture six such blasts every minute of the hour, a few feet away, you will have some idea of what it's like on a lightship during periods of fog.

The first such blast is always startling, even to the man who turns on the switch. He knows when it will begin its series of blasts, yet tenses and jumps ever so slightly when it first sounds. To those unaware, the initial blast can be frightening. A man painting, for example, invariably takes a longer stroke with his brush or dips it deeper into the can. A man writing will break the pencil lead or leave an undisciplined line on the paper. On one occasion a cook, walking aft toward the galley, timed the initial roar of the horn with an acrobatic toss of a pan of potatoes. A man walking along the main deck involuntarily expedites his pace as though suddenly feeling a sharp object jutting into the seat of his trousers. A sleeping man is aroused instantaneously in beads of sweating terror. His head swiftly leaves his pillow, and his nerves are a confusion of activity as he becomes rudely aware of the horn.

Being exceptionally fond of fresh air, I slept with two portholes open. One faced in the direction of the foghorn platform twelve feet aft and ten feet higher than the cabin. Here the piercing effect of the horn is most ear shattering of all. When first assigned to the vessel, I knew not what to expect and twice was taken by surprise. The noise exploded with a dreadful detonation, and I am quite sure L left the bed, horizontally, at least six inches. Whether it was fright or repercussion, I'll never know. It was devastating. It was terrifying. I leaped up, closed the portholes tightly and buried by head in a pillow. The clamor followed and clung tenaciously. My heart beat faster, my blood pressure soared, my eardrums vibrated. Sleep was gone, never to return the remainder of the night.

I soon became used to the invasions of fog and learned to barricade myself from the sound of the horns. The compressor that furnished air for the diaphragms became my ally. When the man on watch in the radio room wished to place the horn in operation, he first had to telephone the engine room for air pressure. The engineer on watch then started the compressor and telephoned the radio room. When an adequate amount of pressure was reached, the horns began. This process consumed about five minutes. I always woke up at the sound of the compressor starting and, after the first couple of times, knew what to do. I would instantly leap out of bed, close the portholes, make certain the doors to the cabin were shut, and insert cotton in my ears (an ample supply being kept available for such times. This defense had its drawbacks, however, for the muffled sound still penetrated the cotton, and I never was able to sleep well under those conditions. The supply of fresh air was drastically reduced, and the room became warm, uncomfortable and stuffy. On warm nights I moved to the wardroom with a pillow and blanket to sleep on the built-in cushions. They were constructed in a sweeping arc to conform to the contour of the ship, and I had to sleep in a similar curved position. Fresh air was obtainable, however, and the discomforts of the wardroom were preferable to those of my cabin.

The crew's berthing space was directly beneath the foghorns. There was a deck hatch above this space, normally kept open for ventilation. The clamor of the horns boomed through this opening to disrupt the sleep of the sleeping crew. On many foggy nights, particularly at the onset of the swirling mist, a white skivvies-clad figure could be seen in motion, frantically closing the hatch to muffle the sound. There were no sound proof bulkheads, however, and the great jarring noises continued, although slightly dulled. A few of the men sleep restlessly, and one or two catnapped, but others found sleep beyond reach. Bunk lights came on, magazines were brought out, and the unhappy night wore on.

Most of us never became completely adjusted to the foghorns at night. Men tossed and turned in bed. Their eyelids sagged. They almost recaptured sleep and then they were suddenly wide awake. The horns wailed on. The night moved slowly. The watch changed.

"What, are you still awake?"

"Yeah. Those damned horns keep me from getting to sleep!"

A glance at another bunk revealed a second sleepless body.

"You awake, too?"

"Yes. Isn't it ever going to clear up?"

Quiet again crept over the bunkroom. It was quiet, that is, except for the insistent chatter of the horn. BEEEE— OOOH. Silence. BEEEE—OOOH. Slowly, ever so slowly the night continued. Sleep did not come. It was snatched away by the signals blasting in the darkness. Thoughts drifted to home. They were interrupted. They returned fleetingly only to be scattered again. The horn will not be denied. Seconds were counted. A three second blast. Two seconds of silence. A three second blast.

"Ah! Now we'll have peace and quiet – for twelve seconds!.. ten, eleven, twelve. BEEEE—OOOH! There we go again. Damn, I wish I could get to sleep!"

It's also interesting to note that sleeping men were awakened just as suddenly by the silence of a horn when it's secured as by the occasion of its first blast.

The intense sound produced by these horns, even though received with a consenting mind, is totally accepted. We did, however, adhere to the philosophy that it was better to live uncomfortably than not to live at all. It was far better to lose sleep than to become involved in a collision with another ship. Then, too, we were doing our job of playing a prominent role in assisting mariners who were navigating in the area.

The dreadful roar had its daytime effect as well, and it did not take long to set ones nerves on edge. It preyed on the mind and attacked the power of concentration. It was upsetting to all forms of activity.

The first blasts would be accepted with a nonchalant shrug of the shoulders.

"Well, I guess we'll have the horns for awhile," was followed by a glance through a porthole to try to determine the probable duration. Everyone would go about his duties with no appreciable change of attitude, for the noise had not yet become a challenge to the senses. An oft repeated query, to which there was no tangible answer, was "I wonder how long they'll be on?" One hoped for an optimistic reply, but who could possibly know how long the fog would remain?

In a couple of hours the crew became conscious of the perseverance of the fog signal. By now it grated on our nerves. One always hoped the fog, and signal, wouldn't last too much longer. Still it persisted, and the terrible constant noise became very disconcerting. You had to try developing enough interest in an activity to offset the paralyzing effect it could have on the mind. You could not allow the horns to dominate you. You had to stop thinking about it. "Ah, but how wonderful it will be when the fog leaves and it's quiet once more!"

The horns reached their maximum volume at the entrance to the wheelhouse (bridge). If the door was opened while the horn was blowing, the vibration was felt as well as heard. The sound flowed through the open door and then could go no further than the bulkheads inside. There it bounced off and cam back out only to be met at the open door and driven inside again as a whirling dervish. The sound was incredibly piercing. Papers on the chart table fluttered, the binnacle cover rattled, handrails vibrated and one has a moment of near panic as the door to the bridge was hurriedly closed. Should a second blast follow before this could be accomplished, the blast reverberated around, over, under, on and through the wheelhouse. It was without doubt the noisiest explosion of sound one experienced aboard the *Buzzards* lightship. Vibrations were felt on the arms, the legs, and the eardrums. It was not a pleasing sensation.

On the main deck, we waited for the second blast of a series, and then scampered to our destination. If we lingered for any reason, we covered our ears with our hands, the forefingers tightly pressed into our ears. One didn't loiter. One remained on deck only if something required immediate attention. If repairs, or necessary work, were to be accomplished in this sector, we used cotton as a protective and muffling agent. The men presented a ludicrous appearance indeed, with a stream of cotton protruding from each side of their head. In the radio room, on the main deck behind the foghorn platform, the noise was resounding to a somewhat lesser degree. It was especially irksome when testing electronic gear, monitoring other stations, working the radio or synchronizing time clocks. The noise from the horn platform drowned out everything else. Radio dispatches, unless repeated, were received with great difficulty. The several tests of electronic and monitoring schedules were superimposed with a tremendous wail of foghorn outbursts. How could anyone remain composed with such blasts in the ear?

Below deck the tone was somewhat subdued in comparison, but still the sound permeates, of that there was no question. Vibrations were not so apparent, but the wail was unmistakable. It became pervasive. It intervened in every form of normal living. We became adjusted to speaking in one of two ways. We learned to shout at one another, and even then we were forced to repeat what we'd said. The most satisfactory method of conversing during fog was with the "interrupted – wait a second" method. In this manner we spoke in a normal tone, stopped at the exact beginning of a foghorn blast, and then when the signal was quiet, continued as though nothing had happened. Sometimes it was stop and go several times before a full sentence was completed. It was less nerve wracking this way; every party to a conversation knows when a sentence was finished and realized that nothing was lost in the exchange.

The uninterrupted din wore on the nerves more and more. Steadily you became less and less unruffled until finally you could not listen and longer. "God, I wish we could secure that [blankety-blank] horn!" You curse the noise and the fog and the ship and your lot. "By – –, I'll sure be happy to get ashore this time on my leave." The horns continued. The sound dimmed your enthusiasm for the everyday routine of life aboard a lightship. It traveled with you everywhere you went, form compartment to compartment, from deck to deck. On the verge of becoming irrational a peace of mind swept over us, and we stopped thinking about the horns and sought relief in being constructive.

Suddenly we became aware that something had drastically changed. Then we heard the dying pulsations of the air compressor, and we realized the horns had been discontinued. The silence was strange, golden. We smiled. We were human again. We stopped shouting. We talked without interruptions. Morale was restored. Life continued. The routine went on. You felt differently toward it and became inspired with freedom from noise. It was strange, too, that shortly upon cessation of the horns the trying conditions under which we had existed were soon forgotten. The memory of the discomfort of the sound failed to linger more than a few moments. We were at peace again, with ourselves, with our fellow man.

The horns provided several amusing and interesting incidents. There was the time an electronics technician tested our horns at the Coast Guard base in Boston on a quiet serene afternoon. The sudden booming noise echoed loudly as it bounced off nearby buildings. Immediately many windows were raised, and peering inquisitive faces appeared. While a minor annoyance to the lightship crew, the test had given unsuspecting residents an awesome jolt. Clem, our senior cook for fifteen months who "just didn't like the sound of foghorns," said the noise and the vibration were so great that afternoon it knocked packages of spaghetti off the shelves of the Hanover Street markets.

Fear of Collision

The third and most disturbing result of fog was the real possibility of collision, a potential danger recognized by all. Rarely a topic of discussion other than at "abandon ship" or "collision" drills, the sole exception was when a ship glided by closely without reducing speed. Then the situation was openly evaluated – pros and cons heard in detail.

Assuming we were struck by a freighter or a tanker, what chance for survival would we have? Our ship certainly was not unsinkable. Lightships have been rammed and sunk before. Even vessels having complex systems of watertight integrity are vulnerable. The luxury liner *Andrea Doria* was sunk by a single blow, and a single blow was all that was necessary to sink our lightship. We realized that, and undoubtedly our primary contention would have been a fight for survival. It is doubtful that our ship could have survived even a glancing collision. It was a question of how long she could remain afloat. Probably not long enough to launch lifeboats. Probably not long enough to bring the wounded out of the engine room or lower decks. We would have tried, of course, but most likely we would have a chance only to gather a life jacket and leap into the water. We might have been able to release life rafts. Then it would be a question of survival. What if the accident occurred during winter with the thermometer below freezing? What if seas were running high? What if fog, rain, snow or sleet prevented a rescue ship from spotting us? How long could one survive in a storm-tossed ocean?

We prepared for such an emergency by holding frequent collision and abandon ship drills. Each man was assigned a duty that he had to be able to perform perfectly. Discipline was a necessity during any emergency, and drills ensured that the men were prepared. When holding collision drills on the lightship, we first made certain that all hands were on the weather deck. Realizing that the time the ship remained afloat may be limited if struck, it was most important to make sure that no one was trapped below. In a typical drill, the ship's emergency alarm was sounded several times. The man sounding the alarm shouted "Collision!" and word was passed throughout the ship as men scurried to their assigned places. They grabbed a life jacket, put it on as they raced topside, and mustered in double ranks on the stern near the dory. A man was issued an individual life jacket the day he came aboard. It was to his keep and care for as long as he was attached to the ship. Life vests, Indian orange in color to be easily seen, were equipped with safety straps, a whistle, and a one-celled flashlight. After the muster and all hands were accounted for, the men assumed their assigned duties for action that would save the ship, unless it was apparent it could not be saved. The crew practiced shoring and bracing bulkheads, pumping flooded compartments, and sealing holes in the hull of the ship. Every man was expected to know the location of each item of damage control equipment and how to use it.

A collision drill usually was followed by orders to "abandon ship." Each man went quickly to the boat to which he was assigned. We had rafts in addition to lifeboats, one on each side of the ship.

There were several instances, recorded in our log, when ships passed close aboard during fog. They ranged from twenty foot pleasure craft to four hundred foot commercial vessels. Sailboats swept so closely around our stern that their rigging brushed our flagstaff. An inbound fishing boat passed within twenty feet during an early evening in September of 1955. The fog was extremely thick at the time, practically zero visibility, yet the engines of the fisherman were carrying him to port as quickly as possible. He appeared out of nowhere and was gone almost immediately as we listened for, but could not detect, his foghorn.

Mariners are expected to use prudence during periods of low visibility. Unfortunately, some were careless, while others were over-confident. This always brings to mind a quote made by a chief boatswain's mate noted for his vast knowledge of seamanship. He said, "There are old skippers and there are bold skippers, but there are no old, bold skippers."

Two Close Calls

Two close calls involving vessels capable of cutting our ship in half served to emphasize the necessity of an efficient watch and to broaden the realization of our position as a potential unwilling target.

At 3:00 P.M. on the afternoon of May 16, 1956, Louis Schaefer, a seaman from Haddonfield, New Jersey, had the radio room watch. Five of us were changing into dress uniforms, for the buoy tender *White Sage* was expected in half an hour to take the liberty party ashore. The remainder of the crew was busy below deck.

At 3:10 P.M. Schaefer knocked excitedly at the door to my cabin. "Skipper, he reported, "there's a large ship around here that's getting closer and closer. I can hear its horn but can't see the ship, and it seems to be getting awfully close."

I ordered him to alert the crew instantly. Within seconds everybody was on deck, and many anxious eyes peered into the fog. We stood on the bow, and the horn of an approaching vessel confirmed his report. There was indeed a big one out there, and she was getting mighty close to us. Her signal dueled with our own foghorn. We strained our eyes, trying to glimpse this monster bearing down on us. It was not necessary to strain our ears. We not only heard the horn but also the echo of our own blasts reverberating off her hull. Often, before and after, we have received an echo from passing ships whose steel construction caused our signal to return to us.

We maintained our nervous vigil for seven or eight minutes until, at 3:18 P.M., a three hundred foot gray hulk appeared. A moment later it was directly off our bow, no more than a ship's length away, a modern military vessel. Crew members on deck showed much interest in us. They were clearly outlined along the starboard rail, for their ship was headed northeastward. They passed directly over, or nearly so, the spot where our own anchor dug into the bottom seventy feet down. We were riding at the five shot mark that day, a length of four hundred and fifty feet.

We exchanged glances with one another and with the men on the other ship. We did not wave to the members of the gray vessel, for we saw no humor in the situation. The navigator had committed the unpardonable sin. He had homed in on our horn. True, the pilot had his ship under control, but several hundred feet is not a great distance at sea. We had performed our own duties to the best of our ability and had used our foghorn as a guide for all shipping interests. We did not, however, appreciate any pilot who allowed his vessel to remain on a course directly towards us until the last split second when he barely had room in which to maneuver.

Much more terrifying is a similar situation occurring in the blackness of a fog-shrouded night. If sound is infinitely more difficult to hear in fog, seeing becomes a virtual impossibility, and both are compounded in darkness.

On July 27, 1956, two days after the sinking of the *Andrea Doria*, I was asleep in my cabin. I awakened with a start and glanced at my watch with the luminous dial. It was fifteen minutes after midnight. I sensed that something was amiss. I was shaking, although the night was warm. I got out of bed to look through my screened port. The fog was impenetrable, and there were no horns operating! I grabbed the sound-powered phone and called the radio room. As the man on watched answered, I heard the beginning strains of the air compressor swinging into action. Simultaneously I heard the roar of a foghorn off our port bow.

"Why aren't the horns on?" I asked with a shout.

"The fog just came in, Captain, ane we're fixing to put them on right away," was the answer.

"Do you hear that ship off our bow?"

"Yes sir, I do. I'm going on deck now."

I slammed the phone back onto the receptacle, dressed hastily, raced outside and peered into the inky darkness. I could see nothing but eddies of wet fog and the beams of our main light as it flashed on and off. The bellow of a foghorn off our port bow was repeated. A strong tide held our bow into the southwest. That meant the ship was coming from seaward and would therefore pass us closely as practicable in order to have a good point of departure as he headed east into Buzzards Bay. At this point our own horns were ready, and it was a colossal relief to hear them. They were like beautiful inspiring music, and how pleasant they sounded. Again I heard the horn to port, and it electrified me.

"Nothing shows on radar, Captain," the watch announced.

Well, no matter. It wouldn't help much anyway. We gazed intently toward the direction of the sound. We saw nothing. Fog swirled. Our foghorns boomed their warning blasts. The suspense was eerie. The incoming ship sounded her horn. Deceptively it seemed to be at our side.

"God," I thought, "she can't miss us." I ran to the alarm lever at the outer bulkhead of the cabin, intending to arouse the crew and get them to the main deck. "This is what we have been drilling for. This is the real thing. I wonder where she will hit us. How long will we stay afloat? Damn! What a night for this to happen!" Numerous thoughts raced through my brain during those few terse seconds. Did I hear a great clanging of bells and a grinding of gears? Is my imagination playing tricks? Are the men on the other ship aware of the drama about to take place?

As my hand touched the lever, a great mass of lights came into view. In that instant I could tell she would miss us. The alarm was not sounded. The ship slithered by, a scant hundred yards away. Distance is deceiving on the water, and doubly so at night. Maybe the vessel merely looked huge, and maybe it was two hundred yards off instead of a hundred. The pilot, if he were concerned, showed it in no way. He did not slack speed, and the vessel passed from view as quickly as it had emerged. It happened in a matter of minutes, perhaps seconds, but I shall always remember it.

On shaky knees I returned to my cabin where I undressed with trembling hands. I admit that I prayed that night. I offered my thanks to God for saving the ship and my crew.

On a less serious note we occasionally became the middle of a tiny city of lights and activity. For reasons known only to those aboard, there were a few times when cabin cruisers, sailboats, fishermen and larger seagoing vessels lingered nearby our vessel waiting for a break in the weather. Our foghorn had a merry time as it became the center of attraction. We had a warm, friendly feeling for those craft, for we knew they were paying attention while we were doing our job. Besides, it was nice to have company for a change.

We have heard tell that lightship sailors who have experienced a particularly foggy tour will continue to talk with a "hitch" after going ashore. That is, talk for the length of time between blasts and then, out of habit, stop when the expected blast is to begin.

Chapter V

"Christmas"

Christmas 1955

Christmas on the *Buzzards* was ushered by twenty-five mile per hour southerly winds with seven foot swells from the same direction. The wind had been increasing steadily since noon of the previous day. The barometer was dropping. Seas were growing. We were on the move, as usual, but only to the motion of ocean and wind. It was like being on a seesaw as the ship rode up and down on an ocean top that alternately rose and fell. We had music, too - the sound of the wind as it twisted and ranted through the rigging.

The previous few days had been pleasant. We made it that way ourselves, for it was the Christmas season. The elements had been kind. Except for a few hours of fog on December 22nd, the wind had been at rest, the sea calm, the visibility excellent. Our cheerfulness had been ruffled fleetingly during that fog when, at 1413 hours, a freighter passed one hundred yards astern, heading north at full bore, obviously in a hurry to reach port for Christmas. Rashness such as that, during thick fog, perturbed us greatly, for the slightest misjudgment on the part of a pilot's calculations could mean instant death to an entire lightship crew. It is doubtful if the freighter's navigator was wished a Merry Christmas that year by anybody aboard the *Buzzards*.

The holiday season had been brightened in a number of ways. William Sherman had returned from liberty on the 15th and was destined to remain aboard during Christmas and New Year's. He had been back several days, gradually working back into the routine of sea life again, before he opened his cloth ditty bag he always carried when traveling.

Taking out an assortment of clean clothing, writing material, toothpaste and soap, he discovered a large green stocking, crammed with candy, fruit, chewing gum, and "silly stuff to draw a laugh" as he termed it. He had been unaware of his surprise as his mother had concealed it between the clothing. The rest of the crew had as much fun as Sherman as they watched him unwrapping. They were, of course, awaiting their allotted portion, for it is the unwritten code of the sea that shipmates share their "pogie bait."

A mess deck table wore an artificial three foot Christmas tree adorned with ornaments and colored lights. It was illuminated at meal times and during the evening, its vivid blues, greens, reds, yellows, and orange generating much cheer as well as capturing much attention. It was beautiful at night with all other lights extinguished that might conflict with its eminence. The variegated coloring threw soft tones of overlaying patterns on the bulkheads. Its glow was warm, friendly, inspiring, if perhaps a bit lonely. It drew many spectators, for we huddled close by at every excuse, drinking coffee, talking, writing letters, or being absorbed in far away thoughts. It made our separation from home less severe, for it was something different - a variance from the cold uniformity of routine existence. Our tree was the single most valuable morale booster on board during those days.

The bulletin board in the recreation room radiated Christmas cheer with cards bearing holiday greetings. The seasonal verses were pleasure giving; their coloring brightened the awful sameness of the compartment.

Three days before Christmas we received mail. The forty-footer from Cuttyhunk Coast Guard station churned alongside to a joyous reception. The men from the island had been to the base at Woods Hole the day before, and thoughtfully remembered their floating neighbors. Fog closed in tightly shortly after their arrival, so they did not linger. With a wave of hands and a "Merry Christmas, everybody," they disappeared to the east. We tackled the mail bag. Letters from home! More greetings! Another package for someone! Human spirits skyrocketed.

The next morning our lookout spotted a gray blob approaching from the north. We knew instantly that our friend Arthur Denault was on his way from Westport Point. Excitement renewed, for Arthur would have more mail form us. How lucky we were! In this season of unpredictable weather we were accustomed to receiving mail only when the tender arrived, every two weeks. The Cuttyhunk boat had interrupted that schedule yesterday. Now, less than twenty-four hours later, we were receiving an encore! How extraordinary! How wonderful! We were not forgotten at all. Everyone was on deck to watch the approaching shape enlarge into the distinct outline of a boat, the *Bridgett Anne*. On and on she came. Now we could see Arthur standing at the wheel. The musical notes of his three-toned horn were captivating. An expert boat handler, he approached the starboard quarter at slow speed, a heaving line was passed, and willing hands hauled the mailbag aboard.

"Thanks, Arthur. Will you come aboard and have a cup of coffee?"

"No thanks, boys. I'm going to fish close to shore this morning. I thought you might enjoy a few more letters, though, so I came out here first. Boy, some of you fellows sure must be in love, judging from the amount of mail you get."

"We certainly appreciate your thoughtfulness, Arthur," we grinned.

"That's all right, boys. Glad to do it for you. I don't think I'll be out again until March, or early April. The weather's too uncertain this time of the year. I'm going sea clamming close to shore. Then if the weather gets bad, I'll be almost home."

"Good luck to you, then. We're certainly grateful for the many favors you've done us."

"O.K., boys. Well, Merry Christmas to you all." The popular fisherman waved, and a broad smile spread over his weatherbeaten face.

"Merry Christmas, Arthur," we responded somewhat sadly as the *Bridgett Anne* departed for the mainland.

Mail was distributed, and everyone retired to his favorite nook or cranny to read without interruption. After that, there was more "pogie bait" to be passed out. Sherman received a fruit cake from his aunt. Herbert Ressler was the recipient of a large box of cookies and candy from warm, sunny Miami. "Gee whiz," said somebody, "Christmas on a lightship isn't so bad after all."

A few telegrams arrived via radio. "Merry Christmas, son. Keeping the tree until you come home."... "Merry Christmas, honey. I love you. Please hurry home."... "we miss you. May your day be happy. Merry Christmas. Love from all."

Christmas Eve the wind shifted from a light northerly air to a fresh southerly breeze. The sky clouded to a full overcast; the lethargy of the sea changed to a growing restlessness.

After the usual movie, which ended at 7:20 P.M., I went to my cabin to read, for the fourth time, letters recently received. Feeling nostalgic, my thoughts naturally were of Christmas and family. I wanted to be as close as possible, and what better way than to retire to my room, alone, and reread the latest news from home with pictures of loved ones before me?

Thirty minutes later I heard a wheelhouse hatch, adjacent to my cabin, being opened quietly. A soft shuffling of feet followed, accompanied by muffled "shhhs." On the verge of challenging the intrusion, I recoiled to an incredibly unmelodious chanting. I broke into a cold sweat, chills ran down my spine, and my hair stood at attention. As a mixture of giggles interspersed the discordant vocal score, my fears liberated and I grinned appreciatively, for I knew what was happening. The crew were singing Christmas carols!

"Silent night. Holy night.
All is calm. All is bright."

The fellows were having sport, of course, but we all laughed, and the carolers were thanked for their enthusiastic performance.

66

Christmas Eve otherwise was like any other night at sea. Television programs carried a holiday theme, to be sure, but nothing else was different. The routine, the watches, the monotony, the wind were unchanged.

0648, Christmas morning: The foghorns began their outcries as all landmarks disappeared in a damp haze. The wind had shifted to the southwest, at twenty-seven knots. Swells of seven foot stature rolled endlessly from the south. A gray overcast greeted early morning viewers. Christmas day! I thought of home, wondering if the children were awake. Yes, of course they would be. What child wouldn't be wide-eyed with excitement early Christmas morning? I hoped they would be pleased with Santa's selections. I listened to the mournful horns for a few minutes. It was impossible to assemble any flowing continuity of thought, so I dressed leisurely and went below for breakfast.

"Merry Christmas, skipper," offered seaman Wheat as we met in a passageway.

"Merry Christmas, Wheat. Rather a noisy one out here."

'Yeah. That's the *Buzzards* station for you. If it isn't rough, it's foggy."

Exchanging pleasantries with the cook, I started to do justice to a plate of bacon, eggs, and toast as Chief Dean nursed a cup of coffee. Suddenly the air was rent with a deep sustained groan. The foghorn had stuck! Instead of the usual characteristics, the awful penetrating sound was continuous, and weakened only as the air supply diminished.

"Is it the horn mechanism or the radio beacon timer that's hung up?"

The radioman answered that for us with a thundering descent of the ladder as he announced, "The horns are stuck. It's not the radio beacon because I checked that."

"I'll get it, then," said Dean resignedly. "It's in the diaphragm, probably. I'll shift over to the other bank of horns." That did it, for the horns on the starboard side worked perfectly, and our usual signal again boomed into space.

"Well," observed Bob as he returned to his coffee. "There goes MY Christmas. It'll be a regular work day for the engineers. Ressler says there's a fuel leak in the port generator, and the switch in number one panel board won't work. I worked on the switch for an hour last night and couldn't do anything with it." He sighed, "I'll try again today, though."

Our Christmas was off to a good start - in reverse. Away from home, fog, wind, rough seas, three mechanical failures already. What next?

0815: Dean, Williams, and I went to the engine room and opened the electrical panel board. Luck was with us, for Williams noticed a loose screw and called it to the attention of Chief Dean.

"That doesn't seem right to me, Chief," he said. "Maybe it's nothing, but you can never tell."

"Yeah, working alone last night with a poor light I didn't see it." The screw was carefully tightened. "Let's see what happens now," he said as he tried the switch. It worked! One down, two to go.

"I'll get Sherman now and look at the foghorn," said Dean. "Got plenty of cotton in the sick bay, Cap, for earplugs?"

0843: More good luck. Land was seen by the lookout. With the annoying horns secured, Dean and Sherman would be able to work with far less irritation and much more efficiency.

1008: Small craft warnings were received and warning flags hoisted. With the westerly winds at thirty-five miles per hour, we had a moderate gale on our hands. The seas grew into impressive eight-footers. The ship pitched violently on a sea that was more white than green. The fog was gone, and a yellow sun broke through a clearing directly above.

Dean reported that a broken valve flange, undoubtedly caused by vibration, had allowed air to escape into the horns. This was the reason, then, for their continuous sounding. Moreover, the crack was such that repairs were not feasible, not on board. This meant that we would have to rely solely

68

on one set of horns. We also would have to notify the district office in Boston by radio and request that a new assembly be shipped as soon as possible.

1130: Still rough and windy. The sun shone brilliantly from a cold blue sky. The engineers announced that the leak in the generator had been repaired. They had been able to fabricate a new line between the fuel injection pump and the filter.

Thus, Christmas morning was history. The engineering log for that day carried a few modest entries that never could possibly describe the feelings of men trying to do a job under the most adverse of conditions. It would never detail the experience of disassembling, examining, and reassembling a heavy piece of equipment high on a metal platform that was in constant movement, up and down, back and forth, as the wind screamed from all corners and fingers ached with pain from the cold. It never would describe the feeling of working on an engine under the same conditions of movement, except that it was in the depths of an engine room where seas thudded against a thin hull a few feet away, grease and oil soiled clothing that made hands and tools slippery, and diesel fumes that tore at lungs and stomach as the men knelt on a steel deck with their heads at ridiculous angles. The "Bible" of the ship, containing a few crisp facts, nothing more, and only those directly involved would ever be aware of the exasperating details.

1200: Christmas dinner, an excellent contribution by Zom, our pocket novel cook. He spared nothing in his efforts to make the meal a pleasant affair. The tables sported green plastic covers of rough weather, the coloring poetically ideal. The traditional turkey served as a center piece on a table heaped with delicacies. It was attended by steaming dishes of dressing, mashed potatoes, mashed turnips, squash, boiled onions, creamed carrots, green peas, and brown gravy. Interjected in every available space were olives, celery, cranberry sauce, sweet mixed pickles, dill pickles, hot biscuits, and condiments. On another table were fruit, nuts, boxes of chocolates and ribbon candy donated by local merchants, plus pies, a huge chocolate cake with vanilla icing, cigars, and cigarettes. It was a banquet befitting kings.

Zom received an abundance of approval, attention, and verbal bouquets. "Good dinner, Zom.".... "Yeah, it's the best meal you ever put out.".... "Zom, you've made Christmas a real festive occasion for us." Zom's eyes twinkled, a winning smile covered his face, and his head was high and proud as he graciously accepted the avalanche of acclaim. After dinner, as a further gesture of gratitude, many hands helped clear the tables, wash dishes, and out away food, Zom not being permitted to lift a finger.

During the afternoon the crew loafed, slept, watched television, and in general, in the words of Sherman, "let their stomach's settle from an overcharge of chow." Two movies were shown, one at 2:00 P.M., the other at 5:30.

Post-dinner lounging invited specific thoughts of home. What a strange way to spend Christmas. Now, if I were home, I would.... Each of us possessed mental fantasies which were at work. They were personal, not to be shared with anyone. We thought of wives, children, parents, relatives, friends, neighbors, acquaintances. How were they enjoying Christmas? Were they thinking of us, on our miserable ship shaking off perpetual driving seas? Did they, too, hear the wind that was whistling, moaning, screaming at everything in its path? Oh, thank God they don't have to live this kind of life. It may be cold and windy at home, but they have an escape. The house does not toss and pitch. The white fireplace spreads warmth and comfort. The decorated tree reflects majestic splendor. Time, hurry up and fly! I know I am wishing part of my life away, but make the days speed into the past! I want to be home. There are so many things I want to do.... That was the general trend of the castle builders fantasy that rickety Christmas afternoon.

1845: The radioman reported trouble with one of the beacons. The precision clock (marine escapement clock) which accurately times the beacons had been erratic, and now was stopped altogether. This necessitated the installation of a spare. The ship pounded, rolled, lurched, climbed, and fell as frenzied as before. The moderate westerly gale still blew. Harassed by the shifting cadence, it took two of us an hour to change clocks.

2400: Christmas was over. Its departure coexisted with the continuing stiffness of the gale. We were not sorry, for we were one day closer to going ashore.

Looking back, a few weeks later, we realized that there WERE those who tried to make it better for us during Christmas. We were eternally grateful to our families and friends for their cards, letters, and gifts; to the merchants who gave us candy and tobacco; to the boys of Cuttyhunk Coast Guard station fro bringing mail during a thick fog; and last but not least to Arthur Denault for his delivery of mail on the twenty-third. Likewise, I was grateful to a fine crew for their spirit of understanding, for the cheerful tree, for the Christmas eve caroling, and for their ability to accept adversity with dignity and a minimum of complaint.

Christmas 1956

This marked the second Christmas for the Buzzards during my tour as Officer in Charge. Not being on board for the holiday, I am indebted to Roger Thoms of Roslindale, Massachusetts for his notes covering activities of the day. They are quoted verbatim, with no additions, deletions, or alterations.

25 December 1956: Christmas on board the *Buzzards* lightship: At 0000 the weather was fair, the sea was calm and the sky cloudy. It was an average night except for one reason; this night was Christmas. Seven people spent Christmas on board. They were Chief Dean, George Sousa, our new cook Ritchie, Ressler, Anderson, Mahoney, and Thomas. Mahoney watched church services on television from 0000 to 0200.

The Christmas tree was situated on top of the television set in the recreation room. Sousa made the stuffing for the turkey. It was good.

71

Nothing much happened in the morning. The weather was fine, though, blue sky, visibility is good, and the temperature is fifty degrees, but there is a moderate breeze which made it a bit chilly. I talked to Chief Dean about the present you gave him. He just laughed.

For dinner we had turkey, sweet and mashed potatoes, peas, corn, stuffing, cranberry sauce, olives, cider, milk, four pies, ice cream, peanuts, assorted nuts, candy.

In the afternoon they showed the movie *Inferno*. We also received small craft warnings around 2:00 P.M.

For supper we had turkey sandwiches. After supper George told me the purpose of a lightship and how ships take their bearing from our station. By supper time the seas were rough, but the visibility was extremely good.

We had a hot water pipe burst in the windlass room, so they secured the hot water. They also showed a movie that night. It was *The Golden Idol*.

Most of the day the crew played checkers or 500 rummy. Everybody watched what they said, as everybody kept from swearing.

Well, skipper, that's all that I can remember on what went on here Christmas day. The decorations for the Christmas tree were made through the combined efforts of Nelson and Ressler.

A later search through the official log revealed no information of an unusual nature. It had been atypical day of unvaried routine.

Chapter VI

"Ship's Routine"

Many have noted, all too frequently, "What do you do on a lightship? You have so much time. It must be a rather good life, with so little to do." This is far from the truth, as this chapter will reveal.

There are two men on watch at a time, one in the radio room and one in the engine room. There is electronic equipment and machinery to be cared for and kept in good running order. There is a constant battle against rust throughout the ship, a battle that knows no end. There is a daily cleaning of the ship similar to that in any large home or public building. There are drills to be practiced, learned until they border perfection. Relaxation comes only after the evening meal and then for only a few hours, for watch standers must have their proper amount of rest.

Watches are of four hours duration. The engineer on watch must keep a constant check on all operating machinery. Fuel lines must be checked frequently, for vibration often cracks or loosens them. Engines must be checked for fuel, oil, water, and any unusual action. Refrigerator motors must receive attention. Bilges must be checked. The engineer must be ready to start or secure air compressors whenever foghorns or the anchor windlass are used. Air, fuel, and water tanks must be checked. A myriad of pipes and valves must be watched for leakage. Soundings of fuel and water tanks must be taken daily, in good weather, and accurately recorded. Preventative maintenance must be carried on continually. Logs must be maintained. The engineer of the watch may not read, other than technical manuals, or involve himself in anything that may tend to distract him from his duties. His is a full-time job.

The radio room watch shoulders a tremendous responsibility. At night he becomes the human radar of the ship, and thus upon him is placed a trust from which there can be no dereliction of duty.

He is responsible for the lives of his shipmates and must keep himself informed of all conditions of weather, ships in the area, and conditions aboard ship. He must turn on the foghorns when visibility is under four miles. He must keep radio beacons properly synchronized, never allowing them to be more than five seconds fast or slow. He has to check the locale frequently for boats or planes that may require assistance. His vigil at the radio must be faultless. He must walk through the ship at least once an hour as a precaution against fire. He has to check the main mooring hourly. He must receive and display all storm warnings. He has to secure all portholes throughout the ship in case of inclement weather. He has to monitor four other lightship beacons every two hours and notify them of any error they unknowingly may be transmitting. He has to turn on the main light an hour before sundown and secure it an hour after sunrise unless visibility is poor. (The main light is kept on even during daylight if the foghorn is in use.) He has to turn on anchor and deck lights at sunset and secure them at sunrise. He has to raise the National Ensign at 8:00 A.M. and lower it promptly at sunset. He has to take a daily sample of sea water (performed in cooperation with a Massachusetts research institution). He is responsible for the cleanliness of the radio room. He has seven logs to maintain. One is the "rough" log in which is recorded a record of miscellaneous events of the day, including weather observations, sea conditions, temperatures, cloud formations, visibility, and barometric pressure. In addition, he has a radio message log; a radio beacon monitoring log in which is recorded readings of every observation of other beacons for which he is responsible; a radio beacon monitoring report which is a neat transcription of the lo;, a shipping log in which is entered the date, name, type, and direction of all passing vessels; a record of storm warnings received and displayed; and a log of the daily surface water temperatures and samples. He has to monitor several buoys in the area, every hour on the hour. Any unusual circumstances which are not fully understood must be reported to the officer-in-charge without delay. It readily can be understood that the radio room watch stander has a strict accountability for his time, as he has many duties which must be effected simultaneously with exactness.

There always is a vast surplus of work on any ship, including a lightship. The war against rust probably is the most wearisome because it is a continual conflict. A few weeks after a steel area has been left in perfect condition telltale smears of brown may begin to appear, again heralding the rust that is breaking through a protective coating. It is like a cancer that has been arrested by a series of operations. Even the smallest patch of rust requires serious respect. Salt water and air, of course, hasten the deteriorating process, particularly to the hull and on the main deck. There, each spot must be treated separately, and it can not be a matter of merely covering it with a coat of paint. Preparation is the most important preliminary to actual painting. The rust area must be chipped with a special hammer; scraped smooth after which the edges must be feathered with sandpaper or other abrasive; an application of wash primer put on, followed by two coats of red lead primer; and, lastly, two coats of the original paint color. The worker must also bear in mind that any area to be painted must be thoroughly clean and free from salt water, dirt, or grease. Rubber gaskets, knife edges of hatches, grease fittings, etc. must NOT be painted. Care must be taken not to spatter or spill paint on the deck or surrounding areas. Brushes must be cleaned before they are stowed in the paint locker, and paint cans must be covered tightly at the end of the day.

Besides painting, bulkheads, pipes, frames, wiring, equipment, etc. must be stenciled. Routine scrubbing of all areas with fresh water is a weekly must. Brass has to be shined. Turnbuckles, threads on porthole dogs or other equipment, electrical socket covers, etc. must be greased.

Boats must be scrubbed and tidied frequently. Equipment in boats must be overhauled and checked. All rigging must be sloshed with a protective coating. Lights must be checked weekly. Vigorous preventative maintenance must be in effect in all divisions of the ship. Anchor chain and windlass equipment must be given special attention. Decks must be waxed, portholes washed, pipes and fittings checked frequently, damage control gear overhauled periodically, ordnance equipment checked and cleaned, and safety practices enforced. Administrative files must be examined systematically. Monthly, quarterly, and annual reports must be submitted on schedule. Stores must be ordered. Personnel problems arrive along with morale problems. Special preparations have to be taken during storms, and a host of other tasks make their appearance. The men were serious when they claimed that when they went home to rest after a twenty-eight day "sojourn" aboard the *Buzzards*.

Our most important duty, not discounting the administration of ship's affairs, was to maintain station. Situated six and eight tenths miles, 153 degrees True from the southern tip of the Massachusetts/Rhode Island boundary, The *Buzzards'* job was to stay there. Daily, when visibility allowed, position was checked by horizontal sextant angles. Gosnold Tower on Cuttyhunk Island was used as the right leg, Gooseberry Neck Tower in Westport, Massachusetts as the middle, and the disestablished Sakonnet lighthouse in Rhode Island as the left leg. Angles obtained were transposed to a chart with the use of a three-armed protractor, position instantly obtained, and we could tell, within a few yards, our distance from the actual center of the charted position of the *Buzzards*. Since our ship stood sentinel duty, in a sense, for all shipping in the vicinity, it was most important that we remained somewhere within our swing area, that is, within two hundred yards of the exact center of the position located on the chart. If, after a storm, we found ourselves outside that area, we picked up anchor and steamed back into the center.

During foul weather, we resorted to radar (after it was installed), but ours was somewhat less accurate, for determining position, than sextant angles. Prior to having radar the only way we could tell if we were dragging was by use of the drift lead. A lead line was dropped near the stern and the line brought forward. If, upon later inspection, the line was found to be leading in a different direction, it was an indication that our anchor was not holding and that we were being dragged off station. It was virtually impossible to tell how badly or how far we were moving from our chartered position, but it was better than nothing. Soundings were of some value, although accurate soundings from a pitching vessel were not easy to obtain. Allowance had to be made for the scope of anchor chain, direction and velocity of wind, plus direction and velocity of the current.

After losing our mooring in extremely rough seas, described in a later chapter, we instantly became alert to any foreign motion or sound of the anchor chain. Even so, we later broke a pawl, and other damage was suffered to our windlass equipment. After that loss of mooring, a professional diver was hired to investigate the bottom. He discovered a series of rocks, one literally a small mountain, close to the anchor. As a result, the ship was relocated to a position one quarter of a mile southwest of the original position. After that, the windlass disturbances disappeared. We dragged during serious storms, but never again did rocks on the bottom foul either anchor or chain.

Military preparedness and smartness, perfected mainly by repeated drills, was another of our duties. On week days we held military and emergency drills. We practiced such exercises as abandon ship, collision, man overboard, fire, fire and rescue, emergency steering, and boat drill. We learned about various types of fires and how to combat them. We learned to work as a team using all emergent and damage control equipment on board. We also studied semaphore, flashing light, International code, first aid, resuscitation, military etiquette, and the like.

Drills became as boring as anything else, and yet the value of these instructions showed handsome dividends late one afternoon in June of 1955. Chief Dean and I were in the radio room. The remainder of the crew were readying the ship for port, as we were to leave in a few days for Boston. Suddenly there was a mad scrambling of feet as someone dashed along deck. The emergency alarm sounded, followed by a loud shout of "Man overboard! Starboard side! Man overboard!"

Dean and I rushed out on deck. Peering over the side, we saw Ronald Balkcom, a seaman from Riverside, Rhode Island, struggling in the water. He and Louis Schaefer had been securing a canvas cover on the pulling surfboat. Balkcom, carelessly working outboard without benefit of a life jacket or lifeline, lost his balance and had fallen into the sea. Schaefer had lost no time in alerting the ship to action.

Fortunately, the water was not rough. Chief Dean tossed a life jacket; someone else threw a ring buoy with a line attached and made fast to the ship; two others released the dory and lowered it to deck level; engineers bounded from the engine room and leaped into the boat which then was lowered to the water's edge; the unhappy seaman was grabbed, pulled aboard, the dory raised to deck level, and, less than three minutes after falling overboard a thoroughly saturated Balkcom was changing his clothing. Every man had done has part perfectly, contributing en masse to the lightning rescue. Balkcom's sole comment concerning his ordeal was made en route from ship to water. An instant before the splash he was heard to utter tow words, "Oh, my!"

Perfection at man overboard drill came the hard way to seaman Wheat, who served as lookout from the bridge. An old life jacket had been thrown over the side to represent the man who, theoretically, had fallen overboard. The emergency alarm was sounded, and the ship sprang to life. Men instantly appeared on deck wearing their orange life jackets. A ring buoy was tossed in the direction of the floating jacket as the dory was manned and quickly lowered.

"Keep pointing at the man in the water, Wheat. Don't take your eyes off of him?"

"Aye, aye, sir."

As the boat crew retrieved the jacket, and then the buoy, it was noted that Wheat was preoccupied with the vapor trail of an overhead jet.

"Wheat," I thundered, "where is the man in the water?"

With a foolish grin Wheat replied, "Oh, he's floated to New Bedford by now. He's having a beer."

Wheat was conspicuous by his absence at movies the following few nights. It seemed that whenever movies were about to begin, the Chief boatswain's mate found a necessary two hour job that could be accomplished only by a man possessing the qualifications of seaman Wheat.

Another seaman who paid the price for inattentiveness was known as "Red." An afternoon session had been partially devoted to the use of rescue breathing apparatus. The men had donned the equipment and had been briefed in procedure, signals, and usage. Following this, I turned the drill period over to Clem Meredith, a huge mild-mannered African American. Clem, formerly a cook, had changed his rating to boatswain's mate. He loathed laxity or listlessness among the men with whom he worked, and now was drill master for the first time. As I handed him a pair of semaphore flags and walked away, "Red" immediately sat down. His posterior had scarcely made contact when he was electrified by a husky uncomplimentary shout from Clem. "Red!" Get your ass off that deck!" Our new drill master meant business.

Infantry drill was enjoyed by almost everyone. It became quite a howl, due to lack of space and the assortment of artillery. Our armory consisted of a .22 caliber rifle, two .30 caliber rifles, and David Oram's 30/30 rifle which was kept in the armory for safekeeping. Drill thus was limited to a group of four participants with three kinds of rifles, as the men took turns at giving and executing commands. During a southwest wind of thirty miles per hour, the results of infantry drill can well be imagined. With the deck pitching up and down the only steady position was that of "Parade, rest." At the command "Attention!" the group would fall to ne side with feet sprawling and a free hand grasping for support, which usually was the man to the left. The poor man on the extreme left had nothing to grab except the pyrotechnic stowage box, and he had to lunge forward to do that. After getting untangled and resuming "Attention!" the next few commands might be executed without incident. It was amazing how they could steady themselves after a few minutes, and none but the most tempestuous of seas could cause further scrambling for balance.

Rowing was a big favorite, when weather permitted. The exercise was healthy, and the men were glad to get away from the ship for a few minutes. To help combat some of the extreme boredom that sometimes existed on lonely week-ends they devised races. During week days they often raced between noon and drill periods, as the engineers challenged the deck force in a course against time around the ship. Always starting near the starboard quarter, they would row around the bow, along the port side, around the stern, and back to the starboard quarter. What compelled them to go always in a counter-clockwise manner nobody quite understood, but the logical explanation is that the dory was lowered from the starboard quarter with the bow of the boat facing the same direction as the bow of the ship; hence, it was the dory's "home" area. Anyhow, the quickest time ever recorded over the oval course was forty-nine seconds by engineers William Sherman and Russell Wood. The teamwork was an inspired effort, and the competitive spirit of the various crews was equal to that of two teams battling in the seventh game of the World Series.

Not all boat drills or rowing exercises were efficient. One day William Mahoney and Herbert Ressler were delegated as boat crew for a man overboard drill. When the dory was waterborne, the hooks were slipped off and the two men started to place their oars in position. The dory, however, had a peculiar starboard list. Each blamed the other as Mahoney and Ressler fumbled with the oars.

"Sit in the middle of the boat, Ressler," suggested Mahoney, the bow oarsman.

"I was just going to tell you to do that," snapped Ressler perplexedly.

Both turned around to see that a boat fall had hooked itself into the port gunwale, holding the dory snugly if unevenly.

Chief Engineman Bob Dean chose a sultry summer afternoon to use the ship's powerboat, which was sporting a new but untested clutch assembly. With Herbert Ressler as his engineer, Dean prepared for the trip. Wearing green bathing trunks, a CPO cap, and dark green sun glasses, he was all set for an afternoon's yachting. The boat was laboriously lowered by Chief Boatswain's Mate George Sousa and his crew, boat falls were cast off, and Chief Dean temporarily became Captain Dean of a twenty-three foot motorboat.

Heading off the port beam, the boat had hardly gotten underway when a shriek was heard from Dean. Holding a broken tiller high above his head, he hollered to Sousa, "hey, George! The tiller's broken! I can't steer!"

The engine was forgotten as the men tried desperately to somehow make use of the disabled tiller. Farther and farther went the boat. Another shriek, much fainter, came from Dean. "Hey, George! We can't fix the tiller!" Ressler, doubled up with laughter, laid upon the engine box in a hysteria of jocundity. Suddenly realizing the boat was by now a half mile from the ship and still going, someone remembered to disengage the clutch. The boat slowed to a drift.

On deck, meanwhile, Sousa wasted no time. Placing a sweep oar in the dory, he ordered two men to row the auxiliary tiller to the powerboat. The dory was lowered, soon reached the powerboat, the oar was handed to Dean, and the dory returned to the ship where the boat falls were hooked and dory and crew hoisted aboard.

All eyes were then on the powerboat, which finally got underway with the steering oar lashed to the stern. Instead of returning to the ship, however, it went on a course which took it even further away. Again it stopped. The oar was unlashed and waved in the air by the two occupants.

"Damn," muttered Sousa, "what in hell is wrong now? Let's lower the dory again. This time I'll go along to give him a hand." Sousa, with a seaman, rowed to the drifting motorboat, by now three quarters of a mile away. Sousa leaped aboard, lashed the oar in a seamanlike fashion so it would steer the boat, then ordered Ressler to help the seaman row the dory back to the ship. He and Chief Dean returned in the powerboat.

Sousa purposely waited until the dory was back. When he saw the men climb aboard ship on the starboard side, he came along the port side and ordered the boat falls lowered. The dory, meanwhile, had been hooked to the starboard falls but had not been raised. All hands were on the port side, for it took brute strength to get the powerboat aboard. After a strain had been taken on the falls, Dean and Sousa climbed a Jacob's ladder to lend a hand on deck. With much puffing and straining and thirty minutes consumption of time the boat finally rested snugly in its cradle.

"I'm sure glad that's over with," sputtered Sousa who was acting Officer in Charge at the time. "Now let's go, fellows, and get the dory up. There'll be no more boating excursions today."

The crew sauntered from port to starboard, looked over the side and exclaimed, almost in unison, "Where's the dory?"

"There she goes!" shouted someone. "She's adrift half a mile off the stern!"

By now, Sousa was starting to burn. The redness crept into his tanned neck, his veins bulged, and he was about to deliver a blistering monologue concerning the seamanship he was witnessing when Ressler volunteered to swim after the errant dory.

"I don't know," mused Sousa, "it's a long ways to swim."

"I don't mind," answered Ressler. "I'm a strong swimmer. I have a Red Cross certificate for life saving, and I've always liked to swim a lot."

"All right," relented Sousa, "but you'll have to wear a life jacket. I won't take any chances."

A moment later the life-jacket clad Ressler hurled himself into the water and started for the dory. The first two hundred yards of his progress were those of an accomplished swimmer. The next couple hundred were somewhat slower, and then it was noted that the swimmer was no closer to the dory than when he had started.

"Damn. The dory's drifting as fast as he's swimming," observed Sousa. "There's only one thing to do. Let's put the powerboat over again."

The now weary crew sped to the port side and, again with great laborious difficulty, succeeded in lowering the heavy powerboat a second time. Sousa and Dean climbed in and headed for Ressler, now laboring in his efforts, although his orange encased figure was easy to spot. He soon was reached and taken aboard, all but exhausted. The dory then was taken in tow, and the procession returned to the ship. As the dory was hooked to the falls at the starboard quarter, Sousa ordered, "Take it away. Only this time, haul it all the way up and secure the thing before you leave."

When that was done, the powerboat jockied to the port pick-up station, hooks were secured, and the thirty minute process of straining and puffing repeated. By the time the boat was nested, lines coiled and equipment stowed, it was 4:40 P.M. The "yachting" had started at 1:00 P.M.. Sousa's crisp comment as he went below decks was, "If those boats are NEVER used again, it'll be too damned soon."

Motion sickness (seasickness on a ship) was a frequent problem, mainly with young seaman or men who had not been at sea for a period of time. Nearly everyone on the *Buzzards*, including myself, was plagued with it at one time or another. Normally it would wear off and disappear after the first day or two. It did take some men several months of concentrated effort before they were able to survive without nausea, and there were a couple who never completely accustomed their minds or bodies to the motion of the sea, becoming seasick during every storm. However, only once was it necessary to request a transfer of a man because of chronic seasickness. Various types of drugstore cures are available for motion sickness, but they simply are not a complete cure-all. The overall problem on the *Buzzards* never was terribly acute.

A typical day aboard our lightship began not at 7:00 or 8:00 in the morning, but at midnight when the first two watch standers, one in the engine room, the other in the radio room, reported to their posts. Chronologically, all days were similar to the following routine:

0000   Relieve the watch (engine room and radio room)
0345   Relieve the watch
0630   Call the cook
0700   Reveille
0715-0730 Breakfast
0730-0800 Make beds, tidy lockers, etc.
0745   Relieve the watch
0800   Morning colors. Commence ship's work
1115   Secure from ship's work
1130   Dinner
1145   Relieve the watch
1300   Drills
1400   Commence ship's work
1545   Relieve the watch
1615   Secure from ship's work
1630   Supper
1730   Movies
1945   Relieve the watch
           Sunset evening colors
2100   Taps

When the newness of lightship duty wears off, a dull monotony creeps in, grows stronger with the passing of time, and finally almost overwhelms a man unless he takes some preventative measure, such as the perusal of a hobby. Everything is the same. You see the same faces and the same bulkheads. You hear the same noises and the same voices. The food begins to taste the same, each meal seemingly no different than the one preceding. Little things irritate, their magnitude overwhelmingly enlarged. Every annoyance appears in the form of a personal affront. There is not one second during the twenty-four hours when you are free from noise. New noises creep in. Electronic signals filter through radio and television programs. The sound of men going up and down ladders becomes a punishing plague. You climb and descend ladders fifty times a day your self, and each trip becomes more wearisome and aggravating. An inoffensive toaster tries the patience because the surrounding lights dim every time it is used. The motion of the ship becomes unbearable, more than flesh and blood can bear without protest. Clouds, pregnant with wind and rain, become cruelly sadistic. Even when the sun breaks through in a wide beaming arc it offers small solace. Days are counted, and they go ever so slowly. Each individual day drags endlessly. Twenty-eight days to go before liberty! Twenty-seven days. After what seems an eternity of mere existence, there are but twenty-six days to wait. Even then you think ahead and realize you are not certain of getting off when the time comes. Weather may well offer interference. Twenty-four days to go. Will it never end? Twenty-three days....

My own day is one of sluggish lethargy, mainly because every single day I realize that I am doing things in exactly the same manner. Up at ten minutes before seven, wash, scrub teeth, brush hair one hundred strokes, listen to news and weather information, fold back my bedding to air. At ten after the hour I go below for breakfast. It's always the same routine. "Good morning." "Nice day today." "How did you sleep?" "How's everything going?" Twenty minutes later I look through the office and arrange my day. Five minutes before 8:00 A.M. I make my bed. (One of the ship's rules is that all bunks must be made no later than 8:00, and I consider mine no exception.) I tear another day off my calendar. I am irritated on Sundays because two days, Saturday and Sunday, are included on one sheet, and I have to wait until Monday to "take a day off." Then I feel better because two days go at once. The day's work commences and occupies the next few hours. At 11:15 I wash and wait for dinner to be served at 11:30. At noon I lie on my bunk to hear more news and weather reports from the radio. Five minutes before 1:00 I prepare for drill. The afternoon passes, and it is time for the evening meal. Then we wait until 5:30 P.M. for the showing of a movie. Two hours later the movie is over, and I go on deck. Fifteen minutes later I go below to watch TV news. Our television does not always work well. Reception is poor, radio beacons and foghorns cause interference, and sometimes the set refuses to operate at all. At 8:00 P.M. I read, write, watch television occasionally, walk the deck. At 10:00 I prepare for bed. Again it is the same routine of washing, scrubbing teeth, brushing the hair a hundred strokes, turning down the blankets and finally making an entrance into the bed. Another day gone, slowly, painfully, and yet tomorrow will be an exact duplicate.

When anyone is asked why he does not like lightship duty, the answer invariable is "because of the terrible boredom. Every day is the same. The only change is when it storms, and then it's worse."

Any variation in the routine was proclaimed with a ringing gladness. Most popular was the arrival of the mail, by any source. Whenever the forty-footer from Cuttyhunk Coast Guard station or the Cutter *White Sage* stopped with mail, it was a cause for great rejoicing. Excitement reigned, for the crew not only received letters from their families and friends but also were able to send off their own at the same time. Mail is the single most important morale factor aboard a lightship. The happiness it brings cannot possibly be overestimated.

Under normal conditions we could not expect mail other than during a regular "tender" trip on every second Thursday. Therefore, any received between trips was an unrestricted bonanza to all. The *White Sage* always was most courteous in that respect. Whenever they worked buoys in our vicinity or passed by, they brought mail to us. We never will be able to repay Mr. Donald Bangs, the Commanding Officer of the ship, or his crew, for the numerous occasions when their unexpected arrival gave all of us such a tremendous lift.

The kindest, most accommodating friend the *Buzzards* ever had was Arthur Denault of Westport Point, Massachusetts. A tall, rugged ex-Marine, Arthur was a fisherman who steered a course that took him close aboard. Catering to fishing parties, he was anxious that his patrons obtain as good a catch as possible. The better fishing grounds were not close to the lightship, yet Arthur never failed to make a wide deviation from his "business" course for the sole purpose of delivering mail, magazines, and newspapers. From the first part of April until mid-December he could be expected on every favorable weekend. During the height of the vacation season, his trips became daily affairs. Every morning his friendly boat, the Bridgett Anne, named after his wife, was the object of much speculation. Trained eyes swept the shoreline on good days, and the gray dot that first appeared off the beach became a source of sparkling soaring spirits. The first man to locate the boat through binoculars would shout, "Denault's boat is on the way!" The outgoing mailbag would be checked as last minute billet-douxs were sealed and addressed. As the boat drew closer and closer, men would pace the deck anxiously, prepare heaving lines and grin at one another. Arthur's cheerful three-toned whistle audibly announced his presence. What a wonderful sight to see this boat a few feet away, the friendly pilot on deck, the mail bags being readied for exchange.

There was no way we could reward Arthur for his many acts of kindness, and he knew it. "Look, fellows," he would explain. "If I didn't want to do it, I wouldn't have to. I realize how lonely it is for you out here, and it makes me feel good to see your smiles when you get mail. So think nothing of it."

In addition to being a steady mailman, Arthur also served as a telegrapher and a mender of lonely hearts. He sent telegrams for us, made telephone calls, purchased cigarettes and postage stamps. His clients gave him a wide assortment of magazines to bring us. He brought daily newspapers, gave us fish, offered to take us fishing, furnished transportation on several occasions, and in general had much to do with making our enforced isolation considerably more bearable. Seeing him approach our vessel was similar to looking at the world through those proverbial rose-colored spectacles. A hard worker, honest, efficient, a lover of his home, well respected in his community, always busy, Arthur Denault gave more of himself than he ever could hope to receive in return. No man assigned to the *Buzzards* lightship will ever forget his generosity or his ability to conceive that another man's loneliness might be important.

Another break in the monotony occurred every two or three weeks when a tender, usually the Coast Guard Cutter *Spar* from Bristol, Rhode Island, delivered fuel and fresh water. Tying astern, they passed a heaving line attached to their hoses, which were rousingly hauled aboard the *Buzzards* by the entire crew. The *Spar* filled our tanks to the brim, usually transferring an average of six thousand gallons of water and two thousand gallons of diesel fuel. This was particularly welcome during winter months, for the added weight was helpful in riding out storms.

Fueling maneuvers did not always go smoothly. I recall two occasions when red faces were the order of the day. The first happened in the thickening twilight of a late winter afternoon. Seas were moderate, but the first couple of tries of the heaving line from the *Spar* missed contact. Connie Wilson, a seaman from Shepherd, Texas, prepared one of our own and heaved it. The wind spoiled his aim and it fell short. As the tender drifted back to make another attempt, Wilson hastily retrieved his line. Coiling it on deck as he hailed it rapidly aboard, he failed to watch for the end, the monkey-fist (a knot used in the end of a heaving line to give it weight), which caught on a railing. Slacking his line slightly, Wilson gave it a quick jerk, and it flew over the railing towards the deck of the *Spar*. The only trouble was that its momentum carried it too far, and it sailed on until it smacked against an object. The object was the left cheek of Ralph Sears, a seaman from greater Boston. Sears wouldn't have minded the pain or the resultant shiner, except that he was due to go ashore the next day. He feared his girl friend would find disfavor with him, accuse him of fighting and not believe his explanation. We were sympathetic, for how could a man possibly explain a lack of defense against a flying missile called a monkey-fist?

The second unhappy incident was caused by haste. It did not result in personal injury, if one discounts the emotions and pride of man. The *Spar* this time was tied astern on a cool, clear morning, their hoses already on our deck. It was customary to notify the tender by radio when we were ready to receive water and then fuel. Both were delivered simultaneously through separate hoses but since it took longer to fill the water tanks, that hose was connected first and the tender notified when to start pumping. Water already had started to drain into our tanks when William Sherman, an engineer from Newport, Rhode Island, reported that all was ready to receive fuel.

"Are you sure, Sherman?" he was asked.

"Yes, all set. You can call them anytime."

Our radio boomed, "Start the fuel."

Soon the fuel could be heard as the first few gallons gurgles through the hose. Almost immediately there was a loud sharp retort not unlike that of a rifle. We looked in the direction of the sound. There stood Sherman, a greasy pipe wrench clutched in a soiled hand.

"Oh, God," he bellowed. "The hose has busted! Tell them to secure the fuel.

"*Buzzards* to *Spar*": "Secure the fuel."

"What happened, Sherman?" I asked.

"Oh, Skipper, darn it all. I was hurrying and forgot to open the valve. It's my fault."

There was nothing to do but notify the tender and drag more hose aboard so the broken section could be disconnected and discarded. Ten minutes passed before the silence was broken by Sherman's, "All set now, Skipper."

"Sherman, are you quite certain everything is ready? Is the valve open this time?"

"Yes it is, Skipper. Come and see."

I accepted his word, and the flow of fuel was resumed. This time there was no loud rifle report signifying a ruptured hose. Not at all. It was replaced by the gushing of fuel oil streaming along the waterways and over the side of the ship.

Immediately upon requesting the *Spar* to secure again, I went forward, looked at Sherman and inquired sternly, "Well, what happened this time?"

"Well, gosh, I guess I tried to hurry too fast again, Skipper. We took that broken section of hose off, hauled in some more, and I thought I connected their line. I guess I must have put the old piece back on instead."

Several months passed before I told the Commanding Officer of the tender the whole truth about the chain of events. It became a legendary joke aboard the *Buzzards*, but extreme care was taken ever after to guard against a repeat performance.

The *White Sage* from Woods Hole, Massachusetts made most of the logistic trips, scheduled every other Thursday. They brought our supplies, mail, and the liberty party. This was another day we all looked forward to, that is, with the exception of the returnees. For a third of the crew it meant liberation from their isolated entity. It meant they could walk on dry land. Their beaming faces were ones of realistic happiness as they boarded the tender. Soon they would be on their way ashore. Everything would seem more cheerful to them. As they approached Woods Hole, the grass would look greener. Houses would seem more trim than usual. When they reached shore, the antics of opposition drivers would be more easily understood. The roads would seem smoother. Wives and sweethearts would look prettier. Home cooked food would taste better. Chairs would be more comfortable. Water would be clearer. Nothing would be offensive to them that first day home.

To another third of the crew, halfway through the four week period themselves, it meant a change of faces, mail, stores to sort and check. They would make light chatter with members of the Sage. Only two more weeks to go! Their valedictory to departing shipmates always was, "Hurry back so we can go ashore!" It was answered with a wild waving of hands and such remarks as, "You can't beat liberty. Nothing LIKE it!"

The regaining third, those just returned, were pitiful to behold. Their bedraggled appearance, relative silence, and immobile features indicated their unspoken feelings. "Twenty-eight days to go. Those two weeks sure went fast. Twenty-eight days to go... an eternity!"

Strangely enough, it was the last week of the twenty-eight days that dragged more than the rest. After three weeks, as time ashore drew near, it became increasingly difficult to concentrate. Naturally enough, thoughts were of home and of plans for the two weeks there. Those mental images overshadowed any desire to think seriously about a lightship until one realized that he still had seven whole days to wait. These symptoms were popularly diagnosed as channel fever, and have been experienced by mariners since ships first were used.

There were other diversions of a strictly on-board type. The nightly showing of movies was timed for the loneliest period of all, the hours between the evening meal and 8:00 P.M. Through the courtesy of the U.S. Navy we received fifteen movies every two weeks. Occasionally, of course, there was a repeat, for there was a limit to the amount and variety of films available. We had several experienced operators on board, so there was no problem in that respect. The poor operator, though, was ever hounded with queries as to the film hen intended to show, for it was his choice whenever he ran the projector.

"What are you going to show tonight?"

"I don't know yet." "Wait and see." "What difference does it make?" "You'll see them all anyway." These were the customary answers.

One little joke never wore out. In response to a request for the title someone would interject, *Tom Mix - In Cement.* It took a year for Sherman to come up with a suitable answer: "Hasn't he gotten that cement mixed yet?"

Interest in movies failed to wane even when we found ourselves without sound projection bulbs. Several times the sound failed completely, but movies were shown on schedule, and we watched in silence. None us being adept in lip reading, Sherman kept a running commentary on what he believed was taking place: "I'll bet they're doing this," or "He's telling the king...."

Clem Meredith approved. "That's right, Sherman," he would state gruffly. "You narrate."

Although television was fairly popular between the hours of 8:00 and 10:00 P.M., nobody became terribly distressed whenever the set suffered a breakdown. The men cursed more at the foghorn or other types of interference than they did when the TV would not operate.

An astonishing number of men pursued correspondence courses to further their education. Even with frequent changes of personnel all but a couple had at least one such course in effect. Courses were available through the Coast Guard and through the United States Armed Forces Institute (USAFI). Several men requested and successfully passed one of college level. Others studied to gain promotion or to prepare themselves for a school. English, economics, philosophy, algebra, and typing were but a few of the USAFI studies in progress. It was gratifying to see the crew so interested in a pursuit of knowledge, and all possible assistance and encouragement were given them.

`Some departures from the awful boredom were insti-gated by the men themselves. We all lacked proper exercises.

There was little room. We could walk one hundred and twenty-nine feet from bow to stern and twenty-nine feet from side to side, but that was all. However, this did not prevent us from using the deck as a recreational area. We enjoyed life from the main deck many times, especially on clear, calm nights. We studied stars and planets. We tried to identify objects or land as far away as possible. On an exceptionally clear night we could see the Brenton Reef Lightship, fourteen miles away. Once or twice, during the day, we could see Squibnocket Beach on Martha's Vineyard, a distance of thirteen miles.

There were inexhaustible inescapable gab sessions, in which all of us participated at one time or other. Lack of women constituted a subject that never ceased to tax the imagination. What idle dreams men invent in order to retain their sanity. The men "imagined" what it would be like to be married to a movie actress or a woman wrestler. Pros and cons of women from all walks of life were heatedly discussed. Although no clear-cut decision was ever reached on any single phase, it was unanimously agreed that women were "interesting."

During one of these assemblies the ship was compared to a human being. The generator, for example, was the throbbing heartbeat. The coursing of electrical power was the life blood. The innumerable wiring was the veins and arteries. Air compressors were the lungs. The foghorn was the booming voice. The radar and man on watch were the eyes. The radio was the ears. The main engine, said somebody, was the legs, for it was there to use when you wanted to get up and go. "By the same token, the anchor is the arms, then," opined another, "for it holds us in place."

"Yeah, remember when we lost our mooring? We had a broken arm that time."

Games of cards, checkers, Monopoly, scrabble, etc. were played once in awhile. Most of the crew liked to read, magazines being the more popular although book-length novels were by no means completely shunned.

The men once became detectives. They tried to solve the riddle of mysterious black smudges that appeared on the decks from the shoes of a person or persons unknown. These created extra work for the deck force, for the smudges were unsightly, and it was necessary to have them removed. They finally were traced to a couple of the crew who wore high black shoes referred to as "boondockers." The marks left by this type of sandal later came to be known as "feetnen." Feetnen in turn branched out to include not only the deck smudges but also the sound created by men who ran up and down ladders with heavy feet.

Coffee breaks became known affectionately as "tete-a-tete" time. These were in addition to "happy hours" held on Wednesday and Sunday nights. Tete-a-tete, on working days, took place at 10:00 A.M. and 2:30 P.M. On many a work day my work was interrupted by a knock on the door followed by, "Tete-a-tete time, Skipper. Your coffee's all poured."

Sometimes at night, in the vicinity of 10:00 P.M., the chiefs and I would drink cocoa in the wardroom. Chief Dean was an excellent connoisseur of the beverage and usually could be talked into making a cup. This mini-party became known as the wardroom party."

One Sunday afternoon I entertained the entire crew in the wardroom. For some reason, we had no rated cook on board during the particular two week period, but Leroy Wilson, boatswain's mate first class from Portland, Maine, furnished the incentive and handled the organization. He made coffee, tarts and turnovers, and notified us when his preparations were complete. It was a jovial caucus and helped us pass an otherwise drab and cheerless windy afternoon.

Traffic jams always amused us. One wouldn't think, with ten men aboard a ship the size of the *Buzzards*, that such an occurrence would be possible. However, it was rather common for men to converge on a single water cooler from three directions. Situated on the recreation deck, the cooler was in a passageway that lead to the mess deck, engineering storeroom and rec. deck. Frequently, men from all three areas developed simultaneous thirsts, Gaston-Alphonso acts ensuing.

The American sense of humor often prevailed when the going was the toughest. How childish life could be and yet so amusing. We grasped at anything for a laugh. I remembered a short pearl of wisdom I had learned many years before. It stated simply, "In mud eels are; in clay none are." It made sense, too, but when delivered with rapidity, it sounded like undecipherable jargon. This argot, mingled with a few timely gestures, could cause a small riot. People would think they were the subjects of some ridiculous sport, or they would look completely bewildered. I twice used the expression.

On December 8, 1955, I left the radio room, ran down a ladder and burst into the wardroom where Bob Dean and Bill Burroughs were having a heated discussion. Looking straight at Chief Dean, I launched into a rapid "In mud eels are; in clay none are." I paused while he looked at me with sheer amazement. "Yes," I continued emphatically, "no more than a hundred yards off the stern!" Dean fidgeted, and not knowing what to do or say, offered a remorseful, "What?" Burroughs caught on.

"That's right. There's a whole bunch of them."

Dean spun his head towards Burroughs, then back at me, with a puzzled expression. Bill and I could contain ourselves no longer and burst into frenzies of laughter.

"Get out of here, both of you damned fools," pleaded a distressed Bob Dean.

Almost a year later I walked through the crew's berthing spaces on a sunny weekend morning. They were talking in veins of the pleasantry of life ashore. An opportune moment had presented itself. "In mud eels are; in clay none are," I said crisply.

"What? ? ? ?"

"Yes, that's true. Off the starboard bow." As the crew flocked to the portholes, I walked away, chuckling. I felt I had diverted attention from their loneliness at that particular moment. It wasn't good for them to be feeling sorry for themselves.

The awful dreary routine becomes so monotonous that men sometimes get into a rut from which they need extensive help in escaping. The extent to which the routine envelops a man can be illustrated by a simple change in the noon menu on October 26, 1956. It was a Friday, but the cook served roast pork instead of the customary fish. One of the men looked at the meat sadly, remarking, "Meat! I thought today was FRIDAY." No one answered, and the man said no more. At the end of the meal he made one final attempt. Shaking his head with defeat he said, "What a disappointment. Ever since I got up this morning I thought it was Friday, but now I find it's only Thursday." The crew laughed and someone answered, "That's the way it goes." The man had become so accustomed to a routine that he had temporarily lost his power of reasoning, and did not have enough confidence in his own convictions to defend his belief that it actually WAS Friday, fish or no fish.

Twice, both on the same day, routine was interrupted by requests for assistance from unfortunate mariners.

At 5:50 A.M. on the morning of May 5, 1956, a dory arrived alongside carrying four weary men. They were the crew members of the eighty-six foot fishing vessel *Palestine* which had met an unhappy ending. Fishing twelve miles south southwest of the lightship, they had struck a floating log or piling, according to their explanation. The ship took on water which rapidly covered the engine. With all pumps rendered useless the crew took their only alternative. They escaped in the vessel's dory, saving only their personal luggage. The weather was good, seas placid, and all night they had rowed, in the general direction of New Bedford until they reached the *Buzzards*. The men were taken aboard, fed and rested. A request was then made for transportation for them and their dory to New Bedford. Two hours later the Coast Guard Cutter CG83388 arrived from the base at Woods Hole, and the men were taken ashore.

At 11:00P.M. that same night, with heavy seas running that had built up steadily all day long from the northwest, a fishing vessel was seen approaching the lightship. As she drew almost alongside, a voice sounded into the wind asking if they would be allowed to tie astern. It was the *Stella Maris*, disabled with salt water that was steadily rising in the base of the engine. A line was quickly thrown, grabbed, secured, and the *Stella Maris* pitched, rolled, tossed violently at the end of an eight inch hawser. Another radio request was made for a patrol boat to tow the disabled vessel to New Bedford, and again the CG83388 arrived on the scene from Woods Hole. With moderate difficulty because of the buffeting wind and mountainous seas, they finally succeeded in relieving us of our hapless tow.

Routine work sometimes raised a laugh, and even that was a change for us. Sherman once was asked what he had accomplished during the forenoon.

"I did some typing in the office and some painting in the engine room," was his rational response.

"Boy, you sure have long arms, then," quipped Ressler. "It's a long reach from the office to the engine room."

"Well, at least I don't maul a typewriter the way YOU do. You hit the keys so hard you BRAND the letters on the paper."

One other change in routine came for us whenever our electronic equipment failed and repairs were beyond our non-professional capacity. The supporting base at Woods Hole furnished qualified technicians to rectify these infrequent failures. Arriving by boat a technician's limited stay offered a new face and a new voice to the scenery. Usually it meant that mail would be received, too, and this prospect ever gladdened hearts and refreshed minds.

Photo courtesy of U.S. Coast Guard

Warrant Officer, USCG
George E. Rongner
Officer in Charge
Buzzards Lightship

Clem Meredith, Cook (l) and Herbert Ressler, Engineman (r)
taken on the fantail of the Buzzards Lightship

Photo courtesy of Richard Nelson, Crew Member

Warrant Officer George E. Rongner (l) entering the bridge
Engineman William Sherman (r)

Buzzards Lightship in Boston after new installation of spare
anchor leading through a pipe rather than carried near the bow

Photo courtesy of U.S. Coast Guard

Chief Engineman Robert J. Dean
Engineering Officer
Buzzards Lightship

New system installed at Boston after the storm of
February 25-26, 1956 as described in Chapter XI

Photo courtesy of U.S. Coast Guard

Dick Nelson, rising colors aboard the Buzzard

Photo courtesy of Ronald Balkcom, Crew Member

Boat Drill

Photo courtesy of Ronald Balkcom

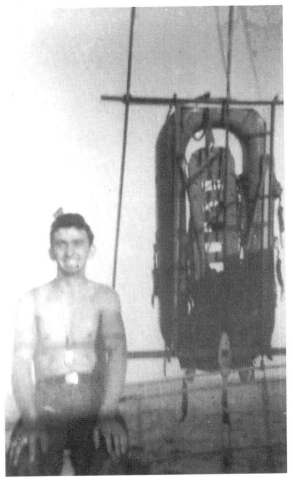

Seaman Ronald Balkcom
Life raft has just been re-installed and attached to the rigging

Original system of carrying the spare anchor on the starboard bow; dangerous if necessary to use in rough weather; used during the storm of February 25-26, 1956

Photo courtesy of U.S. Coast Guard

Boat Drill

Photo courtesy of Ronald Balkcom

Leroy Wilson

Commisaryman 2nd Class Dick Nelson (l) and Engineman Herbert Ressler (r) on the USCGC White Sage, going ashore on leave!

Photo courtesy of Dick Nelson

Engineman Herbert Ressker (l)
and Engineman William Sherman (r)

Photo courtesy of Dick Nelson

Left to right: Seaman Brazal, Chief Mate George Sousa (executive officer). Seaman Ed Juratic, Chief Engineman Al Carter

Photo courtesy of Dick Nelson

Photo courtesy of Dick Nelson

Passing beneath a bridge on the Cape Cod Canal en route to Boston
left to right: Seaman Brazal, Seaman Ed Juratic,
Commissaryman Dick Nelson

Photo courtesy of Dick Nelson

Commissaryman 2nd Class Dick Nelson aboard the USCGC
"White Sage" as it pulls away from the Lightship after delivering
stores and personnel

Photo courtesy of Dick Nelson

At Base Boston for annual servicing

Ronald Balkcom

Photo courtesy of Ronald Balkcom

"Zom" before the galley range

REFERS TO ONE OF THE CₐOOKS, NICKNAMED "ZOM", ALWAYS READING
AND SMOKING A PIPE.

"Hey, George!! The tiller's broken!"

REFERS TO AN INCIDENT WHEN CHIEF ENGINEMAN ROBERT DEAN AND FIREMAN
HERBERT RESSLER TESTED THE POWERBOAT, WHEN CHIEF BOATSWAIN'S
MATE, THE EXECUTIVE OFFICER, WAS IN CHARGE, AND THE TILLER
BROKE.

Cornelius Van Pooper surrounded by green ferns

REFERS TO CONNIE WILSON, BOATSWAIN'S MATE 2ND CLASS, FROM
TEXAS, NICKNAMED "CORNELIUS VAN POOPER", IN AN
INCIDENT THAT INCURRED HIS WRATH WHILE DINING IN
A BOSTON RESTAURANT.

The Herring Gull (Larus Argentatus Smithsonianus)

GULLS, ALWAYS AWAITING THE COOK'S DISPOSALS. NOTE, IN THE DISTANCE, THE COAST GUARD CUTTER WHITE SAGE APPROACHING FROM WOODS HOLE WITH SUPPLIES, MAIL AND THE RETURNING LIBERTY PARTY.

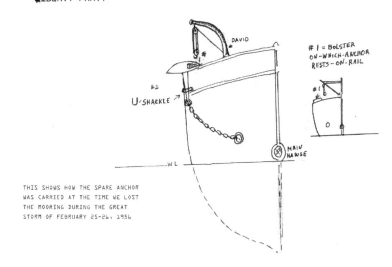

DAVID

#1 = BOLSTER ON-WHICH-ANCHOR RESTS-ON-RAIL

U-SHACKLE

MAIN HAWSE

WL

THIS SHOWS HOW THE SPARE ANCHOR WAS CARRIED AT THE TIME WE LOST THE MOORING DURING THE GREAT STORM OF FEBRUARY 25-26, 1956

SHOWS HOW THE SPARE ANCHOR WAS CARRIED AT THE TIME THE MOORING WAS LOST DURING THE STORM OF FEBRUARY 25-26, 1956

Chapter VII

"Chow Time"

Eating was more than mere necessity on the *Buzzards*. It was a highly popular hobby, for many of the crew lived to eat. It was not unusual or improper that mealtime should produce such ecstacy when one considered that this group of men was thrust into close contact on a ship bobbing at anchor where the same routine was experienced day after day after day. Everyone, except the cooks, looked forward to dinner and supper with delightful anticipation. Breakfast was not such a happy repast, for most men were sleepy and not a little pugnacious at that hour of day. The hand bell, shaken vigorously to proclaim the readiness of a meal, seldom was needed, for the men were not sluggish about being available.

Our commissary supplies were ordered by radio and delivered by buoy tender. Ten days before the return of a liberty party we sent our list of desired items to the Coast Guard base at Woods Hole. They in turn telephoned the catering markets who delivered to the base the day before a scheduled tender trip. The following morning they were loaded onto the tender by the lightship's returnees. When the tender arrived at the lightship, she usually tied astern. Their small boat plied back and forth between tender and lightship until the stores were aboard. All hands pitched in to make short work of the maneuver, for in moderate seas time was an element, and danger of accident or loss of merchandise manifestly presented itself. A small davit was used to handle the heavier bundles; medium ones were hauled aboard with a heaving line; lighter ones were tossed or passed from hand to hand. Following this procedure, a chain was formed by on-board personnel who passed everything through a hatch from the main deck to the second deck and thence to the main hold where it was stowed by the cook in the commissary locker or refrigerator. The complete transfer, from tender to stockroom shelf, consumed forty-five minutes to an hour, depending upon sea conditions.

The cooks prepared their shopping lists subject to approval by the Officer in Charge, who was the commissary officer of the ship. This was a responsibility he could not delegate. A menu was typed a week in advance in the same manner. Details of the menu, however, were known two weeks ahead of time, for it was necessary to order a fourteen day minimum. We always planned to carry at least another ten days rations, for the ways of storms could not be accurately anticipated, and the tender not always was able to arrive on a scheduled date. Our larder occasionally was replenished with fresh fish, gifts from fishermen in the area.

The cuisine was the direct responsibility of the cooks. They were expected to have properly prepared meals on the table at designated hours. The only meal in which punctuality was waved was breakfast, which was served individually from 7:00 to 7:30 A.M. The crew likewise were expected to appear promptly unless they were on watch or detained by necessary or emergent work. Tardy "chow-hounds" on the *Buzzards* were a rarity, but crew members who infrequently were late for meals due to their own lackadaisical carelessness suffered the consequences of cold food or reduced rations, depending upon the kindness of their fellow table squatters.

The job of a cook was most unrewarding, for it was an absolute impossibility to be able to please everyone all of the time. Cooking in rough weather was no cinch either. It was difficult, unpleasant, upsetting, and sometimes nauseating. Nutritive intake usually was voluntarily curtailed at these times. Still, meals had to be ready on time, and always it was assumed that each man would eat a regular portion. The lot of the cook was more pleasant on smooth days, for he did not have to pursue pots and pans across the top of a range; baked potatoes did not roll into a disorderly stack in a corner of the oven; gravy was perfectly willing to remain within the confines of a bowl; tossed salad performed controlled acrobats only.

It seemed, when I first was aboard, that however hard the cook tried to please, rarely was he saluted with a "Thank you" or a "Good meal, Cookie." I often made it a practice to compliment him in front of the crew, and it was gratifying to see the courtesy brush off onto others who followed suit with pleasantries of their own.

Our most unforgettable cook was Clematee Meredith, a husky, big-boned, six foot, one hundred and ninety-five pound African American from Georgia. Clem was mild and unobtrusive in character but frightening in physical stature. The boys were very careful to avoid entanglements with him. Consequently, he seldom was subjected to criticism of his culinary ability. If any adverse thoughts were harbored, they wisely were concealed.

Meredith was methodical, unharried, and highly efficient. His cooking and baking for the day were all but completed by 9:00 A.M. every morning. Up at 6:30 A.M., he wasted little time in reaching the galley to start his daily preparations. There was no confusion or fretting as he shuffled his provender into well balanced meals. He had mastered the intricacies of a prima donna oven that seldom, if ever, pooped along at the desired temperature. Mealtime found him punctual. We could almost set our watches to the summons of his "Come-and-get-it" bell. He gave few extras or side dishes, for in his words, "They don't appreciate what they DO get." Nevertheless, he possessed a genuine interest in his work. He had been to two service schools and had completed two correspondence courses in order to further his knowledge. He was neat and exacting, both with himself and with his job. His galley and mess deck were spotless. Week after week, Saturday inspections found little fault with the commissary spaces when he was aboard.

This popular man with the powerful frame and pleasant disposition became ruffled only by constant inquirers into his proposed bil-de-faire. In answer to an oft-repeated "What's for chow, Clem?" he would halt in his tracks, bristle, stand with arms akimbo, glare squarely at his interrogator and belch, "FOOD!" He did not waste words, although he would diversify his oral counterattack once in awhile with a resigned "Stick around and see."

He had other good answers, too, as when an odor of sauerkraut once permeated the ship. A new seaman, with more courage than sense, sidled up to Meredith and scornfully asked, "Clem, what in the world stinks so much?"

Clem answered, with poetic justice, "That's just your breath blowing back in your face."

No wealth of knowledge was amassed from questioning Clem, but the arrogant Willie W. never seemed to learn, and one day carried his torments too far. The usual question and the usual reply over with, Willie berated the cook with blistering unintelligence, and foolishly used a poor choice of words from his limited vocabulary. Clem, objecting strenuously to the profane abuse, uttered a hoarse cry and gave chase, meat cleaver in hand. Willie didn't stick around. He made haste through a door and ran. Clem didn't mope along either, and the frightened Willie, when he realized his adversary was angry, picked up his feet and put them down with amazing alacrity. Clem followed in hot pursuit, but his terrorized antagonizer gradually lengthened the distance between them. Noting that he would be unable to apprehend his fleeing quarry, the irate cook yelled after him, "Willie, when I get my hands on you, I'll kill you!"

There were not many places on a hundred and thirty foot vessel where a man could hide, yet Willie managed to remain adroitly out of sight. The supper hour came, but Willie, taking no chances of damage to his skull, failed to put in an appearance. Willie loved to eat, too, but the lure of food failed to entice him from his sanctuary. It was just as well, for Clem still was fuming.

Next to consuming quantities of food, Willie loved horizontal drill. At every opportunity he basked in the warmth of his sack. He remained there until the last possible moment in the morning. He returned as soon as he was able, usually for a few minutes preceding dinner. Immediately after, his bunk beckoned again. Most joyous of all was the luxurious knowledge that after the evening meal he could "hit the Pad" until called for watch. It made no difference if he was wide-awake. In that case he would read from a reclining position. The night of his misunderstanding with Clem he made a supreme sacrifice. He did not establish himself in his usual recumbent position. He was too scared. As he remained in hiding, how he must have wished he hadn't asked "What's for chow, Clem?" and then pursued it to such stupid lengths.

Evening wore on. Six o'clock, and the movies had been showing for fifteen minutes. No Willie. Seven o'clock, last reel of film just started. No Willie. Seven-thirty, movies over. Still no Willie. By eight o'clock Clem had regained his composure. Feeling sorry for Willie, he passed word that the thoroughly intimidated lad could return without fear of reprisal. It is understood that Willie learned a valuable lesson that day through bitter personal experience and that future inquiries about Clem's meals were more skillfully fashioned.

One other mild irritant annoyed Clem. Sherman preferred chicken and liver to any other meat. Upon the demolition of meals that included either, he at no time failed to ask, "Are you going to put the left-over meat in the refrigerator, Clem?" Such answers as "No, Sherman, I'm going to sell it back to the store," or "Eat what you want now and don't worry about it," became the established repartee. Clem used to grumble to me, "They're just like little boys. They know the answer, but they just want to hear someone say it."

I chanced to walk through the crew's mess deck a month before Clem's transfer and overheard Sherman ask, Are you going to put the left-over chicken in the refrigerator, Clem?" Clem looked at me and guffawed, "There we go again. You can put THAT in your book, Skipper."

"Zombie" was the direct opposite of Clem in physique. Five feet six inches in height, one hundred and twenty pounds soaking wet, he couldn't have fought his way through a paper bag. Protruding eyeballs and resemblance to a corpse had earned him his nickname, or so claimed older members of the crew. His popularity with his shipmates fluctuated with his moods. At times he tried terribly hard but became discouraged easily if harassed by hostile reviews of his offerings.

Zom, a book lover of the nth degree, was fond of mysteries, westerns, and girlie stories, carrying one with him most of the time. While sometimes it stuck out of a rear pocket, it usually was in his hand. Pipe in mouth with volcanoes of smoke gushing forth, Zom typically stood before the range with his open narrative, paying no heed to coffee boiling over or to vegetables becoming charcoaled. His free hand scratched at a compelling itch as the literary plot blocked out all other mental awareness.

Between meals, when need for alertness was not quite so pressing, a capsized milk crate became his library. From this retreat he rarely ventured forth, as page after page of characters came to life. The boatswain's mate used to wait until Zom was swallowed up with his imaginary adventures before inspecting the mess deck. Zom dreaded the loud "Oh, oh!" which meant that a discrepancy had been found. It wasn't necessary to say anything else. The boatswain's mate might bend down to peek under a toaster where he knew a few crumbs to be located. The exclamation uttered, he continued to peer at the same spot. Zom would sigh heavily, turn his head first at the invader of his solitude and then sharply aside, slam the comers of his book, abdicate his makeshift settee, walk to the counter and brush away the hateful crumbs, all without a word.

Two or three times a week Zom had cake for dessert. Wafer thin, they generally were failures. "They marbleized," said one of the crew. Burned on top, soggy on the bottom, crystallized in the middle, they were so hard that when sliced, the sides glowed with a polished shine. They were awful to look at. "They look like lean-tos," said one man from Maine, an expert in that type of architecture. The edible portions tasted good, though, and there was no more persistent a person than Zom. He kept trying.

Zom frequently suffered from the plots of practical jokers. Late one Sunday night he carefully roasted a small chicken which he intended to consume himself. Erroneous in his belief that he had been undetected, he made the mistake of leaving the tasty tidbit unguarded while he went to his locker in the forward part of the ship. Bill Burroughs and Donald Moore, who had been watching silently from the wardroom, sneaked furtively into the galley and purloined the fowl. Quickly divesting it of legs, wings, and breast they retreated to the wardroom, closed the door, and thoroughly enjoyed an unexpected snack. Zom returned to the galley with a beloved storybook to find little more than an unappetizing carcass. Anguished accusations that followed were dignified only by ribald denials of guilt. No one seemed to have any information on an alleged chicken thief.

Zombie's chile con carne never will be forgotten by the members of the *Buzzards* who were on board for an evening meal in early December of 1955. The menu advertised, very simply, chili and rice. It failed to reveal that the chili would be watery, unsavory, and ghastly. The meal was so bad it became amusing and surprisingly pleasant. Everybody made jokes and laughed good-naturedly. Poor Zom, who usually became grossly irritated at such shenanigans, was unhappy but took his ribbing fairly well. This particular evening's offering was so unpalatable that the Chiefs and I settled for crackers and milk, ordering crackers three different times.

"The crackers are going pretty well at this table to-night," Burroughs said to the cook.

Dean added, "Yes, you toasted them just to the proper shade of brown."

Zom replied, "Gees. I'm glad something pleases you guys tonight."

Donald Moore noted, "I thought there were supposed to be some beans in this stuff. Look at my plate. Five beans in the whole mess!"

Ralph Sears explained, "That's soup. Didn't you ever hear of chili soup?"

"I notice you're shoving it into YOUR stomach, Sears," said Zom sarcastically.

"Yes," answered Sears. "I learned to eat everything at home because my father shoved my face into it if I didn't."

"Hey," shouted Russell Wood, "who stole the bean off my plate?"

And so it went. I did nothing but laugh hysterically. Then Clem started, and finally everybody joined with lengthy, lusty guffaws. Zom grinned, too, but he made certain that chile con carne never again was on his menu.

Men, including cooks, came and went. The stay of one, a nice lad, was of short duration, as he suffered unbearably from motion sickness. A ship was no place for an incurable, and the poor fellow was seasick twelve of his first fourteen days aboard. After a two weeks leave of absence, he returned for six successive days of additional nausea. Confined to his bunk, his health became an anxiety, and we were forced to request his immediate transfer. His merits were unknown to us, for he was unable to remain on his feet long enough to offer samples of his recipes.

Another of our food concocters was Richard Nelson, a tall, slender, blonde, quiet Swedish man from Worcester, MA whose ability in the galley was much better than average. No idler, he was studious, a good organizer, and anxious to advance himself. He endeavored so earnestly to please that, to him, incidental disappointments became catastrophic. He was extremely sensitive to adverse criticism. As Sherman pointed out, "It bent him all out of shape."

Richard inaugurated our "happy hours." In the combat against monotony too great a stress could not be placed on food. Special desserts, if not overdone in frequency, went a long ways toward relieving boredom at the table. Nelson planned a surprise every Wednesday and Sunday night. The first time it was a large spice cake with four generous helpings for each man. Desserts being confined to the noonday meal before this, the change was received with a welcome grinning astonishment. Men began to have cake for supper, they ate it as they watched the night away with television. Watchstanders had some with their night rations. There was cake left over at breakfast time. They had their fill and were not dessert conscious for several more days. Sunday, a slow, unexciting day aboard ship, was enlivened by the evening advent of pizza. And so the "happy hour," conceived and exploited by Nelson, caught the fancy of all and became an established ritual.

Robert Ritchie, a commissary man third class from Chicago, was assigned to the *Buzzards* shortly before I left. My most prominent memory of him involved an incident that occurred on March 5, 1957. He made his first cake and coated it with white icing. Wishing it sufficiently cooled in time for dinner, he carried it to the main deck and, instead of placing it in a secluded spot, left it immediately in front of the ladder leading from the second to the first deck. It was placed in such a position that anyone climbing the ladder would not see the cake until the last possible moment, when his foot already would be descending precariously close. A couple of rumors about Leroy Wilson accidently stepping on it brought a scurry of footsteps as Ritchie hastened to salvage the remains. Noting that his confection was undamaged, he moved it to a location where the crew claimed it was accessible to the gulls.

During dinner, as the cake was being devoured lustily, Wilson had a thought. "Ritchie, are you sure the seagulls didn't splatter this cake?'

"I don't think it would make much difference," replied Ritchie triumphantly.

Eating habits and preferences of food varied considerably. Posture was a source of interest, too. We had "fly-boys," men who sat with their elbows spread to the extent. "When are you going to take off?" from their fellow passengers usually resulted in a strategic withdrawal of the offending forearms. We gad "sprawlers" would could find no comfortable place for their feet, consequently kicking everyone within a wide radius. They were "hunchers,." men who hovered a few inches above their plates and smacked their lips to the withdrawal of their eating tools. This type meant business. Oblivious of their comrades, they heaped their plates as rapidly as possible, posed momentarily with utensil in hand as if to draw a deep breath, and dove in. They were the action boys. "Relaxers" had difficulty in keeping their balance, sitting with elbow on table, head in hand. This sleepy habit was curtailed largely by lack of necessary space. "Fault finders" chronically disliked all manner of food. They considered every meal and almost every part thereof a personal affront. They usually liked bee-bop with their meals, so they could complain about that, too. In lieu of the wholesome foods they found so distasteful aboard ship, these same men, on liberty, would offer no objection to stuffing themselves with greasy hamburgers at the "Slippery Spoon" or "Joe's Slop Shop." Almost without fail, we noticed that these same men were pleased with little else. They seemed to have a grudge against the world. "Conventions," relaxed, mixed food and conversation with confidence. They enjoyed a slow, easy gait spiced with discourse, laughter, and silent amusement of the more perverted methods of food intake. This latter type rarely was afflicted with stomach disorders, having learned the secret of proper mastication. They were far easier to please, perhaps because they were less torn by internal conflict.

Some of the men were identified by specific character-istics. Sherman had an irritating habit of appearing at the table with sleeves unbuttoned. They flapped loosely and generally were soiled from contact with oil or grease. No amount of prodding could cure him. At the end of a meal and frequently en route he raised an unfettered cuff to wipe his mouth. In winter the cuffs were elevated a bit higher to reach his nose. An inspiration evolved done day, and the odious practice was soon to be terminated. Sherman wiped his nose as usual. Someone said, "Sherm, I'm glad to see you carry your napkin with you. That's a good idea, too, attaching it to you so it won't get lost." Sherman was embarrassed and somewhat irked by this effrontery to his dignity. That was the clue! Later the cuff rubbed his nose.

"Sherm, I see you've got your hankie with you."

Sherman glared reproachfully but issued no comment. For a week the mealtime air was filled with, "Sherm, your hankies are cleaner today," Sherm, Im glad you didn't forget your napkins." Forthwith and ever after the sleeves were rolled, carelessly, to be sure, or else were firmly fastened. The razzing had found its mark.

Herbert Ressler was a cake eater non-pareil, the baked sweetened mixture finding much favor with him. On one occasion he had four rectangular sections with his dinner. Leaving the mess deck for a bit of mid-day shut-eye, he drifted back twice, each time for the sole purpose of diminishing the supply of leftover cake. Chief Dean and I watched from the wardroom, but Ressler was unaware of two sets of eyes following the retracing of his footsteps. A few minutes before the afternoon drills he made a third retreat, and for the third time emerged with cake crumbs dropping from his chin. Promptly at one o'clock the alarm buzzer sounded, followed by a shouted order to "ABANDON SHIP!" As the crew took their places on the double, Ressler climbed into his assigned boat with the remains of his eighth piece of cake clamped between his teeth. If he were going to abandon ship, he proposed to do so on a fulls stomach - of cake.

Hoople was a loose-leaf dresser. Being extremely careless in personal grooming and selfish in output of exertion, he habitually slipshodded to the table with shirttail trailing. After being sent from the mess deck three or four times by Chief Burroughs "to get dressed," I issued an order that if he as much as approached the table again with shirttails exposed, they would be cut off. The uprising was quelled.

With twenty-two years of service prepared chicken behind him, Chief Dean concentrated on vegetables whenever fowl was place before him, taciturnly ignoring the winged delicacy. His sole verbal outburst consisted of "Damned dried-up seagull. I've eaten it so much I'm sick of it."

The greatest coffee consumer was the same Willie who was chased into seclusion by Clem. Willie drank twelve to fourteen cups a day. His fellow crewmen explained that excessive coffee drinking made him "soft," for it had no other visible effect as far as their observations were concerned. Basically, Willie was a loner, and perhaps he poured forth his problems over a cup of coffee while commuting with himself.

The most fabulous of all "chow hounds" was Cornelius Van Pooper. He perfected sprinter style eating methods. England had its Roger Bannister who first ran the four minute mile, but we had our Cornelius Van Pooper who perfected the four minute meal. Eating with great gusto (his boon companion), Cornelius electrified us daily with his stashing ability. Noisily inviting attention by earthquaking his tableware, Connie would signal that he was ready. An octopus of arms reaching in all directions, he heaped his plate without undue loss of time. Before the astonished eyes of others who scarcely had settled onto the mess deck stools, enthusiastic shoveling began. Hand to mouth, again and again with staggering rapidity, his timing was punctuated by fork tines solidly meeting dish as the forceful appearing of food ensued. Most of his meat was pre-sliced into nuggets by professional slashes of a hunting knife, that piece of equipment aiding him no end in his quest of the four minute record. By the time the rest of the crew had obtained a helping, and condiments had been politely passed, Connie was through. Rising with a smirk, he made his boisterous way to the galley where he deposited his dishes with unrestrained whoopdedoo. He was proud of his feats of haste and wanted everyone to be witness. Looking around to make sure he was being watched, he dropped his dishes mercilessly to make sure they were heard.

Comments about his exploits were openly expressed. The subject was brought up daily, digested and re-digested. Some marveled. Some were disgusted. Others just shook their heads.

Sherman had many views, gathered from close observation over a matter of months. "I've never yet been able to figure out what he does with all the time he saves," he would say.

Mahoney commented, "He has a system, all right. I don't see how he keeps from hitting himself with the silverware. I sit there and wait for a tooth to fall out."

Sherman added, "Here's how it's done. First you have to develop a disinterest in what people think. Then you have to develop a perfect coordination between mouth and hand. He's got both. The minute his hand is a hair-breath away from his dish his mouth automatically opens."

Connie didn't mind the discussions, for he enjoyed the attention. One day when relieved of the radio watch he sat at the table as Sherman was finishing. Sherman couldn't believe his own eyes as he remained to watch Connie consume four helpings of roast veal, vegetables, and potatoes. No "record" was at stake, yet the food disappeared in relatively short time. Sherman later imparted, "That's what I call REAL gut stuffing! Man!"

Another time Sherman engaged Connie in conversation upon an extraordinary swift completion of a meal. "You don't stop to taste your food," he observed.

Connie retorted, "I'm here to eat."

"Then you must have taste buds inside your stomach."

"TASTE buds! What in hell is that?"

"Just what I said. Everyone has them on his tongue. You're supposed to let the food touch your tongue so you can taste it. YOU just INHALE your food."

"Don't ask me what you're talking about," stormed Cornelius as he stalked out of the compartment. Looking back over his shoulder, he offered, "If any of you guys think you can beat me in eating, just let me know."

"Ow, Damn!" he expostulated as he turned around fast, without looking, and bumped his shin on the water cooler. Of course it wasn't his fault. The water cooler had no business being in the way, in spite of having been securely bolted in the identical spot for a period of years.

"God, what a noisy person," mused Sherman. "You know, I actually think he's proud of his ability as a hit and run eater. And he always makes enough racket so everybody will look up and see him."

"Yeah," added someone else. "You can always tell who's having coffee during coffee break just from the way he stirs it."

"That's right, but you forgot to add how he drops the spoon onto the table and settles the sugarbowl cover back in place."

Eating during a storm was much more difficult and far less enjoyable. Rubber mats kept the tablecloth from becoming a veritable skating rink, so the problem of keeping food from sliding off was not acute. Appetites were not so ravenous, even among the "salts." Gaiety was lacking and food not as interesting. The men had to sit with their feet braced against the motion of the ship. The passing of a platter from hand to hand became somewhat hazardous. A pass at a meatball could be turned instead into an unsuccessful lunge into the spaghetti. Faces infrequently were ashen at the table and green on deck. Under such conditions eating was an art successfully mastered only through experience. Suffice to record here that the return of pleasant weather always was truly appreciated.

Noel Anderson of Ishpeming, Michigan, had no desire whatever for food during rough weather. He tried gallantly, and never completely gave up when seasick. He spent many hours on deck, alternately regurgitating and filling the void with crackers, determined to overcome seasickness. His appearances in the mess deck were the weather vane of sea conditions. Clem Meredith summed it up in his typical observing way. "When it's rough, you can't get him in here, and when it's not, you can't keep him out."

Every two weeks breakfast became the barometer of a situation joyously known as liberty. The meal was rather morose on other days. Some ate breakfast greedily, some were spasmodic, others never bothered to show up for the important meal. Chief Dean, grouchy as a bear early in the morning, awakened slowly with three cups of coffee, no food, and no chatter. Men hardly said "Good morning," to one another. The cooks were equally noncommunicative. On the day the tender was due, a complete about face was enacted. Channel fever engulfed the entire ship. Tables were filled with noisy, hungry men as laughter and gaiety rocked the mess deck. The cook had his hands full as he launched into the rare circumstance of feeding breakfast to a full crew. What a difference, and who could blame them for their buoyant spirits?

Two final incidents bearing a chow-time twang took place outside the mess deck limits. One happened on the ship, the other in Boston. Cornelius Van Pooper was featured in both. The first time, resuscitation drill was being held, and Cornelius attempted to revive an unwilling patient. The rocking cycle involved in the back-pressure, arm-lift method, employed at that time, was to have been completed twelve times a minute, but Cornelius, the renown speed merchant, accelerated himself well beyond the accepted rhythms. "Slow down, there, Van Pooper," shouted the boatswain's mate. "You're not eating!"

Connie was a Texan and proud of it. He acted the part well, spun tall tales and bragged about the splendors of his favorite state. On liberty he dressed like a Texan and thus, on one occasion, regaled in skin tight blue jeans hung from a wide bejeweled belt, fancy cowboy boots, blue denim jacket embroidered with frills and imitation rubies, he strolled into a Boston hotel, ten-gallon hat in hand. Lavishing a two dollar tip onto the head waiter, he was escorted to a vacant table set decorously directly in front of the orchestra. After studying and being unable to understand the menu, he ordered fried chicken which shortly was placed before him in a silver tureen.

Then it began. Sweeping all excess silver into a clattering disarranged heap, he grabbed a fork with one hand and slammed the top of the tureen to the table with the other. Elevating the vessel, he scraped the chicken onto his dinner plate. The tureen top was replaced with a frightening clatter that shattered the nerves of customers in the far away reaches of the huge dining room. His fork flashed into a chicken side, pinioned it to the plate, and a leg was savagely separated from the carcass. With lightening swiftness, the technique possibly learned from watching gulls, the bone was stripped of meat which made a quick passage to Connie's gullet. Again the fork flashed, found its mark unerringly, and a wing followed the same fate.

By this time Connie was the center of attraction. Giggling patrons stopped eating to better view the burlesque. Members of the band interrupted their dinner music to double over in chuckling hysteria. The head waiter, close to apoplexy, sped to the scene. Bent stiffly, he asked, "Good heavens, man. Have you no knowledge of etiquette? Don't you possess any table manners?"

"What in hell do you mean?"

"Don't you know how to eat properly?"

"I eat any damned way I want to. It's the only way I know how."

The short, stout garcon with the this mustache rolled his eyes skyward, tilted his head, gritted his teeth, and raise his palms as if to seek divine guidance. With that he turned and walked briskly away.

Connie later confided, "He looked like he just puffed up and walked off. I didn't give a damn. I kept on eating."

A week later Connie reentered the same hotel, adorned in the same finery. He squandered another two dollar tip to the same head waiter, was recognized instantly and escorted once again to a vacant table. This table was not in front of the band. It was in a dimly lighted retreat surrounded by massive green ferns. Consequently, he was discreetly shielded from the wandering eyes of most other humans.

Connie finished his meal greedily, as usual, and as he prepared to leave, he beckoned to the uneasy waiter.

"What's the idea of all these damned bushes?" he inquired.

"Why, those are ferns," smiled the waiter, relieved that the Texan was leaving.

"What's the idea of putting me behind them?" continued Cornelius.

"That," explained the waiter, "was the only unreserved table available!"

Connie wasn't impressed. "Look, my money talks as loud as anybody else's. The next time I come in here don't you stick me behind any of those damned bushes, you hear?" Without waiting for a reply he strode to the cashier, paid his bill, and vanished into the night.

Chapter VIII

"Indian Summer"

Of the New England seasons, I much prefer September and October, the "Indian summer" months. (Indian summer, in the strict interpretation, comes in November and usually is a few days of warm, sunny weather immediately following the first real cold spell of the season. A loose interpretation, however, allows one to consider Indian summer as the ninth and tenth months of the year.) In any event, the days are sunny; skies are bright with segments of fibrous cirrus or rolls of soft stratocumulus; the air carries an authoritative zing, temperatures are moderately cool. To me, this is most beautiful and inspiring. I awaken on these mornings with a feeling of jubilation and am glad to be alive and a part of the great universe. I bound out of bed joyfully, my mind at peace with the world. I am ready for anything.

I experienced this same gladness of life on the *Buzzards* during the autumns of 1955 and 1956. Many, many days vied for the ultimacy of grandeur, and my notes reveal that such a day was September 26, 1955:

At seven o'clock I awakened to the meow of a cat. A cat? Out here? Closer examination revealed it to be the "party"cry of a herring gull. The cook had discarded some scraps, and the gull was acknowledging his appreciation and possibly inviting friends to join him.

My notes continue. It is a beautiful autumn morning, typical of the season. I can tell the heading of the ship from my bunk on sunny days by the influx of sunlight through the portholes of my cabin. This morning we are headed north because two yellow circles, broken in their roundness only by the dogs that secure the ports, appear on the green bulkhead. A miniature aurora borealis dances on part of the overhead, caused by reflection of bright sun on calm water. Now the ship is headed more northwesterly because three disks appear, the third through the porthole facing toward the stern. The miniature borealis now engulfs the whole overhead in a dazzling display. The sky, seen through the ports, is a friendly deep blue. It is positively fascinating to awaken in this manner. The water, not seen until I arise, is blue except for an area near the ship's rudder where it breaks off in a precise line of demarcation to a deep dark green, as translucent a sea green as ever I have seen.

Day wore on. It was a thrill to breathe the cool fresh undiluted air, so crisply invigorating. The season might be called Indian summer because of the coloring, for Indians liked bright colors. Where or when could one find a more colorful time than autumn in New England?

The fly population was the lone discouraging note of the day. Hundreds of them bombarded the ship, seeking entry. They were the familiar housefly (Musca domestica) and apparently were carried by offshore winds from the mainland. They were a nuisance in flight and at mealtime, but seemed to bite only on the ankles. Swarms of them ultimately fell victim to our electric spray gun.

A dragonfly (order of Odonata) made a visit late in the afternoon. He was a conspicuous part of color himself, with his green forepart, a long slender black body, a blue tail, and transparent wings. I know not whether he was wind-blown in company with the flies or had pursued them. As a youngster, I knew this species as a "darning needle." My dad used to tell me they sewed up the mouths of naughty little boys who used cuss words. Needless to say, the very sight of the insect always terrified me, and my little legs pumped as fast as they could go as I made haste for the shelter of home. I knew he intended to do a stitching job on me, but he had to catch me first. It was surprising to see our visiting dragonfly leave the lightship with so much sewing unaccomplished.

5:00 P.M., same day. There was a light northerly breeze. A few cirrus dotted the sky to the west. To the southeast, Gay Head was clearly visible although an aqua haze projected the island onto a lofty perch. The multicolored cliffs showed resplendent vertical tinges of white, gray, brown, pink, and red. Through binoculars, a lighthouse and a church showed prominently.

To the east lies the island of Cuttyhunk, and the Coast Guard watch tower, on the highest part of the island, is plainly visible to the naked eye. Almost all of the manmade construction lies on the east side of Cuttyhunk where it is sheltered from the cold northwesterly winds of winter. A lone hut to the north and another to the extreme south are, from the lightship, the only buildings capable of being seen. Otherwise, the island looks barren with a burnt brown effect spattered sparsely with evergreen shrubbery. A rocky coast on the west side must have discouraged early pioneers. To this day it still discourages boatmen except the experienced who find exceptionally good striped bass fishing (Roccus saxatilis) amongst the rocks.

To the north lies the mainland, and we are almost directly south of the boundary between Massachusetts and Rhode Island. This evening the coastline has a border of royal blue. Water in the direction New Bedford, close to shore, presents a wide band of white icefield coloring.

To the west and southwest lie the open seas. To the south, the small island of Nomansland infrequently shows itself. Tonight it appears as an island floating in the sky, an optical illusion caused by land haze. Now a cloud bank approaches from the west, obscuring the sun. already a chill is felt in the air. "Old-timers" often refer to days like these as "weather breeders." Perhaps they will be right.

The next few days were calm and peaceful. The ship barely displayed any motion in the serenity of a tranquil sea. The sun shone warmly. Visibility remained unimpaired. Temperatures were normal for the season. I busied myself in my duties, for I had much to learn, and my notes were neglected.

Nothing further of unusual interest impressed me, autumnwise, until the eighth day of the following October, a year later. I was in exceptionally buoyant spirits that morning, for again it was a sunny day keenly alive with an air of fall. A lone auxiliary sloop, bearing the romantic name of *Rapture*, approached from the east, south of Cuttyhunk. Its hull was robin's egg blue, the superstructure varnished. A matching blue dinghy with a bright red bottom was carried on deck. Two large grayish-brown areas showed on the port side where it had chafed, probably at a dock. Two occupants sat in the stern sheets. One appeared to be a girl in new brilliant yellow oilskins while the other, at the tiller, evidently was a male, attired in an olive brown parka. There was an energetic head wind as the rugged little craft chugged slowly along under power. The sea was a mottled green and blue, splattered with whitecaps. The sky was a magnificent deep blue directly above, fading to gray along the horizon.

How I envied those two persons boating alone, enjoying the brisk clearness of the autumn day and the sweet cool taste of invigorating air, unchallenged by man made crafts of speed. The *Rapture* moved slowly into the face of the seas, the bow now down, now up, but gaining with a stubborn determination. At times the greater portion of the green underwater section, nearly to the keel, came into view as a sea swell challenged its right to be on the open ocean. A breaking wave struck the bow with a thud, and a spray of white foam confettied the entire boat and its occupants.

Twenty minutes later the boat was a speck on the distant horizon. A varnished mast wig-wagged its position on the turbulent seascape. I was reminded of the axiom "the best things in life are free," often philosophized in speech and song. The words rang a true note. How wonderful to be able and feel a love of nature, to be able to enjoy her sky, her winds, her seas, her air. Bon voyage, occupants of the *Rapture*!

Three days after the Rapture disappeared beyond the western fringes of vision the small white transparent jellyfish returned in vast numbers. There was no precision or formation to their maneuvers as they floated here and there, moving with the tide, aimlessly, effortlessly. This was on the eleventh of October, and Indian summer was with us in gaudy details. The following days were so glorious we found the sun-drenched deck irresistible, and spent much time there as possible. My pen became imbued with spirit and produced more memoranda.

October 12, Columbus Day, a legal holiday in Rhode Island, a few miles away. Many fishing boats make good usage of the weather by carrying potential Isaac Waltons to the fishing grounds. Tautog (Tautoga onitis) are being caught in abundance at the western entrance to Vineyard Sound. This species is called blackfish in New York and New Jersey, but to Massachusetts residents a blackfish is a small whale, once prized for its oil. The blackfish being caught by anglers near the lightship are edible, weigh from four to fifteen pounds and are no relation to a whale.

4:00 P.M.: The boats scampered toward shore. The tide was running in an easterly direction, and millions of tiny plankton filled the sea as it flowed around us. A few squirrel hake (physics chuss) reportedly broke the surface with jaws agape, relishing the supply of food coming their way. The gulls showed interest neither in the microscopic sea life nor in the hake. Abruptly, twenty minutes later, no further activity was seen. The water cleared. Marine plant and animal life seemingly disappeared.

A few low, lazy southwest swells rocked us gently. The seas began to take on a briskness in spite of a lack of whitecaps. A light air sprang up from the southwest along with feathery cirrus high above more cumbersome alto-cumulus. The lower clouds were arranged in lines like an array of troops marching across the heavens. The horizon, as seen between these regimental forms, had taken on a milky appearance. Distant objects were replaced by a low haze that made them appear as massive floating objects, although features of the landscape ten miles away remained sharp and distinct.

A gull floated by, having sport with a short section of driftwood. He looked proud as he stood with piercing eyes, charting his course. He attempted to wash his beak and feed on plankton, all the while doing knee bends. Soon he tired and elected to swim nearby, possessively guarding his "cabin cruiser."

As night settled upon us, a half moon rose from the east, its reflected earthshine casting a yellow path which fanned across the sea to the distant west. The planet Mars was a bright spectacle in the southeastern sky. The red lights of radio towers on the mainland twinkled prominently. Red, green, and white buoys flashed over the bay. Indeed it was Indian summer day and night.

October 13. 8:15 A.M.: I watched a tanker proceeding in an easterly direction along the Sakonnet coast, it looked grotesque, like two separate objects. To the naked eye it appeared to be a tug with a tow, and only the binoculars revealed it to be one completely attached vessel. One hundred and eighty degrees away Nomansland was visible, suspended in the sky by refraction. The sun again shone brilliantly, all conditions of weather being similar to those of the preceding day.

1:30 P.M.: The sea was a vast mirror. A school of hake swam lazily near our bow. The playful antics of gulls several miles away could be watched in detail. The crew were on deck preparing to launch the dory. From my cabin I could hear them laugh boisterously, contentedly. This weather foments good spirits. We felt lighthearted, carefree. No problem would be too great an obstacle. We were bursting with exuberance. Now the boat has been lowered, and I could hear the slap of an oar as it struck the water, followed by the surge of oars against the tholepins as the dory moved away.

An oak leaf, sans chlorophyl, drifted by. How did it get here? The nearest oak tree is at least five and a half miles from the Buzzards. And that leaf came from seaward! From where? How long had it been waterborne? Why hadn't it been crushed by an irritated sea? How long would it be able to continue in its present state before it perished? Would it ever again be noticed by man? Strange how a simple oak leaf could cause such questioning.

The boys in the dory came alongside. "Skipper, how about us rowing over to Brown's Ledge? We'll take the outgoing mail if you'll let us go." How could I refuse on a day such as this? They started with a burst of enthusiastic dipping of oars. This brief flurry soon abated in frenzy, and they then rowed strongly and steadily. Tinier and tinier they became, but the distance to the cluster of motorboats was greater than the men had anticipated. Through binoculars we could see the rise and fall of their oars, not now as rhythmic or as rapid and probably not nearly so enjoyable as when they first conceived the idea. They remained resolutely determined and finally, later than they had planned and much more tired, they reached their destination.

Half an hour later the *Bridget Ann* approached, with our dory in tow. Our tired oarsmen were joshed good naturedly. "What's the matter? Are you pooped?" "It was too long a row, huh?"

David Oram, from Marblehead, Massachusetts, had a good answer: "Hell, when you get an offer for a ride like this you don't turn it down."

They brought a peace offering, six freshly caught tautog that became our Sunday dinner.

October 14: The sunrise was gorgeous. As it ascended above the island of Martha's Vineyard, it cut a glittering path to our home on the sea. Within a space of ten minutes, immediately upon rising, it presented itself in three colors, changing from red to orange to yellow. A few light ground swells wallowed from the southwest. The gurgling tide aped a mountain brook as it swept around our rudder, rushing toward the northeast.

October 15: The haze that arrived yesterday afternoon still lingered, reducing visibility to less than two miles. Unable to see land, we were subjected to the sound of foghorns. According to the radio, Boston was experiencing smog. On board ship the crew referred to fog as water smoke, and joked about the closest land being only seventy feet away - straight down! Blue skies and warm sunshine pierced the haze vertically but neither horizontally nor obliquely.

October 16: The third successive day of haze. A lone American scoter zig zagged across the path of morning sunlight to the southeast, inches above the water. We were saddened during the afternoon by the death of one of our feathered friends. A pretty yellow and black warbler had been visiting us for several days, becoming quite domesticated as he hopped unconcerned around our feet. At 1:00 P.M. he perched on the rudder quadrant, sunning himself. At 2:00 P.M. we found him dead, inches from his last living perch. Sorrowfully, we buried him at sea.

October 17: We received mail shortly after breakfast. Our friends from Westport Point, en route to their favorite fishing grounds, threw a bag of mail and magazines aboard. It was indeed a moment of rejoicing. It was so pleasant to receive letters from home. After accepting our thanks and well wishes for a bountiful day, the captain of the little boat departed, cautioning, "Don't go nowhere!"

At noon we watched the squirrel hake who still remained close by, always on the shady side of the ship. One was tempted by an apricot pit dropped over the side. He obviously objected to the taste or to the quality of the offering, for he quickly opened his jaws and expelled the stone, swimming away as it slowly sank from sight.

Thirty minutes after sundown, Bob Dean and I were standing near the starboard side of the wheelhouse when we saw a strange cloud approaching. The sky was eighty percent covered with stratocumulus when a low sliver of unbroken cloud approached swiftly from the south. It resembled the vapor trail of a plane except for being dark in color and only a couple of hundred feet above the water. It disappeared as it reached us, and we thought no more of it. Suddenly, a moment later, it reappeared to the north in bold detail against an unclouded sector of sky. It continued its northward course for fully ten minutes before disintegrating. Later we learned that it had indeed been a vapor trail, one that had come to earth. We discovered the answer to this perplexing fragment of cloud by watching the white avenue left by a plane high in the sky to the northwest. As it settled slowly earthward, it darkened and took on similar features to our own stray formation. It was a phenomenon no longer.

The next two days were windy and rough as a north-easter bore down upon us. We had misgivings as to the duration of Indian summer, for winter was beginning to stir and show ugly intentions. We remained below decks much of the time and ventured out only to catch a breath of air or to gaze somewhat dejectedly toward the mainland.

October 20: What has happened to the long northeaster we were supposed to get? It had given up without much of a struggle, for the morning dawned clear. The sun shone without hindrance of cloud. There hardly was a ripple on the water. Our brilliant fall had returned. As we looked north to the mainland, we could see ground fog lying in separate patches over Newport, Westport, and New Bedford, none appearing between the municipalities or over the islands. It was a sight we never before had been invited to witness. Usually fog was everywhere or nowhere.

During mid-morning a dozen whistlers (American goldeneye) skimmed from east to west, distinguished from afar by their black and white markings. Their maneuvers were polished and well executed as they speeded on their way, now fanning, now converging.

In the afternoon we sensed with a sad realism that this would be the last of the lovely Sundays of Indian summer. The ocean was motionless. Warm sunshine sparkled. We could see Squibnocket Beach on Martha's Vineyard, visual perception from this area of the *Buzzards* being most extraordinary. Everyone was on deck. Some sat in the sun, reading. Two others hung washing. I took sextant angles as Leroy Wilson checked me for accuracy.

To the southeast, five miles distant, fourteen boats were counted on Sound Ledge. Sailboats passed on various courses, and we could feel their wake as it gently rocked the ship. On Brown's Ledge, to the southwest, nine more boats had fishing lines dangling over the sides. Off the Sow and Pigs, a rock formation close to Cuttyhunk frequented by schools of striped bass, three skiffs carried fishing enthusiasts. Fifty squirrel hake lingered within the shadows cast by our bow and superstructure. A piece of scrap metal dropped nearby resulted in a flurry of fish heading temporarily for the deeps. Their scare soon ended, and they returned to the surface.

We remained on deck for the duration of the afternoon. The splendor of the warm sun was intoxicating. We were not impregnated with ambition, being contentedly lax, lazy, docile. Our thoughts drifted shoreward, as always, filling us with desire to share the cheery warmth with our loved ones. We were stymied in this aspiration, of course, and could only hope that they, too, were enjoying autumn at her best.

That night was the most beautiful I ever spent on the Buzzards lightship. In early evening, for want of something to do, we watched a silent movie, for the sound track of the projector was inoperative. When monotony comes to the fore, threatening to overwhelm one's mind, he invariably will fight back with everything in his power rather than succumb meekly. Thus it was that we showed the silent film and tried to guess the words that were being spoken. We were dismal flops as lip readers, but the picture filled a void in time. Regardless of the season, the end of a movie was closely followed by a trek to the main deck for a "look around." The night of October 20, 1956, was the ultimate in sheer beauty. The tide being slack, the ocean had not regained motion save for the ripples of the companionable hake. Wind was non-existent. A large yellow moon, just past the full, shown from a cloudless sky, its plains and mountains defined in bold detail. We could see shore lights all the way from West Falmouth on Cape Cod to Point Judith in Rhode Island. The constellations Corona and Bootes were in faint display above the flash of the Brenton Reef Lightship. Cygnas, the swan, was directly overhead. Auriga and the Pleiades were rising from the northeast. Binary stars were almost visible as such. We were loathe to retire from this remarkable setting, but a damp southeast breeze sprang into being, and our "Indian summer" had nearly completed its cycle.

Chapter IX

"Storms"

Clashes with a storm drenched Atlantic are sustained with frequent monotony on a lightship. Riding at anchor more than five miles from the nearest approach of the mainland, the *Buzzards* was subjected to nature's whims from every angle. At times she was merciless; at other times she was kinder, depending on the quarter from which she chose to unleash her belligerency.

The most dreaded storm along the Atlantic seaboard is the northeaster, which often lasts for several days. A southeaster may be more severe but is of shorter duration. Owing to the geographical location of the *Buzzards* station, the easterlies, however, were not usually of any great consequence. The southeaster was, as mentioned above, a short storm, and the contour of the land protected us from the brutal lashings of other easterly storms except one of two or three days onslaught that arrived DIRECTLY from the northeast. 045 degrees on the compass. This true northeaster could be genuinely unpleasant, and caused the ship to drag anchor more than once.

A northwester was almost like human breath being blown on a bathtub sailboat. Wintry winds up to fifty knots sometimes attacked us from that direction, bringing avalanches of snow and freezing rains, yet the sea remained relatively placid, thanks to the protection afforded by the coastline. Swells had no room in which to build to bothersome heights. Wind waves were not particularly frantic or awesome. Snow required the springing to life of our great searching foghorn, but the miserable pitching of wretched ship upon crested wave was absent.

From due west counter-clockwise to the southeast was our exposed sector, form whence wind and wave rolled in for miles across an open sea. Southwest was by far the most ruthless vector for our station. From here the introduction of even the lightest of winds caused an upheaval of ocean that bounced our ship like dishes being washed in a sink. Seas increased rapidly in severity to crash against the hull with shattering impact. Winds howled with various degrees of strength and cadence. The anchor chain sounded like a series of freight cars being coupled together as it strained against the elements. Men became nauseated and miserable. Work reached a virtual standstill as human misery was expounded.

Few people realize what the Coast Guard does for mariners or how so many sometimes suffer for so few. Exposed to the tortures of a southwester, fighting nausea, fighting to stand erect, fighting to eat, fighting to maintain a proper watch, fighting to sleep at night, fighting to retain sensibility even, we stove, on the *Buzzards*, to stay "on station" for the benefit of boating interests. How many, sitting snugly at home before the fireplace on a blustery oppressive night, gave any thought to a crew of men being mauled on a lunging lightship? How many care? I am sure the families of the crew are gravely concerned, but even they can only partially realize the discomforting, sometimes harrowing, ordeal of a pitching vessel, a quaking stomach, sleepless nights, and a most unhappy existence.

The most depressing feeling I ever have known is that of riding out a southwester at night. The ship moves up and down, down and up, up and down with terrible monotony of motion. Some swells are gradual and lazy. Others are steep and harsh. Sleep comes with great difficulty, if at all. Your head aches, a crick appears in the neck, you grit your teeth subconsciously, your stomach is sore, your kidneys and back ache with a dull throbbing. No position in the bunk (or out of it) is comfortable. It is impossible to remain on your side, so you lie on your back, feet braced against the end of the bunk, arms held at the side to assist in remaining as motionless as possible. You almost scream in anguish at the constant upheaval of a ship that tugs at your body in different directions. You feel your weight shifting, being pushed against the head of the bunk, then being dragged towards the foot. To the head, to the foot, over and over and over. Meanwhile, the back feels as though it is being scraped devoid of flesh. The kidney region protests mightily with waves of pain. Subjected to continuous rigors of discomfort and near nausea, minutes seem endless, and a nightmare of eternities dampens one's spirit. Worse yet is the battle to retain the senses. After four days of similar batterings, you are nearly ready for the bughouse, symptoms - mental derangement.

By day you sway back and forth like a cobra, striving to keep your balance. When you are first arising from bed, it is most difficult to remain upright, for you are not used to standing on a moving floor. It is like riding a frenzied twisting subway on foot with no strap to help in staying vertical. You stagger, lurch, grasp for support. If support is not immediately procurable, an involuntary series of short steps follow, continuing until a bulkhead or a locker gets in the way.

An attempt to pull on trousers from a standing position becomes a locomotive duel. It can also be absolutely dangerous. First you get the legs of the trous4rs in a receptive position. Then one foot is elevated and lowered in the direction of the appropriate leg. It may land where intended. It may not come close. You try again. This time the left foot finds the opening, and a trouser leg is pulled over the foot. You think you're all set. You raise the other foot, preparing to insert it in the vacant trouser leg. At that moment the ship lurches. The raised foot quickly seeks support. You are off balance, unable to move the left foot which now has anchored the trousers firmly to the deck. One hand attempts to hold the tops of the trousers while the other gropes frantically for support. If the groping hand is successful, you try again. If not, you take a weird hop or two or three, trying to retain balance. If this fails, you probably will have to pick yourself off the deck, trousers and feet a war of confusion, and renew your undertakings from the beginning. You curse at anything available, usually the first thing that comes to the fore. The weather always is included in the vehement outburst: "Damned son of a bitch of a southwest wind!"

A successful tussle with the trousers paves the way to the washbowl. Standing there, braced firmly against the ship's antics, you try to wash. You lean over to rinse soap from your face or tooth paste from your mouth, and you are in grave danger of pitching into the bowl. You clutch the side, if you are lucky, before bumping your forehead on a water spigot or the medicine cabinet. Again the cuss words scream at the wind, to no avail. The wind screams back as if angered by a meaningless rebuke.

Your day is off to a miserable start. Your frame of mind becomes clouded with a grim tarnished perspective towards everything connected with a maritime theme. The lighter side of life offers no appeal, for you have little sense of mirth for the situation. This inner feeling may, and very often does, continue for the duration of the vessel's rock and roll session.

Stumbling to the mess deck, where breakfast is ready, you find little appeal in the food. You sit at a stool to sip coffee which tastes like anesthesia. As you look through the portholes, the sea, land, and sky seem to be in motion, racing wildly like old film through a projector. You see a snarling ocean crusted with white waves, then the distant land. Then you see nothing but clouds and sky that suddenly evaporate and are buried in a swirling green. The maddened water churns over the whole surface of the porthole, and the clouds reappear as the ship shudders herself back to a temporary evened keel. Your coffee spills, but firmly braced legs prevent you frm falling off the stool. One or two hardy souls may join you for coffee, but most find conditions most repulsive to appetite.

The workday commences half-heartedly as seasick and headachy seamen go about their duties robot like. Decks are not swept thoroughly. Dusty niches remain dusty. Tarnished brass is destined to remain as lusterless as the men. Department heads (men in charge of sections) do not feel inspired to stimulated enterprise themselves as they hold to a stanchion or brace themselves in an office to plan their day's activity. The angry sloshing of water breaking against the hull of the ship interrupts their thoughts, or possibly helps them to formulate a decision. The work list becomes the victim as its magnitude of effort is appreciably diminished, at least for the day at hand.

The cooks unhappily prepare meals, muttering, "They won't eat much today, so there's no use breaking our ass getting things ready." Ingredients are measured somewhat carelessly. Pans slide across the galley range. Liquid is slopped from pots as the cook struggles to keep from falling,

"Damn it. I should have wiped up that grease I spilled on the deck. Stinking damned southwester. Those people who think we have it so frigging easy should come out here and try to cook on a day like this. They'd be puking their guts out."

An ashen face appears at the partitioned hatch above a sign stating "AUTHORIZED PERSONNEL ONLY" and meekly asks if there are any more crackers.

"Yeah, I'll get some when I get a chance. Don't get sick and puke in here. I'll let you know when I bring them up from the storeroom."

The seas continue to plow into us, punching solidly, flinging unnumbered gallons of water and spray. They vessel trembles, pitches, rolls, is struck full force by another onrush of seething turbulence. Bulkheads wail and groan. Loose gear thuds to the deck. Hatches rattle. The bow totters high in the air, the sea drops out from under, the ship falls heavily into the trough. Men hang on for all they're worth. The are dreadfully uncomfortable whether they be sitting, walking, working, or in their bunk. Their bodies are as storm racked as the vessel. Minds are clouded, senses dulled.

How much can human endurance tolerate? How long can a suffering body yield to such unnatural beating? We read about sadism in magazines and in the newspapers. That it exists is known fact. Its barbaric happenings are recorded daily, all over the world. Yet, is such suffering endured so much worse than the torture to body and mind received at the end of an anchor chain during a stout southwest storm, especially when it continues for days?

Little is accomplished on the *Buzzards* during such outbursts of wind and wave. We maintain watches and radio contact. We try to stay as nearly on station as possible, and pride ourselves at our availability to remain on the little spot dictated by the chart. We may drag anchor, grudgingly giving a few yards now and then to the storm. We carefully check the scope and reactions of the chain, for we must know when we are dragging and how badly.

Night finally arrives, and we are glad the day is over. Yet how dismal are the prospects of sleep or untormented rest! What is there to look forward to, other than a change of wind that will come "sometime"? Up and down rides the vessel, back and forth, ever on the move. Another wave, another gust of wind, a rumbling of the anchor chain, vibrations, double vibrations, triple vibrations. Thump! A shower of spray! The vessel raises her bow haughtily as a broken sea gushes desperately along the waterway, seeking escape. Human bodies sustain another jolt to their intricate complex systems. Tempers fall short, far short of desirable acceptance. Unanswered, unheard oaths of damnation are hurled in all directions as men respond to the awful battering in the only way they are able. Night creeps on, ever so slowly. Minutes crawl. Hours become eons. Engine room personnel check their motors, generators, and pumps for signs of vibration, loosened fittings, or cracked pipes. The radio room watch cautiously makes his way along deck, checking boats, rigging, the weather. He has to be careful about venturing too close to the railing, for an unexpected lurch could hurl him into an ocean that is ever ready to carry a tragic victim to Davy Jones. The deck is well lighted. Deck fittings are painted white to minimize their stumbling hazard, but the ocean is fierce. Backed by a strong southwest wind, it is mad.

Southwesters are sneaky. Their position, course, speed, and velocity generally are difficult to accurately forecast. Once in awhile they arrive on schedule. Rarely do they pull any punches by terminating their vigor prior to inflicting great punishment. Often they become a storm near our immediate locale, enlarge rapidly in energy, and rage upon us before we have a chance to really get ready, but then, even a small southwester with limited intensity is vicious on the *Buzzards* station.

Late afternoon of December 9, 1956, was lovely for the season of the year. The murky waters were serene, visibility excellent, and sky littered with dark billowy clouds forming slowly from the northwest ahead of a slight breeze from the same sector. We were contented for many reasons. We were in easy motion, swinging gently from seventy-five fathoms of anchor chain. It was Sunday, which meant the nearness of liberty scheduled four days hence. Radio stations were merry with pre-Christmas happiness, and we were engaged in our own holiday thoughts. We had no storm warnings, light northerly winds being predicted. We were rested. The weekend was nearly at an end, and the working days to follow would pass quickly.

That night we received our first snow. Relaxed in my bunk, I noted the time. It was 10:30 P.M. Large snowflakes swirled beneath the deck light outside the porthole. They resembled insects of summer winging they way hopefully in search of someone to bite. "How beautiful," my mental picture photographed, "to be able to be at home tonight, the mellow warmth of the hearth casting grotesque shadows as one peers through the window at the gathering whiteness. Out here snow brings little joy." My sole emotion was the realization of the coziness of my cabin. I marveled at the two extremes of temperature and conditions separated by the few inches of insulated bulkhead. Flakes that stuck against the glass ports melted almost instantly.

As the snowflakes grew larger, dancing with a heavier concentration of partners, my romantic visions were rudely rearranged by the foghorns that began their shouts of disapproval. As usual, I heard the compressor warming to its task and inserted cotton in my ears. The blasts were expected. Even so, my body tensed perceptibly at the initial onset.

The following noon, December 10th, unconfirmed reports were announced by commercial radio of the possibility of southwest gales within twenty-four hours, carrying winds that possibly would reach sixty miles per hour. One commentator stated bluntly, "We are not concerned with the KIND of weather to be expected tomorrow, but rather with the VELOCITY of the strong winds that are anticipated."

Knowing too well how even a minor southwest skirmish affected our station, we awaited no official confirmation. Sufficient preparations being a splendid risk, we shifted our attention immediately to a pre-hurricane routine. Department heads sent their men to the task of securing all loose gear. Oil levels were checked. The paint locker was given special attention, for it already had suffered a couple of painful experiences with southwesterly mesmerizations. Extra lashings were tightly knotted around the boat covers. The dory, usually suspended over the starboard quarter, was rigged in and secured on deck near the stern. Lifelines were brought to the wheelhouse, ready for use if conditions dictated. The anchor chain was let out to six and a half shots, about six hundred feet. The object of the extra length of chain was not to prevent dragging anchor, but to slow it down as much as possible. These tasks readied, we waited with a mistrusting air of hopeful anticipation that perhaps the storm wouldn't develop into as brisk a showing as hinted.

Small craft warnings were officially displayed at 10:00 P.M. The wind gradually backed to the west, to the southwest, and then to southwest proper. Great rolling swells began their sickish rhythm. Wind waves were born on the puffings of steadily increasing torrents of warm moist air.

By daybreak the roller coaster spasms were consistent. We were in the clutches of our enemy - the southwester. It was Tuesday, December 11th, and the storm, while it never reached the predicted sixty mile per hour range, was destined to last for three days. It interfered with our liberty day routine, which was most disheartening of all. It also interfered with the digestive tracts of several of the crew, and the cook expended extra rations of salt crackers.

At 8:00 A.M. the sea was a dark blue under cover of cloud, brightening to a medium green when Sol turned on his charm. The whole was plentifully dotted with a white meringue. A set of signal halyards slipped from the grasp of a man hoisting storm warnings. They trailed astern, fluttering semi-horizontally from the mainmast. It seemed doubtful if they could be reached until the wind and sea subsided, for it was much too perilous to send a man aloft, up the ratlines. Leroy Wilson came on deck and finally captured the runaway halyards by tossing a heaving line over them. We noticed the brass snaphooks shining brilliantly where they had rubbed against the line during and before their escapade.

At 9:00 A.M. Wilson and I checked our position. The wind blew so fiercely the gusts prevented us from taking sextant angles from the flying bridge, so we huddled on the bow in the protection of the bulwarks. Pitching violently up and down, staggered by the jerking sensation, blown by the wind that made our eyes water, we nevertheless obtained a fix. The sun darted in and out from behind the clouds making Gosnold Tower on Cuttyhunk exceedingly difficult to find in the mirror of the sextant.

A few hardy gulls remained close by, paddling, heads lowered into the direction of the wind. Uncanny judges of broken water, they allowed small wind waves to swamp them, emerging unruffled with a disdainful shaking of beaks. Always, when a large breaker moved upon them, they were able to escape, helicopter style, a flapping of wings carrying them up and away before the arc of water could enact a capture.

A diesel driven fishing boat headed for New Bedford, diving headlong into ten foot seas lashed by forty mile per hour winds. Her bow buried into the troubled green sea as she knifed shoreward, casting torrents of water the length of the vessel that dissolved in cold white spray. Fishermen do not have an easy life. Exposed to all mannerisms of hardships, the contributors of the conventional fish dinner of Friday often earn their wages under trying conditions.

A slashing giant swell broke over our high bow, thudding with terrible energy against the wheelhouse. Water poured off the portholes like torrential rain. On the starboard side a warm sun quickly evaporated the few remaining droplets, leaving encrusted scabs of salt.

It was interesting to stand in the bow, topside, shielded by the bulwarks, watching the ship rise and fall as tons of surly water slammed against the hull. The hawsepipe, from whence the anchor chain leads, ordinarily a few feet above the water's edge, was immersed from sight as the gigantic southwest swells rolled in. As the bow rose sharply, cascades of water, trapped within, panicked its way back through the hawse and windlass room scuppers. A mass of white sudsy lather topped the dull green ocean. A yellow sun illuminated fine spray as arcs of rainbow coloring added to the spectacle. A dozen feet of anchor chain emerged from the sea, shaking itself vigorously like a dog brought in from the rain.

Looking straight down while the bow was forced upward was similar to looking down from a second story window. The ocean seemed far, far away. When a heavy swell lurched against the ship, dipping the bow, the sea rose swiftly toward the railing. Just as suddenly it lowered again. It was like riding in a fast moving elevator where floor levels receded or rushed back, not nearly so smoothly.

I walked to the bow where David Oram and William Sherman were watching the antics of wind, wave, and vessel. Sherman exclaimed, "Skipper, come listen to the echo. Go ahead, Dave. Show him."

Oram stood near the eyes of the ship. With a smile of accomplishment he hollered, "Uuuupppp and dowwwnnnNNNNN," timing his utterances to the motion of the ship. When the bow rose abruptly, he started his "Uuuupppp," and as it fell, he slurred into "dowwwnnnNNNNN." When the *Buzzards* reached midway to the bottom of a storm infested trough, a wall of quarrelsome water rushing towards us captured the end of Oram's "downnnNNN" and hurled it back, greatly magnified in volume.

Again he shouted at the ocean. "Uuuuupppp and dowwwnnnNNNNN. Uuuupppp and dowwwnnnNNNNN." Each time the shouts and echoes blended as one as the ship lunged toward the bottom of the trough of sea water. The onrushing Atlantic hurled back the shouted "dowwwnnnNNNNN" almost as though it had originated it.

Watching the behavior of the anchor chain during these powerful onslaughts, one marvels at its strength, its construction, its ability to hold a heavy vessel in a relatively stationary position. The anchor grabs obstinately onto the bottom as the chain straightens energetically. It is our brake. It is different than applying brakes in an automobile where the forward motion continues at least a few feet and the slowdown is gradual. On a ship the BACKWARD motion is checked, and we are wrenched in the opposite direction.

Time dragged slowly as the lashings continued with nerve wracking monotony. We were existing as hum-drum humans, waiting hopefully, cursing wretchedly, losing interest in our surroundings, thinking of home, hating everything else. Our bodies ached, our nerves were distraught, our minds fought to retain sanity.

At 3:00 A.M. on Wednesday morning the southwester was forty-eight hours old and showing no indications of retreat. I had been unable to sleep. At the point of drifting sweetly into the land of nod the violent shaking fight of ship versus elements rudely alerted me to consciousness. I thought about reading. Reaching for a book, I fell back, exhausted. Still I could not sleep. The fight continued, pounding, sparring, slashing,. I considered getting up and going on deck. The thought of this tired me, too, and the beckoning of slumber slowly closed my eyelids. Not for long. My eyes opened, stared only at the deck lights that were rising, falling irregularly. "I wish I could sleep."

The wearisome seas piled against us. One would strike villainously, vanish. Another, stalking, took its place. The ship pitched, rolled, vomited streams of brine. The wind howled endlessly.

Where does the sound of wind come from and where does it go? Would it still exist, as sound, if there were no one to listen to it? Did it make a continuous roar or scream as it moved above the battering seas? Did its voice become alive only when human receivers were tuned to its transmissions?

We were dragging ever so slightly. I could sense the short distinct nips of the anchor as it alternately dug into ocean floor and wrenched loose. A short series of high seas pummeled us. The anchor chain flailed with supernatural clamor. Severe tugs could be felt as the anchor applied the brakes, giving ground ever so little, unwillingly.

Suddenly I no longer felt the vibration of the anchor imbedding itself. After a few minutes of listening in vain, I became alarmed, dressed and went on deck. The chain was leading properly, so I went below to investigate conditions in the windlass room. Nothing seemed amiss, and a clattering snap of the chain reassured me.

Back on deck. I checked our ranges. For a few panicky seconds it looked as if we were bearing down on a green lighted buoy. This meant only one thing! The anchor chain had given up the struggle, had parted! No. Wait a minute. The ranges do seem normal. Yes, they are. We're holding our own!

I returned to the windlass room to watch and listen to the chain in the hawsepipe. An unexpected rugged clanking of chain followed by an awful shuddering of bulkheads threw me off balance. This indicated the anchor was still doing its share. It was holding. I went back to bed, the anguished pulsating of my heart subsiding to normalcy.

The war of wind and sea rampaged through Wednesday and into Thursday, liberty day. Prospects for getting ashore were grim. Anxious questions originated from everyone. "Do you think they'll be out today?" "What's the chances of a change of wind?" "What's the latest forecast?" "They've been out on rougher days than this, haven't they?"

At 8:00 A.M. the radio bristled with contact from the *White Sage*.

"What are landing conditions at your unit?"

Doubtfully I looked over the side as the ship stood momentarily suspended. As the crest of the wave passed astern, we were spilled shatteringly into the seething trough. There was no doubt in my mind as I reported, regretfully, "Landing conditions are not favorable at this time."

Utterly discouraging in every detail is liberty that is delayed by storm. Spirits are quickly dampened. Everything seems to go wrong. Interest in immediate affairs is unenthusiastic. Waves seem heavier, winds stronger, ship pitches more emphatic.

"What's the latest weather forecast?" is repeated over and over as the miserable crew watch disconsolately over the white spilling seas. If the weatherman makes a boo-boo, he is never forgiven or forgotten.

"That damned bag on TV last night said the winds would shift to north by morning. I've got a good mind to write her a nasty letter."

"Yeah, and some other son of a bitch said it was so windy you'd better hang on to your hat or something. Then he laughed. The stupid ass ought to come out HERE and see if he laughs at the wind. He'd puke his guts out."

More than once bitter remarks were expostulated at a hapless forecaster. No amount of explanation of the difficulties of accurate weather forecasting registered favorably with unhappy men waiting to go ashore.

Sitting at the mess deck tables, the men tastelessly sipped coffee. Their vein of thought, delayed liberty, left and concentration was centered on bracing an elbow or a foot as the compartment tilted, rose, slanted to the opposite side, and fell with a gush. The seas were cursed, the wind was cursed, the duty was cursed. Pre-liberty plans were submerged in a sea of disappointment. Unrestrained laughter and joy were gone, and would return only with a change in sea conditions.

Their thoughts remained on shore leave, their families, their hopes, their expectations. They had been waiting twenty-eight long days for liberty, and the glum prospects of denial were unattractive.

All day long the *White Sage* kept in radio contact with us. Weather forecasters predicted a shift to the north during the afternoon. At 2:30 P.M. the change had not materialized, and Chief Boatswain Bangs radioed that the *Sage* would leave at daylight the next morning for her rendevous. The crew of the *Buzzards*, disappointed, discussed the enforced change in plans. By nightfall the wind did move to the north, and the seas flattened. Night being a dangerous time to transfer men and material at sea, the wisdom of Mr. Bang's orders was soundly justified.

The storm had ended. The following morning minds and bodies quickly recovered from their bruised batterings, and the liberty parties were exchanged. The return to norm was most welcome.

Seasickness became most prominent during a south-wester. The two went hand in hand. Men who withstood punishment without abdominal discontent during other storms fell prey to the southwester. Others were afflicted with headaches, dizziness, profuse perspiration, aching limbs and muscles.

A seasick person feels horrible. He thinks he is ready to die. He likewise thinks that death might, in fact, be a welcome relief. There hardly is a less enjoyable feeling known to all humanity. Yet he receives a minimum of sympathy. Few are sorry for his plight. He is ridiculed, scorned, berated, teased. He is told to "eat some greasy pok chops or spare ribs with sauerkraut" or to "swallow a piece of raw salt pork." All the poor devil asks is to be left alone. He has not requested advice from dieticians who are feeling more fortunate. His squeamish anatomy, his merry-go-round stomach gag at the flow of soothing commentaries. He departs in great haste, his ashen face sweating cold droplets, his hands cupped protectively across a mouth about to expel a gushing torrent of multicolored puke.

Chief Boatswain's Mate George Sousa was prone to a limited leniency with his men. He mad them work and fight against a condition he felt was mainly psychological. If the men made an honest attempt to do a job to the best of their ability, if they cooperated, if they were not goldbricks, if they did not feel sorry for themselves and surrender whole heartedly to seasickness, he rewarded a genuine case with a few hours off duty. There were two stipulations. The afflicted man was expected to stand his watch. He also was expected to go on deck frequently to breathe the open air.

George learned to deal with seasick crewmen through experience. He explained, "Before I got wise to some of them they used to be so sick they couldn't do anything but lay in their bunk. At movie time, however, they'd show up, completely recovered, with a big cigar in their mouth."

The question was debated over and over as to which was worse, fog or a southwester. No answer was wholly convincing. When the foghorns were booming into a curtain of mist, we thought that fog was far more sufferable. When the wind shifted strongly to the southwest, our consensus of opinion shifted with it. Pros and cons were endless. The best cure was to go ashore on liberty and forget both of them.

Not all aspects of southwest storms were morbid, however. Sometimes interesting things happened. For example, there was the spirited dance of the brooms on the fantail. Swabs, deck brushes and corn brooms were kept in a wooden rack lashed against the stern railing on the main deck. The stand which supported them held the handles erect as they were stowed business end up. Once an afternoon wind caught them just right, and they spiraled with a finished locomotion not unlike the star of a ballet executing a pirouette. The performance was repeated tirelessly under a gray overcast of swiftly moving clouds as day shaded into twilight.

A slower coquettish dance was that of the peacoats, whose act was most impressive after dark. The heavy navy blue jackets were hung from a pipe welded between two stanchions in the crew's berthing quarters. A few feet away was the entrance to the wash room, illuminated at night by a red bulb of low wattage. That, plus a second red bulb at the base of the ladder leading to the main deck, were the sole lights permitted in the compartment after taps. The peacoats, swaying noiselessly in the reddened glow, cast fanciful outlandish shadows. They appeared like phantoms in foot lights, endowing the bulkheads with a specter spell of voodooism. It was remindful of Walt Disney's production of *Fantasia* as the distorted shapes bewitched the night.

Southwesterly induced seas had their moments of buffoonery, too. Dick Nelson was blissfully asleep one night, minding his own business, unobtrusive, bothering no one. His bottom bunk, on the port side of the ship close to the bulkhead, was below a pair of portholes that opened on a line with an unoccupied bunk above. Since it was summer and Dick was newly aboard, he saw no reason for securing the ports in spite of the churning swells. A giant ultimately rose from the depths, splashed robustly against the ship, and a sizeable portion fought its way through the circular openings. Frigid wet brine dripping from his face, Dick bounded soggily onto the deck, his sleep shrouded mind envisioning a floundering vessel. Half incensed, half relieved, he awakened to his predicament, cursed silently, and barricaded himself from further moist encroachments, far wiser to the impish ways of the sea.

Cornelius Van Pooper, firmly ensconced in viewing television cowboys on a frosty autumn evening, avidly puffing a steer-figured pipe, soiled feet resting on a gray wastebasket, erupted to life with a howling leap. A southwest sea boiled against a porthole flanking Connie's tilted chair. Seeking ingress, the seething deluge angrily assailed the glass enclosed aperture. Thinking the port was merely ajar, Connie hastily departed the area, megaphoning a yowling, "Oh! Damn!" His chair crashed to the deck, the wastebasket bombed the television stand, a tobacco can clashed with a bulkhead, and Connie's keys were resurrected with clamorous pandemonium as he retreated with his customary hullabaloo.

Mentally salvaging sunken wrecks in the wardroom, Leroy Wilson, hearing the barrage of confusion, hastened to investigate. William Sherman, on watch in the engine room, had been thinking how peaceful it was with Chief Dean, the senior engineer, ashore on liberty. His daydream, not to mention his nerves, was shattered by the blatant uproar. He, too, sped to the scene. Both arrived to find nothing more than Connie, grinning sheepishly, picking up debris scattered by his madcap debacle.

Chief Burroughs never will forget an experience that befell him one squally night. He and Chief Dean were absorbing what sleep they could in their individual staterooms. The ship, meanwhile, swung her bow briefly from the path of the southwest wind. That was all that was necessary as a contrary minded sea charged against the starboard side. Heeling to port, the ship was struck hard by a second powerful mass of water before she could spring back. The first sea awakened the catnapping chiefs. The second, descending upon them with an explosive violence, petrified them. Never before had they felt or heard such a frightful force raking the vessel. Their minds, as they leaped from bed, painted mental images of unappeasable doom. Burroughs thought the ship had been struck by another vessel. Dean, ever thinking of his engine room, was certain that an internal explosion had taken place.

Both chiefs tore at the doors leading from their rooms to the wardroom. Dean scampered out to meet an engineer coming from below.

"What happened?"

"A couple of seas hit us real hard. There's nothing wrong in the engine room, chief."

"What are you doing up here then?"

"I figured the noise would wake you up. I thought I'd let you know that everything was all right down below."

Further discourse was interrupted by a consistent banging on a door. Dean returned to the wardroom and turned on a light to see the bottom of Chief Burroughs' door giving way under a barrage of hammer like blows.

"What's the matter, Bill?" he asked.

"I can't get this dammed door open. I was about to kick it when I heard you come back. See if you can give me a hand with it."

Dean walked over, turned the latch, and easily slid the door sideways. "I don't see anything wrong with it," he volunteered.

"Well, well," expostulated Bill. He laughed and continued, "No wonder I couldn't open it. I thought it swung on hinges like yours. I tried to get out so fast I clean forgot that it slides. I was gonna' smash it if I had to. I wasn't about to have the damned ship sink with me still in that room. What happened, anyway?"

Dean, doubled over with laughter, could scarcely answer. From that time on, Bill Burroughs took no more chances on being trapped. He never again closed the sliding door.

On another occasion Bob Dean awakened during a southwester, scrambled out of bed to make a routine check, and walked past the wardroom table just in time to catch a filled sugar bowl that had slid off the table and was on its way to the deck. Not a grain was spilled.

In spite of a few amusing incidents attributable to the southwester, the relief created by its departure was most cheerful. How grand it was to once again enjoy the healthy aspects of a behaved ocean.

A few other storms left memorable incidents. In mid-September of 1956 there occurred a thunderstorm that swept over the *Buzzards* during a movie. The squall was given little attention, so absorbed were the crew in entertainment. The stroll on deck, the breath of fresh air, the "look around" that always followed a movie had more than the usual interest for us on this particular evening. The heavens had a special show.

To the east, eight or ten miles away, the definite pattern of a waterspout was taking shape. A huge black cone-shaped cloud high in the sky spiraled toward the ocean. The remainder of the sky was gray and black. A few streaks of lightning colored the area adjacent to the unusual coned segment. Larger and larger it grew. Seconds ticked slowly. Gray and black clouds darkened near the water spout in the making. Suddenly, it was no more. The bottom of the cone broadened, the cloud flattened, and it became part of the dull sky, no longer possessing an individual characteristic. Four of us had excitedly watched the rare display which, according to my watch, had lasted for six minutes.

At 9:00 P.M. on April 5, 1957, one of the infrequent full-fledged thunderstorms experienced on the *Buzzards* station took place. The night was foggy and rough. The foghorn moaned reproachfully as the ship rose and fell on five foot seas backed by westerly winds of thirty miles an hour. Rain fell in squalls. Whitecaps were abundant.

I watched from an open porthole on the second deck. The water close to the ship shimmered faintly with the pale reflection of the deck lights. A deep black shadow huddled close to the hull where light was unable to penetrate. The outline of the railing and a ring buoy reached from the shadow in half tones. Raindrops sparkled like diamonds as they sped through the brightness to dissolve in ringlets upon the sea. Pencil shafts of yellow from the main light disappeared into a solid bank of fog.

The sky suddenly was transformed into day as a blinding flash of pale blue lightning intruded. The water became a virescent green speckled with irregular foamy splotches of white. Directly under the white seas were small areas of black that were shielded from the flash of invading light. A white bank of rain became a wall of blue as all shadows disappeared. The rain fell harder, and the surface of the ocean bubbled with springing droplets of silvery condensation. Raindrops struck with such strength they bounded back into the air a few inches. The effect was like a wintry vapor hovering just above a cold ocean top. Distant rumblings of thunder grew louder.

The scintillating impulsions of lightning made my eyes blink. One of the series of flashes revealed a volcanic effect. The green water was topped by a band of fog fifty feet in height, an opening at the summit being ringed by black snarling formations of cloud. It was like viewing a black nebula through a telescope. The fog changed from white to smokey gray and streaked past like a black vapor. Seething seas hissed a hundred yards away.

A following outburst of lightning unveiled a low white arc of fog to port, the highest part of the arc about ten feet above water, the whole about two hundred yards in length. The rest of the area was colored in electric blue. A wide line of foam scampered by as if frightened by the awesome atmosphere.

The next flash lighted the area dimly for half a mile. A pea green sea was mottled lightly with white breaking waves two feet in height, guarding their black bellies. Fog was patchy. A pair of six foot swells slid past, snarling at the effort as the ship plunged and rose sharply.

The lightning grew fainter and sporadic as the squall moved toward the northeast. Rumbles of thunder became less frequent, less angry. The showers of rain were disorganized, a torrent one minute, mist the next. Soon the storm was over and the scene reclaimed by the sea, the fog, the wind, the ship, and the foghorn.

Chapter X

"Personnel"

"It takes all kinds to make a world." How true that was on the *Buzzards*, where our crew was gathered from all over the United States. We had men from Arkansas, California, Florida, Georgia, Maine, Maryland, Massachusetts, Michigan, New Hampshire, New Jersey, New York, Illinois, Ohio, North Carolina, Pennsylvania, Rhode island, South Carolina, Tennessee, and Texas. We had men from many walks of life. Some had been to college, while others possessed an intimate knowledge of adolescence in city slums. We had tall men and short men, some stocky, some slender. We had Caucasians and African Americans. We had men who talked endlessly, weavers of hypothetical plots and situations. Others were quiet. Most wanted to improve themselves. A slender minority, who admitted they were in the Coast Guard to escape the Army, did not care. Most were cooperative and willing to work; a few had to learn, sometimes through woeful experience. Some came from large families. One or two were an only child. Most were clean in hygienic habits, and only a couple, enjoying the restricted use of fresh water, had to be ordered to bathe. We had men of many nationalities: English, French, German, Polish, Irish, Portuguese, Scandinavians, but Americans above all.

This chapter will be devoted to a cross section of the personnel of the *Buzzards* during my tenure, some of their personalities, hobbies, likes, dislikes, and incidents that befell them during the year and a half they were grouped on a lightship that guarded the western approaches to Buzzards Bay and Vineyard Sound.

One of our more unusual individuals was Cornelius Van Pooper. Connie, five feet five inches in height, slender, wiry, lean face with a prominent crooked nose that snorted with impatience, was a hard worker bur decidedly accident prone. His barked shins were a mass of welts, indicating utter disrespect for the raised sections of bulkhead that were located immediately below each hatch. His fingers were cut and bruised. His head was generously sprinkled with bumps, the result of encounters with light fixtures suspended from a low overhead. Connie made a lot of noise everywhere he went. His exact whereabouts could be pinpointed by his haste in traveling up or down a ladder, a raucous clearing of the throat, the slamming of a hatch, the ringing detonation of a spoon dropped onto a table, the rattle of a sugarbowl cover, the preparation for a movie, or a bellowing rendition of "Ain't nothin' but a houn'dog."

In spite of his attention grasping, publicity type tactics, Connie was a good seaman. As he began working toward a boatswain's mate rating, Connie set out to master the mysteries of a bosn pipe, traditionally used in the Navy and Coast Guard to signal certain events of the day. So ardently did he hold rehearsals, the shrill whistling grievously harassed the minds of all, and it became necessary to banish him to the solitary confines of the windlass room where he could attain perfection without risk of provoking a mutiny. That was nothing new for Connie, for two months earlier he had suffered the same indignation with a guitar.

Connie's interests included movies and photography. He learned the intricacies of a movie projector and became the self appointed operator. Gulping his evening mea lin record time, he would dash to the recreation room where, amid fuming clamor, the projector was put in order and reels of film rewound. Connie then would draw up a chair, produce a magazine, and remain as immobile as possible for some fifty minutes until it was time for the "cinema" to open to its patrons. He was making certain that no one else would beat him to the honor of "motion picture operator of the night," for several other men also had received classroom instruction in movie projector operations.

Connie once returned from liberty with an inexpensive camera with flash bulb attachment. striding forth on a shutter clicking expedition, his photographic career came to an abrupt unhappy end. Attempting a candid shot in the crew's berthing quarters, a faulty bulb deprived him of the desired shot. Wrenching the attachment from the camera, he savagely smashed it against the nearest bulkhead. Tossing the remains ignominiously into a waste basket he walked away, smirking as if to say, "There! That'll teach you a damn lesson you won't forget."

His neurotic uprisings were chronic. Whittling a boat plug for a dory, Connie carelessly projected his thumb into the path of a razor-edged knife. With a squeal of anguish he reared back and threw the knife with the strength of a baseball outfielder pegging a ball to home plate. It sailed far overboard to splash into the ocean. Several days later another knife nearly received the same treatment. That time the knife pierced the end of Connie's index finger, and as it was about to sail on a similar journey, somebody close by asked if he could have the knife to use himself. It was meekly surrendered.

Cornelius Van Pooper was not his real name. It was bestowed on him by Leroy Wilson. Connie did not approve of his newly acquired handle and asked Leroy, "Where in hell d'ya get THAT name?"

Leroy replied jovially, "It fits your personality."

Cornelius liked to watch television, usually placing himself about three feet from the picture tube. Slouching in a chair, he used a waste basket as a combination hassock and ash receptacle. Wearing high black shoes, unlaced, he sprawled in luxurious comfort, occasionally flickering a cigarette ash. One night the basket was empty so instead of carefully extinguishing his cigarette he satisfied himself with tossing burning butts like a basketball player. That was fine, until his aim became erratic and a butt dropped cozily inside his shoe. With a yowl of pain, Connie sprang up with a mighty leap. A severe blister and much scrambling later, the aggressive object was removed. Connie's aim thereafter was unerring.

In direct contrast to Van Pooper was the unforgettable William Sherman, a tall, rugged, handsome, slow moving lad of twenty-one years. Talented in many directions, Sherman was subject to lapses of memory, inattentiveness, and tough luck.

Quick on the quip, he had endeared himself to his shipmates by describing a lightship as "nothing but an oversized buoy with a crew."

His memory lapses, however, did not please Chief Dean, his boss in the engineering department. Sherman's unmistakably New England drawled nasal excuses of "I guess I must have forgotten," or "I didn't think about that," irritated Dean considerably. Usually they touched off an explosive verbal blast.

"Sherman," he used to say, "you talk all the time. Your mouth goes like a duck's ass in a mud puddle, but you can't remember a thing. Why don't you pay attention to what you're doing? How many times do you have to be told the same thing over and over again?"

Sherman's inattentiveness was noteworthy during a fueling operation in port. Manning the sounding tape, Sherman's duty was to take repeated measurements and to report when the tank was nearly filled. All went well until Sherman's attention was diverted by a truck lumbering along the dock. Suddenly a geyser of oil shot into the air, and Sherman became the unwilling victim of a diesel bath. As the fluid dripped from his hair, eyelids, nose, clothing and the sounding tape, he hollered, "SHUT IT OFF. THE TANK'S FULL! HEY!! SHUT IT OFF!!" The tank had filled, of course, as Sherman's eyes wandered after the truck, and the oil had nowhere to go except on deck and upon the unfortunate inattentive man standing at the fill pipe.

Sherman's propensity for innocent involvement in difficulties occurred on the very first day of his assignment to the ship. He was shown through the engine room, and the duties of the watch were explained in detail, for assuming responsibility of the watch was the first thing to be learned on the *Buzzards*. Sherman stood the 8:00 P.M. to midnight watch with another engineer, the usual procedure with a new man. One of the duties of that watch was to shift the electrical output from one generator to the other, precisely at midnight. It was simple enough to do. When both generators were running, it meant a short walk to the panel board in the center of the engine room and the engaging of a single switch. Under the guidance of the other member of the watch Sherman undertook this call of duty. He engaged the switch exactly as he was instructed, exactly as it had been done a thousand times previously. This time, however, flying missiles unexpectedly sailed through the air, and the ship was plunged into darkness as the switch mechanism flew apart in all directions. An emergency request for a tender was the sole recourse, for it would be hours before electricity could be restored. All night long the tender remained nearby, her brilliant spotlight focused on the *Buzzards* lightship whose signal was darkened and whose engineers groped for, located, and eventually succeeded in transposing the puzzle of parts into an effective electrical component. Standby batteries were on hand for such an emergency, but their life was limited to a few hours.

A skillful artist, Sherman frequently was called upon to produce diagrams of electrical, water, air, and fuel systems or sketches of a mechanical feature. On such task involved a diagram of the fresh water system in the engine room, and as he and his helper, David Oram, reproduced lines and legend on heavy brown wrapping paper, Oram explained, "We're going to call them brown prints." After the chuckles had subsided, he added, "If you're going to put that in your book, skipper, don't forget that it was me who said that about the brown prints."

According to George Sousa, of Bristol, Rhode Island, Sherman was a real pain during movies because he couldn't sit still. He couldn't seem to figure what he should do with his long legs.

"Try sitting behind him some night," complained Sousa. "His head bobs back and forth, an arm shoots up in the air, then he scratches an ear with his other hand. Worst of all, though, his feet keep moving. First he crosses his legs, then sits straight, then slouches with feet sprawled. Then he puts one foot on the back of somebody's chair until they complain of the smell. I'm all worn out from trying to see around him. I think I'll reserve a seat for him, at the back of the other side of the compartment where he'll be away from everybody."

Sousa had another movie complaint. "Oram always comes back with his hair practically sheared off it's cut so short. It's blond, too, and his head shines in the dark so much I can't see the screen."

One man, whom we shall call Bill, would wear the same work clothes for a startlingly long period of time during his early days on board. He saw no need to waste water, and so his clothing infrequently was subjected to the surprise of being dunked in hot soapy water. Months of taunts ultimately found their way under his skin. "Hey, Bill, when are you going to change oil in those dungarees?"... "Bill, how can you stand all that raunchiness?"... "Do those trousers ever try to run away from you, Bill? I know they can stand all by themselves, but can they run?"

Occasionally we would get a man who was inclined to be lazy. Such a fellow was seaman Wheat, who knew all the shortcuts around work. He seemed to know all the angles, all the stalls to keep a respectable distance between himself and any task involving output of labor. What he failed to realize, for a long while, was that the chief boatswain's mate knew the angles, too. Wheat was arrogant but harmless, and while he contrived schemes to benefit himself solely, it never was at the direct expense of anyone else. He became an avid coffee drinker, consuming innumerable cups daily. It began as a system to separate him momentarily from a paint brush or a chipping hammer. When scheduled coffee breaks were initiated, his coffee consumption became a habit.

Wheat was not with us for very long, but well remembered was the time he was detailed to cover three hand lanterns with red paint. The effort tired him, and he sat down to catch his breath. Only when he arose did he realize that he had sat upon the very objects he had just finished painting. They left a permanent impression upon the seat of his britches vaguely resembling the outline of a huge hand. His mates claimed that he had sat down on the job so often that "Satan had become tired of it, had grabbed him by the arse, and had left his imprint for all to see."

Chief Robert Dean was allergic to noise, particularly vocal or foot induced. The forward bulkhead of his compartment bordered the aft ladder leading from the second to the main deck. Anyone who trod too heavily up and down this avenue became well aware of the necessity of learning to use a lighter step. Woe to the man at night whose "feetnen" were responsible for awakening Chief Dean from a delightful dream. The foghorns seldom bothered him, but the slightest extra pressure of a foot on the ladder roused him to a belligerent pitch of undesirable wakefulness. He could clearly hear any nocturnal voice emissions from the mess deck, and there again the men learned the advantage of being quiet. Dean could deliver a scathing "chewing," which the men showed a positive desire to avoid.

Bob would have made a good salesman of hearing aids. Whenever a radio was bursting forth with unrestricted volume, he would ask the men if they were sure they could hear, or he inquired if their ears had been tested of late. As his irritation progressed over the weeks, he acidly suggested hearing aids for the rock and rollers. He hinted that the aids came in assorted colors to suit individual tastes. The pay-off came when a Sonotone advertisement appeared on the bulletin board. This drew a chuckle which grew to a hearty crescendo the next day at a superimposed announcement inked by one of the crew: "Robert J. Dean, local representative."

Dean was one of our more fabulous letter writing experts, both numerically and in length. He carried on a tremendous correspondence with a host of friends, for Bob enjoyed companionship afloat and ashore. Others frequently composed a longer epistle, or perhaps briefly exceeded his output, but in spite of stiff competition Bob retained the ship's championship. As a composer of billet-doux, he knew no peer.

A good natured man of Irish descent who lived alone (at that time) but did not relish the predicament, Bob was mesmerized with plaudits of married life by Bill Burroughs and myself, our golden opinions of wedded bliss deriving its zest from great happiness. Bill, of medium height, a shade on the stocky side, blonde with a crew haircut, was a North Carolinian.

"Bob," he used to explain, "there's nothin' like married life. NOTHIN'! You can't beat it. You go home, and your wife meets you at the door with a tender kiss. Then you go in and sit down. She brings your slippers to you and your pipe. The pipe is all ready to light because she knows what kind of tobacco you smoke and just how you want the pipe packed. She even has the matches ready. There's nothin' LIKE it!"

"Yes," I would interject, "and when she brings you a cup of steaming hot coffee, you don't even have to put in the sugar and cream because she's already done it. It's ready to drink."

"That's right," Bill would add. "She knows just how you like it. And in the summer when you're hot and thirsty, she brings you a cold can of beer, just at the moment when you want it most. You don't have to ask for it because she can tell by lookin' at you just when you want a can. It's automatic. You sit there and think how good a can of beer would taste, and then you look up. There's your wife with the beer."

"Not only that, Bill," I continued, "but there's nothing like having your wife come up and put her arms around you and call you sweetie and have her tell you how much you mean to her."

"That's absolutely right," said Bill. "She knows just when to do THAT, too. She knows when you need to be cheered. She can tell when you're lonesome and need reassurance."

"Hmmmmmmmm, Bill. You're making me homesick. It's perfectly true, though. I think I'm the happiest husband in the world," I opined. "I LOVE married life."

Bill cut in. "Just a minute, skipper. I think that I'M the happiest husband in the world."

The fidgeting Bob Dean had enough. "Cut it out, both of you guys," he pleaded. "You're making me feel bad enough as it is. I know you're both happy. But don't keep rubbing it in."

Bill would look at me and wink. "There's nothin' like it, Bob. Nothin' in THIS WHOLE WORLD LIKE BEIN' MARRIED!!" His voice rose in a crescendo with the climax occurring on the last word. "The skipper'll tell you the same thing."

"I know it. I know it. Look, let's talk about something else, O.K.?" Bob was impressed but distinctly tired of hearing the same old thing.

"O.K., Bob. The skipper and I just wanted you to know how we felt."

Burroughs would NOT have made a good chaplain, according to the boys in his deck force. Since Bill was executive officer until his transfer, he had to listen to all the prolific lamentations of the crew. One would bewail his lot at having to work on his birthday. Another would complain about the foghorn interrupting his sleep. A third might lodge a grievous complaint about washing paintwork, capping his denunciation with a fuming summit of "Van Pooper just stands around and watches." Bill would listen with a padre air of enraptured reflection, then render the grumbler incommunicative with a slow shake of his head and an uncharitable "NAS-ty break!" Bill possessed two other prosaic rejoinders. "You know it!" was one of his prototypes which left a fault finder coldly insensible from lack of accommodative pity. The other, which completely failed to alleviate the infinite anxiety of a sulking complainer, was,

"Ah feel for yuh, but ah can't reach yuh, so there's no need to kick up a fuss."

Bill liked to expound the virtues of lightship duty. Never acknowledging that life anywhere else had better advantage, he would slap his hands together and assert, "THIS is LIVin'. THIS is REAL-LY LIVing!" The crew were astonished by such glorified enthusiastic acceptance of a life they dreaded. Bob Dean and I weren't fooled. We KNEW he was lying.

Burroughs was an amusing spinner of yarns. His inexhaustible supply helped wile away countless hours of tedious loneliness. Narrating in the first person, his droll tales describing life in North Carolina, especially of the days before becoming a Coast Guardsman, were most hilarious. One of our favorites concerned an encounter with the FBI.

Bill was working in a grocery store in his home town. On his haunches, sorting vegetables, he looked up as a well dressed man walked over and tapped him on the shoulder. With a serious expression the man asked, "Are you William T. Burroughs?"

Bill answered matter of factly, "That's right. What can I do for you?"

The stranger replied, "I'm afraid you'll have to come with me."

Bill was puzzled. "What do you mean, I'll have to go with you?"

The stranger brought forth a wallet which he opened, displaying a shiny business looking badge. "FBI," he explained. "It will be easier if you come quietly without making a fuss. My colleague is outside, sitting in a car. There are some questions we have to ask."

A panic stricken Bill Burroughs trembled visibly as a hundred thoughts flashed through his mind. In his own words, "I knew I was guilty, but I didn't think anybody else knew it." He thought of making a run for it. He could flee through the back door and dash into a nearby orchard. From there he could climb a stone fence and be in the woods before the FBI men had a chance to nab him. No, that would be no good. If they didn't shoot him, they'd catch him later anyhow. Bill thought of his mother. She was getting along in years, and this would be a terrible shock to her. If only there was some way to spare her feelings. If only he could make a deal with this FBI man to keep it quiet. No, that wouldn't do. Then they'd have him on a charge of attempted bribery. What about his young wife at home? She was innocent and had no knowledge of this terrible thing that had just happened to him. What would she think of him? As an afterthought, he realized she could say nothing. "After all, she told me she was nineteen until the day we got the marriage license. Then she admitted she was only seventeen. But that's not helping me now."

"Well?" inquired the stranger, a huge brawny man who could have passed as a professional football player or a wrestler. His hands reached menacingly for his coat pocket. "I hope it won't be necessary to use cuffs."

"I'll go quietly," decided a thoroughly subdued William T. Burroughs. "I'll tell the boss I'm going outside for a few minutes."

"No tricks now," warned the ominous man with the badge.

Bill's boss accepted his explanation, and Bill and the stranger walked into the street and toward a large lack sedan parked nearby. A back door was jerked open, and Bill was motioned ro get in as the stranger climbed into the front seat.

"Why, Bill Burroughs. Ah haven't seen you for a lawng, lawng time. How the hell are yah?" asked the second man in the car.

Bill weakly shook a proffered hand and looked into the face of John Simmons, a lifelong friend he hadn't seen for several years.

"Damn you, John," exclaimed a sweating but relieved Burroughs. "You sure had me scared. That's a hell of a trick to play on a man."

Burroughs and I derived keen delight from an episode involving a train. The *Buzzards* was moored at the Coast Guard base in Boston a few days after losing a mooring in a furious southwest storm. Bill and I boarded the Cape Cod train at the South Station in Boston and headed home for the weekend. At Buzzards Bay, the Budd car destined for Woods Hole was uncoupled and, after a fifteen minute wait, rumbled across the Cape Cod Canal. At that time our families shared a two-apartment house in Woods Hole, Bill and his family living upstairs. The house was no more than a hundred feet from the railroad track, and we considered the possibility of asking the conductor to let us off at our door. In that way, we would be spared the remaining quarter mile ride to the Woods Hole depot. We knew, of course, that our wives were awaiting our arrival at the train station. We thought it would be quite a trick if we could get off the train and sneak inside, unseen. How surprised the wives would be to drive home disappointed only to discover we already were there! It was only a thought, and we chuckled about it and then spoke of other subjects. I forgot about the possibility. Bill did not.

The train disembarked fares at Monument Beach, Pocasset, Cataumet, North Falmouth, and the stop at Falmouth nearly emptied the car of all passengers. As we approached Woods Hole, the final stop, Bill arose and casually meandered to the front of the car. I noted that he was engaged in conversation with the conductor, but gave it little thought for Bill talked to everybody. Closer and closer to Woods Hole churned the wheels. Soon our home would come into view. It was just beyond the next hill. There it is! As we drew abreast, we could see the railroad station ahead. Bill beckoned to me, asking, "Want to get off here, Cap? Let's go." Two hundred yards later the train stopped, a door opened, and out stepped Bill and I.

Our wives, meanwhile, were sitting in their parked autos waiting for the train to pull into the station. They saw the train stop and saw a blue uniformed figure step out. They figured it was the conductor. Then a second blue figure emerged, both walked away, and the train resumed motion.

"It's the boys!" shouted one of the girls. They started their cars, left the parking area, and drove along the road paralleling the railroad tracks, tooting horns madly to attract our attention.

"Pay no attention, Cap," Bill said. "Let's make believe we don't notice them. We'll be in the house before they get there."

We dashed inside our apartments, hastily doffed coats and hats, set aside our luggage, flopped into a chair, and lit a cigar. "Where in the world have you been?" we asked our wives when they came in. "We haven't been home for four weeks, almost sink the ship, and you don't even think enough of us to be in the house when we come home!" we declared with a feigned injured feeling that fooled no one. We laughed about it long afterwards.

Now and then the cooks became unwilling subjects of tomfoolery. Zombie was forever losing his liberty shoes. Working carefully to obtain a sparkling shine, he never failed to leave them unprotected just long enough for a rascally shipmate to hide them. It was a common sight to see Zom, dressed neatly in blue uniform sans shoes, his face deepening in color from red to purple. "Come on, you wise guys. Whoever hid my shoes bring them back before I tell the skipper."

Somebody would ask, "Zom, what's that dangling under the washing machine? It';s something black. You don't suppose anybody would be mean enough to tie your shoes there, do you?"

With bulging eyes, Zombie would quickly retrieve and don his runaway shoes, snapping, "You guys think you're pretty funny, don't you?"

It is understood that the time he found them nailed to the main deck he was so livid with anger he was speechless for several hours, failing to detect the slightest bit of humor in the situation.

Concealment of Zoe's pipe was almost a daily custom, the favorite hiding place being an overhead frame in a dark corner, for Zom wasn't tall enough to see without standing in a chair. He grew accustomed to his hazing and gradually learned to carry his pipe on his person. Whenever he did forget, and allowed it to remain in sight on a vacant bunk or table, he examined it carefully with an acquired suspicion. He had smoked black pepper in his tobacco too often not to be wary.

Clem Meredith, tall and muscular, never failed to return from liberty grizzled, glum, disheartened, sulky. A few days after the numbness of leaving home had been reduced, he became the life of the party. The first day back, though, everyone was careful not to aggravate him as he shuffled slowly on leaden feet.

In July 1956, the *Buzzards* was moored in an East Boston shipyard when Clem came back from liberty. It was a hot summer night, late, as he trudged his way along a deserted dead-end street leading to the shipyard gate. The whites of Clem's eyes showed widely as he interpreted every rustle of a leaf or squeal of a rat as a possible attempt on his life. Dingy apartment buildings rose on either side of the narrow cobblestone road. The few tiny plots of bare ground were quagmires of litter and vermin, as was the sidewalk and street, and the odor of animal excrement mingled with the smell of unattended garbage. A gray curtain that once had been white fluttered softly in the night, through a broken window, possibly reviving Clem's boyhood imagination of ghosts. Every shadow was possible disaster, lurking, waiting, preying. Clem's eyes rolled cautiously from one side to the other. A few empty cars were parked along the sides of the street, and Clem visualized a thug with smoking revolver in each. There was no turning back for him now, though. He could go neither to the left nor to the right. The only direction was straight ahead. As each step carried him closer to safety, he began to feel a hopeful sense of relief.

Clem's progress, however, was being watched. "Hostile" eyes were following and awaiting his approach, for sitting in one of the parked automobiles was one of the men from the *Buzzards*, fully aware of Clem's feelings of panic. Onward trudged the cautious Clem, ever on the lookout for danger. Suddenly a voice from a car spoke firmly, deeply, gutturally, "Hey, boy. Where are you going?" If Clem recognized the owner of the voice, he gave no indication. Disdaining to answer, he broke into a flying gallop and raced full speed ahead, pausing only to look back when he reached the safety of the ship.

Dick Nelson, a tall Swede with typically blonde hair, who replaced Zombie when the latter was transferred, was a cook on board ship and a musician ashore, playing the drum in a dance band. He wasn't able to bring all his equipment aboard to practice, so he contented himself with the sticks. His talents, however, were not fully appreciated as he beat the mess deck tables into submission with his drumsticks as the ship's radio wailed lustily. Dick would discover himself keeping time to a deep silence as the radio mysteriously went off the air in the middle of a performance.

Dick was better than average massager of groceries who remembered everyone's birthday with a traditional cake, replete with colorful icing and greetings of the day. He also had a sense of humor that was used as an avenue of approach by the crew in coercing him into making other pastries. They would warm to the task during coffee break, first making sure that Dick was well within range of their conversation.

"Boy, I'd sure like to have some doughnuts," one would start. "Yeah," a second would add, "and Dick Nelson's just the guy who could make a good tasty batch of them."

"They'd sure taste good after the movie tonight, but then, we can't expect Nelson to work all day."

"What do you mean, work all day? If Dick knew we'd like some doughnuts, he'd break his neck making them for us."

"Yeah, I know. That's the way Dick is. He sure can cook. Boy, I can just taste those doughnuts right now."

"I don't know of anybody I'd rather see cook doughnuts than Dick Nelson because EVERYthing he cooks is so good!"

"That's true. He enjoys making the crew happy, too. Notice how he makes birthday cakes for everybody, and takes such pride in his cooking?"

"Well, gee, I don't know why we're talking like this. I know that if Nelson thought for one minute that we'd like doughnuts that he wouldn't say a word. He'd just go ahead and surprise us with a whole batch of them."

"Oh sure, I know he would, but then, I don't feel like asking him to do extra work."

"It's not the extra work. Dick would love to do it if he only knew that we wanted them so badly. He does such a good job putting out meals, though, that I wouldn't want him to think we didn't like his chow. He sure could make some good doughnuts though, I bet."

Dick Nelson always absorbed the conservation, as intended, then would burst into a pleased fit of snickers and mutter, "How can I refuse after that build-up?"

For all his good intentions, Dick was in trouble one day. A practical joker at times, he was peeling carrots for a stew. One of the galley portholes darkened as a foot stepped through it from outboard. Peering through another open port, Dick saw Ronald Balkcom dressed in a life jacket with safety line attached, wielding a paint brush. It was a warm sunny spring morning, and outside work was in progress. Wearing a sardonic grin, Dick deftly tied a carrot paring to Balkcom's shoelace. When Balkcom noted the addition to his apparel, he shook his foot vigorously. Part of the paring broke and fell into the water. The colored knot remained. Galled, he laid his paint brush aside and painstakingly removed the invasive garbage.

A few ornaments later Balkcom complained loudly, "Cut it out, Dick."

George Sousa, overseeing the deck work, asked, "What's going on, Balkcom?"

"Nelson keeps tying carrot peels to my shoe laces," explained Ronald.

"Come up here," ordered George. "I'll fix him."

In a couple of minutes Sousa said, "All right, Balkcom. Stick your head over the side and holler for Nelson."

Balkcom dutifully complied. Nelson's round sand-colored head emerged through a porthole, turned, and looked up.

Splash! The head withdrew instantly as cold salt water, capsized adroitly from a bucket, irrigated every hair, ferrule, and pore.

"That'll teach you to play grab-ass during working hours," shouted Sousa.

Dick provided us a hobby by saving and washing empty bottles. Romantically we scribbled notes, placed them inside, carefully sealed the tops, and threw the bottles into the sea. Our messages were of the same general type. "Thrown overboard from the *Buzzards Lightship* on (date) by (name). If found, please notify (name) (address)."

Surprisingly enough, more than a few were found by beachcombers who did reply, forwarding details of their discovery. Strangely, every report originated from a locale east to southeast of the ship. The bottles did not travel much more than fifteen miles, although the possibility exists that some were still afloat in the broad reaches of the Atlantic for many months.

Of three such messages dropped by myself, replies were received from two, the first being discovered on Gay Head, ten and a half miles away. Of interest was the time element involved between the originating of the message and the date of discovery. The letter reads:

"I found your letter Saturday, July 21, 1956, around 5:00 on Gay Head Beach, Martha's Vineyard, Mass. I estimate that it could not have been there more than three days. In case you have sent a large number of messages, this one was dropped from the Lightship WAL-511 at 9:05 A.M., Tuesday, December 13, 1955. The bottle containing the message was in excellent condition, but the cap disintegrated when I unscrewed. I have enclosed a map showing where I found it."

Where was this bottle for seven months and eight days? Did it make a quick journey and remain on the beach awaiting discovery? Did it float to and fro, born on the tides of the great ocean most of the time? Perhaps it landed many times and was swept back into the sea by storms or tides to be cast upon another beach. It was the ONLY bottle I tossed overboard during the winter.

On the last day of July 1956 I tried a second message. Significant that time was the speedy reply from the discoverer.

"I picked up your bottle on the beach at Lobsterville on Vineyard Sound Shore, the north shore, in other words, where Menemsha Bight runs for a short distance east and west, on this Friday (August 3, 1956). I think it made a quick trip."

In addition to bottles, we had an incident with a jettisoned can. The water was a pleasant, restful shade of light blue as the round yellow sun shown directly upon it. A few squirrel hake loitered in the shadow of the ship a few inches below the unwrinkled surface. Someone threw an empty peanut tin over the side, first punching a tiny hole in the bottom. The bi-colored can settled slowly as it filled, and when the roof of the sea closed over it, it began to turn end over end. It showed blue, aluminum, blue, aluminum, flashing like a neon sign as it slowly sank from sight, rotating leisurely with an enchanting beauty.

A man with a flair for color combinations was Roosevelt Jackson, an Afro-American engineer. Men were allowed to stow their individual lockers as they wished, with the sole proviso that they be neat and tidy. Jason went a step further, decorating the interior of his with a weird rainbow of soft pastels. Not content with that, his efforts resulted in the engine room workbench sporting brilliant pink drawers, framed with blue.

It was Jackson who brought the wrath of his fellow engineers upon himself, rightfully, one day when he gave the foghorns their morning test. Three engineers were working inside the smokestack, removing soot and grease preparatory to painting when Jackson came to the radio room to ask if he might test the horns. He explained that he had started the air compressor in order to check a new gasket and would like to test the horns at the same time rather than have to start the compressor again later.

Since the horns were located a few feet forward and above the stack, I asked if he had warned the men or had ordered them to stand clear. He assured me that he had. The flick of a switch brought forth the growling agony of a blaring foghorn which instantly was dwarfed by an explosion of righteous indignation that arose from the confines of the stack, for the men STILL WERE INSIDE.

Three very unclean men, looking like coal miners, and close to physical, insensibility, stumbled from the stack. Stupefied from the terrific din, coated generously with soot, their teeth chattered and their hands shook. They showed bitter resentment at the rankling injustice and gnashed their feelings in angry, snarling protest.

"God," later explained William Sherman, "it was awful. It was just like being inside a drum with somebody beating on the outside."

Jackson felt the world was against him, an unpleasant childhood having embittered him. He sought advice from no man and was guilty of minor errors for which there was little excuse, such as the stenciling of engine room equipment which progressed with an alarming rate of misspelled words. I felt like a teacher correcting papers as I ordered entire words removed and re-stenciled in accordance with Webster's suggestions.

Immaculate about his person, Jackson wore spotlessly clean work clothes, ironed by hand. His bedding showed the same faultless quality. In direct contrast was his manner of expressing himself. Possessing a grossly limited vocabulary, his favorite verb was one of four letters. The verb was converted to a descriptive adjective by the addition of "ing," and Jackson used the loathsome expression with a disgusting degree of frequency. He had little control over the junior

179

men in his department, his arrogant foul manner of speech being largely responsible.

Contra positioned to Jackson in command of words and of himself was Ronald Balkcom, who never uttered a single unpleasant word. He was content to express himself without the use of foul invectives and was rousingly respected for it. The closest anyone ever heard him come to swearing was, "Oh, gee." Men used to judge spicy jokes by his reception. If he smiled, someone would say, "It's a clean story. Balkcom smiled." One remarkable change was noted in Balkcom's character. When he first became a member of the *Buzzards*, his prime objects of enjoyment were hunting and fishing. A year later he still enjoyed hunting, but his quest had changed from animals to girls.

During one nine month period, three of the seven men deck force answered to the name of Wilson, and the ship was waggishly referred to as the "Wilson line" during that interim. Three other members of the fourteen man crew had names beginning with the letter "W": Wheat, Willis, and Wood. Only the latter was not a member of the deck department, and not a little confusion resulted in the early stages of this combination. When the "W" men were transferred, nationalities occupied the vacuum of similar oddities, with Swedish strains claiming four places among the crew.

We also had youngsters who were quick thinkers. Three men were sitting in the mess deck engaged in zealous conversation once which concluded as I entered the compartment.

"Keep on talking," I suggested. "If you stop talking when a person enters a room, it's an indication that he's being discussed."

A chorus of noes hailed this repartee. "Skipper," explained one of the embarrassed men, "it's like this. We're waiting to see what YOU want to talk about."

Being a firm believer in punctuality, I once reprimanded two engineers for failure to be at work sharply at 1:00 P.M. Men always have an excuse for their failings, and this one was, "Skipper, we start working late because we have no clock in the crew's quarters. We can't tell what time it is, and if we aren't called until one o'clock, it takes a few minutes to get going."

"But you always secure from work on schedule. I seldom notice any voluntary overtime from you."

"Well, skipper, that's because there IS a clock available in the engine room."

Another man was on the carpet for a disarray of dirty clothing that had been left indifferently in a corner of the laundry room. Since it was a first offense, the ship's orders were explained lengthily to the alleged delinquent. I concluded with, "The apparel found by the boatswain's mate was stenciled with your name. Now I don't think you're the type of person to be flagrantly careless. Possibly someone else put those clothes there, hoping you would be blamed. In any event, I'll bet that you'll be glad to help me catch the guy who IS responsible."

Versed in wardroom procedure, the downtrodden man was in a mood to acquiesce in anything I said. "I'll sure help you catch him, skipper. I'll bet he never leaves clothes all around again, not when I get through with the guy."

When the monotony of life on the lightship became unbearable, the crew derived strength from an assortment of fads and hobbies. Minds grow inactive and corrode without rest or deviation, and the medical science has long suggested hobbies as a highly acceptable form of relaxation, both to body and to mind. Our crew were no different than men anywhere. They needed diversions and changes of pace perhaps more than the average person ashore, for they were limited in their choice. With hardly any room for physical exercise, hobbies became a must.

Some men wrote letters of amazing length. Others solved crossword puzzles, built model planes, made rings on the lathe, read books and magazines, studied correspondence courses, and developed into amateur artists.

Wheat, referred to by the crew as the only man out of step when the saints came marching in, fancied himself a caricaturist of superior ability. Sherman, the truly proficient artist of the ship, was a severe critic, and Wheat objected strenuously to his adverse estimates.

"Wheat," Sherman would offer, "the nose is just a smidgin out of proportion."

"The hell with you," was the habitual reply. "The only thing YOU can draw is flies."

Fads on the *Buzzards* included "roll your own" cigarettes. The lightship cowboys, using teeth and one hand, usually failed utterly in their miserable attempts to roll a decent cigarette, the tobacco pouch thus being discarded early in the experiments and supplanted by "ready-mades."

Another fad was the raising of all manners of beards and mustaches. Most of the beards were of a reddish tint, itched considerably, and did little to improve facial features. A few beards were worn ashore, much to the complete horror of wives and sweethearts. Races up the ratlines were another diversion, performed infrequently as the outcome of a wager for a cigar or a pack of cigarettes.

Pros and cons of lightship duty were a daily topic of conversation, at sea. Some disliked it passionately; others took it in stride. Seldom did anyone take a definite fancy to it. The dislikes stemmed mainly from the boredom, the isolation, the foghorns, the rough weather, and, in winter, infrequent mail deliveries. Secondary peeves were such things as "I hate to scrub decks with steel wool." "I can't wear my cowboy boots." "I don't like everybody asking me what I'm gonna' have for chow." "It's hard to strike for a rating unless you go to school." "I live so close to home I can practically see it. If I'm going to be away, I'd rather be a long ways off." "I'd rather see my girl often or not at all." "We can't use as much water as we could if we were ashore." I don't like the uncertainty of waiting twenty-eight days and then not knowing if the weather will be good so I can get ashore." "I miss reading the daily newspapers. I can't keep up with the comics." "It's like being in jail. You can't go anywhere or play ball or anything like that." "People forget you once you're out here."

The older men usually were steadier and psychologically better equipped for the duty. They realized it did no good to fight it and accepted the life for what it might be worth. As Leroy Wilson used to say, "It all counts on twenty years."

Those who were able to adapt themselves thought of the duty in terms of a "change," and they realized that some benefits did exist. "I like the liberty. When you go ashore, you can stay at home for two weeks and forget all about the job." "You don't have to get up in the middle of the night to go looking for somebody who lost his way in the fog." "I find one thing on this lightship. Everybody works together. There is no cut throating." "I never lock my locker. I leave money laying around and never think about anybody stealing it." "I feel closer to civilization than I did on weather patrol. Also, we get mail more often." "It doesn't make much difference to me. I would just as soon be here as anywhere." "I like the idea of having some time to myself. I can read some of the books I've always wanted to. I never had the time before." "I like the extra time to study my correspondence course. Gee, a man out here has time to study and prepare himself for civilian life." "I don't think too much about it one way or the other." "It's good in this respect. Nobody can sneak up on you or spy to see what you're doing. They have to come by boat, and we're far enough out so that nobody will bother us very often." "I like the way the crew works together. There's hardly ever any fighting over little things that don't amount to anything."

Pros and cons? They are discussed heatedly on every lightship. They always have been. They will cease to be heard on the day the last lightship is withdrawn from active service.

Chapter XI

"The Storm of February 25-26, 1956"

The morning of February twenty-fifth dawned dismally and slowly. It had, in fact, been dismal long before the grayness of morning fully developed, for fog had settled about us in spite of a brisk thirty knot wind from the dreaded southwesterly sector. The horns had chattered incessantly from a 2:30 A.M. awakening, and southwesterly swells mauled us as they pounded against the bow. The ship twisted and bobbed, back and forth, up and down, back and forth, up and down. Decks moaned, rigging whistled, halyards slapped, and the anchor acted oddly as the chain emitted a shrill, metallic scraping behavior. Small craft warnings were in effect, having been posted the previous afternoon.

O800, February 25: Breakfast over, the crew went to work with inspired fervor, in spite of miserable weather and a bellowing fog signal. We were to be relieved in two more days, on February twenty-seventh, by the *Relief* lightship for our annual "in-port" period. We were readying the *Buzzards* for the occasion, and we wanted a clean, orderly shipshape vessel. We wanted more than that even. We wanted ours to be as good as any in the fleet, and every man had worked hard for nine months to achieve that aim. A spirited group, they had become proud of their ship and its appearance. They had painted, scraped, sanded, scrubbed, spliced, shined, drilled, and performed the multitude of tasks assigned a seafarer. Finishing touches were being applied as decks carefully received their fourth coat of wax; bulkheads and ports were cleaned; bright work had been cleared of paint particles, and in its place the brilliant yellowish brass sparkled. The men were careful not to smudge brass or paintwork with fingerprints, heel marks, spillage, or the like.

Pipes, frames, compartments, hatches, and machinery had been cleaned, pained, checked, and stenciled. Grease fittings, water valves, oil valves, and air valves were all painted neatly with proper identifying colors. Bilges were clean and pumped as dry as possible, gear was stowed in its proper place, and tools were in their allotted spots. Spare engine parts were in identified boxes and secured in bins. Fenders, mooring lines, gangway lights, etc. had been checked and readied for use in port.

The entire crew was aboard. The last liberty party had returned on Thursday, and no one had gone ashore as we wanted everyone aboard to assist in taking the ship to Boston. Now it was Saturday, and the crew was looking forward to the half holiday routine of Saturday afternoon. Sunday would be a day of rest for all. Men planned to ready their clothing and personal effects for the nightly liberty to be granted in port. Then, the following day, we would be relieved on station, get underway, and begin our journey. Excitement reigned. Man discussions, mostly of what to do and see in Boston, were commonplace. Even so, not a little conversation was devoted to our "clean, systematic home at sea." It was, to quote one of the men, in "apple-pie order."

"They can't find much fault with us this time," opined one member.

"No siree," added his neighbor at the coffee table. "They should see a big difference in the ship since the last time we were there. Boy, what a mess when we first took station out here."

"Yeah, that's right. Skipper, are you going to ask some of the officers to come down and see the ship before the yard workers start tearing things apart?"

"Absolutely. You fellows have done a tremendous job. I especially want credit to be given you men who did the actual work. I certainly appreciate your endeavors and you cooperation. It is my intention to invite several officers to inspect the ship as soon as possible."

"They'll see a good one, then. Boy! Look at the shine on those decks!"

"Yeah, and how about the brass around those port-holes."

"Don't forget how we cut in the paint on the electrical fixtures, the overhead, and all that sort of thing."

"You know another good thing? In two more days we get relieved. We'll be in Boston during March, which is one of the windiest months in the year. And when we come backout in April, the winter will be over. So actually we have only two more days of winter out here."

"We can stand on our heads and do that!"

"The way this southwester is going, you might be doing just that."

"Gorry, it IS blowing harder. But what do we care? Two more days and we'll be in port."

The observation was partially correct. The wind had increased to thirty-five knots. Visibility had not improved, for we could see no more than half a mile, and the horn had reminded us of half of our predicament. The agitated motion of the ship kept us advised of the other half - the southwest winds. Coffee time ended, remnants of Saturday morning routine cleared, and the weekly inspection took place. Everything was as close to perfection as possible, in our eyes, and it was most gratifying to realize the many changes that had taken effect. It was a thrill, too, to realize that we knew, in our own hearts, that we had a darned nice looking ship. Neither boastful nor naive, we were aware of the simple truth. We had made many improvements, and we were extremely proud of our ability to work together as a team, dedicated to a single aim.

The sole disturbing element that morning, other than the elements of nature, was the activity of the anchor chain. It continued to act most peculiar. There always was a severe strain in bad weather, particularly during southwesters, which could be felt, heard, seen, and sensed whenever the chain tautened suddenly. It was checked frequently during bad weather, but the usual groanings and vibrations were normal signs of an anchor that was holding well. It was routine, previously, but today it was different. It flayed; it frapped; it tightened; it clacked, all with an eerie harsh grating. The anchor pawl, usually snuggling against a link, rode an inch or more vertically, then settled back. This had not happened before, as far as we could recollect. It worried us, even though all else seemed normal and secure. From deck the chain appeared to lead well forward, so we discounted, unfortunately, the possibility of it being caught on a wreck or a crag. As the weather was continually worsening, we lengthened the scope by two shots (one hundred and eighty feet), and now it road with approximately seven shots of chain. The course cacophony continued, however, the pawl continuing to ride up and down. As the tremblings failed to lessen noticeably, we checked the windlass gear at least every ten minutes, sometimes watching it for half an hour at a time.

1200, February 25: The wind mounted in intensity, directly from the southwest, and now blew at an estimated forty-five knots. The anchor chain tremors became more accentuated. The ship was riding high in the water for we were light, our fresh water supply being low. We were down to our last one thousand gallons, and the fore peak tank, situated near the bow area, was empty. We had not requested a tender to replenish our supply because we soon would be in Boston where water would be available from the dock. Also, we had wished to save the busy buoy tender a trip, it seeming like such a waste of effort, time, money, and man hours to ask for something we did not actually need. High in construction, the bow now rose considerably higher than usual, making a huge target for wind and sea, both of which buffeted us mercilessly. The wind blew furiously against the elevated bow, first on one side and then on the other as the ship veered to and fro. Swells slashed against the hull in thudding salvos. Our anchor continued to hold, grudgingly, although the chain clattered in sharp disagreement.

Bill Burroughs, the Chief Boatswain's Mate at that time, did not like the situation. "If that anchor pawl fails, we'll be in a bad spot. There's something wrong, but I can't put my finger on it, unless it's because we're riding so high in the water."

Bob Dean, Chief Engine man, suggested, "Don't you think that's probably the trouble? We have such a high bow anyway, and now that the fresh water tanks are almost empty we're much higher than usual. The wind is pushing us around much more, and it's causing a heavy strain on your anchor. If the tanks were full, I don't think you'd notice it anywhere near as much."

"How about isolating the fore peak tank from the others and filling it with salt water?" I asked. "Is there any reason why that can't be done?" How about it, Bob?"

"We can try," answered the Chief. "We'll get the P-60 (portable fire pump) and see what we can do."

Burroughs added, "I'd sure like to try that and see if it doesn't help."

I ordered the tank filled. Burroughs and Dean sent men to bring the pump, fire hose, suction hose, spanner wrenches, and everything necessary to the operation.

It was not with complete confidence that the task was started. Foremost in our mind was the questionable ability of the pump to lift water far enough, vertically, to reach the fill pipe. It was a long lift for so small a pump, and we had experienced such difficulties before. If it hadn't been for the tremendous slashing of the wintry seas, it would have been a simple matter to lower the dory part way with the pump inside. A short lift then could easily be effected, but that was out of the question today as mighty rollers leaped nearly to the dory itself. If the storm became much worse, it would be necessary to rig it in, that is, take it from the davits and lash it on deck.

An alternative would be to use the pump on the second deck. However, it was a gasoline engine, and we dared not use it below decks except during an extreme emergency. It constantly backfired when first started, and we could picture ourselves fighting a fire as we shuttered violently at the end of the anchor chain.

188

Accordingly, the pump was carried to the bow portion of the main deck and slashed beneath the bulwarks to prevent it from sliding around. Hoses were connected and tightened as the ship's bow reared skyward, then fell with as deafening thud. Spray coated the deck, the men, the pump. Now we had something else with which to contend. The pump would have to be wiped dry and some sort of shelter provided.

1335, February 25: Small craft warnings were changed to southwest storm warnings. The wind continued at forty-five knots. The gray fog-laden atmosphere gave way to rain as large drops fell in a torrential downpour, soaking men to the skin in a matter of minutes. The hastily erected shelter kept most of the salt spray from the pump as the seas continued their deadly assault. The bow moved frenetically up and down and to and fro like a hammock caught in a sudden squall.

"O.K. Let's try her." A pull on the lanyard turned the motor, pump, and magneto. The magneto, in turning, theoretically built up a spark strong enough to ignite the gasoline which started the engine. A mighty tug was taken, the lanyard spun out its full length and disengaged. Nothing happened. A second try produced the same results. A third, fourth, fifth did no better.

"Let's wipe her off again. Bring some more dry rags. Hold that canvas so the salt spray will run off. Hold on! Here comes a big one!"

The bow plunged into a huge sea. Salt water covered the bridge, drenched the men a second time, and gurgled angrily into the waterways. Ressler protected the fire pump by throwing a canvas over it and holding it in place with his body. The water on deck did not quite reach into the pump and quickly dispersed.

"Damned southwesters! Anybody who says this is easy duty ought to come out here when we have a stinking storm like this. He'd soon change his frigging mind. Don't just stand there! Get me some dry rags!" That was in unison, or so it appeared, from several brine enveloped engineers.

More rags arrived, and the pump was dried again, as well as possible with the heavens opened up, spray continually coating the bridge, and the bow rocking, rolling, pitching, vibrating in the furious storm. Another series of yanks on the lanyard brought only a short sputtering, the motor stubbornly resisting every effort.

Donald Moore, engine man first class, studied the situation as wind whistled through his soggy clothing. His shoes, filled with water, failed to warm his feet or add to his comfort. He pranced up and down to stimulate circulation and blew warm air on his frigid fingers. His teeth chattered, but his next order was unmistakably clear and crisp.

"Sherman, the old man's in the windlass room. So bring ne the half inch electric drill with a fitting to accommodate this nut on the end of the crankshaft."

"What are you going to do?" asked Sherman with an irritating drawl.

"Never mind," retorted Moore sharply. "Just hurry up and bring that drill."

Sherman scampered away. Meanwhile, in the engine room, Chief Dean was exiling the forward water tank from the rest of the system, which we would keep clear as long as possible. We did not intend to flood the whole works with salt water unless absolutely necessary, perhaps as a final resort, for we needed drinking water. Dean closed the appropriate valves, and all was in readiness.

In the windlass room Chief Burroughs and I surveyed our situation. We were ready to take on water but still no sound of the fire pump. They were having a difficult time on deck. Small wonder! How much more disagreeable could it be? Windy, rough, foggy, raining, ship continuing to bounce like a fishing cork, a continuous shower of spray. Conditions with the windlass were not encouraging. The chain still appeared to be tending properly, yet the strange springing sensations continued. The pawl was holding, but not properly, as it too continued its odd behavior. From an ordinary slack it suddenly would vibrate into shrill metallic life, and the pawl would bounce slightly upwards. If it failed to hold, the strain soon would be on the windlass brake. We knew that would not hold for long.

"If that damned spare anchor wasn't carried on deck, we'd be able to drop it. With both anchors out we would ride better. At least I'd feel a whole lot better about the situation."

"That's true, and had we known we were going to have such a storm we would have readied it. However, under these conditions it is too dangerous to even make an attempt to get it over. We'd punch a hole in the side of the ship and maybe lose all hands. Then, too, it would be far too dangerous to the fellows who would have to do the work. In this weather, one slip could easily maim someone for life."

At that time the spare anchor of many lightships was carried on the starboard rail. Ours was no different. In order to launch the anchor it was necessary to raise it with a block and tackle, keep the anchor from swinging in ANY direction, rig the davit outboard, let out two shots of anchor chain, then cut a manila strap holding the anchor from the davit. It would barely clear the hull under the best of conditions. With a port roll it easily could penetrate the relatively thin hull, and a gash below the waterline could have most disastrous effects. If undue strain were added due to the rolling and tossing of the ship, a line quickly would chafe and part. Men could be hurt. The anchor would swing on the davit out of control or would crash to the deck. Worse, it might crash into the hull. In rough weather such as this the ship might even be doomed by such an accident, and what chance would men have, in February, battling twelve foot seas? An hour would elapse before help arrived, at the earliest, if indeed we still had means to notify anyone of our plight. Who could struggle that length of time, in a life jacket, in frigid seas like this? Would we not all die of exposure long before aid could arrive? During severe storms, we were strangely alone. We had to survive through common sense, through proper ship handling and good seamanship, through proper upkeep of machinery, hull, and equipment. Besides all that, we still had to maintain our vigilance as an aid to navigation, a visual and accurate aid to all other shipping interests in the area.

Our discussion of the anchor chain situation was interrupted by the coughing of a motor. It died, coughed again, and was silenced. Then it sputtered into life, remained thusly in loud synchronized surges. A chorus of hurrahs filtered through the din. We knew the P-60 was running.

I went on deck. The engineers were smiling and clapping one another on the back, in spite of being soaked and half frozen. The first gallon of water had been pumped. Smoke poured from the exhaust of the P-60. The sound of the motor made a welcome addition to that of the foghorn, the dreary monotonous wind, the sizzling of spilled surf, and the thundering of seas striking against the hull. Then the pump accelerated briskly, the hose flattened, smiles turned to frowns. Suction had been lost. The ship was pitching so heavily the end of the hose had been lifted from the sea. Every swell that lashed against the port bow heeled us to starboard and dragged the hose above the water's edge. The hose was lowered several feet, the pump restarted. The hose filled, and water commenced its flow to the tank. Again suction was lost. The same procedure was followed, with the end of the hose thrust yet deeper into the water, for the ship was rolling heavily. Each wave crest raised the bow, and as it sped on its course, the hose end was again exposed. After several more attempts, it finally was lowered enough so that it remained below the surface. The major problem, as before, was the vertical lift. Each lowering of the hose lengthened the lift. Thus, each subsequent trial was begun with misgivings, the engineers not expecting continued success as the distance now was considerably beyond the usual recommended lift. Good fortune prevailed as the hose ultimately filled, no longer lost ingestion, and the tank was being filled. Everyone was gleeful, that is, as gleeful as one could be when wet, cold, and expose to a stiff southwest storm on a tossing vessel in the middle of winter.

Noticing the drill, I inquired as to its part in the proceedings.

Moore was ill at ease. "We, ah, that is," he faltered, "ah, we had to drill something. No, I'll tell the truth. We

192

used it on the pump to get the shaft to spin fast enough. Otherwise, I don't think we could have gotten it to run."

I was too relieved at the sight of water coursing into our tank to make an issue of it in spite of his disregard of safety procedures. One man was left to watch the P-60 so the others could go below to change into dry clothing. The storm continued, unabated, wind velocity increased slightly, and Chief Burroughs advised that the anchor chain still was misbehaving. We decided to await the filling of the tank before taking further action, and a watch was posted in the windlass room.

1600, February 25: The wind was southwest at forty-five knots, seas were running from the same direction, now fifteen feet in height, visibility had increased to one mile in the fog and rain. The P-60 was secured in its rack near the stern, the fore peak tank having been filled nearly to capacity. We estimated that 4300 gallons had been pumped into it, thus adding seventeen tons of weight to the bow which now was perceptively lower. The difference was immediately noticeable as the ship rode considerably better. Less perpendicular structure was exposed to the angry swells and buffeting winds which continued, nevertheless, to assail us furiously. Strain on the anchor chain was lessened, and it resembled near normalcy in its flayings. It fetched and slackened with more of a grumbling than the metallic ringing that previously had caused so much concern, and the ship did not shudder quite so drastically when the onslaughts of the seas were rebuffed. The anchor pawl settled into place. It was holding. Since the grumblings originating in the windlass room could be heard throughout the vessel, we eased out watch, which was decreased to a thorough check every fifteen minutes. We breathed more easily.

1900, February 25: The wind was still from the southwest at forty-five knots but gusting to fifty, visibility remaining at one mile. The ship was taking a severe pummeling from wind and sea. Discomfort was more acute. There was no agreeable position for the body, whether standing, sitting, or lying horizontally. As the anchor chain began again to absorb painful abuse, I ordered the engine room to make necessary arrangements to get underway at a moment's notice.

Prior to and since this particular storm, many suggestions have been heard of the relative merits of using the ship's engine to assist in removing some of the strain from the anchor. There are heated arguments to this endless debate. Some lightship skippers maintain that they believe they could, if necessary during a gale or hurricane, remove much of the strain by jogging ahead slightly, drifting back, and then jogging ahead again. Others insist that the engines should not be used for this purpose because it is impossible to know when to jog ahead and when to drift back at the precise moment it might be beneficial. At night, particularly, it is exceedingly difficult to tell how much slack is in the chain. It is all well and good to move slowly into the face of a gale, but it is impossible to maintain position in one exact spot on the ocean. Winds are gust;, sequences, height and, power of seas are unreliable; and tidal currents enter the picture.

We had once tried the use of engine during storm, at anchor, and found it wanting. At first we thought it a good idea as we moved slowly into the teeth of the wind. There was no strain whatever on the chain or the anchor. We drifted before the seas and wind. When we THOUGHT (we could not be sure) we were nearly to the end of our scope, we again moved forward. Good fortune could not last forever under these conditions, and suddenly we felt a tremendous pull on the anchor. The chain vibrated madly. The ship shuttered and moaned fiercely. All too soon we had reached the end of the scope. Then the chain and anchor were forced to bear the additional strain of a vessel moving some little distance WITH wind and seas. Not only did it have the normal weight of the ship with which to contend but also the dynamic tension of a MOVING vessel along with it. We immediately secured the engine and kept it on standby. The ship actually rode easier WITHOUT the attempted help.

Hence we did not, on February 25th, make any attempt to use the main engine as a strain preventer or alleviator. We felt that by doing so our condition would be materially worsened. We had several times ridden out storms as severe as the one now engulfing us. Nothing uncommon had happened before; there was no reason to believe it would now. Still, we did not like the mannerisms of the chain. The pawl resumed motion, riding up and down. The chain once more quivered with its metallic ringing urgency.

Not wishing to be unprepared we decided to have the main engine standing by. When a vessel is getting underway from a dock, some fifty minutes was required to build a necessary supply of compressed air. On station, during an emergency, the time could be shortened ten or fifteen minutes. That was because only one bell, or signal to the engine room requiring the use of compressed air, is needed on the open sea. When one is undocking from a narrow slip, with little room to maneuver, a series of bells often is required.

1945, February 25: The storm roared savagely with frightful screams. Visibility remained at one mile, fog and rain remaining constant. The winds were blowing at an estimated seventy-five knots, hurricane force. It happened suddenly. The gusts of fifty-five knots grew to sixty, sixty-five, seventy, seventy-five. Then they were gusts no longer. It was a steady screeching wind that tore from the southwest. Seas towered above us as they grew to twenty feet, then twenty-five, then thirty! All in a space of minutes! Each swell crashed over the bulwarks, flooding the decks. Waterways were not large enough to cope with the newly created rapids, and water spilled over the sides of the hull. The wheelhouse and bridge were swallowed in driven spray. The ship dove heavily, dipped briskly, quivered from port to starboard, from stem to stern. The thud of tons of angry water could be heard everywhere as it fought to drive us to eternity.

In the windlass room the vexing sharp snap of the chain was annoying. The motion of the ship was so distorted, seas so rough, it was difficult to gauge the lead (direction). As Burroughs and I stood there, desperately racking our brains, the pawl flipped upward and completely disengaged. Burroughs leaped forward and threw the pawl back onto the chain, but the broad part of a link was in the way. The pawl lay useless atop the link.

"This is what I call a damned bad storm. We'll have to engage the windlass and take up on it enough to get the pawl back in place," he said. "We'd better do it in a hurry, too. Come on, fellows. You know what to do! Hurry it up!"

It took a matter of seconds to accomplish, as air already had been built to the required pressure, but the pawl engaged did not make us feel a bit optimistic. If it happened once, it was almost sure to happen again.

We watched the pawl a few moments. The wind continued with agonizing fury. Mountainous waves of water cascaded upon us. The sound of the storm rankled on. Half the crew felt nauseated. Supper had been attended by only a few, and even those not affected with nausea had headaches.

The anchor chain became strangely silent. It rattled modestly a few times. There were no sudden tugs. Still, we were headed into the wind and could feel the endless seas breaking against the hull.

2000, February 25: An urgent scurrying of footsteps descending to the windlass room interrupted our observations. It was the radio room watch. "Skipper," he blurted. "The fog hasn't cleared a bit, but I can see the green flasher right off our stern!" The green flasher was a buoy, two miles thirty degrees true from our charted position.

In a group we rapidly ascended the ladder to have a look. There it was! No doubt about it. Less than a mile away the green flashes of light were plainly seen. Not another light was in sight. Fog, rain, and the green light which should not be visible. It could mean only one thing!

"Cap, we're adrift!" shouted Burroughs to make himself heard above the storm.

We both realized it at the same instant. "Bill, send a man to me in the wheelhouse right away. Tell Williams (boatswain's mate) to take two men and release the quadrant immediately. I'll notify the engine room. Come up to the bridge as soon as you can."

Burroughs was on his way. I dashed to the wheelhouse. It took the combined efforts of two of us to open the port hatch. We fought fore breath as the winds flung us from our feet. Safely inside, I rang the engine room. "We're adrift. We want to get underway as soon as the quadrant is cleared. (The quadrant was shackled when not in use to keep the rudder amidships.) Do you have sufficient air pressure?"

"Yes, sir," replied the engineer on watch.

"Very well. Stand by for a signal. Tell Chief Dean to report to the bridge when all is ready."

I then called the radio room. "We're adrift. I'll have a priority message for you in a little while. Meanwhile, secure the horn, radio beacons, and main light. Report to me as soon as you have done so. Is that clear?"

"Yes, sir," ended the conversation.

Seaman Wheat appeared at the bridge. "Seaman Wheat to stand wheel watch, sir."

"Very well. Stand by the wheel. When we get underway, we will steer course 225."

"Aye, aye, sir. Course 225 when underway."

The phone buzzed as Burroughs ran to the bridge. "Deck force ready to get underway, Cap," he yelled into the teeth of the gale.

"Very well. Grab that phone, Bill, and see what it is."

"It's the radio room. He reports all aids to navigation secured. Do you want him to send a dispatch?"

"Not yet. Have him stand by the radio. Tell Williams to bring in the remnants of the anchor chain and notify us how much has been lost."

Chief Dean burst through the hatch. "Engine room is ready, Cap."

"Very well." I rang one bell for approximately half speed ahead. It was answered similarly. We were able to discern the chug-a-bug, chug-a-bug as the main engine sprang to life.

"Course 225, helmsman."

"Course 225, sir," he repeated.

We hoped that curse would keep us nearly head-on to the giant seas that loomed ominously all about us. They rose steeply in our immediate path. They were immense. We gauged them as close to thirty feet and could not have been far off. If anything, we underestimated their actual measurement. The wind was steady, maintaining hurricane velocity. Burroughs and I peered through the ports, trying to see the waves as they approached. The main engine was turning at 400 RPM. We seemed to be barely moving. We increased speed to 450 RPM to get us back close to our regular station. We then planned to settle back to 400 RPM, hoping we might be able to "Heave to" on our approximate established position. The wind screamed incredibly. Perpetual torrents of spray impaired vision as it streamed off the bridge. Steering the ship was a battle, and we sent for a second helmsman. Connie Wilson and Wheat stood side by side, striving to hold the ship on course.

"Come right to 235."

"Come right to 235, sir," the helmsman acknowledged.

Chief Burroughs left the bridge and returned a few minutes later.

"Anchor chain is in the locker, Captain. Williams says we lost about two shots."

"Very well. Please send for the radioman."

":Aye, aye, Captain."

The helmsmen reported the ship falling to the left. "Steering 218, Captain. We're unable to bring her to 235. She's hard over."

"Very well. Chief dean, ring the engine room and ask them if they can give us 475 RPM. I don't want to ring for full speed in these seas."

"Will do. They can set it ahead that much."

The radioman appeared as Dean ordered his engineers to increase speed by 25 RPM. Wheat and Wilson battled the wheel. "Steering 215, Captain. Still falling off."

198

The following priority radio message notified the outside world of our plight:

TO OPERATIONS X LOST MAIN MOORING AND TWO SHOTS ANCHOR CHAIN X UNDERWAY ON OWN POWER X SECURED ALL AIDS TO NAVIGATION X WAL-511 (our number) HOVE TO VICINITY REGULAR STATION X AWAITING MODERATE WEATHER CONDITIONS BEFORE ATTEMPTING TO DROP SPAREANCHOR.

The message was sent to the district office in Boston, the base of Coast Guard operations covering an area from northernmost Maine to Connecticut. The Coast Guard base at Woods Hole was listed as an information addressee.

With the increase in speed, the helm began to answer, "Swinging right, sir, steering 220."

"Very well. Notify me of every 5 degree change in course until you reach 235."

"Notify you of every 5 degrees change in course until we reach 235. Aye, aye."

"Steering 225."

"Steering 230."

"Steering 235."

At last we were headed on our safest course. Most of the seas were met head on or nearly so as they thundered onto the wheelhouse at every dip of the bow. The wind was unrelenting. The barometer, in a period of forty-five minutes, had dropped a staggering o.53 of an inch. The sea looked dark and ominous, and their course was spotted with difficulty. Occasionally one approached a bit from the south or from the west, but most came from due southwest. The rigging emitted shrill outcries as wind and spray raged with distemper. The motion of the ship was mostly up and down. Cross seas struck furiously, however, causing us to roll menacingly until a head sea took over again. The men on the wheel were drenched with sweat as they attempted to steer the ship on 235 degrees. The ship would fall off a bit, return to 235, fall off, return. Never to the right of 235, she fell continuously to the left. Any further increase in speed was inadvisable at the time. Burroughs and I continued to peer through the ports, our eyes growing accustomed to the spray encrusted darkness. We watched huge combers tower momentarily dead ahead, disappear as the bow raised and dipped, then pass into oblivion.

Burroughs answered a buzzer. "Cap. It's the radio room. Woods Hole wants to talk to you on the radio."

"Very well, Bill. Take over for a few minutes."

As I turned my back, he roared, "FULL RIGHT RUDDER!! QUICKLY!! HURRY IT UP!!

Before any answer was forthcoming, a cross sea from the westerly sector struck us heavily along the starboard bow. SLAM! The ship shuddered under the impact and leaned to port. The bow fell off sharply. Burroughs jumped to the wheel to assist the two helmsmen. A second wall of water sped towards us from the same sector, on the heels of its forerunner. It was a dark sinister wave, carrying a cap of white foam driven before it by the wind. Heeled to port as we were, it appeared like a skyscraper, a huge rampart of water bearing down upon us with destruction in view. It would not be denied. There was no escape. We were in a trough and semi-broached. It would catch us full on the starboard beam. Could we escape complete disaster. What if another followed? What if there was a series? Higher and higher it rose. Why were we still heeled to port? Why wouldn't the rudder answer the wheel? It was amazing how so many thoughts could fit through one's mind in a horror stricken second preceding disaster! What were the men thinking as they tugged on the wheel? Burroughs knew the tremendous mass was about to strike. He has seen it the moment he sprang to the wheel. Had the two seamen noticed?

C-R-A-S-H! The terrible sea literally swallowed us. It had struck us broad on the starboard while we were still heeled to port. A thunderous detonation occurred at the moment of assault and for several seconds after. The noise was such it seemed the ship must be disemboweled. Its feral savagery stunned minds and bodies.

It was the worst sea ever taken by the *Buzzards* during our tenure. By rights, the ship should have disintegrated under that hammer blow of sea and wind. The moment when sea met steel was a deafening shock. Salt water spewed everywhere. It had ridden above the starboard railing and emptied onto the deck, onto the superstructure, into the lifeboats. The ship took a thirty degree list.

The internal violence exploded in our ears. Pandemonium broke loose. The sound of dishes, tools, equipment breaking, structures torn loose was everywhere. Lights dimmed, miraculously came back on. The terrific clatter continued as the vessel slowly made her way back to an even keel. Slowly, oh so slowly, she recovered, then rapidly. She turned briskly to starboard, then settled back, upright.

Hanging to a safety railing, I had managed to remain on my feet. A quick glance through the porthole revealed no more westerly monsters close at hand. The seas still ran high from the southwest. I looked at the wheel to ask our heading. NO ONE WAS THERE! Seconds previously there had been three men, braced, frantically turning to starboard. Now they had disappeared. The shock was electrifying but dissipated when I noticed a tangle of struggling humanity on the port extreme of the wheelhouse. The collision with Poseidon had loosened their grip on the wheel and thrown them to the deck. Stunned, they regained their feet, apparently none the worse for their provoking experience. They instantly responded to orders.

"Come right to 235."

"Come right to 235, sir."

"Bill, that sea was something. I've never seen anything like it before."

"Me either, and I hope I never do again. Want me to take a check to see if the ship's all right?"

"Yes, please do. I'll call the engine room and wait for you to get back before I radio Woods Hole."

The engine room reported no casualties to machinery or hull. The storeroom was a "mess," but as far as they could tell, the engines had suffered no ill effects. A quick check had been taken, and the engineers planned to retrace their steps more minutely. A report would be made as soon as possible.

The chart table in the wheelhouse was completely devoid of charts, parallel rules, protractors, dividers, etc. they were in a disheveled heap on deck.

"Steady on 235, sir."

The wind was beginning to moderate, visibility beginning to improve. The seas still were tumultuous, from the southwest. A lone cross sea showed up once in awhile, but was dwarfed by comparison with the grandfather that had clawed at us. A lone star showed overhead. From its position in the overcast sky it probably was Sirius, the dog star. Our situation still was serious, too. Not as dangerously so as a few moments ago, but serious just the same. Sirius, serious. The pair of homonyms intrigued me as I watched the seas and listened to the wind. Remember how one studied Shakespear in high school and didn't like it because the lines never rhymed? The teacher called it blank verse. And remember learning part of "Il Penserosos"? Never liked that, either, at the time. Why? Maybe because it had been drilled and drilled that it was a classic without having it explained WHY. Poetry! Sirius, serious. Ironic, wasn't it? Here you were on a low powered, single screw, difficult to maneuver lightship that lost its mooring in a fierce storm. Your plight is serious. That word again? How could you think of poetry at a time like this?

"What is your heading?"

"231, sir."

Burroughs returned to report no injuries to any crew members. "It's a damned mess down there, though. It'll take a week to clean that place up. You wouldn't believe it if I told you about it, Cap. Why don't you go down and have a look for yourself?"

The engine room reaffirmed their initial report of no casualties to machinery. "We're not taking on any water, as far as we can see. We'll keep checking, though, and keep you informed."

Turning the bridge over to Chief Burroughs, I strode to the radio room to consult with the base at Woods Hole.

"DO YOU NEED HELP?" was their initial transmission.

"NEGATIVE. THE SEAS ARE RUNNING VERY HIGH BUT WE ARE ALL RIGHT. WE TOOK A COUPLE OF BAD ONES AND SOME EQUIPMENT WAS TORN LOOSE. HOWEVER WE ARE NOT LEAKING. THERE IS NO DAMAGE TO MACHINERY. WE ARE HOVE TO IN THE VICINITY OF OUR REGULAR POSITION. IT STILL IS MUCH TOO ROUGH TO ATTEMPT TO DROP THE SPARE ANCHOR. WE PLAN TO AWAIT MORE FAVORABLE CONDITIONS."

"THE DISTRICT IS PLANNING TO SEND THE HORNBEAM TO ASSIST YOU."

"WE DO NOT NEED ASSISTANCE. IT IS NOT UP TO ME TO RUN THE SHOW BUT WE ARE IN NO IMMEDIATE DANGER. WE ARE UNDERWAY AND WAITING ONLY FOR THE SEAS TO MODERATE."

"I ROGER THAT. I WILL INFORM THE DISTRICT OF THE SITUATION. THEY PROBABLY WILL INSIST ON SENDING THE HORNBEAM TO STAND BY YOU."

"ROGER. PLEASE IMPRESS ON THEM HOWEVER THAT WE DO NOT NEED OR DESIRE ANY ASSISTANCE."

"ROGER. OUT."

In the radio room the sole evidence of anything amiss was a capsized waste basket and a few scraps of sodden litter on the deck. The radioman had been able to cling to the mainmast, which passed through the compartment. He was unscathed, reporting that the chair and logs had startled him as much as the sea when they capsized onto the deck.

Outside the radio room, a bit aft, dory equipment was all over. Oars, boat hooks, tholepins, life jackets, had broken their lashings and spilled onto the weather deck. One jacket and an oar were atop the wardroom fidley, three feet above deck level. The dory hung at a grotesque angle from the davits. A cursory inspection showed it to be free from apparent damage.

Ring buoys had been washed overboard. The watertight lantern of one still showed a glob of white light as it rose on the crest of a wave.

I decided to return to the bridge by way of the second deck. Utter chaos greeted me. Our neatly waxed decks shone no longer, the luster having been replaced with white streaked stains. We had leaned so far to port, water had poured through a non-watertight door. There was a twelve inch rising at the top of the ladder leading to the second deck, but in spite of that the seas had risen above it and had deposited gallons of water through the door. The crew were gathering it from the deck with buckets.

In the wardroom, chairs were in disarray against the port bulkhead. Mixed with them were books, magazines, an ash tray, a foul weather jacket. Water had streamed down the rudder post and was sloshing with every motion of the ship. The television, by a miracle, had failed to jump completely from the half inch molding holding it. Coffee had spilled, and its aroma was nauseating as it mingled with strange odors from other portions of the ship.

The office was a jungle of books, publications, calendars, pencils, and a perforator. A capsized trash receptacle rolled to and fro. The typewriter, fortunately, was bolted. The deck contained a goodly portion of sea water, too, for it was directly below the ladder down which the seas had just cascaded.

As I walked forward, the recreation room at first glance showed no mishap except for a group of tumbled chairs, although salt water was there in gallons. Approaching the galley, I noticed that a foam proportioner was missing. Twenty inches in diameter and thirty inches in height, it was held in place by a metal strap. Used to smother electrical or inflammable liquid fires with a mechanical foam, it was stowed near the recreation deck fire main where it could be hooked into the hose with a minimum of delay. Now the strap was broken, and the proportioner had disappeared.

Entering the mess deck, I first noticed the errant proportioner, lashed against a bulkhead. Prior ro coming to rest in that position it had bowled over three stools, each of which had been held in place by four three-inch screws! It also had ripped away a jagged section of linoleum decking and loosened a fourth stool. From that, one can judge the force behind the foam proportioner as it bounded through a hatch onto the mess deck, sweeping everything before it! The stools now had been gathered in a heap and were temporality lashed to a radiator. The trays above the three tables were empty, the condiments spilled on deck. Mayonnaise, pickles, mustard, pepper, sugar, salt, catsup, chili sauce, and horse radish emitted a sickening odor as they mingled with napkins, broken jars, and sea water. They dripped from tables and bulkheads and coated a goodly portion of the deck. The refrigerator was opened to disclose a topsy-turvy of equal proportions.

The galley was a replica of the mess deck, with a few broken dishes joining the hodgepodge. The galley range, which had been secured, nevertheless reeked with the scent of spilled coffee. The pot rolled on its side, its top somewhere in the muddle under foot.

One could scarcely make his way through the ship's library where scattered books were nearly as numerous as hairs on the head. Glass doors, enclosing shelves of novels, had swung open but had not smashed. The editions tumbled out, where they were further distributed in all directions by a submersible pump that had broken loose. Dominoes, playing cards, scrabble figures, a Monopoly game, and a ship model intermingles, enhancing the destructive scene.

Schaeffer, Meredith, and Williams had been standing in the crew's berthing quarters on the starboard side when the giant sea struck. Meredith and Williams had been able to grab a stanchion and hold on. Schaeffer, a rugged one hundred and seventy pound, six foot seaman, was spun off balance and clutched at a locker as his full weight hit against it. The locker, held in place by eight screws, gave way under the impact. Schaeffer and locker, his arms still entwined about it, wound up against the port side of the ship and slid to the deck. More alarmed than hurt, he got to his feet and walked away. Schaeffer, who survived that mishap without injury was, two days later, to fracture his thumb while tossing a heaving line.

In addition to the locker, mattresses, blankets, and pillows were all over the place. When one of the men opened a locker, the contents fell out to a scattered clutter at his feet. Clothing was sodden with hair oil and shaving lotion. A few very wet magazines had ben tossed into a waste basket. The linoleum there was likewise streaked with white where the water had forced its way from the main deck. One porthole was cracked.

On the third deck, the boatswain's locker looked like "Oh, hell, what's the use?" Adjacent to it, the commissary locker was the same where canned goods and dry stores had fallen from shelves in spite of bars designed to hold them securely. Here and there was a jagged jar, with jam spreading like an ink stain.

The most dangerous jumble was in the paint locker where, in spite of previous precautions, cans of paint, thinner, linseed oil, and paint remover had been propelled from lipped shelves. A dozen cans had punctured in the process, and their contents now sloshed several inches deep. The fumes were toxic, so I ordered the hatch firmly secured for the present time.

In the midst of clearing some of the shambles the emergency alarm wailed. Nobody took any chances and made haste topside, life jackets donned. When muster revealed all hands to be present, it was then that we discovered a short circuit had caused the alarm to sound so gravely.

I returned to the bridge. The engine room reported the same type of mess I had witnessed on my abbreviated tour. Tools were on deck, in the bilges, wedged behind a work bench. Pipe fittings, nuts, bolts, electrical components had spilled in all directions. Lockers of various mechanical gear acted in the same manner as the crew's clothing lockers. One opened a door and stood back, not knowing what might leap at him. Drawers in benches had come open, spilling their contents. Decks were dangerously slippery from spilled oil mixed with water. A chain hoist had torn loose, fallen, and broken. Storage batteries had tipped in their racks. Acid overflowed and ran along the decks.

A radio dispatch from Boston to the buoy tender *Hornbeam* was passed to us for information:

"FROM OPERATIONS X CONFIRMING TELEPHONE CONVERSATION X WAL-511 BROKE MOORING X IS UNDER OWN POWER X PROCEED AND RENDER ASSISTANCE AS NEEDED"

I again radioed Woods Hole Base and repeated that, in my opinion, it was not necessary to send anyone to our assistance. We had weathered the worst of the storm which already was showing definite signs of abating.

I was informed that the *Hornbeam* had been ordered as a precautionary measure, particularly in view of the velocity of the storm. Soon another dispatch informed us that the Hornbeam was underway:

"HORNBEAM DEPARTED WOODS HOLE"

Wood, Engine man third class, had been assigned the midnight watch. Making his way to his bunk to attempt a few winks of rest, he observed Clem Meredith braced against a bulkhead. Sitting thusly on deck was the only steady position because the ship still was in exceedingly rough seas. Meredith was cautious. Taking no chances, he had regaled himself in his bright orange life jacket.

Wood laughed and asked, "Clem, what's that you've got on?"

Clem saw little humor in the query and replied, almost sadistically, "What the hell does it look like?"

"We're not going to sink, you know."

"Maybe not. I'm just not taking any chances."

Williams burst in, shaking his head sadly. A tall, slender North Carolinian with strains of Cherokee blood, Williams was renown among the deck force as being a perfectionist with decks. Many a time men had been sent back to scrub and shine them again until they glittered to the Williams standard.

"What a damned mess," observed Williams. "And to think of all the hours we spent on this rust bucket, working to make it look good. We might just as well have sat on our ass for all the good it did. Look at those decks. They'll swear, in the District, that we haven't done a dammed thing out here the past nine months."

"Oh, no, they'll understand. That was a damned bad sea we took. We can't help that."

"I just hope the 'Old man' will hand them a good line when we get there."

"He won't have to. Just tell the truth. This storm was an act of God."

"But why did it have to happen just two days before we're due in port? Just two measly frigging days."

"I didn't like it either, Williams. I worked hard, too, but it was just one of those things."

Williams was not easily convinced. As Boatswain's mate, he was responsible to see that the ship sparkled from bow to stern. As he viewed the conglomeration of scattered gear, the ruined decks, the wet bedding, he felt like crying. In all his nineteen years of service he had never seen so much hard labor go for naught in a twinkling. Sadly disheartened, he nevertheless had his men doing what little they could under the circumstances.

Now, for the first time, we noticed that the weather had cleared. Not a cloud was left in the sky. Visibility was improving all the time although the edge of the sea was a haze of breaking waves and flying spray. In the southwest sky Orion was a beautiful spectacle. To its left, in the south, the visible stars of Canis Major were stunted by Sirius. Higher in the southern sky, still farther to the left as we faced it, Canis Minor, with Procyon, twinkled clearly.

By then we had time to collect our thoughts and to discuss the evening. We could not help thinking of our families, and hoped that news of our predicament had not leaked out. It was unlikely that commercial interests would be aware of the situation, but there always was the grapevine. Sometimes the grapevine was right; more often it was not. What fantastic stories could be dreamed by wandering minds.

We did not realize it, but at that very moment lots of people were discussing our plight. Newscasters on radio and television (we later learned) were describing us somewhat inaccurately. We had lost our mooring and were adrift in heavy seas, or we were battling to maintain our regular vigil. The Coast Guard cutter Hornbeam had been sent to our "rescue." How sensationally and gripping situations sometimes are described when only the barest of details are available.

The grapevine also was intoxicated with excitement. "The *Buzzards* lightship is adrift and in danger of being cast upon the rocks of Cuttyhunk at any moment! They couldn't use their engine, and the *Hornbeam* was speeding to her assistance. In all probability they couldn't get there in time because of very rough seas!"

We were pleased to discover later that our families had not heard any of the fantastic rumors until the following day. By then we were out of danger, and they knew that, too.

By maintaining a speed of 475 RPM we were able to maintain a steady course directly into the face of the seas. Winds had moderated to forty-five miles per hour, and swells diminished to about eighteen feet. We were traveling away from our chartered position at one and a half miles an hour. Realizing it would be almost suicidal to try to come about in such seas, I ordered our course and speed maintained. When, and only when, wind and seas lessened considerably more would we return to our position. What good to go back now when we could not release our spare anchor?

The following message was sent to the Hornbeam:

"STEERING COURSE 235 FROM CHARTERED POSITION X SPEED APPROXIMATELY ONE AND ONE HALF KNOTS X PLAN TO MAINTAIN COURSE AND SPEED UNTIL WEATHER MODERATES."

When the *Hornbeam* did arrive, what a welcome sight she was! How reassuring to have company in time of danger. We felt inspired in spite of the shambles below decks. The storm was abating slowly. No more sheer walls of towering furious Atlantic bore down on us. Seas lessened still further to fifteen feet. Our courage was further bolstered by a cheery message from the *Hornbeam*:

"WILL ESCORT YOU ASTERN AT A DISTANCE OF ONE HALF MILE X IF YOU NEED ANYTHING JUST LET US KNOW."

All night long the *Hornbeam* was our companion. How friendly her running lights, her bulk, her shoulder to shoulder comradeship.

Night wore into the brightness of day. Wind remained in the southwest at twenty-five miles per hour. We waited half an hour, an hour. No further decrease in wind or sea appeared likely, and seas were holding at ten feet in height.

Notifying the *Hornbeam* of our decision, we changed course to 065 degrees and proceeded towards Vineyard Sound. There, between the Elizabeth Islands and Martha's Vineyard, we hoped to make a lee for the deck force to work on the spare anchor. With the change in course we were able to run full speed before the wind and seas.

An hour's run brought the shelter for us, and the crew was able to get the spare anchor over the side. It was no cinch, as the ship still rolled, bobbed, and pushed by swells striking against the stern. The deck pitched much less violently, however, and there was no salt spray coating the bow and bridge every time a wave lashed at us.

The safest procedure, which we followed, was to drop the anchor in comparatively shallow water, then retrieve it in the hawse, steam back to position and then drop it again. It was not accomplished without mishap. Two lengths of chain, a bit more than the depth of the water, were let out. The anchor was hoisted on a davit, the manila strap cut, and the anchor dropped. Instead of falling over the side and splashing into the Sound, as it was supposed to, the lip of the five thousand pound mushroom anchor caught on the bulwarks. There it hung. It took two men with crowbars another five or six minutes to free it. Eventually it slid into the ocean, at the cost of a jagged hole on the starboard bow, eight inches horizontally and fourteen inches vertically. The tear was well above the water line, and a damage control party was able to plug it sufficiently to keep the seas from pounding through.

1120, February 26: The following message ended the ordeal that had begun the previous day:

"TO OPERATIONS X 1120 X WAL-511 ON STATION X RESUMED NORMAL OPERATING CHARACTERISTICS"

The *Hornbeam* had helped station us with her radar, for at that time we were not equipped with that valuable gear. Upon receiving our thanks and assurances that all was well, she departed, and again we were alone, at anchor in a riled ocean.

Three sequels are of interest. During the morning after the storm, the crew were overheard complaining about the water. I couldn't blame them for complaining after what they had been through. But the water??

"What's wrong with the water?"

"Skipper, taste the water in the scuttlebutt, if you will, and see if you don't think it's salty. It tastes peculiar to the rest of us."

It certainly was salty, all right. Somehow, during the storm, valves had jarred open or perhaps had been leaking. In any event, salt water from the peak tank had infiltrated the entire fresh water system. A check of the suspected leakage verified our suspicions, for the water level was down fully a foot. The top of the tank was below the waterline of the ship, and since water seeks its own level, there was only one other place for it to go - into the other tanks.

It was a teasing situation. Everyone imagined himself thirsty. Men who rarely ever stopped at the water fountain now tried it because he knew there was no water fit for drinking. When water was available, the urge for it was not nearly so aggravated.

The crew were not beaten, however, not by a long shot, not as long as the distilled water in the engine room caboys held out. Sampling it cautiously, making a wry face at its flat tasteless content, Moore said, "Well, it's wet. We can use it for coffee and it won't taste so bad." Thus we found ourselves on water hours - distilled water.

The second aftermath refers to newspapers and some of the articles they carried about us. One well known Boston edition referred to us as an UNPOWERED ninety-three foot vessel. They were wrong on two accounts. The engineers stated that the business of the "unpowered" vessel was a low blow. Also, the paper had somewhere lost thirty-seven feet of our length. Another paper wrote that we were off station ONE hour and had to be TOWED back by the Coast Guard cutter *Hornbeam*. Actually we were off station a total of fifteen hours and twenty minutes. Knowing facts, then reading twisted versions, one wonders why some reporters insist on their flair for the sensational. They hurt the press in general and their own newspaper in particular. In fairness to them, however, sensationalism is in popular demand by the listening, watching, and reading public. Who can possibly blame reporters, the, for giving the public what they want?

The third sequence of events occurred at 1930 (7:30 P.M.) Sunday night (February 26), less than twenty-four hours after we first lost our mooring. The *Relief* lightship had left Boston, was coming to take over our station, and had sent an official dispatch:

"DO YOU WISH TO BE RELIEVED TONIGHT?"

Summoning the crew, I asked them if they would care to be relieved that night, that it would mean another sleepless night for practically everyone, and that if they wished to wait until morning we would do so.

Aching bodies and tired minds instantly were alert, and with one loud spontaneous chorus they shouted, "TONIGHT!! TONIGHT!!"

Grinning, I phoned the radioman. "Notify the *Relief* that we we'll be ready to leave as soon as she can get here."

The ship's log that night contained a final entry that warmed our hearts, lifted us from our despondency over the vicious devastation, and caused enthusiastic morale to surge back into our veins:

2305 (February 26): "Secured all aids to navigation. Underway on various courses and full speed. Enroute Coast Guard Base, Boston."

Chapter XII

"The Stars"

With never ceasing boredom, the mind clutches at anything and everything. One becomes aware and alert to every factor of his environment. The smallest events of the day are hoarded and discussed spiritedly at dinner hour. The water is viewed daily, and every change in color, every wave undulation is noted. Away from the complexities of land life where the noises of civilization obscure and blunt the perceptions, one is able to view his surroundings with untrampled senses. Pleasure is derived - must be derived - from the world around him. Soon the waves, the horizon, the whims of nature become inexorably interesting. One's interest in the elements is renewed, and recalled to mind are topics of eighth grade science, particularly astronomy. Away from the sometimes tedious task of textbook studying, a world of imagination and intrigue is opened.

A lightship is an excellent place to observe the wonder world of the evening sky. The disadvantage of deck lights or a rough sea is outweighed by the lack of distractions, hills, trees, houses, humanity, and the hours of reflective opportunity available for such study. Amongst the twenty-eight consecutive duty nights there always are at least a few when conditions are near perfect. A cloudless sky, an unruffled ocean, a windless atmosphere, plus endless hours of sluggish moving time set the stage which transforms the casual observer into an ardent enthusiast.

Learning the names of stars, planets, constellations, and their relative positions in space becomes fascinating. Types of stars, their colors, magnitude, number, distance, and motion fill the viewer with questions, answers, theories. He becomes intensely cognizant of the vastness of the universe.

He wonders about the prospect of peoples on other planets. He considers the possibility of inter-spacial collision, of comets, meteors, explosions, the birth and death of space phenomena. He considers the concept of space itself, whether it be finite or infinite. Endless unanswered questions are projected. Perhaps one day the astronomers will discover the answers, the reasons. Then again perhaps it is intended that some secrets of the universe will remain forever locked from man. The possibilities are inexhaustible.

Richard Nelson, David Oram, William Sherman and myself, the amateur star gazers aboard the *Buzzards*, discussed such topics frequently and fervently. The easiest method, and to us the most interesting, of acquiring knowledge of stars was to associate them with constellations. Ignoring the taunts of Bob Dean and George Sousa who viewed the subject with total disinterest, we would take our reference books to a darkened area of the main deck and peer into the sky. Dean and Sousa always were invited, for we enjoyed their good natured bantering.

"Come on, fellows. We'll show you Perseus or Cassiopeia tonight."

"Cassey who?"

"Cassiopeia."

"No thanks. Not interested."

"Me either, but you'd better not fool around with her. She might have a husband or a boy friend, and he'll send a flying saucer after you!"

Spotting Canis Major (Big Dog) on the eastern horizon in early winter, one of us would holler down the ladder, "Hey, Bob, come on up and see the big dog."

His usual reply indicated his disinterest in the outer universe. "Get out of here! Go drive somebody else crazy, will you?"

"What's the matter, Bob? Aren't you interested in heavenly bodies?"

"Yeah, sure, but not THAT kind."

The four of us learned that in latitude 41 degrees 20 minutes north (the lightship's position), five constellations were visible that were circumpolar in nature. That is, they remained in view as they traveled around the north pole, never rising or setting, and could be seen during all seasons of the year at any time of night. The key to the northern constellations, of course, was Ursa Major, the Big Dipper, one of the brightest and most conspicuous of all. From there it was easy to locate Ursa Minor which contained Polaris, the North Star, and then the constellations Cepheus, Cassiopeia, and Draco.

Sherman triumphantly announced his discovery of Draco with a thunderous shout. "There it is! There's his head! See? Look where I'm pointing! Then he curves around in opposite directions and winds up near the Big Dipper." Such unbridled enthusiasm was generated frequently by all of us at various times as our observations continued through the months.

Winter was the best time to observe and study stars. The cold clear nights offered less interference from atmospheric haze, and the sky was studded with a brilliance of twinkling lights as faint stars and nebulae not visible during other seasons came into view. Many constellations were bright, easily recognizable, and contained first magnitude stars. Orion, the Hunter, was the most conspicuous and most beautiful of the winter constellations. It also was the key that enabled us to locate and identify other stars and formations, including Auriga, Gemini, Canis Major, Canis Minor, the Pleiades, Taurus, Perseus, Pegasus, Andromeda, Aries, and Leo.

From an uncertain beginning our knowledge of the sky began a slow but gradual awakening. What we lacked in qualifications we made up for with enthusiasm. We learned the brighter stars and well defined constellations. Later we learned lesser stars and less distinct constellations. Our self instruction enabled us to associate groups of stars in relation to their diurnal positions. We could tell, at a given hour, where to expect our friends in the land of far away lights. We knew which stars would be rising or setting, which would be directly overhead. We knew what to expect of the Big

Dipper during its revolution. We could separate the planets and know at a glance where they could be found. The heading of the ship no longer confused our observations.

We learned too that the brightness of a moon at or near the full interfered with star gazing. It interfered with a study of the moon itself. We soon discovered that a sky with a quarter moon was most conducive to concentrated learning, for if a night were too dark, hordes of fainter stars twinkled for attention and tended to confuse us.

The long, clear evenings of winter gave way to long, hazy days of late spring, summer, and early fall. Smoky southwesters played havoc with visibility. My associates had watches to stand, the midnight watches becoming a real obstacle as Sherman and Oram went to bed at dusk if they were due to have that particular one. Our available nocturnal hours had been shortened considerably. The nights did not become sufficiently darkened until much later, and the periods between supper and movies now ticked away in daylight. So did the hour between movies and bedtime. No longer did we go on deck in groups of three or four as before. Interest waned, and yet the die had been cast, for we thirsted for more knowledge. Stubbornly we waited for ideal evenings in which to continue our investigation, our schooling. We wanted to know how the summertime skies compared with those of winter. We remained determined in spite of fog, haze, rain, and southwesters.

Our patience ultimately paid dividends, and we were able to identify Cygnus, Lyra, Aquila, Sagitta, Delphinus, Bootes, Corona, Hercules, Scorpius, Sagittarius, and Virgo. While there were innumerable others, we concentrated on those most distinct, colorful, and prominent, as we had during winter, and our efforts afforded us many, many hours of joyous excitement.

By knowing our stars and constellations we were able to spot the visible planets unerringly. Mars, closer to earth in August of 1956 than during the previous fifteen years, was of great interest to us as we watched the reddish planet from August through November when it was very bright in the southeasterly sky near Aquarius, a constellation south of Pegasus.

Without the aid of a telescope we were unable to observe Mars as a disc. We were unable to see its polar caps or its mysterious "canals." We did speculate on its properties, its size (half that of the earth), its length of day (similar to ours), and the ever romantic possibility of life even though it be limited to lichens.

We also identified Venus, Jupiter, Mercury, and Saturn although, as with mars, we had no telescope and were compelled to limit our visual interest in them to their identification and position. Even so, they were subjects of unlimited conjecture, and hours of spirited discussion made our twenty-eight day hibernation more enjoyable.

The night of October 21, 1956, was typical of our main deck gatherings. It was one of the most gorgeous of all nights on the *Buzzard*s. The water was like glass, the sky cloudless. With no wind, the temperature was a warm 69 degrees F. The moon, a day past the full, hovered above Cuttyhunk Island, cutting a golden swathe across a dimpled sea. Cygnus, directly overhead, stood out boldly. Aquila, distinct in the southwest, Bootes and Corona, faint in the northwest, and Hercules, low in the west, were easy to locate. Beautiful Orion was rising above the southeastern horizon. Light from Mars, midway between Pegasus and the 1st magnitude star Fomalhaut, was reflected brightly, and Oram was the first to point out the reddish glow cast from the planet. We again reflected about the possibility of life on our neighboring planets. We wondered if nights there were as beautiful as this. What would our own world look like viewed from Mars? The northern circumpolar constellations, Ursa Major, Ursa Minor, Cephus, Draco, and Cassiopeia, along with Lyra, just west of Cygnus, completed the panorama. It was a night not likely to be soon forgotten. We felt contented, at peace with ourselves and with each other. The awful dreary monotony was temporarily shelved.

Someone suddenly asked, "How far IS space? Does it end or go on and on and on infinitely?

"It HAS to end somewhere."

"Why?"

"Everything has an end somewhere, sometime."

"I don't see why."

"How about death, then? Many people believe in a hereafter, but others feel that death is the absolute end. So why shouldn't space have a definite end?"

"Never thought of it like that, but if space DOES end, what is beyond it? Is it boxed in? If so, by what?"

At this point the non star-gazers, the scoffers, entered the conversation. It was too lovely a night for anyone to remain below decks, and several men had been lounging nearby, disinterested with would-be astronomers. Now, however, they edged closer to our group, hesitating. We could tell they were listening, for their individual chatter had ceased. Their heads were turned slightly so they could catch the trend of our viewpoints. They wished to participate with us, not in locating or naming stars, not in physical properties of the planets. It was the potentiality of life on other worlds that appealed to them as they strolled the mid-autumn deck, a subject that rarely fails to arouse curiosity in man.

"Yes, what about that?" ventured one of them. "How do we know we're not dropping into a big pit in space? Isn't there a possibility that we may hit bottom sometime?"

"Present day man is not yet capable of understanding many questions about the universe or our own planet, he is terribly limited in his scope of knowledge, and has not yet learned to fully utilize his own power of reasoning. The average man, according to one theory, uses a maximum of only thirty percent of his brain potential. So man must find a method of putting his entire intellectual faculties to work."

"What do you think about flying saucers?"

"Based solely on incidents and books I have read on the subject, I would venture to say they exist. Science and the Armed Forces refer to them as unidentified flying objects. Most reports of such objects are proven to be erroneous. Sometimes they are traced to known phenomena, reflection of light, military activities, jet planes, etc. some, totally baseless, are received from crack-pots. However, bona fide sightings seem to be too numerous to be discounted. By that I mean reports that are received from airline pilots, ranking officers of the Armed Forces, etc. the objects not always are round. They have, in some instances, been described as cigar-shaped. Whatever these objects are, if they are from another planet or even from another universe, they are not now warlike. They appear to be content to merely observe us. They resort to great measures to keep out of the way. They do not risk collision, for example, with any of our own limited flying ventures although they have been reported nearby. They evade attempts to intercept or overtake them. I'm not an alarmist, but I certainly have an open mind concerning the possibility of their being for real."

"Could they possibly be something that Russia has perfected, or is working on?"

"I wouldn't think so. These objects approach our atmosphere at tremendous speeds. They are capable of suddenly changing course at sharp angles. Men of our era, neither here nor in Russia, is yet capable of duplicating such speed, nor could his body stand the shock of such acute changes in course at those terrific speeds."

"Who could be flying them? If they're from some other world, could they be anything like us?

"Who knows? One can only guess. It is unlikely that they would resemble humans as we know them. Still, it is not an absolute impossibility. We don't know. Nobody claims to know. There is little doubt that if the objects are manned in the sense that a pilot flies a plane, they are done so by an intelligence far greater than any known on earth."

"Do they travel alone, in pairs, or in groups?"

"They have been observed singly and in formation. The manner in which they travel would seem to indicate that some force or power is directing them."

Food for thought.... A quiet crept over our group, as though everyone was absorbed in a private thought to be jealously guarded from revelation. Stars, planets, the moon, flying objects..... Who knows what the future will bring?

Regular air routes to Mars, perhaps. Meanwhile, average laymen like us have to content ourselves with watching, reading, and listening in order to gather a limited knowledge of space and its great mysteries. One of the finest places to absorb such an acquaintance, of course, is on a lightship.

Chapter XIII

"The New Man"

The assignment of a new man to the *Buzzards* was exciting. The change was refreshing. Everyone wanted to see the fellow the moment he stepped aboard, talk with him, find out something about him. An avalanche of questions invariably greeted him: *What's your name, mate? Where are you from? How did you happen to join the Coast Guard? How'd you happen to be lucky enough to get a lightship? Have you ever been at sea before? Do you have a steady girlfriend? When did you get through boot camp? What are you planning to strike for? Are you a twenty year man?* His answers and actions, carefully scrutinized, are filed in many minds for future reference, for the man is being "sized up." The crew could tell, from the first few minutes of spontaneous third degree, whether the man was likeable, intelligent, scared, an average "Joe," or one who liked to "shit up the troops." A chain reaction is set off from the storehouse of knowledge gleamed from the newcomer, for his replies already have determined the extent of horseplay he must endure. If he is green, or from the hills or the "sticks," any moth-eaten, time-worn prank will do. If he shows traces of higher intelligence, it will take concentrated planning to maneuver him into unsuspected caprice.

The flimflam came later. The man was given a few days of grace in which to settle into the routine of shipboard life, read the ship's orders, learn the responsibilities of his watch, know his way around the ship, acquaint himself with his duties during drill, and, in general, to be indoctrinated in all procedures of military life at sea.

Devoid of suspicion, the greenhorn one day is duped into a trip to the engine room to get a can of oil for the red and green running lights. "Just ask any of the engineers," he is told. "They'll get it for you. Then bring it up here to the bridge. We have to fill these lights before it gets dark."

"All right. I'll get it right away." Off he goes, smartly, for he wishes to impress the boatswain's mate with his desire to please and to remain in good standing.

He innocently reports to an engineer. "The boatswain's mate sent me after the oil for the running lights. Would you show me where to find it, please?"

Taken by surprise, the agent of the engine room asks, "What?"

"I'd like the oil for the red and green running lights. 'Boats' told me you would get it for me."

The light dawns as the engineer's mind ignites. "Oh, yes, I know what you mean. Let's see now. We keep it over here." A number of cans are brought forth, labels studied, the cans replaced in a display of searching pretense. "Gosh, I can't seem to find any. I know we have it somewhere, although there's not much left. Go back and ask him how much he wants. Meanwhile, I'll try to find it."

The trusting man, imbued with a sense of duty, climbs two sets of ladders and winds his way along the main deck. "'Boats,' Oram wants to know how much you want. He says he hasn't got much left."

The boatswain's mate replies, "That's all right. I checked the lights, and we have enough oil for a couple more nights. Go back instead and get the oil for the relative bearings. They're pretty dry and need greasing. And whatever you do, don't let the engineers tell you they don't have any."

A second trip to the engine room follows, and down the two ladders descends the new man. "Oram," he pants upon arrival at his destination, "Boats says he has enough running light oil for a couple more days. Now he wants oil fro the relative bearings."

"O.K. Wait until I put the running oil away." A further reconnoitering of the shelves occurs as the messenger awaits, out of breath. "Hey, Sherman," Oram eventually demands, "Where did you put that oil for the relative bearings?"

"It was right there on the top shelf the last time I saw it. Maybe we're all out of it."

"Oh, I'm pretty sure we have some of it here somewhere."

"Oh, yes, we have some all right. Wait a minute. I think I know where it is. No, it's not under the bench. I'll tell you what. Go back and tell 'Boats' that Sherman and I are going to grease the anchor windlass in a little while and that we'll bring the oil up when we come. Tell him we'll need his key to the anchor watch."

"You'll bring the oil when you come up? O.K. What kind of a key is it you want?"

"The key to the anchor watch. Be sure to tell him because we'll need it in a few minutes."

Back on deck the fatigued greenhorn, by now hating every step in every ladder, breathes heavily as he reports, "They said to tell you they'll bring the oil in a few minutes because they're going to do something to the anchor. Oram says to be sure and tell you he'll need your key to the anchor watch."

"THEY can't seem to find ANYthing! Well, go back and tell them it's too late now anyway. We'll wait until tomorrow. Tell them the key is in the boatswain locker, but I'm not going down there for them or anybody else. That job can wait, too."

The boatswain's mate had another favorite. He once sent a man to the main hold to ask for fifteen feet of lubber's line. (A lubber's line is a thin black line inside a compass that coincides with the heading of a ship.) The new man eagerly complied with the order.

"Fifteen feet of WHAT kind of line?" asked the experienced seaman, sitting among odds and ends of rope, making a fender.

"Lubber's line," replied the earnest recruit.

"You go back and tell the boatswain's mate that I don't know where to find it since its been moved. He has it somewhere because we've been using too much of it. He's the only one who knows where it is."

"But I'll help you look for it if...."

"Don't give me any back talk! You go tell him what I told you."

The deflated recruit turned on his heels and departed. Approaching the boatswain's mate he said, hesitantly, "He wouldn't give me any. From the way he talks I think he knows where it is, but he said to tell you he didn't know where to find it and that you hid it somewhere."

The engineers had a favorite, too. A new fireman was properly introduced to the greasy foul smelling bilges. Loaded with cleaning compound and rags, he would be instructed to do a good job. "Get those bilges spotless. If you find the golden rivet, I'll ask the 'Old man' to give you a three day pass when we get to Boston."

"The golden rivet? What's that, sir?" All chiefs were addressed as "Sir" by a new recruit the first few days aboard.

"Do you mean to say you've never heard of the golden rivet? Why man, ships are put together with rivets just like a house is put together with nails. Only thing is, the very last rivet that goes into ANY ship is made of gold. We haven't been able to find the one on here yet, but we do know that it's somewhere in the bilge."

"Gee! I didn't know that. And what was that you said, sir, about a three day pass? I didn't quite understand what you meant."

"The 'Old man' has promised a three day pass to the man who locates the golden rivet. He has to fill out a report on the condition of all the rivets. But there's a place in the report where he has to pout down the exact location of the golden one. He's tearing his hair out trying to find it. Now, son, if you do a good job on those bilges, you might be the lucky one to find it. You'll have to get them all nice and clean. Otherwise, if there is just a little bit of oil or grease on the golden one, it'll look just like all the rest."

"I'll do my best, sir, I mean chief. I sure like the sound of that three day pass. But how'll the 'Old man' be able to..."

"DON'T YOU EVER refer to the captain of this ship as the 'Old man,' at least not until you're dry behind the ears. Is that clear?"

"Yes sir, chief. I didn't mean nuthin' by it. But how'll the skipper be able to fill out his report if we don't find out where that rivet is?"

"Never mind that, son. It's there somewhere. You just do a good job and see what you can find."

If the new man was a deck worker, he would be told, by a "buddy," to make sure he emptied the white porcelain slop buckets in the chief's compartments. "They have to use the head that's off the rec. deck, and they don't like to bother to walk out there at night. So one of your duties for awhile will be to see that the pots are emptied and cleaned every morning, right after breakfast." Of course, no such equipment existed, but the gullible man would search in vain until sounds of laughter revealed the farce.

A young seaman, if a smoker, would be warned against the use of tobacco without proper authority. "You're not of age, even though you're in the service. Do you have a note from your parents saying that it's all right for you to smoke?"

"Why, no. I didn't think it would be necessary. I never gave it any thought."

"Well, it IS necessary, very much so, on this ship. You'd better go see the boatswain's mate, and he'll ask the chief for you. That's the way we usually do it."

The boatswain's mate, after being asked, would return from the wardroom with a sober expression. "The chief wants to know if you smoke regular sized cigarettes or king size."

"I smoke the regular size, but not very often. I'd just like to smoke once in awhile."

Again the boatswain's mate would disappear, to return shortly with a broad smile. "Good news! The chief says it's all right to smoke three or four a day, but never during working hours. If you smoked king sized, he was going to make you cut them in half."

"Gee, thanks, Boats."

A new cook would be told that the "Old man" liked a snack in bed about an hour before breakfast every morning. Pondering this in his mind, with the horrified realization that he would have to be a very early riser, he would ask, "What does the skipper usually have for his snack?"

This was what the conveyor of the information wanted him to ask. "Two rolls and a turnover!" he would reveal as the crowd of onlookers burst into peals of laughter.

Woe to the new man who first reported on a regular liberty day. This meant that he traveled to the lightship with a third of the vessel's personnel, and en route he would be filled to the brim with sadistic tales of the boatswain's mate's incredible inhumane treatment of all seaman.

"He's probably the toughest boatswain's mate in the Coast Guard. I kid you not. I hate to go back myself," the talk would start.

"Yeah," another would observe sadly. "If it gets much worse, I'm gonna' ask for a transfer. I can't stand much more of it."

"The guy just doesn't have any feelings. He won't give you a chance. Remember the time he gave me four hours extra duty because he couldn't bounce a dime off my sack? I hate his guts!"

"How about the time Smith was sipping coffee and making a noise. The boatswain's mate tore the cup out of Smith's hand and threw it in his face. How many stitches did it take?"

"Five. But what I don't like is the way he stands in back of you all the time you're working, just waiting for you to do something wrong. Gosh, it makes a man nervous just to think about it."

"Yuh, remember the time that Jones was sweeping the deck? The side of his broom hit a chair and knocked some paint off. The boatswain's mate had him paint all the chairs on the ship, on his own time."

"That's nothing. How about the time Smith was empty-ing the waste baskets. It was raining like cats and dogs, and some cigarette ashes stuck to the hull. Smith had to put on a raincoat and a life jacket and go over the side and scrub the whole area. He had to do it during his noon hour, too, and in the rain. It was rough that day. "Spose he'd a'fallen overboard!"

"God, I wish he'd get transferred. You don't hear anything about it, do you?"

""No. He'll stay on there as long as the 'Old man' does. The 'Old man' backs him up every time."

"When do you expect the 'Old man' to get transferred? the new man might ask, timidly.

"Ha, my boy. You've got a long time to wait. He's got at least another year to go on there. It's an eighteen month tour, you know."

"Well, let's not scare this poor kid with all these stories. He'll find out soon enough how it is and be as miserable as we are. Let him live it up for another hour, at any rate."

By this time the new crew member was dismally surveying his predicament. Whatever had possessed him to join the Coast Guard? He rudely revised the limits of his own sanity, previously considered normal. How do they let a man get away with things like that? It doesn't seem possible, in this day and age, yet these men seem sincere and awfully unhappy. Maybe my father knows somebody who knows a Congressman who can help me get a transfer is a probable thought that enters his mind and remains until he finally discovers that the boatswain's mate is "a good guy who simply expects everyone to be on the ball."

Another trick employed by the crew was to act the part of homosexuals. The first night the new man was aboard they would dress in dazzling shorts, multicolored scarves, tams, and tinted glasses, and parade around the crew's quarters.

"You stinka, dollface. You simply must never attempt to outdo me in the wearing of pastels."

"Oh now, my dearie, please don't get upthet. I drethed ethpthially for you. Thay that you like me."

Their attempts were obvious, and the newcomer wasn't usually shaken to any great extent. The crew, meanwhile, had passed a few more tedious moments and had showed their new shipmate that it was not necessary to surrender oneself completely to monotony.

Beloved by all the veterans was the fake dispatch. On the day before liberty, for which the new man had waited twenty-eight days, the radioman would burst into a crowded compartment with a sheet of official looking paper in his hands. "Well, boys, I'm afraid it's bad news. Here, read it yourselves. I've already shown it to the skipper."

The sheet of paper would be grabbed and anxiously read. "Son of a bitch! Listen to this. "HOIST NORTHEAST STORM WARNINGS AT 10:00 P.M. TONIGHT X WINDS OF 45 to 50 MPH WILL BLOW STEADILY THE NEXT THREE OR FOUR DAYS X WEATHER BUREAU BOSTON." The message, of course, would look authentic as it would have a date and time group, an originator, action addresses, and times of delivery and receipt.

The newcomer, who had fomented a bundle of plans during the previous few days, would be crestfallen. His world was shattered. Everything he had planned and hoped for was doomed. Northeast storms for three or four days! "Damn it, anyway! What a stinking life. It's not bad enough that you have to stay out here, in all kinds of weather, for twenty-eight days. No. Then, when you're entitled to go ashore, a damned storm comes along. I'll be so damned glad when my time is up so I can be a civilian again.

"Steady, boy," someone would say in mock sympathy, "It happens to all of us." The muttering of the new man, however, would continue far into the night or until he discovered the fraud.

The same type of deception was enacted at the expense of Robert Ritchie on the eve of his first liberty from the ship. Both cooks could not be off at the same time, and Richard Nelson, the other cook, was due to return the following day. The night the man on watch produced a simulated dispatch. "RICHARD W. NELSON IN USPHS HOSPITAL X

SUFFERED SERIOUS ACCIDENT X DURATION OF HOSPITALIZATION UNKNOWN AT THIS TIME."

"Well, Ritchie," said George Sousa. "I have no choice. I have to keep you aboard."

There followed, from Robert Richie, the greatest production of forceful lamenting condemnations of services life ever compiled on the *Buzzards* lightship. It helped not at all for one of the crew to satire, soothingly, "Look how important you are, Ritchie. The ship can't get along without you."

The same Ritchie occupied the bottom of a double bunk arrangement in the berthing compartment. He had a habit of vaulting into the bunk, Tarzan style. He would grab the top bunk, swing himself inward, and drop. The bottom bunk was held in place by chains hooked into the upper berth which in turn was held in place by chains attached to a padeye welded to the overhead. The man who had the top bunk got awfully tired of the same old jolt every time Ritchie went to his bunk, so one night the crew made elaborate preparations for his advent. They removed the bottom hooks and made the bunk fast with light twine. Then they extinguished all but the red light marking a hatch entrance, crawled into their own beds, and stealthily waited. In short order, Ritchie came bounding along, prepared for nighttime siesta, and vaulted as usual. The result was a falsetto of boisterous merry-making, as a surprised and subdued Ritchie picked himself off the deck.

If a new man displays the slightest interest in ghost stories, it becomes a cue for the crew to secretly discuss arrangements for a visit from a spectre. The 8:00 P.M. to midnight watch is chosen as the ideal hour, for it is late enough to lull the radio room watchstander into a false sense of security and early enough so that the remainder of the crew can be around to witness the activity. To prepare the recruit, he is filled with tales of spirits and ghosts visiting the ship to reclaim the soul of a man who killed himself in a fit of despondency. "Yup, he was sitting right in the radio shack, checking the beacons and radio," the story would unfold. "All of a sudden he went crazy and started hollering and hooting. Finally, he stabbed himself and jumped overboard. There was blood all over the deck, but no trace of the man was ever found. Every year, about this time, his ghost comes back. We don't know what he's looking for, but we think it's his soul. So you'd better holler if you see him. You'll know when he's around because he makes a lot of racket."

Noel Anderson, having been properly indoctrinated with tales of ghosts, took over the 8:00 P.M. watch one night, checked his logs, monitored other beacons as usual, made a few entries, and settled back to think about home and, more especially, of a certain bright-eyed girl about whom he orated at great lengths. His thoughts wandered to the ridiculous saga of the phantom who, according to the crew, was due to revisit the ship some night soon. The corners of his mouth curled into a slight smile. "What do they take me for, a fool?" he mused to himself. Little did he realize that at that very moment a man was quietly climbing the ratlines, ready to cut loose a heavy section of chain that had been lashed there during late afternoon. Nor did he realize that another man was donning a blue face mask similar to the face shields worn by men on duty in the North Atlantic. Neither did he hear the remainder of the crew gathering silently on deck to watch.

At a given signal the line holding the chain was severed, and it fell heavily on the overhead of the radio room.

"WHA-aaaa-CKK!!!"

Anderson bounded from his chair eyes wide apart, his hair standing on end. It sounded as though the main mast had broken and fallen with a tremendous crash onto the radio room. Possibly the new radar installation had somehow let go. Whatever it was, it was something almost supernatural. What a noise! His nerves aquiver, limbs trembling, face ashen, eyes still the size of saucers, heart racing with terror, breath coming in gasps, he turned slowly to steady himself against the desk. His hair started to settle back onto his head when his attention was attracted to a slight movement at the porthole. His head jerked involuntarily in the direction of the motion. He recoiled convulsively at the misshapen face staring at him. His hair again reached for the overhead. His saucer like eyes became platters of panic. He wanted to run. He couldn't. He was petrified. He stood, staring stonily, unable to move a muscle. His heart cried out in mental anguish. It was torture.

Bill Mahoney removed the mask as the crew chimed, amid riotous gales of laughter, "The next time, Andy, you'll believe us when we tell you about ghosts." Anderson does not believe in ghosts now any more than he did before, but never will he forget his visitation from that awful real life apparition on the *Buzzards*.

I thought I knew all of the methods used to make sport with new crew members. Such things as Ensign Charlie Nobel, a bucket of blue steam, cans of striped paint, etc. were commonplace enough. I was, however, quite unprepared for a report carefully placed on my desk on the occasion of a February return from liberty. "What is this?" I asked George Sousa as I picked up an official looking document that had been neatly typed, submitted by (name), and forwarded by George A. Sousa.

"That's a character reference," explained Sousa. "The boys told the new man that the skipper wanted a character reference of every man on board for his personal file. They told him it was one of the first things a man had to do when he came aboard. It was handed to me, so I've forwarded it to you, through proper channels. We both smiled as we read the synopsis.

"CHARACTER REFERENCE OF (name) (Info to Officer in Charge):

A PRANK QUESTIONNAIRE TO A NEW MAN WHO CAME ABOARD

(The following statements were made by "name")

Hobbies: Making models of planes and ships; dancing (polka, 2-step)

School: Got out in senior year of high school (lost interest)

Jobs: Worked for (name) railroad prior to entering Coast Guard. While on leave, I help my father in the tavern business (do not particularly care for this type of business).

Habits: I drink mildly; I get a thrill out of driving at high speeds while on open highways, but am a careful driver; I have a tendency to leave loose gear in the berthing area, but will try to do better in the future.

Readings: Sports magazines and adventure stories.

Movies: I like ancient history pictures best of all.

Astronomy: (This obviously for benefit of the C.O.) NO INTEREST AT ALL.

Women: I like the type that does not run around wild and is boy crazy. The girl that I am going with now I plan to marry.

Foods: I like most Polish dishes, Polish sausage and sauerkraut. Will eat most anything - not fussy.

Opinion of present duty: I like this ship and crew except for a few.

Vacationing: I like to vacation in other states and would like to make my residence in (name of place) when I am married.

Studies: I like to keep up on Studies of American built cars and styles.

Intercourse: I have intercourse approx. 3 times in a period of two weeks.

Sports: I like to swim, ice skate and play football. (Watch baseball games)

Overweight: I have a tendency to over indulge in fattening
foods.

Submitted (Name) (Signed)

Forwarded: (George A. Sousa)
EXECUTIVE OFFICER

For all the pranks played by members of the crew of the
Buzzards, never did they resort to the type of practical joke
that could cause physical harm.

Chapter XIV

"Wildlife"

Lonely though our vigil. We had companionship constantly, being visited by representatives of five families of wildlife - birds, insects, fish, mammals, and reptiles.

Birds

Birds were the more consistent and varied of our neighbors. We positively identified several species of gulls, four sparrows, many warblers, migratory game birds, pigeons, a junco, blue jay, crow, brown thrasher, meadowlark, and a flicker.

Gulls were with us always unless there was a particularly vicious storm. Otherwise, whether it be rain or shine, warm or cold, windy or calm, summer or winter, they screamed their presence. Most common was the herring gull, although he often was accompanied by ring-bills or great black-backs. Scavengers by instinct, they kept the waters clear of all garbage jettisoned from the *Buzzards*. In winter they became so domesticated they almost took food from a hand extended through a porthole. The slightest activity at a port was a signal for the flock, sometimes numbering twenty-five, to scream into action. They would fly within a few feet of an extended hand, not quite daring or willing to be fed in that manner, but scraps tossed into the air would be gathered on the wing and rarely allowed to reach the water.

They must have had wonderful digestive systems, for we have seen them swallow whole the leg of a turkey, with no apparent discomfort. Often they would screech and fight with one another over a single scrap while others floated with the tide until further reconnoitering revealed them to their learned eyes.

In mid-winter, when they could not choose to be fussy, they sometimes were objects of tomfoolery. One of the cooks took some stale bread, coated it liberally with pepper and tabasco sauce, then offered it to the cranky winged Aves. The offering disappeared promptly as usual. An open beak, a gulp, a momentary bulge at the throat, and the bread was gone. The only visible emoticon displayed was the almost instantaneous reopening of the beak which was fervidly rinsed in the cool waters of the ocean. The gull then appeared to gasp for air, submerged his beak again and swished it to and fro. He then was ready for seconds.

One day the men were kidding the cook about :seagull appetites." He had baked cupcakes for dessert, two small ones for each man, and each the size of a quarter. "May as well feed them to the gulls," was one comment.

William Sherman ate his in silence, arose and said, "Cook, cross me off the list. I've eaten MY two cupcakes."

Sousa observed, "Sherman, if you're walking away from the table, I KNOW you've had two."

The favorite roosting spot for the gulls on the *Buzzards* was atop the masts or on the yardarms. They were allowed to remain as long as they did not become careless in their toilet habits. When this occurred and the deck was spotted or washing was splattered, the gulls were requested to take a leave of absence by setting up an artificial vibration in the rigging. They objected to such pulsations and flew away until the rigging once again became stationary under foot. Their return would be brief, for one of the crew would shake a stay or guy, and the vibrating began anew. The birds would come back as many as five or six times before they realized they would be unable to enjoy their comfortable haunt as long as a human was visible underneath.

Of the migratory game birds, a half dozen were positively identified close by, including the American scoter, black duck, American eider, American goldeneye, bufflehead, and Canadian goose. A rare visitor to our locale was the common loon, seen twice in late October, swimming and feeding for a few days.

The first few geese, from the *Buzzards*, were seen in October and then in greater quantities throughout the winter. Flying very high on their spring return to their breeding grounds in the north, the flocks were more heavily populated than in autumn. Following the call of their temporary leader, arranged in a wide "V," they answered his loud call as they surveyed their route. Towards nightfall they cautiously alighted, in silence, where they remained, alternately feeding and resting, until morning. Rarely did they alight on the ocean near the ship, and the only time they flew low was in fog or during a snowstorm.

Of the land birds who ventured to our position, the flicker was the most colorful. On March 22, 1957, Sherman came running to my cabin. It was late morning as he pounded on the door, yelling, "Hey, skipper, come out here quick! There's a crazy mixed up bird out here!" I responded, and flying nervously around the bow and than back to the stern where he rested in the rigging was a flicker. He remained with us a couple of days. Several other times we saw flickers, but their stay was of short duration, probably a brief rest period.

Another handsome bird visited us in October of 1956. Arriving alone and remaining for several hours, a brown thrasher looked us over and then rejected us as a possible nesting place. One other thrasher passed the *Buzzards* in April of 1957.

An elegantly colored blue jay provided us with a sample of nature in the raw one Sunday afternoon in October 1956. Going on deck after the usual mid-morning movie we were astonished to see him hovering near the stern of the ship. Obviously frightened by our attention he flitted about the ship for five minutes, vainly attempting to hide under the fantail. Tiring, or instinctively aware of the futility of escaping the menace of nearby humans, he headed north, toward the mainland. Immediately two gulls charged after him, and within seconds a dozen others joined the fray. The blue jay darted, twisted, swerved, but finally was knocked to the water. Rooting for him to escape, we watched in helpless rage as the underdog was attacked by the swarm of larger birds. It seemed a pity that such a beautiful contribution of nature should suffer such injustice and persecution. Our hearts were in our mouth as the jay splashed into the sea. A chorus of yells shouted their approval as the jay, fighting for his life, managed to regain the flight toward shore, skimming the water. Again the gulls, hovering for the kill, gave chase. Again he was knocked to the water. Miraculously the will to survive spurred him again into flight, and it appeared briefly that he might yet escape. Alas! A third time he was nudged into the water by an angry snapping beak, and this time the gulls were not to be denied. The jay was picked up, dropped, picked up, dropped. Out last view of the hapless jay was that of blue feathers fluttering in the darkening gloom as the gulls fought for his remains. "Bastardly gulls," muttered someone. It summed up the feelings of all.

Another bird that made only a single appearance was the meadowlark. On March 28, 1957, a pretty specimen was seen to arrive from the south, chased by several gulls. The wanderer wisely remained near the ship for an hour, rested, shook off his pursuers, and finally flew north towards shore, alone and unopposed.

The common crow was an uncommon visitor to the lightship. Two singles flew by during September of 1956, unmolested although gulls were nearby. On March 31, 1957, another flew around the ship for an hour, apparently lost in the fog.

A song sparrow came aboard during October of 1956 and again on March 29 and April 8 of 1957. The last one was the tamest and flew through the interior of the ship, from compartment to compartment. He resisted attempts at capture, instinctively fearing the large hands that groped at him. When finally caught, he was released from the stern of the ship, flew a hundred yards in a straight line, circled and returned. Several hours later he was gone.

Discounting the gulls, our most numerous bird visitors were warblers. They arrived in late March and early April on warm days on their way north, then disappeared until late September and October. In early November of 1956, on a cold frosty night, the air was alive with these little creatures. The following morning ice had formed in the waterways and we picked up about fifty bodies of the tiny birds that had perished during the night. Obviously, they died from the cold. Why had not their instinct warned them of the bitter night and urged them to leave swiftly prior to its advent? Why had they chosen to remain on the *Buzzards* to finish their life span? They could have remained warm had they huddles close to the stack or the engine room fidley. The bodies were found on the colder sections of the ship, mostly on the cold bare decks and the frosty waterways.

These attractive birds were quite tame, hopping about the deck and scurrying for safety only when they spotted one of the men within three or four feet. If we sat on deck, they would hop right by us, seeming to realize that we meant no harm. One of them, trapped below decks, visited the wardroom. He hopped inquisitively under our feet as we read, and we all laughed as he slipped on the waxed deck, like a dog who loses traction when he tries to run too fast.

Of all the birds to pass the *Buzzards* the only ones to make noise were the gulls and the American goldeneye. The latter made a whistling sound with his wings, hence the name "whistler." The gulls only orated in any sense of the meaning, and their utterings were shrill and characteristic of someone with a poor disposition. Even so, their harsh outcries were much easier to accept than the booming blast of our own foghorn, and we were happy to have them nearby.

Insects

The housefly (Musca domestica) was the most common of all insects and certainly the most despised. They were a nuisance and a distraction as they buzzed the dinner table and bit our ankles. Porthole screens and periodic spraying kept them to a minimum below decks, but topside they appeared in droves on warm, sunny days. As colder weather approached, they tried desperately to get inside, and it was at this time that they became a problem requiring strict control. Two or three different types of flies were seen on the ship, but the housefly was by far the more numerous. It was difficult to believe they could arrive in such vast numbers on our anchored vessel five miles away from the nearest land, but arrive they did.

The fly was the only actual pest we had, other than a rare visit from a mosquito. The mosquitoes were usually heard before they were seen and were killed before they could do much damage. We had no cockroaches, no silverfish, no bed bugs.

Dragonflies appeared quite often, possibly being there in pursuit of flies. Had they not rested with their wings outstretched they would have been practically invisible on our gray decks. In the air they could hover in one spot like a helicopter and then dart away with lightning rapidity.

Infrequently we had the company of ladybugs, which are harmless, and we always gave them the run of the ship.

Two butterflies fluttered to a landing in our wardroom. The first came on October 8, 1956. He was a large fellow, probably a monarch, and we benefited from his striking beauty for an afternoon and then released him from the main deck. He flew southwesterly, his dainty wings carrying him effortlessly out of sight into a pale blue sky.

The other butterfly, or moth, arrived on the twelfth day of December. We were amazed to see the inch long whitish-gray visitor at that season of the year. He still was there at night on the 14th, but on the following day had disappeared. He apparently was a fall webworm, a web builder who performs his tasks on the leaves of trees and is considered a pest and a nuisance. On the *Buzzards* we were pleased to see ANY form, and he was made welcome.

On October 17, 1956, and again on October 22 the warm sunny autumn afternoons induce two dissimilar bees to fly the air currents to our position. The first was small, less than half an inch in length, bicolored with yellow and brown. His little formidable looking body was brown with yellow stripes, and his wings were a translucent yellow. He probably was a honeybee. Whether he was on a honey gathering expedition or a vacation is difficult to say, for the only known honey on the *Buzzards* was in the salutations of love letters.

The second was a bumblebee, twice the size of the original visitor, hairy, colored with brown and yellow which was distributed differently. His thin delicate wings were more of a brown, and a hourglass figure of brown began on the thorax and ended on the abdomen. Most of the abdomen was yellow except for a single brown stripe. We respected the reputed ability of each and made no attempt to agitate either of the transients.

On a sunny morning in mid April of 1956 I was amazed to find several tiny spiders in the rigging near the bridge, apparently having arrived in the air currents that had carried them from land. This probably was the explanation of the tiny visitors on the lightship, for previously there was not a trace of a member of their species. They did not remain, for the following day they were no longer visible. Whether they perished or abandoned ship I cannot say, but I rather suspect they did not like the looks of our ship and instinctively shoved off to more fertile grounds. (Spiders are included here even though they are not a true insect.)

Fish

In a world where fish supposedly teemed it was most surprising that more varieties were not recorded on the *Buzzards*. During warm days from late spring through autumn the fishing enthusiasts, lead by Ronald Balkcom, frequently fished from the stern of the ship. About all they caught were squirrel hake that failed to tempt anyone, including the gulls.

Squirrel hake were abundant and accepted almost very type of bait. Somewhat resembling a cod, they weighed from one to three pounds, were about eighteen inches long, and were mostly brownish, shading to a dull gray on the belly. Schools of these fish played around the ship from spring until late fall, keeping always on the shady side. On the 8th of December 1956 we saw a school of them feeding near the stern, and this was our last sight of them until the middle of the following March.

A few stragglers of other species were taken by line. On July 29, 1956, Balcom caught thirty-five hake of a different type while Herbert Ressler was catching thirty-three. Balcom also caught one shad (Alosa sapidissima) which weighed about a pound.

Once in a while a tautog (Tautoga onitis) was caught. A member of the wrasse family, it is a good food and game fish. The ones caught from the *Buzzards* weighed from two to three pounds.

One barracuda was taken by line in May 1956. Identified by Arthur Denault as a Northern Barracuda, this fellow was slender and about fifteen inches in length, had a brown mottled belly, a gray back with two dorsal fins, and a mouth containing two rows of sharp vicious teeth. For all its appearance it is not considered dangerous, a vast difference in character from its larger tropical cousin.

On July 29, 1956 we saw our first sand shark (dogfish) (Squalus acanthias). He appeared off the stern of the ship where the crew were catching hake. Cries of "Shark off the stern!"and "Hey! Look at the shark!" sent us running topside to view at first hands this menacing looking member of one of the most primitive forms of life known to man. He swam placidly about the ship for an hour, his dorsal fin cutting through the water like a saw. The crew hurriedly made a shark hook from odds and ends of metallic scrap but were unable to lure him to the bait. Dogfish were sighted quite often during the remainder of the summer, never bothering or accepting bait, but always creating a waver of excitement when their fins first appeared.

Although I never spotted a swordfish (Xiphias gladius) from the *Buzzards*, the crew sometimes saw one during the warm months of summer. Carrying a large "sword" attached to the upper jaw, this fish at first glance to an untrained eye appears as a shark, with its single dorsal fin cutting the water. However, the fin is sharper and taller, and is situated closer to the head. Sometimes they bask near the surface of the water.

A single Sand Dab (Limanda ferruginea) was taken by hook. A member of the flounder family, this one measured about nine inches in length and weighed two pounds.

A sea animal arriving in great quantity was the Moon Jellyfish (Coelenterates). The ones in the vicinity of the lightship were white and about three inches in diameter. They were most notable in August and September, although many were seen as late as October 29 (1956), and a few more stragglers swam by during the first week of November.

One last form of sea life was witnessed from the *Buzzards* on October 12, 1956. The day was clear with blue skies, bright sunshine, and an idle wind. The sea, however, was murky with millions of tiny plankton and algae. Fish rippled the water everywhere as they enjoyed nourishment in festive form. The gulls, too, were active feeders that day. The volume of minute sea life reached a maximum at 4:00 P.M. from an early morning beginning and then gradually cleared until at sundown the water again was blue. It was irresistibly fascinating and the only time I recall having seen that part of the ocean so dense with life.

Mammals

During the last two weeks of March 1957 and the first two weeks of April a Humpback Whale (Megaptera) about forty feet long, gray in color, surfaced playfully nearby almost daily, sounding and sending a small geyser some ten feet high. Ronald Balkcom kept tabs on our huge friend, calling us daily whenever he had the watch to show us a long gray back or a small fountain of water. His "There he is!"

became as familiar as the "Thar she blows!" of the whaling era.

Schools of porpoises (Phocaena) ranged fairly close aboard from April to October, swimming rapidly and leaping from the water as though they had not a care in the world. A single school of these frolicsome black mammals, four to six feet in length, sometimes contained twenty-five aor thirty individuals. They completely ignored the bow area of the lightship, preferring to approach no closer than a quarter of a mile as though scornful of our existence or ability to enjoy life.

Reptiles

On June 12, 1956, at 5:15 A.M., William Mahoney was on watch in the radio room. It was a magnificent summeriesh morning. A light northwest breeze failed to ripple the countenance of a calm sea. The yellow sun shone with a radiant beauty from a cloudless sky. Visibility was limited only by curvature of the earth's surface. The smell of salt air was clean, wholesome, invigorating. As Mahoney surveyed the peaceful scene from the entrance to the radio room, the tranquility was interrupted by a strange "schlurp, schlurp." The phonetics were similar to the happy noises produced by teenagers in a soda shop. Puzzled, Mahoney listened attentively, trying to gauge the direction of the sound. The unusual "schlurp" was repeated. Investigating further, he looked over the side of the ship and saw the biggest turtle he had ever seen in his life. Dull green in color, it measured over six feet in length and "would have covered the wardroom table."

Mahoney called Herbert Ressler, the engineer of the watch. Together they watched the antics of the turtle as it swam close to the ship, in no hurry to go anywhere. They discussed the possibility of awakening George Sousa to suggest that he attempt a capture. Not wishing to incur his wrath unwittingly for an unimportant early morning call they vetoed the idea and dismissed it. The turtle, meanwhile, basked leisurely in the sun for about an hour, then swam easterly and disappeared.

From their description it apparently was a leatherback turtle (Dermochelys coriacea), which is the largest of the sea turtles. Authorities on turtles claim this species sometimes weighs over a ton and outlives all other forms of life. They also claim the turtle has remained virtually unchanged for an estimated one hundred and fifty million years.

This was the only time the ship was visited by any member of the reptile family.

Epilogue

For fourteen months we worked together, suffered together, laughed together, and became a team. The long lonely days and nights crept slowly. Many storms caused terrible discomfort. Boredom always tugged at us, threatening our minds. In spite of these aggravations, we watched our home at sea gradually emerge into a ship of which we could feel proud. More and more we came to feel satisfied that we had made strides in the right direction. The ship was clean, stowage was systematic, rust streaks were at a minimum, equipment was in the best possible condition, and we became more self-dependent. On the 2nd of October, 1956, we were given a bi-annual inspection by the Eastern Area Inspectors from Staten Island, New York. The gist of their report, received several weeks later, is summarized below:

"The organization of this vessel as to adequacy and compliance with regulations, and the assignment of authority and responsibility is evaluated as very good.

The material condition of this unit with regards to maintenance, adequacy of material to perform the operational mission, and operability of equipment is considered very good.

Material condition of the engineering and electronics department is considered satisfactory.

Readiness of personnel, as demonstrated by their knowledge of instruction, military smartness and morale, and the execution of required drills and exercise, is classed as very good.

Administration and internal management of this vessel by the officer in charge is considered to be very good.

Maintenance of ship's files, directives and publications and the submission of required reports and returns is classed as very good.

An effective and continuing safety program is being carried out, and the personnel education program is adequate. In connection with the educational program, it was noted that twelve men out of an on-board complement of fourteen enlisted were either pursuing Coast Guard Institute or USAFI courses.

Menu served in the commuted ration mess is considered more than adequate to assure health and well being.

Administration of finance and supply matters on board this vessel is considered to be very good.

The operational readiness of this vessel is classed as very good.

With due consideration of age and operational assignments, the present condition of this vessel is considered to be very good."

Discrepancies were found, of course, but in general we were thrilled with the report. Our fourteen months of assorted hardships had shown dividends, for we were not alone in thinking that we had survived to reflect credit upon ourselves and upon our ship.

Seven months later I was assigned a change of duty. Looking back, I realize the twenty-one months aboard the *Buzzards* lightship had gone fast. I had learned a lot about ships and men and, I hope, had helped my men cross some of the more difficult hurdles of our secluded and compact existence. It was not without a lump in my throat that I bade farewell to as fine a group of men as I ever have met along the avenues of life.

PUBLICATION G781   **MARCH 2017**

CURRENT FLEETS OF OPERATORS IN THE AREA OF MID AND WEST WALES (CW)
Covering the Areas of Carmarthenshire, Ceredigion, Pembrokeshire, Powys and Swansea.

This publication is part of a series covering the Operators which appear in the PSV Circle News Sheets.
It gives details of the known current fleets of operators in the Areas of Carmarthenshire, Ceredigion, Pembrokeshire, Powys and Swansea, referred to by the PSV Circle as Mid and West Wales (CW), and is correct to News Sheet 926 (March 2017).

CONTENTS

HOW TO INTERPRET THIS BOOK

This book is presented in alphabetical order operator by operator. Each entry is split into two parts. Text in bold refers to Operator Data while ordinary text relates to Vehicle Data.

OPERATOR DATA

Each operator has a heading giving the following information:

(a)   The PGxxxxxxx number at the beginning of each title is the official operator's licence number and is shown on the operator licence discs. After each number there is a code letter which represents the grade of licence held by the operator as follows:- CB = Community Bus (white); I = International (Green); N = National (blue); R = Restricted (orange) or T = Taxi. The colour of the discs is given, where applicable, in brackets.

(b)   In the titles, the portion of the name and address in capital letters is that used for the operator in the PSV Circle News Sheets.

(c)   The next entry (FN:) is the operator's Fleet Name(s) and these are commonly displayed on the vehicles or on the operator's publicity. If no FN: is given, the operator's fleet name is presumed to be the same as its title.

(d)   Operating Centre(s) (OC:) are as reported and in some cases are subject to frequent change.

(e)   Vehicles authorised (VA:) is the maximum number of vehicles that the operator is authorised to use at any one time. It does not necessarily indicate the maximum number of vehicles actually with an operator.

VEHICLE DATA

The vehicle data that follows the operator data is the recorded fleet of each operator. Data is listed in eleven columns, the first of which is often blank. These columns are explained as follows:-

(1)   The first column contains the vehicle's fleet number if fleet numbers are used. It can also contain a status code letter (in lower case) where the vehicle status is other than for normal PCV use ie:- a = ancillary vehicle, tow wagon etc, p = preserved by the licenced operator; r = used for spares; t = trainer; u = unlicenced (used only in the Major Operators allocations section); w = withdrawn; x = non-PSV with the licenced operator; z = with the operator but not used, eg a store shed etc .

VEHICLE DATA (continued)

(2)   The second column contains the vehicle's current registration number. Where a vehicle has previously carried other registration numbers, these are contained in a separate line underneath with the date of re-registration given adjacent to them. Individual lists are presented in vehicle registration order. Where a fleet numbering system is in consistent use that order is adopted.

(3)   The third column is a code signifying the name of the chassis builder. A list of these codes is given on page 3.

(4)   The fourth column is also a code and signifies the chassis model type. A list of these codes is also given on page 3

(5)   The fifth column contains the vehicle's chassis number or, where known, the full 17 character VIN (Vehicle Identification Number).

(6)   The sixth column contains a code and signifies the body builder or minibus converter. A list of these codes is given on page 3.

(7)   The seventh column contains the body builder's body or conversion number if these numbers are allocated. Where the field is blank, no numbers are allocated.

(8)   The eighth column is a complex descripter indicating the vehicle's seating capacity and certain other information. The descripter will start with one of the codes B, C, CH, DP, H, L, M or O deciphered as follows:-.

B indicates a single decker bus or a coach-built minibus of a bus-type style. It is followed by the number of seats and the position of the door - C (centre), D (dual, typically front and centre), F (front) or R (rear). One or more of the special fitment codes L - wheelchair accessible via a lift or T- fitted with a toilet may follow.

C indicates a single decker coach or a coach-built minibus to a coach style. It is also followed by the number of seats and the door position, followed by fitment codes if applicable.

CH indicates a double decker built to coach standards. It is followed by two numbers of seats seperated by a slash with the first being the upper deck capacity and the second being the lower deck capacity. On odd occasions, only one capacity will be given and this means that the seating split is unknown. The seating capacity is again followed by the door position and fitment codes.

DP indicates a dual purpose vehicle. The data that follows is similar to C.

F indicates a double decker bus with a front-mounted engine but with a full front, rather than the normal half front/half bonnet. It is followed by the same information as CH. This code is rarely used.

H indicates a double decker bus. It is followed by the same information as CH.

L is also rarely used and indicates a double decker bus built to the old low bridge design. The data that follows is the same as CH.

M indicates a minibus typically converted from a van or crewbus design and up to and including 16 seats. It is followed by the exact number of seats where known.

O indicates an open top double decker. The data that follows is the same as CH.

PO indicates a part open / part closed top double decker. The data that follows is the same as CH.

(9)   The ninth column lists the date the vehicle was new. Prior to 4/81 this date is the month of issue of the vehicle PSV licence. Since that date, where possible, this is the date of effective taxation.

(10) The tenth column contains the vehicle's previous operator where this is known, or indicates that the vehicle was new or newly converted. The previous operator's name is followed by a code signifying the area or county in which they were formerly based.

(11) The last column gives the month of issue of either the first PSV licence to the current operator (before 4/81) or of the date of arrival with the current operator. Where a precise date is not known the date is preceded by the word 'by' or 'c' (circa).

YOU CAN UPDATE THESE LISTS

You can update these lists on a monthly basis by subscribing to the PSV Circle's News Sheet 8. For details of costs and membership details, please write to the PSV Circle, 4B Crown House, Linton Road, BARKING, IG11 8HG or visit our website www.psv-circle.org.uk.

This publication was compiled by Nick Eyles and Ian Kirby.

CHASSIS & BODY CODES

Listed below are those codes used for space saving reasons in this G List. These are part of a more comprehensive list used by the PSV Circle in their News Sheets and other publications.

CHASSIS

AD	Alexander Dennis	SLF	Super Low Floor	Bxr	Boxer
Dt	Dart	Jv	Javelin	Rt	Renault
SLF	Super Low Floor	Lt	Lancet	Mtr	Master
E20D	Dart	EOS	EOS	Tc	Trafic
Env	Enviro	Fd	Ford	Sca	Scania
Jv	Javelin	Tt	Transit	Sn	Seddon
Tt	Trident	FR	Freight Rover	Ta	Toyota
AEC	A.E.C.	Sa	Sherpa	Tbs	Transbus
Bm	Bridgemaster	Ft	Fiat	Dt	Dart
Re	Reliance	Do	Ducato	SLF	Super Low Floor
As	Ayats	Ibs	Irisbus	Env	Enviro
Asn	Autosan	Io	Iveco	Jv	Javelin
Au	Neoplan (Auwärter)	Ka	Setra (Kassbohrer)	Tmsa	TemSA
Ba	Bova	KL	King Long	VH	Van Hool
BBd	Blue Bird	Ld	Leyland	VDL	V.D.L.
Bd	Bedford	LDV	L.D.V.	Vo	Volvo
Bl	Bristol	Cy	Convoy	VW	Volkswagen
BMC	B.M.C (Turkey)	Max	Maxus	Ce	Caravelle
Cr	Commer	Pt	Pilot	Crf	Crafter
Avr	Avenger	MAN	M.A.N.	Tr	Transporter
Ctn	Citroen	MB	Mercedes-Benz	Vx	Vauxhall
Rly	Relay	MCW	Metro Cammell Weymann	Mov	Movano
DAF	D.A.F.	Nn	Nissan	Viv	Vivaro
Ds	Dennis	Oe	Optare	Ytg	Yutong
Dt	Dart	Pt	Peugeot		

BODY

ACl	Autobus/Autobus Classique	FGy	Frank Guy	Pn	Plaxton
AD	Alexander Dennis	FR	Freight Rover	PMT	P.M.T.
Ar	Alexander	GM	GM Coachwork	PR	Park Royal
ArB	Alexander (Belfast)	HC	Hispano Carrocera	Prem	Premier
As	Ayats	Hdw	Holdsworth	Pt	Peugeot
Asn	Autosan	Hn	Harrington	PVB	Pentagon
Au	Neoplan (Auwärter)	Ind	Indcar	RB	Reeve Burgess
AVB	Advanced Vehicle Builders	Ir	Irizar	RH	Robin Hood
Ba	Bova	Is	Ikarus	RKC	Red Kite Conversions
BBd	Blue Bird	Jb	Jubilee	Roh	Rohill
Bds	Bedwas	Jay	Jaycas	Rt	Renault
Bf	Berkhof	Je	Jonckheere	Se	Steedrive
Blbd	Bluebird	Ka	Setra (Kassbohrer)	SCC	SC Coachbuilders
BMC	B.M.C. (Turkey)	KL	King Long	Sds	Saunders
Bs	Beulas	KVC	Kilbeggan Vehicle Convs.	Sit	Sitcar
CD	Chassis Developments	LCB	Leicester Carriage Builders	Sm	Smit
Ce	Carlyle	LHE	L.H.E.	Ssd	Sunsundegui
Cen	Central Coachcraft	Ld	Leyland	Stan	Stanford
Co	Salvador Caetano	LDV	L.D.V.	SwCh	Swansea Coachworks
Cpt	Concept	May	Mayflower	TBP	T.B.P.
Csd	Courtside	MB	Mercedes-Benz	Tbs	Transbus
Ctn	Citroen	MCW	Metro Cammell Weymann	Tmsa	TemSA
Cym	Cymric	Me	Mellor	Treka	Treka Bus
Cys	Crystals	MinO	Minibus Options	UVG	U.V.G.
DAF	D.A.F.	Ml	Marshall	UVM	UV Modular
DC	Devon Conversions	MM	Made to Measure	VH	Van Hool
Do	Dormobile	Mpo	Marcopolo	VW	Volkswagen
Du	Duple	MWr	Metro-Wilker	Vx	Vauxhall
Ech	Eurocoach	My	Massey	Vxl	Vehixel
ECW	Eastern Coach Works	NC	Northern Counties	Wh	Whittaker
EL	East Lancs	Nuk	NuTrack	Wk	Willowbrook
EOS	EOS	NWCS	North West Coach Sales	WS	Wadham Stringer
Eurm	Euromotive	O&H	Oughtred & Harrison	Wt	Wright
Fd	Ford	Oe	Optare	Ytg	Yutong
Fer	Ferqui	Oly	Olympus		

MID AND WEST WALES (CW)

PG1043352/I: 1ST CHOICE Transport Limited, The Transport Depot, Sandy Road, LLANELLI, Carmarthenshire, SA15 4DP. OC: as address. VA: 25.

	Reg		Chassis	Chassis No		Body	Body No		Seats		Last Owner	
	NSU 572	Vo	B10M-62	YV31M2B17TA044233	Pn	9512VUM4340		C53F	1/96	Thomas, Neath (CC) 56	9/10
			(ex N 61 MDW 9/10, K 19 DJT 8/10, N 61 MDW 2/07)									
	TJY 761	Vo	B10M-62	YV31MA618YA051705	Bf	4139		C49FT	4/00	Mordecai, St Helens (MY)	8/11
	WNN 734	Vo	B10M-62	YV31MA614VC060420	Pn	9712VUP6703		C51FT	5/97	Veolia Cymru (CC) 74049	5/11
	4691 HP	Vo	B12B	YV3R8G1285A101833	Je	27202		C49FT	3/05	Hookways, Meeth (DN) HK01	9/11
			(ex SF 05 XYX 11/09, HSK 647 1/08)									
w	M765 CWS	Vo	B10M-62	YV31M2BX1RA041531	Pn	9412VUP2626		C70F	12/94	First Devon & Cornwall (DN) 20435	8/06
	P234 BFJ	Vo	B10M-62	YV31MA618TA045900	Pn	9612VUP5746		C49FT	10/96	First Devon & Cornwall (DN) 20444	8/06
			(ex TJY 761 7/14, P234 BFJ 12/07)									
w	P295 HKU	MB	609D	WDB6680632N044235	Cys	M1584		C24F	2/96	Bell & Cook, Middlesbrough (CD)	2/11
	R516 SCH	BBd	CSRE3700	1BAGKBSA2WF080508	BBd	F121415		B60F	2/98	Silk, North Walsham (NK)	7/11
	R517 SCH	BBd	CSRE3700	1BAGKBSA4WF080509	BBd	F121416		B60F	2/98	Silk, North Walsham (NK)	7/11
	R176 VWN	Ds	Jv	SFD721BR3TGJ21869	Pn	9712HFM6259		C70F	4/98	First Cymru (CW) 21146	1/11
	R178 VWN	Ds	Jv	SFD721BR3TGJ21880	Pn	9712HFM6261		C70F	4/98	First Cymru (CW) 21148	1/11
	R 3 WCT	Vo	B10M-62	YV31MA616VC060578	Bf	3611		C49FT	2/98	Wombwell Coach, Wombwell (SY)	3/10
			(ex R908 ULA 8/04)									
	S 99 CCH	Vo	B7R	YV3R6B518WA000576	Pn	9812TCM9471		C57F	1/99	Arlott, Beenham (BE) 9	9/10
			(ex CNZ 3833 8/02, S 99 CCH 1/02)									
	W381 PRC	Vo	B10M-62	YV31MA610YA052136	Pn	0012VUS2181		C51FT	4/00	Veolia Cymru (CC) 74051	6/11
	W117 TJF	Vo	B7R	YV3R6B518XA001177	Pn	9912TCM1086		C57F	8/00	Arlott, Beenham (BE) 6	8/11
	X 5 PCL	Ibs	391E.12.35	ZGA662P000E003064	Bs	00.094		C49FT	2/01	Veolia Cymru (CC) 74011	7/11
	Y 63 RBK	Ds	Jv	SFD721BR4XGJ22294	SCC	4111/2000		C70F	5/01	Roots, Mayford (SR)	1/11
	CF 51 JAO	Ds	Jv	SFD721BR41GJ22354	Pn	0212GFM4497		C54F	-/02	Devonport Royal Dockyard (MoD)	8/13
			(ex HJ 51 VVL 8/13)									
	KP 51 SYF	Vo	B10M-62	YV31MA610WC060996	Pn	9812VUP9720		C70F	2/02	TGMGroup (LN)	8/11
	WX 51 AJY	Vo	B12M	YV3R9H4111A000181	Pn	0112TJT4206		C49FT	9/01	First Cymru (CW) 20512	4/11
	YM 51 WGO	Ds	Jv	SFD721BR41GJ22342	Pn	0212GFM4490		C55F	1/02	Algar, Llanelli (CW)	9/10
			(ex AE 51 LRY 8/14)									
	CF 02 XAA	Ds	Jv	SFD721BR41GJ22395	Pn	0212GFM4533		C55F	-/02	MoD (X)	8/11
			(ex VO 02 HMV 8/13)									
	YO 52 FHG	Ds	Jv	SFD721BR41GJ22396	Pn	0212GFM4536		C55F	9/02	Algar, Llanelli (CW)	by11/10
			(ex HF 52 WAU 6/14)									
	CT 03 RTX	Tbs	Jv	SFD741BE54GJ22434	Tbs	0312GRX4838		C57F	5/03	Stephenson, Tholthorpe (NY)	8/11
			(ex TRN 772 2/15, CT 03 RTX 3/13, 2732 RH by1/13)									
	OO 03 GAR	Ibs	397E.12.35	ZGA7B2P000E000259	Bs	02.107		C49FT	3/03	Smith Newbiggin-by-the-Sea (ND)	9/10
	WX 03 ZFG	Vo	B12M	YV3R9F8143A000953	Tbs	0312TJT4805		C70F	5/03	First Cymru (CW) 20534	8/11
	FX 53 GYK	Ibs	150E24	ZCFA1LJ0102381142	Vxl			B68F	9/03	Denbighshire County Council (CN) 28378	8/11
	GB 04 LLC	Vo	B7R	YV3R6G7104A007349	Tbs	0412THX5538		C53F	4/04	Hallmark (LN) 11401	9/10
	FJ 54 ZDD	Vo	B12B	YV3R8G11X4A015526	Pn	0412TKL5650		C49FT	10/04	Premiere, Nottingham (NG) 972	9/11
	FJ 54 ZDH	Vo	B12B	YV3R8G1114A015575	Pn	0412TKL5688		C49FT	10/04	Premiere, Nottingham (NG) 973	9/11
	KE 54 HEJ	MB	O814D	WDB6703742N114109	Pn	048.5MAE5435		C33F	10/04	Three Star, Luton (BD)	2/11
	YN 05 XZR	Vo	B7R	YV3R6G7235A105429	Pn	0512TLX6020		C57F	7/05	Jones, Pwllheli (CN)	9/11
	YX 05 AVU	MB	O814D	WDB6703742N116993	ACl	1882		C33F	5/05	Barnard, Kirton-in-Lindsey (LI)	5/11
			(ex TLT 48 3/11, YX 05 AVU 2/06)									
	NB 06 XKZ	Ds	Jv	SFD741BR55GJ22577	Pn	0612GRX6636		C53F	-/06	Unknown MoD Contractor (MoD)	8/11
			(ex ?? ?? ??? 8/16)									

PG1104660/T: Amran Uddion AHMED, 181 Lon Dolafon, NEWTOWN, Powys, SY16 1QY.
FN: Ahmed Taxi. **OC:** as address.

No vehicles currently recorded.

PG1101143/N: ALGAR Travel Limited, The Transport Depot, Sandy Road, LLANELLI, Carmarthenshire, SA15 4DP.
OC: as address. **VA:** 8.

P 26 BUS	Ds	Jv	SFD721BR3WGJE2157	Pn	9812GHM8886	C55F	by2/99	Jenkins, Pontypool (CS)	4/16
			(ex S841 SUH 5/16, ???? ??? -/??)						
YR 03 KPH	Tbs	Jv	SFD741BR53GJ22451	Tbs	0312GRX5146	C70F	by8/03	1st Choice, Llanelli (CW)	by10/16
			(ex ST 03 PNV by7/14)						
YO 53 ZNC	Tbs	Jv	SFD741BR53GJ22453	Tbs	0312GRX5148	C53F	12/03	1st Choice, Llanelli (CW)	by9/16
			(ex ?? ?? ??? 5/14)						
YN 56 DYX	Vo	B7R	YV3R6G72X6A113593	Pn	0612TLX6547	C53F	9/06	OFJ Connections,	
								Stanwell (LN)	8/16

PG2001697/N: Sarah Lilian BELL, Rhosyn Gwyn, TRECWN, Haverfordwest, Pembrokeshire, SA62 5XP.
OC: as address. **VA:** 16

New application currently pending.

PG1010816/N: Malcolm Philip BEVAN, 210 Llanllienwen Road, CWMRHYDYCEIRW, Morriston, Swansea, SA6 6NB.
FN: Malcolm Bevan Coaches. **OCs:** as address; EVD Commercials, Cramic Way, Port Talbot, SA13 1JU;
DJ Thomas Coaches Limited, Nuberian Works, Milland Road Industrial Estate, Neath, SA11 1NJ. **VA:** 3.

No vehicles currently recorded.

PG1040772/R: Brian Hugh BEVAN, Cware Farm, FELINFOEL, Llanelli, Carmarthenshire, SA14 8EZ.
FN: Bens Buses. **OC:** as address. **VA:** 2.

YP 07 OJD	Fd	Tt	WF0DXXTTFD7D20025	Fd		M16	6/07	-?-, -?-	1/09

PG0007110/N: Robert Norman BOWDEN, Lower Gelli, Golfa, CYFRONYDD, Powys, SY21 9BB.
FN: RN Bowden. **OC:** as address. **VA:** 4.

w S906 KGD	MB	O814D	WDB6703732N074843	Onyx 303		C24F	11/98	Collison, Stonehouse (SW)	12/00
BT 55 LUH	Fd	Tt	WF0EXXTTFE5K22724	Fd		M14	11/05	-?-, -?-	9/08
YP 06 FON	Fd	Tt	WF0EXXTTFE6S27154	Fd		M16	5/06	-?-, -?-	10/07

PG0007527/I: Richard Wilson BOWEN, Churchill Drive, Barnfields, NEWTOWN, Powys, SY16 2LH.
FN: Central Travel. **OC:** Unit 43 Mochdre Industrial Estate, Mochdre, Newtown, SY16 4LE. **VA:** 4.

D 7 CTL	MB	515CDI	WDB9066572S187058	Stan		M16	9/06	Back Roads, Chiswick (LN)	11/14
			(ex EY 57 FHL)						
G 7 CTL	Sca	K124IB	1835986	VH	33381	C49FT	4/00	Keenan, Bellurgan (EI)	9/10
			(ex W403 WRE 1/13, 00-KK-2226 5/11)						
Y 7 CTL	Sca	K114IB4	YS4K4X20001841176	VH	36065	C49FT	5/02	Simpson, Rosehearty (SN)	8/13
			(ex AIG 9385, YR 02 ZZN)						

PG0006682/I: William George BRIGGS, Elba Crescent, Fabian Way, CRYMLYN BURROWS, Swansea, SA1 8QQ.
OC: as address. **VA:** 7.

PSU 610	MAN	10.220	WMAL53ZZZ1Y077195	Ind	4.673	C33FT	4/02	MCT, Motherwell (SW)	9/14
			(ex R 12 MCT 3/15, SL 02 OXG 11/12, PSU 610 9/12, SL 02 LZL 11/04, 02-KK-2088 4/04)						
RIG 6293	MAN	18.310	WMAA51ZZZ3S001187	Noge	N.5079	C55F	9/04	Swallow, Rainham (LN)	5/16
			(ex YN 54 JUT 6/16)						

BRIGGS, CRYMLYN BURROWS (continued)

RIG 6294	Ds	Jv	12SDA2156/1512	WS	-?-	C70F	by7/96	Watermill Coaches,
			(ex SW 02 FGY 6/16, N639 UMO by4/04)					Fraserburgh (SN) 8/15
RIG 6295	Ds	Jv	12SDA2156/1516	WS	-?-	C70F	by7/96	Watermill Coaches,
			(ex SW 02 VFX 6/16, N959 LEG by4/04)					Fraserburgh (SN) 8/15
RIG 6296	Ds	Jv	10SDA2120/826	WS	3839/93	DP57FA	8/93	Bell, Eastergate (WS) 6/16
			(ex L486 XOU 6/16, 74 KK 50 10/03, L954 KBE 8/03, 74 KK 50 6/02)					
W605 PTO	Oe	M920	VN6408	Oe	6408	B33F	5/00	Summercourt Travel,
			(ex OUI 8952 9/15, W605 PTO 10/12)					Summercourt (CO) 34 9/15
ME 02 YBN	Ds	Jv	SFD721BR41GJ22391	Pn	0212GFM4528	C70F	-/02	Lainton, Gorton (GM) 7/16
			(ex ?? ?? ?? 2/14)					
w SK 02 VOG	MB	O817L	WDB6764642K292323	Leinster		C33F	5/02	Edinburgh Castle Coaches,
								Edinburgh (SS) 4/03
MX 05 EKY	Oe	X1200	SAB28000000000010	Oe		B42F	4/05	Konectbus (NK) 401 10/16
YN 05 BUH	MAN	13.220	WMAA53ZZZ3S001535	Noge -?-		C35FT	3/05	Bell, Eastergate (WS) 8/16
w BX 55 FYD	MB	616CDI	WDB9056132R573631	Koch		B25F	10/05	Glamorgan Bus, Cwmbach (CC) 4/13
SK 06 FBO	MB	Tourino	WEB44420323000018	MB		C32FT	6/06	Parnell, Honiton (DN) 9/1●
			(ex LL 06 CEL 6/16, SK 06 FBO 10/09, B 18 DWA 8/07, SK 06 FBO by3/07, B 14 DWA 1/07, B 18 DWA 1/07)					
SK 07 FOV	MB	616CDI	WDB9056132R922558	UNVI 34232		C23F	4/07	Going Forth, Edinburgh (SS) 4/12
			(named Amy)					
YX 07 AYL	MB	O815D	WDB6703742N122622	Fer	8619	C33F	5/07	Radical Travel, Edinburgh (SS) 4/12
			(named Julie)					
YX 08 HGE	MB	618D	WDB6683532N132391	Onyx 848		C24F	5/08	Fisher, Edinburgh (SS) 9/14
			(ex T 11 BUD 7/14, YX 08 HGE 8/08) (named Taylor)					

PG1027639/l: BRODYR JAMES Cyfyngedig, Glanyrafon Garage, LLANGEITHO, Tregaron, Ceredigion, SY25 6TT.
OCs: as address; Heulfryn, Bronant, Aberystwyth, Ceredigion, SY23 4TF. VA: 17.

MSU 923	Ta	XZB50R	TW1FC518006000011	Co	F0730471002	C22F	6/07	Lewis, Llanrhystud (CW) 8/1●
			(ex BX 07 BHD 2/16)					
6738 UN	Vo	B10M-62	YV31MA615WC060752	Pn	9812VUS0924	C50F	3/98	Shearings (CH) 924 5/0●
			(ex R924 YBA 4/07)					
329 UWL	Ds	Jv	8.5SDA1926/679	Pn	918HFA0617	C35F	5/92	new 5/9●
w F434 DUG	Vo	B10M-60	YV31MGD11KA020874	Pn	8912VCAP0832	C53F	4/89	Brooks, Ryarsh (KT) 6/0●
M796 EUS	MB	609D	WDB6680632N025031	Jb		DP24F	4/95	Welsh Gold, Dolgellau (YCN) 6/0●
w M 61 WKA	MB	709D	WDB6690032N020873	Ar	AM117/794/9	B23F	8/94	Arriva North West (MY) 61 7/0●
M 65 WKA	MB	709D	WDB6690032N021899	Ar	AM117/794/13	B25F	8/94	Arriva North West (MY) 65 7/0●
N281 MRN	Vo	B10M-62	YV31M2B13SA043532	Pn	9512VUM4208	C57F	2/96	Harrison, Morecambe (LA) 7/0●
			(ex 5108 VX 2/00, N892 AEO 10/97)					
w P 25 WTN	Fd	Tt	SFAEXXBDVETC86086	Fd		M14	8/97	Northgate (Y) 7/0●
T712 UOS	Vo	B10M-62	YV31MA613XC061027	Je	25003	C53F	3/99	Park, Hamilton (SW) 5/0●
			(ex HSK 643 11/01)					
BX 53 AAN	Ta	BB50R	TW1FG518405500294	Co	F023071014	C21F	9/03	new 9/0●
WA 53 ONL	Ds	Jv	SFD721BR41GJ22372	Pn	0212GFM4593	C53F	5/02	Lawrence & Harding,
								St Ann's Chapel (CO) 6/0●
FH 06 OPR	VDL	SB4000	XMGDE40PS0H013604	Mpo	OF.1321	C53F	3/06	Holmeswood,
			(ex L 60 LTL 6/15, FH 06 OPR 3/14, 06-KE-4889 7/09)					Holmeswood (LA) 9/1●
FJ 06 URP	Vo	B12B	YV3R8G1275A106862	Co	F053043020	C49FT	6/06	new 6/0●
GL 06 PUL	AD	Jv	SFD245BR55GJ22581	Pn	0610GTX6515	C41F	6/06	Pulhams,
								Bourton-on-the-Water (GL) 2/1●
MX 06 ULT	MAN	14.280	WMAA67ZZZ3S001556	Co	F033051004	C36FT	5/06	Lainton, Gorton (GM) 10/1●
AA 07 ASH	VDL	SB4000	XMGDE40PS0H014784	Bf	5497	C53FLT	7/07	Lewis, Llanrhystud (CW) 9/1●
BX 07 KWE	LDV	Cy	SEYZMVFZGDN112545	Excel -?-		M16	3/07	Flockhart, Bonnyrigg (SS) 11/1●
BV 57 MLO	Asn	A1012T	SUAED5CGP7S620288	Asn		C70F	9/07	Lewis, Llanrhystud (CW) 8/1
YN 57 BXJ	AD	Jv	SFD341BR55GJ22584	Pn	0610GXT6895	C41F	9/07	new 9/0●
CU 09 AEM	AD	Jv	SFD755BR68GJ22618	Pn	0812JAX7752	C57F	3/09	new 3/0

PG1028811/I: BRODYR WILLIAMS Limited, Bryneglur Garage, 30 Llannon Road, UPPER TUMBLE, Llanelli, Carmarthenshire, SA14 6BW. OC: as address. VA: 15.

36	JSV 472	EOS	E180Z	YA9CF2N22TB128178	EOS	T/8178		C51FT	4/97 Gordon, Leslie (SE)	8/00
			(ex P897 PWW 8/00)							
40	7 WTJ	Vo	B10M-62	YV31M2B10TA044882	Pn	9612VUP4700		C49FT	3/96 Holdsworth,	
			(ex N253 KFR 11/04)						Great Harwood (LA) 253	11/04
44	EAZ 8418	DAF	SB3000	XMGDE33WS0H004890	Pn	9612DRP5026		C53F	5/96 Adams, Walsall (WM)	6/06
			(ex N984 FWT 6/06, B 19 DAF 4/04, N984 FWT 3/02)							
46	3201 MY	VDL	SB4000	XMGDE40XS0H011534	VH	37097		C49FT	4/05 Guideissue, Biddulph (ST)	9/07
			(ex YJ 05 PZB 1/08)							
49	490 ENU	Vo	B12M	YV3R9F8103A000898	Pn	0212TJT4765		C57F	11/02 Viscount (CM) 53003	12/10
			(ex GU 52 WSX 1/11)							
50	RIL 2220	Vo	B12M	YV3R9F8183A000907	Pn	0212TJT4769		C57F	12/02 East Midland (DE) 53007	6/11
			(ex GU 52 WTE 7/11)							
51	CN 53 NWC	Vo	B12M	YV3R9F8184A011651	Tbs	0312TJT5234		C44FT	12/03 Laser Minicoach,	
									Llanharry (CC)	8/11
53	FN 03 BUS	Vo	B12M	YV3R9F8183A001099	Bf	4680		C49FT	4/03 Sim, Boot (CA)	4/15
			(ex FN 03 DXL 11/12, 219 DLV 10/12, FN 03 DXL 1/12)							
54	LLZ 5719	Vo	B10M-62	YV31MA612XC061164	Je	25144		C53F	4/99 Jeffs, Helmdon (NO)	12/15
			(ex T719 UOS 4/05, HSK 650 11/01)							
55	YN 07 KHH	Vo	B7R	YV3R6G7256A115882	Pn	0612TLS6847		C70F	4/07 Festival Travel, Kirkliston (SS)	7/16
	P550 CLJ	Vo	B10M-62	YV31MA612VA046513	Pn	9712VUM6085		C70F	3/97 Thomas, Neath (CC) 57	8/13
			(ex LUY 742 8/13, P550 CLJ, A 9 EXC)							
	CE 11 RSO	Fd	Tt	WF0DXXTTFDBC30208	Fd			M16	3/11 Ysgol Gyfun Plasmawr,	
									Cardiff (XCC) E001331	6/14
	MX 11 EVU	VW	Crf	WV1ZZZ2EZ86012018	?			M16	7/11 Gorslas Minibuses,	
									Upper Tumble (CW)	11/16
	BX 14 KPZ	KL	XMQ6900	LA6R1DSE5DB105332	KL			C31FT	5/14 new	5/14

PG1074173/I: BROOK MINIBUSES Limited, Brook Garage, Clifton Street, LAUGHARNE, Carmarthen, Carmarthenshire, SA33 4QG. OC: as address. VA: 10.

SH 04 MVF	Fd	Tt	WF0EXXGBFE3T64978	Fd	M16	4/04 Arnold Clark (Y)	6/10
CE 05 UFX	Fd	Tt	WF0EXXTTFE5J21412	Fd	M16	3/05 Focus Training, Perivale (LN)	1/13
FY 05 UBL	Fd	Tt	WF0EXXTTFE4K75312	Fd	M16	4/05 Hammond, Ferryhill (DM)	7/14
NJ 06 NLM	Fd	Tt	WF0EXXTTFE5E58070	Fd	M16	3/06 -?-, -?-	11/11

PG0007419/N: Nigel Wyn BROWN, 15 High Street, BUILTH WELLS, Powys, LD2 3DN.
FN: Browns of Builth. OCs: Tynrheol, Hundred House, Builth Wells, LD2 3TE; The Service Station, Garth, Builth Wells, LD4 4BA. VA: 21.

z	u/r	Ta	HZB50R	TW043PP5009000420	Co	6511101	C21F	6/96 USAF, Alconbury (X)	10/14
			(ex USAF 2999 by12/05)						
z	AIG 6553	Ds	Jv	12SDA2136/1417	Co	658017	C67F	8/96 Baig & Nash, Worcester (WO)	10/12
			(ex P177 ANR 10/05)						
z	FIL 4033	Ld	PSU5D/5R	8031308	Du	235/5444	DP61F	4/82 Millward, Sheffield Park (SY)	9/01
			(ex WGV 866X 7/88)						
z	LUI 5809	Vo	B10M-61	YV3B10M6100007158	Pn	8412VZH1C16N	C53F	2/84 Pike, Bolsover (DE)	12/03
			(ex A640 UGD 4/03, 789 CLC 8/97, A640 UGD by3/92)						
z	MSV 372	Fd	R1114	BCRSAT422580	Du	223/4547	C53F	5/83 Ace, Aintree (MY)	12/07
			(ex NCA 520Y 8/89)						
	OCZ 8829	Oe	M850	SAB19000000000938	Oe		B25F	2/03 Ulsterbus (NI) 1829	3/13
	OCZ 8830	Oe	M850	SAB19000000000939	Oe		B25F	2/03 Ulsterbus (NI) 1830	2/13
z	OJI 5267	Bd	YMT	LW452344	Du	217/2606	C53F	3/82 Tricky Tykes,	
			(ex BRO 585X 4/92)						Pencarreg (XCW) by3/14
w	PIL 6827	Bd	YNT	ET105235	Pn	8411NTP1C042	C53F	10/84 Pike, Bolsover (DE)	12/03
			(ex B548 NDG 8/98)						
z	PJI 8329	Bd	YLQ	FW455873	Pn	7710QC003AM	C45F	9/77 Pike, Bolsover (DE)	12/03
			(ex UVO 246S 9/98)						
z	TIL 5412	Bd	YNT	SKFYNT3NZHT101796	Du	8754/0479	C53F	2/88 Langley, St Arvans (CS)	7/09
			(ex E753 HJF by11/01)						

BROWN, BUILTH WELLS (continued)

	Reg		Model	Chassis			Body	Seating	Date	Operator	Date
w	URN 989	Bd	J2SZ10		190586	Pn	642329	C20F	5/64	Miles, Gelligaer (CS)	5/85
	VXT 571	Vo	B10M-62	YV31M2B17RA040224		Co	358006	C53F	3/94	Harrington, Kynpersley (ST)	2/16
	(ex L 38 CAY 12/01)										
z	XIL 7241	Vo	B6-41	YV3R36E12MM005011		Co	259001	C35F	2/93	Campbell Coaches,	
										East Kilbride (SW)	10/10
	(ex K 3 MCT 7/06, K698 RNR 9/95)										
r	XJI 9612	MCW	MF158/11		MB9851	MCW		B31F	9/88	Davies, Merthyr Tydfil (CS)	6/03
	(ex F192 YDA 4/99)										
z	938 HNM	Vo	B10M-62	YV31M2B19RA040225		Co	358007	C53F	3/94	Harrington, Knypersley (ST)	2/16
	(ex L 39 CAY 12/01)										
	487 VYA	Vo	B10M-62	YV31M2B18RA040197		Co	358003	C53F	3/94	Harrington, Knypersley (ST)	2/16
	(ex L 35 CAY 12/01)										
z	ADY 229B	Bd	VAS1		1800	Du	1171/60	C29F	7/64	-?-, -?- (V)	by12/06
z	ANY 376B	Bd	SB13		94495	Du	1170/98	C41F	5/64	Hobbs, Cefn Hengoed (P)	3/02
w	BHY 942C	Bd	J2SZ10		218483	Pn	652956	C20F	3/65	Bryant, Bristol (GL)	4/80
z	LAW 102F	Bd	VAM70		7861878	Du	1215/28	C45F	1/68	Wat's Dyke School,	
										Wrexham (XCN)	12/93
z	LEL 40F	Bd	VAM70		7854288	Du	1215/16	C36F	9/67	Rugeley Rosettes JB (XST)	12/93
z	XOT 919J	Bd	VAS5		1T483157	Pn	712076	C29F	1/71	British Airways Club,	
										Cranford (XLN)	5/85
z	LUR 510L	Bd	VAL70		2T473363	Pn	732402	C53F	5/73	Duffy, Macclesfield (P)	9/10
z	NCJ 800M	Bd	YRQ		CW454300	Du	267/1106	C45F	8/73	Staples, Leominster (HR)	1/97
z	PVJ 300M	Bd	YRQ		DW454056	Du	415/2102	C45F	5/74	Staples, Leominster (HR)	1/97
z	RTA 693M	Bd	YRQ		CW454348	Du	415/2029	C45F	11/73	Crowther, Booker (BK)	12/00
	(ex 645 CJD by2/90, SNK 246M 5/87)										
z	YVO 278M	Bd	YRT		DW451019	Pn	418/3674	C53F	2/74	Brutonian, Bruton (SO)	8/88
z	DRF 118N	Bd	YRT		DW455534	Pn	7411TX515	C53F	8/74	Boulton, Cardington (SH)	10/93
z	JDW 555N	Bd	YRQ		EW452601	Pn	7510QC069	C45F	6/75	Boulton, Cardington (SH)	10/93
z	REP 999N	Bd	YRQ		DW455634	Pn	7410QC037	C45F	8/74	Conwy Borough Council,	
										Llandudno (CN)	7/00
z	PFT 70R	Bd	YLQ		FW455859	Pn	7710QCM041	C45F	6/77	Crowther, Booker (BK)	12/00
w	FYA 201T	Bd	YLQ		JW451393	Pn	916/2258	C45F	3/79	Coombs Group, Weston (SO)	11/95
z	KRN 120T	Ld	PSU3E/4R		7806591	Du	834/5337	C49F	5/79	Evington Scouts (XLE)	1/02
z	DKG 270V	Bd	YMT		JW454259	Pn	8011TC020	C53F	1/80	Crowther, Booker (BK)	12/00
r	NNW 374V	Bd	YMT		HW452163	Pn	8011TC161	C53F	6/80	Perry, Macclesfield (CH)	9/00
z	EAA 829W	Bd	YMQ		KW452629	Du	015/2133	C45F	8/80	Coombs Group,	
										Weston (SO) 29	11/95
z	KVO 687W	Bd	YMQ		KW453678	Pn	8010QC038/S	C45F	10/80	Pike, Bolsover (DE)	12/03
w	BWT 340X	Bd	VAS5		LW452761	Du	211/1000	C31F	3/82	Motley, Blazefield (NY)	8/03
	(ex SVN 6X 10/03)										
z	LFT 6X	Ld	TRCTL11/2R		8102156	Du	8778/0506	C57F	2/82	Blaengwawr School, Aberaman (CC	
	(ex JIJ 3737 10/97, LFT 6X 12/87 - re-bodied 10/87, originally carried Pn body, number 8211LTS5X508)										2/0-
w	URA 481X	Bd	YMP		CT103445	Du	215/2150	C45F	7/82	Glover, Ashbourne (DE)	2/0-
r	BNC 344Y	Sn	Pe 7		73326	Wk	812661	C43FT	8/82	Andy Dixon, Brynmenyn (XCC)	9/03
w	CEJ 939Y	Bd	VAS5		CT103003	Du	212/1053	C29F	9/82	Evans, Tregaron (CW)	6/0
w	FBV 827Y	Bd	VAS5		DT102002	Du	312/1050	C29F	6/83	Porteous, Anlaby (EY)	11/0
z	UUY 460Y	Bd	YMP	SKFYMP2DZDT101489		Pn	8310MQB1B801	DP45F	5/83	dog transporter,	
										Llanybydder (XCW)	by2/1
w	A511 LPP	Bd	YMP		DT105037	Pn	838MQP1C008	C35F	8/83	Culverbeck, Berinsfield (OX)	9/9
r	A855 OVJ	Bd	CFL		DV613212	Se	1723/3	M12	1/84	new	1/8-
r	A387 XTG	Bd	CF		GV615070	Do	1787 706 84	M12	7/84	Price, Llanvihangel	
										Crucomey (CS)	6/9
z	B360 AVS	Bd	YNT	SKFYNT3NZET106901		Pn	8511NTP2C008	C53F	5/85	Langley, St Arvans (CS)	7/0
z	C152 SRT	Fd	R1115	BCRSCB23953		Pn	8511FDP2C006	C53F	9/85	Lets Go, Manselton (CW)	4/0
w	D110 CRE	FR	Sa (Opel)		AN275178	PMT	6050	DP16F	11/86	PMT (ST) 110	10/9
z	D611 GCD	Bd	YMP	SKFYMP2DZHT100819		Pn	878MSP3C014	C33F	6/87	Roberts, Lewdown (DN)	by2/0
	(ex FWV 690 by6/00, D777 ALR by9/93)										
r	D658 NNE	MCW	MF151/3		MB8931	MCW		B23F	4/87	Balcomb, Canvey (EX)	8/0
z	D461 PON	MCW	MF150/14		MB9112	MCW		B23F	6/87	Crowther, Booker (BK)	12/0
z	D462 PON	MCW	MF150/14		MB9113	MCW		B23F	6/87	Crowther, Booker (BK)	12/0
z	D469 PON	MCW	MF150/14		MB9120	MCW		B23F	6/87	Crowther, Booker (BK)	12/0
z	D470 PON	MCW	MF150/14		MB9121	MCW		B23F	6/87	Crowther, Booker (BK)	12/0
w	D335 UGA	Au	N122/3		86 129 19	Au		CH57/20CT	10/86	Blackburn Private Hire,	
										Gorton (GM)	6/0
	(ex LSK 613 10/94, D324 NWG 1/94)										

BROWN, BUILTH WELLS (continued)

	Reg	Make	Model	Chassis No	Body	Body No	Seating	Date	History	Date
w	E737 EVJ	Bd	YMP	GT103957	Pn	878MQP3C001	C35F	9/87	new	9/87
r	E606 HTF	MCW	MF158/8	MB9836	MCW		B--F	6/88	Reading (BE) 606	1/02
z	E132 KYW	MCW	MF150/38	MB9008	MCW		B25F	10/87	Apollo, Cardiff (CC)	9/02
r	E261 REP	MCW	MF150/16	MB9094	MCW		B25F	8/87	Cardiff (CCz)	9/96
w	E262 REP	MCW	MF150/16	MB9095	MCW		B25F	8/87	Cardiff (CCz)	9/96
r	E269 REP	MCW	MF150/16	MB9102	MCW		B25F	8/87	Cardiff (CCz)	9/96
r	E270 REP	MCW	MF150/16	MB9103	MCW		B25F	8/87	Cardiff (CCz)	9/96
w	E148 TBO	MCW	MF150/79	MB9577	MCW		DP23F	3/88	Heath, Hinckley (LE)	9/02
r	E149 TBO	MCW	MF150/79	MB9578	MCW		DP23F	3/88	Cardiff (CC) 049	4/96
r	E812 UDT	MCW	MF150/15	MB9086	MCW		B23F	8/87	Cardiff (CCz)	9/96
z	E673 WWD	Ld	TRCTL11/3LZ	TR00012	Pn	8712LMMOD32E	B54F	9/87	Silcox, Pembroke Dock	
									(CW) 204	7/16
w	E134 YUD	DAF	MB230LT615	XLACA02LT00304255	Pn	8812DVH3C05N	C53F	4/88	Langley, St Arvans (CS)	7/09
z	F192 PNR	DAF	SB2305DHS585	XLRDE23HS0E318927	Co	858055	C53F	3/89	Gillie, Aylesham (KT)	by5/09
r	F617 UBV	MCW	MF159/3	MB10016	MCW		B31F	9/88	Fazakarley, Birmingham (WM)	9/01
z	F101 YWO	MCW	MF150/104	MB9966	MCW		DP25F	10/88	Hancock, Gilwern (CS)	9/02
r	F107 YWO	MCW	MF150/103	MB9955	MCW		DP23F	9/88	Davies, Merthyr Tydfil (CS) 4	6/03
w	G777 WFC	Oe	MR09	VN2009	Oe	2009	B25F	6/90	City of Oxford (OX) 777	8/99
w	H169 OTG	Oe	MR01	VN1047	Oe	1047	B31F	12/90	Cardiff (CCz)169	3/00
	H802 WNP	Ds	Jv	8.5SDA1925/653	Pn	918HEA2404	C35F	6/91	Worcestershire County Council,	
									Worcester (WO) 3561	2/05
	H803 WNP	Ds	Jv	8.5SDA1925/652	Pn	918HEA2405	C33FL	6/91	Worcestershire County Council,	
									Worcester (WO) 3562	2/05
z	J 20 CCG	MB	411CDI	WDB9046632R547172	Koch		M16	9/03	Cresswell, Moira (DE)	7/12
w	J449 MDB	DAF	400	XLRZMYFEACN900019	MM		M16L	9/91	Tim's Travel, Sheerness (KT)	9/01
w	J100 OMP	DAF	SB2305DHTD585	XLADE23HC00314107	Pn	9012DFA2091	C57F	9/91	Tanners Croft, Redditch (WO)	9/97
z	K440 BMO	Ds	Jv	10SDA2119/748	Bf	2197	C36FT	1/93	A2B Taxis, Trispen (CO)	2/14
			(ex SEL 23 2/06, K440 BMO 9/03, A 13 HLC 7/03, K440 BMO by2/97)							
	K201 GRW	Ds	Jv	12SDA2101/662	Co	150206	C70F	3/93	Weale, Llandegley (CW)	5/15
z	K101 UJR	Ds	Jv	10SDA2120/706	WS	3773/92	DP46FA	9/92	Munro's, Jedburgh (SS) 955	by3/14
			(ex 74 KK 34 8/04, K601 FSH 9/03, 74 KK 34 by6/01)							
z	K183 YDW	Oe	MR01	VN1255	Oe	1255	B31F	8/92	Langley, St Arvans (CS)	7/09
w	L482 GTX	Oe	MR15	VN1617	Oe	1617	B31F	7/94	Deeble, Upton Cross (CO)	10/10
			(ex L104 GBO 1/09)							
w	L732 PRP	LDV	400	SEYZMNFEACN939515	?		M14	2/94	Northamptonshire County	
									Council (XNO)	11/05
w	M302 OTF	Ds	Jv	8.5SDA2137/998	Bf	2592	C35F	10/94	Village Green, Shobdon (HR)	12/13
w	M 2 WHC	MAN	18.370	WMAA510193W024773	Co	450005	C49FT	3/95	Dick, Slough (BE)	4/01
r	N507 BEG	LDV	400	SEYZMYSEADN002944	LDV		M16	7/96	-?-, -?-	by5/09
w	N 5 DMW	MAN	11.190	WMA4691845G098696	Co	559003	C35F	1/96	Lamont, Glenboig (SW)	10/10
z	N281 GSC	LDV	400	SEYZMYSEACN973069	LDV		M16	5/96	-?-, -?-	5/08
w	N373 PNY	MB	709D	WDB6690032N042420	ArB	M58480596	B25F	5/96	Langley, St Arvans (CS)	7/09
w	N374 PNY	MB	709D	WDB6690032N042519	ArB	M58490596	B25F	5/96	Langley, St Arvans (CS)	7/09
	N209 WMS	Ta	HZB50R	TW043PB5009000257	Co	551008	C21F	10/95	Owens, Four Crosses (CW)	10/09
w	P380 AFJ	LDV	Cy	SEYZMNFEEDN008178	Cys	-?-	M16L	2/97	Devon County Council	
									(XDN) 05-2751	8/06
w	P171 ANR	Ds	Jv	12SDA2136/1414	Co	658016	C53F	8/96	Aron, Hayes (LN)	4/02
			(ex 420 DWX 12/00, P171 ANR 2/00)							
	P174 ANR	Ds	Jv	SFD731BR3TGJ31803	Co	658092	C53F	2/97	Village Green, Shobdon (HR)	12/13
w	P779 BJF	Ds	Jv	SFD731BR3TGJ31804	Co	658093	C53F	3/97	New Concept, Glasgow (SW)	3/09
			(ex GDZ 879 9/03, P779 BJF 4/03)							
z	P212 CAY	Ta	BB50R	TW043BB5000001005	Co	651124	C14F	3/97	Avis, Hayes (LN) 12	8/08
z	P575 GCF	Ds	Jv	12SDA2136/1376	Bf	2926	C57F	2/97	Weale, Llandegley (CW)	7/13
z	P720 VFC	LDV	Cy	SEYZMYSEADN003570	LDV		M16	9/96	-?-, -?-	by5/09
	P779 WDE	Ds	Jv	SFD731BR3TGJ31964	Co	758503	C51FT	5/97	Silcox, Pembroke Dock	
			(ex 9195 PU 6/16, P779 WDE 5/13)						(CW) 179	7/16
w	R 94 GNB	LDV	Cy	SEYSLWSEEDN020794	LDV		M16	9/97	-?-, -?-	10/03
			(ex -?- 10/03)							
w	R162 GNW	DAF	SB3000	XMGDE33WS0H005584	Pn	9712DSS6447	C53F	4/98	Shamrock, Pontypridd (CS)	5/06
w	R812 XBA	Io	49.10	ZCF04970005127270	MinO		M16L	8/97	Manchester Minibus Agency,	
									Ardwick (GM)	11/09
z	S499 CDE	MB	614D	WDB6683532N076650	Onyx 314		C24F	10/98	Edwards, Tiers Cross (CW)	7/12
w	T872 JBC	MAN	24.400	WMA4740538W035065	Noge N-2749		C49FT	3/99	Bennett, Hayes End (LN)	2/09

BROWN, BUILTH WELLS (continued)

	Reg										
w	V488 LGM	LDV	Cy	SEYZNVSHEDN051202	LDV		M16	3/00	Herdman, Clyro (CW)		11/08
	W208 CDN	DAF	SB2750	XMGDE23RS0H007540	Sm	3990	C45F	4/00	Airlinks (LN) 1164		7/03
z	W425 CWX	Oe	MR17		VN2332	Oe	2332	B29F	4/00	Henderson, Hamilton (SW)	10/10
z	X200 CEC	Oe	M850		VN6483	Oe	6483	B28F	9/00	Dumfries & Galloway Council (SW) 105041	2/16
	Y165 AJF	Vo	B12(T)	YV3R2A216YA008835	Pn	0012VHS3106	C53F	4/01	Cummer, Galway (EI)		4/04
			(ex 01-G-3470 1/04)								
	YJ 51 EOB	LDV	Cy	SEYZMNFJEDN073039	Crest	LDV1047	M16	9/01	Herdman, Clyro (CW)		3/16
w	YL 51 ZTH	Oe	Alero	SAB21000000000220	Oe		B16F	12/01	-?-, -?-		1/08
w	YP 52 BSV	Oe	Alero	SAB21000000000301	Oe		B12F	10/02	Doncaster Community, Doncaster (SY) 88	10/08
w	YP 52 JWK	Oe	Alero	SAB21000000000319	Oe		B13F	1/03	Greenwood & Drury, Fleetwood (LA)	2/07
	OF 03 OFO	MB	O814D	WDB6703742N109845	Tbs	038.5MXV5051	DP33F	4/03	new		4/03
	VX 04 ULV	MB	O814D	WDB6703742N112562	Pn	048.5MAE5385	C33F	5/04	new		5/04
	KX 55 RYY	Oe	M950SL	SAB19000000002122	Oe		B33F	1/06	Davies, Llanidloes (CW)		2/13
w	YJ 55 JEO	LDV	Cy	SEYZMVSZGDN112027	LDV		M16	10/05	Leeds Teaching Hospitals (XWY)	9/10
	YJ 55 JHK	LDV	Cy	SEYZMVSZGDN111836	LDV		M16	10/05	Leeds Teaching Hospitals (XWY)	9/10
	BX 06 EFP	Ibs	397E12.43A.C	ZGA7B2A100E002669	Bs	05.210	C53F	4/06	Dero's, Killarney (EI)		6/14
			(ex 06-KY-3498 10/12)								
	BX 06 EHZ	MAN	A51	WMAA51ZZ25C005786	Bs	05.076	C59FT	by9/06	Kavanagh, Urlingford (EI)		4/11
			(ex 06-D-41090 by4/11)								
	YJ 06 FXY	Oe	M780	SAB19000000002439	Oe		B23F	6/06	new		6/06
	YJ 57 YCM	Oe	M810SL	SABDNGAF07R192967	Oe		B27F	12/07	Dudley Metropolitan Borough Council (XWM) V1734	9/13
			(ex YJ 57 XWL c1/08)								
	BX 62 BWZ	KL	XMQ6800	LA6R1CSB8BB204160	KL		C30F	11/12	Harrington, Kynpersley (ST)	4/16
	YJ 62 FYS	Oe	M9600SR	SABTW3AF0CS290480	Oe		B33F	9/12	Britannia Parking, Bournemouth (DT) 15	3/16

PG1066022/R: David Gerard BROWN, Rhydnewydd, SARNAU, Llandysul, Ceredigion, SA44 6PX.
FN: David Brown Minibus Travel. **OC:** Unit 4 Tanygroes, Rhoshill, Cardigan, SA43 2TP. **VA:** 1.

No vehicles currently recorded.

PG1103020/I: Ernest George BRYAN, 23 Fifth Avenue, PENPARCAU, Aberystwyth, Ceredigion, SY23 1RE.
FN: Bryans Coaches. **OC:** Llys Eifion Yard, Ponterwyd, Aberystwyth, SY23 3AG. **VA:** 3.

No vehicles currently recorded.

PG1121955/T: Alison BURROWS, 3 The Rise, TREFONEN, Llandrindod Wells, Powys, LD1 5YD.
FN: Dragon Taxi. **OC:** as address.

No vehicles currently recorded.

PG0007573/I: BYSIAU CWM TAF Valley Coaches Limited, Penrheol, Ciffig, WHITLAND, Carmarthenshire, SA34 0NH.
FN: Bysiau Cwm Taf / Taf Valley Coaches. **OC:** as address; The Garage, King Edward Street, Whitland, SA34 0AA; Waun Fach, Login, Whitland, SA34 0UX. **VA:** 30.
PG1022208/N: David Clive & Heather Rose Edwards, Penrheol, Ciffig, Whitland, Carmarthenshire, SA34 0NH.
FN: Bysiau Cwm Taf / Taf Valley Coaches. **OC:** as address. **VA:** 4.

	Reg									
	ENZ 7605	Ds	Jv	SFD741BR54GJ22518	Pn	0512GRX5906	C53F	-/05	Unknown MoD Contractor (MoD)	10/15
			(ex YU 05 ZKX 11/15, HV 05 AYG 10/15)							
	VIL 8705	Ds	Jv	SFD721BR3TGJ31786	Bf	3266	C70F	10/97	Johnson, Hodthorpe (DE)	8/04
			(ex R118 OEB 8/11, ESU 307 12/02)							

BYSIAU CWM TAF, WHITLAND (continued)

XAE 695	Sca	K94IB	YS2K4X20001848889	Ir	151503	C70F	1/05	Go-Goodwins, Eccles (GM)	9/13
		(ex YN 54 OCG 10/13)							
279 NDE	Vo	B10M-62	YV31MA61X1A053106	Pn	0112VUL3871	C53F	1/02	Hedingham (EX) L323	10/09
		(ex EK 51 JBE 3/10)							
E 14 TAF	MB	O816D	WDB6703742N135484	Sit	2497	C29F	6/10	Williams, Brecon (CW)	9/15
		(ex WA 10 CFO 8/16)							
E 16 TAF	Vo	B9R	YV3S5P727DA160548	Pn	CP37/05	C49FT	5/13	Logan, Dunloy (EI)	3/16
		(ex YN 13 GXE 3/16)							
w N543 SJF	Vo	B10M-62	YV31M2B1XTA045179	Je	24030	C53F	5/96	Clarke, Lower Sydenham (LN)	6/06
		(ex N 50 TAF 8/16, N543 SJF 2/07)							
N 50 TAF	Ds	Jv	SFD741BR54GJ22550	Pn	0512GHRX6207	C53F	8/05	Unknown MoD	
		(ex YU 05 ZKW 8/16, FY 05 GXD 9/15)						Contractor (MoD)	4/16
T 5 TAF	MB	311CDI	WDB9036632R172672	?		M16	10/00	Bevan, Cwmrhydyceirw (CW)	12/14
		(ex X371 DKF 12/14, T 7 WYS 7/14, X371 DKV 4/10)							
Y619 GFM	Ds	Dt SLF	SFD322BR1YGW14974	Ml	C39.659	B41F	3/01	Silcox,	
								Pembroke Dock (CW) 47	7/16
Y551 XAG	Ds	Dt SLF	SFD212AR11GW25770	Pn	0110.1HJB4117	B30D	7/01	London United (LN) DPS551	6/13
MX 53 ZWD	MB	O814D	WDB6703732N111952	Onyx	639	C24F	12/03	Hicks, Drefach (CW)	2/13
YK 04 KWD	Oe	M1020	SAB19000000001540	Oe		B37F	7/04	Lloyd, Bagillt (CN)	6/16
YN 04 LXK	Oe	M950	SAB19000000001227	Oe		B33F	3/04	Lloyd, Bagillt (CN)	6/16
YN 04 XYW	Oe	M850	SAB19000000001464	Oe		B27F	4/04	Llew Jones, Llanrwst (CN)	12/15
YU 05 ZBG	Ds	Jv	SFD741BR55GJ22548	Pn	0512GRX6138	C53F	6/05	Unknown MoD	
		(ex BU 05 THZ 10/15)						Contractor (MoD)	10/15
BC 55 TAF	Vo	B9R	YV3S5M1228A129060	Pn	0812.3TFR7953	C57F	4/09	JAK, Keighley (WY)	6/14
		(ex YM 09 TOU 3/16, 09-MN-593 2/14)							
BC 06 TAF	Vo	B12B	YV3R8G1236A114314	Pn	0612TKT6613	C53FT	9/06	G-Line Holidays, Lytham (LA)	4/13
		(ex YN 56 DYT 5/13)							
BC 07 TAF	VW	Tr	WV2ZZZ7HZ8H153767	VW		M8	6/08	Edwards, Llantwit Fardre (CC)	4/14
		(ex CP 08 NFN 8/16)							
BC 57 TAF	Vo	B12B	YV3R8G1217A116922	Pn	0712TKT6889	C49FT	9/07	new	9/07
YJ 58 FFN	VDL	SB200	XMGDE02FS0H015868	Pn	0812LCA7722	B35F	9/08	Silcox, Pembroke Dock	
								(CW) 59	6/16
YM 09 TNZ	Vo	B9R	YV3S5M1279A129475	Pn	0812.3TFR7954	C70F	4/09	Matthews, Inniskeen (EI)	6/14
		(ex 09-MN-594 2/14)							
YN 10 FKW	MB	O816D	WDB6703742N139250	Pn	108.5MBJ8603	C33F	6/10	Evans, Milford Haven (CW)	9/13
BC 12 TAF	Vo	B9R	YV3S5P721CA152525	Pn	BP03/01	C49FT	4/12	new	4/12
YX 62 FDG	AD	E20D	SFD7E1AR6CGY13244	AD	C232/1	B39F	1/13	Alexander Dennis,	
								Guildford (Qd)	11/13
BC 13 TAF	VDL	FHD2 129.365	XNL501E100D002427	VDL		C??F	7/13	new	7/13
YX 14 RZE	AD	E20D	SFD1D1AR6DGY14143	AD	D258/4	B29F	6/14	Mid Wales, Penrhyncoch (CW)	6/16
BC 15 TAF	VDL	FHD2 129.365	XNL501E100D004334	VDL		C55FT	5/15	new	5/15
BC 66 TAF	Vo	B8R	YV3T7U520GA175364	Pn	FL13/01	C59F	9/16	new	9/16

PG1061595/R: CSA Site Services Limited, Unit 2, Llanelli Gate, DAFEN, Llanelli, Carmarthenshire, SA14 8LQ.
FN: CSA Recruitment. OCs: as address; Merc Tech Limited, 138 Heol Y Gors, Cwmbwrla, Swansea, SA5 8LT;
Ty Alban, Palace Avenue, Llanelli, SA15 1NA. VA: 2.

OO 03 CSA	Fd	Tt	WF0TXXTTPT4D05080	Fd	M??	9/04	-?-, -?-	6/12
		(ex WX 54 BFA 7/12)						
OO 54 CSA	Fd	Tt	WF0DXXTTFD9D14588	Fd	M16	3/10	Day's Rental, Swansea (YCW)	8/12
		(ex CV 10 KLS 8/12)						
x OO 05 CSA	MB	111CDI	WDF63960323288922	MB	M5	11/06	private owner	6/09
		(ex FV 56 GWA 8/09)						
x OO 06 CSA	MB	111CDI	WDF63960323237406	MB	M5	5/06	private owner	7/09
		(ex KD 06 UER 7/09)						
EJ 09 MXY	Fd	Tt	WF0DXXTTFD9B15508	Fd	M16	7/09	-?-, -?-	3/14

PG1125880/N: CALL A CAB (Carmarthenshire) Limited, 58 Maesyfelin, PONTYBEREM, Llanelli, Carmarthenshire, SA15 5ET. OC: Oakfield Garage, Llannon Road, Pontyberem, Llanelli, SA15 5NB; Brook Garage, Clifton Street, Laugharne, Carmarthen, Carmarthenshire, SA33 5DR. VA: 10.

w	YEZ 6636	MAN	11.220	WMAA469229G113867	Bf	3251	C33FT	6/97	Laser Minicoach, Llanharry (CC)	2/11
			(ex P103 CCK 10/09, P 5 HWD by11/01)							
x	K 11 NTJ	Pt	Bxr	VF3ZAAMFA17522339	Pt		M8	12/05	private owner	c8/13
	T529 EUB	Vo	B10M-62	YV31MA613XC061125	Pn	9912VUP0529	C48FT	4/99	Laser Minicoach, Llanharry (CC)	4/14
			(ex WSU 873 by10/05, T529 EUB 4/03)							
	T936 KEC	MB	O814D	WDB6703742N076486	Pn	988.5MZE9662	C33F	4/99	Chris Cars, Carmarthen (CW)	2/15
			(ex B 13 MPB 8/13, T936 KEC 9/09)							
w	W488 EOL	MB	614D	WDB6683532N087763	Crest	M560	C24F	5/00	Jenkins, Pontypool (CS)	3/12
	W347 VOD	MAN	13.220	WMAA530263G134986	Bf	3907	C41F	4/00	Easyway, Pencoed (CC)	8/13
	LK 03 GXX	Io	50C13	ZCFC5090005415742	Me	3816	M16L	4/03	Westfield Community Centre, Hinckley (XLE)	3/14
			(ex GO 03 WMS 10/08, LK 03 GXK 8/07)							
x	OY 03 EJA	MB	313CDI	WDB9036622R495063	AVB		M8	5/03	Kate Williams, Carmarthen (XCW)	11/11
	RG 53 GXA	MB	614D	WDB6683532N105888	Crest	-?-	C24F	10/03	Clarke, Biddenden (KT)	12/13
			(ex W 29 WJW 11/13)							
	FH 05 OYE	Io	50C13	ZCFC5090005528208	Me	12230	B16FL	8/05	Shropshire Council, Shrewsbury (SH) N4232	1/14
	BT 06 RBV	VW	LT35	WV1ZZZ2DZ6H035531	?		M16	8/06	PFB Self Drive, Birmingham (YWM)	12/08
	GN 56 LVD	LDV	Max	SEYL6PFB20N210604	?		M11	12/06	Patient Transport Services, London (XLN)	8/14
	CN 08 CVS	Rt	Mtr	VF1NDD1L638611631	Rt/Tawe		M16	4/08	Homeward Bound, Winterbourne (DT)	3/15

PG1144882/R: Ann-Marie CARROLL, Tyrddol, CENARTH, Newcastle Emlyn, Carmarthenshire, SA38 9JU. FN: AMC Travel. OC: as address. VA: 1.

No vehicles yet recorded.

PG0005006/I: CASTLE Garage Limited, Market Square, LLANDOVERY, Carmarthenshire, SA20 0AA. OCs: High Street, Llandovery, Carmarthenshire, SA20 0AA; Bridge Street Depot, Llandovery, Carmarthenshire, SA20 0AA. VA: 24.

w	JIL 8032	MB	811D	WDB6703032N020532	WS	4561/94	B31F	8/94	Wren, Carlin How (CD)	8/04
			(ex M983 CYS 8/04)							
w	NIL 9367	MB	814D	WDB6703132N042991	Pn	968.5MMY5175	C33F	8/97	Rojay, Wigan (GM)	4/14
			(ex R738 EGD 5/11)							
w	E327 NTC	MB	811D	WDB67030320865795	RH	11170	C29F	3/88	Marksman, Gatwick (WS)	12/9
			(ex DJ 8143 5/09, 100 OX 8/06, E992 JLF 2/94, WET 342 1/90, E499 JLK 1/89)							
w	L190 MAU	MB	811D	WDB6703032N014142	Do	52553 634 93	DP33F	8/93	Compass, Worthing (WS)	5/0
			(ex UTH 1S 9/08, L190 MAU 5/04)							
w	P570 APJ	MB	709D	WDB6690032N042941	PN	967.6MHV5988	B27F	9/96	Stephenson, Tholthorpe (NY) 2705	2/1
	P690 HND	MB	O814D	WDB6703742N053159	Pn	9785MXV6846	DP33FL	4/97	Codling, Hartlepool (CD)	10/1
w	R892 SHY	Fd	Tt	WF0LXXBDVLVK86503	May		M16	3/98	-?-, -?-	10/0
			(ex K 4 DAF 9/10, R892 SHY 10/04)							
	T433 EBD	MB	O814D	WDB6703742N081991	Pn	988.5MXV1119	B29F	3/99	Collins, Roch (CW)	1/1
z	T 91 JBA	MB	O814D	WDB6703742N080335	Pn	988.5MXV0666	B31F	3/99	GHA, Ruabon (CN) 1011	6/1
w	V116 GWP	MB	O814D	WDB6703732N085866	Onyx	377	C24F	7/99	Parnell, Dunkeswell (DN)	8/0
	Y 83 PAE	MB	108CDI	VSA63819423371094	?		M8	3/01	private owner	12/0
	Y129 TBF	MB	O814D	WDB6703742N090625	Pn	008.5MXV2822	B31F	4/01	Pickford, Chippenham (WI)	7/1
x	NX 51 ZZS	MB	110CDI	VSA63819423391528	MB		M8	10/01	-?-, -?-	7/1
	BD 02 SVA	LDV	Cy	SEYZMVSYGDN087155	?		M16	7/02	-?-, -?-	12/1
	BU 02 XPL	LDV	Cy	SEYZMVSYGDN085953	LDV		M16	5/02	-?-, -?-	8/0
	CX 02 EBU	MB	O814D	WDB6703742N103711	Pn	028.5MAV4604	B33F	6/02	Evans, Tregaron (CW)	8/1
	HJ 02 OPU	LDV	Cy	SEYZMVSYGDN082388	LDV		M16	4/02	U-Drive, Bournemouth (XDT)	8/0
w	RY 02 XMP	LDV	Cy	SEYZMVSYGDN087839	LDV		M16	7/02	Burnt Tree, Harlescott (XSH)	8/0
	FH 52 ETO	Io	65C15	ZCFC65A0005367657	TransLinc		B20FL	1/03	Essential Fleet, Lincoln (LI) 073.250	6/1

CASTLE, LLANDOVERY (continued)

	Reg			Chassis		Body			Date	History	
	SL 52 BBX	MB	O814D	WDB6703732N105987	Leinster		C24F		10/02	Thomas, Lee (LN)	2/16
w	YP 52 DWW	LDV	Cy	SEYZLWSYGDN090118	LDV		M8		12/02	-?-, -?-	12/13
z	WX 03 JDK	MB	413CDI	WDB9046122R482946	UVM -?-		B16FL		4/03	Bristol City, Brislington (XGL) 481/54	9/16
	DC 53 EYK	Fd	Tt	WF0TXXGBFT3P66164	Fd		M8		1/04	-?-, -?-	8/14
	KR 53 WHG	LDV	Cy	SEYZMVSZGDN101367	LDV		M16		2/04	Lawson, Corby (NO)	1/13
	YJ 53 WMV	LDV	Cy	SEYZMVSYGDN098799	LDV		M16		2/04	Williams K, St Georges (SH)	12/12
	KE 04 JVH	MB	413CDI	WDB9046122R623364	UVM 9773		B16FL		8/04	Go Ride, Brightlingsea (XEX)	6/16
	AE 54 POJ	LDV	Cy	SEYZMVSZGDN108818	LDV		M16		12/04	Turner, Edgware (LN)	4/13
z	FJ 54 LOD	Io	50C13	ZCFC5090005432192	O&H -?-		M16L		9/04	Church Stretton Area Ring & Ride (XSH) N1761	10/16
	CU 05 FYX	LDV	Cy	SEYZMVSZGDN110796	LDV		M16		5/05	Neath Port Talbot Council (XCC) FM28	by7/14
	CU 05 HPZ	Io	50C13	ZCFC5090005527956	?		B16FL		9/05	Neath Port Talbot Council (XCC) 209	6/16
z	CN 55 NKM	MB	411CDI	WDB9046122R893719	UVM -?-		B15FL		2/06	Carmarthenshire Council (XCW) 766047	6/16
	HX 55 ADU	Fd	Tt	WF0VXXBDFV5R51785	?		M8L		11/05	-?-, -?-	7/13
z	BX 06 JXW	MB	O814D	WDB6703732N121697	Me 4284		B16F		3/06	Sandwell Metropolitan Borough Council (XWM) BS170	1/16
	MV 06 KTL	Fd	Tt	WF0VXXBDFV6Y07111	?		M5L		7/06	-?-, -?-	1/13
z	AV 11 LKF	Fd	Tt	WF0BXXBDFBBD04822	Fd		M8		5/11	-?-, -?-	5/16
x	YB 12 UOK	Fd	Tt	WF0BXXBDFBCK40172	Fd		M8		7/12	-?-, -?-	1/16

PG1129715/I: CELTIC TRAVEL (Llanidloes) Limited, New Street, LLANIDLOES, Powys, SY18 6EH.
OC: as address; Unit 1 Parc Hafren Industrial Estate, Llanidloes, SY18 6RB; Mount Lane Car Park, Mount Lane, Llanidloes, SY18 6EY; Coach Parking Ground, Smithfield Market Site, Llanidloes, SY18 6DY; Pant Garage, Staylittle, Llanbrynmair, SY19 7BU. VA: 37.

	Reg			Chassis			Body			Date	History	
w	NJI 4736	Ld	TRCTL11/3RZ	8500524	Du	8590/0040		C70F		4/86	G&A, Trethomas (CS)	8/03
w	RJI 8603	Vo	B10M-60	YV31MGD1XKA021523	Pn	8912VCB1184		C53F		4/89	Warren, Neath (CC)	10/02
			(ex C911 FMP 1/94)									
w	TJI 1684	Vo	B10M-61	YV3B10M6100007121	Pn	8512VPP2C031		C55F		2/85	Moore, Sturminster Newton (DT)	6/03
			(ex B250 NUT 2/95)									
	349 LVO	Ld	PD2/40	573387	PR	B33335		O27/28R		7/58	Mac Tours (SS) 21	8/09
			(ex TRN 662A 12/10, LST 873 2/09, TRN 662A 9/91, CEO 952 c4/86)									
w	A646 GLD	Vo	B10M-61	YV3B10M6100004183	Pn	8312VTP1C013		C51F		7/84	Moore, Sturminster Newton (DT)	6/03
w	A606 UGD	Vo	B10M-61	YV3B10M6100005865	VH	11053		C70F		1/84	Park, Hamilton (SW)	5/88
w	F377 MCA	Vo	B10M-60	YV31MGD10KA020476	Pn	8912VCAP0829		C53F		4/89	Meredith, Malpas (CH)	6/00
			(ex WAW 367 5/00, F432 DUG by3/93)									
	H 73 DVM	Vo	B10M-50	YV31MGC10MA026248	ArB	B32010191		B68F		2/91	Arriva Midlands North (ST) 3304	8/08
			(named Emma)									
w	J215 NNC	Vo	B10M-60	YV31MGD18MA027601	VH	30908		C53F		1/92	National Holidays Coaches (EY) 90	3/02
			(ex 349 LVO 12/10, J215 NNC 3/08)									
w	J 52 SNY	Ld	TRCL10/3ARZM	TR00869	Pn	9012LCJ2334		C70F		8/91	Perry, Bromyard (HR) 162	8/03
			(ex J222 BUS 7/03, J 52 SNY 11/01)									
	L 66 CEL	Ds	Jv	10SDA2156/1168	WS	4730/95		C46F		3/95	Skills, Nottingham (NG) 56	10/09
			(ex M631 VRB 10/09, PUJ 925 9/09, M631 VRB 10/05, -?-, 11/03, 27 AY 77 by9/03)									
x	L 88 CEL	Vx	Viv	W0LF7BCA63V616192	Vx			M8		3/03	Action Cars, Pontefract (YWY)	6/09
			(ex BV 03 HWR 7/09, A 2 BHU by6/09, BV 03 HWR by5/09)									
	L222 CEL	Vo	B10M-62	YV31M2B14TA044397	VH	32525		C53F		1/96	Saxon, Stainforth (SY)	9/12
			(ex N715 UVR 7/13, 226 LRB 8/08, N715 UVR by3/04)									
	L333 CEL	Vo	B10M-62	YV31M2B19RA040919	VH	31837		C57F		5/94	Bysiau Cwm Taf, Whitland (CW)	8/12
			(ex L705 PHE 7/13, ENZ 7605 8/12, L705 PHE 9/04)									
	L555 CEL	Rt	Mtr	VF1FDCUM633013807	Tawe			M16		8/05	Mistry, Leicester (LE)	5/07
			(ex DX 05 GEJ 2/09)									
	N887 HSX	Ds	Jv	12SDA2157L/1290	WS	4963/95		C70F		9/95	New Adventure Travel, Cardiff (CC)	10/14
			(ex BHZ 9542 8/10, N887 HSX 4/05, EC 57 AA 8/04, M352 LBC by8/03, EC 57 AA by12/01)									
w	P350 JND	Vo	B6RLE	YV3R3A919VC006161	Ar	9613/41		B36F		3/97	Bysiau Cwm Taf, Whitland (CW)	7/12

CELTIC TRAVEL, LLANIDLOES (continued)

	Reg			Chassis No			Body	Date	Owner	
w	P236 WHB	Fd	Tt	WF0EXXBDVEVP48833	Fd		M8	by7/97	private owner	4/00
xw	R301 WSD	Fd	Tt	SFAEXXBDVEVC80957	Fd		M8	11/97	Jones, Llanidloes (CW)	10/06
	T 32 JBA	MB	O814D	WDB6703732N081031	Pn	998.5MXV0579	B31F	4/99	Travel Wright, Newark on Trent (NG) SL1	9/12
w	V 20 PJC	MB	O814D	WDB6703732N083610	Pn	998.5MXV1229	B31F	9/99	C&R Travel, Abertillery (CS)	4/13
	(ex V992 DNB by4/00)									
	Y235 BAW	Ds	Jv	SFD721BR4YGJ22325	Pn	0012GFM2910	C57F	-/01	Silcox, Pembroke Dock (CW) 243	7/16
	(ex ???? ??? 9/13)									
	Y863 TGH	Ds	Dt SLF	SFD112AR11GW15576	Pn	019.3HEB3789	B29F	3/01	Doyle, Alfreton (DE)	7/14
	Y252 YSO	Ds	Jv	SFD721BR4YGJ22323	Pn	0012GFM2908	C57F	by8/01	Lex (MoD)	6/14
	LL 52 CEL	Vo	B12M	YV3R9F8173A000784	Pn	0212TJT4735	C53F	10/02	First Devon & Cornwall (DN) 20532	6/10
	(ex WV 52 HVF 10/10, WV 52 HVE 12/02)									
	HJ 03 KVM	Vx	Mov	VN1F9CML528101766	?		M16	3/03	private owner	5/07
	LL 53 CEL	Ds	Jv	12SDA2152/1172	WS	4719/95	C70F	3/95	Fleet Support, Portsmouth (HA) 1/04	
	(ex M772 XHW 10/10, 16 RN 60 1/04, M516 LWN 11/03, 16 RN 60 by1/04)									
	NA 53 BZF	Fd	Tt	WF0EXXGBFE3S32868	Fd		M16	9/03	-?-, -?-	9/07
w	LL 04 CEL	Ds	Jv	12SDA2157L/1127	WS	4701/94	C70F	1/95	MoD (X)	9/04
	(ex M239 XWS 7/13, CX 63 AA 9/04, M116 LBC 5/04, CX 63 AA by7/01)									
	CN 54 HFB	Oe	M990	SAB19000000001557	Oe		B35F	9/04	Anslow, Garndiffaith (CS)	4/16
w	EY 54 NXJ	Fd	Tt	WF0PXXBDFP4C65673	Fd		M8L	9/04	Group Taxibus, Chelmsford (EX) 44	8/07
	BX 05 FFC	AD	Env	SFD213AR15GG10146	AD	5302/1	B52F	7/05	Go-Goodwins, Eccles (GM)	6/11
	NA 55 XFT	Fd	Tt	WF0EXXTTFE5A52563	Fd		M16	10/05	-?-, -?-	9/08
	CT 06 EBT	Vo	B12M	YV3R9G1256A111623	Pn	0612.8TZL6385	C50FT	3/06	Brown, Thorp Arch (WY)	3/15
	DT 06 EBT	Vo	B12M	YV3R9G1276A111624	Pn	0612.8TZL6386	C50FT	3/06	Brown, Thorp Arch (WY)	3/15
x	BD 56 ONR	Rt	Tc	VF1FLGHA66V278886	Rt		M5	12/06	-?-, -?-	by6/14
	YN 07 EXU	Sca	K114IB4	YS2K4X20001856890	Ir	103570	C49FT	7/07	Williams, Brecon (CW)	9/13
x	BV 57 UBE	LDV	Max	SEYL6P6B20N211464	LDV		M14	9/07	new	9/07
x	KD 57 FHX	Vx	Viv	W0LJ7BHB68V603661	Vx		M8	9/07	Mar Taxis, Mansfield (YNG)	9/13
x	PK 57 YYA	Rt	Tc	VF1JLBHB68V309811	Rt		M8	10/07	M&S Airport Transfers, Wyre (X??)	8/12
	YN 57 MBX	MB	O816D	WDB6703742N128998	Pn	078.5MBJ7359	C20FT	10/07	Logan, Dunloy (NI)	4/12
x	SB 08 BSO	Rt	Tc	VF1JLAHA68V324959	Rt		M8	5/08	Lex Leasing (Y)	9/11
	YN 09 HRD	Vo	B12BT	YV3R8M9269A132765	Pn	0914TAA8211	C52FT	4/09	Logan, Dunloy (NI)	9/12
	LL 60 CEL	Vo	B9R	YV3S5P725BA144510	Pn	1012.8SAZ8747	C53FT	1/11	new	1/11
	(named *Marymair*)									
x	NX 60 UNZ	Rt	Tc	VF1FLBHA6AV389801	?		M8	9/10	-?-, -?-	9/13
x	DS 11 AXC	Fd	Tt	WF0BXXBDFBAG87539	Fd		M8	4/11	Day's Rental, Swansea (YCW)	9/13
	BG 61 SXV	Vo	B7RLE	YV3R6R625CA153170	Wt	AG948	B44F	1/12	new	1/12
	BG 61 SXW	Vo	B7RLE	YV3R6R629CA153186	Wt	AG949	B44F	1/12	new	1/12
	BG 61 SXX	Vo	B7RLE	YV3R6R627CA153445	Wt	AG950	B44F	1/12	new	1/12
x	DE 61 GZB	Vx	Viv	W0LJ7BHBSBV657185	Vx		M8	9/11	-?-, -?-	5/16
x	BD 62 AUN	Vx	Viv	W0LJ7B7BSCV645756	Vx		M8	11/12	new	11/12
	CU 13 AEM	Wt	StLt WF	SA9DSRXXX13141229	Wt	AH661	B37F	7/13	new	7/13
	CU 13 AEO	Wt	StLt WF	SA9DSRXXX13141230	Wt	AH662	B37F	7/13	new	7/13
	LL 16 CEL	Ytg	ZK6938HQ	LZYTCTE67F1069360	Ytg		C35F	7/16	new	7/16
	LL 66 CEL	Ytg	ZK6938HQ	LZYTCTE65G1027027	Ytg		C35F	11/16	new	11/16

PG1105601/I: CERBYDAU CENARTH Cyf, The Workshop, CENARTH, Newcastle Emlyn, Carmarthenshire, SA38 9JP.
OC: as address. VA: 23.

Reg			Chassis No			Body	Date	Owner	
JIG 6713	Ds	R405	SFD152BR11GC10163	Co	FN13043031	C49FT	4/04	Premiere, Nottingham (NG) 953	9/12
(ex FN 04 FSG 10/12)									
LUI 8320	MB	O814D	WDB6703532N065385	ACl	1490	C24F	4/98	Burrows, Chasetown (ST)	10/13
(ex R 8 HCT 10/13, R908 EDO 4/01)									
RIG 2717	MB	O814D	WDB6703742N098402	ACl	1795	C25F	10/01	Hughes, Widnes (CH)	8/16
(ex FX 51 BVF 3/16, K200 RAP 12/15, FX 51 BVF 5/12)									
SUI 8105	DAF	SB3000	XMGDE33WS0H005585	Pn	9712DSP6448	C55F	5/97	Watts, Bonvilston (CC)	2/07
(ex P169 RWR 12/10)									
SUI 8106	Ds	Jv	SFD321BR4VGJ42093	Bf	3652	C54F	8/98	Reynolds, Maerdy (CC)	12/05
(ex S218 AWP 12/10, S 3 BUS 6/03, S 1 BUS 6/03, S 3 BUS 6/00)									

CERBYDAU CENARTH, CENARTH (continued)

	Reg	Make	Model	Chassis	Body	BodyNo	Seats	Date	Previous owner	Date
	UIJ 412	Ds	Jv	11SDL2133/903	Pn	9311HZM1457	C47F	1/94	Orkney Coaches (SN) 59153	12/09
			(ex L153 BFV 4/05)							
	WJZ 4093	Ka	S315GT-HD	WKK62725223000282	Ka		C49FT	1/06	Gaw, Stewarton (SW)	9/14
			(ex BX 55 FYV 12/14)							
	R 91 WFV	Ds	Jv	SFD721BR3VGJ31957	Co	758501	C70F	10/97	Holmeswood,	
			(ex R 3 HWD 10/04)						Holmeswood (LA)	9/07
w	T416 KAG	Ds	Dt SLF	SFD322AR1WGW12826	Pn	9810.7HLB0092	B39F	2/99	Premiere, Nottingham	
									(NG) 3316	10/11
	T101 XDE	Ds	Jv	SFD737BR4WGJ42155	Pn	9812GMP9752	C53F	5/99	Jones, Llanrwst (CN)	8/11
w	T102 XDE	Ds	Jv	SFD737BR4WGJ42215	Pn	9812GPM9753	C55F	5/99	Llew Jones, Llanrwst (CN)	10/11
	V630 EEJ	Rt	Mtr	VF1FDCCL521347226	Cym	-?-	M16	12/99	new	12/99
x	EJ 51 WGJ	Rt	Tc	VF1FLBCA62V115450	Cym	RT1250	M7L	1/02	new	1/02
	WJ 51 BUS	Fd	Tt	WF0XXXTTFX6A24196	?		M16L	3/07	converted from a van	6/15
			(ex BN 07 ONV 11/15)							
	YM 51 WGK	Ds	Jv	SFD721BR41GJ22341	Pn	0212GFM4489	C55F	-/02	VT Aerospace (MoD)	1/14
			(ex AE 51 HHD 10/13)							
	KU 02 YBF	Ds	Dt SLF	SFD2B2CR31GW16262	SCC	4246/02	B??F	4/02	Olympus/SM Coaches,	
									Harlow (EX)	7/11
	FP 53 GWN	LDV	Cy	SEYZMVSZGDN101240	LDV		M16	12/03	Rafi, Findern (DE)	11/07
	CR 04 ABX	Ds	Jv	SFD741BR54GJ22507	Pn	0412GRX5653	C55F	9/04	Unknown MoD	
			(ex ?? ?? ??? 11/14)						Contractor (MoD)	c10/14
	CR 04 AUM	Ds	Jv	SFD741BR54GJ22508	Pn	0412GRX5654	C53F	-/04	Unknown MoD	
			(ex SJ 04 EOH 11/14)						Contractor (MoD)	by11/14
	AT 54 LCT	BMC	1100FE	NMC111TKCRD100001	BMC		B60F	9/04	Cushing & Littlewood, Acle (NK)	7/12
	YN 54 WCW	Ds	Jv	SFD741BR54GJ22517	Pn	0412GRX5678	C70F	10/04	PMP, Luton (BD)	8/11
	FL 05 ETO	Ft	Do	ZFA24400007500748	?		M8	3/05	Hemstock, Edenthorpe (SY)	9/07
x	CT 55 LHC	Fd	Tt	WF0TXXBDFT5D82085	Fd		M8	12/05	new	12/05
	HJ 55 MOU	Fd	Tt	WF0EXXTTFE5P00978	Fd		M16	9/05	-?-, -?-	5/15
	YJ 57 BSZ	Tmsa	Safari	NLTRHT87R01050010	Tmsa	0A02189	C57F	9/07	Brown, South Kirkby (WY)	12/16
	YN 08 FEK	MB	O816D	WDB6703742N127880	Ind	6572	C33F	3/08	Carr, Maghull (MY)	2/10
	BX 09 LLE	KL	XMQ6127	LA6R1HSJ68B102112	KL		C49FT	6/09	new	6/09
	YN 61 AWJ	AD	Jv	SFD765BR7AGJ22657	Pn	1012JBX8646	C70F	9/11	new	9/11
	YN 61 AWM	AD	Jv	SFD765BR7AGJ22658	Pn	1012JBX8647	C70F	9/11	new	9/11
	YG 65 ASU	Ytg	ZK6129HQ	LZYTMTF65E1034441	Ytg		C51FT	11/15	new	11/15

PG1095527/N: CHRIS CARS Limited, Station Approach, CARMARTHEN, Carmarthenshire, SA31 2BE.
FNs: Chris Cars Limited; Coracle Coaches of Carmarthen. OC: as address; Carmarthenshire Tyre, Alltycnap Road, Johnstown, Carmarthen, SA31 3RY. VA: 9.
PG1147391/I: CORACLE Coaches Limited, Station Approach, CARMARTHEN, Carmarthenshire, SA31 2BE.
OC: Carmarthen Athletic RFC, Athletic Park, Alltycnap Road, Johnstown, Carmarthen, SA31 3QY. VA: 3.

	Reg	Make	Model	Chassis	Body	BodyNo	Seats	Date	Previous owner	Date
	D 1 DUX	Vo	B12M	YV3R9F8152A000524	Bf	4482	C51FT	5/04	Bysiau Cwm Taf,	
			(ex CN 04 RHY 12/15, XAE 695 10/12, CN 04 RHY 3/12)						Whitland (CW)	3/14
	J 14 CCG	Vo	B12M	YV3R9F8132A000599	Pn	0212TJL4575	C70F	5/02	Morris Travel,	
			(ex FP 02 YDJ 6/09)						Carmarthen (CW)	7/16
	K 19 DUX	Ka	S415GT-HD	WKK63213123102061	Ka		C56FT	9/06	Bysiau Cwm Taf,	
			(ex AF 56 MMF 1/16, CB 55 TAF 12/14, AF 56 MMF 2/14)						Whitland (CW)	12/14
	K 20 DUX	Ibs	397E.12.31	ZGA7B2N000E001103	Pn	0412EBT5600	C49FT	3/05	Courtesy, Chadderton (GM)	11/13
			(ex YN 05 UUJ 12/15, M 77 YEL 10/12, YN 05 UUJ 3/12, T 4 JBT 3/11, YN 05 UUJ 3/10)							
	N209 HWX	Vo	B10M-62	YV31M2B12TC060134	Pn	9612VUP5040	C55F	4/96	Bysiau Cwm Taf,	
			(ex ENZ 7605 8/15, N209 HWX 8/13, N 60 CLC 10/12, YDL 435 3/09, N209 HWX 12/05,						Whitland (CW)	8/15
									B 19 GOO c6/04, N209 HWX 8/01)	
w	N230 HWX	Vo	B10M-62	YV31M2B12TC060103	Pn	9612VUP4751	C53F	3/96	Warren, Neath (CC)	4/10
	R161 LDE	Vo	B10M-62	YV31MA616WA048945	Pn	9812VUP8456	C49FT	3/98	Jones, Login (CW)	8/11
			(ex 834 TDE 8/11, R161 LDE 10/05)							
	R965 RCH	Vo	B10M-62	YV31MA610VA046137	Pn	9612VUP6026	C49FT	4/98	Bysiau Cwm Taf,	
									Whitland (CW)	10/15
	Y506 TGJ	Vo	B10M-62	YV31MA615YA051810	Pn	0012VUT2138	C57F	4/01	Bysiau Cwm Taf,	
									Whitland (CW)	7/13
	NE 04 FOF	Tbs	Jv	SFD741BR54GJ22500	Tbs	0412GRX5655	C53F	-/04	Unknown MoD	
			(ex SJ 04 EZV 10/14)						Contractor (MoD)	10/14

CHRIS CARS, Carmarthen (continued)

	AF 07 MMM	Ka	S415GT-HD	WKK63213123102852 Ka		C51FT	3/07 Isaac & Morgan,	
			(ex GM 03 BUS 9/16, AF 07 MMM 3/14)				Lampeter (CW)	10/16
x	DN 13 YFR	Vx	Viv	W0LJ7B7BSDV621729 Vx		M8	5/13 -?-, -?-	9/14

PG0006671/N: Peter John COMLEY, 25 Saron Road, CAPEL HENDRE, Carmarthenshire, SA18 3LG.
FN: Ammanford Bus Hire. OC: as address. VA: 5.

w	KLZ 3471	Vo	B10M-62	YV31M2B10RA041635 VH	31848	C53F	9/94 Davies, Llanelli (CW)		2/14
			(ex MIL 2979 1/11, E911 AFM 10/10, M 8 SKY 9/10)						
	LIB 2880	VW	LT46	WV1ZZZ2DZ2H031035 Me	3681	M16L	9/02 Ammanford Taxis,		
			(ex FN 52 XTV 7/10)				Ammanford (CW)		3/15
w	R505 UEC	MAN	11.220	WMA4692290G113852 Bf	3250	C35F	8/97 Hornsby, Ashby (LI) B56		2/06
			(ex 7455 RH by7/03, R505 UEC by5/02)						
	T141 LAF	MB	614D	WDB6683532N075604 ACl	1570	C24F	3/99 Courtney, Bracknell (BE)		2/06
			(ex T 2 CCL 1/06)						
	BD 51 UNK	Io	45C13	ZCFC459000D169892 Crest IV1201		M16L	1/02 Howorth, Bancffosfelen (CW)		11/11
	FD 53 UOB	MB	614D	WDB6683532N111845 Me	3930	B16FL	1/04 Bakewell Community Transport		
							(XDE) CT4	2/11	
w	VK 05 LNN	Fd	Tt	WF0EXXTTFE5U35166 Fd		M16	3/05 private owner		1/07
w	EK 57 DGZ	Fd	Tt	WF0DXXTTFD7Y08288 Fd		M16	10/07 -?-, -?-		11/08

PG1117790/I: COOKSON TRAVEL Limited, Hope Cottage, HOPE, Leighton, Welshpool, Powys SY21 8HF.
OC: as address. VA: 18.

w	FIL 4164	Ld	TRCTL11/3R	8301060 VH	11294	C57F	4/84 Beeston, Hadleigh (SK)		8/04
			(ex A143 RMJ 9/88)						
	FSU 803	Vo	B10M-61	YV3B10M6100007362 VH	11263	C53F	3/84 Dukes Travel, Berry Hill (GL)		6/02
			(ex A643 UGD 1/88)						
w	GDZ 885	Ld	TRCTL11/3RZ	8400985 VH	11766	C51F	3/85 MASS, Anston (SY)		4/05
			(ex B327 AMH 7/89)						
	JBZ 2078	DAF	MB200DKFL600	234130 VH	10876	C53F	4/83 Manoharan, Ramsgate (KT)		11/06
			(ex FNF 417Y 6/93)						
	JUI 5015	Vo	B10M-60	YV31MGD15LA023214 VH	14057	C53F	2/90 Avon Valley, Snitterfield (WK)		2/12
			(ex G383 RHR 6/99)						
	LUI 9375	MAN	16.290	WMA4702354W021917 Je	22886	C51FT	3/93 Jarvis, Aberaman (CC)		7/09
			(ex K217 CBD 5/02)						
	MIL 2034	Vo	B10M-60	YV31M2A1XMA025842 VH	30688	C57F	1/91 Lawson, Corby (NO)		8/13
			(ex H168 DVM by1/11, IIL 7077 by3/10, H168 DVM 5/00)						
	MUI 7828	Vo	B10M-61	YV3B10M6100007479 VH	11331	C53F	4/84 Godward, South Woodham		
			(ex A 37 DTV 3/03)				Ferrers (EX)		2/03
	REZ 5216	Vo	B10M-61	YV31MGD19HA013583 VH	12601	C70F	2/87 Warrington Coachways,		
			(ex D546 MVR 8/08, 15 RED 3/08, D546 MVR 9/02, WNR 63 1/00, D546 MVR 2/92)				Warrington (CH)		8/10
w	RJI 2717	DAF	MB200DKTL600	224008 VH	10608	C53F	5/82 Fellows, Bradley (WM)		4/04
			(ex HAS 914X 6/93, 318 DHR 3/90, XJS 971X 7/84, 279 AUF 6/84, XJS 971X by4/84)						
w	RJI 2722	DAF	MB200DKVL600	243016 Du	8462/0430	C49FT	2/85 Red Dragon, Newtown (CW)		c10/07
			(ex B999 YFR 9/93)						
	TUI 3639	Vo	B10M-62	YV31M2B13SA043711 VH	32268	C53F	3/96 Skill, Nottingham (NG) 42		11/05
			(ex N499 PYS 2/12, A 3 HEX by1/12, SIL 9542 11/06, N499 PYS 7/00, KSK 984 11/98)						
	WDZ 4127	Ld	TRCTL11/3R	8301042 VH	11532	C57F	9/84 Aldershot Coaches,		
			(ex B 88 AMH 3/97)				Aldershot (HA)		4/04
z	WJI 1721	Vo	B10M-46	YV31MGC11JA018350 Pn	889.5VNP3C004	C39F	8/88 Hamer, Newtown (CW)		12/12
			(ex F 30 NLE 2/98)						
	WSV 418	Ld	TRCTL11/3RZ	8400412 VH	11771	C55F	3/85 Three C's, Nedging Tye (SK)		3/10
			(ex B379 FHK 4/03, 436 VVT 9/96, B551 VWT 5/95)						
	XIL 3680	Vo	B10M-60	YV31MGD12LS025688 VH	30465	C70F	3/92 Kinch, Minety (WI)		1/13
			(ex J867 JNS 8/03)						
	757 FFR	Vo	B10M-62	YV31M2B1XSA041941 VH	32071	C46FT	2/95 Cape, Lane End (BK)		7/14
			(ex 5202 AD 9/12, M260 TRJ 7/11, BSV 216 6/11, M260 TRJ 12/08, 3402 FM by5/05, M666 KVU 6/01,						
							M260 TRJ by1/01, SPR 35 by12/00)		
	317 LDV	Vo	B10M-61	YV3B10M6100009620 VH	11862	C53F	8/85 Leon, Stafford (ST)		7/07
			(ex C334 FSU 12/88)						

COOKSON TRAVEL, HOPE (continued)

z	C674 BCR	Ld	TRCTL11/3R	8301420	VH	11534	C53F	2/86 Watkins, Cefn Coch (CW)	by9/13
			(ex SEL 813 by12/02, C674 BCR 7/87)						
	H175 DVM	Vo	B10M-60	YV31M2A16MA025899	VH	30695	C70F	1/91 Premier, Blyth (ND) 13	1/15
			(ex 16 RED 9/07, H175 DVM 4/05, NIL 6342 by12/04, H175 DVM 6/97)						
w	J432 NCP	DAF	SB2305DHS585	XLRDE23HS0E332336	VH	30524	C55F	6/92 Scottish Borders Council (XSS)	8/05
	M105 PRS	MAN	11.190	WMA4691558G091012	Co	459001	C33F	9/94 Crute, Gobowen (SH)	6/11
			(ex A 14 PSV 8/10, M105 PRS 3/08, AIG 9403 6/07, M105 PRS 5/06)						
	P966 DNR	Ta	BB50R	TW043BB5000001046	Co	651135	C21F	5/97 Hewens, Laugharne (CW)	11/07
	P647 RND	Vo	B10M-62	YV31M2B16TA045311	VH	32621	C53F	8/96 Wheeler, Kendal (CA)	3/15
			(ex J 55 SOM 5/06, C 9 SOM 12/05, P314 UBD 8/04, OFE 486 by7/03, P169 OBD -/??,						
								N 85 DVV by1/02, L 1 ONC	8/00)
	R946 YNF	Vo	B10M-62	YV31MA616WC060808	Je	24799	C51FT	4/98 Goodsir & Hughes,	
			(ex 102 UTF 7/12, R946 YNF 7/07)					Holyhead (CN)	3/13
	T113 JBA	Vo	B10M-62	YV31MA611XC061060	VH	33515	C53F	3/99 Snowdon,	
								Easington Colliery (DM)	9/13
	FE 52 HFP	Io	CC80.E18M/P	SBCA80D0002351687	Ind	4586	C29F	10/02 Young, Romsley (WO)	4/16
			(ex M 50 MCT 6/09, FE 52 HFP 8/07)						
w	VU 05 XLJ	Fd	Tt	WF0EXXTTFE5J15028	Fd		M14	3/05 -?-, -?-	1/10
	CN 55 ZYW	Fd	Tt	WF0EXXTTFE5K15203	Fd		M16	11/05 -?-, -?-	2/09
	DV 55 APU	Fd	Tt	WF0EXXTTFE5K21087	Fd		M16	12/05 Staffordshire County Council	
								(XST) Q6029	3/15

**PG1147391/I: CORACLE Coaches Limited, Station Approach, CARMARTHEN, Carmarthenshire, SA31 2BE.
OC: Carmarthen Athletic RFC, Athletic Park, Alltycnap Road, Johnstown, Carmarthen, SA31 3QY. VA: 3.**

See combined entry under PG1095527/N: Chris Cars, Carmarthen (page 15).

**PG1097035/R: Robert W CROOK, 24 Pine Crescent, Clasemont, MORRISTON, Swansea, SA6 6AR.
FN: Wilcox Mini Travel. OC: as address. VA: 1.**

CP 10 JUH	Fd	Tt	WF0DXXTTFDAT14496	Fd	M16	6/10 Day's Rental, Swansea (YCW)	9/13

**PG1068365/R: Stephen CUTAJAR, 105A Penfilia Road, BRYNHYFRYD, Swansea, SA5 9HT.
FN: Swallow Travel. OC: 19 High Street, Gorseinon, Swansea SA4 4BX. VA: 2.**

xw	BD 52 WEJ	MB	110CDI	WDF63809423504125 Jubilee	M8	1/03 -?- (taxi), Swansea (YCW)	8/08
	EO 52 VGT	Fd	Tt	WF0EXXGBFE2B26118 Fd	M14	11/02 Houlihan, Swansea (CW)	8/13
	SA 04 BUS	Fd	Tt	WF0EXXTTFE5M55474 Fd	M16	3/05 Lewis, Tirdeunaw (CW)	9/13
			(ex CP 05 AEE 11/13, X 2 BUS 9/13, CP 05 AEE 2/07)				
	EX 07 OAJ	Fd	Tt	WF0DXXTTFD7L66874 Fd	M16	7/07 -?-, -?-	4/14
x	MF 07 TXW	Fd	Tt	WF0SXXBDFS6R56975 Fd	M8	3/07 -?-, -?-	6/13
	WG 07 XWO	Fd	Tt	WF0DXXTTFD7E41585 Fd	M16	7/07 Llanrhidian Parks,	
						Gower (XCW)	1/14
	YE 62 EOO	Fd	Tt	WF0BXXBDFBCE44516 Fd	M8	10/12 new	10/12

**PG1049614/I: CYMRU COACHES Limited, Suites 1 – 4 Prospect Park, Queensway, Swansea West Industrial Park,
FFORESTFACH, Swansea, SA5 4ED. OC: as address. VA: 26.**

w	AIG 7943	Sca	N113DRB	YS4ND4X2B01833002	EL	27610	H47/31F	11/99 Veolia Cymru (CC) 65005	6/11
			(ex V307 EAK 10/05)						
w	JUI 7461	DAF	SB3000	XMGDE33WS0H004257	VH	31958	C51F	3/95 Taylor, Barrow-on-Soar (LE)	5/09
			(ex A 7 UOD 2/02, JUI 7461 1/01, M736 RCP 8/99)						
	B 12 CYM	Vo	B12BT	YV3R8L2267A117992	Je	27913	C49FT	3/07 Procter, Leeming Bar (NY)	8/13
			(ex FJ 07 AEA 3/15, OIA 419 6/13, FJ 07 AEA 3/11)						
	C 12 CYM	Vo	B12M	YV3R9G1144A011887	Ssd	B-2934	C53F	5/05 -?-, -?-	11/05
			(ex FJ 05 APK 3/15)						
	C 14 CYM	Vo	B12BT	YV3R8L2297A118330	Je	27915	C57FT	3/07 Procter, Leeming Bar (NY)	8/14
			(ex FJ 07 AEC 3/15, 904 YUF 4/13, FJ 07 AEC 1/12)						
	R555 GSM	Vo	B10M-62	YV31MA617VA046488	Co	658098	C70F	10/97 Mayne, Buckie (SN)	5/09
	V810 EFB	Vo	B6BLE	YV3R3A913XC010063	Wt	B283	B36F	10/99 First South West (CO) 48210	11/15

CYMRU COACHES, FFORESTFACH (continued)

	Reg		Type	Chassis	Body	Seats			Previous owner	Date
z	W811 PFB	Vo	B6BLE-55	YV3R3A913YC010162 Wt	B554		B36F	3/00	First South West (CO) 48211	12/15
	W831 PFB	Vo	B6BLE-55	YV3R3A914YC010199 Wt	B572		B35F	5/00	First South West (CO) 48231	12/15
	YN 51 MKF	Sca	L94IB	YS4L4X20001838230 Ir	94078		C72F	9/01	Veolia Cymru (CC) 74030	6/11
	LG 02 KHO	Vo	B7TL	YV3S2G5132A002062 Wt	F15		H41/22D	5/02	London General (LN) WVL15	5/02
	LG 02 KHR	Vo	B7TL	YV3S2G5192A002079 Wt	F17		H41/22D	5/02	London General (LN) WVL17	5/02
w	CP 03 YSG	Fd	Tt	WF0EXXGBFE3Y08741 Fd			M16	7/03	Day's Rental, Swansea (YCW)	9/06
	YV 03 YVF	MB	O814D	WDB6703742N108598 Pn	038.5MAE5037		C33F	5/03	Mills, Kilpin (EY)	1/11
				(ex 03-KK-2537 by9/08)						
	YN 04 GLF	Sca	K114IB4	YS2K4X20001848262 Ir	101695		C46FT	8/04	Veolia (WM) NXL7	6/11
	SF 05 XCW	Vo	B12M	YV3R9G12X5A102835 Je	27213		C53F	3/05	McGinley, Gortahork (EI)	4/15
				(ex 05-DL-5942 8/14, SF 05 XCW 5/07, KSK 953 11/06)						
	YN 05 GZA	Sca	K114EB4	YS2K4X20001851337 Ir	102272		C49FT	8/05	Irvine, Law (SW)	12/12
	YU 05 ZKE	Ds	Jv	SFD741BR54GJ22526 Pn	0512GRX5912		C70F	3/05	Unknown MoD	
				(ex WK 05 HFZ 3/16)					Contractor (MoD)	3/16
	YU 05 ZKR	Ds	Jv	SFD741BR54GJ22536 Pn	0512GRX5924		C70F	4/05	-?-, -?-	3/16
				(ex WA 05 YBD 10/15)						
	SF 06 MFO	Vo	B12M	YV3R9G1206A110587 Je	27514		C49FT	3/06	McGinley, Gortahork (EI)	4/15
				(ex 06-DL-6344 4/15, SF 06 MFO 3/08, LSK 444 3/08, SF 06 MFO 6/06)						
	FJ 07 VWU	Vo	B12B	YV3R8L2247A119787 Je	28041		C53F	4/07	SMS, Towcester (NO)	9/15
				(ex Y 80 SMS 5/15, FJ 07 VWU 3/14)						
	PX 07 EAA	Vo	B12BT	YV3R8L2267A119452 Pn	0715TAR7025		C63FLT	4/07	Stagecoach Scotland	
									(SE) 50423	3/13
	NH 57 DCF	Fd	Tt	WF0SXXBDFS7U44104 Fd			M8	1/08	-?-, -?-	by5/13
	PN 57 RVT	MB	O816D	WDB6703742N129273 Pn	078.5MBJ7370		C33F	11/07	First Stop,	
									Bury St Edmunds (SK)	c10/16
	EL 08 BUS	Vo	B12BT	YV3R8L3248A125962 Je	28600		C53FT	4/08	Callinan, Claregalway (EI)	8/14
				(ex 08-G-9926 by8/14, EL 08 BUS 8/10)						
	EU 08 BUS	Vo	B12BT	YV3R8L3248A125959 Je	25859		C53FT	4/08	Callinan, Claregalway (EI)	6/14
				(ex 08-G-9925 6/14, EU 08 BUS 8/10)						
	FJ 08 KMK	Sca	K340EB6	YS2K6X20001859164 Co	F073043059		C61FLT	7/08	New Adventure Travel,	
				(ex H 6 KFJ 6/13, FJ 08 KMK 10/11)					Cardiff (CC)	8/13
	SK 08 BZY	Ibs	397E.12.33	ZGA7B2N100E000012 Pn	0812.8ECL7679		C61F	8/08	Simpson, Rosehearty (SN)	11/16
				(ex B 21 DWA 11/10)						
	SN 08 ODA	Ibs	397E.12.33	ZGA7B2N100E000466 Pn	0812.8ECL7438		C61F	8/08	Seaward, Harlesden (LN)	11/16
				(ex B 20 DWA 1/11)						
	SF 09 GWM	MB	515CDI	WDB9066572S349114 Onyx	882		M16	8/09	Gibson Direct, Renfrew (SW)	12/15
	YN 10 FZT	Vo	B9R	YV3S5P726AA140030 Pn	1012.6SAA8554		C53F	5/10	Shaw, Carnforth (LA)	9/16
				(ex 7132 ET 8/16, YN 10 FZT 3/15)						
	YN 10 FZV	Vo	B9R	YV3S5P72XAA140404 Pn	1012.6SAA8556		C53F	5/10	Shaw, Carnforth (LA)	9/16
				(ex 4122 YG 8/16, YN 10 FZV 3/15)						

PG1125628/R: DH TAXIS (Swansea) Limited, Office 1 & 2 Garngoch Workshops, Phoenix Way, Garngoch Industrial Estate, GORSEINON, Swansea, SA4 9WF. FN: Phoenix Travel. OC: as address. VA: 2.

Reg		Type	Chassis	Body	Seats		Previous owner	Date
WA 51 ZSD	VW	LT46	WV1ZZZ2DZ2H011443 GM		M15L	1/02	Barnes, Basingstoke (HA)	3/14
CP 03 YSK	Fd	Tt	WF0EXXGBFE3T08739 Fd		M16	7/03	Taylor, Llansamlet (CW)	3/14

PG0006747/I: Kevin & Sharon DAVIES, 80 Glyn Road, Lower Brynamman, BRYNAMMAN, Carmarthenshire, SA18 1ST. FN: Cerbydau Gareth Evans. OC: as address. VA: 12.

Reg		Type	Chassis	Body	Seats		Previous owner	Date
C 20 GEC	MB	616CDI	WDB9056132R815284 ?		M16	6/06	Mullany, Watford (HT)	10/09
			(ex YX 06 DXL 12/10)					
L 20 GEC	MB	1223L	WDB9702582L018676 Fer	-?-	C35F	8/06	Laser Minicoach,	
			(ex YX 06 DZC 5/12)					Llanharry (CC)	8/11
S 23 CGE	Vo	B10M-62	YV31MA6111A053687 Co	F013043004	C74F	3/02	Premiere, Nottingham (NG) 955	8/11
			(ex RG 02 ONN 5/13, M 18 YEL 8/11, RG 02 ONN 5/10, B 12 PTL 4/09, RG 02 ONN 3/08, 5877 MW 1/07)					
S 23 GEC	Sca	K114IB4	YS2K4X20001848987 Ir	151516	C57F	2/05	Guideissue, Knypersley	
			(ex CU 54 PAO 5/13, 8399 RU 9/12)					(ST) 189	9/12
AK 02 LPX	Sca	K114IB4	YS4K4X20001842403 Ir	150947	C70F	6/02	Day & Ellwood, Chatteris (CM)	8/11
AK 02 LPY	Sca	K114IB4	YS4K4X20001842407 Ir	150948	C70F	6/02	Day & Ellwood, Chatteris (CM)	8/11
SC 04 OOL	Sca	K94IB	1847867 Ir	151423	C70F	5/04	Williams, Brecon (CW)	11/07

DAVIES, BRYNAMMAN (continued)

BX 55 NZP	Asn	A1012T	SUAED5CPP5S620187	Asn		B70F	11/05	new	11/05
BX 55 NZR	Asn	A1012T	SUAED5CPP5S620188	Asn		B70F	11/05	new	11/05
KU 55 FLJ	Fd	Tt	WF0EXXTTFE5P80395	Fd		M16	9/05	private owner	6/06
YN 57 GAA	Sca	K94IB	1858148	Ir	-?-	C70F	1/08	new	1/08

PG1109101/I: DAVIES of Lampeter Limited, Brynmeddyg, Victoria Terrace, LAMPETER, Ceredigion, SA48 7DF.
FN: Vincent Davies. OC: as address. VA: 14.

x	ONZ 1332	Rt	Tc	VF1JLAHA6AV367868	Rt		M8	3/10 -?-, -?-	by7/14
w	YIL 3167	MB	709D	WDB6690032N020338	Pn	947MHV2411	B23F	5/94 Davies & Jones,	
								Letterston (CW)	3/12
w	M421 VYD	Vo	B10M-62	YV31M2B16SA042682	VH	32235	C53F	5/95 Dawlish Coaches,	
								Dawlish (DN)	10/04
w	M702 YSF	Vo	B10M-62	YV31M2B14RA041699	VH	31852	C53F	1/95 John Martin, Midsomer Norton	
		(ex XIL 5452 10/05, M702 YSF 3/04, GSV 351 7/98, M441 ECS 2/97, KSK 949 10/96)							(SO)	2/06
	P226 YGG	Vo	B10M-60	YV31MA613TA045903	VH	32674	C53F	3/97 Stainton, Kendal (CA)	10/06
		(ex KSK 977 11/99)								
xw	T 59 MKL	MB	108CDI	WDB63809423212509	?		M7L	5/99 -?-, -?-	1/05
w	X998 JOH	MB	614D	WDB6683532N090623	Excel -?-		C24F	9/00 Embling & Barker,	
								Maidenhead (BE)	5/03
w	KR 51 PBU	MB	311CDI	WDB9036632R355399	?		M16	1/02 Evans, Tregaron (CW)	9/09
	MX 04 ULP	VW	LT46	WV1ZZZ2DZ4H018759	?		M??	3/04 -?- Church, -?- (X??)	8/11
	YN 04 HHT	Ds	Jv	SFD741BR53GJ22489	Tbs	0312GRX5200	C53F	3/04 Turbostyle, Crawley (WS)	9/12
	CX 54 JFN	MB	O814D	WDB6703732N113710	KVC		C24F	11/04 Bevan, Cwmrhydyceirw (CW)	12/14
		(ex B 13 MPB 11/14, YN 54 XXO 9/14, J111 LMW 9/14, YN 54 XXO 6/13)								
	WX 54 NPO	MB	311CDI	WDB9036632R607686	?		M16	9/04 Hicks, Llanelli (CW)	11/09
	DK 05 OGB	MB	311CDI	WDB9036632R729854	?		M16	8/05 Hicks, Drefach (CW)	7/10
	MX 55 VJU	MB	311CDI	WDB9036322R759574	Oly		M12	11/05 MCH, Uxbridge (LN)	4/11
		(ex MCH 96 2/11, MX 55 VJU 8/06)								
	YN 07 DUA	MB	O816D	WDB6703742N099100	Pn	068.5MBE6929	C33F	3/07 Bevan, Cwmrhydyceriw (CW)	3/14
	YN 57 DVC	MB	515CDI	WDB9066572S188813	KVC		M16	9/07 Knight, Warnham (WS)	4/16
		(ex FPN 259 2/10, YN 57 DVC 8/08)								
	YN 08 AWG	Ibs	397E.12.45	ZGA7B2T000E000674	Bs	07.126	C49FL	4/08 Barnes, Swindon (WI)	2/16
		(ex DH 08 AND 3/14, YN 08 AWG 4/13)								
x	YP 08 KSK	Vx	Viv	W0LJ7BMA68V646541	Vx		M8	4/08 Jones, Pontrobert (CW)	11/13
	FE 13 XJL	Fd	Tt	WF0DXXTTFDDJ36241	Fd		M16	3/13 Shropshire Council	
								(SH) N2269	7/16
	FE 13 XJM	Fd	Tt	WF0DXXTTFDDJ36263	Fd		M16	3/13 Shropshire Council	
								(SH) N2268	7/16
	YP 13 VLK	Fd	Tt	WF0DXXTTFDDU68538	Fd		M16	7/13 Shropshire Council	
								(SH) N2288	7/16

PG1060966/I: DAVIES Coaches Limited, 65 Stepney Street, LLANELLI, Carmarthenshire SA15 3YA.
OCs: Unit 12, Crofty Industrial Estate, Penclawdd, Swansea SA4 3RS; Crosshands Training Park, Cwmgwili,
Carmarthenshire SA14 6PP. VA: 40.

BRZ 9743	MB	O814D	WDB6703742N092037	Pn	018.5MXV4048	C33F	7/01 Hicks, Drefach (CW)	6/13
	(ex Y852 SDD 10/13)							
CCZ 2214	Vo	B10M-62	YV31MA616WA048122	Co	758546	C70F	5/98 Silverdale (London),	
	(ex R497 UFP 11/11)						Watford (HT)	11/11
CLZ 1803	Ds	Jv	12SDA2157/1273	WS	4960/95	C57F	8/95 Thomas, Neath (CC) 90	7/16
	(ex N823 OAE 10/16, N 14 CJT 7/16, N823 OAE 3/08, EC 54 AA 5/03)							
HIG 2499	Vo	B10M-62	YV31MA615VA046361	Bf	3228	C51FT	3/97 Creigiau Travel,	
	(ex P808 WWO 4/14, L 19 CTL 7/12, P808 WWO 10/09,					Capel Llanilltern (CC)	10/13
	DJI 8003 8/09, P808 WWO 2/04)							
JIG 8580	Ds	Jv	12SDA2152/1110	WS	4693/94	C57F	1/95 Turner, Bristol (GL)	4/08
	(ex M165 XHW 4/13, PUI 9422 2/13, M165 XHW 6/08, CX 57 AA 7/02, M812 ALC by7/02, CX 57 AA by7/02)							
JIL 2433	As	A18-12A/T	VS936VG232A031419	As	20205	C53FT	5/03 Stolzenberg & Morgan,	
	(ex HF 03 OLT 1/15)						Maesteg (CC)	12/14
JIL 7657	As	A18-12A/T	VS936VG232A031417	As	20203	C51FT	7/03 Stolzenberg & Morgan,	
	(ex AJ 03 LXD 2/15)						Maesteg (CC)	12/14

DAVIES, LLANELLI (continued)

Reg	Make	Chassis	Chassis No		Body No	Body	Date	Operator	
JUI 5931	Vo	B10M-62	YV31MA612WC060868	Pn	9812VUP8546	C53F	3/99	Guideissue, Knypersley (ST) 6	1/12
		(ex T 64 MUX 10/14, 3275 RU 5/10)							
KIG 1256	Vo	B10M-62	YV31MA615XC061076	Co	858548	C53F	5/99	Silverdale London,	
		(ex T366 AJF 10/12)						Watford (HT)	5/12
KXA 394	Vo	B10M-62	YV31M2B14TA045050	VH	32554	C48FT	2/96	Hills Services,	
		(ex N716 CYC 12/09)						Stibb Cross (DN)	10/09
KXI 318	Vo	B10M-55	YV31MA718YA051881	VH	33830	C49FT	5/00	Roselyn Coaches, Par (CO)	8/13
		(ex W704 YBD 10/13, NUF 276 by8/13, W704 YBD 1/11, 668 PTM by1/11)							
MHZ 1556	Vo	B12M	YV3R9F8192A000476	BF	4444	C50FT	6/02	Silver Star, Caernarfon (CN)	10/14
		(ex KC 02 EEY 5/10)							
NJI 1256	Sca	K94IB	YS2K4X20001846078	Ir	151323	C57F	3/04	Little, Ilkeston (DE)	3/16
		(ex FN 04 BSU 4/16)							
OBF 706	Sca	K94IB	YS2K4X20001846758	Ir	151325	C57F	3/04	Little, Ilkeston (DE)	3/16
		(ex FN 04 BSV 7/16)							
OIB 3520	Ds	Jv	10SDA2120/710	WS	3778/92	C46F	9/92	Morris Travel,	
		(ex K496 SUS 11/07, 74 KK 39 by1/03)						Carmarthen (CW)	6/11
OIL 9262	Sca	K94IB	YS2K4X20001846062	Ir	151321	C57F	3/04	Little, Ilkeston (DE)	3/16
		(ex FN 04 BRX 6/16)							
PIL 9276	DAF	SB3000	XMGDE33WS0H006040	Pn	9712DRM7221	C53F	1/98	Arriva Kent & Surrey	
		(ex R903 BKO 2/16)						(KT) 2903	8/15
PUI 9422	Ds	Jv	10SDA2156/1175	WS	4733/95	C40F	5/95	Stozenberg & Morgan,	
		(ex M375 EBX 2/13, 27 AY 80 8/11)						Maesteg (CC)	12/12
REZ 9461	Vo	B10M-62	YV31MA616XA050096	Co	858542	C49FT	5/99	Silverdale London,	
		(ex T362 AJF 7/12)						Watford (HT)	6/12
RJI 2714	DAF	SB3000	XMGDEE3WS0H007438	VH	33225	C51FT	7/99	Going My Way, Cheadle (ST)	6/14
		(ex T209 XVO 6/15, 815 DYE 10/14, T209 XVO 3/12, 815 DYE 3/10, T209 XVO 12/08)							
SIL 6477	Ds	Jv	10SDA2120/704	WS	3770/92	DP54F	8/92	Morris Travel,	
		(ex K714 PHU 11/07, K154 WDV 12/02, 74 KK 31 by12/02)						Carmarthen (CW)	4/11
SUI 4533	MB	O814D	WDB6703732N087100	Me	3202	B24FL	11/99	Greenwich Service Plus,	
		(ex V586 NOF 8/12)						Woolwich (LN)	7/12
SUI 8190	Vo	B10M-62	YV31MA611XC061365	VH	33569	C49FT	3/00	Daishs Coaches, Torquay (CO)	7/13
		(ex W209 JBN 11/10)							
SUI 8194	Vo	B10M-62	YV31MA615WA048676	Pn	9812VUS7797	C49FT	2/98	Daishs Coaches, Torquay (DN)	4/13
		(ex R257 DWL 11/10, R 9 OXF 11/05)							
TIL 5703	Ds	Jv	12SDA2131/993	Pn	9412HKM2502	C67F	1/95	Collins, Roch (CW)	by2/15
		(ex M710 HBC 9/12)							
z TIL 8886	Ds	Jv	SFD213BL37GJ11756	UVG	5404/96	C47F	10/96	Hayward, Carmarthen (CW)	10/14
		(ex P420 YEU 10/12, ?? ?? ?? by10/12)							
TUI 3630	MB	O814D	WDB6703732N087133	Me	3201	B24FL	11/99	Greenwich Service Plus,	
		(ex V583 NOF 8/12)						Woolwich (LN)	7/12
TUI 7063	Ds	Jv	12SDA2122/733	WS	3796/92	C70F	11/92	Castleton, South Bank (CD)	7/15
		(ex K583 PHU 8/12, 74 KK 97 6/03, K151 ACY by6/03, 74 KK 97 by6/03)							
WEZ 9874	Vo	B10M-62	YV31MA618XA050097	Co	858543	C49FT	5/99	Silverdale London,	
		(ex T363 AJF 7/12)						Watford (HT)	6/12
WTL 642	Vo	B10M-62	YV31MA611XC061284	Je	25322	C53F	3/00	Shaw, Carnforth (LA)	4/13
		(ex W851 AAY 8/13, 824 HAO 3/11, W851 AAY by7/05)							
YIL 4432	Vo	B10M-62	YV31MA61XWA048124	Co	758547	C53F	5/98	Silverdale London,	
		(ex R498 UFP 11/11)						North Acton (LN)	11/11
852 YYC	Sca	K113CRB	YS4KC4X2B01827680	Bf	3188	C49FT	2/97	Collins, Roch (CW)	by2/15
		(ex P126 JHE 7/15, RJI 2714 5/15, P126 GHE 8/10, LIL 9715 10/08, P126 GHE 4/02)							
z F407 OSR	Ds	Jv	8.5SDL1903/373	Pn	898HBA0765	C35F	5/89	Brodyr James,	
		(ex GSU 378 10/99, F407 OSR 7/91)						Llangeitho (CW)	10/11
z G492 XWS	Ld	TRCTL11/3LZM	TR00787	Pn	8912LTF1604	DP54F	10/89	Eurotaxis, Siston Common (GL)	4/07
		(ex 03 KJ 25 6/97)							
w G826 XWS	Ld	TRCTL11/3LZM	TR00788	Pn	8912LTF1607	DP70F	11/89	Turner, Bristol (GL)	6/08
		(ex KXI 318 10/13, G826 XWS 3/09, 6486 LJ 4/08, G826 XWS 7/03, 03 KJ 28 3/98)							
w G524 YAE	Ld	TRCTL11/3RZ	TR00951	Pn	8912LMF1593	DP68F	11/89	Morris Travel,	
		(ex CLZ 1803 5/13, G524 YAE 7/07, 03 KJ 47 6/99)						Carmarthen (CW)	5/11
w G525 YAE	Ld	TRCTL11/3RZ	TR00822	Pn	8912LMF1591	DP68F	10/89	Morris Travel,	
		(ex OBF 706 2/15, G525 YAE 7/07, 03 KJ 40 6/99)						Carmarthen (CW)	6/11
J222 BER	Ds	Jv	12SDA2152/1246	WS	4949/95	DP70F	7/95	Watermill Coaches,	
		(ex M303 YWE 12/07, EC 43 AA by1/03)						Fraserburgh (SN)	10/16

DAVIES, LLANELLI (continued)

w	K818 HUM	Vo	B10M-60	YV31M2B11PA031242 VH	31718		C55F	3/93	Evans, Carmarthen (CW)	8/07
			(ex JUI 5931 10/14, K818 HUM 4/99)							
	K619 KWT	Vo	B10M-62	YV31M2B14PA031249 VH	31725		C48FT	3/93	Lakeland, Hurst Green (LA)	11/12
			(ex FDZ 362 11/12, K619 KWT 3/99, WA 3399 12/96, K801 HUM 11/95)							
	L 20 PNY	MB	O814D	WDB6703742N076977 Pn	978.5MZE9667		C33F	3/99	Thomas, Neath (CC)	7/16
			(ex T781 LCS 9/09)							
w	L388 YNV	Ds	Jv	12SDA2131/985 Pn	9412HKM2730		C70F	7/94	Jones, Gawsworth (CH) J11	4/13
			(ex CLZ 1803 6/16, L388 YNV 5/13, GJZ 6100, L388 YNV, WYR 562, L388 YNV, A 8 CLN)							
	M788 ASL	Ds	Jv	12SDA2152/1252 WS	4955/95		DP70F	7/95	Watermill Coaches,	
			(ex EC 49 AA 12/03)						Fraserburgh (SN)	10/16
	M796 ASL	Ds	Jv	12SDA2152/1243 WS	4953/95		DP70F	7/95	Watermill Coaches,	
			(ex EC 47 AA 12/03)						Fraserburgh (SN)	10/16
w	M649 KVU	Vo	B10M-62	YV31M2B14RA041685 VH	31874		C51F	1/95	Rambler, Hastings (ES) 23	4/09
			(ex NJI 1256 3/16, M649 KVU 6/09, JDY 673 6/09, M649 KVU 1/03)							
w	M411 TWF	Au	N116/3	WAG301162SSM22850 Au	116416		C48FT	3/95	Davies, Pontyberem (CW)	12/12
			(ex G 15 UKY 9/12, M411 TWF 2/05, A 5 BKE by1/04, M411 TWF 5/99, M422 TWF c3/96)							
w	P790 GHN	Vo	B10M-62	YV31MA61XTC060192 Je	24193		C53F	2/97	Hilton, Newton-le-Willows (MY)	10/13
			(ex RUI 5159 11/16, P790 GHN 4/14)							
w	P 37 PPO	Vo	B10M-62	YV31M2B16TC060122 Pn	9612VUP5089		C53F	5/96	Durbin, Patchway (GL)	1/12
			(ex OIL 9262 3/16, L400 SGB 10/10, N857 AHP 2/09, OIL 9262 2/09, N857 AHP 7/06, 96-D-25768 5/99)							
	P717 RWU	DAF	SB3000	XMGDE33WS0H005183 Is	350T1PT1GB0018 C70F			8/96	Brodyr Williams,	
									Upper Tumble (CW) 43	c3/16
	Q424 CHH	Ds	Jv	10SDA2156/1345 WS	4982/95		C41F	10/95	Speldhurst, Bedford (BD)	3/16
			(ex EB 87 AA 7/05, N152 OJD by2/05, ER 87 AA by2/05)							
w	T 4 WCT	Vo	B10M-62	YV31MA616XC061071 Bf	3785		C49FT	4/99	Creigiau Travel,	
			(ex T 74 JKG 5/04)						Capel Llanilltern (CC)	1/12
	V220 EAL	BBd	RE	1BAGKBSA6XF091990 BBd			DP60F	10/99	Collins, Roch (CW)	10/14
			(ex OBF 706 7/16, V220 EAL 2/15)							
	W512 KDS	Ka	S315GT-HD	WKK32600001015061 Ka			C44FT	5/00	Davies, Brynamman (CW)	7/16
			(ex L 1 GEC 6/16, B 6 PRE 9/10, W512 XDS 7/06)							
	DC 51 WAL	Ka	S315GT-HD	WKK62725213000132 Ka			C49FT	2/02	Pewsey Vale, Pewsey (WI)	7/14
			(ex BD 51 YMJ 7/14, T 9 PVC 9/12, BD 51 YMJ 12/09, A 20 YAL 8/09, BD 51 YMJ 1/07)							
	DC 02 WAL	Ds	Jv	SFD721BR41GJ22393 Pn	0212GFM4530		C70F	-/02	Lex (MoD)	6/15
			(ex CF 02 XJZ 9/15, ?? ?? ??? 6/15)							
	DC 52 WAL	MB	O814D	WDB6703742N099100 ACl	1810		C27F	9/02	Davies, Lampeter (CW)	4/14
			(ex FY 52 LFX 7/14)							
	DC 03 WAL	Au	N316SHD	WAG2031663ND34240 Au	ND34240		C53F	4/03	Stolzenberg & Morgan,	
			(ex YN 03 AXF 4/15, N600 PEG 3/15, YN 03 AXF 7/13, 9920 MT 3/13, YN 03 AXF 10/07)						Maesteg (CC)	12/14
z	LK 03 HYG	Io	65C15	ZCFC65A0005381584 FGy	8895		B24FL	3/03	Grey, Swansea (CW)	by3/15
	DC 04 WAL	Ds	Jv	SFD741BR55GJ22555 Pn	0512GRX6192		C53F	-/05	Lex (MoD)	7/15
			(ex YU 05 ZJX 10/15, GK 05 VNY 7/15)							
	DC 54 WAL	Fd	Tt	WF0EXXTTFE5M55475 Fd			M12	3/05	James, Porthyrhyd (CW)	7/14
			(ex CP 05 AEL 9/14, N 2 DAJ by7/14, CP 05 AEL 10/05)							
x	YA 05 YXC	Vx	Viv	W0LF7BBB55V653147 Vx			M8	7/05	-?-, -?-	1/09
			(ex JIL 2433 1/15, YA 05 YXC 1/10)							
	PO 55 GGY	LDV	Cy	SEYZNVFZGDN111402 Cpt			M16	9/05	Bevan, Cwmrhydyceirw (CW)	3/15
	DC 07 WAL	Fd	Tt	WF0DXXTTFD7D28689 Fd			M16	5/07	James, Porthyrhyd (CW)	7/14
			(ex CP 07 LBX 8/14)							
	DC 57 WAL	MB	O816D	WDB6703742N127342 Me	4467		C30F	9/07	new	9/07
	DC 09 WAL	Fd	Tt	WF0DXXTTFD9P82492 Fd			M16	5/09	-?-, -?-	12/09
			(ex AD 09 CLX 8/14)							
	DC 60 WAL	MB	O816D	WDB6703742N140899 Pn	108.5MBJ8713		C33F	11/10	new	11/10
	DC 62 WAL	Vo	B9R	YV3S5P722CA157202 Pn	CP08/01		C53F	9/12	new	9/12

PG1006863/R: Thomas Paul DAVIES, 18 Blaen Nant, Swiss Valley, LLANELLI, Carmarthenshire, SA14 8HB.
FN: Paul Davies Minibus Hire. **OC:** as address; 18 Blaen Nant, Swiss Valley, Llanelli, SA14 8HB. **VA:** 2.

	EX 53 UPG	Fd	Tt	WF0EXXGBFE3Y10666 Fd			M16	9/03	St John's School,	
									Porthcawl (XCC)	1/15

PG1078025/R: Michael Alan DAVIES, 51 Rhyd-y-Fro, LLANGADOG, Carmarthenshire, SA19 9HW.
FN: Llangadog Cabs.   **OC:** as address.   **VA:** 2.

Y254 XBN	Fd	Tt	WF0EXXGBFE1B76965	Fd		M14	7/01 -?-, -?-		6/07
ML 54 XBR	Fd	Tt	WF0DXXTTFD8A53245	Fd		M16	6/08 Afford Rent a Car,		
								Fenton (YST)	9/12

PG1012782/R: Arwyn DAVIES, Heniarth Farm, LLANGYNIEW, Welshpool, Powys, SY21 0JR.
FN: Arwyn's.   **OC:** as address.   **VA:** 2.
PG1148618/R: Arwyn & Elaine DAVIES, Penybryn, LLANGYNIEW, Welshpool, Powys, SY21 0JS.
FN: A & E Hire.   **OC:** as address.   **VA:** 1. [PENDING]

xw BT 52 VYE	MB	108CDI	WDF63819423519140	MB		M8	2/02 -?-, -?-		11/12
BU 04 MFP	LDV	Cy	SEYZNVFZGDN101300	?		M16	6/04 King, Stickney (LI)		9/08
x FP 06 XCJ	Fd	Tt	WF0PXXBDFP6S20451	Fd		M8	5/06 -?-, -?-		10/12
x BD 07 GYS	Rt	Tc	VF1FLAHA67V303061	Rt		M8	6/07 -?-, -?-		1/15

PG1054834/N: Brian DAVIES & Son Limited, West View Garage, OLD CHURCH STOKE, Montgomery, Powys, SY15 6DH.   **OC:** as address.   **VA:** 4.

No vehicles currently recorded.

PG0007079/I: Robert Neal DAVIES, 24 Grugos Avenue, PONTYBEREM, Llanelli, Carmarthenshire, SA15 5AF.
FN: PTS Travel.   **OC:** Coalbrook Road, Pontyberem, SA15 5HU.   **VA:** 2.

AFZ 9708	Sca	K114EB4	YS2K4X20001840833	Ir	94848	C49FT	4/92 Snowdon,		
	(ex YL 51 ZTS 7/10)							Easington Colliery (DM)	4/14
R 3 CJT	Vo	B10M-62	YV31MA619VA047447	Je	24570	C49FT	8/97 Laser Minicoach,		
								Llanharry (CC)	7/12
R453 SKX	DAF	SB3000	XMGDE33WS0H006036	Pn	9712DSM7217	C53F	11/97 Hayward, Carmarthen (CW)		1/17

PG0007003/R: Susan Mary DAVIES, SCURLAGE, Rhossilli, Swansea, SA3 1BA.
FN: The Countryman.   **OC:** The Countryman, Scurlage, Rhossili, Swansea, SA3 1AY.   **VA:** 1.

No vehicles currently recorded.

PG0006769/N: Vernon & Anne Meryl Gwenydd DAVIES, Station Yard, SENNYBRIDGE, Powys, LD3 8RR.
FN: Leith's of Sennybridge.   **OC:** as address.   **VA:** 2.

No vehicles currently recorded.

PG0006613/N: Mary Christine DAVIES, The Garage, TALYBONT-ON-USK, Powys, LD3 7JD.
FN: Talgarth Travel.   **OC:** as address.   **VA:** 8.

KUI 1744	Fd	Tt	WF0EXXGBFE3M40614	Fd		M16	3/04 private owner		9/07
	(ex EX 04 HCF 5/13)								
J 6 VEP	MB	614D	WDB6683532N105458	Excel 0297		C20F	8/02 Marriott, Clayworth (NG)		4/16
	(ex YO 02 LDN 5/16, S 7 BUS 7/07)								
w M135 KHO	VW	LT28	WV2ZZZ21ZRH005191	DC	415L	M12	3/95 converted from a van		10/98
w X271 ACB	VW	LT46	WV1ZZZ2DZ1H012094	P&L		M16	10/00 Wood Norton Hotel (YHW)		5/03
xw LN 51 NJO	VW	Tr	WV1ZZZ70Z2H091422	?		M8	2/02 private owner		9/07
w VU 51 GGK	MB	614D	WDB6683532N092863	Onyx 461		C24F	1/02 Myrtle Tree, Bristol (GL)		3/09
	(ex KUI 1744 5/13, VU 51 GGK 4/09)								
w MV 03 HZG	LDV	Cy	SEYZMVSYGDN095954	LDV		M16	5/03 Sixt (Y)		3/06
x RK 53 EHH	VW	LT35	WV1ZZZ2DZ4H008770	AVB		M14	1/04 National (Y)		5/06
NC 04 TJZ	Fd	Tt	WF0EXXGBFE3M46835	Fd		M16	6/04 Hertz (Y)		6/08
WA 04 MHE	MB	O815D	WDB6703742N110517	Sit	1926	C29F	5/04 Office & Transport Services,		
	(ex 573 LCV 2/13, WA 04 MHE 4/10)							Constantine (CO)	3/13

DAVIES, TALYBONT-ON-USK (continued)

w LJ 07 PYL	VW	Crf	WV1ZZZ2EZ76034942 Stan -?-		M16L	7/07	London Hire,	
							Rotherhithe (XLN)	10/11
BU 08 BVG	VW	Crf	WV1ZZZ2EZ86027995 KVC		M10	4/08	TGM Group (LN)	11/12

PG0005805/I: D.G. DAVIES & G.R. & M.A. JONES, Summerdale Garage, Haverfordwest Road, LETTERSTON, Pembrokeshire, SA62 5UA. FN: Summerdale Coaches. OC: as address. VA: 10.

FSU 827	Vo	B12M	YV3R9F8193A000933 Pn	0212TJT4770	C57F	12/02	East Midland (DE) 53008		3/11
		(ex GU 52 WTF 3/11)							
JIL 2284	Vo	B10M-62	YV31M2B18TA044029 Pn	9512VUP4450	C53F	2/96	Brown, Roecliffe (NY)		12/07
		(ex N937 RBC 12/07, WIJ 551 10/06, N937 RBC 9/05)							
JIL 4438	Vo	B10M-62	YV31MA619WC060981 Pn	9812VUP8778	C70F	5/99	Thomas, Neath (CC) 64		8/14
		(ex T 11 VCC 8/14, T149 OWB 10/99)							
JIL 4812	Vo	B10M-62	YV31MA618VA046774 Pn	9712VUP6430	C53F	3/97	Guideissue, Biddulph (ST) 33		9/05
		(ex P746 HNT 9/06, 3563 RU by2/05)							
JIL 6511	MB	O814D	WDB6703742N115339 Pn	048.5MAE5729	C33F	4/05	Gibson Direct, Renfrew (SW)		4/13
		(ex SF 05 FNV 6/13)							
JIL 7591	Vo	B10M-62	YV31M2B10SA043231 Pn	9512VUP3675	C53F	12/95	Lochs Motor Transport,		
		(ex N760 AHP 3/11, 95-D-41601 5/99)						Leurbost (SN)	3/11
w NIL 7042	Vo	B10M-60	YV31MGD18MS026023 Pn	9112VCS0273	C49FT	4/92	Coach Hire, Blackpool (LA)		9/08
		(ex 366 EKH 6/07, NIL 7042 9/04, J423 HDS 5/98, 813 VPU 12/97, J423 HDS 3/94)							
TIL 2744	Vo	B12B	YV3R8G1255A102597 Pn	0412TKL5785	C53F	12/04	Harrison, Morecambe (LA) 931		3/12
		(ex YN 54 WWC 4/12, 7121 RU 1/12, YN 54 WWC 6/10)							
w F150 RFH	Vo	B10M-61	YV31MGD15JA016292 Pn	8812VMH3C799	C57F	10/88	Pulham, Bourton (GL)		8/04
		(ex TIL 2744 4/12, F150 RFH 9/04, LDD 488 2/03, F150 RFH 1/93)							
z G648 UHU	MB	609D	WDB66806320963230 MM		C26F	8/89	McChrystal, Kirkintilloch (SW)		1/04
w M572 SRE	MB	709D	WDB6690032N022596 Pn	947MHV2875	B24F	11/94	PMT (ST) 572		4/02
w N378 PTG	MB	412D	WDB9044122P541375 Bds	42483	B16FL	3/96	Morris, Pencoed (CC)		8/03
T544 BBR	MB	O814D	WDB6703742N077156 Pn	988.5MZE9664	C33F	6/99	Parnell, Honiton (DN)		9/15
		(ex K999 HEM 8/15, T544 BBR 1/15, 927 NOF 9/13, T544 BBR 3/09, T 2 STX 7/05)							
w W102 ODE	LDV	Cy	SEYZMNFHEDN055882 LDV		M14L	7/00	Collins, Roch (CW)		10/02
w GN 53 NWP	LDV	Cy	SEYZMVSYGDN099777 ?		M16L	11/03	Thanet Communty,		
							Broadstairs (KT)	4/11
CU 04 EHT	LDV	Cy	SEYZNVFYGDN103748 LDV		M16	6/04	Collins, Roch (CW)		9/14
CV 55 FVD	Fd	Tt	WF0EXXTTFE5C03802 Fd		M16	2/06	CSA, Llanelli (CW)		8/12
		(ex OO 04 CSA 8/12, CV 55 FVD 7/09)							
WA 06 CDY	Vo	B12M	YV3R9F8206A109553 VH	33935	C53FT	3/06	Chalfont, Southall (LN)		10/13

PG1141202/R: The DEVELOPMENT COMPANY UK Limited, The Old Stables, 6A Dark Street, HAVERFORDWEST, Pembrokeshire. SA61 2DS. OC: as address; Newgale Lodge, The Whitehouse, Penycwm, Haverfordwest, SA62 6LA. VA: 1.

No vehicles yet recorded.

PG1104724/N: Vito DI-CATALDO, 947 Carmarthen Road, FFORESTFACH, Swansea, SA5 4AB. FN: Alpha Travel. OC: as address. VA: 3.

LX 61 BDV	Rt	Mtr	VF1MEN4JE45847268 Rt		M16	12/11	-?-, -?-	by9/15
LX 61 DGF	Rt	Mtr	VF1MEN4JE46130788 Rt		M16	11/11	Shrewsbury House School,	
							Surbiton (XLN)	9/16

PG1141037/N: Michael, Andrew & Carol DUGGAN, 36 Heol y Nant, CLYDACH, Swansea, SA 6 5HB. FN: Clydach Taxis / Brian E. Duggan & Sons. OCL as address. VA: 6.

GF 05 MEV	Fd	Tt	WF0EXXTTFE5R41308 Fd		M16	8/05	-?-, -?-	9/09
CP 10 EYZ	Fd	Tt	WF0DXXTTFD9E38895 Fd		M16	5/10	Bevan, Cwmrhydyceirw (CW)	10/14

PG1104667/T: Malcolm Peter DUST, Farleigh, Beaufort Road, LLANDRINDOD WELLS, Powys, LD1 5EE.
FN: Pro-Cabs. OC: as address.

No vehicles currently recorded.

PG0007155/R: Robert Leslie EARLAND, Glanyrafon, Heol Geidd, CWMGIEDD, Ystradgynlais, Powys, SA9 1LP.
FN: Rob's Mini Bus. OC: as address. VA: 2.

w	P767 XDE	LDV	Pt	DN014395 LDV		M12	by7/97 -?-, -?-	by4/07
	(ex -?- 6/05)							
w	T306 JKY	LDV	Cy	SEYZLWSJEDN051812 LDV		M16	8/99 -?-, -?-	6/06
x	V 20 WES	MB	316CDI	WDB9036622R321185 ?		M12	10/01 -?-, -?-	12/08
	(ex YN 51 KKO 12/08)							

PG0006917/R: Reginald Thomas & Susan Carole EBREY, 28 St Martins Road, MONKTON, Pembroke, Pembrokeshire, SA71 4NG. FN: Monkton Cars. OC: Monkton Cars Workshop, Hundleton Coach Works, Hundleton, Pembrokeshire, SA71 5AA. VA: 2.

No vehicles currently recorded.

PG1035092/R: David Eirwyn EDWARDS, Halfen, Llanfihangel, LLANFYLLIN, Powys, SY22 5JE.
FN: DE Edwards. OC: as address. VA: 2.

w	X694 AAV	Fd	Tt	WF0EXXBDVEYC12166 Fd		M14	12/00 Sockett & Jones, Meifod (CW)	10/08
	X214 GBH	Fd	Tt	WF0EXXBDVEXM65730 Fd		M14	12/00 London Underground (XLN)	10/05

PG1117401/I: EDWARDS Bros (Tiers Cross) Limited, The Garage, Broad Haven Road, TIERS CROSS, Haverfordwest, Pembrokeshire, SA62 3BZ. FN: Edwards Tiers Cross. OC: as address. VA: 23.
PG0006194/I: Robert William EDWARDS, The Garage, Broad Haven Road, TIERS CROSS, Pembrokeshire, SA62 3BZ. FN: Edwards Tiers Cross. OC: as address. VA: 4.

	KUI 9600	Vo	B10M-60	YV31M2B11PA031905 Pn	9312VCM1300		C53F	8/93 Bevan, Cwmrhydyceirw (CW)	8/08
			(ex L 46 CNY 7/08)						
	891 VDE	Vo	B10M-62	YV31MA61XYA051804 Pn	0012VUT2134		C51FT	6/00 Sihota, Southall (LN)	5/12
			(ex W800 BCL 5/12, 593 CCE 10/07, W800 BCL 5/06)						
	P703 GPA	Ds	Jv	SFD721BR3TGJ31787 Bf	3267		C53F	3/97 Bysiau Cwm Taf,	
			(ex L 7 PSV 5/16, P703 GPA 3/16, P 4 BAN 2/10)					Whitland (CW)	7/16
	P100 SDE	Vo	B10M-62	YV31MA619VA046413 VH	33005		C57F	5/97 O'Shea, Ballyheigue (EI)	2/04
			(ex P199 PYB 3/04, 97-KY-1750 by2/04)						
	P325 TGS	MB	811D	WDB6703032N047706 MI	C16.454		DP33F	3/97 Chambers, Bures (SK)	2/06
w	T374 JJC	MB	O814D	WDB6703742N081056 Pn	998.5MXV0975		B31F	4/99 Harrington, Bedworth (WK)	2/13
	V390 SVV	MB	O814D	WDB6703742N084389 Pn	998.5MXV1267		B29F	9/99 Pickford, Chippenham (WI)	7/12
			(ex J108019 by2/08, V390 SVV 12/06, V309 SVV c9/00)						
w	X291 ABU	Ds	Dt SLF	SFD612BR1XGW14332 Ar	9941/3		B29F	12/00 Bodman, Worton (WI)	6/11
	X764 ARP	MB	311CDI	WDB9033632R152308 NWCS			C16F	9/00 Somerbus, Paulton (SO)	9/04
	X936 DYB	Ba	FHD12-370	XL9AA18CG18003933 Ba			C51FT	4/01 Rover European, Horsley (GL)	6/16
			(ex K 18 AND 6/16, X936 DYB 8/08, K 18 AND 2/08)						
	X851 VAF	MB	614D	WDB6683532N089181 ACl	1761		C24F	9/00 Courtney, Bracknell (BE)	2/06
			(ex X 9 CCL 2/06)						
	Y493 YFP	Ds	R	SFD131BR1YGC10118 Bf	4244		C57F	7/01 Maude, Barnard Castle (DM)	11/13
			(ex G 14 ELY 8/08, ESU 374 12/02)						
	WV 02 AXK	LDV	Cy	SEYZLWSYGDN086940 LDV			M8	6/02 -?-, -?-	12/11
	VO 03 VUY	Vo	B7R	YV3R6G7183A004875 Pn	0212THX4752		C57F	6/03 Francis, Eastington (GL)	9/14
			(ex 03-G-7670 11/06)						
	MP 53 ZBY	Tbs	Jv	SFD741BR53GJ22465 Pn	0312GRX5163		C53F	-/04 Unknown MoD	
			(ex ?? ??? ??? 7/14)					Contractor (MoD)	9/14
	LS 04 UPE	Fd	Tt	WF0EXXGBFE4B86482 Fd			M16	6/04 Hewens, Laugharne (CW)	1/13
	VX 04 KTG	MB	O814D	WDB6703742N112589 Pn	048.5MXV5375		DP33F	6/04 new	6/04
	YN 04 WTJ	Vo	B12M	YV3R9F8144A011808 Pn	0412TJT5554		C53F	5/04 Longmynd, Lea Cross (SH)	4/16

EDWARDS, TIERS CROSS (continued)

HX 54 BHP	MB	616CDI	WDB9056132R575582	Me	-?-		B18F	11/04	Somerbus,	
									Midsomer Norton (SO)	5/15
CN 55 ZTP	Fd	Tt	WF0EXXTTFE5U47024	Fd			M16	9/05	Hewens, Laugharne (CW)	8/14
CU 06 KND	Ibs	397E.12.31	ZGA7B2N000E002389	Pn	0512EBL6142		C53F	3/06	Reays, Wigton (CA)	6/14
		(ex M 30 YEL 4/13, CU 06 KND 9/10, BC 06 TAF 6/10)								
RE 06 RDE	MB	O814D	WDB6703742N121651	Pn	068.5MAE6376		C33F	4/06	new	4/06
YN 06 JFE	MB	413CDI	WDB9046632R874436	KVC			M16	4/06	Hutchinson, Easingwold (NY)	9/11
w YJ 09 EXV	Oe	M710SE	SABCN2AB09R193380	Oe			B23F	3/09	Acorn, Fishguard (CW)	5/11
VX 59 HFH	Ft	Do	ZFA25000001410853	?			M16	12/09	-?-, -?-	4/10
PX 10 GPF	Vo	B12B	YV3R8M92XAA138279	Pn	1012.8TPL8522		C53FT	5/10	Hodgson, Barnard Castle (DM)	5/14
		(ex HC 10 BUS 5/14)								
YJ 10 EXU	Oe	M710SE	SABCN2AB0AL193557	Oe			B23F	4/10	Silcox, Pembroke Dock	
									(CW) 36	6/16
YN 11 FTZ	Ibs	397E.12.33	ZGA7B2N100E001506	Pn	1113.1EDR8691		C57F	6/11	Collier, Earith (CM)	4/15
MX 12 CFU	Wt	StLt WF	SA9DSRXXX11141046	Wt	AE487		B33F	3/12	Eastwood, St Ives (CO)	6/16
MX 13 BCE	Wt	StLt WF	SA9DSRZZZ12141150	Wt	AH002		B33F	3/13	new	3/13

**PG1022208/N: David Clive & Heather Rose EDWARDS, Penrheol, Ciffig, WHITLAND, Carmarthenshire, SA34 0NH.
FN: Taf Valley Holidays. OC: as address. VA: 4.**

See combined entry under PG0007573/I: Bysiau Cwm Taf, Whitland (page 10).

**PG1107005/R: Wynne EDWARDS, 13 Gough Road, YSTALYFERA, Swansea, SA9 2NB.
FN: Wyn Edwards Mini Bus Services. OC: Woodland Service Station, Wind Road, Ystradgynlais, Swansea,
SA9 2JX. VA: 1.**

BW 51 WYN	Fd	Tt	WF0SXXBDFSAU75017	Fd		M8	10/10	new	10/10
BW 54 WYN	Ft	Do	ZFA25000001746685	Ft		M16	5/10	-?-, -?-	4/15
		(ex HX 10 ABV 5/15)							
BW 55 WYN	Fd	Tt	WF0HXXTTGHFC75073	Fd		M8	5/15	new	5/15
		(ex YK 15 WPF 5/15)							
CU 08 AZF	Ft	Do	ZFA25000001454524	?		M8	6/08	-?-, -?-	8/09

**PG1081133/R: Peter EGLITIS, Unit 5 Viking Way, Winch Wen Industrial Estate, SWANSEA, SA1 7DA.
FN: Eastside Cabs. OC: as address. VA: 2.**

x PO 13 YCU	Vx	Viv	W0LJ7B7BSDV604665	Vx		M8	5/13	new	5/13

**PG1148541/I: ELLIS Passenger Transport Limited, Ty Elwyn, LLANLLWCH, Carmarthen, Carmarthenshire, SA31 3RN.
OC: Nantyci Farm, Llysonnen Road, Carmarthen, Carmarthenshire, SA33 5DR. VA: 2
PG1116360/R: Michael Anthony RHYS-ELLIS, 1 Llygad Yr Haul, LLANGUNNOR, Carmarthenshire, SA31 2LB.
FN: Ellis (EPT) Passenger Transport. OC: as address. VA: 1.**

M 15 EPT	MB	413CDI	WDB9046632R577867	Onyx 683		M16	2/04	Buzzlines, Hythe (KT)	11/12
		(ex VX 53 AVF 4/13)							
M 55 EPT	Ds	Jv	SFD321BR4WGJ22185	Pn	9810GDM9710	C41F	by2/99	Hicks, Drefach (CW)	1/17
		(ex S354 UPW 11/16, BIG 8773 by11/16, S354 UPW by2/12)							

**PG1065474/R: John Christopher ELMS, Sunnydene, LOWER FREYSTROP, Haverfordwest, Pembrokeshire,
SA62 4LB. FN: Top-notch Limousines. OC: as address. VA: 2.**

No vehicles yet recorded.

PG0006889/R: Mrs. Buddug EVANS, Cartrefle, LLANGADFAN, Powys, SY21 0NW.
OC: as address. VA: 2.

MJ 61 XFN	Fd	Tt	WF0DXXTTFDBS16161 Fd		M13	12/11 Afford Rent-a-Car,	
						Fenton (YST)	1/15
x AF 62 OZN	Fd	Tt	WF0BXXBDFBCD43957 Fd		M8	9/12 -?-, -?-	4/13

PG1057567/N: EJ EVANS & Sons Limited, Coach Depot, Thornton Industrial Estate, MILFORD HAVEN, Pembrokeshire, SA73 2RR. FN: Evans Coaches. OCs: as address; Lyndhurst, 22 Waterloo Road, Hakin, Milford Haven, SA73 3PB. VA: 14.

R 9 BBC	Vo	B10M-62	YV31MA617VC060461 VH	33406		C49F	3/98 Thompsons, Framlingham (SK)	9/09
R711 KGK	Ds	Jv	SFD731BR4VGJ22113 Bf	3640		C53F	4/96 Lewis, Whitland (CW)	9/05
R160 LDE	Vo	B10M-62	YV31MA61XWA048883 Pn	9812VUP8455		C49FT	3/98 Lewis, Whitland (CW)	11/11
(ex 526 AFE 11/09, R160 LDE 10/05)								
V 29 RCC	MB	O816D	WDB6703742N132912 UNVI OF596			C29F	8/08 Rainham Coach,	
(ex YN 08 OFU 4/15)							Gillingham (KT)	1/16
CV 02 JVG	Vo	B10M-62	YV31MA6131A053383 Pn	0112VUL3573		C49FT	3/02 Jones, Login (CW)	8/15
(ex 521 WDE 8/15, CV 02 JVG 1/07)								
TE 02 EVS	MB	516CDI	WDB9066572S669373 EVM			C22F	7/12 MCH, Uxbridge (LN)	9/14
(ex X111 MCH 11/14, RX 12 HBG 3/13)								
RG 53 GSV	Vo	B12M	YV3R9F8172A000573 Bf	4488		C53F	9/03 Hodge, Sandhurst (BE)	9/14
(ex 1598 PH 8/14)								
YN 06 RVT	Vo	B7R	YV3R6G7226A112891 Pn	0612TLX6529		C57F	4/06 Thornes, Hemingbrough	
(ex ABT 1K 2/12, YN 06 RVT 2/11)								
(NY) 151 8/12								
WJ 11 XFM	Fd	Tt	WF0DXXTTFDAR52113 Fd			M16	3/11 Vospers Car Hire,	
							Plymouth (YDN)	12/13
YY 63 KTE	MB	O816D	WDB6703742N146632 Pn	CC24/1		C31F	9/13 new	9/13
CV 15 LXX	VW	Tr	WV2ZZZ7HZFH119654 VW			M8	4/15 new	4/15
PE 66 EJE	MB	923F	WDB9670232L975783 Erd	-?-		C33F	9/16 new	9/16

Note. Prior to 5/06, vehicles were licensed to PG0006575/N: Edward John & Philip Evans, Steynton.

PG0007566/R: Mary EVANS, Journeys End, Heol Las Road, TALGARTH, Powys, LD3 0PH.
FN: Evans Taxis. OC: as address. VA: 2.

No vehicles currently recorded.

PG1019693/I: EVANS Coaches Tregaron Limited, Old Station Yard, TREGARON, Ceredigion, SY25 6HX.
OC: as address. VA: 12.

OIL 9685	Vo	B10M-62	YV31M2B11TA044244 VH	32300		C67F	3/96 County, Brentwood (EX)	9/14
(ex 5189 RU 10/14, N523 PYS 10/08, 823 NMC 10/08, N523 PYS 3/99, HSK 650 12/98)								
TUI 9870	Ds	Jv	12SDA2155/1392 Bf	2861		C70F	3/96 Bysiau Cwm Taf,	
(ex N 2 BJT 6/14, N 11 LON 10/01)							Whitland (CW)	2/14
6053 NE	Vo	B10M-62	YV31MA612YA052008 VH	33589		C53F	6/00 Nefyn Coaches, Nefyn (CN)	3/14
(ex W159 RYB 5/14, J 20 RGO 3/14, RNZ 1042 5/12, W159 RYB 3/12)								
z D434 BCJ	Bd	YNT	SKFYNT3NZFT109688 Pn	8711NTP3C033		C53F	4/87 Birchnall, Norwich (NK)	6/13
T420 JNE	MB	614D	WDB6683532N080441 ?			C16FL	3/99 Hicks, Drefach (CW)	6/15
VK 51 LKM	MB	311CDI	WDB9036632R311339 ?			M16	9/01 Grantham, Hailey (OX)	by8/13
YS 02 YYG	Ds	Jv	SFD721BR41GJ22392 Pn	0212GFM4702		C70F	6/02 Rowbotham,	
							Kerswell Green (WO)	8/11
HV 52 WSU	Ds	Dt SLF	SFD2BACR32GW16825 SCC	4336/02		B33F	11/02 Tellings Golden Miller (LN)	8/11
x LT 54 WSJ	Ta	He	JT121JK1100020598 Ta			M8	9/04 Bysiau Cwm Taf,	
							Whitland (CW)	12/16
VX 05 BVL	MB	O814D	WDB6703742N113023 Me	3959		C33F	3/05 Lewis, Whitland (CW)	10/11
AE 06 ZCK	MB	O814D	WDB6703742N119899 Ech			C33F	8/06 Parnell, Dunkeswell (DN)	3/13
EJ 06 OKV	MB	311CDI	WDB9036632R878291 Elite			M16	5/06 Mountain Goat,	
(ex M 60 ATS 10/15, EJ 06 OKV 3/10)							Windermere (CA)	10/15

EVANS, TREGARON (continued)

YJ 59 NOU	Oe	M950SL	SABFN5AFEAL193597 Oe		B32F	2/10 new	2/10
SE 64 JAE	Oe	M900SR	SABSW3AF0ES290868 Oe		B32F	1/15 new	1/15
AE 66 VEJ	Oe	V1152MC	SAB4HD2A1GS400149 Oe		B40F	1/17 new	1/17

PG0006253/N: Harold Rupert EVANS, Waterloo Villa, Waterloo Place, Salop Road, WELSHPOOL, Powys, SY21 7HE.
FN: Harry Evans. **OC:** as address. **VA:** 5.

BG 12 HPF	Fd	Tt	WF0DXXTTFDCG27171 Fd		M16	5/12 Hertz (Y)	6/15

PG0007198/R: Edward James EYNON, Glan Gwaun, PONTFAEN, Fishguard, Pembrokeshire. SA65 9SG.
FN: Eynons Coaches. **OC:** as address. **VA:** 1.

No vehicles currently recorded.

PG1134553/R: Simon William FENTON, 43 Pencaerfenni Lane, CROFTY, Swansea, SA4 3SD.
FN: Gower Adventures. **OCL:** as address. **VA:** 2.

CV 57 WKH	Rt	Mtr	VF1NDD1L638123062 ?		M16	10/07 -?-, -?-	5/14

PG1127013/I: FFOSHELIG Coaches Limited, Maes y Prior, St Peters, CARMARTHEN, Carmarthenshire, SA33 5DS.
OC: as address. **VA:** 14.

DSU 772	Vo	B10M-62	YV31MA6121A052693 VH	33618		C49FT	10/02 Richmond, Barley (HT)	8/10
		(ex EJ 52 UYS 9/10, 649 ETF by5/10)						
XUD 367	Vo	B10M-62	YV31M2B17SA042416 Je	23584		C53F	4/95 Davies, Llanelli (CW)	2/15
		(ex M326 KRY 8/16, JIL 7657 2/15, M326 KRY 9/10, DSU 772 8/10, M326 KRY 3/01)						
B 6 PRE	Vo	B7R	YV3R6G7113A005494 Je	28546		C53F	6/03 Hilton, Newton-le-Willows (MY)	8/09
		(ex WD 03 WVW 9/10, 03-KY-2698 by6/07)						
V 2 FOS	Vo	B7R	YV3R6K6259A130424 Ssd	B.4953		C44F	5/09 Priory City of Lincoln	
							Academy, Lincoln (XLI)	7/14
		(ex FN 09 AOA 7/14)						
X847 XDE	Ds	Jv	SFD725BR4YGJ22331 Pn	0012GFM3280		C70F	2/01 Jones, Login (CW)	8/11
FF 05 BUS	Ka	S416GT-HD	WKK63213423100968 Ka			C53FT	2/06 Lodge, High Easter (EX)	8/11
		(ex BV 55 FPN 9/16, 46 AEW by8/16, BV 55 FPN 10/11)						
SF 55 PSY	MB	O814D	WDB6703742N117496 Pn	058.5MXW5928		DP29FL	10/05 Chapman,	
							New Stevenston (SW)	8/13
YJ 55 YGX	Oe	M850SL	SAB19000000002133 Oe			B23F	11/05 Compass, Worthing (WS)	9/14
DS 56 FOS	Vo	B7R	YV3R6K6247A121078 Pn	0712TWX7282		C57F	-/07 Snaith, Otterburn (ND)	8/15
		(ex YV 07 PVJ 9/15, NU 07 YGH 8/14)						
RE 57 FOS	AD	Jv	SFD745BR55GJ22600 Pn	0712GRX7305		C57F	9/07 new	9/07
YJ 59 NNY	Oe	M710SE	SABCN2AB09L193556 Oe			B21F	1/10 new	1/10
DS 11 FOS	MB	O816D	WDB6703742N141419 Pn	118.5MBJ8755		C33F	4/11 new	4/11
RE 65 FOS	MB	Tourismo	WEB63241523000570 MB			C55F	1/16 new	1/16

PG1103625/R: Anthony Kenneth FIRKINS, 611a Birchgrove Road, GLAIS, Swansea, SA7 9EN.
FN: Arrow Minicoaches. **OC:** Arrow Motor Services, Upper Bank, Pentrechwyth, Swansea, SA1 7DB. **VA:** 2.

xw CU 54 HXB	LDV	Cy	SEYZMVSZGDN107558 LDV		M16	1/05 Craig-y-Nos School,	
						Swansea (XCW)	10/13
EJ 08 XHH	Fd	Tt	WF0DXXTTFD8B89846 Fd		M16	5/08 Hopkins, Glais (CW)	11/12
HS 16 FRN	Fd	Tt	WF0HXXTTGHFS16615 Fd		M11	7/16 new	7/16

PG0000421/I: FIRST CYMRU Buses Limited, Heol Gwyrosydd, Penlan, Swansea SA5 7BN.   *(First)*
FNs: De Cymru / South Wales; First Cymru Coach Hire; Clipiwr Cymru / Cymru Clipper.
OCs: [BGD]   Unit 38, Aneurin Bevan Avenue, Brynmenyn Industrial Estate, Bridgend, CF32 9SZ.
        [HAV]   Units 1 & 2, Withybush Trading Estate, Withybush Road, Haverfordwest, SA62 4BS.
        [LLA]   Pentregethin Road, Ravenhill, Swansea, SA5 7BN.
        [MAE]   Plot 4, Heol Ty Gwyn Industrial Estate, Maesteg, CF34 0BQ.
        [PT]   Acacia Avenue, Sandfields Estate, Port Talbot, SA12 7DP.
        [RAV]   Pentregethin Road, Ravenhill, Swansea, SA5 7BN.
        [TYC]   40 Pontardulais Road, Tycroes, SA18 3QD.
Also at   Ex Quarry Park, Ludchurch, Narberth, SA67 8HZ.
        Pembroke Port, The Royal Dockyard, Pembroke, SA72 6TD.
        Brynyhyfryd Garage, Penrhyncoch, Aberystwyth, SY23 3ES.
        [res]   reserve fleet
VA: 412.

19000 S 90 FTR	Vo	B7LA	YV3R7G8123A001532	Wt	H454		AB40D	5/06	Wright, Ballymena (Q)	9/09
(ex YK 06 CZN 9/09)										
19029 S100 FTR	Vo	B7LA	YV3R7G7246A109486	Wt	K367		AB40D	7/06	First York (NY) 19029	5/09
(ex YJ 06 EKT 5/09)										
19030 S 10 FTR	Vo	B7LA	YV3R7G7246A111500	Wt	K857		AB40D	1/08	First Coaches (GL) 19030	7/09
(ex CU 57 AJV by1/13)										
19032 S 20 FTR	Vo	B7LA	YV3R7G7226A111589	Wt	K859		AB40D	1/08	First Coaches (BD) 19032	9/09
(ex CU 57 AJX 9/09)										
19033 S 80 FTR	Vo	B7LA	YV3R7G7276A111779	Wt	K860		AB40D	5//07	new	5/07
(ex YN 07 SYJ 4/09)										
19034 S 30 FTR	Vo	B7LA	YV3R7G7236A111780	Wt	K861		AB40D	1/08	First Coaches (BD) 19034	9/09
(ex CU 57 AJY 9/09)										
19035 S 40 FTR	Vo	B7LA	YV3R7G7296A112075	Wt	K862		AB40D	5/07	new	5/07
(ex CU 57 AKG 4/09)										
19036 S 50 FTR	Vo	B7LA	YV3R7G7206A112076	Wt	K863		AB40D	10/07	new	10/07
(ex CU 57 AKJ 4/09)										
19037 S 60 FTR	Vo	B7LA	YV3R7G7216A112099	Wt	K864		AB40D	10/07	new	10/07
(ex CU 57 AKN 5/09)										
19038 S 70 FTR	Vo	B7LA	YV3R7G7246A112100	Wt	K919		AB40D	10/07	new	10/07
(ex CU 57 AKK 7/09)										
20323 YN 57 BVW	Vo	B7R	YV3R6K6258A122953	Pn	0712TWS7404		C70FL	10/07	new	10/07
(named Afon Llwchwr/*River Loughor*)										
20324 YN 57 BVX	Vo	B7R	YV3R6K6278A122954	Pn	0712TWS7405		C70FL	10/07	new	10/07
(named Afon Afan/*River Afan*)										
20325 YN 57 BVY	Vo	B7R	YV3R6K6238A122997	Pn	0712TWS7406		C70FL	10/07	new	10/07
(named Afon Mellte/*River Mellte*)										
23319 YN 55 PXK	Sca	K114EB4	YS2K4X20001849221	Ir	102574		C49FT	12/05	First Hampshire & Dorset	
(named Afon Ogwr/*River Ogmore*)									(HA) 23319	5/13
23320 YN 55 PXL	Sca	K114EB4	YS2K4X20001849229	Ir	102577		C49FT	12/05	First Hampshire & Dorset	
(named Afon Taf/*River Taff*)									(HA) 23320	1/13
23321 YN 06 CGU	Sca	K114EB4	YS2K4X20001849235	Ir	102578		C41FT	5/06	First Hampshire & Dorset	
(named Afon Nedd/*River Neath*)									(HA) 23321	1/13
23323 YN 06 CGX	Sca	K114EB4	YS2K4X20001849270	Ir	102781		C41FT	5/06	First Hampshire & Dorset	
(named *Afon Tawe/River Tawe*)									(HA) 23323	1/13
32037 W807 EOW	Vo	B7TL	YV3S2C61XYC000314	Ar	9954/10		H49/29F	4/00	First Somerset & Avon	
									(SO) 32037	9/15
32041 W811 EOW	Vo	B7TL	YV3S2C619YC000322	Ar	9954/09		H49/29F	4/00	First Somerset & Avon	
									(SO) 32041	9/15
32042 W812 EOW	Vo	B7TL	YV3S2C610YC000323	Ar	9954/07		H49/29F	4/00	First Somerset & Avon	
									(SO) 32042	9/15
32044 W814 EOW	Vo	B7TL	YV3S2C616YC000326	Ar	9954/12		H49/29F	4/00	First Somerset & Avon	
									(SO) 32044	9/15
33061 LN 51 GKU	Ds	Tt	SFD136BR21GX21820	Pn	7602		H39/22F	12/01	First South Yorkshire	
									(SY) 33061	12/16
33062 LN 51 GKV	Ds	Tt	SFD136BR21GX21819	Pn	7603		H39/22F	12/01	First South Yorkshire	
									(SY) 33062	1/17
33063 LN 51 GKX	Ds	Tt	SFD136BR21GX21822	Pn	7604		H39/22F	12/01	First South Yorkshire	
									(SY) 33063	1/17

FIRST CYMRU (continued)

33064	LN 51 GKY	Ds	Tt	SFD136BR21GX21817	Pn	7605	H39/22F	12/01	First South Yorkshire	
									(SY) 33064	1/17
41381	X381 HLR	Ds	Dt SLF	SFD212AR1YGW15306	MI	C39.674	B31F	11/00	Centrewest (LN) 41381	10/09
41386	X386 HLR	Ds	Dt SLF	SFD212AR1YGW15359	MI	C39.679	B31F	12/00	Centrewest (LN) 41386	10/09
41391	X391 HLR	Ds	Dt SLF	SFD212AR1YGW15366	MI	C39.684	B31F	11/00	Centrewest (LN) 41391	1/10
41392	X392 HLR	Ds	Dt SLF	SFD212AR1YGW15398	MI	C39.685	B31F	11/00	Centrewest (LN) 41392	1/10
41489	LT 02 ZFA	Ds	Dt SLF	SFD6B2CR31GW16470	MI	C39.846	B25F	6/02	Centrewest (LN) 41489	12/09
41491	LT 02 ZFC	Ds	Dt SLF	SFD6B2CR31GW16472	MI	C39.848	B25F	7/02	Centrewest (LN) 41491	12/09
41719	W719 ULL	Ds	Dt SLF	SFD212AR1YGW14492	MI	C39.619	B33F	7/00	First Capital East (LN) 41719	10/09
41727	W727 ULL	Ds	Dt SLF	SFD212AR1YGW14565	MI	C39.628	B28F	7/00	First Bristol (GL) 41727	12/14
42569	P569 BTH	Ds	Dt SLF	SFD112BR1TGW10302	Pn	969.2HWN5536	B31F	10/96		10/96
42600	CU 54 HYK	AD	Dt SLF	SFD1BACR44GW18164	AD	-?-	B31F	2/05	new	2/05
42601	CU 54 HYL	AD	Dt SLF	SFD1BACR44GW18166	AD	4234/3	B31F	2/05	new	2/05
42602	CU 54 HYM	AD	Dt SLF	SFD1BACR44GW18170	AD	-?-	B31F	2/05	new	2/05
42603	CU 54 HYN	AD	Dt SLF	SFD1BACR44GW18167	AD	4234/4	B31F	2/05	new	2/05
42604	CU 54 HYO	AD	Dt SLF	SFD1BACR44GW18168	AD	4234/6	B31F	2/05	new	2/05
42605	CU 54 HYP	AD	Dt SLF	SFD1BACR44GW18169	AD	4234/5	B31F	2/05	new	2/05
42606	CU 54 HYR	AD	Dt SLF	SFD1BACR44GW18171	AD	4234/7	B31F	2/05	new	2/05
42607	CU 54 HYT	AD	Dt SLF	SFD1BACR44GW18172	AD	4234/8	B31F	2/05	new	2/05
42608	CU 54 HYV	AD	Dt SLF	SFD1BACR44GW18173	AD	-?-	B31F	2/05	new	2/05
42609	CU 54 HYW	AD	Dt SLF	SFD1BACR44GW18174	AD	4234/9	B31F	2/05	new	2/05
42610	CU 54 HYX	AD	Dt SLF	SFD1BACR44GW18175	AD	4234/13	B31F	2/05	new	2/05
42611	CU 54 HYY	AD	Dt SLF	SFD1BACR44GW18176	AD	-?-	B31F	2/05	new	2/05
42612	CU 54 HYZ	AD	Dt SLF	SFD1BACR44GW18177	AD	4234/12	B31F	2/05	new	2/05
42613	CU 54 HZA	AD	Dt SLF	SFD1BACR44GW18178	AD	-?-	B31F	2/05	new	2/05
42614	CU 54 HZB	AD	Dt SLF	SFD1BACR44GW18179	AD	-?-	B31F	2/05	new	2/05
42674	CU 53 APO	Tbs	Dt SLF	SFD3CACR43GW87466	Tbs	3052/1	B31F	11/03	new	11/03
42675	CU 53 APV	Tbs	Dt SLF	SFD3CACR43GW87467	Tbs	3052/2	B31F	11/03	new	11/03
42676	CU 53 APX	Tbs	Dt SLF	SFD3CACR43GW87470	Tbs	3052/3	B31F	11/03	new	11/03
42677	CU 53 ASO	Tbs	Dt SLF	SFD3CACR43GW87471	Tbs	3052/4	B31F	11/03	new	11/03
42678	CU 53 ARZ	Tbs	Dt SLF	SFD3CACR43GW87472	Tbs	3052/5	B31F	11/03	new	11/03
42679	CU 53 ARX	Tbs	Dt SLF	SFD3CACR43GW87473	Tbs	3052/6	B37F	11/03	new	11/03
42680	CU 53 ARO	Tbs	Dt SLF	SFD3CACR43GW87474	Tbs	3052/7	B37F	11/03	new	11/03
42681	CU 53 ARF	Tbs	Dt SLF	SFD3CACR43GW87476	Tbs	3052/9	B37F	11/03	new	11/03
42682	CU 53 APZ	Tbs	Dt SLF	SFD3CACR43GW87477	Tbs	3052/10	B37F	11/03	new	11/03
42683	CU 53 APY	Tbs	Dt SLF	SFD3CACR43GW87489	Tbs	3052/11	B37F	11/03	new	11/03
42684	CU 53 AUP	Tbs	Dt SLF	SFD3CACR43GW87490	Tbs	3052/12	B37F	12/03	new	12/03
42685	CU 53 AUO	Tbs	Dt SLF	SFD3CACR43GW87491	Tbs	3052/13	B31F	12/03	new	12/03
42686	CU 53 AUT	Tbs	Dt SLF	SFD3CACR43GW87492	Tbs	3052/14	B31F	12/03	new	12/03
42687	CU 53 AUU	Tbs	Dt SLF	SFD3CACR43GW87493	Tbs	3052/15	B31F	12/03	new	12/03
42688	CU 53 AUV	Tbs	Dt SLF	SFD3CACR43GW87494	Tbs	3052/16	B31F	12/03	new	12/03
42689	CU 53 AUW	Tbs	Dt SLF	SFD3CACR43GW87495	Tbs	3052/8	B31F	12/03	new	12/03
42690	CU 53 AUX	Tbs	Dt SLF	SFD3CACR43GW87507	Tbs	3052/17	B31F	12/03	new	12/03
42691	CU 53 AUY	Tbs	Dt SLF	SFD3CACR43GW87508	Tbs	3052/18	B31F	12/03	new	12/03
42692	CU 53 AVB	Tbs	Dt SLF	SFD3CACR43GW87509	Tbs	3052/19	B37F	12/03	new	12/03
42693	CU 03 BHV	Tbs	Dt SLF	SFD3CACR33GW87253	Tbs	3017/1	B37F	8/03	new	8/03
42694	CU 03 BHW	Tbs	Dt SLF	SFD3CACR33GW87254	Tbs	3017/2	B37F	8/03	new	8/03
42861	CU 53 AVJ	Tbs	Dt SLF	SFD3CACR43GW87510	Tbs	3052/20	B37F	12/03	new	12/03
42862	CU 53 AVK	Tbs	Dt SLF	SFD3CACR43GW87511	Tbs	3052/21	B37F	12/03	new	12/03
42863	CU 53 AVL	Tbs	Dt SLF	SFD3CACR43GW87512	Tbs	3052/22	B37F	12/03	new	12/03
42864	CU 53 AVM	Tbs	Dt SLF	SFD3CACR43GW87518	Tbs	3052/23	B37F	12/03	new	12/03
42865	CU 53 AVN	Tbs	Dt SLF	SFD3CACR43GW87519	Tbs	3052/24	B37F	12/03	new	12/03
42866	CU 53 AVO	Tbs	Dt SLF	SFD3CACR43GW87520	Tbs	3052/25	B37F	12/03	new	12/03
42867	CU 53 AVR	Tbs	Dt SLF	SFD3CACR43GW87521	Tbs	3052/26	B37F	12/03	new	12/03
42868	CU 53 AVP	Tbs	Dt SLF	SFD3CACR43GW87522	Tbs	3052/27	B37F	12/03	new	12/03
42869	CU 53 AVV	Tbs	Dt SLF	SFD3CACR43GW87534	Tbs	3052/28	B37F	12/03	new	12/03
42870	CU 53 AVT	Tbs	Dt SLF	SFD3CACR43GW87535	Tbs	3052/29	B37F	12/03	new	12/03
42877	SF 05 KWY	AD	Dt SLF	SFD3CACR44GW18053	AD	4225/1	B37F	3/05	First Glasgow (No.2)	
									(SW) 42877	12/07
42878	SF 05 KWZ	AD	Dt SLF	SFD3CACR44GW18054	AD	4225/2	B37F	3/05	First Glasgow (No.2)	
									(SW) 42878	12/07
42879	SF 05 KXA	AD	Dt SLF	SFD3CACR44GW18055	AD	4225/3	B37F	3/05	First Glasgow (No.2)	
									(SW) 42879	12/07

FIRST CYMRU (continued)

42880 SF 05 KXB	AD	Dt SLF	SFD3CACR44GW18056	AD	4225/4	B37F	3/05	First Glasgow (No.2)	
								(SW) 42880	1/08
42881 SF 05 KXC	AD	Dt SLF	SFD3CACR44GW18057	AD	4225/5	B37F	3/05	First Glasgow (No.2)	
								(SW) 42881	1/08
42882 SF 05 KXD	AD	Dt SLF	SFD3CACR44GW18058	AD	4225/6	B37F	3/05	First Glasgow (No.2)	
								(SW) 42882	1/08
42883 SF 05 KXE	AD	Dt SLF	SFD3CACR44GW18059	AD	4225/7	B37F	3/05	First Glasgow (No.2)	
								(SW) 42883	12/07
42884 SF 05 KXH	AD	Dt SLF	SFD3CACR44GW18060	AD	4225/8	B37F	3/05	First Glasgow (No.2)	
								(SW) 42884	12/07
42912 WX 05 RVW	AD	Dt SLF	SFD3CACR44GW18083	AD	4226/18	B37F	3/05	First Somerset & Avon	
								(SO) 42912	9/12
42913 WX 05 RVY	AD	Dt SLF	SFD3CACR44GW18084	AD	4226/19	B37F	3/05	First Somerset & Avon	
								(SO) 42913	9/12
43836 SN 53 ESV	Tbs	Dt SLF	SFD6BACR33GW87227	Tbs	3022/2	B29F	10/03	new	10/03
43837 SN 53 ESU	Tbs	Dt SLF	SFD6BACR33GW87226	Tbs	3022/1	B29F	10/03	new	10/03
43838 SN 53 ESY	Tbs	Dt SLF	SFD6BACR33GW87315	Tbs	3022/3	B29F	10/03	new	10/03
43839 SN 53 ETD	Tbs	Dt SLF	SFD6BACR33GW87316	Tbs	3022/4	B29F	10/03	new	10/03
43840 SN 53 ETE	Tbs	Dt SLF	SFD6BACR33GW87317	Tbs	3022/5	B29F	10/03	new	10/03
43841 SN 53 ETF	Tbs	Dt SLF	SFD6BACR33GW87318	Tbs	3022/6	B29F	10/03	new	10/03
43850 WK 06 AEE	AD	Dt SLF	SFD6BACR45GW88584	AD	5239/1	B29F	3/06	First Devon & Cornwall	
								(DN) 42850	6/11
43851 WK 06 AEF	AD	Dt SLF	SFD6BACR45GW88585	AD	5239/2	B29F	3/06	First Devon & Cornwall	
								(DN) 42851	6/11
43852 WK 06 AFU	AD	Dt SLF	SFD6BACR46GW88686	AD	5239/3	B29F	3/06	First Devon & Cornwall	
								(DN) 42852	6/11
43853 WK 06 AFV	AD	Dt SLF	SFD6BACR46GW88687	AD	5239/4	B29F	3/06	First Devon & Cornwall	
								(DN) 42853	6/11
43901 SN 03 LGG	Ds	Dt SLF	SFD4DBER33GW47247	Tbs	3024/1	B41F	6/03	new	6/03
43902 SN 03 LGK	Ds	Dt SLF	SFD4DBER33GW47258	Tbs	3024/3	B41F	6/03	new	6/03
43903 SN 03 LGJ	Ds	Dt SLF	SFD4DBER33GW47248	Tbs	3024/2	B41F	6/03	new	6/03
44500 WA 56 EBZ	AD	Dt	SFD321AR16GY10106	AD	6204/1	B38F	9/06	First Devon & Cornwall	
								(DN) 44500	5/11
44501 CU 08 ACY	AD	Dt	SFD361AR27GY10551	AD	7229/1	B38F	4/08	new	4/08
44502 CU 08 ACZ	AD	Dt	SFD361AR27GY10552	AD	7229/2	B35F	3/08	First Beeline (BE) 44502	12/15
44503 CU 08 ADO	AD	Dt	SFD361AR27GY10553	AD	7229/3	B35F	4/08	First Beeline (BE) 45503	12/15
44504 CU 08 ADV	AD	Dt	SFD361AR27GY10554	AD	7229/4	B35F	4/08	First Beeline (BE) 45504	12/15
44505 CU 08 ADX	AD	Dt	SFD361AR27GY10555	AD	7229/5	B35F	3/08	First Beeline (BE) 45505	12/15
44552 YX 13 AEV	AD	E20D	SFD8D1AR6DGY13422	AD	C252/1	B33F	3/13	new	3/13
44553 YX 13 AEW	AD	E20D	SFD8D1AR6DGY13523	AD	C252/2	B33F	3/13	new	3/13
44554 YX 13 AEY	AD	E20D	SFD8D1AR6DGY13524	AD	C252/3	B33F	3/13	new	3/13
44555 YX 13 AEZ	AD	E20D	SFD8D1AR6DGY13525	AD	C252/4	B33F	3/13	new	3/13
44556 YX 13 AFA	AD	E20D	SFD8D1AR6DGY13526	AD	C252/5	B33F	3/13	new	3/13
44557 YX 13 AFE	AD	E20D	SFD8D1AR6DGY13527	AD	C252/6	B33F	3/13	new	3/13
44558 YX 13 AKU	AD	E20D	SFD8D1AR6DGY13528	AD	C252/7	B33F	3/13	new	3/13
44559 YX 13 AKV	AD	E20D	SFD8D1AR6DGY13529	AD	C252/8	B33F	3/13	new	3/13
44568 YX 63 LLJ	AD	E20D	SFD7E1AR6DGY13914	AD	D233/9	B36F	9/13	First Beeline (BE) 44568	9/14
44570 YX 63 LKU	AD	E20D	SFD7E1AR6DGU13939	AD	D232/2	B37F	11/13	new	11/13
44573 YX 13 BNA	AD	E20D	SFD8D1AR6DGY13639	AD	D203/1	B33F	5/13	new	5/13
44574 YX 13 BNB	AD	E20D	SFD8D1AR6DGY13640	AD	D203/2	B33F	5/13	new	5/13
44575 YX 13 BND	AD	E20D	SFD8D1AR6DGY13641	AD	D203/3	B33F	5/13	new	5/13
44576 YX 13 BNE	AD	E20D	SFD8D1AR6DGY13642	AD	D203/4	B33F	5/13	new	5/13
44577 YX 13 BNF	AD	E20D	SFD8D1AR6DGY13643	AD	D203/5	B33F	5/13	new	5/13
44578 YX 13 BNJ	AD	E20D	SFD8D1AR6DGY13644	AD	D203/6	B33F	5/13	new	5/13
44579 YX 13 BNK	AD	E20D	SFD8D1AR6DGY13645	AD	D203/7	B33F	5/13	new	5/13
44580 YX 13 BNL	AD	E20D	SFD8D1AR6DGY13646	AD	D203/8	B33F	5/13	new	5/13
44581 YX 13 BNN	AD	E20D	SFD8D1AR6DGY13647	AD	D203/9	B33F	5/13	new	5/13
44582 YX 63 ZUD	AD	E20D	SFD7E1AR6DGY14034	AD	-?-	B37F	12/13	new	12/13
44583 YX 63 ZVA	AD	E20D	SFD7E1AR6DGY14035	AD	-?-	B37F	12/13	new	12/13
44584 YX 63 ZVB	AD	E20D	SFD7E1AR6DGY14036	AD	-?-	B37F	12/13	new	12/13
44585 YX 63 ZVC	AD	E20D	SFD7E1AR6DGY14037	AD	-?-	B37F	12/13	new	12/13
44586 YX 63 ZVD	AD	E20D	SFD7E1AR6DGY14038	AD	-?-	B37F	12/13	new	12/13
44587 YX 63 ZVE	AD	E20D	SFD7E1AR6DGY14044	AD	-?-	B37F	12/13	new	12/13

FIRST CYMRU (continued)

44588	YX 63 ZVF	AD	E20D	SFD7E1AR6DGY14045	AD	-?-	B37F	12/13	new	12/13
44589	YX 63 ZVG	AD	E20D	SFD7E1AR6DGY14046	AD	-?-	B37F	12/13	new	12/13
44590	YX 63 ZVH	AD	E20D	SFD7E1AR6DGY14047	AD	D229/9	B37F	12/13	new	12/13
44591	YX 63 LHK	AD	E20D	SFD7E1AR6DGY14049	AD	D230/1	B37F	12/13	new	12/13
44592	YX 63 LHL	AD	E20D	SFD7E1AR6DGY14050	AD	D230/2	B37F	12/13	new	12/13
44593	YX 63 LHM	AD	E20D	SFD7E1AR6DGY14051	AD	D230/3	B37F	12/13	new	12/13
44594	YX 14 RWN	AD	E20D	SFD7E1AR6DGY14052	AD	-?-	B39F	4/14	new	4/14
44595	YX 14 RWO	AD	E20D	SFD7E1AR6DGY14053	AD	-?-	B39F	4/14	new	4/14
44602	YX 14 RUC	AD	E20D	SFD7E1AR6DGY14148	AD	-?-	B39F	3/14	new	3/14
44603	YX 14 RUH	AD	E20D	SFD7E1AR6DGY14149	AD	-?-	B39F	4/14	new	4/14
44604	YX 14 RUJ	AD	E20D	SFD7E1AR6DGY14150	AD	-?-	B39F	4/14	new	4/14
44605	YX 14 RUO	AD	E20D	SFD7E1AR6DGY14151	AD	-?-	B39F	4/14	new	4/14
44606	YX 14 RUR	AD	E20D	SFD7E1AR6DGY14152	AD	-?-	B39F	4/14	new	4/14
44607	YX 14 RUU	AD	E20D	SFD7E1AR6DGY14153	AD	-?-	B39F	4/14	new	4/14
44608	YX 14 RUV	AD	E20D	SFD7E1AR6DGY14154	AD	-?-	B39F	4/14	new	4/14
44609	YX 14 RUW	AD	E20D	SFD7E1AR6DGY14155	AD	-?-	B39F	5/14	new	5/14
44610	YX 14 RUY	AD	E20D	SFD7E1AR6DGY14156	AD	-?-	B39F	5/14	new	5/14
44611	YX 14 RVA	AD	E20D	SFD7E1AR6DGY14157	AD	-?-	B39F	5/14	new	5/14
44612	YX 14 RVC	AD	E20D	SFD7E1AR6DGY14158	AD	-?-	B39F	5/14	new	5/14
44613	YX 14 RVE	AD	E20D	SFD7E1AR6DGY14159	AD	D261/12	B39F	7/14	First Games Transport (SW) 44613	8/14
44614	YX 14 RVF	AD	E20D	SFD7E1AR6DGY14160	AD	D261/13	B39F	7/14	First Games Transport (SW) 44614	8/14
44615	YX 14 RVJ	AD	E20D	SFD7E1AR6DGY14161	AD	D261/14	B39F	7/14	First Games Transport (SW) 44615	8/14
44616	YX 14 RVK	AD	E20D	SFD7E1AR6DGY14162	AD	D261/15	B39F	7/14	First Games Transport (SW) 44616	8/14
44617	YX 14 RVL	AD	E20D	SFD7E1AR6DGY14163	AD	D261/16	B39F	7/14	First Games Transport (SW) 44617	8/14
44618	YX 14 RVM	AD	E20D	SFD7E1AR6DGY14164	AD	D261/17	B39F	7/14	First Games Transport (SW) 44618	8/14
44619	YX 14 RVN	AD	E20D	SFD7E1AR6DGY14165	AD	D261/18	B39F	7/14	First Games Transport (SW) 44619	8/14
44620	YX 14 RVO	AD	E20D	SFD7E1AR6DGY14166	AD	D261/19	B39F	7/14	First Games Transport (SW) 44620	8/14
44621	YX 14 RVP	AD	E20D	SFD7E1AR6DGY14167	AD	D261/20	B39F	7/14	First Games Transport (SW) 44621	8/14
44622	YX 14 RVR	AD	E20D	SFD7E1AR6EGY14182	AD	-?-	B39F	4/14	new	4/14
44623	YX 14 RVT	AD	E20D	SFD7E1AR6EGY14183	AD	-?-	B39F	4/14	new	4/14
44624	YX 14 RVU	AD	E20D	SFD7E1AR6EGY14184	AD	-?-	B39F	4/14	new	4/14
44625	YX 14 RVV	AD	E20D	SFD7E1AR6EGY14185	AD	-?-	B39F	4/14	new	4/14
44626	YX 14 RVW	AD	E20D	SFD7E1AR6EGY14186	AD	-?-	B39F	4/14	new	4/14
44627	YX 14 RVY	AD	E20D	SFD7E1AR6EGY14188	AD	-?-	B39F	4/14	new	4/14
44628	YX 14 RVZ	AD	E20D	SFD7E1AR6EGY14189	AD	-?-	B39F	4/14	new	4/14
44629	YX 14 RWE	AD	E20D	SFD7E1AR6EGY14190	AD	-?-	B39F	4/14	new	4/14
44630	YX 14 RWF	AD	E20D	SFD7E1AR6EGY14191	AD	-?-	B39F	4/14	new	4/14
44631	YX 14 RWJ	AD	E20D	SFD7E1AR6EGY14192	AD	-?-	B39F	4/14	new	4/14
44632	YX 14 RWK	AD	E20D	SFD7E1AR6EGY14187	AD	-?-	B39F	4/14	new	4/14
44633	YX 64 VPJ	AD	E20D	SFD7E1AR6EGY14425	AD	E245/1	B39F	9/14	new	9/14
44634	YX 64 VPK	AD	E20D	SFD7E1AR6EGY14426	AD	E245/2	B39F	10/14	new	10/14
44635	YX 64 VPL	AD	E20D	SFD7E1AR6EGY14427	AD	E245/3	B39F	10/14	new	10/14
44636	YX 64 VPM	AD	E20D	SFD7E1AR6EGY14428	AD	E245/4	B39F	10/14	new	10/14
47629	SN 15 ADO	Wt	StLt DF	SA9DSRXXX15141985	Wt	-?-	B37F	4/15	new	4/15
47630	SN 15 ADU	Wt	StLt DF	SA9DSRXXX15141986	Wt	-?-	B37F	4/15	new	4/15
47631	SN 15 ADV	Wt	StLt DF	SA9DSRXXX15141987	Wt	-?-	B37F	4/15	new	4/15
47632	SN 15 ADX	Wt	StLt DF	SA9DSRXXX15141988	Wt	-?-	B37F	4/15	new	4/15
47633	SN 15 ADZ	Wt	StLt DF	SA9DSRXXX15141989	Wt	-?-	B37F	4/15	new	4/15
47634	SN 15 AEA	Wt	StLt DF	SA9DSRXXX15141990	Wt	-?-	B37F	4/15	new	4/15
47635	SN 15 AEB	Wt	StLt DF	SA9DSRXXX15141991	Wt	-?-	B37F	4/15	new	4/15
47636	SN 15 AEC	Wt	StLt DF	SA9DSRXXX15141992	Wt	-?-	B37F	4/15	new	4/15
47637	SN 15 AED	Wt	StLt DF	SA9DSRXXX15141993	Wt	-?-	B37F	4/15	new	4/15
47638	SN 15 AEE	Wt	StLt DF	SA9DSRXXX15141994	Wt	-?-	B37F	4/15	new	4/15
47639	SN 15 AEF	Wt	StLt DF	SA9DSRXXX15141995	Wt	-?-	B37F	4/15	new	4/15

FIRST CYMRU (continued)

47640	SN 15 AEG	Wt	StLt DF	SA9DSRXXX15141996	Wt	-?-	B37F	4/15 new	4/15
47641	SN 15 AEJ	Wt	StLt DF	SA9DSRXXX15141997	Wt	-?-	B37F	4/15 new	4/15
47642	SN 15 AEK	Wt	StLt DF	SA9DSRXXX15141998	Wt	-?-	B37F	4/15 new	4/15
47659	SN 65 OKO	Wt	StLt DF	SA9DSRXXX15141185	Wt	AM502	B37F	9/15 new	9/15
47660	SN 65 OKP	Wt	StLt DF	SA9DSRXXX15141186	Wt	AM503	B37F	10/15 new	10/15
47661	SN 15 ABK	Wt	StLt DF	SA9DSRXXX15141963	Wt	-?-	B37F	4/15 new	4/15
47662	SN 15 ABO	Wt	StLt DF	SA9DSRXXX15141964	Wt	-?-	B37F	4/15 new	4/15
	(named *William Gammon*)								
47663	SN 15 ABU	Wt	StLt DF	SA9DSRXXX15141965	Wt	-?-	B37F	4/15 new	4/15
	(named *Susan Miles 1959 – 2016*)								
47664	SN 15 ABV	Wt	StLt DF	SA9DSRXXX15141966	Wt	-?-	B37F	4/15 new	4/15
	(named *Ivor John Allchurch MBE*)								
47673	SL 15 RVO	Wt	StLt DF	SA9DSRXXX15141005	Wt	-?-	B37F	5/15 new	5/15
	(named *Sir Harry Secombe*)								
47674	SL 15 RVP	Wt	StLt DF	SA9DSRXXX15141007	Wt	-?-	B37F	5/15 new	5/15
	(named *Red Lady of Paviland*)								
47675	SL 15 RVR	Wt	StLt DF	SA9DSRXXX15141008	Wt	-?-	B37F	5/15 new	5/15
	(named *John Henry Vivian*)								
47676	SL 15 RVT	Wt	StLt DF	SA9DSRXXX15141009	Wt	-?-	B37F	5/15 new	5/15
	(named *Dylan Thomas*)								
47677	SL 15 RVU	Wt	StLt DF	SA9DSRXXX15141010	Wt	-?-	B37F	5/15 new	5/15
47678	SL 15 RVV	Wt	StLt DF	SA9DSRXXX15141011	Wt	-?-	B37F	5/15 new	5/15
47679	SL 15 RVW	Wt	StLt DF	SA9DSRXXX15141012	Wt	-?-	B37F	5/15 new	5/15
47680	SL 15 RVX	Wt	StLt DF	SA9DSRXXX15141013	Wt	-?-	B37F	5/15 new	5/15
47681	SL 15 RVY	Wt	StLt DF	SA9DSRXXX15141014	Wt	-?-	B37F	5/15 new	5/15
47682	SL 15 RWX	Wt	StLt DF	SA9DSRXXX15141075	Wt	AM344	B37F	6/15 new	6/15
47683	SL 15 XWY	Wt	StLt DF	SA9DSRXXX15141076	Wt	AM345	B37F	6/15 new	6/15
47684	SL 15 XWZ	Wt	StLt DF	SA9DSRXXX15141077	Wt	AM346	B37F	5/15 new	5/15
47685	SL 15 XXA	Wt	StLt DF	SA9DSRXXX15141078	Wt	AM347	B37F	5/15 new	5/15
49002	YJ 13 HMD	Oe	V1080	SABWW4AC0DS320639	Oe		B36F	5/13 new	5/13
49003	YJ 13 HME	Oe	V1080	SABWW4AC0DS320640	Oe		B36F	5/13 new	5/13
49004	YJ 13 HMF	Oe	V1080	SABWW4AC0DS320641	Oe		B36F	5/13 new	5/13
49005	YJ 13 HMG	Oe	V1080	SABWW4AC0DS320642	Oe		B36F	5/13 new	5/13
49006	YJ 13 HMH	Oe	V1080	SABWW4AC0DS320643	Oe		B36F	5/13 new	5/13
49007	YJ 13 HMK	Oe	V1080	SABWW4AC0DS320644	Oe		B36F	5/13 new	5/13
49008	YJ 13 HMU	Oe	V1080	SABWW4AC0DS320645	Oe		B36F	6/13 new	6/13
49009	YJ 13 HMV	Oe	V1080	SABWW4AC0DS320646	Oe		B36F	6/13 new	6/13
49010	YJ 13 HMX	Oe	V1080	SABWW4AC0DS320647	Oe		B36F	6/13 new	6/13
49301	YJ 13 HLR	Oe	V1170	SABXW4AC0DS320630	Oe		B40F	5/13 new	5/13
49302	YJ 13 HLU	Oe	V1170	SABXW4AC0DS320631	Oe		B40F	5/13 new	5/13
49303	YJ 13 HLV	Oe	V1170	SABXW4AC0DS320632	Oe		B40F	5/13 new	5/13
49304	YJ 13 HLW	Oe	V1170	SABXW4AC0DS320633	Oe		B40F	5/13 new	5/13
49305	YJ 13 HLX	Oe	V1170	SABXW4AC0DS320634	Oe		B40F	5/13 new	5/13
49306	YJ 13 HLY	Oe	V1170	SABXW4AC0DS320635	Oe		B40F	5/13 new	5/13
49307	YJ 13 HLZ	Oe	V1170	SABXW4AC0DS320636	Oe		B40F	5/13 new	5/13
49308	YJ 13 HMA	Oe	V1170	SABXW4AC0DS320637	Oe		B40F	5/13 new	5/13
49309	YJ 13 HMC	Oe	V1170	SABXW4AC0DS320638	Oe		B40F	5/13 new	5/13
53058	VX 53 OEV	Oe	M850	SAB19000000001277	Oe		B26F	11/03 First Potteries (ST) 53058	1/17
53059	VX 53 OEN	Oe	M850	SAB19000000001250	Oe		B26F	10/03 First Potteries (ST) 53059	1/17
53060	VX 53 OEO	Oe	M850	SAB19000000001251	Oe		B26F	10/03 First Potteries (ST) 53060	12/16
53063	VX 53 OET	Oe	M850	SAB19000000001254	Oe		B26F	11/03 First Potteries (ST) 53061	12/16
53707	MX 58 KZA	Oe	M710SL	SABCN2AN08R193126	Oe		B21F	12/08 new	12/08
53708	MX 58 KZB	Oe	M710SE	SABCN2AB08R193300	Oe		B21F	1/09 new	1/09
53711	YJ 60 LRN	Oe	M780SE	SABDN2AB0AL193724	Oe		B26F	12/10 Edwards, Tiers Cross (CW)	7/16
53802	WX 05 RRV	Oe	M850SL	SAB19000000001720	Oe		B26F	4/05 First Hampshire & Dorset (HA) 53802	8/12
53804	WX 05 RRZ	Oe	M850SL	SAB19000000001722	Oe		B26F	4/05 First Somerset & Avon (SO) 53804	3/12
62189	W591 RFS	Vo	B10BLE	YV3R4A517YA006534	Ar	9919/15	B44F	6/00 First Bristol (GL) 62189	5/16
62208	W596 RFS	Vo	B10BLE	YV3R4A519YA006566	Ar	9959/20	B44F	7/00 First Bristol (GL) 62208	5/16
63079	SN 14 DTX	Wt	StLt DF	SA9DSRXXX13141310	Wt	-?-	B41F	3/14 new	3/14
63080	SN 14 DTY	Wt	StLt DF	SA9DSRXXX13141311	Wt	-?-	B41F	3/14 new	3/14
63081	SN 14 DTZ	Wt	StLt DF	SA9DSRXXX13141312	Wt	-?-	B41F	3/14 new	3/14

FIRST CYMRU (continued)

Fleet No	Reg		Type	Chassis No		Body	Seats	Date	Notes		Date
63082	SN 14 DUA	Wt	StLt DF	SA9DSRXXX13141313	Wt	-?-	B41F	3/14	new		3/14
63083	SN 14 DUH	Wt	StLt DF	SA9DSRXXX14141420	Wt	-?-	B41F	4/14	new		4/14
63084	SN 14 DUJ	Wt	StLt DF	SA9DSRXXX14141421	Wt	-?-	B41F	4/14	new		4/14
63085	SN 14 DUU	Wt	StLt DF	SA9DSRXXX14141422	Wt	-?-	B41F	4/14	new		4/14
63086	SN 14 DUV	Wt	StLt DF	SA9DSRXXX14141423	Wt	-?-	B41F	4/14	new		4/14
63087	SN 14 DUY	Wt	StLt DF	SA9DSRXXX14141424	Wt	-?-	B41F	4/14	new		4/14
63088	SN 14 DVB	Wt	StLt DF	SA9DSRXXX14141425	Wt	-?-	B41F	4/14	new		4/14
63089	SN 14 DVC	Wt	StLt DF	SA9DSRXXX14141426	Wt	-?-	B41F	4/14	new		4/14
63090	SN 14 DVF	Wt	StLt DF	SA9DSRXXX14141446	Wt	-?-	B41F	4/14	new		4/14
63091	SN 14 DVG	Wt	StLt DF	SA9DSRXXX14141428	Wt	-?-	B41F	4/14	new		4/14
63092	SN 14 DVH	Wt	StLt DF	SA9DSRXXX14141429	Wt	-?-	B41F	4/14	new		4/14
63093	SN 14 DVJ	Wt	StLt DF	SA9DSRXXX14141430	Wt	-?-	B41F	4/14	new		4/14
63094	SN 14 DVK	Wt	StLt DF	SA9DSRXXX14141431	Wt	-?-	B41F	4/14	new		4/14
63095	SN 14 DVL	Wt	StLt DF	SA9DSRXXX14141432	Wt	-?-	B41F	4/14	new		4/14
66350	MV 02 VEA	Vo	B7L	YV3R7G6162A001115	Wt	F113	B41F	7/02	First Somerset & Avon (SO) 66350		9/16
66351	MV 02 VEB	Vo	B7L	YV3R7G6112A001118	Wt	F114	B41F	7/02	First Somerset & Avon (SO) 66351		9/16
66716	WX 54 XDA	Vo	B7RLE	YV3R6G7235A102482	Wt	H581	B43F	12/04	First Somerset & Avon (SO) 66716		3/13
66717	WX 54 XDD	Vo	B7RLE	YV3R6G7245A102510	Wt	H584	B43F	12/04	First Somerset & Avon (SO) 66717		3/13
66718	WX 54 XDB	Vo	B7RLE	YV3R6G7265A102508	Wt	H582	B43F	12/04	First Somerset & Avon (SO) 66718		3/13
66944	WX 55 TZF	Vo	B7RLE	YV3R6G6296A108922	Wt	H837	B43F	12/05	First Hampshire & Dorset (HA) 66944		10/15
66945	WX 55 TZG	Vo	B7RLE	YV3R6G6206A108923	Wt	H838	B43F	12/05	First Hampshire & Dorset (HA) 66945		10/15
66953	WX 55 TZP	Vo	B7RLE	YV3R6G6256A109193	Wt	H846	B43F	12/05	First Hampshire & Dorset (HA) 66953		10/15
66958	WX 55 TZV	Vo	B7RLE	YV3R6G6206A109490	Wt	H851	B43F	12/05	First Somerset & Avon (SO) 66958		10/12
66960	WX 55 TZY	Vo	B7RLE	YV3R6G6246A109492	Wt	H853	B43F	12/05	First Somerset & Avon (SO) 66960		10/12
66961	WX 55 TZX	Vo	B7RLE	YV3R6G6266A109493	Wt	H854	B43F	12/05	First Somerset & Avon (SO) 66961		10/12
67091	YX 65 RHY	AD	E20D	SFDDMABR8FGYA5153	AD	F249/1	B41F	9/15	new		9/15
67092	YX 65 RHZ	AD	E20D	SFDDMABR8FGYA5154	AD	F249/2	B41F	10/15	new		10/15
67093	YX 65 RJJ	AD	E20D	SFDDMABR8FGYA5155	AD	F249/3	B41F	10/15	new		10/15
67094	YX 65 RJO	AD	E20D	SFDDMABR8FGYA5156	AD	F249/4	B41F	10/15	new		10/15
67095	YX 65 RJU	AD	E20D	SFDDMABR8FGYA5157	AD	F249/5	B41F	10/15	new		10/15
67431	SL 63 GBF	AD	E30D	SFD1C8AR2DGG30965	AD	D317/1	B42F	12/13	new		12/13
67432	SL 63 GBO	AD	E30D	SFD1C8AR2DGG30966	AD	D317/2	B42F	12/13	new		12/13
67433	SL 63 GBU	AD	E30D	SFD1C8AR2DGG30967	AD	D317/3	B42F	12/13	new		12/13
67434	SL 63 GBV	AD	E30D	SFD1C8AR2DGG30968	AD	D317/4	B42F	12/13	new		12/13
67435	SL 63 GBX	AD	E30D	SFD1C8AR2DGG30969	AD	D317/5	B42F	12/13	new		12/13
67436	SL 63 GBY	AD	E30D	SFD1C8AR2DGG30970	AD	D317/6	B42F	12/13	new		12/13
67437	SL 63 GBZ	AD	E30D	SFD1C8AR2DGG30971	AD	D317/7	B42F	12/13	new		12/13
67438	SL 63 GCF	AD	E30D	SFD1C8AR2DGG30982	AD	D317/8	B42F	12/13	new		12/13
67439	SL 63 GCK	AD	E30D	SFD1C8AR2DGG30973	AD	D317/9	B42F	12/13	new		12/13
67501	M626 XWS	Ds	Jv	12SDA2157L/1126	WS	4705/54	C54F	1/95	Munden S, Bristol (GLq)		9/05
				(ex CX 67 AA 8/05)								
68506	CU 54 CYZ	BMC	1100FE	NMC111TKCRD200013	BMC		B60F	9/04	new		9/04
69231	MX 56 AEZ	Vo	B7RLE	YV3R6G72X6A115537	Wt	AA017	B43F	10/06	First Manchester (GM) 69231		10/08
69232	MX 56 AFA	Vo	B7RLE	YV3R6G7216A115538	Wt	AA018	B43F	10/06	First Manchester (GM) 69232		10/08
69233	MX 56 AFE	Vo	B7RLE	YV3R6G72X6A115649	Wt	AA019	B43F	10/06	First Manchester (GM) 69233		10/08
69234	MX 56 AFF	Vo	B7RLE	YV3R6G7266A115650	Wt	AA020	B43F	10/06	First Manchester (GM) 69234		10/08
69235	MX 56 AFJ	Vo	B7RLE	YV3R6G7266A115955	Wt	AA021	B43F	11/06	First Manchester (GM) 69235		10/08
69236	MX 56 AFK	Vo	B7RLE	YV3R6G7286A115956	Wt	AA022	B43F	10/06	First Manchester (GM) 69236		10/08
69237	MX 56 AFN	Vo	B7RLE	YV3R6G7226A115953	Wt	AA023	B43F	10/06	First Manchester (GM) 69237		10/08
69238	MX 56 AFO	Vo	B7RLE	YV3R6G7246A115954	Wt	AA024	B43F	10/06	First Manchester (GM) 69238		10/08
69239	MX 56 AFU	Vo	B7RLE	YV3R6G72X6A115957	Wt	AA025	B43F	10/06	First Manchester (GM) 69239		12/08
69240	MX 56 AFV	Vo	B7RLE	YV3R6G7236A116013	Wt	AA026	B43F	11/06	First Manchester (GM) 69240		12/08

69241	MX 56 AFY	Vo	B7RLE	YV3R6G7256A116014	Wt	AA027	B43F	11/06 First Manchester (GM) 69241	12/08
69242	MX 56 AFZ	Vo	B7RLE	YV3R6G7276A116015	Wt	AA028	B43F	11/08 First Manchester (GM) 69242	12/08
69243	MX 56 AGO	Vo	B7RLE	YV3R6G7216A116060	Wt	AA029	B43F	10/06 First Manchester (GM) 69243	12/08
69244	MX 56 AGU	Vo	B7RLE	YV3R6G7236A116061	Wt	AA030	B43F	10/06 First Manchester (GM) 69244	12/08
69249	YJ 07 WFR	Vo	B7RLE	YV3R6K6297A120198	Wt	AA899	B43F	6/07 First Devon & Cornwall	
								(DN) 69249	4/12
69250	YJ 07 WFS	Vo	B7RLE	YV3R6K6207A120199	Wt	AA900	B43F	6/07 First Devon & Cornwall	
								(DN) 69250	4/12
69251	YJ 07 WFT	Vo	B7RLE	YV3R6K62X7A120288	Wt	AA901	B43F	6/07 First Devon & Cornwall	
								(DN) 69251	4/12
69252	YJ 07 WFU	Vo	B7RLE	YV3R6K6297A120329	Wt	AA902	B43F	6/07 First Devon & Cornwall	
								(DN) 69252	4/12
69301	CU 08 AHN	Vo	B7RLE	YV3R6K6208A127137	Wt	AB783	B44F	5/08 new	5/08
69302	CU 08 AHO	Vo	B7RLE	YV3R6K6208A127140	Wt	AB784	B44F	5/08 new	5/08
69303	CU 08 AHP	Vo	B7RLE	YV3R6K6208A127283	Wt	AB785	B44F	5/08 new	5/08
69304	CU 08 AHV	Vo	B7RLE	YV3R6K6258A127280	Wt	AB786	B44F	5/08 new	5/08
69305	CU 08 AHX	Vo	B7RLE	YV3R6K6238A127326	Wt	AB787	B44F	5/08 new	5/08
69380	HY 09 AJX	Vo	B7RLE	YV3R6K6209A132615	Wt	AD120	B41F	3/09 First Hampshire & Dorset	
								(HA) 69380	11/13
69381	HY 09 AKG	Vo	B7RLE	YV3R6K6299A132614	Wt	AD121	B41F	3/09 First Hampshire & Dorset	
								(HA) 69381	11/13
69382	HY 09 AOU	Vo	B7RLE	YV3R6K6209A132713	Wt	AD122	B41F	3/09 First Hampshire & Dorset	
								(HA) 69382	11/13
69383	HY 09 AZA	Vo	B7RLE	YV3R6K6299A132712	Wt	AD123	B41F	3/09 First Hampshire & Dorset	
								(HA) 69383	11/13
69384	HY 09 AKF	Vo	B7RLE	YV3R6K6279A132675	Wt	AD124	B41F	3/09 First Hampshire & Dorset	
								(HA) 69384	11/13

FIRST CYMRU - Fleet Allocation / Check List

19000	w	42601	TYC	42715	BGD	44502	RAV	44594	TYC	44635	RAV	44929	BGD	63084	PT
19029	w	42602	RAV	42861	HAV	44503	RAV	44595	TYC	44636	RAV	49002	BGD	63085	PT
19030	RAV	42603	RAV	42862	HAV	44504	RAV	44602	BGD	47629	MAE	49003	BGD	63086	PT
19032	w	42604	RAV	42863	LLA	45505	RAV	44603	RAV	47630	MAE	49004	BGD	63087	PT
19033	w	42605	RAV	42864	LLA	44552	RAV	44604	RAV	47631	MAE	49005	BGD	63088	PT
19034	RAV	42606	RAV	42865	HAV	44553	RAV	44605	RAV	47632	MAE	49006	BGD	63089	PT
19035	w	42607	RAV	42866	RAV	44554	RAV	44606	RAV	47633	MAE	49007	BGD	63090	PT
19036	RAV	42608	RAV	42867	HAV	44555	RAV	44607	RAV	47634	BGD	49008	BGD	63091	PT
19037	w	42609	RAV	42868	HAV	44556	RAV	44608	RAV	47635	BGD	49009	BGD	63092	PT
19038	RAV	42610	RAV	42869	HAV	44557	RAV	44609	RAV	47636	MAE	49010	BGD	63093	PT
20323	RAV	42611	LLA	42870	RAV	44558	RAV	44610	RAV	47637	BGD	49301	PT	63094	MAE
20325	RAV	42612	TYC	42877	HAV	44559	RAV	44611	RAV	47638	PT	49302	PT	63095	MAE
23319	RAV	42613	LLA	42878	HAV	44568	BGD	44612	RAV	47639	PT	49303	PT	66350	RAV
23320	RAV	42614	RAV	42879	HAV	44570	MAE	44613	RAV	47640	PT	49304	PT	66351	RAV
23321	RAV	42674	PT	42880	HAV	44573	RAV	44614	RAV	47641	PT	49305	PT	66716	TYC
23323	RAV	42675	PT	42881	HAV	44574	RAV	44615	RAV	47642	PT	49306	PT	66717	TYC
32037	w	42676	PT	42882	HAV	44575	RAV	44616	RAV	47659	PT	49307	PT	66718	LLA
32041	w	42677	RAV	42883	HAV	44576	RAV	44617	RAV	47660	PT	49308	PT	66944	RAV
32042	w	42678	RAV	42884	HAV	44577	RAV	44618	RAV	47661	RAV	49309	PT	66945	RAV
32044	w	42679	HAV	42912	LLA	44578	RAV	44619	RAV	47662	RAV	53058	RAV	66953	RAV
33061	PT	42680	RAV	42913	LLA	44579	RAV	44620	RAV	47663	RAV	53059	RAV	66958	PT
33062	PT	42681	RAV	43836	BGD	44580	RAV	44621	RAV	47664	RAV	53060	PT	66960	PT
33063	PT	42682	HAV	43837	RAV	44581	RAV	44622	RAV	47673	RAV	53063	LLA	66961	PT
33064	PT	42683	RAV	43838	PT	44582	BGD	44623	RAV	47674	RAV	53707	LLA	67091	RAV
41381	PT	42684	RAV	43839	LLA	44583	BGD	44624	RAV	47675	RAV	53708	LLA	67092	RAV
41386	PT	42685	PWE	43840	LLA	44584	BGD	44625	RAV	47676	PT	53711	HAV	67093	RAV
41391	PT	42686	PWE	43850	PWE	44585	BGD	44626	RAV	47677	RAV	53802	PT	67094	RAV
41392	PT	42687	PWE	43851	PWE	44586	BGD	44627	RAV	47678	RAV	53804	PT	67095	RAV
41397	PT	42688	PWE	43852	PT	44587	BGD	44628	RAV	47679	PT	62189	t	67431	TYV
41489	PT	42689	PWE	43853	PT	44588	BGD	44629	RAV	47680	PT	62208	t	67432	RAV
41491	MAE	42690	PT	43901	RAV	44589	BGD	44630	RAV	47681	PT	63079	PWE	67433	RAV
41719	PT	42691	PWE	43902	RAV	44590	BGD	44631	RAV	47682	PT	63080	PWE	67434	RAV
41727	PT	42692	PWE	43903	RAV	44591	BGD	44632	RAV	47683	PT	63081	PWE	67435	RAV
42569	w	42693	RAV	44500	RAV	44592	BGD	44633	RAV	47684	PT	63082	PWE	67436	RAV
42600	LLA	42694	HAV	44501	RAV	44593	BGD	44634	RAV	47685	PT	63083	PT	67437	RAV

FIRST CYMRU - fleet allocation / checklist (continued)

67438 TYC	69232 PT	69237 LLA	69242 TYC	69251 LLA	69304 LLA	69383 TYC
67439 TYC	69233 PT	69238 RAV	69243 LLA	69252 LLA	69305 LLA	69384 TYC
67501 w	69234 PT	69239 TYC	69244 LLA	69301 TYC	69380 TYC	
68506 RAV	69235 PT	69240 TYC	69249 LLA	69302 TYC	69381 TYC	
69231 PT	69236 PT	69241 LLA	69250 LLA	69303 TYC	69382 TYC	

PG0006900/I: Thomas John **FREEMAN**, Coach Centre, Alltycnap Road, Cillefwr Industrial Estate, Johnstown, **CARMARTHEN**, Carmarthenshire, SA31 3QY. **FN:** Morris Travel. **OC:** as address. **VA:** 29.

See combined entry under PG0007563/I: Morris Travel, Carmarthen (page 55).

PG1077224/R: Nigel Stuart **GARDINER**, 64 Wern Terrace, **PORT TENNANT**, Swansea, SA1 8NT. **FN:** Gardiner Mini Travel. **OC:** Carlton Business Centre, rear of 49 Carlton Terrace, Swansea, SA1 6AF. **VA:** 2.

No vehicles currently recorded.

PG1128948/R: Geoffrey Howard & Rosalind Ann **GARRATT** and Aubrey Charles & Clare **FRY**, Racquety Lodge, **HAY-ON-WYE**, Powys, HR3 5RS. **FN:** Paddles & Pedals. **OC:** as address. **VA:** 2.

No vehicles yet recorded.

PG0006970/N: Peter **GILBERT**, Grasmere, Christopher Road, Skewen, Neath, SA10 6LE. **FN:** Chauffeur Travel. **OC:** Arrow Motor Services, Kemys Way, **SWANSEA**, SA6 8QF. **VA:** 6.
PG0007537/N: Rosemarie **GILBERT**, Grasmere, Christopher Road, Skewen, Neath, SA10 6LE. **FN:** Chauffeur Travel. **OC:** Arrow Motor Services, Kemys Way, **SWANSEA**, SA6 8QF. **VA:** 3.

	GJZ 1056	LDV	Cy	SEYZMVSYGDN097583	?	M16	8/03 new	8/03
	KJI 609	MB	711D	WDB6693632N023863	Onyx -?-	C24F	6/94 Di-Cataldo, Fforestfach (CW)	8/13
				(ex L854 FPB 9/13)				
	T337 SBX	Rt	Mtr	VF1FDCCM519619138	Cym 99/2992	,14	6/99 Penny, Cilfrew (CC)	7/12
				(ex L 6 PNY 4/10, T337 SBX 3/06)				
	BD 02 ODL	LDV	Cy	SEYZMVSYGDN087275	LDV	M16	6/02 Capehorn & Partners, Par (CO)	3/06
	CN 04 XCW	Rt	Mtr	VF1PDMVL531625538	Me 12030	M16	7/04 new	7/04
	CN 04 XFU	Rt	Mtr	VF1PDMVL531597590	Me 12047	M16	8/04 new	8/04
	CN 04 XFX	Rt	Mtr	VF1PDMVL531597588	Me 12045	M16	8/04 new	8/04
	DX 54 KJN	Rt	Mtr	VF1FDCUM632248976	Tawe	M16	12/04 Forge Travel, Maesteg (CC)	6/16
x	EO 54 WLA	Fd	Tt	WF0TXXTTFT4K71482	Fd	M8	9/04 -?-, -?-	8/12
	CN 55 EYW	Rt	Mtr	VF1PDMUL532906974	Tawe	M16	9/05 new	9/05
	CN 55 EYX	Rt	Mtr	VF1PDMUL632906970	Tawe	M16	9/05 new	9/05
	CN 55 LUJ	Rt	Mtr	VF1NDDUL634801850	Tawe	M16	2/06 new	2/06
x	SL 08 TFX	Rt	Tc	VF1JLAHA68V324798	Rt	M8	4/08 -?-, -?-	10/08
	CV 12 CLX	Fd	Tt	WF0DXXTTFDBP15213	Fd	M16	3/12 Day's Rental, Swansea (YCW)	5/16
	YJ 12 CWA	Io	45C18	ZCFC45A310D435629	Onyx 948	M16	3/12 new	3/12

PG0006151/I: Richard Geraint **GITTINS**, Ty Faeldref, **DOLANOG**, Welshpool, Powys, SY21 0LQ. **OC:** The Coach Garage, Dolanog, Powys, SY21 0LQ. **VA:** 3.

	FIG 2925	MB	O814D	WDB6703742N096718	ACl 1781	C29F	1/01 Lambeth, Reddish (GM)	10/09
				(ex X959 HFU 5/08)				

PG1026616/N: **GORSLAS MINI BUSES** Limited, 6 Waungoch, **UPPER TUMBLE**, Llanelli, Carmarthenshire SA14 6BX. **OC:** Brynteg Garage, Llannon Road, Upper Tumble, Llanelli, SA14 6BT. **VA:** 6.

x	AE 07 BYX	LDV	Max	SEYL6P6E20N212766	LDV	M14	6/07 Pete's Airlink, Catherington (HA)	8/16
	BV 57 UOU	LDV	Max	SEYL6P6B20N211955	LDV	M14	11/07 -?-, -?-	7/08

GORSLAS MINI BUSES, UPPER TUMBLE (continued)

MX 58 EKV	LDV	Max	SEYL6FFE20N224926	LDV	M16	10/08	Whitegate Travel,	
							Anderton (CH)	8/10
MX 13 EPN	VW	Crf	WV1ZZZ2EZD6007286	?	M16	3/13	new	3/13
YX 14 FZN	VW	Crf	WV1ZZZ2EZE6203980	Excel	M16	4/14	new	4/14
x CK 64 DTF	Fd	Tourneo	WF03XXTTG3EU42900	Fd	M8	10/14	new	10/14
YK 64 WXD	Fd	Tt	WF0HXXTTGHEB79819	Fd	M17	10/14	new	10/14
PO 16 VZZ	MB	516CDI	WDB9066572P200432	?	M16	3/16	new	3/16

PG1021984/N: GOWER MINI Travel Limited, White Lodge, Swansea Road, GORSEINON, Swansea, SA4 4LQ.
OC: as address. VA: 8.

G 1 BUS	MB	516CDI	WDB9061552N566452	Fer	C19F	4/14	new	4/14
CU 14 LXG	Fd	Tt	WF0DXXTTFDDM12276	Fd	M16	3/14	Day's Rental, Swansea (YCW)	9/15
CU 14 MDV	Fd	Tt	WF0DXXTTFDDM12797	Fd	M16	3/14	Day's Rental, Swansea (YCW)	9/15
CV 14 YZA	Fd	Tt	WF0DXXTTFDDK00288	Fd	M16	6/14	Day's Rental, Swansea (YCW)	3/16
CP 64 RDV	MB	516CDI	WDB9061552N574367	Fer	C16F	9/14	new	9/14
		(ex X 5 LDG 1/16)						
YJ 65 FDL	Io	50C15	ZCFC145A105000684	?	C19F	10/15	new	10/15

PG1099400/R: Jason Damian GOWER & Robert Miles O'NEIL, 42 Maes y Capel, PEMBREY, Burry Port,
Carmarthenshire, SA16 0EG. FN: Coastal Mini Coaches. OC: Ashburnham Road, Pembrey, Burry Port, SA16 0TH.
VA: 2.

JDG 46V	LDV	Cy	SEYZNVFZGDN111637	Excel 765	M16	11/06	Gooden, Erdington (WM)	3/16
		(ex BX 56 AYT 4/16)						
JA 53 GOW	Fd	Tourneo	WF03XXTTG3GC72464	Fd	M7	8/16	new	8/16
		(ex VA 16 UWK 8/16)						
CD 54 TAL	MB	311CDI	WDB9066352S128616	?	M16	11/06	-?-, -?-	7/10
		(ex KM 56 ZGP 7/13)						
CD 55 TAL	MB	513CDI	WDB9066552S430966	SwCh	M16	12/09	-?-, -?-	3/14
		(ex WR 59 RXM 3/14)						
w VF 06 BYN	LDV	Cy	SEYZNVFZGDN111472	Oly	M16	3/06	Bamber, Runcorn (CH)	8/14
		(ex JDG 46V 4/16, VF 06 BYN 9/14, D 19 ANT by8/14)						
CV 60 XBD	Fd	Tt	WF0SXXBDFSAM75542	Fd	M8	10/10	-?-, -?-	1/11

PG0006898/N: James Lewis GREY, 29 Convent Street, WAUN WEN, Swansea, SA1 2BX.
FN: Jim Grey. OC: Kings Head Motors Limited, 449 Middle Road, Gendros, Swansea, SA5 8EH. VA: 6.

x CV 08 DCU	Fd	Tt	WF0SXXBDFS7M52811	Fd	M8	3/08	Day's Rental, Swansea (YCW)	9/10

PG1130240/R: Elwyn & Ursula GRIFFITHS, Waen Glapiau, LLANFAIR CAEREINION, Welshpool, Powys, SY21 0DR.
FN: Elwyn's. OC: as address. VA: 2

w BJ 03 FML	LDV	Cy	SEYZMVSZGDN095629	LDV	M16	5/03	Yates & Humphreys,	
							Woodchurch (MY)	5/11
w YX 54 HNE	LDV	Cy	SEYZNVFZGDN106567	Excel 563	M16	1/05	SW Travel, St Austell (CO)	5/13
DX 05 ZKT	Io	45C13	ACFC459000D260237	Elite	M16	5/05	Williams, Wednesfield (WM)	10/14
		(ex BAG 699S 5/11)						
HN 62 EDK	Fd	Tt	WF0DXXTTFDCY69058	Fd	M16	10/12	Green Urban, Northolt (LN)	4/16

PG1055607/I: GWYNNE PRICE Transport Limited, 38 Heol Llanelli, TRIMSARAN, Kidwelly, Carmarthenshire,
SA17 4AA. OC: as address. VA: 18.

HIL 2395	Vo	B10M-62	YV31MA6101A053504	Pn	0112VUT3868	C53F	6/01	Longmynd, Lea Cross (SH)	2/15
		(ex Y798 UDT 4/15)							
w OIB 3523	Ld	TRCTL11/2RH	8400778	Pn	8511LTP2X515	C49F	2/85	Evans, Tregaron (CW)	2/99
		(ex B275 KPF 3/91)							
YLZ 9777	Vo	B10M-62	YV31MA61X1A052683	Pn	0012VUT3101	C49FT	4/02	Yardley, Yardley (WM)	10/13
		(ex YS 02 UGY 1/11)							

GWYNNE PRICE, TRIMSARAN (continued)

	Reg	Type	Chassis	Chassis no		Body	Body no	Seat	Date	History	Date
w	KSP 809X	Ld	TRCTL11/3R	8101149	Pn	8212LTS5C01N		C53F	5/82	Evans, Tregaron (CW)	6/94
			(ex 7722 SR 2/91, VHD 322X 10/85)								
w	JNM 756Y	Ld	TRCTL11/3R	8200805	Pn	8312LTP1C049		C50F	5/83	Lewis, Llanrhystud (CW)	9/97
			(ex HIL 2395 4/15, JNM 756Y c3/91)								
w	RTG 332Y	Ld	TRCTL11/3R	8200886	Je	18536		C49FT	4/83	Thomas, Tonypandy (CC)	3/87
w	A 3 VPC	Ld	TRCTL11/3R	8301033	Pn	8412LTP1C016		C57F	4/85	Evans, Tregaron (CW)	7/94
			(ex B742 CCV 4/95)								
w	D589 MVR	Ld	TRCTL11/3RZ	8600441	Pn	8712LZP3C015		C53F	3/87	Roberts, Burry Port (CW)	8/04
w	E440 AJL	Ds	Jv	12SDA1907/189	Pn	8812DAP3C009		C70F	5/88	Walker, Riseley (BD)	2/06
w	H 7 CPC	Ds	Jv	12SDA1919/624	Pn	9012HCA2010		C57F	9/90	Titchen, Benfleet (EX)	3/98
			(ex H302 FSK 3/98)								
w	L567 XTC	Ds	Jv	12SDA2122/905	WS	3879/93		DP70F	12/93	MoD (X)	6/05
			(ex 75 KK 21 6/05, L908 CDW by6/05, 75 KK 21 5/94)								
	P743 AHR	Ds	Jv	SFD723BR3TGJ21941	UVG	5600/97		C70F	4/97	MoD (X)	8/05
			(ex P359 OUM 8/05)								
	P803 XTA	Vo	B10M-62	YV31M2F13TC060315	Pn	9612VUM5794		C70F	10/96	Stagecoach Devon (DN) 52343	7/12
	P178 YFC	Ds	Jv	SFD721BR3TGJ21592	UVG	5482/96		C57F	10/96	MoD (X)	6/05
			(ex -?- 6/05)								
w	R 38 BYG	LDV	Cy	SEYZMNFJEDN029158	Cpt			M16	5/98	new	5/98
w	R180 EOT	MB	O814D	WDB6703742N072032	RH	1.121		C25F	4/98	Shamrock, Pontypridd (CC)	4/04
	R 82 SEF	Vo	B10M-62	YV31MA516VA047391	Pn	9712VUM7129		C51F	8/97	Andrews (SY) 52462	8/11
			(ex 1975 HE 5/11, R 82 SEF 1/08)								
	S275 LRY	Ds		SFD731BR4VGJ22054	SCC	4001/98		C69F	9/98	West, South Woodford (LN)	6/14
			(ex J 3 BUS 3/14, S275 LRY 10/02)								
	W794 AEP	MB	O814D	WDB6703742N090120	Pn	008.5MZE3154		C27F	-/00	MoD (X)	2/13
			(ex ???? ??? 2/13)								
	Y 11 HMC	Ds	R	SFD112BR1YGC10121	Pn	0112GWL3721		C49FT	4/01	Vamplew, Dolanog (CW)	1/15
w	CV 02 GZB	LDV	Cy	SEYZMNFJEDN073437	Cym	-?-		M16	4/02	Roberts, Burry Port (CW)	8/04
	LV 52 KTN	VW	LT46	WV1ZZZ2DZ3H005879	Stan	-?-		M16L	9/02	London Borough of Hammersmith & Fulham, Fulham (LN) 2717	8/10
	WC 52 DMW	MB	1836RL	WEB63420323000001	MB			C49FT	9/02	Williams, Brecon (CW)	3/07
	WC 52 JLW	MB	1836RL	WEB63420323000002	MB			C49FT	9/02	Williams, Brecon (CW)	1/08
	EK 03 VPN	Fd	Tt	WF0EXXGBFE3D26634	Fd			M14	4/03	-?-, -?-	1/13
	VO 03 BZU	LDV	Cy	SEYZMVTZGDN091909	LDV			M12	6/03	-?-, -?-	3/10
	PO 53 OXF	MAN	18.360	WMAA51ZZZ3S001471	Mpo	1.03.R.952		C49FT	11/03	Holmeswood, Holmeswood (LA)	1/08
	HF 05 JPY	MB	O815D	WDB6703742N116709	Sit	TR12UK29		C27F	5/05	Sea View, Parkstone (DT) 721	7/11
	MX 09 BCZ	VW	Crf	WV1ZZZ2EZ96009344	Excel	990		M16	3/09	Airport Services UK, Kendal (CA)	4/13
	DX 59 FHD	Asn	A1012T	SUAED5CGT7S620354	Asn			C70F	10/09	new	10/09
	PO 59 CPV	MAN	SU353F	WMAA91ZZ37C009613	Mpo	OF.1521		C55F	10/09	new	10/09
	FJ 61 EYC	Vo	B9R	YV3S5P725CA152169	Co	F113043142		C70F	1/12	Dunn, Heanor (DE) 4042	8/16
	FJ 61 EYD	Vo	B9R	YV3S5P729CA152238	Co	F113043143		C48FLT	1/12	Dunn, Heanor (DE) 4043	8/16
	PO 61 KBP	MAN	SU293F	WMAA91ZZXBC016230	HC	450.002		C70D	11/11	new	1/11
	PO 12 EOP	MAN	SU293F	WMAA91ZZ1BC016231	HC	450.001		C70D	4/12	new	4/12
	YD 66 AXR	Ytg	ZK6938HQ	LZYTCTE66G1027487	Ytg			C32FT	9/16	new	9/16

PG1068602/N: Brian Selwyn & Angela Rose HAMER, 22 Brynglas Avenue, Barnfields, NEWTOWN, Powys, SY16 2QB. FN: Angela's Travel. OCs: as address; Unit L, Mochdre Industrial Estate, Newtown, SY16 4LE. VA: 5.

No vehicles currently recorded.

PG1109054/N: Phillip Christopher & Patricia Denise HARLEY, Gaer Farm, HUNDRED HOUSE, Llandrindod Wells, Powys, LD1 5RU. FN: Gaer Farm Buses. OC: as address. VA: 10.

	Reg	Type	Chassis	Chassis no		Body	Body no	Seat	Date	History	Date
	C 13 PCH	Sca	L94IB	YS4L4X20001834074	Ir	91845		C49F	1/99	Lewis, Greenwich (LN)	8/14
			(ex S357 SET 9/14, 111 JMN c8/14, FSU 661 9/06, S357 SET 1/04, 99-D-8471 by8/02)								
	P 13 PCH	Fd	Tt	WF0PXXBDFP3J14290	Fd			M11	10/03	Wood, Builth Wells (CW)	by3/14
			(ex FG 53 KXD 6/10)								
x	DU 05 FMZ	Fd	Tt	WF0TXXTTFT4S81146	Fd			M8	3/05	-?-, -?-	12/12
	GY 59 UPB	Fd	Tt	WF0DXXTTFD9G64011	Fd			M16	11/09	-?-, -?-	11/13

HARLEY, HUNDRED HOUSE (continued)

BN 10 HTY	Fd	Tt	WF0DXXTTFDAL58957 Fd		M16	3/10 -?-, -?-		4/13
YR 10 FUH	Fd	Tt	WF0DXXTTFD9E34017 Fd		M16	4/10 Sixt Kenning (X)		2/13
x DY 12 FCD	Vx	Viv	W0LJ7BHB6CV612941 Vx		M8	3/12 -?-, -?-		12/12
x DY 12 FFK	Vx	Viv	W0LJ7BHB6CV611909 Vx		M8	3/12 LOCOG (XLN)		12/12

PG0007174/R: Phillip Wayne HARRIS, 2 Picton Lane, SWANSEA, SA1 4AF.
FN: Yellow Cabs. OCs: as address; 100 Clase Road, Morriston, Swansea, SA6 8DY. VA: 2.
PG1122462/R: Katy & Zoe HARRIS, 2 Picton Lane, SWANSEA, SA1 4AF.
FN: ZK Cars. OC: 2 – 3 Tontine Street, Swansea, SA1 5BP. VA: 2.
PG1088843/R: PW & EK HARRIS TAXI HIRE Limited, 2 Picton Lane, SWANSEA, SA1 4AF.
FN: PW & EK Harris Taxi Hire. OC: 100 Clase Road, Morriston, Swansea, SA6 8DY. VA: 2.
PG1023182/R: Zoe HARRIS, 2 Picton Lane, SWANSEA, SA1 4AF.
FN: Zoe Harris Taxi Hire. OC: Yellow Cabs, 100 Clase Road, Morriston, Swansea, SA6 8DY. VA: 2.

VCD 519	Fd	Tt	WF0DXXTTFD6B66509 Fd		M16	11/06 -?-, -?-		5/12
			(ex WA 56 FYZ 5/12)					
CE 03 UON	Fd	Tt	WF0EXXGBFE2G31519 Fd		M16	3/03 -?-, -?-		2/11
CV 54 XOC	Fd	Tt	WF0EXXTTFE4D11047 Fd		M16	9/04 Grey, Waun Wen (CW)		10/16
EX 07 NYT	Fd	Tt	WF0DXXTTFD7L66877 Fd		M16	7/07 -?-, -?-		5/14

PG1023130/N: M HAYWARD and Daughter (South Wales) Limited, Cwmau Bach, St Peters, CARMARTHEN, Carmarthenshire, SA31 3RR. OC: as address. VA: 4.

xw C171 GVU	Ld	TRCTL11/3RZ		8500815 WS	1174/86	B54F	7/86 Davies, Brynamman (CW)		7/11
		(ex 69 KE 47 10/96)							
w N113 VWN	Ds	Jv	12SDA2153/1399 Pn	9512HCP3831		C44FT	5/96 Morris Travel,		
							Carmarthen (CW)	c7/12	
P 26 SMC	Ds	Jv	12SDA2136/1337 Pn	9612HBM5831		C57F	8/96 London Borough of Barking &		
							Dagenham, Dagenham (LN) TF15	6/14	
P837 XAG	Vo	B10M-62	YV31MA612VA047368 Pn	9712VUP6769		C53F	7/97 Watts Coaches,		
		(ex A 15 EYC 6/12, P837 XAG 4/03)					Bonvilston (CC)	11/16	
R907 BKO	DAF	SB3000	XMGDE33WS0H006046 Pn	9712DRM7225		C53F	1/98 Arriva Kent & Surrey (KT) 2097	3/15	
z R341 LPR	Sca	K113CRB	YS4KC4X2B01827512 Ir	8804		C49FT	9/97 Dealtop, Plymouth (DN)		12/16
T 34 CNN	Sca	L94IB	YS4L4X20001834154 Ir	150337		C57F	3/99 Stagecarriage,		
		(ex T 3 AOL by10/11, T 34 CNN 3/03)					Grangetown (CD)	7/16	
z X574 AAK	MB	614D	WDB6683532N094088 Excel 0107	,		C24F	10/00 Chris Cars, Carmarthen (CW)		1/17

PG0005951/I: Gwynfa Margaret & Paul HERDMAN, Hom Garage, CLYRO, Powys, HR3 5JL.
FN: Herdman Coaches. OCs: as address; The Old Station, Three Cocks, Powys, LD3 0SD. VA: 26.
PG1135249/I: HERDMAN COACHES Limited, Little Hom, CLYRO, Powys, HR3 5JL.
OC: as address; The Old Station Yard, Three Cocks, LD3 0SD. VA: 26.

z JIL 8324	Bd	YNV	FT700325 Du	8592/0058		C61F	5/86 Weale, Llandegley (CW)		1/05
		(ex C346 VNR 2/95)							
VNT 22	DAF	SB3000	XMGDE33WS0H004845 Is	350T1PS1GB0013		C55F	5/96 Perrett, Shipton Oliffe (GL)		9/00
		(ex N998 FWT 1/03)							
w WJI 2839	Bd	YNT	FT106257 Pn	8611NTP2C020		C53F	5/86 R&R, Warminster (WI)		5/04
		(ex C288 NFV 2/98, XMR 558 by1/98, C288 NFV 3/93)							
z WMJ 29	Ds	Jv	SFD721BR4YGJ22317 Pn	0012GFM2906		C57F	-/00 Lex (MoD)		8/13
		(ex ?? ?? ??? 11/13)							
YAZ 150	Ds	Jv	SFD721BR4YGJ22329 Pn	0012GFM2914		C57F	-/00 Lex (MoD)		8/13
		(ex Y144 BPF 3/13)							
z 417 XAF	Ds	Jv	SFD321BR4XGJ22286 Pn	9910GFM1241		C43F	-/00 Unknown MoD		
		(ex ?? ?? ??? 11/13)						Contractor (MoD)	8/13	
w C433 HHL	Bd	YNT	ET107219 Pn	8611NTP1C001		C53F	11/85 Kerfoot-Davies, Dyserth (CN)		4/99
w D659 WEY	Bd	YNT	FT107194 Pn	8611NTP2C020		C53F	9/86 Taylor, Tintinhull (SO)		12/04
		(ex 610 LYB 3/94, D933 XWP 4/93)							
w G667 NWX	Ds	Jv	8.5SDA1915/432 Du	8884/0959		C37F	4/90 Lainton, Clayton (GM)		5/04
H840 DDL	Ds	Jv	11SDL1923/646 Wt	M165		B65F	4/91 Perry, Bromyard (HR)		5/06
r H248 XHX	DAF	400	CN881197 DAF			M16	9/90 Class Event, Brackley (YNO)	by9/00	
w K106 JCJ	Rt	Tc	08858283 Hdw			M11	by7/93 MoD (X)		8/16
		(ex -?- 8/96)							

HERDMAN, CLYRO (continued)

	Reg	Chassis	Type	Chassis No	Body	Body No	Seats	Date	History	
z	N602 CVP	Ds	Jv	120SDA2156/1365	WS	4990/95	C47F	11/95	Williams, Brecon (CW)	9/14
				(ex ER 95 AA by8/03)						
z	N 82 OYN	LDV	400	CN965781	LDV		M16	12/95	Keen, Battersea (YLN)	by12/98
	N 42 YJW	Io	59-12	ZCFC5980002163026	MI	C31.164	DP25F	3/96	Langley, St Arvans (CS)	5/09
z	P724 BPR	DAF	SB3000	XMGDE33WS0H005680	Is	TRA3502TIPVIGB0053	C70F	5/97	Veolia Cymru (CC) 72001	4/11
	P719 JYA	Ba	FLD12-270	XL9AA12JGT6003694	Ba		C70F	8/96	Warren, Neath (CC)	12/10
w	P658 ROU	Io	59E12	ZCFC5980102191818	LCB	500	DP19F	9/96	Huyton Travel, Huyton (MY) 2	3/07
	P803 YHB	Ds	Jv	SFD213BR3TGJ11937	UVG	5555/97	C57F	3/97	Isaac & Morgan,	
				(ex P123 KHK 6/07)					Lampeter (CW)	8/12
	R506 CNP	MB	O814D	WDB6703732N067037	Pn	987.8MWV8291	B29F	6/98	Ryan, Langridge (SO)	6/10
z	R225 OSH	LDV	Cy	SEYZNHPJEDN029327	Me	02913	B16FL	7/98	Deeble, Upton Cross (CO)	5/11
	R746 RTN	LDV	Cy	SEYZMYSHEDN035500	LDV		M16	5/98	Owen, Hereford (YHW)	1/02
z	S288 AOX	Oe	M850	VN6099	Oe	6099	B27F	2/99	West Midlands (WM) 288	5/11
w	T290 UOX	Oe	M850	VN6101	Oe	6101	B27F	4/99	West Midlands (WM) 290	5/11
w	T306 UOX	Oe	M850	VN6136	Oe	6136	B27F	5/99	West Midlands (WM) 306	5/13
w	T309 UOX	Oe	M850	VN6139	Oe	6139	B27F	5/99	West Midlands (WM) 309	5/13
w	T315 UOX	Oe	M850	VN6145	Oe	6145	B27F	7/99	West Midlands (WM) 315	5/11
w	T318 UOX	Oe	M850	VN6148	Oe	6148	B27F	7/99	West Midlands (WM) 318	5/11
w	V259 DRB	Oe	M920	VN6342	Oe		B33F	2/00	Nottingham (NG) 259	3/15
w	W637 CUA	LDV	Cy	SEYZMVSHEDN058572	Jay		M16	3/00	Network Rentals, Putney (YLN)	7/01
	W 80 HOD	Ka	S315GT-HD	WKK32600001015086	Ka		C49FT	6/00	Sanders, Holt (NK)	10/12
				(ex OGR 647 by10/12, W 80 HOD 5/10)						
w	AF 02 SDZ	LDV	Cy	SEYZMNFJEDN080585	CSm		M16	4/02	Travel For All, Clitheroe	
									(LA) TFA09	9/10
	LG 02 DKY	LDV	Cy	SEYZMVSZGDN085673	LDV		M16	6/02	Target Vehicle Rental,	
									Oxford (YOX)	1/05
r	BL 52 OVK	LDV	Cy	SEYZMVSZGDN092968	LDV		M16	1/03	Bowen, Newtown (CW)	7/12
	FD 03 YOH	Ibs	397E.12.35	ZGA7B2P000E000142	Bs	02.067	C49FT	7/03	Active, West Molesey (SR)	5/10
	YX 03 FCN	Tbs	Jv	SFD741BR52GJ22427	Tbs	0212GRX4797	C70F	4/03	Leicestershire County	
									Council (XLE) YB2	11/13
	VX 04 JZT	Oe	M850	SAB19000000001320	Oe		B31F	4/04	Worcestershire County Council,	
									Worcester (WO) 5013	3/15
w	YN 04 DXU	LDV	Cy	SEYZMVSZGDN104541	LDV		M16	6/04	Weale, Disserth (CW)	1/15
w	PO 54 MJU	LDV	Cy	SEYZNVFZGDN106277	Cpt		M16	9/04	Whitegate Travel,	
									Anderton (CH)	1/08
z	WX 54 LHT	LDV	Cy	SEYZMVS37DN106337	LDV		M15	9/04	Lawrence Weston Community	
									Transport (XGL)	11/10
	YN 54 OCC	Sca	K94	YS2K4X20001848875	Ir	151499	C70F	1/05	Newport (CS) 21	4/13
	YN 54 OCD	Sca	K94IB	YS2K4X20001848864	Ir	141500	C70F	1/05	Newport (CS) 22	6/13
w	PN 05 PZR	LDV	Cy	SEYZNVFZGDN108997	Cpt		M16	3/05	Whitegate Travel,	
									Anderton (CH)	1/08
	YN 05 RCF	Fd	Tt	WF0AXXGBFA3C58158	Fer	-?-	C16F	3/05	Johnson, Hodthorpe (DE)	3/06
	FM 55 RRO	Ka	S315GT-HD	WKK62725223000252	Ka		C53F	1/06	Garrett & Saunders,	
				(ex N 1 WET 1/12, JP 55 WET 1/11)					Groby (LE)	11/15
	YJ 55 LPZ	MB	416CDI	WDB9046632R817284	?		M16	9/05	Queen Elizabeth Grammar	
									School, Wakefield (XWY)	3/16
z	YJ 06 HSZ	LDV	Cy	SEYZMVSZGDN112188	LDV		M16	3/06	-?-, -?-	10/11
	YN 06 MXZ	MB	O814D	WDB6703742N122345	Pn	068.5MAE6445	C33F	4/06	Star, Erdington (WM)	12/11
	YX 06 DHA	LDV	Cy	SEYZMVSZGDN113394	LDV		M16	3/06	Guest, Winsford (CH)	9/10
	MX 57 UOD	LDV	Max	SEYL6PFE20N221780	?		M11	12/07	Hodgson & Rhodes,	
									Morley (WY)	12/12
	MX 08 GWM	LDV	Max	SEYL6PFE20N221790	LDV		M16	4/08	Restall, Hayes (LN)	1/13
	PN 09 JXU	LDV	Max	SEYL6PFE20N223055	LDV		M16	3/09	Transcare Services,	
									Keighley (WY)	1/16

PG1010635/I: Roger Charles HEWENS, Rosegwyn, Pendine Road, LAUGHARNE, Carmarthenshire, SA33 4TT.
FN: Laugharne Travel.　OCs: as address;　Unit 11A, Parc Owen Industrial Estate, Station Road, St Clears,
SA33 4BP.　VA: 5.

IIG 9294	MB	O814D	WDB6703742N117767	Pn	058.5MXW6006	C33F	2/06	Burghfield Mini Coaches,		
		(ex SF 55 FVR 10/11)						Burghfield (BE)	8/14
L 7 PSV	VW	Crf	WV1ZZZ2EZ86005279	KVC		M10	10/07	Serenity, Redditch (WO)	1/15
		(ex BF 57 LFZ 5/16)							
M 93 BOU	Ta	HZB50R	TW043PB5050000109	Co	451035	C21F	8/94	Young, Radstock (SO)	1/16
RX 05 EOY	MB	413CDI	WDB9046632R763154	Eurm 13441/3 05		M14	4/05	-?-, -?-	10/12
DK 55 BVC	MB	614D	WDB6683522N118987	?		B16FL	10/05	Corvedale Community	
								Minibus, Ludlow (XSH)	by11/16
RP 06 AMY	MB	413CDI	WDB9046632R872967	?		M16	by8/06	Philip, Alford (SN)	8/15
		(ex SK 06 FDJ 3/08)							
SF 06 FSP	MB	O814D	WDB6703742N121226	Onyx 778		C24F	6/06	Brunswick Cars,	
								North Cheam (LN)	4/14
x YP 09 GPZ	Fd	Tt	WF0BXXBDFB9J40958	Fd		M8	5/09	-?-, -?-	11/13
		(ex V 7 TTS 2/15, YP 09 GPZ by11/13)							

PG1097839/R: Nigel Mark HICKS, 7 Meadow Park, BURTON, Milford Haven, Pembrokeshire, SA73 1NZ.
FN: A2B Mini Bus Hire.　OC: as address.　VA: 2.

w W892 PAP	Fd	Tt	WF0AXXBDVAXU55651	CD	B14FL	3/00	Howells, Pontnewynydd (CS)	4/09
WX 02 ELW	MB	311CDI	WDB9036632R351295	?	M16	4/02	Little Bus, Leominster (HR)	7/12
MX 54 VWK	MB	313CDI	WDB9036632R602162	Cpt	M16	11/04	Evans, Milford Haven (CW)	9/14
DK 07 BWU	MB	313CDI	WDB9066352S155902	?	M14	8/07	National Blood Transfusion	
							Service (X)	3/13
YK 16 UGC	Fd	Tt	WF0HXXTTGHGR03687	Fd	M16	6/16	new	6/16

PG0007431/N: John A G HICKS, Rose Cottage, Mynyddcerrig, DREFACH, Llanelli, Carmarthenshire, SA15 5BD.
FN: Glyn's Mini Bus Hire.　OC: as address.　VA: 4.

J 20 AGH	MB	313CDI	WDB9036632R432655	?	M16L	9/02	Stone, Wilton (WI)	10/10
		(ex FN 52 KBF 10/10)						
MT 04 EHC	MB	313CDI	WDB9036632R608398	Oly	M12	5/04	Back Roads, Chiswick (LN)	8/11
YN 54 SZC	MB	614D	WDB6683532N114136	Onyx 670	C24F	9/04	Vallance,	
							Annesley Woodhouse (NG)	5/14
CV 55 MFM	MB	O814D	WDB6703742N118332	Pn	058.5MAE6094	C33F	9/05	Evans, Carmarthen (CW)	7/11
		(ex FF 05 BUS 7/11)						
SF 56 GOP	MB	311CDI	WDB9036632R877697	Onyx 759B	M16	11/06	Hewens, Laugharne (CW)	10/13
GX 64 FOU	MB	516CDI	WDB9066572S910608	EVM	C22F	11/14	new	11/14

PG1073342/R: Malcolm HIER & Raymond EVANS, 5 Eagles Place, BLAENYMAES, Swansea, SA5 5NS.
FN: South Wales Transport Preservation Group.　OC: Unit D, SA1 Business Park, Langdon Road, Swansea,
SA1 8DB; Unit 12, Hastie's Yard, 72 Morfa Road, Swansea, SA1 2EP.　VA: 5.

KXW 495	AEC	Rt III	09614013	Sds	H30/26R	8/50	Tamkin, Leighton Buzzard (P)	8/13
SWO 986	Bl	MW6G	135125	ECW 9932	C39F	5/58	SWTPG (P)	10/08
UCY 837	AEC	Bm	B3RA041	PR B43233	H41/31RD	10/59	SWTPG (P)	10/14
WNN 191	AEC	Re	2MU3RV3083	Hn 2309	C41F	7/60	SWTPG (P)	10/08
WNO 484	Bl	KSW5G	98174	ECW 6489	O33/28R	11/53	SWTPG (P)	10/08
FTH 991W	Vo	B58-61	16710	Pn 8112VC045	C53F	6/81	SWTPG (P)	10/08
		(ex OUF 359W by10/08, 789 CLC by3/92, FTH 991W 12/87)						

PG1130007/N: Michael & Catherine HILTON, 8 Greenwood Place, PORTMEAD, Swansea, SA5 5HQ.
FN: MJN Travel.　OC: Nantyffin Road South, Swansea Enterprise Park, Llansamlet, Swansea, SA7 9RD.　VA: 1.

BF 58 ABN	Fd	Tt	WF0DXXTTFD8D80545	Fd	M16	9/08	Northbourne Park School,	
							Betteshangar (XKT)	10/13

PG1147410/I: Paul Ian HODGES, 6 Queen Street, NEW QUAY, Ceredigion, SA45 9PY.
FN: P & S Travel. OC: Maesteg, Plwmp, Llandysul, Ceredigion, SA44 6HE. VA: 5.

S222 PST	VW	Crf	WV1ZZZ2EZ86005277	KVC		M10	11/07	Lewis, Llanrhystud (CW)	10/16
KX 07 HDH	Vo	B12B	YV3R8G1257A116681	Pn	0612TKL6788	C53F	4/07	Hartlepool Council, Hartlepool (CD)	11/16
		(named *Sophie Mogan*)							
KX 59 CYE	Vo	B12M	YV3R9M925AA137697	Pn	0912.8TXL8466	C50FT	1/10	Lucketts, Watford (HT)	11/16
		(named *Stephanie Ann*)							

PG1128562/T: Neil Francis HOLDER, Bridge House, HOWEY, Llandrindod Wells, Powys, LD1 5PT.
FN: Adey's Cars. OC: as address.
PG2000501/R: Joyce & Neil Francis HOLDER, Bridge House, HOWEY, Llandrindod Wells, Powys, LD1 5PT.
OC: as address. VA: 2. [PENDING]

x	FL 07 CBX	Fd	Tt	WF0XXXBDFX6R59453	Fd	M8	3/07	-?-, -?-	7/11
	BG 12 HMD	Fd	Tt	WF0DXXTTFDCF24270	Fd	M16	5/12	-?-, -?-	4/15
	HV 12 MHN	Fd	Tt	WF0DXXTTFDCB61342	Fd	M16	3/12	-?-, -?-	11/15
x	LK 14 YBD	Vx	Viv	W0LJ7B7B2EV621258	Vx	M8	4/14	new	4/14

PG1105437/R: Ian David HOPKINS, 4 Graig Court, Graig Road, GLAIS, Swansea, SA7 9JF.
OC: as address. VA: 1.

No vehicles currently recorded.

PG0007130/R: Delyth Patricia HOWELL, Dringarth, YSTRADFELLTE, Powys, CF44 9JE.
FN: DP Howell & Sons. OC: as address. VA: 2.

x	LR 05 NGG	Vx	Viv	W0LF7BCA65V627351	Vx	M8	5/05	-?-, -?-	8/15

PG1106685/R: Terry HOULIHAN, 41 Rodney Street, SWANSEA, SA1 3UA.
OC: Driver Training (Wales), Swansea Lime, Nantyffin South, Llansamlet, Swansea, SA7 9RG. VA: 2.

	H 8 ULA	Fd	Tt	WF0DXXTTFD8J62939	Fd		M16	6/09	-?-, -?-	8/14
		(ex OY 09 ZXO 8/14)							
	H 10 ULA	Fd	Tt	WF0DXXTTFD6M38469	Fd		M16	9/06	Ramsey School, Halstead (XEX)	11/11
		(ex EX 56 SGU 6/12)							
	EO 52 EEK	Io	40C13	ZCFC4090005393747	Me	11652	M16	1/03	London Borough of Barking & Dagenham, Dagenham (LN) TE66	11/14
x	PN 06 NXM	Nn	Primastar	VSKF4BCA6UV170097	Versa		M8	6/06	-?-, -?-	2/10

PG1065632/R: Wayne HOWELLS, 21 Cae Castell, LOUGHOR, Swansea, SA4 6UJ.
FN: H&H Travel. OC: 35 Heol Gwenallt, Gorseinon, Swansea, SA4 4JP. VA: 1.

EX 03 WVC	Fd	Tt	WF0EXXGBFE2G29005	Fd	M16	3/03	-?-, -?-	12/08
DV 56 LNK	Fd	Tt	WF0DXXTTFD6R81590	Fd	M16	11/06	Worts, Long Sutton (LI)	2/11

PG1007508/R: Nick & Sophie HURST, Parcynole Fach, MATHRY, Fishguard, Pembrokeshire, SA62 5HN.
FN: Preseli Venture. OC: as address. VA: 2.

No vehicles currently recorded.

PG0006513/I: David Granville ISAAC & Menna Wyn MORGAN, Pontfaen Garage, South Lodge, Pontfaen Road, LAMPETER, Ceredigion, SA48 7JL. FNs: G&M Coaches; Bysiau G&M. OC: as address. VA: 12.

W342 MKY	Sca	K124IB4	YS4K4X20001836975	Ir	93319	C49FT	5/00	Ace Travel, Beeding (WS)	6/16
		(ex AEZ 1361 3/16, W342 MKY 3/05)							
GM 02 BUS	MB	O816D	WDB6703742N147983	IM	-?-	C33F	5/13	new	5/13
YN 06 NZO	Sca	K94IB	1853938	Ir	151616	C57FL	4/06	new	4/06
WU 56 HXZ	Fd	Tt	WF0DXXTTFD6U11567	Fd		M16	9/06	Thrifty (Y)	6/11
YN 07 DVM	Ibs	397E.12.35	ZGA7B2P000E002914	Pn	0612EBT6438	C53F	3/07	new	3/07
SN 08 OPU	Ibs	397E.12.35	ZGA7B2N100E000467	Pn	0812ECL7437	C61F	5/08	Eve, Dunbar (SS)	8/11
		(ex EV 08 EVE 6/11, N 1 EVE 8/10, YN 08 NXV 4/09)							
YX 58 BNN	MB	515CDI	WDB9061552N343690	Fer	-?-	C19F	9/08	BM Coaches, Hayes (LN)	5/14
YX 58 BWE	MB	613D	WDB6683532N133450	Onyx	870	C24F	10/08	Barnwell School, Stevenage (XHT)	5/15
x CA 09 BFL	Rt	Tc	VF1JLAHA69V350917	Rt		M8	6/09	-?-, -?-	5/13
x CV 61 RLZ	Fd	Tt	WF0SXXBDFSBE07055	Fd		M8	9/11	MITIE, Telford (XSH)	4/13
YJ 16 UTG	Ytg	ZK6129H	LZYTCTE68F1046878	Ytg		C35F	3/16	new	3/16
YX 66 WNG	Vo	B8R	YV3T7U529GA179073	Pn	GL05/01	C59F	9/16	new	9/16

PG0007469/R: David Arthur JAMES, Wig Farm, PORTHYRHYD, Carmarthenshire, SA32 8PS. FN: Arthur's Minibus Hire. OC: as address. VA: 2.

No vehicles currently recorded.

PG0006893/R: Keith JAMES, 1 Capitol Buildings, Gurnos Road, YSTRADGYNLAIS, Swansea, SA9 2JS. FN: JJ's Taxi & Minibus Hire. OC: as address. VA: 1.

No vehicles currently recorded.

PG1030520/N: AC JENKINS Bus and Airport Services Limited, Unit 10 Llys Caer Felin, FELINFACH, Fforestfach, Swansea, SA5 4HH. OC: as address. VA: 25.
PG1116945/N: Alec JENKINS FLEET HIRE Limited, 260 Dunvant Road, DUNVANT, Swansea SA2 7SR. OC: Merc Tech, 138 Heol Y Gors, Cwmbwrla, Swansea, SA5 8LT. VA: 2.

CV 06 DXZ	Fd	Tt	WF0EXXTTFE5C79230	Fd		M16	3/06	Day's Rental, Swansea (YCW)	9/08
CV 56 LBY	Fd	Tt	WF0DXXTTFD6M30254	Fd		M16	9/06	Day's Rental, Swansea (YCW)	1/09
FT 07 KLZ	Fd	Tt	WF0DXXTTFD7D11342	Fd		M16	7/07	-?-, -?-	9/09
FV 07 EOS	Fd	Tt	WF0DXXTTFD7K89203	Fd		M16	7/07	-?-, -?-	9/09
CV 57 ATZ	Fd	Tt	WF0DXXTTFD7Y11972	Fd		M16	9/07	-?-, -?-	12/07
CV 57 HMK	Fd	Tt	WF0DXXTTFD7Y11405	Fd		M16	9/07	Day's Rental, Swansea (YCW)	4/10
CP 09 OKG	Fd	Tt	WF0DXXTTFD8Y35884	Fd		M16	7/09	Day's Rental, Swansea (YCW)	9/10
CV 09 VTU	Fd	Tt	WF0DXXTTFD8Y35889	Fd		M16	4/09	Day's Rental, Swansea (YCW)	8/10
CV 59 XFY	Fd	Tt	WF0DXXTTFD9C71445	Fd		M16	10/09	Neath Port Talbot Council (CC) H3551	5/12
CP 10 WKN	Fd	Tt	WF0DXXTTFD9D31029	Fd		M16	7/10	-?-, -?-	10/13
x CV 61 RLO	Fd	Tt	WF0SXXBDFSBL10615	Fd		M8	9/11	new	9/11
CP 12 LCC	Fd	Tt	WF0DXXTTFDCC52150	Fd		M16	7/12	Day's Rental, Swansea (YCW)	8/16
CP 12 LCM	Fd	Tt	WF0DXXTTFDCC52183	Fd		M16	7/12	Day's Rental, Swansea (YCW)	11/13
CV 12 CKO	Fd	Tt	WF0DXXTTFDBP31845	Fd		M16	3/12	Day's Rental, Swansea (YCW)	4/13
x CV 12 CPZ	Fd	Tt	WF0SXXBDFSCB27805	Fd		M8	3/12	new	3/12
x CV 12 YDP	Fd	Tt	WF0SXXBDFSBU19831	Fd		M8	5/12	new	5/12
CV 62 DAO	Fd	Tt	WF0DXXTTFDCC52205	Fd		M16	9/12	new	9/12
x CV 62 VBK	Fd	Tt	WF0BXXBDFBCL46270	Fd		M8	9/12	Day's Rental, Swansea (YCW)	7/13
x CU 13 HZZ	Fd	Tt	WF0SXXBDFSCT54118	Fd		M8	3/13	new	3/13
CU 13 JBX	Fd	Tt	WF0DXXTTFDCY71189	Fd		M16	3/13	-?-, -?-	8/16
CU 13 JBY	Fd	Tt	WF0DXXTTFDCS80395	Fd		M16	3/13	-?-, -?-	12/15
CU 13 JEJ	Fd	Tt	WF0DXXTTFDCY71609	Fd		M16	3/13	Day's Rental, Swansea (YCW)	6/14
x CV 13 DWE	Fd	Tt	WF0SXXBDFSDP61967	Fd		M8	6/13	Day's Rental, Swansea (YCW)	3/15
CU 63 DJE	Fd	Tt	WF0XXXTTFXDB47919	Fd		M16	9/13	new	9/13

JENKINS, FELINFACH (continued)

	CU 63 DKD	Fd	Tt	WF0DXXTTFDDM12567 Fd	M16	9/13 new		9/13
x	CU 63 DKE	Fd	Tt	WF0SXXBDFSDP61623 Fd	M8	9/13 new		9/13
	CU 14 LVX	Fd	Tt	WF0DXXTTFDDM13647 Fd	M16	3/14 new		3/14
x	CP 15 DXZ	Fd	Tourneo	WF03XXTTG3FL69279 Fd	M8	6/15 Day's Rental, Swansea (YCW)		6/16

PG0007126/R: John Thomas JONES, Happy Union Inn, ABBEY-CWM-HIR, Llandrindod Wells, Powys, LD1 6PH.
FN: JT Jones & Sons. **OC:** as address. **VA:** 1.

No vehicles currently recorded.

PG1098924/R: Lee JONES, 216 Cefn Road, BONYMAEN, Swansea, SA1 7JE.
FN: A Star Mini Travel. **OC:** as address. **VA:** 1.

x	HY 61 VLF	Rt	Tc	VF1JLAHASBV417735 Rt	M8	9/11 -?-, -?-		5/13

PG1038331/N: S J JONES School Run Limited, 33 Holbrook Road, BROAD HAVEN, Haverfordwest, Pembrokeshire, SA62 3HZ. **OC:** Unit 3, Portfield, Haverfordwest, Pembrokeshire, SA61 1DY. **VA:** 15.

AD 02 HCE	LDV	Cy	SEYZMVSZGDN087501 LDV	M16	6/02 -?-, -?-		2/06

PG0005823/I: Decima Eileen JONES, Central Garage, CRYMYCH, Pembrokeshire, SA41 3RJ.
FN: DJ Jones & Son. **OC:** as address. **VA:** 1.

YJ 05 YVY	LDV	Cy	SEYZMVSZGDN110929 LDV	M16	6/05 Practical (Y)		9/08

PG0006183/I: Myrddin & Meirion JONES, Old Shellmax Depot, Station Road, LLANDEILO, Carmarthenshire, SA19 6NG. **FN:** Jones International. **OC:** as address. **VA:** 6.

MJI 1940	Ld	TRCTL11/3RZ	8500594 VH 12037	C53F	3/86 Hayward, Carmarthen (CW)		6/13
		(ex C342 DND 7/13, MJI 2050 by12/07, C342 DND 4/02)					

PG0006524/N: David Eurig & Ellis JONES, 10 Maes-yr-eglwys, LLANSAINT, Carmarthenshire, SA17 5JE.
OC: as address. **VA:** 3.

w	M139 PBU	MB	410D	WDB6114682P404852 Me 01958	M15	3/95 Gee, Clayton (WY)		9/05
			(ex RIL 5127 3/16, M139 PBU 7/01)					

PG0007232/I: Michael Anthony JONES, Coach Park, LLANSILIN, Powys, SY10 7QB.
FN: Llansilin Motor Services. **OC:** as address. **VA:** 1.

No vehicles currently recorded.

PG0006507/R: John Evan JONES, Cledlyn Garage, Cwrtnewydd, LLANYBYDDER, Carmarthenshire, SA40 9YH.
OC: as address. **VA:** 1.

No vehicles currently recorded.

PG0005052/I: JONES Motors (Login) Limited, Isfryn, LOGIN, Carmarthenshire, SA34 0UX.
OC: as address. **VA:** 30.

YDE 679	AD	Jv	SFD745BR55GJ22595 Pn 0712GRX7315	C53F	9/07 new		9/07
		(ex CU 57 AKF 1/16)					
963 CDE	Vo	B10M-61	YV31MKC18HA014342 EL 38001	DP70F	5/87 new		5/87
		(ex D963 HDE 1/93 - re-bodied 7/01; originally carried Du 8693/0423)					

JONES, LOGIN (continued)

834 TDE	Vo	B12B	YV3R8M9258A128043	Pn	0812TML7863	C49FT	6/08 Cooper's Tourmaster,	
			(ex YN 08 OWF 9/16, NSU 462 3/16, YN 08 OWF)				Bedlington (ND)	8/16
521 WDE	AD	R	SFD152BR24GC10197	Pn	0512GXT6015	C49FT	3/06 new	3/06
			(ex CU 06 ABX 1/16)					
CV 55 AEU	Vo	B7R	YV3R6G7235A105446	Pn	0512TLX6037	C57F	9/05 new	9/05
CU 56 AXO	Vo	B7R	YV3R6G7276A113955	Pn	0612TLX6600	C57F	1/07 new	1/07
CU 59 AHF	Oe	M710SE	SABCN2AB09L193521	Oe		B19F	11/09 new	11/09
CU 11 ERO	MB	O816D	WDB6703742N140879	Pn	108.5MBJ8712	C33F	5/11 new	5/11
CP 61 LFJ	Fd	Tt	WF0SXXBDFSBJ17829	Fd		M8	1/12 new	1/12
TJ 65 TCJ	MB	921L	WDB9670232L927067	Erd	-?-	C33F	1/16 new	1/16
CJ 16 CEJ	Vo	B8R	YV3T7U527GA176740	Pn	FP13/01	C53FT	3/16 new	3/16

PG0007117//R: Elwyn William JONES, Ael-y-bryn, NEW INN, Pencader, Carmarthenshire, SA39 9AZ.
FN: Eden Tours. OC: as address. VA: 2.

x KJZ 8580	VW	Tr	WV2ZZZ7HZ6X005060	VW		M8	9/05 -?-, -?-	3/08
			(ex CX 55 VNS 4/08)					

PG0007423/R: Dafydd Lewis JONES, Dros Y Nant, PONTROBERT, Meifod, Powys, SY22 6JR.
FN: DL Jones. OC: Frondeg, Pontrobert, Meifod, SY22 6JN. VA: 2.

x DLJ 17T	Vx	Viv	W0L3J7710FV632256	Vx		M8	4/15 new	4/15
			(ex CX 15 XVR 5/15)					
YR 55 UOT	Fd	Tt	WF0TXXBDFT5M32508	Fd		M8	9/05 -?-, London (YLN)	11/11

PG1104007/I: Robert John & Sarah Marie JONES, Tynant, Tynygraig, YSTRAD MEURIG, Ceredigion, SY25 6AE.
FN: RJ Jones Travel. OC: as address. VA: 6.

RIL 1015	Vo	B10M-62	YV31MA610TA045910	VH	32679	C53F	3/97 Hollinswood, Biddulph (ST)	3/16
			(ex P219 YGG 6/09, LSK 495 11/99, LSK 444 3/98)					
w L705 CNR	DAF	SB3000WS601	VLVDE33WS0H003544	Co	358024	C49FT	4/94 Lewis, Llanrhystud (CW)	6/14
			(ex MSU 923 4/15, L705 CNR 8/09)					
S 40 RJJ	MB	1836RL	WEB63420323000046	MB		C49FT	5/04 Jones, Burley Gate (HR)	4/12
			(ex BX 04 NCA 8/12)					
S400 RJJ	Ka	S415HD	WKK62941123102556	Ka		C49FT	1/08 Austin, Earlston (SS)	5/14
			(ex SN 57 VPL 6/14, KNL 665 6/11)					
SA 52 AXV	MB	O814D	WDB6703732N104506	Essbee		C24F	9/02 Evans, Tregaron (CW)	9/14
x DS 12 FDG	Vx	Viv	W0LJ7B7BSCV630986	Vx		M8	6/12 -?-, -?-	2/14
YJ 64 HEV	Ytg	ZK6129H	LZYTATF65D1049514	Ytg		C51FT	12/14 Pelican Engineering,	
							Castleford (Qd)	3/15
BF 15 JVW	Fd	Tt	WF0HXXTTGHEG43466	Fd		M17	3/15 Flora Motor Hire, Aston (YWM)	4/16

PG1095921/N: Phillip Andrew JONES & Sarah Elizabeth SINGLETON-JONES, Grey Gables, PEN-Y-MYNYDD,
Trimsaran, Carmarthenshire, SA15 4RN. FN: PA Jones. OC: as address. VA: 1.

No vehicles currently recorded.

PG1143319/I: JONES INTERNATIONAL Travel Limited, Old Shellmex Depot, Station Road, LLANDEILO,
Carmarthenshire, SA19 6NG. OC: as address. VA: 4.

NJI 656	Ka	S315GT-HD	WKK62725213000133	Ka		C49FT	1/02 Grindle, Cinderford (GL)	6/16
			(ex BU 51 FXF 1/17)					
NJI 787	Sca	L94IB	YS4L4X20001835123	Ir	92608	C49FT	7/99 Jones, Llandeilo (CW)	by11/17
			(ex T412 OWA 9/15, 149 WX 6/15, T412 OWA 3/09, UTT 806 10/07, T412 OWA 3/07,					
							99-D-55118 3/03, T412 OWA 7/99)	

PG1077023/R: KILVEY Mini Travel Limited, 33 Granville Road, ST THOMAS, Swansea, SA1 8DY.
OC: as address. VA: 2.

	CV 55 EAW	Fd	Tt	WF0EXXTTFE5C88979 Fd	M16	11/05	Day's Rental, Swansea (YCW)	1/10
	KV 56 FMD	Fd	Tt	WF0DXXTTFD6P52467 Fd	M16	10/06	Royal Russell School, Croydon (XLN)	2/12
x	CV 11 BBF	Fd	Tt	WF0BXXBDFBAR83362 Fd	M8	3/11	Day's Rental, Swansea (YCW)	5/13

Note. Prior to by12/10, this operator was named Penlan Cabs, St Thomas.

PG1147436/R: KNIGHTON TAXIS Limited, 3 Pontfaen Meadow, KNIGHTON, Powys LD7 1LA.
OC: as address. VA: 1.

No vehicles yet recorded.

PG1136681/N: KRISLYN Motors Limited, 139 Coalbrook Road, GROVESEND, Swansea, SA4 4GP.
OC: as address. VA: 6.

See combined entry under PG1010939/N: Morgan, Grovesend (page 53).

PG1112337/N: LAKELINE of Powys Limited, Ebran-ddu, FELINDRE, Knighton, LD7 1YU.
OC: as address. VA: 4.

w	DX 53 HFL	LDV	Cy	SEYZMVSZGDN099773 LDV	M16	12/03	Powys County Council (XCW)	1/08

PG1122171/T: Arthur LAWRENCE, The Stables, PENYBONT, Llandrindod Wells, Powys, LD1 5SY.
FN: Al's Taxi Service. OC: as address.

No vehicles currently recorded.

PG1006269/N: LETS GO Travel (Wales) Limited, 152 Manselton Road, MANSELTON, Swansea, SA5 8PW.
FN: Lets Go. OCs: Units 9 & 10 Aztec Business Centre, Queensway, Swansea West Industrial Park, Fforestfach, Swansea, SA5 4DJ; Building 1, Aztec Business Centre, Queensway, Swansea West Industrial Park, Fforestfach, Swansea, SA5 4ED. VA: 18.
PG1094238/N: SWANSEA BUS Limited, 308 Townhill Road, Mayhill, SWANSEA, SA1 6PD.
FN: Swansea Bus. OC: Aztec Business Centre, The Queensway, Fforestfach, Swansea, SA5 4DJ. VA: 6.
PG1109836/N: M&J TRAVEL Limited, 152 Manselton Road, MANSELTON, Swansea, SA5 8PW.
OC: Aztec Centre, The Queensway, Fforestfach, SA5 4DJ; Unit 9A Prospect Park, Queensway, Fforestfach, Swansea, SA5 4ED. VA: 6.

	1	MIG 1723	Ds	Jv	SFD721BR41GJ22399 Pn	0212GFM4537	C70F	-/02	Unknown MoD Contractor (MoD)	c12/13
		(ex CT 02 PBO 3/14, ?? ?? ??? 1/14)								
	2	MIG 1724	Ds	Jv	SFD721BR41GJ22410 Pn	0212GFM4690	C55F	-/02	Unknown MoD Contractor (MoD)	c12/13
		(ex CT 02 PBU 3/14, ?? ?? ??? 1/14)								
w	2	SUI 2033	Ds	Jv	SFD115BR3TGJ11847 UVG	5436/96	C35F	c1/97	MoD (X)	9/06
		(ex P838 XDE 8/09, JL 66 AA 9/06, P840 AFX by3/06, JL 66 AA by3/01)								
	3	MIG 1726	Ds	Jv	SFD721BR41GJ22375 Pn	0212GFM4508	C55F	-/02	Lex (MoD)	1/14
		(ex CT 02 PBV 3/14, ?? ?? ??? 2/14)								
	4	MIG 1725	Ds	Jv	SFD721BR41GJ22369 Pn	0212GFM4504	C55F	-/02	Lex (MoD)	1/14
		(ex CT 02 PBX 3/14, ?? ?? ??? 2/14)								
	5	MIG 1727	Ds	Jv	SFD721BR41GJ22345 Pn	0212GFM4493	C55F	-/02	Lex (MoD)	1/14
		(ex CP 51 ZBE 3/14, MU 51 FDJ 1/14)								
	6	CP 51 ZBR	Ds	Jv	SFD721BR41GJ22350 Pn	0212GFM4492	C55F	by2/02	Lex (MoD)	5/14
		(ex ?? ?? ??? 6/14)								
	6	YN 53 EJX	MB	O814D	WDB6703742N111850 Tbs	048.5MXV5368	B31F	1/04	Pickford, Chippenham (WI)	12/12
	7	HIG 6242	Ds	Jv	SFD113BR3TGJ11835 UVG	5431/96	C35F	c1/97	Your Travel, Kirkby (XMY)	2/10
		(ex P119 UFM 5/10, JL 61 AA by2/10)								
w	7	K915 TBX	Ds	Jv	SFD0570210G000825 WS	3838/93	C46F	9/93	MoD (X)	5/06
		(ex WTL 526 11/10, K915 TBX 2/07, 74 KK 49 5/06)								
	7	CT 02 PCF	Ds	Jv	SFD712BR41GJ22384 Pn	0212GFM4523	C55F	-/02	Lex (MoD)	7/14
		(ex ?? ?? ??? 8/14)								

LETS GO, MANSELTON (continued)

8	MUI 4147	Ds	Jv	10SDA2156/1360	WS 4987/95	DP53F	11/95	MoD (X)	9/02
	(ex N840 KBX 10/06, ER 92 AA 9/02)								
9	WJY 760	Ds	Jv	12SDA2157/1153	WS 4717/94	C70F	2/95	Welham Travel,	
	(ex M427 XHW 9/12, CX 79 AA by4/03, M275 VUD 11/02, CX 79 AA by11/02)							Welwyn Garden City (HT)	9/12
10	HIG 6244	Ds	Jv	12SDA2152/1179	WS 4721/95	C70F	3/95	Bodman, Worton (WI)	11/09
	(ex M241 XWS 3/10, M240 LYK 3/04, 16 RN 62 11/03, M420 LYK by11/03, 16 RN 62 by10/03)								
11	SJ 51 EEN	DAF	FA45-150	XLRAE45CE0L227423	Nuk	B25FL	11/01	Windy Corner, Pencader (CW)	7/11
12	HIG 6245	Ds	Jv	SFD531BR3TGJ61885	Au 3000012	C67F	11/97	Howells, Dunstable (BD)	7/07
	(ex R133 KWS 3/10, R 30 ARJ 4/02)								
w 12	SUI 2034	Ds	Jv	SFD113BR3TGJ11834	UVG 5436/96	B35F	c1/97	MoD (X)	8/06
	(ex N176 LBX 9/09, JL 60 AA 9/06, P314 TBW by7/06, JL 60 AA by6/01)								
14	SUI 2037	Ds	Jv	8.5SDA2126/986	WS 4283/94	C36F	3/94	Cook, Swayfield (LI) 3	11/09
	(ex L 15 BUS 12/09, L864 WAV 4/02, 47 KL 55 by4/02)								
15	SUI 2814	Ds	Jv	10SDA2120/851	WS 3853/93	C57F	11/93	Midway, Crymych (CW)	11/09
	(ex L715 KTH 11/09, 74 KK 64 2/02)								
16	SUI 2812	Ds	Jv	8.5SDA2126/969	WS 4282/94	C47F	3/94	Webber, Blisland (CO)	10/09
	(ex L779 ECV 10/09, LUI 9965 7/08, L779 XCV 6/02, L166 XUS by10/01, 47 KL 54 by10/01)								
17	SUI 3854	Ds	Jv	SFD0513250G001406	WS 5008/95	C41F	12/95	MoD (X)	2/11
	(ex S779 TUH 6/11, ES 13 AA 2/11)								
18	HIG 9708	Ds	Jv	10SDA2156/1317	WS 4971/95	C47F	10/95	Turbostyle, Crawley (WS)	8/11
	(ex N884 RGA 2/12, ER 76 AA 4/01)								
21	SUI 3951	Ds	Jv	8.5SDA2169/1454	WS 5019/96	C45F	1/96	Lawrence,	
	(ex N759 PAE 9/10, ER 44 AA 905)							Weston-super-Mare (SO)	9/10
22	WIL 6744	Ds	Jv	12SDA2122/956	WS 4273/94	C54F	1/94	MoD (X)	9/10
	(ex L370 GTX 1/11, 47 KL 47 9/10)								
23	SUI 3855	Ds	Jv	12SDA2122/741	WS 3800/92	C54F	12/92	MoD (X)	10/10
	(ex K307 DHB 6/11, 75 KK 01 3/11)								
25	WTL 526	Ds	Jv	12SDA2122/726	WS 3790/92	C54F	11/92	MoD (X)	10/10
	(ex K304 CHB 5/11, 74 KK 91 10/10)								
27	P782 WOS	Ds	Jv	SFD213BR3TGJ11888	UVG 5538/96	C57F	2/97	Tamworth Bus & Coach,	
	(ex JL 71 AA 5/04, P528 SUS by4/00, JL 71 AA by4/00)							Tamworth (ST) 174 1/13	
	YN 05 WDX	BMC	1100FE	NMC111TKCRD200061	BMC	B55FL	4/05	Your Travel, Kirkby (XMY)	1/17

PG0007100/I: Michael Pryce LEWIS, The Rectory, CASTLE CAEREINION, Welshpool, Powys, SY21 9AL.
OC: as address. VA: 4.

DK 07 BWV	MB	313CDI	WDB9066352S155900	?	M13	8/07	-?-, -?-	11/12
SB 08 UOF	Fd	Tt	WF0DXXTTFD8G82743	Fd	M16	7/08	Freeway, Chesterfield (YDE)	11/12
KN 12 UTU	Ctn	Rly	VF7YCTMFC12158151	?	M14	3/12	-?-, -?-	11/12
KN 12 UTX	Ctn	Rly	VF7YCTMFC12158810	?	M14	3/12	LOCOG (XLN)	11/12

PG0006997/N: Gaynor Mary & David Benjamin LEWIS, Esgairhir Isaf, Heol Henfwlch, CARMARTHEN,
Carmarthenshire, SA33 6AD. FN: D&G Lewis. OC: as address. VA: 4.

CV 55 DDO	LDV	Cy	SEYZMVFZGDN104230	?	M16	10/05	new	10/05
MX 07 OPH	Io	40C12	ZCFC408100D317354	?	M16	7/07	Cunniff, Normanton (WY)	4/13

PG1128873/N: Robert John LEWIS, 43 High Street, LLANELLI, Carmarthenshire, SA15 2RF.
OC: Brynteg, Llwynhendy Road, Llanelli, SA14 9BN. VA: 2.

YN 53 ZDD	MB	311CDI	WDB9036632R533147	?	M14	11/03	Evans, Tregaron (CW)	6/14

PG1008935/I: Gwyn Richard LEWIS, Bryneithin Yard, LLANRHYSTUD, Ceredigion, SY23 5DN.
FN: Lewis's Coaches. OC: as address. VA: 30.

w	GIG 7594	Ds	Jv	12SDA2122/899	WS	3875/93	DP70F	12/93	Goldstraw, Leek (ST)	8/11
				(ex L473 XOU 10/11, 75 KK 17 5/03, L167 OAH by5/03, 75 KK 17 by5/03)						
w	KSK 930	Vo	B10M-62	YV31MA612WC060790	Je	24795	C50F	5/98	Caldew, Dalston (CA)	3/09
				(ex R 28 XAO 9/09, 695 CWR 5/06, 472 HKE 2/06, R942 YNF 10/05)						
w	MMR 740R	Bd	VAS5		FW454741	Pn	76PJK058	C29F	8/76	Shaftesbury & District (DT)	8/98
w	B792 MGV	Bd	YNT		ET105086	Du	8420/0346	C53DL	9/84	Chambers, Bures (SK)	9/97
w	E 11 GRL	DAF	SB3000	XMGDE33WS0H006557	Is	350T1PW1GB0104	C53F	5/98	Morton, Chineham (HA)	8/10
				(ex R164 GNW 1/12)						
z	S250 XUY	Ds	Dt SLF	SFD322BR1WGW12552	Pn	9810.7HLB9565	B39F	10/98	Glenferry, Little Island (EI)	by7/13
w	V286 HBH	Ds	Dt SLF	SFD612BR1XGW14058	Pn	998.8GKB1803	B29F	1/00	Lloyds Coaches,	
									Machynlleth (CW)	8/15
w	X469 AEJ	Ctn	Rly	VF7233J5216007755	?		M12	2/01	Ceredigion Council	
									(XCW) 3726	by7/13
w	X166 BNH	Ds	Dt SLF	SFD322BR1YGW14689	MI	C39.615	B37F	9/00	Stagecoach in the Fens	
									(LI) 33303	9/12
w	X167 BNH	Ds	Dt SLF	SFD322BR1YGW14690	MI	C39.616	B37F	9/00	Musterphantom (HA) 599	9/12
w	X168 BNH	Ds	Dt SLF	SFD322BR1YGW14691	MI	C39.617	B37F	9/00	Stagecoach in the Fens	
									(LI) 33304	8/13
z	X746 LOK	LDV	Cy	SEYZMVSJEDN066703	LDV		M16	9/00	-?-, -?-	8/15
w	FB 51 AAU	MB	412CDI	WDB9044632P884415	KVC		M16	4/99	Romdrive,	
				(ex H 1 WET 1/08, 99-D-18919 9/02)					Melton Mowbray (LE)	4/08
w	BU 53 UJX	Rt	Mtr	VF1FDCNM527454164	O&H		M12	1/04	East Midlands Ambulance	
									Service (XNG) 8933	12/12
w	BX 55 SSU	LDV	Cy	SEYZMVSZGDN112463	LDV		M16	11/05	Davies, Lampeter (CW)	8/16
w	CN 56 BTU	Io	50C14	ZCFC50A1005618948	Brecon		M15L	12/06	WRVS, Ross-on-Wye (XHR)	4/15

PG1029703/I: EJ LEWIS and Sons Limited, The Garage, MAENCLOCHOG, Clynderwen, Pembrokeshire, SA66 7LB.
OC: as address. VA: 13.

	IUI 4166	Vo	B10M-62	YV31MA619VA046136	Pn	9612VUP5874	C57F	1/98	Jackman, Willand (DN)	12/13
				(ex R762 OVN 6/09)						
w	HBX 972X	Bd	YMT		KW451261	Du	120/2956	B53F	8/81	Jones, Login (CW)	8/99
w	E239 NDE	Vo	B10M-61	YV31MKC19JA017448	Du	8793/0659	C53FT	4/88	Jones, Login (CW)	9/04
				(ex 526 FDE 9/04, E239 NDE 1/93)						
w	G978 ARV	MB	709D	WDB6690032P041507	Ar	AM81/2589/98	B23F	7/90	Sussex Coastline (WS) 848	by5/02
	J 10 CCG	MB	O814D	WDB6703742N088636	ACI	1740	DP31F	7/00	St Andrews Executive Travel,	
				(ex W 33 GEF 10/10, W 11 JRT by9/10, W346 XEE 10/09,					St Andrews (SE)	9/12
				W 33 GEF by7/09, W346 XEE 7/04)						
	L 4 PNY	MB	614D	WDB6683532N117077	Crest	-?-	C23F	6/05	Thomas, Neath (CC)	7/16
				(ex BX 05 VNK 8/13)						
	M453 LJF	MB	709D	WDB6690032N029492	ArB	M34140395	B29F	5/95	Nottingham (NG) 29	11/01
	P421 JDT	Ds	Jv	12SDA2155/1242	Pn	9412HBM3591	C70F	8/96	Lets Go, Manselton (CW) 9	10/12
				(ex MHR 677 10/12, P421 JDT 2/07)						
	P162 RWR	DAF	SB3000	XMGDE33WS0H005634	Is	350T1CV1GB0041	C70F	5/97	Wilkins, Cymmer (CC)	8/11
				(ex SIL 5864 1/07, P162 RWR 5/05)						
	R200 STL	Vo	B10M-62	YV31MA615WA048869	Co	858513	C49FT	6/98	Veolia Cymru (CC) 74039	11/11
				(ex PSU 612 2/05, R200 STL 10/02)						
	S703 RWG	Ds	Jv	SFD721BR3WGJE2175	Pn	9812GHM9634	C70F	11/98	Shaw, Carnforth (CA)	9/11
	S610 VAY	Ds	Jv	SFD721BR3VGJ52052	Mpo	1.97.R.314	C55F	1/99	Wilts & Dorset (DTz)	9/11
	V133 ESF	MB	O814D	WDB6703742N085687	Pn	998.5MZE1603	C33F	10/99	Glenesk Travel, Edzell (SE)	5/16
				(ex BXI 850 7/10, V133 ESF 6/05)						
	HG 06 FLD	Fd	Tt	WF0EXXTTFE6Y19266	Fd		M16	3/06	-?-, -?-	8/11
x	YB 56 HAE	Fd	Tt	WF0BXXBDFB6M41030	Fd		M8	1/07	Streamline Taxis, York	
									(YNY) 736	10/13

PG1110841/R: Steve LEWIS, 1017 Llangyfelach Road, TIRDEUNAW, Swansea, SA5 7HS.
FN: Tango Mini Travel. OC: as address. VA: 1.

	X 2 BUS	Fd	Tt	WF0TXXGBFT3Y89660	Fd		M8	7/03	-?-, -?-	8/13
				(ex CP 03 VDZ 9/13)						

PG1085518/I: LEWIS RHYDLEWIS Cyf, Penrhiwpal Garage, RHYDLEWIS, Llandysul, Ceredigion, SA44 5QG.
FN: Lewis Rhydlewis. OC: as address. VA: 20.

	FIW 563	Ds	Jv	SFD721BR3XGJE2273 Pn	9912GHM1097	C70F	8/99	Moffat & Williamson,
				(ex NIA 9896 8/16, T206 OWG 8/14)				St Fort (SE) 7/14
	MIB 3230	Ds	Jv	SFD721BR41GJ22407 Pn	0212GFM4692	C55F	-/02	Lex (MoD) 8/14
				(ex 600 KPU 8/16, CT 02 PCO 8/14, ?? ?? ??? 8/14)				
	NIA 9778	Ds	Jv	SFD721BR4WGJ22138 Pn	9812GFM8466	C53F	5/98	Slack, Matlock (DE) 7/14
				(ex R411 YWJ 8/14)				
	779 HCY	Tbs	Jv	SFD741BR53GJ22463 Tbs	0312GRX5162	C53F	-/03	Unknown MoD
				(ex YO 53 ZMV 8/14, ?? ?? ??? 5/14)				Contractor (MoD) 7/14
w	143 HDH	Cr	Avr IV	94A0359 Du	1121/7	C41F	by12/60	Central, Walsall (WM) 3/62
w	C996 NAL	Bd	YMP	SKFYMP2DZFT106714 Pn	8510MQP2C002	C45F	9/85	Lewis, Llangeitho (CW) 8/97
				(ex FIW 563 10/14, C996 NAL c5/98)				
	G744 YDE	Ds	Jv	8.5SDA1915/448 Pn	898HFA1223	C35F	9/89	Jones, Login (CW) 1/06
				(ex NIA 8778 8/16, G744 YDE 9/08, 521 WDE 1/06, G744 YDE 4/99)				
w	L 43 VRW	Vo	B10M-62	YV31M2B16RA041073 Pn	9412VUP2178	C57F	6/94	Shaw, Coventry (WM) 6/00
				(ex TCG 4 2/16, L 43 VRW by3/02, HST 11 5/00, L 43 VRW by5/99)				
	R925 LAA	Vo	B10M-62	YV31MA617WC060705 Pn	9712VUM7271	C57F	12/97	Elcock, Madeley (SH) 2/09
				(ex A 12 EXC 10/00)				
	R705 MNU	Vo	B10M-62	YV31MA611VA046762 Pn	9712VUM6247	C57F	10/97	Lewis, Whitland (CW) 11/11
				(ex WYM 675 7/09, R705 MNU 8/06)				
	R706 MNU	Vo	B10M-62	YV31MA618VC060467 Pn	9712VUM8089	C70F	2/98	Felix, Stanley (DE) 2/06
	R 6 PSW	Ds	Jv	SFD721BR4WGJ22139 Pn	9712GFM8471	C53F	4/98	Winson, Loughborough (LE) 56 2/09
	W 1 TSL	Ka	S315GT-HD	WKK32600001015030 Ka		C49FT	3/00	new 3/00
	X469 DYA	Io	49-10	ZCFC4970005131307 Oly		C19F	10/00	Meyers, Llanpumpsaint (CW) 4/06
	Y 2 TSL	Ka	S315GT-HD	WKK32600001015111 Ka		C49FT	5/01	Scottish Coaches,
				(ex Y882 THS 2/02)				Edinburgh (SS) 2/02
	YK 03 OAD	Fd	Tt	WF0EXXGBFE2A22556 Fd		M14	3/03	private owner 2/09
	FX 53 FRJ	MB	O814D	WDB6703742N109843 ACl	1847	C33F	10/03	Bysiau Cwm Taf,
								Whitland (CW) 8/16
	BX 55 OGJ	BMC 850		NMC850RKTRD300073 BMC		C35F	9/05	new 9/05
	CE 55 GZC	Fd	Tt	WF0EXXTTFE5M60896 Fd		M16	9/05	new 9/05
	BN 58 HJZ	Fd	Tt	WF0DXXTTFD8K38681 ?		M16	9/08	-?-, -?- 6/09
	YK 59 WYY	Fd	Tt	WF0DXXTTFD9A50073 Fd		M16	9/09	new 9/09
	LR 60 BUS	MB	O816D	WDB6703742N139217 Pn	108.5MBJ8618	C29F	9/10	new 9/10
	WF 61 JJE	Fd	Tt	WF0DXXTTFDBY78176 Fd		M16	10/11	new 10/11
	EE 64 SNE	Fd	Tt	WF0HXXTTGHEJ14686 ?		M16	9/14	new 9/14

PG2001514/R: LEWIS TAXIS Cyf, Bryneithin, LLANRHYSTUD, Ceredigion, SY23 5DN.
OC: as address. VA: 1.

New application currently pending.

PG1146975/N: LLANWYRTYD WELLS Community Transport Limited, Tunnel Site, Cefn Llewellyn, CILMERY, Builth Wells, Powys, LD2 3FL. OC: as address. VA: 6.

New application currently pending.

PG0007582/R: William Graham LLOYD, Uluru, GLASBURY, Hereford, Powys, HR3 5NT.
FN: Glasbury Taxis. OC: as address. VA: 2.

	LK 04 KYY	Io	40C13	ZCFC4090005421091 Stan		M14L	6/04	Buchanan,
				(ex N 3 DKT 2/14, LK 04 KYY 8/13)				Stretton Sugwas (HR) 11/14
	CK 58 NYL	Fd	Tt	WF0DXXTTFD8Y26894 Fd		M16	10/08	Brecon Car Hire (YCW) 2/15

PG1073397/R: Jeremy LLOYD, 27 Station Street, KIDWELLY, Carmarthenshire, SA17 4UT.
FN: JC Travel. OC: Davies Bros Yard, Pembrey Road, Kidwelly, SA17 4TF. VA: 1.

	WX 03 DYN	Rt	Mtr	VF1FDCUM528183753 ?		M16	4/03	Williams, Essington (ST) 12/14
				(ex BAZ 1751 12/14, WX 03 DYN 9/11)				

Celebrating their 15th anniversary in 2017 Cookson Travel, Hope are a familiar site in the Welshpool area operating a number of contracts in the area. They also operate a thriving private hire business as shown by MAN M105 PRS seen in Chester in August 2015. (Graham Ashworth)

Cymru Coaches, Fforestfach were based in Skewen but in 2012 moved their depot back to the Fforestfach district of Swansea. Being new to Parks, Hamilton (SW) Volvo/Jonckheere SF 06 MFO has operated in Scotland, Eire and Wales. (Nick Eyles)

Since being formed in 1999 the business of Davies, Llanelli have expanded rapidly from their initial Leyland Leopard. In 2011 they opened a depot in Crofty on the Gower Peninusla to operate a number of contracts in the area. Volvo/Plaxton DC 62 WAL is seen approaching the NEC in December 2014. (Tony Hunter)

When Silcox, Pembroke Dock ceased operating Edwards, Tiers Cross expanded the number of services operated in the Milford Haven and Haverfordwest areas. In addition to their Wright StreetLites they also use this Mellor bodied Mercedes HX 54 BHP which is seen taking a rest in Haverfordwest during June 2016. (Nick Eyles)

Although the active fleet of Evans, Tregaron currently consists of only 15 vehicles, it has a large throughput of vehicles due to its dealership activities. One of the newest vehicles in the fleet is this Optare Solo M900SR, SE 64 JAE, which was photographed departing from Aberystwyth for its home town. (Dick White)

First Cymru operate a large number of services throughout South West Wales with routes stretching as far as Cardiff and Aberystwyth. A number of express routes are branded as Clipiwr Cymru/Cymru Clipper and have this pleasant blue and gold livery. This is demonstrated by Wright bodied Volvo WX 55 ZTY which is seen on one of the routes linking Neath and Swansea in February 2017. (Nick Eyles)

In 2016 First Cymru relaunched route 227 between Neath and Margam via Port Talbot with higher frequencies. In connection with this the buses used on this service were repainted with orange fronts as illustrated by Wright Streetlite SL 15 RWX seen leaving Neath Bus Station in February 2017. (Nick Eyles)

In 2015 Jones, Login celebrated its 50th anniversary. The following year two new vehicles were delivered, the smaller of which was TJ 65 TCJ seen in the revised white based fleet livery now being applied to existing members of the fleet. It was seen in Shrewsbury during the summer of 2016. (Nick Eyles)

Bearing the Swansea Bus-com branding and looking quite smart in its bright blue livery, Lets Go, Manselton ex-MOD (via Cooke, Swayfield(LI)) Wadham Stringer-bodied Dennis Javelin number 14, SUI 2037 was photographed near its home depot on the Aztec Business Park at Fforestfach. (Dick White)

Dolgellau is the location of this photograph of Lloyds Coaches, Machynlleth's SCC-bodied Dennis Dart. This is a much-travelled vehicle; it was new in 2006 to SM Coaches, Harlow(EX), went to Irvine, Law(SW) in 2007, returned to Essex with Hunn, Debden in 2012 and spent just over a year with Peoplesbus, Liverpool(MY) before arriving at Lloyds in January 2015. (Dick White)

Double deck buses are not a frequent site in the area of this book but to cope with loadings on routes that service Aberystwyth University Mid Wales, Penrhyncoch operate two. New to the operator, SN 65 OFH is seen in Aberystwyth Bus Station in August 2016 prior to departing on one of the many bus routes operated by the company in and around the town. (Nick Eyles)

The Marshall Capital-bodied Dennis Dart SLF have been a familiar sight in south west Wales for many years with dozens of them in the fleet of First Cymru. Morris Travel of Carmarthen also have two of the breed having been acquired ex London Central in 2009. They can usually be found operating the Tesco free bus service in their home town and T406 AGP was photographed entering that town's bus station. (Dick White)

Based very close to the Powys/Shropshire border Owens, Four Crosses celebrate their 45th anniversary in 2017. In addition to operating town services in Welshpool and Newtown the company operates a large holiday programme under its Travelmaster Holidays brand. Having always a white, red and blue livery the company has modified it slightly for 2016 as shown by Neoplan OU 16 ERK seen approaching Wembley in August 2016. (Ken Lansdowne)

Rhiew Valley, Berriew operates a fleet which is half-and-half minibuses and coaches. The coaches are fairly elderly but well presented as shown by B 3 RYM, a Van-Hool T8-bodied Scania K113CRB which was new to Galvin of Dunmanway in the Irish Republic in 1995, registered 95-G-4711. It was photographed in Welshpool. (Dick White)

Richards, Cardigan operate a large network of services around the south west coast of Wales. In 2015 the company started to operate one of the TrawsCymru network of services, the T5 from Haverfordwest to Aberystwyth. Seen in Aberystwyth having completed the 3hour 15 minute long route is YJ 15 AWP showing the green and white livery applied to all vehicles operating on the TrawsCymru network. (Nick Eyles)

Some of the services provided by South Wales Transport, Morriston require higher capacity vehicles such as SK 15 GXW seen leaving Neath Bus Station in February 2017 on the half hourly circular service to Caewathan. (Nick Eyles)

PG1106541/N: LLOYDS COACHES Limited, Old Crosville Garage, Heol Y Doll, MACHYNLLETH, Powys, SY20 8BH.
OCs: as address; Lodge Farm, Tre'r Ddol, Machynlleth, Powys, SY20 8QD; Old Station Yard, Heol y Doll, Machynlleth, SY20 8BL; Arriva Train Wales, Heol Y Doll, Machynlleth, SY20 8BL; Unit 3 Salop Leisure, Treowain Enterprise Park, Forge Road, Machynlleth, SY20 8EG; Arran Road, Dolgellau, LL40 1LA. VA: 38.

	HIG 3853	Sca	K114IB4	YS2K4X20001844638	Ir	151180		C55F	6/03	Mayne, Warrington (CH) 53	4/16
			(ex YN 03 WRW 8/09)								
w	JIG 9474	Vo	B10B-58	YV3R13F13RA001321	Wt	S281		B49F	10/94	Beeston, Hadleigh (SK)	10/11
			(ex M528 WHF 10/11)								
w MMM825	JIG 9476	MB	O814D	WDB6703732N078024	Pn	987.8MXV9864	B29F	11/98	Owen, Nefyn (CN)	9/09
			(ex S825 MMC 10/11)								
z	LUI 6233	Oe	M850		VN6078	Oe	6078	B30F	1/99	Premiere, Nottingham	
			(ex S103 LBL 11/09)							(NG) 2203	3/13
z	LUI 7627	Oe	M850		VN6102	Oe	6102	B27F	4/99	Premiere, Nottingham	
			(ex T291 UOX 6/11)							(NG) 2291	3/13
	NIL 9774	Sca	K114IB4	YS2K4X20001842642	Ir	150961		C55F	7/02	Mayne, Warrington (CH) 52	4/16
			(ex YS 02 XDX 1/09)								
	PDZ 181	Ds	Dt SLF	SFD612BR1XGW13462	Pn	998.8GKB1408	B30F	8/99	Cardiff (CC) 150	12/13
	RAZ 5171	Sca	K114IB4	YS2K4X20001842253	Ir	150960		C55F	7/02	Mayne, Warrington (CH) 51	4/16
			(ex YS 02 XDW 1/09)								
	WIL 4343	MB	O814D	WDB6703732N068764	Pn	977.8MWV7931	B29F	5/98	Williams, Porthmadog (CN)	by6/12
			(ex R814 YJC 1/08)								
w EXV648	WLZ 5648	Vo	B10M-62	YV31MA617YA051520	Pn	9912VUP1643	C49FT	12/99	East Yorkshire (EY) 41	5/07
			(ex V841 JAT 10/11, 787 EYC 4/07, V841 JAT 10/04)								
CVV649	WLZ 5649	Vo	B10M-62	YV31MA618YA052076	Pn	0012VUL2175	C49FT	9/00	Bysiau Cwm Taf,	
			(ex X 92 HFP 10/11, 279 NDE 11/07, X 92 HFP 1/05)						Whitland (CW)	1/08
	C 22 BUS	MB	O814D	WDB6703742N117664	Pn	058.5MAE5896	C29F	4/05	O'Grady, Dublin (EI)	8/15
			(ex KT 05 XFJ 9/15, 05-D-39965 8/15)								
w	M410 UNW	Vo	B10B-58	YV3R13F11RA001270	Ar	AF19/294/1	B51F	9/94	Arriva Yorkshire (WY) 410	9/08
r	N585 CKA	Vo	B10B-58	YV3R13F1XSA002150	Wt	U181	B49F	9/95	Arriva Merseyside (MY) 6585	c6/12
	N661 FKL	Ds	Jv	12SDA2152/1511	WS	5222/96	C70F	2/96	Country Lion,	
			(ex K 70 CLN 2/14, ?? ?? ?? -/??)						Northampton (NO)	3/14
	N202 UHH	MB	709D	WDB6690032N035204	ArB	M37.270995	B25F	10/95	Nefyn Coaches, Nefyn (CN)	8/13
z	N329 XRP	MB	709D	WDB6690032N044492	Ar	9526/231	B25F	6/96	Williams, Porthmadog (CN)	8/11
w	P212 JKL	MB	709D	WDB6690032N045620	Pn	967.6MHV6154	B27F	11/96	Nefyn Coaches, Nefyn (CN)	8/13
	P215 TGP	Ds	Jv	SFD731BR3TGJ21572	Pn	9612HIP5623	C49FT	2/97	S&S Travel Services,	
			(ex MHS 5P 2/10, P215 TGP 4/05)						Oldham (GM)	9/14
r MMM813	P222 WYN	MB	O814D	WDB6703732N068736	Pn	977.8MWV7928	B29F	5/98	Arriva North West (MY) 0313	1/07
			(ex R813 YJC 2/08)								
z	S251 JUA	DAF	DB250	XMGDE02RS0H007050	Ar	9724/50	H45/21F	1/99	Arriva Midlands (LE) 4778	12/16
w MMM588	T588 SKG	MB	O814D	WDB6703742N084253	Pn	998.5MXV1123	B31F	7/99	Swindon & District (WI) 42568	10/10
z	V280 HBH	Ds	Dt SLF	SFD612BR1XGW14058	Pn	998.8GKB1799	B29F	12/99	Arriva The Shires (HT) 3280	c1/16
z	V285 HBH	Ds	Dt SLF	SFD612BR1XGW14103	Pn	998.8GKB1805	B29F	1/00	Arriva The Shires (BD) 3285	5/15
z	V652 LWT	DAF	DB250	XMGDE02RS0H007374	Ar	9828/4	H45/24F	9/99	Go-Coachhire, Swanley (KT)	6/15
	V654 LWT	DAF	DB250	XMGDE02RS0H007370	Ar	9828/2	H45/24F	9/99	Go-Coachhire, Swanley (KT)	6/15
	V109 MVX	Ds	Dt SLF	SFD212BR1XGW13853	Pn	9910.1HJB1556	B33F	11/99	Stagecoach	
										(South) (WS) 34109	1/15
w	V 67 SVY	Vo	B10BLE	YV3R4A519XA005383	Ar	9910/13	DP43F	11/99	Thames Travel,	
			(ex V 3 JJL 11/03)						Wallingford (OX) 67	2/12
	W966 JNF	MB	O814D	WDB6703732N087101	Pn	998.5MXV0588	B33F	4/00	Yelloway, Chadderton (GM)	4/16
			(ex M 80 YEL 4/16, W966 JNF 10/14)								
	Y161 OTL	MB	O814D	WDB6703742N090834	Pn	008.5MXV3150	B33F	4/01	Translinc, Lincoln (LI) 068.050	5/12
	DS 51 YJO	Ds	Jv	SFD721BR41GJ22358	Pn	0112GFM4499	C55F	-/01	MoD (X)	5/13
			(ex VO 51 FPJ 12/12, FY 51 BPO by10/12)								
SDC02	EK 51 XXA	Ds	Dt SLF	SFD6B2CR31GW16120	Pn	0143/1	B29F	2/02	Ace, Aintree (MY) 714	1/13
			(ex 02-D-18250 by9/10)								
xw	YA 02 CBD	Fd	Tt	WF0LXXGBFL2L65850	?		M5L	7/02	Nefyn Coaches, Nefyn (CN)	by12/11
z	CX 52 YLV	LDV	Cy	SEYZMVSYGDN089857	LDV		M16	11/02	Williams, Porthmadog (CN)	by3/11
SDC03	LC 03 WYN	Tbs	Dt SLF	SFD6BACR33GW87101	Tbs	2096/1	B29F	3/03	Stones, Leigh (GM)	5/09
			(ex MP 03 DTZ 11/09, B 1 BUS 3/09)								
z	YJ 03 WXG	Fd	Tt	WF0AXXGBFA2A18479	CD	36565	C15FL	3/03	Summercourt Travel,	
										Summercourt (CO)	3/12
x	AD 53 PZA	Fd	Tt	WF0EXXGBFE3M48554	Fd		M16	1/04	private owner	1/08

LLOYDS COACHES, MACHYNLLETH (continued)

	Reg		Model	Chassis	Body	Body№	Type	Date	Owner/Notes	Date
x	YH 53 GHO	Fd	Tt	WF0EXXGBFE3R48711	Fd		M5L	9/03	-?-, -?-	8/09
	BX 04 CRV	Oe	M920	SAB19000000001472	Oe		DP??F	9/04	South Staffordshire College (XST)	7/12
	CN 04 NFM	Oe	M850	SAB19000000001562	Oe		B27F	7/04	Evans, Tregaron (CW)	12/14
	KT 04 BUS	MB	O530	WEB62804023103583	MB		B42F	3/04	Western Greyhound, Summercourt (CO) 206	2/14
			(ex WK 04 WKE 11/13, KT 04 BUS 4/10)							
x	MV 04 SZC	Fd	Tt	WF0TXXGBFT3M30428	Fd		M8	3/04	Mach Taxis, Machynlleth (YCW)	3/13
xw	CV 54 ZTB	Fd	Tt	WF0PXXBDFP4Y02176	Fd		M8	1/05	-?-, -?-	by2/09
	DX 54 CMU	LDV	Cy	SEYZMVSZGDN106013	LDV		M16	9/04	Clettwr, Tre'r Ddol (CW)	7/11
	YN 54 DCE	MB	O814D	WDB6703742N113609	Pn	048.5MSW5469	B33F	9/04	Hodder, Charlton-on-Otmoor (OX)	9/16
	FX 05 GCO	VW	LT46	WV1ZZZ2DZ5H019985	Me	4121	M14L	4/05	Rolling Solutions, Crewe (CH) L4	3/15
	VX 05 BVU	MB	O814D	WDB6703742N118764	Pn	058.5MXV6085	B29FL	8/05	Garratt & Sanders, Grobe (LE)	3/13
			(ex UK 05 BUS 3/13, VX 05 BVU by3/13)							
z	DK 55 BEY	MB	411CDI	WDB9046632R848828	?		M16	10/05	-?-, -?-	6/11
x	LX 55 ACZ	Ctn	Rly	VF7ZBAMNB17622025	Stan		M8L	9/05	-?-, -?-	5/14
	EU 06 KDJ	AD	Dt	SFD6BACR45GW88373	SCC	4518	B28F	5/06	Peoplesbus, Liverpool (MY)	1/15
	LC 06 WYN	Vo	B12B	YV3R8G1216A113386	Pn	0612TKT6541	C57F	4/06	new	4/06
x	SH 06 FZX	Fd	Tt	WF0EXXTTFE6S22898	Fd		M16	6/06	Argyle & Bute Council (XSW) 22062	5/12
	WX 06 UTJ	MB	411CDI	WDB9046122R948078	UVM	10980	B16FL	6/06	Milton Keynes Community Transport (XBK)	6/15
r	YJ 06 FYA	Oe	M850	SAB19000000002447	Oe		B32F	5/06	GHA, Ruabon (CN) 1381	10/16
x	AJ 56 HMF	Fd	Tt	WF0BXXBDFB6M40876	Fd		M8	11/06	Babyshambles, Fort William (YSN)	3/14
	KX 56 HCY	MB	413CDI	WDB9046122R715704	Pn	056.5MSW5799	B16FL	9/06	Town & Country, Chesterfield (DE) 22	9/14
CMM07	LC 07 WYN	MB	O814D	WDB6703742N125852	Pn	068.5MBE6922	C29F	3/07	new	3/07
	LL 07 WYN	MB	313CDI	WDB9066352S543340	?		M??	4/11	-?-, -?-	8/14
			(ex DE 11 WWD 3/15)							
x	NG 07 HNA	Fd	Tt	WF0SXXBDFS6R58278	Fd		M8	5/07	TES 2000, Colchester (YEX)	9/12
x	NM 07 ORP	Fd	Tt	WF0SXXBDFS6R58271	Fd		M8	7/07	-?-, -?-	3/14
x	CN 08 BPY	MB	311CDI	WDB9066332S302469	?		M8L	8/08	Powys Council (XCW)	9/14
x	GN 08 XUK	Rt	Tc	VF1JLAHA68V330042	Rt		M8	8/08	-?-, -?-	5/16
	LC 08 WYN	Vo	B12B	YV3R8L2298A127045	Pn	0812.3TMR7762	C49FT	5/08	new	5/08
x	BG 58 AHO	Vx	Viv	W0LJ7BHB69V615404	Vx		M8	1/09	Mach Taxis, Machynlleth (YCW)	3/13
	MX 58 GYK	Io	50C15	ZCFC50A2005706155	JDC		M16L	9/08	Essential Fleet, Lincoln (LI)	9/16
	LL 09 WYN	MB	313CDI	WDB9066352S570626	?		M??	7/11	-?-, -?-	2/15
			(ex DA 11 YMD 4/15)							
	SY 09 DSO	MB	O816D	WDB6703742N135416	Pn	088.5MBJ8124	C30F	4/09	D&E Coaches, Inverness (SN)	4/16
			(ex S 5 YST 5/12, BU 51 DEC 4/11, YN 09 AOP 7/09)							
	BW 11 KGE	MB	313CDI	WDB9066352S558906	?		M??	8/11	-?-, -?-	9/16
x	CY 11 EMX	Fd	Tt	WF0BXXBDFBBL08810	Fd		M8	6/11	Mach Taxis, Machynlleth (YCW)	3/13
x	CY 11 GNK	Fd	Tt	WF0SXXBDFSBD04042	Fd		M8	6/11	Mach Taxis, Machynlleth (YCW)	3/13
	LC 61 WYN	AD	E400MMC	SFD911BR2FGX18701	AD	F435/1	H45/22F	3/16	new	3/16
SDC61	LL 61 WYN	AD	Dt	SFD1A1AR5AGY11690	AD	A207/11	B28F	9/11	new	9/11
	LC 62 WYN	AD	E400MMC	SFD911BR2FGX18702	AD	F435/2	H45/22F	3/16	new	3/16
x	KP 14 ZDK	MB	312CDI	WDB9066352S897801	?		M8	5/14	converted from a van	10/15
	LC 14 WYN	VDL	FHD2 129-365	XNL501E100D002890	VDL		C53FT	3/14	new	3/14
	YJ 14 BCV	Oe	8900SR	SABSN3AF0ES290766	Oe		B30F	4/14	new	4/14
	YJ 14 BCX	Oe	8900SR	SABSN3AF0ES290875	Oe		B30F	4/14	new	4/14
	YJ 14 BCY	Oe	V1100	SABWW3AC0ES320703	Oe		B39F	4/14	new	4/14
	YJ 14 BCZ	Oe	V1170	SABXW4AC0ES320704	Oe		B42F	4/14	new	4/14
	SN 15 ETD	Sca	N280UD	YS2N4X20001893518	AD	E453/1	H47/27F	6/15	GHA, Ruabon (CN) 3001	11/16
	SN 15 ETE	Sca	N280UD	YS2N4X20001893516	AD	E453/2	H47/27F	6/15	GHA, Ruabon (CN) 3002	11/16
	SN 15 ETF	Sca	N280UD	YS2N4X20001893517	AD	E453/3	H47/27F	6/15	GHA, Ruabon (CN) 3003	11/16
x	YD 15 JNJ	Fd	Tourneo	WF03XXTTG3EP62438	Fd		M8	3/15	new	3/15
x	YD 15 JNL	Fd	Tourneo	WF03XXTTG3FD14633	Fd		M8	5/15	new	5/15
	LC 65 WYN	MB	921L	WDB9670232L943846	Erd	-?-	C33F	9/15	new	9/15
	YJ 65 EUM	Oe	V1080MC	SAB4HB2A0FS400081	Oe		B38F	1/16	new	1/16
	YJ 65 EUN	Oe	V1080MC	SAB4HB2A2FS400082	Oe		B38F	1/16	new	1/16
	BU 16 UYL	Vo	B11R	YV3T2U825FA171304	Je	37316	C53FT	3/16	new	3/16

LLOYDS COACHES, MACHYNLLETH (continued)

BU 16 UYM	Vo	B11R	YV3T2U828GA174618	Je	37379	C53FT	3/16 new		3/16
YJ 16 DYT	Oe	V1080MC	SAB4HB2A4FS400083	Oe		B38F	3/16 new		3/16
YY 16 YJT	AD	E20D	SFD7E1AR6GGY15505	AD	F2A7E/06	B39F	7/16 new		7/16
YY 16 YJU	AD	E20D	SFD7E1AR6GGY15506	AD	F2A7E/07	B39F	7/16 new		7/16
YY 16 YJV	AD	E20D	SFD7E1AR6GGY15509	AD	F2A7E/10	B39F	7/16 new		7/16
YY 16 YJW	AD	E20D	SFD7E1AR6GGY15621	AD	G204B/04	B39F	7/16 new		7/16
YY 16 YJX	AD	E20D	SFD7E1AR6GGY15440	AD	F293B/02	B39F	7/16 new		7/16
LC 66 WYN	Oe	M9250SR	SABLDB2A8GS291300	Oe		B30F	9/16 new		9/16
YS 66 YFC	Fd	Tt	WF01XXTTG1GS00397	Fd		M8	12/16 new		12/16
YS 66 YFD	Fd	Tt	WF01XXTTG1GY88756	Fd		M8	12/16 new		12/16

PG1109836/N: M&J TRAVEL Limited, 152 Manselton Road, MANSELTON, Swansea, SA5 8PW.
OC: Aztec Centre, The Queensway, Fforestfach, SA5 4DJ; Unit 9A Prospect Park, Queensway, Fforestfach, Swansea, SA5 4ED. VA: 6.

See combined entry under PG1006269/N: Lets Go, Manselton (page 45).

PG1110303/R: Norman MASON, Rocky Hollow, Providence Hill, NARBERTH, Pembrokeshire SA67 8RE.
FN: Pembrokeshire Elite Travel. OC: as address. VA: 1.

YN 04 XZK	Oe	Alero	SAB21000000000444	Oe		B15F	5/04 -?-, -?-		2/11
EF 65 BWC	MB	313CDI	WDB9066372P216679	?		M16	1/16 new		1/16

PG1099890/N: Darren Norman MASON, Llys Y Blodau, Spring Gardens, WHITLAND, Carmarthenshire, SA34 0HR.
FN: Narberth Mini Bus Travel. OC: Old Transport Yard, Llawhaden, Narberth, SA67 8DS. VA: 4.

FY 02 LEU	MB	O814D	WDB6703742N096792	ACI	1780	C29F	3/02	Mawley Oak,	
								Cleobury Mortimer (SH) 292	12/15
w　KP 05 OWF	Fd	Tt	WF0EXXTTFE5M66198	?		M16	5/05	Dorset Vehicle Rentals,	
		(ex WLT 852 8/11, FY 02 LEU 5/03)						Dorchester (YDT)	12/08
MD 55 NNA	Fd	Tt	WF0EXXTTFE5G70180	Fd		M14	1/06	Sutton, Rothbury (ND)	3/10
NA 06 BWD	Fd	Tt	WF0EXXTTFE6Y05124	Fd		M16	3/06	Hertz (Y)	2/10
MX 56 KYR	Io	35C12	ZCFC408100D317354	?		M16	2/07	Lynx, Keighley (WY)	2/12
		(ex L111 YNX 2/12, MX 56 KYR 3/07)							
YX 07 AWV	MB	1323L	WDB9702682L123796	Fer	N000F624	C37FT	11/06	Silcox,	
		(ex YX 56 AFV 3/07)						Pembroke Dock (CW) 197	8/16
EX 16 DXA	MB	516CDI	WDB9066572P220081	SwCh		M16	4/16 new		4/16

PG1143737/N: Colin Andrew MATTHEWS, 43 North Road, CARDIGAN, Ceredigion, SA43 1LS.
FN: C M Travel. OC: Cottage Stores, Tanglwst, Capel Iwan, Newcastle Emlyn, SA39 8NH.

No vehicles yet recorded.

PG1074373/R: David Harold MATHIAS, 1 Mwrwg Road, LLANGENNECH, Llanelli, Carmarthenshire, SA14 8UA.
FN: DM Cabs. OC: Smith Arms, 1 Pontardulais Road, Llangennech, Llanelli, SA14 8YE. VA: 1.

LM 12 JVC	Ft	Do	ZFA25000002050778	?		M16	7/12 -?-, -?-		9/12

PG1082032/I: MERLIN's Coach Tours Limited, 8 Robert Owen Gardens, PORT TENNANT, Swansea, SA1 8NP.
OC: M&J Motors, St David's Road, Llansamlet, Swansea, SA6 8QL. VA: 2.

w　Y307 HUA	DAF	SB3000	XMGDE33WS0H008953	VH	33280	C49FT	6/01	Smith, Ashington (ND)	4/13
w　SA 02 UMU	Io	120E18	ZCFC1ED1102373299	LCB	3675	C36F	7/02	Briggs, Crymlyn Burrows (CW)	4/15
w　DX 03 WAA	LDV	Cy	SEYZMVSYGDN095691	LDV		M16	6/03	Gilbert, Pentrechwyth (CW)	6/11

PG0006160/I: MID WALES Motorways (1963) Limited, Brynhyfryd Garage, PENRHYNCOCH, Ceredigion, SY23 3ES.
OC: as address. VA: 34.

	H 13 MWT	VDL	SB4000	XMGSE40XS0H013520	VH 37170		C53F	4/06 new		4/06
			(ex YJ 06 LEF 3/14)							
	J 12 MWT	MB	O816D	WDB6703742N127699	Pn 078.5MBE7144	C29F		7/07 new		7/07
			(ex YN 07 OYX 3/14)							
	N 12 MWT	AD	Jv	SFD755BR68GJ22627	Pn 0812JAX8016	C57F		4/09 new		4/09
			(ex YN 09 DXW 7/15)							
	N 14 MWT	Vo	B7R	YV3R6R628BA143439	Pn 1012TTX8738	C57F		10/11 London Mini, Isleworth (LN)		7/15
			(ex YN 61 EOV 2/16)							
w	R 4 MHL	Ds	Jv	SFD721BR3VGJ22034	UVG 5677/97	C69F		1/98 Corbel, Edgware (LN)		9/04
	S 12 MWT	AD	Jv	SFD765BR7AGJ22651	Pn 1012JBX8589	C57F		7/10 new		7/10
			(ex YN 10 HJO 7/15)							
w	T 68 JBA	Ds	Dt SLF	SFD612BR1WGW13201	Pn 998.8GKB0906	B29F		6/99 Torrence,		
									West Cornforth (DM)	c1/10
	T 12 MWT	Vo	B12M	YV3R9F8193A001077	Pn 0312TJL4784	C48FT		3/03 National Holidays (EY) 587		1/14
			(ex MX 03 AET 3/14)							
	152 SA 52 MYR	Ds	Dt SLF	SFD6BACR32GW86793	Pn 2023/2	B29F		2/03 Compass, Worthing (WS)		9/12
	252 SA 52 MYS	Ds	Dt SLF	SFD6BACR32GW86794	Pn 2023/3	B29F		2/03 Compass, Worthing (WS)		9/12
	YN 53 EHZ	Vo	B7R	YV3R6G7103A006424	Tbs 0312THX5125	C70F		9/03 Weaver, Newbury (BE)		2/07
			(ex X 70 OXF 1/07, YN 53 EHZ 5/06, NDZ 70 7/05, YN 53 EHZ 9/03)							
	YN 04 WTC	Vo	B7R	YV3R6G7194A007351	Tbs 0412THX5563	C70F		5/04 Weaver, Newbury (BE)		2/07
			(ex NBZ 70 10/06, YN 04 WTC 7/05)							
	YN 04 WTD	Vo	B7R	YV3R6G7104A007500	Tbs 0412THX5564	C70F		5/04 Weaver, Newbury (BE)		2/07
			(ex NDZ 70 10/06, YN 04 WTD 7/05)							
x	KR 06 TVO	VW	Tr	WV2ZZZ7HZ4X032827	VW		M7	5/06 Bowen, Tamworth (ST)		1/13
	LX 08 ECY	Sca	N230UD	SZAN4X20001861564	Sca 413381	H41/22D		8/08 Green Transport, Hockley (WM)		2/14
	YN 60 BYV	AD	Jv	SFD765BR7AGJ22652	Pn 1012JBX8559	C70F		9/10 new		9/10
	CA 11 MWT	VH	T916	YE2916SS351D54091	VH 54091		C49FT	11/11 new		11/11
	YN 61 EOW	Vo	B7R	YV3R6R624BA143440	Pn 1012TTX8739	C57F		10/11 London Mini, Isleworth (LN)		8/15
	262 YX 62 FCA	AD	E20D	SFD7E1AR6CGY13281	AD C230/4	B39F		1/13 new		1/13
	162 YX 62 FWA	AD	E20D	SFD1D1AR6CGY13163	AD C230/6	B29F		1/13 new		1/13
	YJ 13 GWP	VH	TX15	YE2X15SH249D54928	VH 54928		C49FT	7/13 new		7/13
	MK 63 XAC	AD	E20D	SFD1D1AR6DGY13899	AD D235/3	B29F		1/14 Howard, Great Sankey (CH)		11/14
	YJ 14 CFL	VH	TX15	YE2X15SH249D55049	VH 55049		C42FT	3/14 Fishwick, Leyland (LA)		4/16
	YJ 64 FUW	VH	TX15	YE2X15SH249D55273	VH 55273		C49FT	11/14 new		11/14
	164 YX 64 VRJ	AD	E20D	SFD7E1AR6EGY14444	AD E242/3	B35F		10/14 GHA, Ruabon (CN) 1403		9/16
	YY 15 CMZ	AD	E20D	SFD1D1AR6EGY14795	AD E277/2	B29F		3/15 GHA, Ruabon (CN) 1472		9/16
	115 YY 15 FZE	AD	E20D	SFD8E1AR6EGY14451	AD E243/4	B33F		4/15 new		4/15
	165 SN 65 OFH	AD	E40D	SFD4DSBRFFGXD8525	AD F428/1	H45/32F		9/15 new		9/15
	365 YX 65 RVN	AD	E20D	SFD7E1AR6FGY15126	AD F224/5	B39F		1/16 new		1/16
	265 YX 65 RWN	AD	E20D	SFD7E1AR6FGY15125	AD F224/4	B39F		12/15 new		12/15

PG1007524/R: Andrew John MIDDLETON, 1 High Street, ST DAVIDS, Pembrokeshire, SA62 6SA.
FN: The TYF Group. OC: as address. VA: 2.

No vehicles currently recorded.

PG1085409/I: MIDWAY Motors (Crymych) Limited, Midway Garage, CRYMYCH, Pembrokeshire, SA41 3QU.
FN: Midway Motors / Rees of Crymych. OC: as address. VA: 15.

DW 3420	Vo	B10M-62	YV31MA611WA049050	Co 858523		C70F	1/99 Kavanagh JJ, Urlingford (EI)		12/04
		(ex 99-W-11 12/04)							
HIG 6246	Ds	Jv	SFD213BR3TGJ11818	UVG -?-		C45F	-/96 Lets Go, Manselton (CW) 4		5/12
		(ex P877 GEJ 3/10, -?- 2/06)							
YIL 1202	MB	O814D	WDB6703742N067594	Pn 978.5MXV7661	B31F		12/97 Bysiau Cwm Taf,		
		(ex R940 AMB 2/16, FIL 2688 by2/16, R940 AMB -/??)						Whitland (CW)	9/14
YTH 317	Ka	S416GT-HD	WKK32600001015099 Ka			C51FT	4/06 Ferris, Nantgarw (CC)		2/15
		(ex FB 06 OHR 3/15, SIL 9126 5/11)							
1885 FM	Rt	Mtr	VF1FDCCM522630926	Cym -?-		M16	4/01 Davies, Cardigan (CW)		1/07
		(ex Y845 BEJ 3/07)							
250 DBX	Ka	S416GT-HD	WKK63213423106975 Ka			C49FT	3/09 Hemmings Coaches,		
		(ex HM 09 HEM 2/14)						Holsworthy (DN)	2/14

MIDWAY, CRYMYCH (continued)

w	267 HNU	Bl	MW6G		139121 ECW 10474		DP43F	5/59	Western National (CO) 3002	1/79
w	269 HNU	Bl	MW6G		139123 ECW 10476		DP43F	5/59	Western National (CO) 3009	4/78
w	XNK 200X	Fd	R1014	BCRSAT422760	Pn	8210FTB1B809	B47F	10/81	UH Ventures,	
									Hatfield (HT) OV303	11/93
	A 17 CCG	Ds	Jv	12SDA2136/1522	Pn	9612HBM5939	C57F	9/96	Ridler, Dulverton (SO)	10/11
	(ex P553 KSD 7/12, JNZ 3477 9/10, P553 KSD by11/06, LJI 978 3/00, P553 KSD 1/99)									
w	C453 CWR	Vo	B10M-61	YV31MED1XGA011568	Pn	8612VZH2C789	C48FT	3/86	Denison, Otley (WY)	7/89
	(ex YTH 317 11/06, C453 CWR 4/92)									
w	F966 HGE	Vo	B10M-60	YV31MGD19KA021237	Pn	8912VCB1301	C57F	4/89	Owen, Nefyn (CN)	9/06
	(ex YIL 1202 11/12, F966 HGE 3/04, HIL 6584 c10/03, F966 HGE by1/92)									
w	G541 JBV	Ds	Dt	9SDL3002/103	Du	8911/1097	B39F	8/89	Reg, Hertford (HT)	11/03
w	L356 YNR	Ds	Jv	12SDA2131/867	Pn	9312HKM1774	C53F	11/93	Safeguard, Guildford (SR)	7/02
	(ex NGL 371 1/14, L356 YNR 7/02)									
	M 20 BWS	Vo	B12M	YV3R9F8162A000628	Pn	0212TJL4578	C53F	5/02	Cresswell, Moira (LE)	5/12
	(ex FP 02 YDN 7/12, A 17 CCG, FP 02 YDN)									
r	R348 ENT	Ds	Jv	SFD721BR3TGJ21837	Pn	9612HFM6176	C53F	1/98	Munden, Bristol (GL)	11/03
	T589 SKG	MB	O814D	WDB6703742N084214	Pn	998.5MXV1122	B31F	7/99	Lets Go, Manselton (CW) 6	10/09
	(ex SUI 2037 10/09, T589 SKG 9/09)									
z	T208 UEB	LDV	Cy	SEYZMVSHEDN051829	LDV		M16	8/99	Octobus UK, Pendine (CW)	by3/11
x	V902 HCR	Vx	Mov	YN1F9AED520930679	Vx		M8	12/99	-?-, -?-	10/08
	W 4 JJL	Vo	B10M-62	YV31MA613YA051935	VH	33582	C49FT	5/00	Longstaff, Mirfield (WY)	4/08
x	CU 52 GPO	Vx	Viv	W0LF7BCA63V060659	AVB		M8	11/02	new	11/02
	BX 54 EDP	Ka	S315GT-HD	WKK62725223000260	Ka		C49FT	2/05	Pullmanor, Herne Hill (LN) 213	6/10
	YN 07 OTX	VW	Crf	WV1ZZZ2EZ76026307	VW		M16	7/07	Hardhill Private Hire,	
									Edinburgh (SS)	1/15
	(ex 400 BTM 2/11, YN 07 OTX 4/07)									
x	KD 57 EXP	Vx	Viv	W0LJ7BHB68V602290	Vx		M8	9/07	Collins, Roch (CW)	8/14
	YN 57 DWA	MB	O816D	WDB6703742N127486	Ind	6504	C33F	9/07	Express Cabs, Maidstone (KT)	10/13
	MM 10 WAY	Vo	B12M	YV3R9L224AA138182	Je	29455	C53FT	3/10	Solus, Tamworth (ST)	7/16
	(ex GK 10 BZF 9/16, G 13 BSO 6/15, GK 10 BZF 12/13, LSK 555 4/13)									

PG1090706/R: David John MORDECAI, 11 Gwendraeth Place, BONYMAEN, Swansea, SA1 7BZ.
OC: Viking Court, Viking Way, Winch Wen, Swansea, SA1 7DA. VA: 2.

No vehicles currently recorded.

PG0005778/I: Hannah Jayne & Michael Vaughan MORGAN, 72 Cwmfelin Road, BYNEA, Llanelli, Carmarthenshire, SA14 9LR. FN: T&M Private Hire. OC: as address. VA: 1.

w	F130 RBX	Rt	Tc	VF1T4X80001287540	GM		M8	9/88	private owner	2/99
w	G337 NCW	Rt	Tc	VF1T4X30501347280	CWr	903199	M8L	3/90	Birkett, Sabden (LAx)	12/97
	M 20 MVM	Io	50C13	ZCFC5090005429772	?		B16FL	5/04	Sutton Community	
									Transport (XLN)	8/10
	(ex LK 04 CJU 8/11)									

PG1010939/N: Christopher Lynn and Susan Lorraine MORGAN, 139 Coalbrook Road, GROVESEND, Swansea, SA4 4GP. FN: Krislyn Commercials. OCs: as address; Bryn-yr-Awad Farm, Grovesend, Swansea, SA4 4UJ. VA: 12.
PG1136681/N: KRISLYN Motors Limited, 139 Coalbrook Road, GROVESEND, Swansea, SA4 4GP. OC: as address. VA: 6.

r	P 8 KMT	Fd	Tt	WF0EXXGBFE4B86610	Fd		M16	5/04	Cutajar, Brynhyfryd (CW)	8/13
	(ex RA 04 YGP 2/10)									
w	P529 YOD	Fd	Tt	SFALXXBDVLTG80346	?		M16	3/97	-?-, -?-	11/04
w	T 1 GMK	Fd	Tt	WF0LXXBDVLWR70944	Fd		M14	3/99	Pickering, Hull (EY)	4/07
w	T257 JVF	Fd	Tt	WF0EXXBDVEXY35139	Fd		M11	6/99	-?-, -?-	7/06
	EO 52 EEJ	Io	40C13	ZCFC4090005393747	Me	11652	M16	1/03	DH Taxis, Gorseinon (CW)	2/16
	KU 52 ZKM	Fd	Tt	WF0EXXGBFE2U21410	Fd		M14	10/02	CJ Contract, Barry (CC)	6/09
	HY 03 TZX	Fd	Tt	WF0EXXGBFE2A16737	Fd		M16	3/03	Ghuman, Reading (BE)	8/10
	AJ 04 RYV	Fd	Tt	WF0EXXGBFE4B86588	Fd		M16	5/04	Machnik, Streatham (LN)	4/13
	PN 54 OTP	Fd	Tt	WF0EXXGBFE3U14466	Fd		M16	9/04	-?-, -?-	11/10

MORGAN, GROVESEND (continued)

EN 55 HNJ	Fd	Tt	WF0EXXTTFE6L72916 Fd		M14	1/06 Felsted School (XEX)	3/14
SD 55 VBO	Fd	Tt	WF0EXXTTFE5M68225 Fd		M14	10/05 Car Parks, Luton Airport (BD)	9/11
WJ 55 CFZ	Io	45C14	ZCFC45A100D283882 Csd		M15L	10/05 Swindon Dial-a-Ride	
						(XWI) R17	9/14
AY 56 XHL	Fd	Tt	WF0PXXBDFP6S17988 Fd		M11	9/06 69ers, Houghton Regis (BD)	9/12

PG1140616/N: Paul MORGAN, 2 Heol Gerrig, TREBOETH, Swansea, SA5 9BP.
FN: Swansea Limousine Hire.   OC: Nantyffin Road South, Swansea Enterprise Park, Swansea, SA7 9RG. VA: 4.

YP 52 BPV	Oe	Alero	SAB21000000000313 Oe		C16F	12/02 Tinsley, Maesbury Marsh (SH)	3/16
YN 04 ABK	Oe	Alero	SAB21000000000437 Oe		B16F	7/04 Peyton Travel, Bridgend (CC)	11/14
CP 05 OHU	Fd	Tt	WF0EXXTTFE5M49455 Fd		M16	6/05 Driver Training,	
						Llansamlet (XCW)	7/11

PG1012786/I: RE MORRIS & Sons Limited, The Garage, LLANRHAEADR-YM-MOCHNANT, Oswestry, Powys,
SY10 0AD. FN: Tanat Valley. OCs: as address; The Garage, Pentrefelin, Llangedwyn, SY10 9LE; Station Yard,
Kerry Road, Abermule, Powys, SY15 6NH. VA: 38.

102	SK 02 UFG	MB	O815D	WDB6703742N094315 Sit 1643	C27F	3/02 Longmynd, Lea Cross (SH)	5/07
103	YN 03 ULC	MB	614D	WDB6683222N109136 FGy -?-	B16FL	6/03 Chesterfield Community	
						Transport (XDE) 14	8/11
155	MX 55 EVC	MB	413CDI	WDB9046632R809951 Tawe	M16	9/05 Williams, Newtown (CW)	11/16
194	YRC 194	Ld	PSUC1/1	617649 Ar 6832	DP41F	6/62 Yarnell, Sawley (P)	3/08
			(ex OWJ 170A 8/02, YRC 194 9/84)				
203	YN 53 ELC	Oe	M850	SAB19000000001242 Oe	B27F	9/03 West Norfolk Community	
						Transport, Kings Lynn (NK)	1/15
206	MX 57 CDN	Oe	M950	SABFWMAE07L192463 Oe	B29F	9/07 Shaw, Carnforth (LA)	1/13
207	MX 07 BBK	Oe	M950	SABFWJAE06R192604 Oe	DP31F	3/07 Alton Towers, Alton (ST) 11	5/09
208	YJ 62 FDK	Oe	M970SL	SABTN3AF0CS290563 Oe	B34F	1/13 new	1/13
209	YJ 62 FDP	Oe	M970SL	SABTN3AF0CS290564 Oe	B34F	1/13 new	1/13
210	YJ 13 HKT	Oe	M970SL	SABTN3AF0DS290556 Oe	B31F	3/13 new	3/13
260	DU 60 LOJ	AD	Dt	SFD3B1AR59GY11407 AD 9215/4	B37F	12/10 Lloyds Coaches,	
			(ex LC 60 WYN 12/15)			Machynlleth (CW) SDC60	1/16
271	YJ 57 YCB	Oe	V????	SABWWJAC08L320056 Oe	B38F	2/08 Webberbus, Bridgwater (SO)	11/16
272	YJ 58 CEK	Oe	V1110	SABWWJAC08L320121 Oe	B38F	10/08 Webberbus, Bridgwater (SO)	11/16
274	KX 54 NKG	Tbs	Env	SFD113AR13GG10129 Tbs 3040/3	B44F	9/04 Nicoll, Laurencekirk (SN)	12/15
280	YJ 59 GHV	Oe	X1200	SABMW6AS09L280142 Oe	B40F	11/09 Peoplesbus, Liverpool	
						(MY) 0701	10/15
281	SP 58 DPE	Oe	V1110	SABWWJAC08L320095 Oe	DP45F	11/08 Maytree, Bolton (GM)	3/13
282	SP 58 DPF	Oe	V1110	SABWWJAC08L320094 Oe	DP45F	11/08 Smith, Coupar Angus (SE)	3/13
283	MX 09 YWV	Oe	V1110	SABWWJAC09L320237 Oe	B29F	9/07 Herd, Lowgill (CA)	1/13
			(ex APO 110S 12/12)				
w 285	R985 SSA	Vo	B10L	YV3R5A511WA001114 ArB UL14.03	B43F	1/98 McColl Coaches, Dumbarton	
			(ex 97-D-59003 10/09)			(SW) 2016	8/11
288	YN 08 NXM	Vo	B7RLE	YV3R6K6128A126630 Pn 0812TGA7783	B45F	5/08 Alton Towers, Alton (ST) 016	2/13
301	R 1 STW	Ds	Jv	SFD721BR3VGJ22032 UVG 5673/97	C69F	12/97 Mid Wales, Penrhyncoch (CW)	3/09
w 303	R 3 PHL	Ds	Jv	SFD721BR3VGJ22033 UVG 5678/97	C69F	12/97 Mid Wales, Penrhyncoch (CW)	3/09
304	P211 RUM	DAF	SB3000	XMGDE33WS0H005612 Is 350T1PV1GB0025	C68F	3/97 Williams, Newtown (CW)	11/16
			(ex P 2 HWD 7/13, P211 RUM 4/09)				
305	W736 PPR	DAF	SB3000	XMGDE33WS0H008121 Is TSB350T1PY1GB0142	C70F	7/00 Williams, Newtown (CW)	11/16
			(ex W 4 HWD by2/13, W736 PPR 1/11)				
306	R 6 SGT	Ds	Jv	SFD721BR3VGJ22035 UVG 5679/97	C69F	1/98 Mid Wales, Penrhyncoch (CW)	3/09
380	803 HOM	Vo	B10M-50	YV31MGC15MA026259 ArB B32120291	B70F	3/91 Woods, Standish (GM)	8/11
			(ex H 84 DVM 8/11)				
415	P115 HCF	Ds	Jv	SFD731BR3TGJ41397 Bf 3225	C53F	4/97 Westbus, Hounslow (LN)	9/99
438	R 38 GNW	DAF	SB3000	XMGDE33WS0H005597 VH 32850	C49FT	5/98 Bull, Pytchley (NO) 20	1/16
			(ex 490 EYC 6/15, R 38 GNW 4/08)				
455	YN 55 WPP	MB	1018L	WDB9702472K959794 UNVI 33952	C34F	10/05 Jones, Llanfaethlu (CN)	5/15
			(ex 4 WA by8/06, YN 55 WPP 5/06)				
470	WA 03 EYM	Ba	FHD12-340	XL9AA18P330003732 Ba	C70F	3/03 Reynolds, Maerdy (CC)	5/13
472	WJ 52 MTU	Ba	FHD12-340	XL9AA18P230003699 Ba	C51FT	3/03 Filers Travel, Ilfracombe (DN)	6/14

MORRIS, LLANRHAEADR-YM-MOCHNANT (continued)

	Reg	Make	Model	Chassis No.	Body	Seats	New	History	Date
	473 A 15 TVC	Ibs	391E.12.35	ZGA662P000E002823	Bs 00.021	C49FT	5/00	Phillips, Brynmenyn (CC)	10/11
	(ex W735 PPR 9/12)								
	477 GX 07 NVE	Ba	FHD127.365	XL9AA38R733003419	Ba	C55FT	5/07	Andybus Dauntsey (WI)	6/14
	(ex AJ 07 BUS 4/14)								
	571 R871 MDY	DAF	DB250	XMGDE02RS0H006471	Oe 8636	H48/29F	6/98	Eastbourne (ES) 13971	2/11
	573 R873 MDY	DAF	DB250	XMGDE02RS0H006473	Oe 8638	H48/29F	6/98	Eastbourne (ES) 13973	1/12
	574 YJ 03 UML	DAF	DB250	XMGDE02PS0H010795	Oe 8765	H47/27F	4/03	Go West (NK) 13989	8/16
	575 LW 05 PJO	Ds	Tt	SFD148BR65GX33609	EL 54602	H47/27F	5/05	Isle of Man (IM) 18	10/14
	(ex HMN 221A 10/12)								
x	758 BX 58 OJJ	LDV	Max	SEYL6RXH21N230047	LDV	M8	9/08	National Car Rental (Y)	8/13
w	942 N 42 MJO	Vo	B10M-62	YV31M2B10TC060083	Bf 3028	C27FT	4/96	United Counties (NO) 52036	4/08
	(ex 9737 VC 9/03, N 42 MJO 2/99)								
r	DCZ 4820	Oe	M850	VN6311	Oe 6311	B26F	3/00	Stena Line, Birkenhead (XMY)	11/15
r	NWR 421A	Ld	PSUC1/11	626935	Roe G05746	B45F	10/63	Winter, Darton (P)	10/15
	(ex 434 MDT 2/91)								
z	T637 EUB	DAF	DB250	XMGDE02RS0H006494	Oe 8683	H48/29F	7/99	Arriva Yorkshire (WY) 637	10/15
r	T639 EUB	DAF	DB250	XMGDE02RS0H006496	Oe 8685	H48/29F	8/99	Arriva Yorkshire (WY) 639	10/15

PG0007563/I: MORRIS TRAVEL Limited, Coach Centre, Alltycnap Road, Cillefwr Industrial Estate, Johnstown, CARMARTHEN, Carmarthenshire, SA31 3QY. OC: as address. VA: 32.

PG0006900/I: Thomas John FREEMAN, Coach Centre, Alltycnap Road, Cillefwr Industrial Estate, Johnstown, CARMARTHEN, Carmarthenshire, SA31 3QY. FN: Morris Travel. OC: as address. VA: 29.

	Reg	Make	Model	Chassis No.	Body	Seats	New	History	Date
	GIL 3274	Oe	M850	VN6519	Oe 6519	B27F	12/00	new	12/00
	(ex X382 VVY 6/06, TIL 1990 by6/06, X382 VVY 4/04)								
	PJI 7230	Ld	TRCTL11/3LZM	TR00768	Pn 8912LTF1600	DP68F	11/89	Eurotaxis,	
								Siston Common (GL)	5/07
	(ex G783 XWS 6/07, 03 KJ 21 7/98)								
	YHA 116	Vo	B7R	YV3R6B51X1A002614	Pn 0012TCM4163	C57F	12/01	Berry, Blunsden (OX)	11/11
	(ex YN 51 WHK 12/11)								
	264 ACA	Vo	B12M	YV3R9F8173A000896	Pn 0212TJT4748	C57F	1/03	National Express (LN) CO42	10/12
	(ex ST 52 GZD 10/14)								
w	A695 DCN	Ld	TRCTL11/3RZ	8301203	Pn 8412LTH1C769	C53F	2/84	Hayward, Carmarthen (CW)	3/05
	(ex GIL 5103 7/04, LXI 4455 12/96, A695 DCN by8/96, GSU 347 3/90, A 31 FVN by12/87)								
w	L253 NFA	MB	709D	WDB6690032N022348	WS 4551/94	B29F	6/94	Wardle, Norton (ST)	10/03
	M378 EBX	Ds	Jv	10SDA2156/1159	WS 4726/95	C57F	3/95	MoD (X)	9/11
	(ex 27 AY 43 by9/11)								
	P912 GEJ	Ds	Jv	SFD213BR3TGJ11877	UVG 5549/96	C57F	c2/97	MoD (X)	4/06
	(ex JL 93 AA 5/06)								
	P915 GEJ	Ds	Jv	SFD213BR3TGJ11910	UVG 5548/96	C57F	c2/97	MoD (X)	4/06
	(ex JL 92 AA 4/06)								
	P924 GEJ	Ds	Jv	SFD213BR3TGJ11816	UVG 5438/96	C57F	-/96	MoD (X)	4/06
	(ex ?? ?? ?? 5/06)								
	T406 AGP	Ds	Dt SLF	SFD112BR1XGW13426	MI C39.378	B28F	7/99	London Central (LN) DML6	3/09
w	T106 KGP	Ds	Dt SLF	SFD612BR1WGW12963	MI C39.349	B26F	5/99	London Central (LN) DMS6	3/09
z	V247 BNV	Ds	Dt SLF	SFD612BR1XGW13946	Pn 998.8GKB1467	B29F	10/99	Countryliner, Uckfield	
								(ES) DP13	5/13
z	V 69 GEH	Oe	M850	VN6213	Oe 6213	B27F	9/99	Graham, West Auckland	
								(DM) OS7	8/15
w	V527 JBH	Ds	Dt SLF	SFD212BR1XGW13698	Pn 9910.1HJB1298	B31D	9/99	London Sovereign	
								(LN) SDP527	c12/09
w	W137 ULR	Ds	Dt SLF	SFD212AR1YGW14619	Pn 0010.1HJB2575	B39F	5/00	St John's College,	
								Southsea (XHA)	6/14
	KP 51 SXV	Ds	Dt SLF	SFD6B2CR31GW15992	Pn 0126/2	B29F	12/01	Countryliner, Uckfield	
								(ES) DP20	4/13
	KP 51 SYC	Ds	Dt SLF	SFD6B2CR31GW16016	Pn 0126/8	B29F	12/01	Countryliner, Uckfield	
								(ES) DP22	4/13
	MP 51 BUZ	Oe	M850	SAB19000000000660	Oe	B27F	10/01	Evans, Carmarthen (CW)	c10/13
	(ex B 15 EDC 11/09, MP 51 BUZ 1/07)								
x	CV 02 VOJ	LDV	Cy	SEYZMVSYGDN083644	LDV	M8	12/02	John, Whitland (CW)	by4/13
	(ex 02-C-9949 by2/04)								
	KF 52 TZL	MB	O814D	WDB6703732N105952	Pn 028.5MXV4897	DP33F	9/02	S&S Travel Services,	
								Darwen (LA)	9/12

MORRIS TRAVEL, CARMARTHEN (continued)

YM 52 TOU	Oe	M850	SAB19000000001067 Oe			B27F	1/03	Leven Valley,	
								Stockton-on-Tees (CD) 52	5/15
GX 03 AZL	Tbs	Dt SLF	SFD6BACR32GW87037 Tbs	2083/20		B29F	4/03	Southdown PSV,	
								Copthorne (WS)	2/16
CA 53 APH	Vo	B7R	YV3R6G7104A006914 Tbs	0312THX5227		C53F	2/04	Airport Parking,	
								Copthorne (WS)	10/13
SN 53 ETR	Tbs	Dt SLF	SFD6BACR33GW87401 Tbs	3041/5		B29F	11/03	Compass, Worthing (WS)	2/16
CN 04 XES	Rt	Mtr	VF1PDMVL531597378 Me	12040		M16	7/04	new	7/04
CN 04 XEV	Rt	Mtr	VF1PDMVL531597379 Me	12048		M16	7/04	new	7/04
GX 04 BEU	Vo	B7R	YV3R6G7144A007502 Pn	0412THX5566		C53F	6/04	Airport Parking,	
								Copthorne (WS)	10/13
YU 04 XJM	Tbs	Jv	SFD745BR54GJ22502 Tbs	0412GRX5603		C70F	7/04	PMP, Luton (BD)	8/11
YU 04 XJN	Tbs	Jv	SFD745BR54GJ22503 Tbs	0412GRX5604		C70F	7/04	PMP Recruitment,	
								Pontnewydd (CS)	8/11
YN 54 WCV	Ds	Jv	SFD741BR54GJ22516 Pn	0412JRX5678		C70F	10/04	PMP, Luton (BD)	8/11
MX 06 ACO	Oe	M850	SAB19000000002196 Oe			B25F	5/06	Holsworthy, Dolton (DN)	8/15
MX 06 BTO	Oe	M920	SAB19000000002215 Oe			B34F	6/06	Glasgow Prestwick,	
								Glasgow (SW)	1/08
BX 56 XAL	Asn	A1012T	SUAED5CPP5S620186 Asn			C68F	9/06	Ffoshelig, Carmarthen (CW)	8/15
			(ex DS 56 FOS 8/15, BX 56 XAL 4/09)						
DX 59 FHE	Asn	A1012T	SUAED5CGT7S620351 Asn			C70F	2/10	new	2/10
DX 59 FHF	Asn	A1012T	SUAED5CGT7S620348 Asn			C70F	2/10	new	2/10
DX 59 FHG	Asn	A1012T	SUAED5CGT7S620349 Asn			C70F	2/10	new	2/10
YJ 59 GGV	Oe	M810	SABDNJAF09L193522 Oe			B24F	10/09	new	10/08
YJ 59 GGX	Oe	M810	SABDNJAF09L193523 Oe			B24F	10/09	new	10/09
YJ 59 GGY	Oe	M1020	SABGNJAF09L193524 Oe			B36F	10/09	new	10/09
YJ 59 GGZ	Oe	M1020	SABGNJAF09L193525 Oe			B36F	10/09	new	10/09
YJ 59 NPX	Oe	M1020	SABGN4AF0AL193595 Oe			B36F	1/10	new	1/10
YJ 59 NPY	Oe	M1020	SABGN4AF0AL193596 Oe			B36F	2/10	new	2/10

PG1141623/R: NATIONWIDE Executive Travel Limited, The Sundowner, NEW HEDGES, Tenby, Pembrokeshire, SA70 8TR. OC: as address. VA: 2.

KX 14 LZA	MB	513	WDB9066552S896314 ?		M16	6/14 -?-, -?-		1/15

PG1136235/I: Louise NICHOLLS, 8A Broad Street, HAY-ON-WYE, Powys, HR3 5DB. OC: as address; Wyecliff, Hay-on-Wye, Powys, HR3 5RS. VA: 2.

No vehicles yet recorded.

PG1076006/R: William NUNNS, Welsh Border Motor Spares, Unit 1 The Fox Complex, Severn Road, WELSHPOOL, Powys, SY21 7AZ. FN: Will Nunns. OC: as address. VA: 2.
PG1125931/R: William NUNNS Limited, 1 The Fox Complex, Severn Road, WELSHPOOL, Powys, SY21 7AX. OC: as address. VA: 2.

x	FOH 561	Fd	Tt	WF0EXXTTFE5B20331 Fd		M16	6/05	Stubbs, Westhoughton (GM)	5/12
				(ex RV 05 YCC 7/12)					
x	W 2 NUN	Fd	Tt	WF0TXXGBFT3S32989 Fd		M8	8/03	-?-, -?-	6/12
				(ex DL 03 CCY 10/12)					
	W111 NUN	Fd	Tt	WF0EXXTTFE4S78040 Fd		M14	1/05	-?-, -?-	5/10
				(ex PJ 54 VCA 5/11)					
	DU 03 HWY	Fd	Tt	WF0EXXGBFE3K75041 Fd		M16	3/03	Leek College of Further Education	
								(XST)	6/12
	BP 08 MKF	Fd	Tt	WF0DXXTTFD8K47735 Fd		M16	8/08	-?-, -?-	10/13
x	BD 10 XEV	Fd	Tt	WF0DXXTTFD9K06905 Fd		M16	7/10	Hartpury College,	
								Hartpury (XGL)	by4/15
	AY 15 OUU	Fd	Tt	WF0HXXTTGHFK01190 Fd		M17	5/15	Midland Van Rentals,	
								Gloucester (YGL)	7/16

PG1084223/R: OCS Group UK Limited, .Optimum Fleet, Second Floor, 3 Herdman Square, Spinningfields, Manchester, M3 3EB. OC: DVLA, Longview Road, CLASE, Swansea, SA6 7JL. VA: 2.

CV 62 CXB	Fd	Tt	WF0DXXTTFDCK79635	Fd	M16	9/12	Day's Rental, Swansea (YCW)	6/13
CV 62 CXC	Fd	Tt	WF0DXXTTFDCK79555	Fd	M16	9/12	Day's Rental, Swansea (YCW)	6/13
BP 15 MYM	Vx	Viv	W0L2J7210FV638458	Vx	M8	7/15	new	7/15

PG1056890/N: OCTOPUS UK Limited, Morfa Bay Adventure Centre, PENDINE, Carmarthenshire, SA33 4PH. OC: as address. VA: 4.

RF 52 RHV	Fd	Tt	WF0EXXGBFE2R88802	Fd	M16	11/02	Parker, Ellesmere Port (CH)	3/11
NA 03 OJG	Fd	Tt	WF0EXXGBFE3K89747	Fd	M14	4/02	Beeston Self Drive, Nottingham (YNG)	11/13
AE 55 NLF	LDV	Cy	SEYZMVSVGDN113324	LDV	M16	12/05	-?-, -?-	3/09

PG0007530/I: OWENS of Oswestry Coaches Limited, 36 Beatrice Street, Oswestry, Shropshire, SY11 1QG. FNs: Owen's Coaches; Travelmaster Holidays. OC: Unit 3, Foxen Manor Business Park, FOUR CROSSES, Powys, SY22 6ST. VA: 24.

E 2 MMO	Vo	B12B	YV3R8G1235A106454	Pn	0512TKL6106	C57F	8/05	new	8/05
		(ex YN 05 XZG 2/13)							
E 10 OWN	MB	515CDI	WDB9061552N318312	Fer	6	C16F	5/07	Whitegate Travel, Anderton (CH)	9/13
		(ex YX 07 AWH 7/16)							
E 11 OWN	Ka	S416GT-HD	WKK63213423102263	Ka		C49FT	8/06	Romdrive, Melton Mowbray (LE)	5/11
		(ex BU 06 HSX 5/11, H 1 WET 2/11, BU 06 HSX 6/08)							
E 12 OWN	Vo	B12B	YV3R8G12X5A103633	Pn	0512TKL5917	C49FT	3/05	Henshaw, Moreton-in-Marsh (GL)	6/15
		(ex YN 05 HVR 10/16)							
E 14 OWN	MB	Tourismo	WEB63203623000076	MB		C45FT	6/09	new	6/09
		(ex BG 09 JJO 10/15)							
H 8 JEO	Ds	R410	SFD152BR23GC10178	Pn	0312GXT4804	C55F	4/03	Alfa, Euxton (LA) 25	3/13
		(ex PN 03 POA 3/13)							
H 7 RSO	Ds	R410	SFD152BR23GC10177	Pn	0312GXT4803	C57F	4/03	Alfa, Euxton (LA) 24	3/13
		(ex PN 03 PFX 3/13)							
T213 EAG	Ds	Jv	SFD721BR3WGJE2235	Pn	9912GHM0695	C70F	3/99	Cochrane, Armadale (SS)	9/16
		(ex R298 DWR 2/08)							
W709 PTO	Vo	B10M-62	YV31MA617WC060901	Pn	0012VUM8773	C53F	5/00	Swiftsure, Burton-upon-Trent (ST)	5/12
EF 03 FEK	Fd	Tt	WF0EXXGBFE2B30995	Fd		M16	6/03	-?-, -?-	11/13
BX 54 VUE	BMC	1100FE	NMC111TKCRD200045	BMC		B60F	12/04	new	12/04
YN 06 RVO	MB	O814D	WDB6703742N122604	Pn	068.5MAE6534	C29F	4/06	new	4/06
x BG 57 LPV	Rt	Tc	VF1JLBHB68V312629	Rt		M8	11/07	new	11/07
BV 57 MTK	BMC	900	NMC900LKKRD200009	BMC		B27F	10/07	new	10/07
BV 57 MTO	BMC	900	NMC900LKKRD200011	BMC		B27F	10/07	new	10/07
x DY 08 UEE	Vx	Viv	W0LJ7BHB68V645771	Vx		M8	3/08	Serco, Ruislip (LNx)	5/12
YJ 08 PHN	Oe	M780SE	SABDN2AB08R192994	Oe		B22F	5/08	Worcestershire County Council, Worcester (WO) 5105	2/16
x DV 58 HWT	Vx	Viv	W0LJ7BHB69V610383	Vx		M8	12/08	John Townsend Trust, Margate (XKT)	4/16
x DV 58 HZD	Vx	Viv	W0LJ7BHB69V610444	Vx		M8	11/08	John Townsend Trust, Margate (XKT)	4/16
FG 10 WEN	MB	Tourismo	WEB63203623000110	MB		C41FT	5/10	new	5/10
ML 61 CXE	Au	N2216/3SHDL	WAGP22ZZ9CT017548	Au		C61FT	11/11	Bennett, Uxbridge (LN) 1	5/14
YJ 61 CKD	Oe	M780SE	SABDN2AB0BL193814	Oe		B23F	11/11	new	11/11
YN 61 EPX	MB	O816D	WDB6703742N140924	Pn	108.5MBJ8703	C29F	9/11	Tate's Travel, Low Barugh (SY)	3/16
BJ 62 VOO	MB	Tourismo	WEB63203623000223	MB		C45FT	12/12	new	12/12
YJ 62 EPL	BMC	750	NMC750RKDRD100019	BMC		C26F	9/12	new	9/12
YJ 13 HKO	Oe	M780SE	SABDN2AB0DS290565	Oe		B23F	3/13	new	3/13
YJ 13 HKP	Oe	M780SE	SABDN2AB0DS290566	Oe		B23F	3/13	new	3/13
x DL 14 BWE	Vx	Viv	W0LJ7B7B2EV637025	Vx		M8	6/14	-?-, -?-	12/14
BG 15 OSX	MB	Tourismo M	WEB63247523000389	MB		C55FT	4/15	new	4/15

OWENS, FOUR CROSSES (continued)

x	DY 15 XDH	Vx	Viv	W0L3J7718FV627618 Vx		M8	6/15 -?-, -?-		10/15
	YC 15 WCM	Ytg	ZK6938HQ	LZYTCTE69E1056706 Ytg		C32FT	5/15 new		5/15
	YC 15 WCN	Ytg	ZK6129HQ	LZYTMTF62E1062200 Ytg		C51FT	5/15 new		5/15
	BJ 16 KYS	MB	Tourismo M	WEB63247523000748 MB		C51FT	5/16 new		5/16
	OU 16 ERK	Au	N2216/3SHDL	WAGP22ZZ3GT023786 Au -?-		C59FT	7/16 new		7/16

PG0004797/N: OWENS Motors Limited, Temeside House, Station Road, KNIGHTON, Powys, LD7 1DT.
OC: Quarry Garage, Skyborry Road, Knighton, Powys, LD7 1DW. VA: 12.

	IIG 4463	MB	O814D	WDB6703742N113631 Pn	048.5MAE5437	C29F	6/04	Bugler, Clutton (SO)	3/16
			(ex YN 04 WSY 5/15)						
	NLZ 1718	Vo	B10M-62	YV31M2B12SA043215 Pn	9512VUM3653	C70F	2/97	McGowan, Neilston (SW)	8/07
			(ex P118 UAT 9/04)						
	VJI 2779	Vo	B10M-62	YV31M2B1XTA045151 Je	24053	C55F	5/96	Price, Newcastle-on-Clun (SH)	4/12
			(ex N 91 SKG 1/05, SIL 1324 3/04, N 91 SKG 9/03)						
	J 20 OML	Vo	B12M	YV3R9F8124A011922 Co	F043043006	C53F	11/05	SMS, Towcester (NO)	8/14
			(ex FJ 55 BXR 9/14, Y 70 SMS 8/14, FJ 55 BXR 1/13)						
	J 30 OML	Vo	B10M-62	YV31MA619WC060852 Pn	9812VUM8459	C53F	4/98	Elcock, Madeley (SH)	3/10
			(ex R921 LAA 3/10, A 13 EXC 10/00)						
	AV 02 KYJ	MB	O814D	WDB6703742N091967 Pn	018.5MXV4486	B31F	3/02	Mulley, Ixworth (SK)	3/16
	YN 05 XZF	MB	O814D	WDB6703742N116733 Pn	058.5MAE5952	C33F	7/05	Essential Fleet, Lincoln (LI)	9/15
x	BL 06 NDD	Fd	Tt	WF0TXXBDFT6L02255 Fd		M7	7/06	Kenilworth Vehicle Rental (YWK)	3/09
	LX 57 OUG	Rt	Mtr	VF1JLBHB67V307147 Rt		M8	9/07 -?-, -?-		5/14
	YT 58 BHV	Fd	Tt	WF0DXXTTFD8D82035 Fd		M16	10/08	Stevens, Ebbw Vale (CS)	4/13
	CP 10 HFX	Fd	Tt	WF0DXXTTFD9D30896 Fd		M16	7/10 -?-, -?-		4/14
x	YP 11 NNR	Fd	Tt	WF0BXXBDFBBE06583 Fd		M8	5/11 -?-, -?-		2/13

PG1081285/R: Wayne Floyd George PANAYIOTIOU, 19 Maes Yr Haf, LLANELLI, Carmarthenshire, SA15 3NF.
FN: Wayne's Minibus Hire. OC: Andrew Street Garage, Andrew Street, Llanelli, SA15 3YW. VA: 2.

w	V563 DTN	Fd	Tt	WF0LXXBDVLXS44804 May		M16	9/99	Castle, Llandovery (CW)	1/10
	FL 52 STZ	Fd	Tt	WF0EXXGBFE2B17815 Fd		M16	10/02	Adams, Sirhowy (CS)	7/14
	EK 62 HFZ	Fd	Tt	WF0DXXTTFDCD19522 Fd		M16	9/12 -?-, -?-		1/13
	HK 15 FHV	Fd	Tt	WF0HXXTTGHFE54840 Fd		M16	5/15 -?-, -?-		1/16

PG1115883/R: PETERS Taxi Limited, Tre Garth, MACHYNLLETH, Powys, SY20 8HT.
OC: Unit 9 Treowain Enterprise Park, Forge Road, Machynlleth, Powys, SY20 8EG. VA: 2.

	NJ 06 JYE	Fd	Tt	WF0EXXTTFE5A47915 Fd		M14	5/06	Target Vehicle Rentals, Banbury (YOX)	12/12

PG0006187/N: Alun Bowen PHILLIPS, Parsonage Farm, TRECWN, Pembrokeshire, SA62 5TN.
OC: as address. VA: 30.

w	HJZ 9973	MB	709D	WDB6690032N014047 Pn	937MHV1551	DP25F	9/93	Brimm, Quedgley (GL)	4/07
			(ex L817 SAE 1/05)						
w	B280 KTV	Fd	Tt	SFAPXXBDVPES74166 Do -?-		B8FL	6/85 -?-, -?-		8/98
w	N210 MBW	Pt	Bxr	VF3232B5215242127 G&M -?-		M8L	6/96	Mole Valley Dial-a-Ride (XSR)	6/05
w	N552 REW	LDV	400	SEYZMYSEACN964913 LDV		M16	3/96	Budget (Y)	11/98
w	N 82 XTF	Ft	Do	ZFA23000005170930 ?		M?L	3/96	Hereford & Worcester Ambulance Service (XHW) 546	8/05
w	P787 EJM	Ft	Do	ZFA23000005324459 O&H -?-		M8L	1/97	Royal Berkshire Ambulance (BE) 635	9/05
w	P792 EJM	Ft	Do	ZFA23000005325228 O&H -?-		M8L	2/97	Hereford & Worcester Ambulance Service (XHW) 568	9/06
w	P796 EJM	Ft	Do	ZFA23000005332163 O&H -?-		M??L	2/97	Royal Berkshire Ambulance Service (XBE)	8/08
w	P741 PLX	LDV	Cy	SEYZLNSEEDN011833 LDV		M16	by7/97 -?-, -?-		6/05
xw	R956 HNJ	VW	Tr	WV2ZZZ70ZWH100755 VW		M8L	3/98	private owner	4/02
w	R409 NCF	Ft	Do	ZFA23000005397217 O&H -?-		M7L	12/97	West Yorkshire Ambulance Service (XWY) 494	1/06

PHILLIPS, TRECWN (continued)

	Reg	Make	Body	Chassis		Body	Type	Date	Operator	Date
w	R206 WOB	LDV	Pt	SEYZKRSDCDN028123	LDV		M8	12/97	Royal Mail (RM) 7780491	9/03
w	T 41 DGB	LDV	Cy	SEYZMVSHEDN050485	LDV		M16	6/99	Enterprise (Y)	3/02
w	T741 MNE	LDV	Cy	SEYZMVSHEDN046987	LDV		M16	5/99	Cheshire Vehicle Rentals (YCH)	10/02
w	T744 MNE	LDV	Cy	SEYZMVSHEDN047898	LDV		M16	5/99	Cheshire Vehicle Rentals (YCH)	10/02
w	T748 RDE	LDV	Cy	SEYZMVSHEDN047414	?		M16	7/99	Pembrokeshire County Council (XCW)	4/08
w	V196 LFJ	LDV	Cy	SEYZMVFHEDN056206	G&M	2706	M12	1/00	Devon County Council (XDN) 2430	1/08
	W665 FCT	Fd	Tt	WF0EXXBDVEXJ51182	Fd		M14	6/00	-?-, -?-	8/09
w	W128 MWG	LDV	Cy	SEYZMVSHEDN061510	LDV		M16	4/00	Sixt (Y)	5/03
w	W386 NDE	LDV	Cy	SEYZMNFHEDN059406	?		M16	3/00	Pembrokeshire County Council (XCW)	4/08
w	W682 PTN	LDV	Cy	SEYZMVSHEDN062618	LDV		M16	6/00	Willhire (Y)	11/03
w	W356 WNS	LDV	Cy	SEYZMYSHEDN056362	LDV		M8	5/00	Boulevard Self Drive, East Kilbride (YSW)	1/04
w	W598 XDM	LDV	Cy	SEYZMVSHEDN063243	LDV		M16	6/00	Sixt (Y)	3/03
w	W129 YOR	LDV	Cy	SEYZMVSHEDN058421	LDV		M16	3/00	-?-, -?-	6/07
w	W237 YVE	LDV	Cy	SEYZMVSHEDN063766	LDV		M16	7/00	Budget-Jaeban (Y)	8/05
w	X378 KRX	Ft	Do	ZFA23000005933203	O&H -?-		M??L	1/01	Royal Berkshire Ambulance Service (XBE)	8/08
	DA 51 XVJ	Rt	Mtr	VF1FDCNL525884785	?		M??	2/02	-?-, -?-	3/11
w	VX 51 VTO	Rt	Mtr	VF1FDCGL525222516	O&H -?-		M8L	10/01	Great Western Ambulance, Chippenham (XWI)	5/11
w	VX 51 VTT	Rt	Mtr	VF1FDCGL525222519	O&H -?-		M8L	10/01	Great Western Ambulance, Chippenham (XWI)	3/11
	CE 02 SDO	LDV	Cy	SEYZMVSYGDN082316	LDV		M16	3/02	Shropshire Council, Shrewsbury (SH) N4555	2/13
	CE 02 UZD	Rt	Mtr	VF1FDBNH526310921	?		M12L	5/02	VEST, Cardiff (XCC)	8/11
w	LC 02 NCY	Ctn	Rly	BF7231A3216166768	?		M12	5/02	-?-, -?-	9/07
w	SG 52 WZC	VW	LT46	WV1ZZZ2DZ3H012232	?		M16L	1/03	-?-, -?-	5/09
	CN 03 MTK	MB	311CDI	WDB9036622R499537	?		M14	4/03	-?-, -?-	8/12
	YN 03 OXK	Rt	Mtr	VF1FDCML527557384	?		M??L	3/03	Yorkshire Ambulance Service, (XWY) 526	9/10
	RX 04 SXR	Io	50C13	ZCFC509000D233213	Eurm -?-		M??L	5/04	London Borough of Merton (XLN) 428	by7/12
	RX 04 YDJ	Io	50C13	ZCFC509000D233214	Eurm -?-		M??L	5/04	London Borough of Merton (XLN) 411	4/10
	OU 54 DVF	Rt	Mtr	VF1FDCVL532807426	?		M??L	2/05	Hereford & Worcester Ambulance Service (XWO)	2/12
	OU 54 DVY	Rt	Mtr	VF1FDCVL532807440	?		M??L	2/05	Hereford & Worcester Ambulance Service (XWO)	2/12
	HX 05 EHP	Io	40C13	ZCFC409000D236851	Stan		M12L	3/05	Elmbridge Community Transport, Esher (XSR)	6/10
	NM 05 BJU	Fd	Tt	WF0EXXTTFE5A52246	?		M16	8/05	-?-, -?-	2/09
	FJ 55 KNY	Io	45C14	ZCFC45A1005562220	?		M16	12/05	-?-, -?-	8/13
	FJ 55 KUW	Io	50C13	ZCFC5090005513464	Me	12275	B16FL	12/05	Shropshire Council, Shrewsbury (SH) N1770	11/13
	FJ 06 LXW	Io	50C14	ZCFC50A1005556522	Me	4402	B16FL	4/06	Shropshire Council, Shrewsbury (XSH) N4239	3/15
	CN 57 FPG	Ibs	50C15	ZCFC50A2005680137	?		M16	11/07	-?-, -?-	2/09

PG1071612/N: Simon Edward PRICE, The Tan Yard, South Street, RHAYADER, Powys, LD6 5BH.
FN: Simon Price Cars. OC: as address. VA: 8
PG1090107/T: Simon Edward PRICE, The Tan Yard, South Street, RHAYADER, Powys, LD6 5BH.
FN: Simon Price Cars. OC: as address.
PG1128938/T: Simon PRICE, The Tan Yard, South Street, RHAYADER, Powys, LD6 5BH.
FN: Simon Price Cars. OC: as address.

	Reg	Make	Body	Chassis		Body	Type	Date	Operator	Date
xw	PL 04 LFR	Fd	Tt	WF0TXXTTFT4B02078	Fd		M8	6/04	private owner	1/08
SP09	BK 07 HRG	Fd	Tt	WF0DXXTTFD7K05754	Fd		M16	4/07	-?-, -?-	1/12

PRICE, RHAYADER (continued)

x	KD 07 EYL	Fd	Tt	WF0BXXBDFB7C77994	Fd		M8	3/07 -?-, -?-	12/09
	SD 07 WOX	Fd	Tt	WF0DXXTTFD7D07211	Fd		M16	3/07 Arnold Clark (Y)	1/13
	ST 07 VPG	Fd	Tt	WF0DXXTTFD7Y01025	Fd		M16	7/07 -?-, -?-	10/11
	CN 57 HTK	LDV	Max	SEYL6RXE20N222091	LDV		M16	12/07 Thrifty (Y)	1/13
	CN 57 HXD	LDV	Max	SEYL6RXE20N222111	LDV		M16	11/07 Thrifty (Y)	1/13
x	YY 08 DUV	Fd	Tt	WF0BXXBDFB8G82931	Fd		M7	5/08 South Cave Car &	
								Van Hire, Brough (XNY)	5/13
x	VE 12 KFY	Fd	Tt	WF0BXXBDFBCC39899	Fd		M8	6/12 -?-, -?-	11/15
x	MT 62 NHP	Fd	Tt	WF0XXXTTFXCR86269	Fd		M8	11/12 new	11/12
	YS 63 VPD	Fd	Tt	WF0DXXTTFDDA28303	Fd		M16	12/13 -?-, -?-	10/15

PG0006861/N: Michael Clifford PROSSER, Roberts Transport Yard, St Davids Road, Swansea Enterprise Park, MORRISTON, Swansea, SA6 8QL. FN: Kim's Coaches. OC: as address. VA: 3.

w	K155 EJB	Ds	Jv	12SDA2122/739	WS	3797/92		B67FA	11/92 Gemini, Swansea (CW)	8/07
				(ex 74 KK 98 4/99)						
w	M 44 CJT	Ds	Jv	12SDA2157/1141	WS	4708/94		C70F	2/95 Turner, Bristol (GL)	2/12
				(ex CX 70 AA 10/05, M463 SMO 12/03, CX 70 AA by7/01)						
	N966 OAE	Ds	Jv	12SDA2157/1284	WS	4961/95		C57F	8/95 Turner, Bristol (GL)	2/12
				(ex EC 55 AA 3/04)						
	MX 55 OKD	LDV	Cy	SEYZMVSZGDN112253	LDV			M16	9/05 Parnell, Dunkeswell (DN)	2/14

PG0007122/I: David Anthony PYE, Benthall Farm Buildings, Alberbury Road, FORD, Shrewsbury, SY5 9NA. FN: Worthen Travel. OCs: Station Road, Abermule, Powys, SY15 6NH; Spar Car Park, Welshpool, SY21 7AS; Porth Llifior, Berriew, Welshpool, Powys, SY21 8QH. VA: 6.

Note. Vehicles are recorded in the Shropshire Other Operators section of News Sheet 4 as Pye, Ford. See also G647 Page 28.

PG1091420/R: RCS Vehicles Limited, Clara Cottage, Bridge Street, ST CLEARS, Carmarthenshire, SA33 4EE. OC: as address. VA: 2.
PG1146435/R: Robert C. SCOURFIELD, Clara Cottage, Bridge Street, ST CLEARS, Carmarthenshire, SA33 4EE. FN: RCS Minibuses. OC: Unit 1 Parc Owen Industrial Estate, St Clears, Carmarthen, SA33 4BP. VA: 1.

	CR 55 GBU	Fd	Tt	WF0EXXTTFE5A58939	Fd		M14	11/05 -?-, -?-	1/14
	LK 06 TZD	Vx	Mov	VN1N9DVL536038414	?		M14	8/06 Unknown MoD contractor	
				(ex ?? ?? ??? 5/11)					Contractor (MoD)	9/11
	WX 06 SZF	MB	411CDI	WDB9046632R902229	O&H		M16L	4/06 North Somerset Council	
								(XSO) 410-02	10/15
	BL 63 LHK	Fd	Tt	WF0DXXTTFDDM13647	Fd		M16	3/14 new	3/14

PG1144486/N: David and Carol REES, 2 Cae Canfas Cottages, PONTYATES, Llanelli, Carmarthenshire, SA15 5UE. FN: DR Taxis, Minibus & Coach Hire. OC: as address; Unit 4.3 Trostre Industrial Park, Trostre, Llanelli, SA14 9UU. VA: 8.

w	C 10 DRT	MB	O814D	WDB6703742N061996	ACl	1434		C33F	5/97 Ishfaq, Cullingworth (WY)	4/12
				(ex P850 ADO 4/12)						
	L972 KDT	Vo	B10M-60	YV31M2B1XPA032275	VH	31753		C55F	2/94 Davies, Llanelli (CW)	8/13
				(ex WTL 642 8/13, J 4 FTH 2/11, L972 KDT 2/06, JIL 7900 1/01, L972 KDT 5/98)						
	R463 LFM	MB	O814D	WDB6703742N070914	Pn	988.5MXV8106		C31F	1/98 Pickford, Chippenham (WI)	11/15
				(ex R 10 ARE 6/04)						
	R 50 PCE	Ds	Jv	SFD721BR3VGJ51961	Mpo	1.97.R.306		C57F	10/97 Hughes, Llandudno (CN)	8/13
				(ex HNZ 3909 8/15, R 50 PCE 11/09)						
	R715 TRV	Ds	Jv	SFD721BR3VGJ22011	UVG	5664/97		C70F	11/97 Tinsley, Maesbury Marsh (SH)	8/15
	R650 VNN	Ds	Jv	SFD721BR3TGJ51792	Mpo	1.97.R.296		C69F	2/98 Cosgrove, Dundee (SE)	9/16
				(ex USY 858 8/05, R650 VNN 3/03)						
w	X736 AHT	Io	59-12	ZCFC5980105272231	FGy			B24FL	10/00 Morgan, Bynea (CW)	6/14
	Y163 GKJ	VW	LT46	WV1ZZZ2DZ1H017021	Crest	VW1011		M16L	7/01 -?-, -?-	4/16
	Y944 NYA	Io	49-10	ZCF04970005278149	G&M			M13L	3/01 Somerset Council	
									(XSO) 133-99	8/14
x	YT 02 XPN	Fd	Tt	WF0LXXGBFL1C24950	Fd			M8	3/02 Salford Van Hire (XGM)	5/08

REES, PONTYATES (continued)

	CV 03 SFK	Fd	Tt	WF0EXXGBFE3C60732	Fd		M16	3/03	St Michael's School, Bryn (CW)	6/15
	AE 04 RJZ	LDV	Cy	SEYZMVSZGDN104312	LDV		M16	6/04	Beeline Taxis, Dorchester (YDT)	1/13
x	PO 55 VLN	Rt	Mtr	VF1FDAVD534613733	Versa		M7	11/05	-?-, -?-	4/16
	YJ 07 LGA	LDV	Max	SEYL6RXH20N216072	LDV		M16	6/07	-?-, -?-	by8/12
x	SA 57 SVG	Fd	Tt	WF0BXXBDFB7K84699	Fd		M8	9/07	Vines, Droitwich (WO)	9/14
			(ex P 20 STC by11/09, SA 57 SVG 12/07)							
	LJ 08 LBF	LDV	Max	SEYL6PFD20N224053	Eurm		M6L	3/08	Olympic, Wimbledon Park (LN) 186	8/15
x	CV 60 WCN	Vx	Viv	W0LJ7BMA6BV616914	Vx		M8	10/10	Tywi Tours, Llandynydd (YCN)	1/13
x	CV 65 LXE	Rt	Tc	VF1JL000753784080	Rt		,M8	10/15	-?-, -?-	7/16
x	CV 65 LYC	Rt	Tc	VF1JL000153614295	Rt		M8	12/15	-?-, -?-	7/16

PG1071976/R: Claire Louise & Ceri Wyn REES, Glanyrafon, RHYDYWRACH, Llanfallteg, Whitland, Powys, SA34 0UJ. FN: Dragons Wheels. OC: as address. VA: 2.

No vehicles currently recorded.

PG1073569/R: Richard Wayne REYNOLDS, 2 Kildare Street, MANSELTON, Swansea, SA5 9PH. FN: Rainbow Travel. OC: 479 Carmarthen Road, Cwmdu, Swansea, SA5 8LL. VA: 1.

No vehicles currently recorded.

PG1050194/N: RHIEW VALLEY Motors Limited, Henfaes Garage, BERRIEW, Welshpool, Powys, SY21 8BG. OC: as address. VA: 9.

w	PXI 6717	DAF	MB230DKFL615		288486	VH	12948	C55F	3/87	Royston, Eckington (DE)	4/03
			(ex D216 YCW 5/93)								
	B 3 RVM	Sca	YS4KC4X2B01822912	VH	31351			C49FT	3/95	Bowen, Newtown (CW)	1/09
			(ex D 7 CTL 2/09, UIL 7812 12/07, M544 TOC 5/02, 95-C-4711 5/01)								
w	E264 AJC	Vo	B10M-61	YV31NGD17HA014361	Je	20475		C53F	3/88	Clynnog & Trefor, Trefor (CN)	4/02
			(ex HSU 548 5/01, E264 AJC 1/96, A 7 KMP 9/95, E773 YJC 3/95)								
w	E980 KJF	Ds	Jv	11SDL1905/113	Du	8778/0512		C53F	4/88	Evans, Welshpool (CW)	8/05
			(ex JSK 328 9/97, E980 KJF 1/96)								
w	E502 VNT	Fd	Tt	SFAZXXBDVZHY92216	Fd			M14	8/87	private owner	11/94
	F461 YOK	Ds	Jv	11SDA1906/337	Pn	8811DAP3C007		C53F	10/88	Evans, Welshpool (CW)	8/05
w	L 58 VLX	Fd	Tt	SFALXXBDVLRL1988	Cym	95/1764		M14	2/94	converted from a van	12/95
w	N224 MUS	Fd	Tt	SFALXXBDVLSY22557	?			M14	1/96	Easton, Stoneyburn (SS)	by3/03
	P614 CUX	Fd	Tt	SFAEXXBDVETK87242	Fd			M14	8/96	converted from a van	10/96
			(ex MAZ 1905 10/96)								
	BG 12 HPC	Fd	Tt	WF0DXXTTFDCG27157	Fd			M16	5/12	Hertz (Y)	4/15

PG1116360/R: Michael Anthony RHYS-ELLIS, 1 Llygad Yr Haul, LLANGUNNOR, Carmarthenshire, SA31 2LB. FN: Ellis (EPT) Passenger Transport. OC: as address. VA: 1.

See combined entry under PG1148541 Ellis, Llanllwch on page).

PG0005878/I: WJM, RM & DN RICHARDS, Moylgrove Garage, Pentood Industrial Estate, CARDIGAN, Ceredigion, SA43 3AG. FNs: Richards Brothers; Brodyr Richards. OCs: as address; Bus Depot, Cardigan Road, Newport, SA42 0LU; Bus Depot, Moylgrove, Cardigan, SA43 3BW; Plot 12 Feidr Castell, Fishguard, SA65 9BB. VA: 70. PG1134488/I: RICHARDS Bros Limited, Moylgrove Garage, Pentood Industrial Estate, CARDIGAN, Ceredigion, SA43 3AG. OC: as address; Unit 12 Feidr Castell, Fishguard, SA65 9BB; Bus Depot, Moylegrove, SA43 3BW; Coach Depot, Cardigan Road, Newport, SA42 0LU. VA: 66.

MDE 666	Bd	OB		140900	Du	49265	C29F	8/50	Cobus, Bridlington (P)	10/12
RBO 284	DAF	SB3000DKVF601	XLVDE33KT0H002912	VH	31469		C51FT	3/93	Coupland & Cronin, Rossall (LA)	4/94
		(ex K530 RJX 5/13)								
RBO 350	DAF	SB3000	XMGDE33WS0H009352	VH	33187		C49FT	2/02	Selwyns, Runcorn (CH) 91	9/11
		(ex YJ 51 EKY 11/12, 352 STG 8/11, YJ 51 EKY 8/10)								

RICHARDS, CARDIGAN (continued)

	Reg	Make	Model	Chassis	BodyMkr	BodyNo	Seats	Date	Owner / Location	Date
w	YEZ 6561	DAF	SB3000DKV601	XLVDE33KT0H001749	VH	30580	C51FT	5/92	Movereturn, Pontycymer (CC)	1/12
				(ex J787 KHD 11/09, LIB 9415 2/06, J787 KHD 5/03)						
	YIL 3191	DAF	SB3000	XMGDE33WS0H006043	Pn	9712DRM7228	C53F	1/98	Chalkwell, Sittingbourne (KT)	8/13
				(ex R910 BKO 2/09)						
	708 WPG	Vo	B7R	YV3R6G7143A004789	Pn	0212THX4741	C57F	3/03	GHA, Ruabon (CN) 4001	9/16
				(ex HM 03 GSM 9/12)						
w	JTM 114V	Bd	YMT	JW458103	Du	020/2951	B55F	6/80	Stanley, Hersham (SR)	7/85
w	F138 LJO	DAF	SB3000DKV601	XLRCE33KS0E325387	Pn	8912DHB1483	C57F	4/89	City of Oxford (OX) 138	5/98
w	G112 PGT	MB	811D	WDB6703032P017077	Ar	AM42/790/5	B32F	4/90	City of Oxford (OX) 712	3/00
w	H931 DRJ	Vo	B10M-60	YV31M2A15MA025733	Pn	9012VCA2208	C70F	1/91	Capital, West Drayton (LN)	9/97
w	H 81 MOB	Ds	Dt	8.5SDL3003/258	Ce	C25.136	B28F	10/90	Petes Travel, West Bromwich (WM)	4/03
w	H 95 MOB	Ds	Dt	8.5SDL3003/228	Ce	C25.117	B28F	10/90	Arriva Merseyside (MY) 1135	9/02
	J785 KHD	DAF	SB3000DKV601	XLVDE33KT0H000371	VH	30547	C57F	4/92	Eastville, Bristol (GL)	2/08
				(ex B 10 MWT 5/03 J785 KHD 5/01)						
	K235 AHG	DAF	SB3000DKVF601	XLVDE33KT0H002916	VH	31473	C53F	3/93	Arriva The Shires (BD) 413	9/08
				(ex 1606 UK 10/04, K517 RJX 10/98)						
	K874 GHH	MB	709D	WDB6690032N005286	ArB	M1104	B25F	6/93	Stagecoach (North West) (CA) 40037	7/03
	K508 RJX	DAF	SB3000DKVF601	XLVDE33KT0H002908	VH	31465	C53F	3/93	Arriva The Shires (BD) 414	9/08
				(ex SEL 853 by8/08, K508 RJX 9/00)						
w	M197 CDE	MAN	11.190	WMA4691456G088495	Oe	4070	B40F	8/94	new	8/94
	M680 DDE	MB	811D	WDB6703032N023526	MI	C16.322	B31F	2/95	new	2/95
w	M817 GFT	Ds	Dt	9.8SDL3040/2174	MI	C37.041	B40F	10/94	Go West Midlands (WM) 710	1/08
	M 13 KCT	MB	609D	WDB6680632N026939	ACl	1204	DP24F	9/94	Crest Tonbridge (KT)	3/07
	M 10 RCC	MB	814D	WDB6703132N030360	ACl	1239	C33F	2/95	Davies & Jones, Letterston (CW)	3/08
	N254 DUR	MB	709D	WDB6690032N025784	MI	C19.353	B27F	8/95	Coulson, Chadwell St Mary (EX)	3/07
	N960 LDE	DAF	SB3000	XMGDE33WS0H004843	Is	350T1PS1GB0011	C55F	6/96	new	6/96
w	N509 LUA	DAF	SB3000	XMGDE33WS0H005041	Is	350T1PT1GB0013	C53F	7/06	London Coaches (Kent), Northfleet (KT)	10/03
				(ex YDE 350 11/15, N509 LUA 10/03)						
	P771 BJF	Ds	Jv	SFD721BR3TGJ21753	Co	667009	C70F	1/97	Silcox, Pembroke Dock (CW) 237	7/16
				(ex 804 SHW 6/16, P771 BJF 5/12, TIL 1260 3/10, P771 BJF 8/01)						
	P916 DEJ	DAF	SB3000	XMGDE33WS0H005618	VH	32841	C70F	5/97	new	5/97
	P106 HCH	MB	O814D	WDB6703732N062339	Ar	9538/6	B29F	6/97	Go West Midlands (WM) 774	1/08
	P508 NWU	Oe	L1070	VN9071	Oe	9071	B40F	2/97	Trent (DE) 900	3/10
	P901 PWW	DAF	SB220	XMGDE02LT0H004013	NC	4812	B49F	8/96	Speedlink (WS) 901	9/98
	P903 PWW	DAF	SB220	XMGDE02LT0H004019	NC	4818	B49F	8/96	Speedlink (WS) 903	9/98
	P501 RYM	Ds	Dt SLF	SFD112BR1TGW10420	Pn	969.2HEZ6094	B30F	11/96	Evans, Carmarthen (CW)	2/11
w	P 97 SDE	LDV	Cy	SEYZMNFFADN001076	Cym	96/2010	M16	10/96	new	10/96
w	P260 SDE	Ds	Dt	SFD412BR5TGD13409	MI	C37.138	B40F	11/96	new	11/96
	S353 CFS	MB	O814D	WDB6703732N078076	Pn	988.5MXV9857	B31F	1/99	Whitegate Travel, Anderton (CH)	6/15
	T343 FWR	Oe	M850	VN6157	Oe	6157	B29F	3/99	New Adventure Travel, Cardiff (CC)	7/11
	T923 MAW	LDV	Cy	SEYZMNFJEDN037713	Cen		M16	4/99	Copas, Buckingham (BK)	6/08
	T564 PNV	Ds	Dt SLF	SFD322BR1XGW13270	Pn	9910.7HLB0963	B37F	12/99	Thames Travel, Wallingford (OX)	7/08
				(ex 99-D-80595 by9/03)						
	T510 RDE	DAF	SB3000	XMGDE33WS0H006566	VH	33210	C49FT	3/99	new	3/99
	T941 RDE	MB	614D	WDB6683532N079167	ACl	1618	C24F	4/99	new	4/99
	V251 BNV	MB	O814D	WDB6703742N087064	Pn	998.5MXV1916	B31F	11/99	Bevan, Cwmrhydyceirw (CW)	12/14
z	V723 GGE	MB	O814D	WDB6703742N084294	Pn	998.5MXV1353	B33F	9/99	Silcox, Pembroke Dock (CW) 48	7/16
	W894 NDE	DAF	SB3000	XMGDE33WS0H008098	VH	33246	C51FT	5/00	new	5/00
	X241 ABU	Ds	Dt SLF	SFD466BR1XGW30321	Ar	9942/1	B42F	10/00	new	10/00
w	X805 AVN	LDV	Cy	SEYZMNFJEDN064003	Crest	LDV763	M16	9/00	Robinson, Seaton Delaval (ND)	8/04
	X319 CBT	Oe	M850	VN6499	Oe	6499	B30F	12/00	GHA, Ruabon (CN) 1319	9/16
	X711 JGU	Ds	Dt SLF	SFD322BR1XGW14262	Pn	0010.7HLB1847	B39F	9/00	Felix, Stanley (DE)	9/07
w	X673 OKH	LDV	Cy	SEYZMNFJEDN064641	Cen		M16	9/00	Copas, Buckingham (BK)	1/08
w	X534 XDE	LDV	Cy	SEYZMNFJEDN058991	Cym	-?-	M16	9/00	new	9/00
	Y753 HVY	MB	O814D	WDB6703742N089364	Pn	008.5MXV2673	B31F	4/01	Pickford, Chippenham (WI)	8/15
	Y741 OBE	MB	O814D	WDB6703742N093425	ACl	-?-	C29F	4/01	Rainbow, Plompton (NO)	8/13

RICHARDS, CARDIGAN (continued)

Reg	Make	Model	Chassis	Body	Body No	Seat	Date	Operator	Date
KX 51 UDH	MB	O814D	WDB6703742N089117	Pn	008.5MXV2395	B31F	9/01	Pickford, Chippenham (WI)	7/16
CV 02 JSU	DAF	SB3000	XMGDE33WS0H009349	VH	33200	C51FT	3/02	new	3/02
NU 02 OSO	LDV	Cy	SEYZMVFJEDN081050	Crest	1242	M16	3/02	Heffernan, West Harrow (LN)	2/11
RB 02 DAF	DAF	SB120	XMGDE12BS0H009553	Wt	F254	B39F	7/02	new	7/02
BF 52 KKH	MB	614D	WDB6683532N105887	Crest	M1399	C24F	11/02	McAllister, Kirkintilloch (SW)	11/02
			(ex UNZ 3153 5/16, BF 52 KKH 9/14, ML 51 LEE 4/11, BF 52 KKH 2/07)						
PN 03 UCG	Vo	B12M	YV3R9H4131A000134	Je	25959	C53F	3/08	Shaw, Carnforth (LA)	12/12
			(ex OW 5371 3/12, PN 03 UCG 3/07)						
RB 03 DAF	DAF	SB4000	XMGDE40XS0H009584	VH	37011	C51FT	3/03	new	3/03
SF 03 ABX	Vo	B7R	YV3R6G7143A004663	Pn	0212THX4708	C57F	3/03	Bowman, Craignure (SW)	8/11
SN 03 DZL	Tbs	Env	SFD113AR11GG10106	Tbs	0182/1	B45F	4/03	Transbus, Falkirk (Qd)	3/04
KX 53 SJV	Vo	B12B	YV3R8F8163A012895	Pn	0312TKL5100	C70F	2/04	Hartlepool Council, Hartlepool (CD)	12/15
SN 53 KKZ	Tbs	Env	SFD113AR12GG10113	Tbs	0182/10	B45F	12/03	Transbus, Falkirk (Qd)	8/04
YN 53 ELH	Oe	L1180	SAB18000000000596	Oe		B41F	9/03	Optare, Crossgates (Qd)	2/04
YO 53 OVD	Oe	M1020	SAB19000000001202	Oe		B37F	2/04	Optare, Crossgates (Qd)	8/04
CU 04 AKP	VDL	SB120	XMGDE12BS0H010297	Wt	F748	B38F	4/04	new	4/04
CU 04 AKV	VDL	SB120	XMGDE12BS0H010283	Wt	F734	B38F	4/04	new	4/04
PN 04 UXE	LDV	Cy	SEYZNVFZGDN100181	?		M16	6/04	Soul, Fareham (HA)	9/15
			(ex P 4 AVE 3/07, PN 04 UXE 9/04)						
BX 54 FRF	LDV	Cy	SEYZNVFZGDN100660	?		M16	9/04	new	9/04
KT 05 XAW	LDV	Cy	SEYZMVFXGDN105278	LDV		M16	3/05	Hester, Darlaston (WM)	11/14
			(ex M 11 MSP 10/13)						
YX 05 DJK	MB	O814D	WDB6703742N117643	ACl	885	C33F	6/05	Hutchinson, Easingwold (NY)	3/11
YJ 55 BJK	Oe	X1200	SAB28000000000028	Oe		B41F	12/05	First Cymru (CW) 64502	1/10
YJ 55 BKE	Oe	X1260	SAB28000000000017	Oe		B41F	9/05	new	9/05
YJ 55 BKF	Oe	X1260	SAB28000000000018	Oe		B41F	9/05	new	9/05
YJ 55 BKN	Oe	X1200	SAB28000000000023	Oe		B41F	10/05	Arriva Cymru (CN) 2863	5/12
CT 06 PBZ	LDV	Cy	SEYZNVFZGDN111921	?		M16	8/06	Culcheth Travel, Culcheth (CH)	11/13
			(ex SK 04 BGK c7/14)						
CX 06 AGO	MB	616CDI	WDB9056132R573242	Koch		B24F	4/06	Hoskins, Skewen (CC)	3/15
YJ 06 LFS	VDL	SB4000	XMGDE40XS0H012315	VH	37126	C53F	4/06	Landtourer Coaches, Brighton Hill (HA)	2/07
YJ 06 LFU	VDL	SB4000	XMGDE40XS0H012331	VH	37147	C53F	4/06	Wickson, Walsall Wood (WM)	7/11
YJ 06 YRO	Oe	X1260	SABNWSZS06L280049	Oe		B41F	8/06	Arriva Cymru (CN) 2869	5/12
YJ 06 YRY	Oe	X1200	SABMWSZS06L280047	Oe		B41F	7/06	Arriva Cymru (CN) 2867	5/12
YJ 06 YRZ	Oe	X1260	SABNWSZS06L280048	Oe		B41F	8/06	Arriva Cymru (CN) 2868	5/12
CX 56 AOJ	MB	616CDI	WDB9056132R584473	Koch		B24F	10/06	Hoskins, Skewen (CC)	3/15
YJ 57 BSY	Tmsa	Safari HD	NLTRHT87R01050003	Tmsa	0A02115	C51FT	9/07	An, Kingston upon Thames (LN)	12/15
YJ 08 DLE	VDL	SB4000	XMGDE40PS0H015758	VH	37183	C53F	5/08	Hatton, St Helens (MY)	7/13
YX 08 HCA	AD	Dt	SFD361AR27GY10591	AD	7241/3	B37F	4/08	Arriva Yorkshire (WY) 1097	12/09
YJ 09 CWR	VDL	SB200	XMGDE02FS0H016502	Wt	AB127	B44F	5/09	new	5/09
YJ 09 CXR	VDL	SB4000	XMGDE40PS0H016543	VH	37204	C51FT	3/09	new	3/09
YJ 09 EXW	Oe	M710SE	SABCN2AB09R193381	Oe		B24F	3/09	new	3/09
YJ 09 EXX	Oe	M710SE	SABCN2AB09R193382	Oe		B24F	3/09	new	3/09
YJ 09 EXZ	Oe	M710SE	SABCN2AB09R193383	Oe		B24F	3/09	new	3/09
YJ 09 OUC	Oe	M710SE	SABCN2AB09L193503	Oe		B19F	7/09	new	7/09
YJ 09 OUD	Oe	M710SE	SABCN2AB09L193504	Oe		B19F	7/09	new	7/09
YJ 59 GFU	Oe	V1100	SABWWJAC09L320224	Oe		B38F	9/09	new	9/09
DX 10 DZW	Asn	A1012T	SUAED5CGT7S620353	Asn		C70F	6/10	Lewis, Llanrhystud (CW)	9/16
YJ 60 GDV	VDL	SB200	XMGDE02FS0H018315	Wt	AC950	B41F	9/10	new	9/10
YJ 60 GFK	VDL	SB4000	XMGDE40PS0H018189	VH	37217	C49FT	10/10	new	10/10
YJ 61 JHZ	Oe	M710SE	SABCN2AB0BS193840	Oe		B19F	2/12	new	2/12
KX 62 BOF	MB	O816D	WDB6703742N145849	Pn	CC09/01	C31F	9/12	Edwards, Llantwit Fardre (CC)	8/16
YJ 62 JZR	VDL	SB200	XMGDE02FS0H020661	Wt	AF557	B44F	12/12	Reays, Wigton (CA)	2/14
BJ 14 KTK	Vo	B7RLE	YV3R6R628EA164232	MCV	NB574	B44F	4/14	new	4/14
YJ 14 CCV	VDL	SB200	XMGDE02FS0H021131	MCV	NB528	B44F	4/14	new	4/14
YJ 14 CDZ	VH	TX16	YE2X16SH249D55224	VH	55224	C53F	8/14	new	8/14
YY 64 TXW	AD	E20D	SFD1D1AR6EGY14697	AD	E266/03	B29F	1/15	JJ Travel, Coatbridge (SW)	1/17
YY 64 TXZ	AD	E20D	SFD1D1AR6EGY14696	AD	E266/2	B29F	1/15	new	1/15
KX 15 BMO	Oe	M790SER	SABDN3AB0ES291053	Oe		B23F	3/15	Cleveland & Redcar Council, Dormanstown (CD)	1/17

RICHARDS, CARDIGAN (continued)

YJ 15 APY	Oe	MC1150	SAB5HD2AXFS400038	Oe		B41F	4/15 new		4/15
YJ 15 AWP	Oe	MC1150	SAB5HD2A4FS400035	Oe		B41F	4/15 new		4/15
YJ 15 AWR	Oe	MC1150	SAB5HD2A6FS400036	Oe		B41F	4/15 new		4/15
YJ 15 AWU	Oe	MC1150	SAB5HD2A8FS400037	Oe		B41F	4/15 new		4/15
YJ 15 ERU	VH	TX16	YE2X16SH249D55586	VH	55586	C53FT	4/15 new		4/15
YK 16 SRU	VDL	FHD2-129.370	XNL501E100D005529	VDL		C57FT	7/16 new		7/16
YK 16 UFV	Fd	Tt	WF0XXXTTGXES82061	Fd		M16	3/16 new		3/16

PG1118239/N: RIGHT DIRECTION Solutions CIC, Unit 3 Caerbont Enterprise Park, Caerbont, SWANSEA, SA9 1SW. OC: as address. VA: 5.

No vehicles yet recorded.

PG1138060/N: ST MICHAEL'S SCHOOL (Bryn) Limited, White Lodge, Swansea Road, GORSEINON, Swansea, SA4 4LQ. OC: as address; St Michael's School, Bryn, Llanelli, SA14 9TU. VA: 10.

CU 13 JCY	Fd	Tt	WF0DXXTTFDCY71154	Fd	M16	3/13 Gower Mini, Gorseinon (CW)	12/15
CU 13 JDZ	Fd	Tt	WF0DXXTTFDCY71570	Fd	M16	3/13 Gower Mini, Gorseinon (CW)	by4/16
CU 13 JFF	Fd	Tt	WF0DXXTTFDCY71558	Fd	M16	5/13 Gower Mini, Gorseinon (CW)	9/15
CU 63 YHC	Fd	Tt	WF0DXXTTFDDM12613	Fd	M16	9/13 Gower Mini, Gorseinon (CW)	6/15
CU 63 YNZ	Fd	Tt	WF0DXXTTFDDC54210	Fd	M16	11/13 Gower Mini, Gorseinon (CW)	9/15

PG1086821/R: Spencer Beynon SAUNDERS, 9 Bargoed Terrace, PONTHENRI, Llanelli, Carmarthenshire, SA15 5PW. FN: SBS Mini Bus Hire. OC: as address. VA: 1.

E 9 SBS	MB	311CDI	WDB9036632R773980	?	M16	4/05 Hicks, Drefach (CW)	10/15
		(ex YN 05 CTX 11/15)						
x N 6 SBS	Fd	Tt	WF0BXXBDFBAR83714	Fd	M8	3/11 -?-, -?-	7/12
		(ex CV 11 BBK 8/12)						

PG0007546/N: SEALYHAM Activity Centre Limited, WOLFSCASTLE, Haverfordwest, Pembrokeshire, SA62 5NF. OC: as address. VA: 3.

w P215 ORJ	LDV	Cy	SEYZMYSEEDN018322	?	M16	6/97 Neath Port Talbot CBC, Neath (XCC)	7/06
w P865 WDE	LDV	Cy	SEYZMYSEADN003309	LDV	M16	6/97 Sealyham Activity Centre, Wolfscastle (YCW)	9/01
HG 04 HVS	Pt	Bxr	VF3ZCPMNC17302913	RKC	M16	6/04 Darlington Council (XDM)	11/14
HG 05 USF	Fd	Tt	WF0EXXTTFE5P77561	Fd	M16	5/05 Ellesmere College, Ellesmere (XSH)	5/15

PG1090056/T: Wayne Douglas SHEPPARD, Capel Farm, LLANGORSE, Brecon, Powys, LD3 7UL. FN: A2B. OC: as address.
PG1134200/I: W. D. & A. S. SHEPPARD Limited, Capel Farm, LLANGORSE, Brecon, Powys, LD3 7UL. FN: A2B. OC: as address. VA: 6.

BJ 54 ZFW	Fd	Tt	WF0EXXTTFE4E14708	Fd	M16	10/04 -?-, -?-	7/07
DY 05 DFP	Fd	Tt	WF0VXXBDFV4S09542	Fd	M14	6/05 new	6/05
NL 55 OTB	Fd	Tt	WF0EXXTTFE5A52554	Fd	M16	9/05 -?-, -?-	1/09
x SB 56 VWH	Vx	Mov	VN1F9C2L636893339	?	M8	12/06 -?-, -?-	11/12
x VO 57 XZK	Fd	Tt	WF0XXXBDFX7S24839	Fd	M8	9/07 -?-, -?-	4/08
GU 09 DLX	Fd	Tt	WF0DXXTTFD8L13366	Fd	M16	3/09 Cransley School, Great Budworth (YCH)	3/15
BN 10 HPC	Fd	Tt	WF0DXXTTFDAL55545	Fd	M16	3/10 -?-, -?-	3/13
x WV 61 WSU	Fd	Tt	WF0BXXBDFBCB27423	Fd	M8	2/12 Holloway, Shirehampton (GL)	2/15
NA 12 KZF	Fd	Tt	WF0DXXTTFDCA02061	Fd	M16	5/12 -?-, -?-	6/15

PG1070893/R: Anthony John SKINNER, Ty Capel, PENNANT, Llanbrynmair, Powys, SY19 7BL.
FN: AJ Contracts. OC: 103 Glanclegyr, Llanbrynmair, SY19 7DH. **VA: 2.**

x	FL 55 FXG	Vx	Viv	W0LF7BCA66V612922 Vx	M8	11/05	Pyne, Southgate (LN)	5/15
x	BX 08 NHJ	LDV	Max	SEYL2KFD20N227827 LDV	M8	8/08	Royal Mail, North Division
							(X) 7751008	9/13
x	YJ 08 TVF	Rt	Tc	VF1FLAHA68V324924 Rt	M5	6/08	-?-, -?-	2/13
	BX 58 OBS	LDV	Max	SEYL6RXH21N229246 LDV	M16	9/08	Europcar (Y)	10/11
x	KU 58 YJB	Vx	Viv	W0LF7BMC68Y726200 ?	M8	9/08	-?-, -?-	5/15
	MX 61 HSV	Rt	Mtr	VF1MEN4JE45847285 Rt	M16	10/11	-?-, -?-	8/14

PG1112480/R: Jamie SMITH, 4 Heol Llanelli, PONTYATES, Llanelli, Carmarthenshire, SA15 5TU.
FN: Rwyth Cabs. OC: Unit 21 Ponthenry Industrial Estate, Ponthenry, Llanelli, SA15 5RA. **VA: 1.**

No vehicles currently recorded.

PG1043409/N: SOUTH WALES TRANSPORT (Neath) Limited, Unit 2 Ferryboat Close, Swansea Enterprise Park,
MORRISTON, Swansea, SA6 8QN. **OC:** as address. **VA: 40.**

E 11 OSO	Vo	B9R	YV3S5P724CA157024 Pn	CP05/01	C55F	2/13	Morrison, Whiteness (SN)	11/15
		(ex SW 62 NUU 1/16, GSU 404 9/15)						
M100 SWT	Vo	B12M	YV3R9L2228A124419 Je	28650	C53FT	3/08	Bryans Coaches, Denny (SE)	9/14
		(ex SF 08 VVG 3/16, E 11 OSO 1/16, SF 08 VVG 9/14, 2 WR 3/10)						
SG 03 ZEX	Vo	B12M	YV3R9F8102A000656 Je	26290	C51FT	3/03	Keith's, Blucher (TW)	4/13
		(ex K 11 KCL 4/13, SG 03 ZEX 3/10, HSK 656 9/05)						
CN 54 HFG	Vo	B12B	YV3R8F8225A101665 Je	27190	C49FT	1/05	Veolia Cymru (CS) 76010	11/11
KE 05 MMJ	MB	O814D	WDB6703742N118287 Pn	058.5MAE5999	C28F	5/05	Ultimate Highland,	
							Edinburgh (SS)	8/13
LX 05 GKD	Ctn	Rly	VF7ZAAMFA17562951 Stan		M8L	8/05	London Hire, Bermondsey (LN)	9/14
SF 05 XDE	Vo	B12M	YV3R9L2228A102585 Je	27206	C51FT	3/05	York Pullman, Strensall	
		(ex R 3 YPB 2/14, SF 05 XDE 1/13, LSK 830 11/06)					(NY) 316	2/14
SJ 06 AXA	Vo	B12M	YV3R9G1206A109939 Je	27507	C53FT	3/06	NCB, Edstaston (SH)	2/14
		(ex C 6 NCB 2/14, SJ 06 AXA 4/10, 2 RWM 7/08)						
CN 56 LSL	Vo	B12BT	YV3R8L2227A117813 Pn	0715TAR7001	C65FLT	2/07	Midland Red (South)	
							(WK) 54001	9/15
CN 07 BAO	Vo	B12BT	YV3R8L2227X120295 Pn	0715TAR7035	C65FLT	5/07	Midland Red (South)	
							(WK) 54004	7/15
CN 07 BAU	Vo	B12BT	YV3R8L2227A120372 Pn	0715TAR7037	C65FLT	5/07	Corbel, Stonebridge Park (LN)	7/16
CN 07 BBE	Vo	B12BT	YV3R8L2207A120421 Pn	0715TAR7040	C65FLT	5/07	Midland Red (South)	
							(WK) 54007	7/15
DC 07 FLZ	Vo	B12M	YV3R8G12861111618 Vo	P056367	C51FT	3/07	Taw & Torridge, Merton (DN)	10/14
AE 08 DJZ	AD	Dt SLF	SFD1HFCR56GW18965 MCV	MCV-241	B32F	4/08	new	4/08
MX 59 AVM	AD	Dt	SFD1A1AR59GY11327 AD	9211/3	B29F	10/09	Powells Bus, Hellaby (SY) 5901	6/14
MX 59 AVY	AD	Dt	SFD141AR49GY11242 AD	8259/4	B29F	12/09	Padarn Bus, Llanberis (CN)	6/14
YN 10 ACF	MB	O816D	WDB6703742N138556 Pn	108.5MBJ8449	C29F	3/10	Williams, Cambourne (CO)	6/15
AB 60 MTB	Vo	B12M	YV3R9M928AA137712 Pn	1012TVL8506	C53F	9/10	Baker, Moreton-in-Marsh (GL)	10/15
CV 60 HVZ	Fd	Tt	WF0DXXTTFDAM83368 Fd		M16	9/10	Day's Rental, Swansea (YCW)	7/15
EB 60 MTB	Vo	B12M	YV3R9M925AA137828 Pn	1012TVL8505	C53F	9/10	Baker, Moreton-in-Marsh (GL)	10/15
MX 60 BXF	AD	Dt	SFD361AR49GY11446 AD	9207/3	B37F	9/10	Comhairle, Stornoway	
							(SN) B145	6/14
MX 60 BXG	AD	Dt	SFD361AR49GY11448 AD	9207/5	B37F	9/10	Comhairle, Stornoway	
							(SN) B146	6/14
BX 11 GVA	Vo	B7R	YV3R6R621BA145789 Pn	1112TTS8806	C53FL	3/11	Whitelaws, Stonehouse (SW)	8/16
BX 11 GWA	Vo	B7R	YV3R6R628BA145790 Pn	1112TTS8807	C57FL	3/11	Woodstows,	
							Kidderminster (WO)	8/16
MX 12 JXT	Wt	StLt WF	SA9DSRXXX12141091 Wt	AG077	B??F	6/12	NSL, Ealing (LN) WB2	10/12
YN 12 BWH	Vo	B9R	YV3S5P722CA157314 Pn	10/01	C57F	8/12	Armstrong,	
							Castle Douglas (SW)	10/15
MX 13 AZW	AD	E20D	SFD1D1AR6DGY13567 AD	C254/1	B29F	6/13	new	6/13
MX 13 BAA	AD	E20D	SFD1D1AR6CGY13270 AD	C240/7	B29F	3/13	new	3/13
MX 13 BAO	AD	E20D	SFD1D1AR6CGY13276 AD	C240/3	B29F	4/13	new	4/13
MK 63 WZV	AD	E20D	SFD1D1AR6DGY13722 AD	D202/1	B29F	9/13	new	9/13

SOUTH WALES TRANSPORT, MORRISTON (continued)

MK 63 WZW	AD	E20D	SFD1D1AR6CGY13162	AD	C230/5	B29F	10/13 new		10/13
KX 64 AAY	MB	O816D	WDB6703742N150549	Pn	DC38/04	C29F	9/14 OFJ Connections,		
								Stanwell (LN)	9/15
SK 15 GXW	AD	E20D	SFD7E1AR6FGY14875	AD	E287/1	B39F	4/15 new		4/15
SK 15 GXZ	AD	E20D	SFD7E1AR6FGY14909	AD	E287/5	B39F	5/15 new		5/15
SN 15 LRV	AD	E20D	SFD1D1AR6FGY14857	AD	E276/10	B29F	4/15 new		4/15
YX 15 XMR	AD	E20D	SFD8E1AR6EGY14450	AD	E243/3	B33F	3/15 new		3/15
YJ 66 AOU	Oe	M7900SE	SABJCB2A1GS291312	Oe		B23F	10/16 new		10/16

PG1022903/I: Stephen SQUIRES, 9 Danygraig Road, PORT TENNANT, Swansea, SA1 8LY.
FNs: Abertawe Travel. OC: Lockhead Road, Lingsdock, Swansea, SA1 8FT. VA: 3.

A 8 TEV	Sca	K113TRB	YS4KT6X2B01828561	Ir	9457	C49FT	5/98 Turner, Bristol (GL)	9/07
			(ex R278 RRH 11/16, R 90 CJT 3/07, R278 RRH 10/01)						
w L 18 ATS	Rt	Mtr	VF1FDCCM517962098	Cym -?-		M14	7/86 Gemini, Swansea (CW)	7/05

PG0005979/I: Nancy STOCKHAM, 19 Plas Derwen, LLANGATTOCK, Crickhowell, Powys, NP8 1HY.
OC: Old Timber Yard, Gilwern Road, Llangattock, NP8 1HW. VA: 6.

w JUI 3850	Vo	B10M-60	YV31M2A1XKA022677	Pn	8912VCB1673	C53F	8/89 Powell, Lapford (DN)	4/06
			(ex G117 XRE 2/99)						
w ABW 186X	Ld	TRCTL11/3R	8100832	Pn	8212LTS5C001	C53F	2/82 Evans, Tregaron (CW)	8/96
			(ex WIA 5409 4/09, ABW 186X 7/98, CSU 432 by6/96, MMR 847X 7/92)						
w P 63 MKR	Io	49-10	ZCFC497010D051816	Eurm 61617		M16L	4/97 Blaenau Gwent County		
								Borough Council (XCS)	5/06
w WJ 52 LFT	Io	40C11	ZCFC407100D187658	Csd		M8L	9/02 Somerset County Council, Taunton		
								(SOx) 135-99	6/11
WJ 52 XCK	Io	45C11	ZCFC457100D205608	Csd		M16L	2/03 Darch, Pentre (CC)		11/11

PG1082007/R: Clive Bernard SULLIVAN, 3 Clifton Court, TREBOETH, Swansea, SA5 7DT.
FN: Dolphin Mini Travel. OC: Ford Sports & Social Club, 815 Llangyfelach Road, Treboeth, Swansea, SA5 9AX.
VA: 2.

No vehicles currently recorded.

PG1094238/N: SWANSEA BUS Limited, 308 Townhill Road, Mayhill, SWANSEA, SA1 6PD.
FN: Swansea Bus. OC: Aztec Business Centre, The Queensway, Fforestfach, Swansea, SA5 4DJ. VA: 6.

See combined entry under PG1006269/N: Lets Go, Manselton (page 45).

PG1145287/R: Peter & Kathleen M. E. SZPADT, Brynlleine, Pentre'r Bryn, LLANDYSUL, Ceredigion, SA44 6JY.
FN: PJ & KME Enterprises. OC: as address. VA: 1.

No vehicles yet recorded.

PG0006593/I: Gareth THOMAS, Towy Garage, LLANGADOG, Carmarthenshire, SA19 9LU.
FN: Thomas Brothers. OCs: as address. VA: 5.
PG1147366/N: THOMAS Bros Coaches Limited, Towy Garage, Station Road, LLANGADOG, Carmarthenshire,
SA19 1LU. OC: as address. VA: 5.

w G593 NUX	Ld	TRCTL11/3RZ	TR00819	Pn	8912LMF1599	DP53F	10/89 Davies, Brynamman (CW)	9/05
			(ex 03 KJ 45 6/98)						
w M 38 GRY	MB	709D	WDB6690032N025909	Danescroft		C24F	1/95 Davis, Minchinhampton (GL)	3/10
M974 NFU	Ka	S250	WKK13400001015010	Ka		C53F	6/95 Safeguard, Guildford (SR)	12/08
			(ex 159 FCG 9/07, M974 NFU 2/01)						
P339 VWR	Vo	B10M-62	YV31MA619VA047013	Pn	9712VUP6463	C50F	5/97 National Holidays		
								Coaches (EY) 934	3/07
P351 VWR	Vo	B10M-62	YV31MA612VA047094	Pn	9712VUP6475	C53F	5/97 Cottrell, Mitcheldean (GL)		8/07

THOMAS, LLANGADOG (continued)

CU 51 UAH	LDV	Cy	SEYZMVSYGDN081129	LDV		M16	-/02 Unknown MoD	
							Contractor (MoD)	6/10
GU 52 WTD	Vo	B12M	YV3R9F8103A000903	Pn	0212TJT4768	C57F	12/02 East Midland (DE) 53006	7/11
GU 52 WTJ	Vo	B12M	YV3R9F8123A000935	Pn	0212TJT4772	C57F	12/02 East Kent (KT) 53010	7/11
VU 03 VVZ	Vo	B12M	YV3R9F8103A001369	Tbs	0312TJT5109	C57F	8/03 East Midland (DE) 53015	7/11
YN 55 KMA	MB	O814D	WDB6703742N118698	Pn	068.5MAE6098	C29F	9/05 Cropper, Guiseley (WY)	12/08
HG 57 OHP	Fd	Tt	WF0DXXTTFD7U78017	Fd		M16	12/07 -?-, -?-	9/10
RX 57 BVM	LDV	Max	SEYL6P6A20N210147	LDV		M14	9/07 -?-, -?-	9/10

PG1109031/N: Jonathan Lee VAMPLEW, Maes Yr Eglwys, DOLANOG, Welshpool, Powys, SY21 0LQ.
FN: Delta Services. OC: Delta Services, The House of Two Souls, Llangyniew, SY21 0JY. VA: 2.

DU 16 JHA	MB	516CDI	WDB906657GP232322	Cento Bus -?-		C22F	3/16 new	3/16
DX 66 HTG	MB	516CDI	WDB906657HP298494	Cento Bus 906BB50		C22F	9/16 new	9/16

PG1116313/I: Dan Mihail VINTILA, 3 Mackworth Terrace, ST THOMAS, Swansea, SA1 8BH.
FN: FDV Transport / Welsh Limos. OC: Kearns Storage, Llys Kearns, Jersey Marine, Swansea, SA1 8QL;
Cape Horner, Miers Street, St Thomas, Swansea, SA1 8BH. VA: 3.

J 7 GBE	MB	411CDI	WDB9046632R332680	?		M15	-/02 Stratton, Hendon (TW)	4/13
Y484 WCE	VW	LT46	WV1ZZZ2DZ1H032001	Wnr		M13L	7/01 Country Cousins,	
							Ilfracombe (DN)	9/12

PG0005871/R: Graham James WALKER, Glascoed, RHYDLEWIS, Ceredigion, SA44 5SP.
FN: Cambrian Bird Holidays. OC: as address. VA: 1.

w G477 ERF	MB	609D	WDB6680632P005251	PMT 9194		B12F	5/90 PMT (ST) 477	5/00

PG1037454/R: David Joseph WALTERS, 25 Christopher Rise, PONTLLIW, Swansea, SA14 9EN.
FN: DJ Walters. OC: as address. VA: 1.

No vehicles currently recorded

PG1141506/R: Pete WARD, Trehenlliw Farm, Whitesands Road, ST. DAVIDS, Pembrokeshire, SA62 6PH.
FN: The Real Adventure Company. OC: as address. VA: 1.

No vehicles yet recorded.

PG1013740/I: Thomas Allen & Sian Eiriona WATKIN, Maes-y-coed, CEFN COCH, Welshpool, Powys, SY21 0AB.
FN: AW Coaches. OC: Brodawel Garage, Wesley Street, Llanfair Caereinon, Powys, SY21 0RX. VA: 14.

RBZ 5358	Sca	K113CRB	YS4KC4X2B01827742	VH	32157	C70F	1/97 Milligan, Mauchline (SW)	12/12
			(ex P101 GHE 10/03, RDU 4 by8/00, P101 GHE by9/99)					
A 17 HOF	Sca	K113CRB	1828327	VH	32711	C49F	2/97 Hellyers, Fareham (HA)	9/07
			(ex P102 GHE 8/02)					
H154 DVM	Sca	K113CRB	1818214	VH	30649	C49FT	1/91 Shearings (GM) 154	5/94
K807 HUM	Vo	B10M-60	YV31M2B1XPA031160	VH	31707	C49FT	3/93 Mayfield, Darfield (SY)	3/13
			(ex NXI 536 by8/06, K807 HUM 3/99)					
P991 HWF	Ds	Jv	SFD531BR3TGJ61564	Au	5006303	C49FT	8/96 Hughes,	
							Llanfair Caereinion (CW)	7/04
T 20 DGE	Sca	K124IB4	1834276	VH	33341	C49FT	5/99 A&P Travel, Osbournby (LI)	8/11
FG 03 JCJ	Io	CC80.E18M/P	SBCA80D0002351686	Ind	4.717	C29F	4/03 Regent, Whitstable (KT)	4/09
SN 04 GKF	MB	O814D	WDB6703732N109173	KVC		C24F	3/04 Irving, Dalston (CA)	4/13
			(ex NES 551E 9/07, SN 04 GKF 3/06)					
CT 09 LCT	Sca	K340EB4	YS2K4X20001860629	VH	36144	C53F	4/09 Leons, Stafford (ST) 179	2/16

PG0007112/N: Martin Jonathan WEALE, Coedmawr, DISSERTH, Builth Wells, Powys, LD2 3TG.
FN: Weales Wheels. OCs: The Grading Station, Llanddewi Ystradenny, Powys, LD1 6SE; St Davids Cottage, Llanddewi Ystradenni, LD1 6SF. VA: 12.

	M554 YSG	Ds	Jv	10SDA2156/1165	WS	4728/95	C57F	2/95 Graham, Appleby (CA)	4/13
				(ex 27 AY 75 2/04, L243 MGY by2/04, 27 AY 75 by2/04)					
	R602 ENP	Ds	Jv	SFD213BR4VGJ12049	UVG	5807/97	C57F	by8/98 Herdman, Clyro (CW)	4/08
				(ex P415 ACW 3/08)					
z	R713 TRV	Ds	Jv	SFD721BR3VGJ22004	UVG	5645/97	C57F	8/97 Veolia Cymru (CS) 72023	by11/11
w	S609 VAY	Ds	Jv	SFD721BR3VGJ52051	Mpo	1.97.R.313	C67F	1/99 Crossgates, Crossgates	
								(CW) 72012	9/12
	T230 GOJ	Ds	Jv	SFD731BR4VGJ42092	Bf	3638	C49FT	5/99 Evergreen, Blackheath (WM)	4/06
	V285 BAN	Ds	Jv	SFD721BR3WGJE2188	Pn	9912GHM0223	C53F	-/99 MoD (X)	1/13
				(ex ?? ?? ??? 1/13)					
	V255 WAB	Ds	Jv	SFD721BR3WGJE2212	Pn	9912GHM0492	C55F	12/99 MoD (X)	7/12
				(ex V603 PCP 7/12)					
z	W109 MWG	LDV	Cy	SEYZMVSHEDN062010	LDV		M16	5/00 Sixt Kenning (Y)	5/12
	CT 02 PBF	Ds	Jv	SFD721BR41GJ22383	Pn	0212GFM4516	C55F	-/02 Lex (MoD)	8/13
				(ex ?? ?? ??? 10/13)					
	AD 54 MXB	Fd	Tt	WF0EXXTTFE4T05624	Fd		M16	1/05 Herdman, Clyro (CW)	12/11
	CN 54 GXO	LDV	Cy	SEYZMVSYGDN106323	LDV		M16	12/04 Monmouthshire Council,	
								Raglan (CS)	10/12
	YN 55 KNB	MB	O814D	WDB6703732N119679	Pn	057.8MXW6170	B28FL	9/05 Travelbility,	
								Weston-Super-Mare (SO)	4/15
	FJ 57 GCV	Io	50C15	ZCFC50A2005654094	Me	-?-	M11L	10/07 Shropshire Council	
								(SH) N1782	1/15

PG0005791/I: Clifford WEAVER, 148 Aberdyberthi Street, HAFOD, Swansea, SA1 2NF.
FN: Weavers Mini Coaches. OC: 134A Eaton Road, Brynhyfryd, Swansea, SA5 9JU. VA: 4.

w	F 53 YAB	FR	Sa	XLRZKWTN77BN84288	FR		M8	by7/89 MoD (X)	10/97
w	H406 HKE	Rt	Mtr	VF6FB30A501310644	Jb		M14	8/90 Leyshon, Pyle (CC)	10/97
				(ex H 3 BRT 9/95, H388 OUY 10/94)					
w	N982 JBX	Rt	Mtr	VF1FB30AH14101300	Cym	RM96/1840	M16	4/96 Grenitote Travel,	
								Grenitote (SN)	by6/10
w	P709 CTA	LDV	Pt	SEYZKRSDCDN013576	LDV		M8	3/97 Royal Mail (RM) 6780233	11/02
w	R738 AOE	LDV	Cy	SEYZMYSJEDN032060	LDV		M16	3/98 Lets Go, Manselton (CW)	8/03
w	W467 XCS	LDV	Pt	SEYZKSFXCDN058667	LDV		M8	3/00 White, Cumnock (XSW)	9/07
w	FC 04 NSU	LDV	Cy	SEYZMUSYGDN103372	LDV		M16	-/04 MoD (X)	2/10
w	SF 05 LJO	Pt	Bxr	VF3ZAAMFA17332457	Allied		M14	7/05 -?-, -?-	2/12
	CX 57 LCJ	LDV	Max	SEYL6P6D20N212358	LDV		M14	12/07 -?-, -?-	3/13
	BX 58 UMF	LDV	Max	SEYL6RXH20N232583	LDV		M15	2/09 Royal Mail (RM) 8753004	7/12

PG0005881/I: WILLIAMS Motors (Cwmdu) Limited, Cambrian Way, BRECON, Powys, LD3 7BE.
OCs: as address; Crescent Garage, Cwmdu, Powys, NP8 1RU. VA: 34.

	TH 1451	IH	SL-34		41234	Agenda Coachworks	B20F	by12/31 Davies, Pencader (CW)	8/99
						(replica body fitted 8/00)			
z	IAZ 6421	Ka	S215HD	WKK17900001035031	Ka		C49FT	4/83 Max Services, Lowestoft (SK)	7/07
				(ex URL 149Y 4/96, YOR 456 12/95, OFB 606Y 3/85)					
	MIB 552	Sca	K114IB	YS2K4X20001845223	Ir	95874	C53F	9/03 Campbell, Lesmahagow (SW)	2/11
				(ex FX 53 BTY 9/14, 445 UXM 12/07, FX 53 BTY 7/07)					
	WIL 2645	Ds	Jv	SFD721BR4WGJ22182	Pn	9810GDM9707	C39FT	10/98 Grey, Witchford (CM)	3/06
				(ex S327 FVE 4/06, ESU 374 3/06, G 16 ELY 4/05, ESU 369 1/02)					
	WIL 3944	Ba	FHD10-340	XL9AA16P230003213	Ba		C41F	5/02 Ingleby, York (NY)	3/15
				(ex YD 02 PXE 5/15)					
w	WSU 259	Ka	S215H	WKK17900001015028	Ka		C53F	4/86 Landtourers, Farnham (SR)	12/93
				(ex C209 UPC 5/90)					
	226 DMW	Ka	S315GT-HD	WKK62725223000297	Ka		C53F	5/05 City Circle, Bonyrigg (SS) 6	6/09
				(ex BX 05 UVP 3/15)					
	299 DMW	Au	N316SHD	WAG2031621BD32107	Au	3160852	C51FT	7/01 Stolzenberg, Maesteg (CC)	5/08
				(ex Y137 HWE 6/08)					
	B 10 PRE	Ka	S415GT-HD	WKK63213123104164	Ka		C48FT	6/07 Prestige Tours, Renfrew (SW)	4/10

WILLIAMS, BRECON (continued)

	P548 PNE	MB	O814D	WDB6703732N064050	Pn	977.8MWV7019	B27F	7/97	GHA, Ruabon (CN) 1013		9/16
				(ex P 3 GHA 12/15, P548 PNE 6/05)							
	Y326 YUT	Ds	Jv	SFD721BR4XGJE2278	SCC	4032/99	C70F	7/01	Norse Eastern, Norwich		
									(NK) 7113		7/16
z	FJ 51 JYA	Ds	Jv	SFD721BR41GJ22336	SCC	4211/01	C70F	12/01	Norse, Norwich (NK) 7124		11/16
z	FJ 51 JYC	Ds	Jv	SFD721BR41GJ22338	SCC	4213/01	C70F	1/02	Norse, Norwich (NK) 7126		11/16
	CX 02 EBV	MB	O814D	WDB6703742N099038	Pn	018.5MAE4551	C33F	6/02	Isaac & Morgan,		
									Lampere (CW)		10/13
	WA 53 SGX	MB	O815DT	WDB6703742N104928	Sit	1816	C33F	1/04	new		1/04
	YX 53 HFR	Tbs	Jv	SFD745BR53GJ22457	Pn	0312GRX5150	C70FL	11/03	Leicestershire County		
									Council (XLE) YB4		2/14
	SK 04 OOL	Sca	K94IB			1847872	lr	151424	C70F	6/04	Buzzlines, Hythe (KT)	11/07
	HM 05 GSM	MB	O815D	WDB6703742N113345	Sit	2017	C33F	3/05	Clegg & Brooking,		
									Middle Wallop (HA)		9/15
	MT 05 SSO	Fd	Tt	WF0EXXTTFE5R25946	Fd		M14	6/05	Pontins, Hemsby (YSK)		1/13
	WN 05 ELJ	Fd	Tt	WF0EXXTTFE5U42045	Fd		M16	4/05	Enterprise (Y)		7/07
	YN 05 AUT	Io	CC100E	ZCFA1AF1102410894	Ind	5378	C29F	3/05	new		3/05
	VX 55 FWF	MB	O814D	WDB6703742N117745	Me	4106	C33F	9/05	Taylors Travel, Parkend (GL)		6/16
	YN 56 FGA	Sca	K94IB	YS2K4X20001853957	lr	151016	C70F	9/06	Jackson, Blackpool (LA)		9/08
	YN 07 DVC	MB	O816D	WDB6703742N125995	Pn	068.5MBE6927	C33F	3/07	Brown, Thorp Arch (WY)		1/15
	FJ 58 AHG	Sca	K340EB4	YS2K4X20001861676	Co	F083043010	C70F	1/09	Luckett, Fareham (HA) 495349	9/16
	BJ 59 OHW	MB	Tourismo	WEB63203623000082	MB		C53F	1/10	Pullmanor, Herne Hill (LN) 231	12/16
	MX 59 FJD	Ibs	45C15	ZCFC45A2005766031	Tawe		M16	9/09	new		9/09
	YJ 10 DLE	Tmsa	Safari HD	NLTRHT97R01010023	Tmsa	OA03938	C57F	6/10	Lever, Motcombe (DT)		2/11
	YR 10 HBY	Fd	Tt	WF0BXXBDFB9E59017	?		M8	3/10	Neath Port Talbot Community		
									Transport, Neath (XCC)		6/16
	WA 11 HXL	Ba	FHD127.365	XL9AA38RB34003974	Ba		C54FT	6/11	Hillier, Foxham (WI)		9/14
	BX 61 DXG	Vo	B9R	YV3S5P720BA149470	Je	30117	C53FT	9/11	Reynolds, St Albans (HT)		1/16
	YN 12 BRZ	Ibs	397E.12.33	ZGA7B2N100E001502	Pn	1113EDR8898	C61F	4/12	Weaver, Newbury (BE)		4/15
	BU 13 ZUD	MB	Tourismo	WEB63203623000224	MB		C49FT	3/13	new		3/13
	OU 14 SRX	Au	N2216/3SHDL	WAGP22ZZ1ET020821	Au	P220767	C61FT	5/14	Bennett, West Drayton (LN)		6/16
	OU 14 SRY	Au	N2216/3SHDL	WAGP22ZZ3ET020822	Au	P220768	C61FT	5/14	Bennett, West Drayton (LN)		6/16
	YN 14 EDR	SCa	K360IB4	YS2K4X20001888878	lr	141621	C51FT	7/14	new		7/14
	YG 65 ARX	Ytg	ZK6938H	LZYTCTE63F1029549	Ytg		C32FT	11/15	new		11/15
	RX 16 XET	MB	516CDI	WDB9061552N641845	EVM		C19F	3/16	Lewis, Llanrhystud (CW)		12/16

PG1132243/N: Griffith Alun & Eurig Dylan WILLIAMS, Graigwen, FELINGWM, Carmarthen, Carmarthenshire, SA32 7PR. FN: Brodyr Williams. OC: as address; Derwendeg, Llansawel, Llandeilo, SA19 7PE. VA: 10.

w	CU 54 AFJ	LDV	Cy	SEYZMVSZGDN106284	LDV	M16	9/04	-?-, -?-	3/09
	CU 54 AFX	LDV	Cy	SEYZMVSZGDN106274	LDV	M16	9/04	new	9/04
x	CV 07 HNK	Fd	Tt	WF0BXXBDFB6A67738	Fd	M8	3/07	-?-, -?-	3/08
	CV 11 HRC	Fd	Tt	WF0DXXTTFDAA78623	Fd	M16	3/11	Day's Rental, Swansea (YCW)	8/12
	CV 11 HRD	Fd	Tt	WF0DXXTTFDAA78606	Fd	M16	3/11	Day's Rental, Swansea (YCW)	12/11
x	CV 61 FFW	Rt	Tc	VF1JLBHBSBV418547	Rt	M8	9/11	new	9/11
x	DY 12 FGD	Vx	Viv	W0LJ7BHB6CV613090	Vx	M8	3/12	-?-, -?-	11/12
x	YP 62 GDF	Fd	Tt	WF0BXXBDFBCL45792	Fd	M8	10/12	-?-, -?-	2/14
x	DY 13 HFS	Fd	Tt	WF0BXXBDFBCY49540	Fd	M8	3/13	-?-, -?-	2/15
	EX 13 UFA	Fd	Tt	WF0DXXTTFDCT19332	Fd	M16	3/13	-?-, -?-	7/13
	CV 14 TZA	Fd	Tt	WF0DXXTTFDDK89327	Fd	M16	4/14	Day's Rentals, Swansea (YCW)	11/14
	CV 14 TZC	Fd	Tt	WF0DXXTTFDDK89411	Fd	M16	4/14	Day's Rentals, Swansea (YCW)	11/14

PG1031525/N: Geoff WILLIAMS Minibuses Limited, Haulfryn, The Square, KERRY, Newtown, Powys, SY16 4NU. OC: as address. VA: 11.

	YP 06 FSA	Fd	Tt	WF0EXXTTFE6S24587	Fd	M16	4/06	-?-, -?-	10/09
	BG 07 NMU	Fd	Tt	WF0DXXTTFD7D19068	Fd	M16	4/07	Solihull College (XWM)	11/11
x	PL 07 ENU	Rt	Tc	VF1JLBHA67V294670	Rt	M8	7/07	new	7/07
x	YR 07 OPN	Fd	Tt	WF0SXXBDFS6R56996	Fd	M8	3/07	Exchange Self Drive,	
									Doncaster (YSY)	10/08

WILLIAMS, KERRY (continued)

x	FV 08 MMF	Fd	Tt	WF0BXXBDFB7P55905	Fd	M8	5/08 -?-, -?-	4/09
	YK 08 JDU	Fd	Tt	WF0DXXTTFD8B85497	Fd	M16	3/08 -?-, -?-	4/09
x	VA 10 AZW	Fd	Tt	WF0SXXBDFS9C53872	Fd	M8	7/10 -?-, -?-	3/14
x	LJ 60 HTL	Fd	Tt	WF0XXXTTFXAS89974	Fd	M8	9/10 -?-, -?-	3/14
x	AK 11 PFY	Fd	Tt	WF0XXXTTFXBD69918	?	M8L	4/11 -?-, -?-	11/11
x	AK 11 PHV	Fd	Tt	WF0SXXBDFSBC89793	Fd	M8	4/11 -?-, -?-	11/11
x	AJ 12 HDL	Fd	Tt	WF0SXXBDFSCG36328	Fd	M8	6/12 -?-, -?-	1/13

PG1074485/I: WINDY CORNER Limited, Windy Corner Garage, PENCADER, Carmarthenshire, SA39 9HP.
FN: Windy Corner Coaches. OC: as address. VA: 24.

w	IIG 1495	Ds	Jv		11SDL2133/1068	Pn	9411HZM2828	C51F	1/95 Orkney Coaches (SN) 59107	12/09
				(ex M107 CCD 9/10, 520 PXR 5/09, M107 CCD 8/04)						
	VIL 9216	Ds	Jv		SFD721BR4VGJ22059	SCC	4003	C69FL	6/99 Holmeswood,	
									Holmeswood (LA)	1/09
				(ex T706 SUT 1/09, 629 LFM by1/09, T706 SUT 10/07)						
	WDR 598	AD	Jv		SFD755BR68GJ22605	Pn	0812JAX7740	C70F	5/08 new	5/08
				(ex YN 08 DNJ 8/16)						
	WSV 465	Ka		S315GT-HD	WKK62725223000186	Ka		C49FT	2/04 Watts Coaches,	
									Bonvilston (CC)	2/15
				(ex YO 53 VSA 3/15, 04-C-7881 3/13)						
w	E 67 HVL	Ds	Jv		12SDA1907/132	Pn	8812DAP3C014	C53F	4/88 Haines, Frampton West (LI)	2/05
				(ex FIL 8156 10/04, DAZ 4302 1/00, E174 FFW 5/95)						
w	L866 ENP	Ds	Jv		8.5SDA2126/977	WS	3896/94	B36F	2/94 Alansway, Heathfield (DN) 7	7/07
				(ex JPY 505 10/06, L866 ENP 3/04, 75 KK 58 by1/03)						
	L 7 WXM	MAN	18.350		WMAA51ZZZYW038812	Mpo	1.01.R.730	C57F	6/02 Wheelers Travel,	
									North Baddesley (HA)	6/12
				(ex FN 02 HGZ 8/09)						
	N 6 STA	MB	Tourismo		NMB63203623000006	MB		C49FT	7/07 McLeans Coaches,	
									Witney (OX)	3/11
				(ex BX 07 NLY 5/16)						
	R 13 WCC	MB	Tourismo		NMB63203623000007	MB		C49FT	7/07 McLeans Coaches,	
									Witney (OX)	8/10
				(ex BX 07 NLZ 7/16)						
	R 14 WCC	MB	Tourismo		WEB63203623000132	MB		C53F	1/11 Symphony Chauffeurs,	
									Hounslow (LN)	5/16
				(ex BD 60 XSR 6/16, Y 50 SYM by5/16, BD 60 XSR 2/14)						
	V663 FPO	Ds	Jv		SFD721BR4VGJ22060	UVG	4004	C70F	9/99 Holmeswood, Holmeswood (LA)	1/14
z	W359 XKX	DAF	SB3000		XMGDE33WS0H008112	Pn	0012DSM2381	C53F	7/00 Hayward, Carmarthen (CW)	6/15
	Y351 ATR	Vo			WDR 598 8/16, Y351 ATR 9/10, 01-D-60731 5/05)		F013043008	C49FT	7/01 Warrington, Swanmore (HA)	4/06
z	Y541 TGA	DAF	FA45-150		XLRAE45CE0L222207	Nuk		B25FL	7/01 Glasgow City Council (XSW)	4/11
z	SF 51 PSZ	DAF	FA45-150		XLRAE45CE0L227031	Nuk		B25FL	9/01 Glasgow City Council (XSW)	5/10
z	SF 51 PTO	DAF	FA45-150		XLRAE45CE0L227244	Nuk		B25FL	10/01 Glasgow City Council (XSW)	5/10
	SJ 51 EEO	DAF	FA45-150		XLRAE45CE0L227598	Nuk		B24FL	2/02 Glasgow City Council (XSW)	5/10
	EA 04 LMV	Fd	Tt		WF0EXXGBFE4B86423	Fd		M16	4/04 Hewens, Laugarne (CW)	9/11
w	???? ???	Ds	Jv		11SDA1906/376	Pn	8911HEA1225	C53F	11/89 Bysiau Cwm Taf,	
									Whitland (CW)	9/09
				(ex TIL 8886 by10/12, VBX 144 by11/08, G951 WNR by11/99)						

Note: Y351 ATR row — (ex WDR 598 8/16, Y351 ATR 9/10, 01-D-60731 5/05), Vo B10M-62 YV31MA6161A053197 Co F013043008 C49FT 7/01 Warrington, Swanmore (HA) 4/06

PG1106134/N: Stephen & Benjamin WOOD, 5-6 Church Street, WELSHPOOL, Powys, SY21 7DL.
FN: Border Mobility. OC: Unit 16, The Quarry, Brook Street, Welshpool, Powys, SY21 7NA. VA: 2.

No vehicles currently recorded.

PG1140977/R: WOODHILL Care Limited, Woodfield Nursing Home, COXHILL, Narberth, Pembrokeshire, SA67 8EH.
OC: as address. VA: 1.

No vehicles yet recorded.

PG1053763/I: Donald James & Donald Myrddin WOOLFE, 3 Banc-y-Ddraenen, Capel Hendre, AMMANFORD, Carmarthenshire, SA18 3SR. FN: Don's Coaches. OCs: Unit 7 Llys Glas, Parc Amanwy, New Road, Ammanford, SA18 3EZ. VA: 3.

w	DNZ 2581	Ld	TRCTL11/3RZ		8700043	Du	8790/0544	C57F	3/88 Langston & Fenner,	
			(ex E162 TVR 6/13)						Steeple Claydon (BK)	11/12
w	V 2 EFA	MB	O814D	WDB6703742N079569	RH	1.127		C24F	10/99 Hayward, Carmarthen (CW)	3/13

PG1036776/N: Thomas Peter & Margaret Ann WRIGHT, Min yr afon, Coronation Terrace, Bridge Street, LLANFYLLIN, Powys, SY22 5AZ. FN: Wrights Private Hire. OC: as address; The Workshop, Bridge Street, Llanfyllin, Powys, SY22 5AU. VA: 7.

x	SW 02 OHW	Fd	Tt	WF0TXXBDFT6S17691	Fd		M8	8/06 -?-, -?-	5/15
			(ex FT 06 GPU 9/15)						
xw	PE 54 YYU	Fd	Tt	WF0TXXTTFT4L29943	Fd		M8	9/04 U-Drive, Parkstone (YDT)	6/07
	PF 07 EKR	VW	Tr	WV1ZZZ7HZ7H121653	VW		M8	6/07 -?-, -?-	8/10
x	DY 57 URL	Vx	Viv	W0LF7BHB67V653671	Vx		M8	9/07 Burnt Tree, Shrewsbury (YSH)	8/10
x	DS 09 OPJ	Vx	Viv	W0LJ7BHB67V631111	Vx		M8	7/09 -?-, -?-	11/09
x	NU 09 LZH	Fd	Tt	WF0BXXBDFB8E21823	Fd		M8	6/09 -?-, -?-	8/12
x	HK 59 PZE	MB	313CDI	WDB9066352S429305	?		M8	1/10 -?-, -?-	9/12
x	CV 10 HAS	Fd	Tt	WF0SXXBDFS9K54876	Fd		M8	3/10 Day's Rental, Swansea (YCW)	8/13
x	AF 63 EKM	Fd	Tt	WF01XXTTG1DK69455	Fd		M8	11/13 -?-, -?-	6/14
x	AF 14 YOO	Fd	Tourneo	WF03XXTTG3ES81417	Fd		M8	3/14 -?-, -?-	10/14

MID AND WEST WALES NON-PSV OPERATORS (XCW)

ABERAERON COMPREHENSIVE SCHOOL, South Road, ABERAERON, Ceredigion, SA46 0DT.
3641 NG 56 UWP Fd   Tt   WF0DXXTTFD6P47412 Fd   M16   12/06 -?-, -?-   11/09

ABERYSTWYTH UNIVERSITY, Penglais, ABERYSTWYTH, Ceredigion, SY23 1NG.

ABERYSTWYTH UNIVERSITY STUDENT'S UNION, Penglais, ABERYSTWYTH, Ceredigion, SY23 1NG.

ALL WALES AMBULANCE Service, The Old School, CWMLLYNFELL, Swansea, SA9 2WD.

AMAZON Swansea, Ffordd Amazon, CRYMLYN BURROWS, Jersey Marine, Swansea, SA1 8QX.
NG 57 GZM Fd   Tt   WF0SXXBDFS7S26960 Fd   M8   11/07 -?-, -?-   7/14

APPLE BLOSSOM CLEANING, Unit 12, Rushacre Enterprise Park, NARBERTH, Pembrokeshire, SA67 7ET.
NH 06 FPY Fd   Tt   WF0EXXTTFE6Y16148 ?   M14   7/06 Anchor Self Drive,
                                                                     Leeds (YWY) 7/12

ASHLEY COURT Care Home, 70-74 New Road, LLANELLI, Carmarthenshire, SA15 3DR.
CN 05 ONJ MB   411CDI   WDB9046632R815456 ?   M15L   8/05 Bryn Helyg, Bynea (XCW) by7/16

BARCHESTER Hafan-y-Coed Care Home, Nightingale Court, Coed Cae Road, LLANELLI, Carmarthenshire, SA15 1HU.
HN 59 EVK Rt   Mtr   VF1FDB2H642021681 Atlas   M??   10/09 -?-, -?-   11/14

BISHOP GORE SCHOOL, De-la-Beche Road, SKETTY. Swansea, SA2 9AP.
CP 56 FXZ Fd   Tt   WF0DXXTTFD6R89924 Fd   M16   11/06 Day's Rental, Swansea (YCW) 11/09

BLACK MOUNTAIN ACTIVITIES, THREE COCKS, Brecon, Powys, LD3 0SD.
w R312 VUJ LDV Cy   SEYZMYSHEDN033553 LDV   M16   4/98 Edgecliff High School.
                                                                  Kinver (XST) 7/09
w W573 PPB LDV Cy   SEYZMVSJEDN061227 ?   M16   6/00 BTC Rentals,
                                                              Wokingham (YBE) 6/07
KX 55 EJF LDV Cy   SEYZMVSYGDN113069 LDV   M16   11/05 Tring School (XHT)   4/09

BLACK MOUNTAIN VENTURES Limited, 18 High Street, CRICKHOWELL, Powys, NP8 1BD.
YJ 06 HTU LDV Cy   SEYZMVSZGDN112286 LDV   M8   3/06 Herdman, Clyro (CW)   6/13

BLUESTONE LEISURE PARK, CANASTON WOOD, Narberth, Pembrokeshire, SA67 8DE.

BRAIN INJURY Rehabilitation TRUST, Ty Aberdafen, The Avenue, LLANELLI, Carmarthenshire, SA15 2DP.
NX 16 BFF Vx   Mov   W0LMWS601GB107915 ?   M4L   8/16 new   8/16

BRECON & DISTRICT DISABLED CLUB, Red Kite House, Rich Way, BRECON, Powys, LD3 7EH.
FN: Brecon Dial-a-Ride.
WX 54 SWN Rt   Mtr   VF1FDCUL632139553 ?   M??   9/04 new   9/04
LJ 09 MJE Ctn Rly   VF7YDBMFC11626998 ?   M??L   4/09 new   4/09
LJ 11 DWG Ctn Rly   VF7YCBMFC11886204 Stan -?-   M??L   3/11 new   3/11
MX 12 HLN Pt   Bxr   VF3YCTMFC12099849 ?   M11L   3/12 -?-, -?-   7/16
WA 62 GWK Ctn Rly   VF7YCTMFC12320834 Csd -?-   M10L   2/13 new   2/13

BRECON MOUNTAIN RESCUE, Ffrwdgrech Industrial Estate, BRECON, Powys, LD3 8LA
SH 06 XEU Fd   Tt   WF0TXXBDFT6L03859 Fd   M8   5/06 Renfrewshire Council (XSW) 7/14

BRITISH RED CROSS, Ganolfan Dyffryn Dyfi, Forge Road, MACHYNLLETH, Powys, SY20 8EU.
AE 06 NNU Rt   Mtr   VF1FDCUL635357611 Csd -?-   M12L   3/06 new   3/06
AE 56 LCT Rt   Mtr   VF1FDCML636155605 ?   M??   9/06 new   9/06

BRYN HELYG Care Home, 64 Cwmfelin Road, BYNEA, Llanelli, Carmarthenshire, SA14 9LR.

BRYN ILLTYD Residential Home, Heol y Mynydd, PEMBREY, Burry Port, Carmarthenshire, SA16 0AJ.
FY 02 XZR Rt   Mtr   VF1FDCNL527051769 Cym   M6   8/02 new   8/02

BRYNLLYWARCH HALL SCHOOL, KERRY, Newtown, Powys, SY16 4PB.

BUILTH WELLS HIGH SCHOOL, College Road, Builth Wells, Powys, LD2 3BW.

BWS BLOOMFIELD, Bloomfield House, Redstone Road, NARBERTH, Pembrokeshire SA67 7EP.

CU 58 CUW	lbs	50C15	ZCFC50A2005726162 Brecon		M16L	9/08 new	9/08

BWS Y BOBL, St. David's & Peninsula Community Bus Group, ST DAVID'S, Pembrokeshire.

LJ 58 NUU	VW	Crf	WV1ZZZ2EZ96006880	?	M15L	9/08 new	9/08

CAMAU BACH, Boulevard De Saint Brieuc, ABERYSTWYTH, Ceredigion, SY23 1PD.

CP 02 OAM	Fd	Tt	WF0EXXGBFE2J11039 Fd		M16	6/02 Mudiad Ysgolion Meithrin,	
						Pontprennau (XCC)	by9/15

CAREW HOCKEY CLUB, The Club House, Bird Lane, CAREW, Pembrokeshire.

HX 56 UER	LDV	Max	SEYL6P6A20N210059 LDV		M14	2/07 -?-, -?-	10/12

CARMARTHEN BREAKTHRO' GROUP, Station Road, NANTGAREDIG, Carmarthen, Carmarthenshire, SA32 7LQ.

X287 VDY	Fd	Tt	WF0LXXGBFLYC19063	?	M??	12/00 new	12/00

CARMARTHENSHIRE County COUNCIL, County Hall, Carmarthen, Carmarthenshire, SA31 1JP.

760036	CN 58 APU	MB	211CDI	WDB9066112S354794	?	M7	12/08 new	12/08
760037	CN 58 APO	MB	211CDI	WDB9066112S353302	?	M7	12/08 new	12/08
760038	CN 58 APK	MB	211CDI	WDB9066112S350463	?	M7	12/08 new	12/08
761012	CN 08 HHU	MB	111CDI	WDF63960323430096	?	M7	7/08 new	7/08
761013	CN 08 HHV	MB	111CDI	WDF63960323430097	?	M7	7/08 new	7/08
763011	CV 09 RVX	Fd	Tt	WF0DXXTTFD9U74183	Fd	M14	3/09 new	3/09
764032	CN 54 MMJ	MB	411CDI	WDB9046632R721718	UVM -?-	B16FL	12/04 new	12/04
764070	CV 10 NVT	Fd	Tt	WF0DXXTTFD9D18946	Fd	M16	3/10 new	3/10
764076	YD 11 WDA	Fd	Tt	WF0DXXTTFDAA71945	Fd	M16	3/11 new	3/11
764077	YD 11 WDE	Fd	Tt	WF0DXXTTFDAA75148	Fd	M16	3/11 new	3/11
764078	YH 11 UCJ	Fd	Tt	WF0DXXTTFDAB36759	Fd	M16	3/11 new	3/11
764080	GN 56 FCM	Io	45C14	ZCFC45A100D317563	Eurm -?-	M16	10/06 new	10/06
764083	CE 12 WFD	Fd	Tt	WF0DXXTTFDCB57681	Fd	M16	3/12 new	3/12
765019	GN 60 CDZ	Ft	Do	ZFA25000001740958	?	M12L	10/09 new	10/09
766039	CN 04 WMT	MB	411CDI	WDB9046122R665451	UVM -?-	B16FL	8/04 new	8/04
766040	CN 04 WLZ	MB	411CDI	WDB9046122R664673	UVM -?-	B16FL	8/04 new	8/04
766056	CU 06 BVZ	Fd	Tt	WF0LXXTTFL5D34298	O&H -?-	M15L	3/06 new	3/06
766058	CN 57 HRZ	MB	511CDI	WDB9061532N365320	UVM -?-	B10FL	1/08 new	1/08
766059	CN 57 HRG	MB	511CDI	WDB9061532N366151	UVM -?-	B16FL	1/08 new	1/08
766060	CN 57 HRF	MB	511CDI	WDB9061532N364694	UVM -?-	B16FL	2/08 new	2/08
766062	CN 57 HRD	MB	511CDI	WDB9061532N366151	UVM -?-	B16FL	1/08 new	1/08
766067	CV 11 JXW	Fd	Tt	WF0DXXTTFDBC29546	Fd	M16	3/11 new	3/11
z	YJ 61 JHY	Oe	M710SE	SABCN2AB0BS193839	Oe	B19F	2/12 Lewis, Llanrhystud (CW)	8/16
	CP 62 GUF	Fd	Tt	WF0DXXTTFDCY61152	Fd	M16	12/12 Day's Rental,	
							Swansea (YCW)	by11/14
	CU 13 JHA	Fd	Tt	WF0DXXTTFDCS07153	Fd	M16	3/13 Day's Rental, Swansea (YCW)	1/14
	CU 13 JHE	Fd	Tt	WF0DXXTTFDDJ44591	Fd	M16	4/13 -?-, -?-	1/14
	CU 13 JVP	Fd	Tt	WF0DXXTTFDDJ43946	Fd	M16	6/13 -?-, -?-	4/14
	CE 63 LSL	MB	513CDI	WDB9066552S848966	Treka -?-	M12L	12/13 new	12/13
	CE 63 LSN	MB	513CDI	WDB9066552S848967	Treka -?-	M12L	12/13 new	12/13
	CE 63 LSZ	MB	513CDI	WDB9061552N548773	Treka -?-	B12FL	10/13 new	10/13
	CE 63 LTN	MB	513CDI	WDB9061552N548499	Treka -?-	B14FL	10/13 new	10/13
	CE 63 LTT	MB	513CDI	WDB9061552N548500	Treka -?-	B15FL	10/13 new	10/13
	CE 63 LTU	MB	513CDI	WDB9061552N548775	Treka -?-	B14FL	11/13 new	11/13
	CE 63 LTV	MB	513CDI	WDB9066552S838513	Treka -?-	M12L	12/13 new	12/13
	CE 63 LTX	MB	513CDI	WDB9066552S838514	Treka -?-	B14FL	12/13 new	12/13
	CU 64 UHR	Fd	Tourneo	WF03XXTTG3EU39495	Fd	M8	9/14 new	9/14
	CV 64 GHN	Fd	Tt	WF0HXXTTGHEP63031	Fd	M16	9/14 new	9/14
	CU 15 PDO	Fd	Tt	WF0HXXTTGHEJ11722	Fd	M16	3/15 new	3/15
	CV 16 DFU	Fd	Tt	WF0HXXTTGHGA16376	Fd	M17	4/16 new	4/16
	LV 16 HDU	MB	513CDI	WDB9066572P279297	Treka -?-	M12L	6/16 new	6/16
	LV 16 HEU	MB	513CDI	WDB9066572P279299	Treka -?-	M12L	6/16 new	6/16
	LV 16 HFD	MB	513CDI	WDB9066572P279300	Treka -?-	M12L	6/16 new	6/16

CARMARTHENSHIRE COUNCIL (continued)

LV 16 HJY	MB	513CDI	WDB9766572P278730	Treka -?-	M15L	7/16 new		7/16
LV 16 HJZ	MB	513CDI	WDB9066572P278732	Treka -?-	M15L	7/16 new		7/16
LV 16 HKB	MB	513CDI	WDB9066572P278731	?	M15	7/16 new		7/16
LV 16 HKE	MB	513CDI	WDB9066572P278729	Treka -?-	M12L	7/16 new		7/16
LV 16 HKF	MB	513CDI	WDB9066572P279301	Treka -?-	M15L	6/16 new		6/16

CARTREF AEL-Y-BRYN Care Home, Pen-Y-banc Road, AMMANFORD, Carmarthenshire, SA18 3HS.

ML 02 PNO	LDV	Cy	SEYZMVSYGDN087610	LDV	M16	7/02 Moss Side Training Centre (XGM)	6/10
AE 55 EBM	lo	50C13	ZCFC5090005514296	?	M??L	9/05 Breakspeare School, Abbots Langley (XHT) E76-1960	12/15

CASTLE SCHOOL, CRESSELLY, Kidwelly, Pembrokeshire, SA68 0SP.

CELTIC CANOES, GLASBURY, Long Barn, Felindre, Talgarth, Powys, LD3 0TE.

w R878 PWN	Fd	Tt	WF0LXXBDVLVG75590	?	M16	11/97 Grange Centre, Hay-on-Wye (XCW)	2/08

CELVAC ENVIRONMENTAL SOLUTIONS, The Salterns, TENBY, Pembrokeshire, SA70 8EP.

SF 56 HYB	LDV	Max	SEYL6P6A20N211537	LDV	M14	12/06 -?-, -?-	6/09

CEREDIGION County COUNCIL, Aberystwyth.

3741 CV 02 LSX	VW	LT35	WV1ZZZ2DZ2H017025	Cym-?-	M11	3/02 new	3/02
3742 CV 02 LSY	VW	Tr	WV1ZZZ2DZ2H060762	Cym-?-	M8L	3/02 new	3/02
3747 CU 04 LXC	VW	LT46	WV1ZZZ2DZ5H001573	Tawe	M14L	8/04 new	8/04
3748 CU 04 LXB	VW	LT46	WV1ZZZ2DZ5H001864	Tawe	M14L	8/04 new	8/04
3754 CU 05 FTK	VW	LT46	WV1ZZZ2DZ5H023362	Tawe	M15L	5/05 new	5/05
3757 CV 55 FFH	VW	LT46	WV1ZZZ2DZ6H008385	Tawe	M14L	1/06 new	1/06
3758 CU 06 ELO	VW	Tr	WV2ZZZ7HZ6H109832	Tawe	M8	6/06 new	6/06
3762 CU 07 HYC	VW	Crf	WV1ZZZ2EZ76035936	Brecon	M11L	8/07 new	8/07
3763 CP 57 MDX	VW	Crf	WV1ZZZ2EZ86020512	Stan -?-	M15L	1/08 new	1/08
3766 CU 59 FYV	VW	Crf	WV1ZZZ2EZ86013077	Stan -?-	M15L	2/10 new	2/10
3767 CU 59 FYW	VW	Crf	WV1ZZZ2EZA6016401	Stan -?-	M15L	2/10 new	2/10
3768 CU 10 EUW	VW	Crf	WV1ZZZ2EZA6016404	Stan -?	M15L	3/10 new	3/10
3769 CU 10 EUX	VW	Crf	WV1ZZZ2EZA6016403	Stan -?-	M15L	3/10 new	3/10
3770 CU 10 EUY	VW	Crf	WV1ZZZ2EZA6016405	Stan -?-	M15L	3/10 new	3/10
CU 64 ZBE	VW	Crf	WV1ZZZ2EZE6036497	?	M5L	11/14 new	11/14

CHRIST COLLEGE, Bridge Street, BRECON, Powys, LD3 8AF.

T 20 CCB	Fd	Tt	WF0DXXTTFDDX67469	Fd	M16	5/14 -?-, -?-	12/14
T 21 CCB	Rt	Mtr	VF1NDD1L638093138	Brecon	M15	8/07 new	8/07
T 22 CCB	Rt	Mtr	VF1NDD1L638093214	Brecon	M15	8/07 new	8/07
T 23 CCB	Rt	Mtr	VF1NDD1L638093235	Brecon	M15	8/07 new	8/07
T 24 CCB	Rt	Mtr	VF1NDD1L638093273	Brecon	M15	8/07 new	8/07
T 25 CCB	Fd	Tt	WF0DXXTTFD9G52725	Fd	M15	12/09 -?-, -?-	8/15
			(ex WL 59 HLO 9/15)				
T 26 CCB	Fd	Tt	WF0DXXTTFDDC67776	Fd	M16	5/14 -?-, -?-	12/14
			(ex BD 14 OLH 2/15)				
HK 05 ZMZ	Fd	Tt	WF0EXXTTFE5B01973	Fd	M16	7/05 new	7/05
			(ex T 25 CCB 9/15, HK 05 ZMZ 8/07)				

CLASE PRIMARY SCHOOL, Rheidol Avenue, Clase, SWANSEA, SA6 7JX.

CV 59 PXP	Fd	Tt	WF0DXXTTFD9G60897	Fd	M16	11/09 new	11/09

COLEG CEREDIGION, Llanbadarn Fawr, ABERYSTWYTH, Ceredigion, SY23 3BP.
OCs: as address; Park Place, Cardigan, Ceredigion, SA43 1AB

KJ 56 XRK	Fd	Tt	WF0DXXTTFD6U02053	Fd	M14	11/06 -?-, -?-	4/10

COLEG ELIDYR Care Home, RHANDIRMWYN, Llandovery, Carmarthenshire, SA20 0NL.

CP 05 MTE	Fd	Tt	WF0EXXTTFE5P77553	Fd	M14	5/05 new	5/05
SK 62 AKO	Vx	Viv	W0LJ7B7BACV643270	?	M8	10/12 new	10/12
SN 62 EAP	Vx	Viv	W0LJ7B7BADV603172	?	M8	1/13 new	1/13

COLEG SIR GÂR, Graig Campus, Sandy Road, LLANELLI, Carmarthenshire, SA15 4DN.
OCs: as address; Ammanford Campus, Station Road, Ammanford, Carmarthenshire SA18 3TA; Jobs Well Road Campus, Carmarthen, SA31 3HY; Pibwrlwyd Campus, Carmarthen, SA31 2NH; Gelli Aur Farm, Llandeilo, Caarmarthenshire, SA32 0NJ.

EX 53 UPK	Fd	Tt	WF0EXXGBFE3C58113 Fd		M16	9/03 -?-, -?-		11/06
CP 56 BWU	Fd	Tt	WF0DXXTTFD6B69491 Fd		M16	10/06 new		10/06
CK 59 KGG	Fd	Tt	WF0DXXTTFD9G60863 Fd		M16L	10/09 new		10/09
CP 59 VEY	Fd	Tt	WF0DXXTTFD9E49181 Fd		M16	2/10 new		3/10
CP 62 GVC	Fd	Tt	WF0DXXTTFDCS07188 Fd		M16	2/13 Day's Rental, Swansea (YCW)		11/13
CP 62 GVG	Fd	Tt	WF0DXXTTFDCS00105 Fd		M16	2/13 Day's Rental, Swansea (YCW)		11/13
CU 13 JJL	Fd	Tt	WF0DXXTTFDCT11877 Fd		M16	3/13 new		3/13

CROSFIELD HOUSE Nursing HOME, Dark Lane, RHAYADER, Powys, LD6 5DB.

CV 55 FFL	VW	LT46	WV1ZZZ2DZ6H007094 ?		M8L	12/05 new	12/05

DOLEN TEIFI Community Bus, Old Post Office, New Street, LLANDYSSUL, Ceredigion, SA44 4OJ.

NX 57 GDA	Io	50C15	ZCFC50A2005670718 ?		B15FL	9/07 Burnt Tree (Y)	1/11
CV 12 PHJ	Ft	Do	ZFA25000002085830 ?		M14L	3/12 Hanes Llandoch, St. Dogmaels (XCW)	9/16
CV 62 CXD	Fd	Tt	WF0DXXTTFDCD02626 Fd		M16	9/12 new	9/12
WA 15 DXL	Pt	Bxr	VF3YETMFC12729923 GM		M13L	3/15 new	3/15
WA 15 DXM	Pt	Bxr	VF3YETMFC12729017 GM		M16L	3/15 new	3/15

DRIVER TRAINING WALES, Natyffin Road South, Enterprise Park, LLANSAMLET, Swansea, SA7 9RG.

w K957 TBX	Ds	Jv	10SDA2120/821 WS	3834/93	C41F	7/93 Let's Go, Morriston (CW) 8		9/08
			(ex 74 KK 45 9/06)					

DUKE OF EDINBURGH'S AWARD SCHEME, Oak House, 12 The Bulwark, BRECON, Powys, LD37 7AD.

CP 59 HDK	Fd	Tt	WF0DXXTTFD9D14731 Fd		M16	1/10 new	1/10

EAST RADNORSHIRE DAY CENTRE, Old Schoool, Scottleton Street, PRESTEIGNE, Powys, LD8 2BL.

EF 57 NKA	Pt	Bxr	VF3YCBMFC11313608 Stan -?-		M??L	12/07 new	12/07
HX 62 HDU	Pt	Bxr	VF3YEHMFC12245812 RKC		M13L:	10/12 new	10/12

FASTNET LINE, SWANSEA.

T544 HNH	Ds	Dt SLF	SFD612BR1XGW13210 Pn	998.8KGB0971	B29F	5/99 JP, Middleton (GM)		by6/10

FOOTHOLD Regeneration Village, Burry Road, LLANELLI, Carmarthenshire, SA15 2DS.

FRIENDS OF YOUNG DISABLED, 300 Carmarthen Road, Cwmbwrla, SWANSEA SA5 8NS.

DN 04 DKA	Fd	Tt	WF0PXXBDFP4G55596 Fd		M11	6/04 Blue Cedars Day Care Centre, Edgbaston (XWM)	9/15

GLASBURY HOUSE OUTDOOR Education CENTRE, on B4350, west of GLASBURY-ON-WYE, Powys, HR3 5NW.

YB 09 FNU	Fd	Tt	WF0DXXTTFD9R32693 Fd		M16	8/09 new	8/09

GOWER COLLEGE SWANSEA, Tycoch Road, SKETTY, Swansea, SA2 9EB.

CU 07 CDV	LDV	Max	SEYL6RXE20N216718 LDV		M14	6/07 new	6/07
CU 57 HXS	LDV	Max	SEYL6RXH20N222671 LDV		M16	12/07 new	12/07
CU 09 FFY	LDV	Max	SEYL6RXE21N232331 LDV		M14	3/09 new	3/09
CU 10 CCX	Fd	Tt	WF0XXXTTFXAY69707 Fd		M16	7/10 new	7/10

GOWERTON SCHOOL, Cecil Road, GOWERTON, Swansea SA4 3DL.

YR 09 OFT	Fd	Tt	WF0DXXTTFD8L18446 Fd		M16	3/09 nwe	3/09

GREEN LINKS Community Interest Company, Pembroke Comprehensive School, Bush Hill, PEMBROKE, Pembrokeshire, SA71 4RL.

BD 54 ZNT	Fd	Tt	WF0EXXTTFE4Y61989 Fd		M14	12/04 -?-, -?-	9/10

GRWP NPTC, Llandloes Road, NEWTOWN, Powys, SY16 4HU.

w PN 02 LZD	Rt	Mtr	VF1FDCML526255801 ?		M16	3/02 Powys County Council (XCW)	by3/10
CY 57 MTK	Fd	Tt	WF0DXXTTFD7M25760 Fd		M16	4/08 Powys Council (XCW)	6/12

GWENLLIAN Education Centre, Hillfield Villas, KIDWELLY, Carmarthenshire, SA17 4UL.
KE 03 XFB	LDV	Cy	SEYZMVSZGDN093316 LDV	M8	6/03 Wembley High Technology College, North Wembley (XLN)	4/15

GWENT BOXING Club, Dyfed Avenue, SWANSEA, SA1 6NF.
CV 02 LRY	Fd	Tt	WF0EXXGBFE1A48548 Fd	M14	4/02 Quality Vehicle Hire, Manselton (YCW)	11/11

GWERNYFED High SCHOOL, THREE COCKS, Brecon, Powys, LD3 0SG.
LG 11 MKU	Fd	Tt	WF0DXXTTFDAR57575 Fd	M16	3/11 -?-, -?-	3/13

HAFAL Charitable TRUST, Suite C2, Britannic House, Britannic Way, LLANDARCY, Swansea, SA10 6EL.
CP 07 AOE	Ft	Do	ZFA25000001139251 ?	M8L	4/07 new	4/07

HAKIN UNITED Association Football Club, Observatory Field, Heathfield Terrace, Hakin, MILFORD HAVEN, Pembrokeshire, SA73 3ES.

HAY & DISTRICT Dial-a-Ride, Council Offices, Broad Street, HAY-ON-WYE, Powys, HR3 5BX.
WA 14 FSP	Ctn	Rly	VF7YETMFC12566834 ?	M14L	3/14 new	3/14

HEATHERTON SPORTS PARK, St. Florence, TENBY, Pembrokeshire, SA70 8RJ.

HENGOED Court CARE HOME, Cefn Hengoed Road, WINCH WEN, Swansea, SA1 7LQ.
S 10 HCP	Rt	Mtr	VF1PDMVL532694338 ?	M14	2/05 Laurandy Centre, Wick (YSN)	3/15
			(ex BX 54 FOJ 3/15)			
w VU 02 KPY	Rt	Mtr	VF1FDCML526161925 O&H -?-	M??L	5/02 WMSNT, Birmingham (WM)	8/07
w YR 52 WNJ	Oe	Alero	SAB21000000000296 Oe	B16F	9/02 Llew Jones, Llanrwst (CN)	9/12
			(ex S 10 HCP 9/13, YR 52 WNJ 10/12)			

HILLSIDE RESIDENTIAL & Care Home, Ffynone Road, SWANSEA, SA1 6DE.
NX 58 CNA	Io	50C15	ZCFC50A2005726480 ?	M16L	9/08 Connect, South Shields (TW) C19	8/12

IEUENCTID CAMBRIA YOUTH, Gamallt Pentre Uchaf, TREGARON, Ceredigion, SY25 6NF.

IRISH FERRIES, PEMBROKE DOCK.
2 A 2 WLS	Ld	TRCTL11/3LZ	TR00022 Pn 8712LMMOD42EB54F		9/87 Silcox, Pembroke Dock (CW) 201	8/14
			(ex E628 WWD 5/04, 87 KF 28 by3/97)			
3 E149 ODE	Ld	TRCTL11/3LZ	TR00038 Pn 8712LMMOD49EB71F		9/87 Silcox, Pembroke Dock (CW) 216	8/14
			(ex 87 KF 35 11/97)			

JIREH EVANGELICAL CHURCH, Castle Street, LOUGHOR, Swansea, SA4 6TB.
NA 06 BVM	Fd	Tt	WF0EXXTTFE6Y04740 Fd	M16	3/06 Hertz (Y)	10/16

JISHIN Karate Acdemy, Units 1 – 3 Meadow Street, Heol-y-Gors, Townhill, SWANSEA, SA1 6RZ
YD 60 OJV	Fd	Tt	WF0DXXTTFDAM80031 Fd	M16	9/10 JCB Acdemey, Rocester (XST)	4/16

JOHNSTOWN PRIMARY School, Heol Salem, JOHNSTOWN, Carmarthen, Carmarthenshire, SA31 3HS.
W366 YTU	LDV	Cy	SEYZMVSHEDN060367 LDV	M16	3/00 -?-, -?-	8/11

KEYSTONE Education Trust, Sway Road, MORRISTON, Swansea, SA6 6JA.
2 OU 12 DOJ	MB	311CDI	WDB9066332S682972 ?	M12	7/12 new	7/12

KILVROUGH MANOR, Outdoor Education CENTRE, PARKMILL, Gower, SWANSEA, SA3 2EE.
WR 06 YYV	VW	LT35	WV1ZZZ2DZ6H034248 G&M -?-	M8L	9/06 new	9/06
WA 08 PFJ	VW	Crf	WV1ZZZ2EZ86031439 G&M -?-	M15	5/08 new	5/08

LRC DRIVER TRAINING, Trostre Industrial Estate, LLANELLI, Carmarthenshire, SA14 9UU.
L478 GTX	Ds	Jv	10SDA2120/827 WS 3840/93	C40F	9/93 Flynn, Carmel (CN)	3/13
			(ex G 4 FLN 2/13, L478 GTX by9/11, 74 KK 51 2/11)			

The LAMB INN, HERMON, Pembrokeshire, SA36 0DS.
w YM 07 ENX	Fd	Tt	WF0BXXBDFB7L16015 Fd	M8	7/07 -?-, -?-	1/11

LAMPHEY PRIMARY SCHOOL, Lamphey, Pembrokeshire, SA71 5NW.
CV 07 PZA Fd Tt WF0DXXTTFD6G36338 Fd M16 3/07 new 3/07

LLANDOVERY COLLEGE, Queensway, Llandovery, Carmarthenshire, SA20 0EE.
CU 62 CFL Rt Mtr VF1MEN4JE45847271 ? M14 9/12 new 9/12
CU 62 DCO Rt Mtr VF1MEN4JE47558665 ? M14 9/12 new 9/12

LLANDOVERY YMCA, Gerwyn House, Market Square, LLANDOVERY, Carmarthenshire SA20 0AB.
MT 64 PNK Pt Bxr VF3YDTMFC12732437 ? M16 11/14 new 11/14

LLANGENNITH HALL COMMUNITY BUS, Llangennith, Swansea, SA3 1HU.
CU 05 FTN VW LT46 WV1ZZZ2DZ5H020662 ? M15L 3/05 -?-, -?- 7/12

LLANIDLOES Dial-a-Ride, Town Hall, Great Oak Street, LLANIDLOES, Powys, SY18 6BN.

LLANDRINDOD WELLS COUNTY PRIMARY SCHOOL – CEFNLLYS, Spa Road East, LLANDRINDOD WELLS, Powys, LD1 5WA.
RX 58 DJV LDV Max SEYL6RXE21N229985 LDV M16 9/08 -?-, -?- 12/13

LLANDYSSUL PADDLERS CENTRE, Wilkes Head Square, Pont Tyeli, LLANDYSSUL, Carmarthenshire.
CP 12 YXM Fd Tt WF0DXXTTFDCD03717 Fd M16 8/12 new 6/12

LLANWRTYD WELLS COMMUNITY TRANSPORT, c/o Cefn Llewelyn, Cilmeri, Builth Wells, Powys, LD2 3FL.
PJ 53 OEP LDV Cy SEYZMVSYGDN099358 LDV M16 11/03 new 11/03
  (ex UCZ 9270 11/03)
w YU 04 WMV LDV Cy SEYZMVFYGDN105440 Onyx 686 M16 8/04 new 8/04
NX 54 BPZ Io 40C13 ZCFC409000D260293 O&H -?- M15L 2/05 Oswestry Community Action, Oswestry (XSH) 1/15
FY 07 XTB Fd Tt WF0DXXTTFD7D30518 Fd M16 4/07 Veola Cymru (CC) 10/11

LLWYN-YR-EOS SCHOOL, Penparcau, ABERYSTWYTH, Ceredigion, SY23 1SH.

LLYS NEWYDD RESIDENTIAL HOME; Heol Lotwen, CAPEL HENDRE, Ammanford, Carmarthenshire, SA18 3RP.
YJ 62 CYL Rt Mtr VF1MAF4BE47814858 O&H -?- M2L 11/12 new 11/12

LLYS GWYN RESIDENTIAL HOME 21 Caecerrig Road, PONTARDDULAIS, Carmarthenshire, SA4 8PE.
M 18 LYS Rt Mtr VF1FDCVL534284934 O&H -?- M9L 10/05 Lewis Day Medical Services
  (ex YX 55 FKP 5/13) (XLN) 3/13

LONGFIELDS ASSOCIATION, 6 Bethany Lane, West Cross, SWANSEA, SA3 5TL.
LX 55 CCU MB 614D WDB6683532N119315 ? B6FL 1/06 new 1/06

MoD OUTWARD BOUND CENTRE, Cwrt-y-Gollen Camp, CRICKHOWELL, Powys.
BU 10 LNA Fd Tt WF0DXXTTFDAS12277 Fd M16 7/10 ne 7/10
BU 10 MJK Fd Tt WF0DXXTTFDAS12065 Fd M14 7/10 new 7/10

MAES-Y-LADE Outdoor CENTRE, TREGOYD, Talgarth, Powys, LD3 0SS.
EK 09 XRB Fd Tt WF0DXXTTFD9P82700 Fd M14 8/09 new 8/09

MAINPORT ENGINEERING, The Pembroke Enterprise Centre, 1 London Road, PEMBROKE DOCK, Pembrokeshire, SA72 4RS.
BU 07 SJO LDV Max SEYL6RXH20N218069 ? M14 8/07 -?-, -?- 5/10

MANORBIER COMMUNITY TRANSPORT, The Grange, Manorbier, Tenby, Pembrokeshire, SA70 7TY.
CV 62 VFS Fd Tt WF0DXXTTFDCS80070 Fd M16 1/13 Pembrokeshire Council (XCW) by10/14

MENTER CWM GWENDRAETH, 11-17 Heol Coalbrook, PONTYBEREM, Carmarthenshire, SA15 5HU.
WL 60 FWG Ctn Rly VF7YDTMFC12131823 Csd M12L 3/12 new 3/12
WA 12 FFS Ctn Rly VF7YDTMFC12131823 Ctn M?? 3/12 new 3/12

MID & WEST WALES FIRE & RESCUE SERVICE, Lime Grove Avenue, CARMARTHEN, Carmarthenshire, SA31 1SP.

CU 03 AHV	Ds	Dt SLF	SFD2CACR32GW16682 EL	C43801	B--F	by8/03 new		by8/03
CU 04 AET	Fd	Tt	WF0EXXGBFE3P67624 Fd		M16	3/04 new		3/04
CU 58 FZR	Rt	Mtr	VF1NDD1L640699772 ?		M14	1/09 new		1/09
CU 62 AOS	MB	519CDI	WDB9066552S635227 ?		M8	10/12 new		10/12
CU 62 AOW	MB	519CDI	WDB9066552S635228 ?		M8	10/12 new		10/12

MILFORD HAVEN SCHOOL, Steyton Road, Milford Haven, Pembrokeshire, SA73 1AE.

MV14009 GN 55 OEP	lo	40C12	ZCFC408100D286006	Eurm -?-	M12L	11/05 new	11/05

MORRISTON COMPREHENSIVE SCHOOL, Heol Maes Eglwys, Cwmrhydyceirw, Swansea, SA6 6NH.

GN 58 EWG	lo	35S12	ZCFC358300D398137	Eurm -?-	M13L	11/06 -?-, -?-	2/11

MYRDDIN Special Needs and Autistic Unit, Ysgol Myrddin, Heol Disgwylfa, CARMARTHEN, Carmarthenshire, SA31 1TE.

763002 X263 VDY	Fd	Tt	WF0LXXGBFLYC19801	Cons	M14L	9/00 new	9/00

NATIONAL TRUST, Dinefwr, LLANDEILO, Carmarthenshire, SA19 6PF

BV 57 UAH	LDV	Max	SEYL6RXH20N219287 LDV		M16	9/07 -?-, -?-	7/09

NEV'S DOORSTEP CHALLENGE, Matrix Alpha, Northern Boulevard, Swansea Enterprise Park, SWANSEA SA6 8RE.

NA 13 AEE	Fd	Tt	WF0DXXTTFDDM01049 Fd		M16	4/13 new	4/13

NEWTOWN & District DIAL-a-RIDE, The Old Brewhouse, Ladywell Centre, NEWTOWN, Powys, SY16 1AF.

EG 03 FBD	Fd	Tt	WF0VXXGBFV3E86096 ?		M6L	8/03 new	8/03
LF 06 PWN	VW	LT35	WV1ZZZ2DZ6H013927 Stan -?-		M15L	3/06 London Borough of Croydon	
						(XLN)	10/12
CE 10 HPY	Ctn	Rly	VF7YDDMFC11584682 Ctn		M11	3/10 -?-, -?-	1/11

OAKWOOD LEISURE PARK, Canaston Bridge, NARBERTH, Pembrokeshire, SA67 8DE.

GF 59 GTU	Fd	Tt	WF0DXXTTFD9C79283 Fd		M16	10/09 new	10/09

OLCHFA SCHOOL, Gower Road, SKETTY, Swansea, SA2 7AB.

KP 05 XWL	VW	LT35	WV1ZZZ2DZ5H031986 VW		M14L	6/05 -?-, -?-	3/06

ORIELTON Field Studies Centre, PEMBROKE, Pembrokeshire SA71 5EZ.

PEMBROKESHIRE COLLEGE, HAVERFORDWEST, Pembrokeshire, SA61 1SZ.

GX 53 LLR	Fd	Tt	WF0LXXGBFL3T64039	Eurm -?-	M14L	2/04 new	2/04

PEMBROKESHIRE County COUNCIL, County Hall, Haverfordwest.

MV13022 CP 57 OKZ	Fd	Tt	WF0DXXTTFD7M25815 Fd		M16	1/08 new		1/08
MV13051 CV 59 ZGE	Fd	Tt	WF0DXXTTFD9C81234 Fd		M16	10/09 new		10/09
MV13052 CP 59 TYT	Fd	Tt	WF0DXXTTFD9C81539 Fd		M16	1/10 new		1/10
MV13053 CV 10 YJW	Fd	Tt	WF0DXXTTFD9E50148 Fd		M16	4/10 new		4/10
MV13054 CV 10 YJX	Fd	Tt	WF0DXXTTFD9K04364 Fd		M16	4/10 new		4/10
MV13055 YT 12 YBD	Fd	Tt	WF0DXXTTFDCB60716 Fd		M16	4/12 new		4/12
MV14013 GN 55 OEG	lo	40C12	ZCFC408100D272610	Eurm -?-	M12L	11/05 new		11/05
MV14046 GN 05 LMV	lo	35S12	ZCFC3581000265615	Eurm -?-	M12L	5/05 new		5/05
MV14056 CU 59 FJK	lo	50C15	ZCFC50A2005774739	Brecon	M12L	12/09 new		12/09
MV14057 CU 59 FJY	lo	50C15	ZCFC50A2005774484	Brecon	M12L	12/09 new		12/09
MV14058 CU 60 UKY	Fd	Tt	WF0XXXTTFXAR56969	Eurm -?-	M8L	1/11 new		1/11
MV14059 YX 11 FTE	VW	Tr	WV3ZZZ7JZBX013823	Blbd -?-	B14F	8/11 new		8/11
MV14060 YX 11 FTF	VW	Tr	WV3ZZZ7JZBX013819	Blbd -?-	B14F	8/11 new		8/11
MV14061 YX 11 FTJ	VW	Tr	WV3ZZZ7JZBX013804	Blbd -?-	B14F	8/11 new		9/11
MV14062 YX 11 FTK	VW	Tr	WV3ZZZ7JZBX013838	Blbd -?-	B14F	8/11 new		8/11
MV14063 GN 60 FXJ	MB	513CDI	WDB9066552S459755	Eurm 17556	M15L	10/10 Euromotive, Hythe (Qd)		11/11
MV35009 DX 10 DXP	Asn		A1012T SUAED5CGT7S620355 Asn		B70F	3/10 new		3/10
MV35010 DX 10 DXR	Asn		A1012T SUAED5CGT7S620356 Asn		B70F	3/10 new		3/10
MV63003 CV 60 RSY	Fd	Tt	WF0XXXTTFXAU75154	Brecon	M8L	9/10 Day's Rental, Swansea (YCW)		11/11
MV63006 CV 09 AEP	Fd	Tt	WF0SXXBDFS8Y30713 Fd		M8	3/09 Day's Rental, Swansea (YCW)		9/10
MV64002 CN 06 ERV	MB	311CDI	WDB9036622R911995	O&H -?-	M10L	6/06 new		6/06
CN 55 AKG	MB	411CDI	WDB9046122R819449 ?		M16L	9/05 new		9/05
CN 55 AKJ	MB	411CDI	WDB9046122R823178 ?		M16L	9/05 new		9/05

PEMBROKESHIRE COUNCIL (continued)

CN 06 BZU	MB		411CDIWDB9046632R892482	UVM -?-	B1FL	3/06 new		3/06
CU 58 CHF	Fd	Tt	WF0DXXTTFD8D65236	Fd	M16	9/08 new		9/08
CU 58 CUG	Io	35C12	ZCFC3584005706829	?	B??F	9/08 new		9/08
CU 58 CUH	Ibs	50C15	ZCFC50A2005726161	?	B16F	9/08 new		9/08
CU 58 CUX	Ibs	50C15	ZCFC50A2005726163	?	B16F	9/08 new		9/08
YP 59 OCU	Fd	Tt	WF0DXXTTFD9C80482	Fd	M16	10/09 -?-, -?-		1/14
CN 13 AOA	MB		513CDI WDB9066572S758495	?	B15FL	3/13 new		3/13
CN 13 AOB	MB		513CDI WDB9066572S758494	?	B15FL	3/13 new		3/13
CV 13 BVB	Fd	Tt	WF0DXXTTFDDJ37819	Fd	M16	5/13 new		5/13
YX 13 BWM	Ft	Do	ZFA25000002335868	Blbd	B16F	5/13 new		5/13
YX 13 BWN	Ft	Do	ZFA25000002354011	Bbld -?-	B16F	5/13 new		5/13
CU 63 DJZ	Fd	Tt	WF0DXXTTFDDM12507	Fd	M16	9/13 new		9/13
CU 63 DYG	Fd	Tt	WF0DXXTTFDDG31200	Fd	M16	9/13 new		9/13
CP 15 DWE	Fd	Tt	WF0HXXTTGHFL64933	Fd	M16	6/15 new		6/15

PEMBROKESHIRE VOLUNTARY TRANSPORT, 'Puffins', 9 Cedar Close, East Moor Park, CUFFERN, Pembrokeshire, SA62 6HR.

VE 06 KKJ	Rt	Mtr	VF1FDCUL635996004	?	M??	7/06 new	7/06
WA 58 GFK	Rt	Mtr	VF1FDC1L640390229	Csd	M12L	10/08 -?-, -?-	12/12
WX 12 CGY	Rt	Mtr	VF1MAF4DR47161739	Csd	M11L	7/12 new	7/12
BX 13 SYP	Rt	Mtr	VF1MAF4BE48321958	?	M13L	4/13 new	4/13

PENDARREN HOUSE, Pursuits CENTRE, LLANGENNY, Crickhowell, Powys, NP8 1HE.

HJ 02 HDX	Fd	Tt	WF0LXXGBFL1U43167	RKC	M16	3/02 new	3/02
YN 59 BLF	MB	O813D	WDB6703742N135214	Pn -?-	B28FL	9/09 new	9/09
HJ 12 TFO	Fd	Tt	WF0DXXTTFDBU70785	RKC	M16	3/12 new	3/12
CE 14 WPD	Fd	Tt	WF0DXXTTFDDD18415	Fd	M16	4/14 ewn	4/14
EJ 15 NYK	Fd	Tt	WF0HXXTTGHFE54817	Fd	M16	6/15 new	5/15

PENGLAIS HIGH SCHOOL, Waun Fawr, ABERYSTWYTH, Ceredigion, SY23 3AW.

HY 57 UME	Pt	Bxr	VF3YCDMFC11127089	RKC	M16	9/07 new	9/07

PENIEL GREEN CARE HOME, 216 Peniel Green Road, LLANSAMLET, Swansea, SA7 9BD.

PENMAES SCHOOL, Canal Road, BRECON, Powys, LD3 7HL.

GX 57 DXB	Fd	Tt	WF0XXXTTFX7Y04184	?	M??	12/07 new	12/07
GN 62 BXB	Ft	Do	ZFA25000002246807	Eurm	M16L	11/12 new	11/12

PENYRHEOL COMPREHENSIVE SCHOOL, Pontarddulais Road, GORSEINON, Swansea, SA4 4FG.

HJ 55 KPZ	Pt	Bxr	VF3ZCPMNC17668823	?	M16	9/05 new	9/05

PLAS PENCELLI OUTDOOR CENTRE, Pencelli, BRECON, Powys, LD3 7LX.

YP 58 YLK	Fd	Tt	WF0DXXTTFD8S49649	Fd	M14	2/09 new	2/09
YP 61 PZK	Fd	Tt	WF0DXXTTFDBT24442	Fd	M15	12/11 new	12/11
CE 12 BAO	Fd	Tt	WF0DXXTTFDBT37415	Fd	M16	4/12 new	4/12
CE 12 BBK	Fd	Tt	WF0DXXTTFDBP37424	Fd	M16	3/12 new	3/12

POWYS County COUNCIL, County Hall, Llandrindod Wells.

X 68 KKG	MB	815L	WDB9702232K508180	?	ML	2/01 new	2/01
Y947 GEU	Rt	Mtr	VF1FDCCL524725845	Csd -?-	M12L	3/01 new	3/01
CN 03 MWA	MB	814D	WDB6703232N107618	?	ML	4/03 new	4/03
AE 53 KWJ	LDV	Cy	SEYZMVSZGDN098742	LDV	M16	10/03 Hertz (Y)	9/05
DX 53 HFO	LDV	Cy	SEYZMVSZGDN099827	LDV	M16	12/03 new	12/03
CN 04 BUW	MB	814D	WDB6703232N111699	?	ML	3/04 new	3/04
CV 04 VLJ	MB	311CDI	WDB9036622R641497	?	M9L	3/04 new	3/04
WD 04 WUK	Fd	Tt	WF0EXXGBFE4B86609	Fd	M16	7/04 -?-, -?-	4/07
CU 54 JPO	Io	40C13	ZCFC459000D260295	?	M16	1/05 new	1/05
CU 54 JYC	Io	40C13	ZCFC459000D260296	?	M16	1/05 new	1/05
CU 54 JYP	Io	40C13	ZCFC459000D260297	?	M16	1/05 new	1/05
CN 06 EOU	MB	814D	WDB6703232N121590	?	ML	4/06 new	4/06
CU 06 BWZ	Io	45C14	ZCFC45A1005575754	?	M16L	3/06 new	3/06
WA 06 HNU	Rt	Mtr	VF1FDCUL635393868	?	M10	4/06 new	4/06
CU 57 EVX	Io	45C15	ZCFC45A200S350892	Eurm 15121	M16	9/07 new	9/07

POWYS COUNCIL (continued)

PN 57 HYB	Rt	Mtr	VF1FDC1L638017546 O&H -?-	M12L	10/07 new		10/07
PN 57 HYC	Rt	Mtr	VF1FDC1L638017541 O&H -?-	M12L	10/07 new		10/07
PN 57 HYF	Rt	Mtr	VF1FDC1L638017538 O&H -?-	M12L	10/07 new		10/07
PN 57 HYG	Rt	Mtr	VF1FDC1L638017535 O&H -?-	M12L	10/07 new		10/07
CE 08 FJC	Ctn	Rly	VF7YDBMFC11410745 ?	M10	5/08 new		5/08
CU 58 CJY	lo	50C15	ZCFC50A200D395069 ?	M11L	9/08 new		9/08
CU 58 CNJ	lo	50C15	ZCFC50A200D395070 ?	M2L	1/09 new		1/09
YS 09 FYH	Fd	Tt	WF0DXXTTFD9B12392 Fd	M14	7/09 new		7/09
CN 10 AWG	MB	513CDI	WDB9061552N425101 UVM -?-	B15FL	7/10 new		7/10
CN 12 CWU	MB	513CDI	WDB9061552N511682 Treka -?-	B15FL	3/12 new		3/12
CN 12 CWV	MB	513CDI	WDB9061552N511282 Treka -?-	B15FL	3/12 new		3/12

POWYS Transport TRAINING Agency (Minibus Training & Hire), Unit 30, Ddole Road Enterprise Park, LLANDRINDOD WELLS, Powys, LD1 6DF.

LD 09 CXW	Ctn	Rly	VF7YDBMFC11624813 Csd -?-	M15	5/09 new	5/09

PRESELI COMMUNITY TRANSPORT, The Old School, BWLCHYGROES, Llanfyrnach, Pembrokeshire, SA35 0DP.

Y356 BGD	VW	LT46	WV1ZZZ2DZ2H001421 FGy -?-	M15L	8/01 Glasgow City Council (XSW)	5/08
CN 07 CBO	MB	511CDI	WDB9066552S132066 O&H -?-	M??L	3/07 new	3/07
CN 08 HJX	MB	511CDI	WDB9066552S309962 O&H -?-	M14L	8/08 new	8/08
MX 11 JJU	Rt	Mtr	VF1MAFFDC44688647 VCL	M??L	4/11 new	4/11

RECTORAL BENEFICE OF TENBY, The Rectory, Church Park, Tenby, Pembrokeshire, SA70 7EE.

CN 07 RYF	Rt	Mtr	VF1NDD1L637577628 Rt	M15	5/07 -?-, -?-	12/07

RHAYADER COMMUNITY SUPPORT Links, The Arches, West Street, RHAYADER, Powys.

PK 54 RZD	Pt	Bxr	VF3ZCPMNC17487440 ?	M14L	10/04 -?-, -?-	by12/10

RHYDYGORS Special SCHOOL, Llansteffan Road, Johnston, CARMARTHEN, Carmarthenshire, SA31 3QU.

764025	HG 04 LZD	Fd	Tt	WF0EXXGBFE4B88625 Fd	M16	3/04 -?-, -?-	8/04

RIVER STROKES Kayak SCHOOL, Unit 1 Greenfields Business Park, HAY-ON-WYE, Powys, HR3 5FA.

ST HELENS PRIMARY School, Vincent Street, Sandfields, SWANSEA, SA1 3TY.

ST JOHN LLOYD SCHOOL, Havard Road, LLANELLI, Carmarthenshire, SA14 8SD.

X312 CTH	LDV	Cy	SEYZMVSHEDN064077 LDV	M16	11/00 Carmarthenshire Council		
						(XCW) 764030	9/09

ST JOSEPH'S CATHEDRAL SCHOOL, Caepistyll Street, SWANSEA, SA1 2BE.

CV 59 JOU	Fd	Tt	WF0DXXTTFD9R32654 Fd	M16	9/09 new	9/09
CP 12 LDE	Fd	Tt	WF0DXXTTFDCC52070 Fd	M16	7/12 Day's Rental, Swansea (YCW)	5/13
HJ 15 NNL	Fd	Tt	WF0HXXTTGHEM52728 Fd	M16	4/15 new	4/15

STAYLITTLE OUTDOOR CENTRE, STAYLITTLE VILLAGE, LLanbrynmair, Powys, SY19 7BU.

YD 07 HNG	Vc	Mov	VF7233J55215115792 Autotrim	M16	8/95 -?-, -?-	by3/11
CP 09 AXJ	Fd	Tt	WF0DXXTTFD8S45455 Fd	M16	5/09 -?-, -?-	by3/11

SWANSEA CITY COUNCIL, County Hall, Swansea.
OC: Swansea West Business Park, Kingsway, Fforestfach, Swansea.

123	CP 08 UCS	Fd	Tt	WF0DXXTTFD8C22911 Fd	M16	6/08 new	6/08
1169	CV 09 TYU	Fd	Tt	WF0DXXTTFD8S44174 Fd	M16	4/09 new	4/09
1191	CV 59 JPO	Fd	Tt	WF0DXXTTFD9R32551 Fd	M16	9/09 new	9/09
1192	CV 59 JNU	Fd	Tt	WF0DXXTTFD9R32628 Fd	M16	9/09 new	9/09
1217	CP 59 VEX	Fd	Tt	WF0DXXTTFD9E48150 Fd	M16	2/10 new	2/10
1221	CP 59 WGG	Fd	Tt	WF0DXXTTFD9E48581 Fd	M16	2/10 new	2/10
1222	CP 59 TXX	Fd	Tt	WF0DXXTTFD9E41614 Fd	M16	2/10 new	2/10
1223	CP 59 HHL	Fd	Tt	WF0DXXTTFD9E48640 Fd	M16	2/10 new	2/10
1224	CP 59 UAZ	Fd	Tt	WF0DXXTTFD9E48610 Fd	M16	2/10 new	2/10
1271	CP 10 JZD	Fd	Tt	WF0DXXTTFDAT21975 Fd	M16	6/10 new	6/10
1303	GN 57 CLV	lo	45C15	ZCFC45A200D331259 ?	B16F	9/07 new	9/07
1304	GX 09 KBF	Fd	Tt	WF0XXXTTFX9M76951 ?	M16	6/09 new	6/09

SWANSEA COUNCIL (continued)

1307 CU 10 BZJ	Ibs	CC150E.25	ZCFA1LJ0302512373	Vxl	B--F	3/10	new		3/10
				(playbus)					
1315 CV 52 HHJ	LDV	Cy	SEYZMVSZGDN089271	LDV	M16	1/03	new		1/03
1316 GX 07 FHR	Fd	Tt	WF0XXXTTFX7C62668	?	M16	3/07	new		3/07
1322 CP 64 NZT	Fd	Tt	WF0HXXTTGHEG49445	Fd	M16	2/15	-?-, -?-		1/16
1330 CP 60 ANX	Fd	Tt	WF0DXXTTFDAB28356	Fd	M16	11/10	new		11/10
1353 CT 60 HRX	Fd	Tt	WF0DXXTTFDAA66999	Fd	M16	1/11	-?-, -?-		2/16
1354 CV 11 EYP	Fd	Tt	WF0DXXTTFDAA67157	Fd	M16	3/11	-?-, -?-		4/13
1355 CK 04 VYY	Fd	Tt	WF0EXXGBFE4B86514	Fd	M16	4/04	new		4/05
1356 BX 59 LZE	Rt	Tc	VF1FLAHA69V355475	Rt	M8	10/09	-?-, -?-		5/15
1359 CU 56 ATN	Rt	Mtr	VF1FDCML636364696	?	M8L	11/06	new		11/06
1360 CU 07 ARZ	Rt	Mtr	VF1FDC1L637245974	?	M11L	5/07	new		5/07
1361 CN 61 DFA	MB	513CDI	WDB9066572S598321	Eurm -?-	M15L	10/11	new		10/11
1362 CN 61 DFK	MB	513CDI	WDB9066572S598787	Eurm -?-	M15L	10/11	new		10/11
1363 CN 61 DFC	MB	513CDI	WDB9066572S598792	Eurm -?-	M15L	10/11	new		10/11
1364 CN 61 DFL	MB	513CDI	WDB9066572S598790	Eurm -?-	M15L	10/11	new		10/11
1365 CN 61 DFO	MB	513CDI	WDB9066572S598788	Eurm	M3L	10/11	new		10/11
1366 CN 61 DFD	MB	513CDI	WDB9066572S598791	Eurm -?-	M15L	10/11	new		10/11
1367 CN 61 DFE	MB	513CDI	WDB9066572S598789	Eurm -?-	M15L	10/11	new		10/11
1368 CN 61 DFJ	MB	513CDI	WDB9066572S600224	Eurm -?-	M15L	10/11	new		10/11
1369 CN 61 DFG	MB	513CDI	WDB9066572S601941	Eurm -?-	M15L	10/11	new		10/11
1370 CN 61 DFF	MB	513CDI	WDB9066572S600225	?	M15L	10/11	new		10/11
1371 CU 61 AXF	Io	50C14	ZCFC50A310D452596	?	B15FL	10/11	new		10/11
1372 CU 61 AXG	Io	50C14	ZCFC50A310D452597	?	B15FL	10/11	new		10/11
1374 CP 61 SJX	Fd	Tt	WF0BXXVDFBCR29712	Fd	M8	2/12	new		2/12
1378 CV 60 FYW	Fd	Tt	WF0DXXTTFDAM79283	Fd	M16	9/10	Neath Port Talbot Council	
								(XCC) H3549	9/12
1418 CU 09 HFK	VW	Crf	WV1ZZZ2EZ96016546	Brecon	M15L	3/09	new		3/09
1420 CU 09 HFM	VW	Crf	WV1ZZZ2EZ96015496	Brecon	M15L	3/09	new		3/09
1421 CU 09 HFN	VW	Crf	WV1ZZZ2EZ96017729	Brecon	M15L	3/09	new		3/09
1422 CU 09 HFO	VW	Crf	WV1ZZZ2EZ96015505	Brecon	M15L	3/09	new		3/09
1424 CU 09 HFR	VW	Crf	WV1ZZZ2EZ96019999	Brecon	M15L	5/09	new		5/09
1425 CU 09 HFV	VW	Crf	WV1ZZZ2EZ96017685	Brecon	M15L	3/09	new		3/09
1427 CU 09 HFS	VW	Crf	WV1ZZZ2EZ96017502	Brecon	M15L	5/09	new		5/09
1429 CU 09 HFP	VW	Crf	WV1ZZZ2EZ96017326	?	M15L	5/09	new		5/09
1440 CU 56 ACZ	Rt	Mtr	VF1FDCUL635997398	?	M12	9/06	new		9/06
1441 CU 56 ACY	Rt	Mtr	VF1FDCUL635997353	O&H -?-	M11L	3/06	new		3/06
1446 CP 05 CWF	Ctn	Rly	VF7ZBPMNB17543410	Tawe	M8L	4/05	new		4/05
1447 CP 05 CWG	Ctn	Rly	VF7ZCPMNC17554539	Tawe	M14L	4/05	new		4/05
1477 CV 12 CMY	Fd	Tt	WF0DXXTTFDBP15776	Fd	M16	5/12	-?-, -?-		11/14
1489 WA 13 FSO	Ctn	Rly	VF7YCTNFC12382086	Csd	M8L	6/13	new		6/13
1498 WA 13 FSS	Ctn	Rly	VF7YCTMFC12378076	Csd	M8L	6/13	new		6/13
1499 WA 13 FSP	Ctn	Rly	VF7YCTMFC12378033	Csd	M8L	6/13	new		6/13
1526 HV 03 SXX	Fd	Tt	WF0EXXGBFE2A21210	Fd	M16	3/03	SHB Self Drive,	
								Southampton (YHA)	8/13
1540 CU 13 EUK	Ibs	50C15	ZCFC50A4205953978	?	B15FL	8/13	new		8/13
1541 CU 13 EUJ	Ibs	50C15	ZCFC50A4205953805	?	M15L	8/13	NEW		8/13
1544 CU 13 EUE	Ibs	50C15	ZCFC50A4205953804	?	B15FL	8/13	new		8/13
1545 CU 13 EUF	Ibs	50C15	ZCFC50A4205953977	?	B15FL	8/13	new		8/13
1546 CU 13 EUH	Ibs	50C15	ZCFC50A4205954344	?	B??F	8/13	new		6/13
1549 CU 13 EUC	Ibs	50C15	ZCFC50A4205954121	?	B15FL	8/13	new		8/13
1552 CU 63 DPY	Fd	Tt	WF0DXXTTFDDB62713	Fd	M16	9/13	new		9/13
1553 CV 63 HRD	Ibs	50C15	ZCFC50A4205958178	?	B15FL	9/13	new		9/13
1565 CU 02 ZCJ	VW	Tr	WV1ZZZ70Z1H154963	Cym-?-	M8L	5/02	new		5/02
1567 CV 63 HRJ	Ibs	50C15	ZCFC50A4205958412	?	B15FL	9/13	new		9/13
1568 CV 52 GXL	Rt	Mtr	VF1PDMML527614153	?	M13L	12/02	-?-, -?-		12/10
1575 CV 63 HRF	Ibs	50C15	ZCFC50A4205958879	?	B15FL	10/13	new		10/13
1598 CV 63 HRE	Ibs	50C15	ZCFC50A4205958618	?	B15FL	9/13	new		9/13
1802 CU 63 DXY	Fd	Tt	WF0DXXTTFDDG31163	Fd	M16	10/13	-?-, -?-		8/14
1803 CV 63 HRG	Ibs	50C15	ZCFC50A4205959120	?	B15FL	10/13	new		10/13
1813 CV 63 SWN	Fd	Tt	WF0DXXTTFDDK83561	Fd	M16	1/14	-?-, -?-		3/15
1815 CV 60 OGN	Fd	Tt	WF0DXXTTFDAU76736	Fd	M16	9/10	-?-, -?-		4/14
1818 CV 06 DXR	Fd	Tt	WF0EXXTTFE5C79232	Fd	M16	3/06	Day's Rental, Swansea (YCW)	3/08

SWANSEA COUNCIL (continued)

1820 BX 58 OLC	LDV	Max	SEYL6RXH21N230886	LDV	M16	10/08	Europcar (Y)	4/14
1821 GX 09 JYK	Fd	Tt	WF0XXXTTFX9J63510	?	M16	4/09	new	4/09
1822 GU 52 RNY	Fd	Tt	WF0LXXGBFL2J88562	?	M16	9/02	new	9/02
1830 CP 14 LAO	lo	50C15	ZCFC50A400D526235	?	B15FL	8/14	new	8/14
1840 CU 65 PDO	lo	50C15	ZCFC150A305052587	?	B15FL	12/15	new	12/15
1844 CU 65 ORO	Fd	Tt	WF0HXXTTGHFL75475	Fd	M16	9/15	new	9/15
1845 CU 65 OSO	Fd	Tt	WF0HXXTTGHFL75503	Fd	M16	9/15	new	9/15
1850 CU 65 BJK	lo	50C15	ZCFC150A005067645	Eurm -?-	M14L	1/16	new	1/16
1851 CU 65 BJO	lo	50C15	ZCFC150A505067642	Eurm -?-	M14L	1/16	new	1/16
1852 CU 65 BJX	lo	50C15	ZCFC150A905067644	Eurm -?-	M14L	2/16	new	2/16
1853 CU 65 BJV	lo	50C15	ZCFC150A705067643	Eurm -?-	M14L	1/16	new	1/16
1854 CU 65 BJY	lo	50C15	ZCFC150A205067646	Eurm -?-	M14L	2/16	new	2/16
1855 CV 16 HJD	lo	50C15	-?-	Eurm -?-	M14L	3/16	new	3/16
1856 CV 16 HJG	lo	50C15	ZCFC150A005069430	Eurm -?-	M15L	3/16	new	1/16
1857 CV 16 HJJ	lo	50C15	ZCFC150A405069429	Eurm -?-	M14L	3/16	new	3/16
1858 CV 16 HJE	lo	50C15	ZCFC150A405069432	Eurm -?-	M14L	3/16	new	3/16
1859 CV 16 HJF	lo	50C15	ZCFC150A205069431	Eurm -?-	M15L	3/16	ewn	3/16
1862 CU 14 MLE	Fd	Tt	WF01XXTTG1EL49026	Fd	M8	3/14	-?-, -?-	4/16
AF 53 EUU	MAN	14.220	WMAA66ZZZ3H002815	MCV MCV-002 (playbus)	B--F	11/03	Simonds, Diss (NK)	8/10
CU 09 HFT	VW	Crf	WV1ZZZ2EZ96015495	Brecon	M15L	3/09	new	3/09

SWANSEA CITY FOOTBALL CLUB, Liberty Stadium, Landore, Swansea, SA1 2FA.

CP 12 KZA	Fd	Tt	WF0DXXTTFDCC51774	Fd	M16	7/12	Day's Rental, Swansea (YCW)	by5/13

SWANSEA SILVER RHYTHMAIRES JAZZ BAND, WINCH WEN, Swansea.

K200 SSR	Ds	Jv	12SDA2159/1295 Pn 9512HCP4331		C49FT	1/96	Rigby, Altham (LA)	10/12
			(ex N300 EST 10/12)					

SWANSEA UNIVERSITY COLLEGE OF MEDICINE, Grove Building, Swansea University, Singleton Park, Swansea, SA2 8PP.

MJ 12 LZG	Fd	Tt	WF0DXXTTFDCG28139	?	M16	5/12	new	5/12
MJ 12 LZR	Fd	Tt	WF0DXXTTFDCG28143	?	M16	5/12	new	5/12

THE BUS STOP (static café), Ferry Terminal, PEMBROKE DOCK, Pembrokeshire.

TWN 933S	Bl	VRT/SL3/501	VRT/SL3/1363 ECW 23233		H--/--F	5/78	Greens Motors, Haverfordwest (CW)	c6/11

THE PRINCE's TRUST, PEMBROKE DOCK, Pembrokeshire.

DN 11 MXE	Fd	Tt	WF0DXXTTFDBC30156	Fd	M16	4/11	new	4/11

TIRABAD Residential Education CENTRE, LLANGAMMARCH WELLS, Powys, LD4 4DS.

HG 09 UCW	Fd	Tt	WF0DXXTTFD9B04843	Fd	M16	8/09	enw	8/09
HG 09 ZTX	Fd	Tt	WF0DXXTTFD9B04786	Fd	M16	9/09	new	9/09
HG 09 ZTY	Fd	Tt	WF0DXXTTFD9B05136	Fd	M16	9/09	new	9/09

TORESTIN Residential & CARE HOME, TIERS CROSS, Pembrokeshire, SA62 3DB.

FN 54 EXZ	Rt	Mtr	VF1FDBVE532355975	?	M2L	11/04	-?-, -?-	2/09

TREBOETH GOSPEL HALL, 788-790 Llangyfelach Road, TREBOETH, Swansea, SA5 9EH.

CT 60 HNF	Fd	Tt	WF0DXXTTFDAA78998	Fd	M16	1/11	Day's Rental, Swansea (YCW)	8/16

TY MAIR CARE HOME, 12 Y-Gaer, LLANELLI, Carmarthenshire, SA14 8AG.

B 12 TYM	LDV	Cy	SEYZMVSZGDN089329	?	M16	9/02	Swansea Industrial Components, Penclawdd (YCW)	8/05
			(ex CV 52 HGY 8/05)					

UNIVERSITY OF WALES TRINITY ST DAVID, Mount Pleasant, SWANSEA, SA1 6ED.
OCs: as address; College Road, Carmarthen, Carmarthenshire, SA31 3EP; College Street, Lampeter, Ceredigion, SA48 7ED.

NU 09 LWF	Fd	Tt	WF0DXXTTFD9P87116 Fd		M16	5/09	new	5/09
YR 62 OLJ	Fd	Tt	WF0DXXTTFDCL35258 Fd		M16	11/12	new	11/12
YR 62 OLM	Fd	Tt	WF0DXXTTFDCL35223 Fd		M16	11/12	new	11/12
YT 62 RZU	Fd	Tt	WF0DXXTTFDCK61476 Fd		M16	9/12	new	9/12

Gwersyll URDD GOBAITH CYMRU, LLANGRANNOG (Welsh League of Youth Holiday Centre), Sgio, Llangrannog, Ceredigion, SA44 6AE.

HN 05 NLR	Fd	Tt	WF0EXXTTFE5U42074 Fd		M16	4/05	-?-, -?-	4/09

USK HOUSE Day HOSPICE, Bridge Street, Llanfaes, BRECON, Powys, LD3 8AH.

CE 08 FJA	Ctn	Rly	VF7YDBMFC11360328 ?		M??	4/08	new	4/08

VALERO ENERGY, Pembroke Oil Refinery, MILFORD HAVEN, Pembrokeshire, SA71 5SJ.

R837 PRG	Vo	B10BLE	YV3R4A518WA004000 Wt	A8	B44F	4/98	Go Northern (TW) 4837	8/14
R849 PRG	Vo	B10BLE	YV3R4A517WA004120 Wt	A98	B44F	4/98	Go North East (TW) 4849	8/14
R620 VEG	Ds	Dt SLF	SFD212BR1WGW12172 MI	C39.223	B31F	5/98	Ensign, Purfleet (EX) 720	5/12
X226 FBB	Ds	Dt SLF	SFD466BR1YGW35404 Pn	0011.3HAB3394	B41F	1/01	Go Northern (TW) 8226	8/14
Y154 NLK	Ds	Dt SLF	SFD212AR11GW15723 Pn	0110.1HJB4060	B30D	6/01	Metroline (LN) DLD190	11/11
Y159 NLK	Ds	Dt SLF	SFD212AR11GW15729 Pn	0110.1HJB4144	B30D	6/01	Metroline (LN) DLD196	11/11
Y261 NLK	Ds	Dt SLF	SFD212AR11GW15725 Pn	0110.1HJB4139	B30D	7/01	Metroline (LN) DLD191	11/11
Y263 NLK	Ds	Dt SLF	SFD212AR11GW15726 Pn	0110.1HJB4141	B30D	7/01	Metroline (LN) DLD193	11/11
Y265 NLK	Ds	Dt SLF	SFD212AR11GW15728 Pn	0110.1HJB4143	B30D	7/01	Metroline (LN) DLD195	11/11
NK 51 MKN	Ds	Dt SLF	SFD466BR11GW45908 Ar	0130/6	B41F	11/01	Go North East (TW) 8239	8/14

WELSH Regional VETERINARY CENTRE, Gelli Aur/Golden Grove College, CARMARTHEN, Carmarthenshire, SA32 8NJ.

LM 54 PLX	VW	Tr	WV2ZZZ7HZ5X015320 ?		M8	1/05	-?-, -?-	9/07

WEST STREET CHRISTIAN CENTRE, West Street, GORSEINON, Swanasea, SA4 4AF.

Y863 LHU	Fd	Tt	WF0EXXGBFE1B51557 Fd		M14	5/01	-?-, -?-	2/16

WEST WALES AMBULANCE, 26 Commercial Row, PEMBROKE DOCK, Pembrokeshire, SA72 6JN.

Glyn WILLIAMS, PENTWYNMAWR.

S148 KNK	Vo	OLY-50	YV3YNA411WC029092 NC	6272	H--/--F	8/98	Souter Foundation, Perth (XSE)	3/15

WOODLANDS Outdoor EDUCATION CENTRE, GLASBURY ON WYE, Powys, HR3 5LP.

WA 57 PZT	VW	Crf	WV1ZZZ2EZ86021990 ?		M16	1/08	new	1/08
WA 08 PFG	VW	Crf	WV1ZZZ2EZ86031416 ?		M16	6/08	new	6/08
WA 09 MJJ	VW	Crf	WV1ZZZ2EZ96034082 ?		M16	6/09	new	6/09

Y RHALLT Care HOME, Salop Road, WELSHPOOL, Powys, SY21 7DJ.

YMCA Outdoor Education Centre, Pen-y-Cwm, Brawdy, NEWGALE, Pembrokeshire, SA62 6LA.

YSGOL BRO DINEFWR, Heol Myrddin, FFAIRFACH, Llandeilo, Carmarthenshire, SA19 6PD.

766066 GX 60 RJZ	Fd	Tt	WF0DXXTTFDAR56072 Fd		M16	12/10	Ysgol Tre-Gib, Ffairfach (XCW)	9/16

YSGOL BRO GWAUN, Heol Dyfed, FISHGUARD, Pembrokeshire, SA65 9DT.

GN 55 OEL	Io	45C11	ZCFC45A100D272025 Eurm	-?-	M12L	11/05	new	11/05

YSGOL BRO PEDR, Peterwell Terrace, LAMPETER, Ceredigion, SA48 7BX.

YSGOL BRO TEIFI, B4624, LLANDYSUL, Ceredigion, SA44 4JN.

YSGOL CEDEWAIN, Plantation Lane, NEWTOWN, Powys, SY16 1LH.

YSGOL CRUG GLAS Special School, Croft Street, SWANSEA, SA1 1QA.

6635 GK 52 GXB	Io	40C11	ZCFC407100B153922 ?		M14	10/02	-?-, -?-	10/04

YSGOL DYFFRYN AMAN, Margaret Street, Ammanford, Carmarthenshire, SA18 2NW.

764069 CN 58 AFE	MB	511CDI	WDB9066552S314175	O&H -?-	M15L	9/08 new		9/08
764079 CN 11 AZP	MB	313CDI	WDB9066352S558465	MB	M16	5/11 new		5/11

YSGOL GYFUN GYMUNEDOL PENWEDDIG, Ffordd Llanbadarn, Llangawsai, ABERYSTWYTH, Ceredigion, SY23 3QN.

YSGOL GYFUN EMLYN, NEWCASTLE EMLYN, Carmarthenshire SA38 9LN.

BV 07 FHU	Fd	Tt	WF0DXXTTFD7K02577	Fd	M16	4/07 Carmarthenshire Council		
						(XCW) 764066	11/10

YSGOL GYFUN GWYR, Talbot Street, Gowerton, SWANSEA, SA4 3DB.

1331 CP 60 ANR	Fd	Tt	WF0DXXTTFDAB29112	Fd	M16	11/10 new	11/10

YSGOL GYMUNEDOL CWMTAWE (Cwmtawe Community School), Parc Ynysderw, Ffordd Parc, Ynysderw Road, PONTARDAWE, Swansea SA8 4EG.

CU 04 HKJ	Fd	Tt	WF0EXXGBFE3M36957	Fd	M16	5/04 Neath Port Talbot Council	
						(XCC) S12 by3/14	

YSGOL GYNRADD GYMRAEG LON LAS, Walters Road, LLANSAMLET, Swansea, SA7 9RW.

HF 52 YST	Pt	Bxr	VF3ZCPMNC17131368	RKC	M16	11/02 Royal Welch Fusiliers ACF,	
						Kinmel Bay (XCN)	11/09

YSGOL HENRY RICHARD, Lampeter Road, Tegfan, Tregaron, Ceredigion, SY26 6HG.

3749 CU 04 LXA	VW	LT46	WV1ZZZ2DZ5H001712	Tawe	M14L	8/04 Ceredigion Council (XCW)	3/13

YSGOL MAESYDDERWEN, Tudor Street, YSTRADGYNLAIS, Swansea, SA9 1AP.

X357 JKJ	Fd	Tt	WF0LXXBDVLYC06875	?	M12L	10/00 new	10/00

YSGOL NANT-Y-CWM, LLANYCEFN, Clunderwen, Carmarthenshire, SA66 7QJ.

YSGOL NANTGAREDIG, Station Road, NANTGAREDIG, Carmarthenshire, SA32 7LG.

CV 11 HRN	Fd	Tt	WF0DXXTTFDAU75618	Fd	M14	3/11 Day's Rental, Swansea (YCW)	7/13

YSGOL UWCHRADD ABERTEIFI, Park Place, CARDIGAN, Ceredigion, SA43 1AD.

YSGOL Y FELIN, Ynyswen, FELINFOEL, Carmarthenshire, SA14 8BE.

BX 58 OCZ	LDV	Max	SEYL6RXH21N229396	LDV	M16	9/08 National Car Rental (Y)	3/13
CP 62 GNK	Fd	Tt	WF0DXXTTFDCY61146	Fd	M16	11/12 new	11/12

YSTRADGYNLAIS COMMUNITY CAR SCHEME, 3 Temperance Lane, YSTRADGYNLAIS, Powys, SA9 1JP.

YSTRADOWEN COMMUNITY CENTRE, 38 New Road, CYMLLYNFELL, Swansea, SA9 2YY.

KP 62 TGU	Fd	Tt	WF0DXXTTFDCY69156	Fd	M16	10/12 -?-, -?-	5/13

YSTWYTH COMMUNITY TRANSPORT GROUP (Community Bus Licence CB000297) Lisburne House, PONTRHYDYGROES, Ceredigion, SY25 6DQ.

CU 05 FTJ	VW	LT46	WV1ZZZ2DZ5H023769	Tawe	M10L	5/05 Ceredigion Council	
						(XCW) 3755 by7/13	
BX 55 CXC	MB	410CDI	WDB9046632R808678	?	M14L	9/05 -?-, -?-	1/11
SF 10 NRJ	VW	Crf	WV1ZZZ2EZA6016641	Verve	M15L	8/10 Glasgow City Council	
						(XSW) 204G	5/15
CN 60 FGD	VW	Crf	WV1ZZZ2EZB6013305	?	M??	1/11 -?-, -?-	2/13
CU 60 UJV	VW	Crf	WV1ZZZ2EZB6013729	?	M11L	1/11 new	1/11
SF 11 FYS	Pt	Bxr	VF3YCBMFC11393516	?	M12	4/11 -?-, -?-	by3/13
WA 14 GGZ	Pt	Bxr	VF3YETMFC12513091	GM	M16	4/14 new	4/14
WA 14 GHK	Pt	Bxr	VF3YETMFC12516202	GM	M16	4/14 new	4/14

-?-, LLANELLI area.

CU 03 BGY	Rt	Mtr	VF1PDMUL528817337	O&H -?-	M?	8/03 Foothold, Llanelli (XCW)	9/14

-?- SCHOOL, SWANSEA area.

GX 10 HVL	Fd	Tt	WF0XXXTTFXAS10205	Fd	M16L	6/10 new	6/10

MID & WEST WALES (CW) - REGISTRATION / PAGE NUMBER INDEX

REGISTRATION / PAGE NUMBER INDEX (continued)

REGISTRATION / PAGE NUMBER INDEX (continued)

REGISTRATION / PAGE NUMBER INDEX (continued)

WX 03 DYN 48	MP 53 ZBY 24	HG 04 HVS 64	CU 54 HYN 29	CU 05 FTN 77	YU 05 ZKE 18
WX 03 JDK 13	MX 53 ZWD 11	HG 04 LZD 80	CU 54 HYO 29	CU 05 FYX 13	YU 05 ZKR 18
WX 03 ZFG 4	NA 53 BZF 14	KE 04 JVH 13	CU 54 HYP 29	CU 05 HPZ 13	YX 05 AVU 4
YH 53 GHO 50	PJ 53 OEP 77	KT 04 BUS 50	CU 54 HYR 29	DK 05 OGB 19	YX 05 DJK 63
YJ 03 UML 55	PO 53 OXF 37	LK 04 KYY 48	CU 54 HYT 29	DU 05 FMZ 37	
YJ 03 WXG 49	RG 53 GSV 26	LL 04 CEL 14	CU 54 HYV 29	DX 05 ZKT 36	AE 55 EBM 74
YK 03 OAD 48	RG 53 GXA 12	LS 04 UPE 24	CU 54 HYW 29	DY 05 OFP 64	AE 55 NLF 57
YN 03 OXK 59	RK 53 EHH 22	MT 04 EHC 40	CU 54 HYX 29	FF 05 BUS 27	BC 55 TAF 11
YN 03 ULC 54	SN 53 ESU 30	MV 04 SZC 50	CU 54 HYY 29	FH 05 OYE 12	BT 55 LUH 5
YR 03 KPH 5	SN 53 ESV 30	MX 04 ULP 19	CU 54 HYZ 29	FL 05 ETO 15	BW 55 WYN 25
YV 03 YVF 18	SN 53 ESY 30	NC 04 TJZ 22	CU 54 HZA 29	FX 05 GCO 50	BX 55 CXC 84
YX 03 FCN 39	SN 53 ETD 30	NE 04 FOF 15	CU 54 HZB 29	FY 05 UBL 7	BX 55 FYD 6
	SN 53 ETE 30	PE 54 YYU 71	CU 54 JPO 79	GF 05 MEV 23	BX 55 NZP 19
AD 53 PZA 49	SN 53 ETF 30	PL 04 LFR 59	CU 54 JYC 79	GN 05 LMV 78	BX 55 NZR 19
AE 53 KWJ 79	SN 53 ETR 56	PN 04 UXE 63	CU 54 JYP 79	HF 05 JPY 37	BX 55 OGJ 48
AF 53 EUU 82	SN 53 KKZ 63	RX 04 SXR 59	CV 54 XOC 38	HG 05 USF 64	BX 55 SSU 47
BU 53 UJX 47	VX 53 OEN 32	RX 04 YDJ 59	CV 54 ZTB 50	HK 05 ZMZ 74	CD 55 TAL 36
BX 53 AAN 6	VX 53 OET 32	SA 04 BUS 17	CX 54 JFN 19	HM 05 GSM 69	CE 55 GZC 48
CA 53 APH 56	VX 53 OEV 32	SC 04 OOL 18	DC 54 WAL 21	HN 05 NLR 83	CN 55 AKG 78
CN 53 NWC 7	WA 53 ONL 6	SH 04 MVF 7	DX 54 CMU 50	HX 05 EHP 59	CN 55 AKJ 78
CU 53 APO 29	WA 53 SGX 69	SK 04 OOL 69	DX 54 KJN 35	KE 05 MMJ 65	CN 55 EYW 35
CU 53 APV 29	YJ 53 WMV 13	SN 04 GKF 67	EO 54 WLA 35	KP 05 OWF 51	CN 55 EYX 35
CU 53 APX 29	YN 53 EHZ 52	VX 04 KTG 24	EY 54 NXJ 14	KP 05 XWL 78	CN 55 LUJ 35
CU 53 APY 29	YN 53 EJX 45	VX 04 JZT 39	FJ 54 LOD 13	KT 05 XAW 63	CN 55 NKM 13
CU 53 APZ 29	YN 53 ELC 54	VX 04 ULV 10	FJ 54 ZDD 4	LR 05 NGG 41	CN 55 ZTP 25
CU 53 ARF 29	YN 53 ELH 63	WA 04 MHE 22	FJ 54 ZDH 4	LW 05 PJO 55	CN 55 ZYW 17
CU 53 ARO 29	YN 53 ZDD 46	WD 04 WUK 79	FN 54 EXZ 82	LX 05 GKD 65	CR 55 GBU 60
CU 53 ARX 29	YO 53 OVD 63	YK 04 KWD 11	HX 54 BHP 25	MT 05 SSO 69	CT 55 LHC 15
CU 53 ARZ 29	YO 53 ZNC 5	YN 04 ABK 54	KE 54 HEJ 4	MX 05 EKY 6	CV 55 AEU 44
CU 53 ASO 29	YX 53 HFR 69	YN 04 DXU 39	KX 54 NKG 54	NM 05 BJU 59	CV 55 DDO 45
CU 53 AUO 29		YN 04 GLF 18	LM 54 PLX 83	OO 05 CSA 11	CV 55 EAW 45
CU 53 AUP 29	AE 04 EJZ 61	YN 04 LXK 11	LT 54 WSJ 26	PN 05 PZR 39	CV 55 FFH 74
CU 53 AUT 29	AJ 04 RYV 53	YN 04 NHT 19	ML 54 XBR 22	RX 05 EOY 40	CV 55 FFL 75
CU 53 AUV 29	BU 04 MFP 22	YN 04 WTC 52	MX 54 VWK 40	SF 05 LJO 68	CV 55 FVD 23
CU 53 AUW 29	BX 04 CRV 50	YN 04 WTD 52	NX 54 BPZ 77	SF 05 KWY 29	CV 55 MFM 40
CU 53 AUX 29	CK 04 VYY 81	YN 04 WTJ 24	OO 54 CSA 11	SF 05 KWZ 29	DK 55 BEY 50
CU 53 AUY 29	CN 04 BUW 79	YN 04 XYW 11	OU 54 DVY 59	SF 05 KXA 29	DK 55 BVC 40
CU 53 AVB 29	CN 04 NFM 50	YN 04 XZK 51	PK 54 RZD 80	SF 05 KXB 30	DV 55 APU 17
CU 53 AVJ 29	CN 04 WLZ 73	YU 04 WMV 77	PN 54 OTP 53	SF 05 KXC 30	EN 55 HNJ 54
CU 53 AVK 29	CN 04 WMT 73	YU 04 XJM 56	PO 54 MJU 39	SF 05 KXD 30	FJ 55 KNY 59
CU 53 AVL 29	CN 04 XCW 35	YU 04 XJN 56	WX 54 LHT 39	SF 05 KXE 30	FJ 55 KUW 59
CU 53 AVM 29	CN 04 XES 56		WX 54 NPO 19	SF 05 KXH 30	FL 55 FXG 5
CU 53 AVN 29	CN 04 XEV 56	AD 54 MXB 68	WX 54 SWN 72	SF 05 XCW 18	FM 55 RRO 39
CU 53 AVO 29	CN 04 XFU 35	AE 54 POJ 13	WX 54 XDA 33	SF 05 XDE 65	GN 55 OEG 78
CU 53 AVR 29	CN 04 XFX 35	AT 54 LCT 15	WX 54 XDB 33	VK 05 LNN 16	GN 55 OEI 83
CU 53 AVP 29	CR 04 ABX 15	BD 54 ZNT 75	WX 54 XDD 33	VU 05 XLJ 17	GN 55 OEP 39
CU 53 AVT 29	CR 04 AUM 15	BJ 54 ZFW 64	YN 54 DCE 50	VX 05 BVL 26	HJ 55 KPZ 79
CU 53 AVV 29	CU 04 AET 78	BW 54 WYN 25	YN 54 OCC 39	VX 05 BVU 50	HJ 55 MOU 15
DC 53 EYK 13	CU 04 AKP 63	BX 54 EDP 53	YN 54 OCD 39	WN 05 ELJ 69	HX 55 ADU 13
DX 53 HFL 45	CU 04 AKV 63	BX 54 FRF 63	YN 54 SZC 40	WX 05 RRV 32	KU 55 FLJ 9
DX 53 HFO 79	CU 04 EHT 23	BX 54 VUE 57	YN 54 WCV 56	WX 05 RRZ 32	KX 55 EJF 72
EX 53 UPG 21	CU 04 HKJ 84	CD 54 TAL 36	YN 54 WCW 15	WX 05 RVW 30	KX 55 RYY 10
EX 53 UPK 75	CU 04 LXA 84	CN 54 GXO 68	YX 54 HNE 36	WX 05 RVY 30	LX 55 ACZ 50
FD 53 UOB 16	CU 04 LXB 74	CN 54 HFB 14		YA 05 YXC 21	LX 55 CCU 75
FP 53 GWN 15	CU 04 LXC 74	CN 54 HFG 65	BX 05 FFC 14	YJ 05 YVY 43	MD 55 NNA 51
FX 53 FRJ 48	CV 04 VLJ 79	CN 54 MMJ 73	CE 05 UFX 7	YN 05 AUT 69	MX 55 EVC 54
FX 53 GYK 4	DC 04 WAL 21	CU 54 AFJ 69	CN 05 ONJ 72	YN 05 BUH 6	MX 55 OKD 60
GN 53 NWP 23	DN 04 DKA 75	CU 54 AFX 69	CP 05 CWF 81	YN 05 GZA 18	MX 55 VJU 19
GX 53 LLR 78	EA 04 LMV 70	CU 54 CYZ 33	CP 05 CWG 81	YN 05 RCF 39	NA 55 XFT 14
JA 53 GOW 36	FC 04 NSU 68	CU 54 HXB 27	CP 05 MTE 74	YN 05 WDX 46	NL 55 OTB 64
KR 53 WHG 13	GB 04 LLC 4	CU 54 HYK 29	CP 05 OHU 54	YN 05 XZF 58	PO 55 GGY 21
KX 53 SJV 63	GX 04 BEU 56	CU 54 HYL 29	CU 05 FTJ 84	YN 05 XZR 2	PO 55 VLN 61
LL 53 CEL 14		CU 54 HYM 29	CU 05 FTK 74	YU 05 ZBG 11	SD 55 VBO 76

REGISTRATION / PAGE NUMBER INDEX (continued)

REGISTRATION / PAGE NUMBER INDEX (continued)

REGISTRATION / PAGE NUMBER INDEX (continued)

OPERATING NAMES AND FLEET NAMES

The following is a list of operating names and fleet names for operators in the Mid & West Wales area (CW) who display a name other than their official one. This list is correct to News Sheet 877 (February 2013).

Name	Operator's Title
AJ Contracts	Skinner, Pennant
AMC Travel	Carroll, Cenarth
A W Coaches	Watkins, Cefn Coch
A2B	Sheppard, Llangorse
A2B Mini Bus Hire	Hicks, Burton
A&E Hire	Davies, Llangyniew
A Star Mini Travel	Jones, Bonymaen
Abertawe Travel	Squires, Port Tennant
Adey's Cars	Holder, Howey
Al's Taxi Services	Lawrence, Penybont
Alpha Travel	Di-Cataldo, Fforestfach
Ammanford Bus Hire	Comley, Capel Hendre
Angela's Travel	Hamer, Newtown
Arrow Minicoaches	Firkins, Glais
Arthur's Minibus Hire	Jones, Porthyrhyd
Arwyn's	Davies, Llangyniew
Ben's Buses	Bevan, Felinfoel
Border Mobility	Wood, Welshpool
Brodyr Williams	Williams, Felingwm
Bysiau G & M	Isaac & Morgan, Lampeter
C M Travel	Matthews, Cardigan
Cambrian Bird Holidays	Walker, Rhydlewis
Central Travel	Bowen, Newtown
Cerbydau Gareth Evans	Davies, Brynamman
Chauffeur Travel	Gilbert, Swansea
Clydach Taxis	Duggan, Clydach
Coastal Mini Coaches	Gower & O'Neil, Pembrey
Coracle Coaches of Carmarthen	Chris Cars, Carmarthen
D M Cabs	Mathias, Llangennech
D R Taxis, Minibus & Coach Hire	Rees, Pontyates
Delta Services	Vamplew, Dolanog
Dolphin Mini Travel	Sullivan, Treboeth
Don's Coaches	Woolfe, Ammanford
Dragon Taxi	Burrows, Trefonen
Dragons Wheels	Rees, Rhydywrach
EPT Passenger Transport	Rhys-Ellis, Llangunnor
Eastside Cabs	Eglitis, Llansamlet
Eden Tours	Jones, New Inn
Elwyn's	Griffiths, Llanfair Caereinion
FDV Transport	Vintila, St Thomas
G & M Coaches	Isaac & Morgan, Lampeter
Gaer Farm Buses	Harley, Hundred House
Glasbury Taxis	Lloyd, Glasbury
Glyn's Mini Bus Hire	Hicks, Drefach
Gower Adventures	Fenton, Crofty
H & H Travel	Howells, Loughor
JC Travel	Lloyd, Kidwelly
JJ's Taxi & Minibus Hire	James, Ystradgynlais

Kim's Coaches	Prosser, Morriston
Krislyn Commercials	Morgan, Grovesend
Laugharne Travel	Hewens, Laugharne
Leith's of Sennybridge	Davies, Sennybridge
Llangadog Cabs	Davies, Llangadog
Llansilin Motor Services	Jones, Llansilin
MJN Travel	Hilton, Portmead
Monkton Cars	Ebrey, Monkton
Morris Travel	Freeman, Carmarthen
Narberth Mini Bus Travel	Mason, Whitland
PJ & KME Enterprises	Szpadt, Llandysul
PTS Travel	Davies, Pontyberem
P & S Travel	Hodges, New Quay
Paddles & Pedals	Garratt & Fry, Hay-on-Wye
Pembrokeshire Elite Travel	Mason, Narberth
Phoenix Travel	DH Taxis, Gorseinon
Preseli Venture	Hurst, Mathry
Pro-Cabs	Dust, Llandrindod Wells
Rainbow Travel	Reynolds, Manselton
Rees of Crymych	Midway, Crymych
Rob's Mini Bus	Earland, Cwmgiedd
Rwyth Cabs	Smith, Pontyates
SBS Mini Bus Hire	Saunders, Ponthenri
South Wales Transport Preservation Group	Hier & Evans, Bonymaen
Summerdale Coaches	Davies & Jones, Letterston
Swallow Travel	Cutajar, Brynhyfryd
Swansea Limousine Hire	Morgan, Treboeth
T & M Private Hire	Morgan, Bynea
Taf Valley Coaches	Bysiau Cwm Taf, Whitland
Talgarth Travel	Davies, Talybont-on-Usk
Tanat Valley	Morris, Llanrhaeadr-ym-Mochnant
Tango Mini Travel	Lewis, Tirdeunaw
The Countryman	Davies, Scurlage
The Real Adventure Company	Ward, St Davids
The TYF Group	Middleton, St Davids
Top-notch Limousines	Elms, Lower Freystrop
Travelmaster Holidays	Owens, Four Crosses
Vincent Davies	Davies, Lampeter
Wayne's Minibus Hire	Panayiotiou, Llanelli
Weales Wheels	Weale, Disserth
Welsh Limos	Vintila, St Thomas
Wilcox Mini Travel	Crook, Morriston
Worthen Travel	Pye, Ford
Yellow Cabs	Harris, Swansea
ZK Cars	Harris, Swansea

APPENDIX 1

COUNTY CODE / NEWS SHEET / AREA INDEX

BD	5	Bedfordshire	LI	5	Lincolnshire
BE	3	Berkshire	LN	1	Greater London
BK	5	Buckinghamshire	MY	6	Merseyside
CA	6	Cumbria	NG	4	Nottinghamshire
CC	8	South Central Wales	ND	7	Northumberland
CD	7	Cleveland	NI	9	Northern Ireland
CH	6	Cheshire	NK	5	Norfolk
CI	3	Channel Islands	NO	5	Northamptonshire
CM	5	Cambridgeshire	NY	7	North Yorkshire
CN	8	North Wales	OX	3	Oxfordshire
CO	3	Cornwall	Qd	BJ	Dealer/Manufacturer demonstrator
CS	8	South East Wales	RM	BJ	Royal Mail
CW	8	Mid & West Wales	SE	9	Scotland East
DE	4	Derbyshire	SH	4	Shropshire
DM	7	Durham	SK	5	Suffolk
DN	3	Devon	SN	9	Scotland North
DT	3	Dorset	SO	3	Somerset
EI	8	Irish Republic	SR	2	Surrey
ES	2	East Sussex	SS	9	Scotland South
EX	2	Essex	ST	4	Staffordshire
EY	7	East Yorkshire	SW	9	Scotland West
GL	3	Gloucestershire	SY	7	South Yorkshire
GM	6	Greater Manchester	TW	7	Tyne & Wear
HA	2	Hampshire	WI	3	Wiltshire
HT	5	Hertfordshire	WK	4	Warwickshire
HO	4	Herefordshire	WM	4	West Midlands
IM	6	Isle of Man	WR	4	Worcestershire
IS	3	Isles of Scilly	WS	2	West Sussex
IW	2	Isle of Wight	WY	7	West Yorkshire
KT	2	Kent	X	BJ	National non-PCV
LA	6	Lancashire	Y	MB	Non-PSV Minibuses
LE	4	Leicestershire			

Discovered a mistake ? A missing vehicle ? A withdrawn vehicle ? Know of an Operating Centre
that is not given ?   These lists are only as up to date as readers' reports.

If you can add anything on any operator covered in this publication
please send your comments to:-

The PSV Circle, Unit 1R, Leroy House, 436 Essex Road, London N1 3QP

or by e-mail: post.office@psv-circle.org.uk